The Great Ideas

Detail of *Alexander Hamilton,* oil painting by John Trumbull,
in the Yale University Art Gallery

The Great Ideas Today

1975

Encyclopædia Britannica, Inc.

Chicago • London • Toronto • Geneva • Sydney • Tokyo • Manila • Johannesburg • Seoul

The Great Ideas Today 1975

The lines by Ezra Pound on p. 7 are from THE CANTOS OF EZRA POUND,
Copyright 1948 by Ezra Pound. Reprinted by permission of New Directions
Publishing Corporation.

Reprinted by permission of Harcourt Brace Jovanovich, Inc., and Faber and
Faber Limited: "At the Indian Killers' Grave," by Robert Lowell, from
LORD WEARY'S CASTLE, copyright 1946, 1974, and POEMS 1938–1949.

Reprinted by permission of Farrar, Straus & Giroux, Inc., and Faber and Faber
Limited are: "Skunk Hour" and "Commander Lowell" from LIFE STUDIES
by Robert Lowell, Copyright © 1956, 1959 by Robert Lowell; "Dream Song 40"
from 77 DREAM SONGS and "Dream Songs 145, 179, 223, 261" from HIS TOY,
HIS DREAM, HIS REST by John Berryman, Copyright © 1959, 1962, 1963,
1964, 1965, 1966, 1967, 1968, 1969 by John Berryman; "Vers de Société" from
HIGH WINDOWS by Philip Larkin, Copyright © 1974 by Philip Larkin.

Reprinted by permission of Faber and Faber Limited: "Sunny Prestatyn" and
"Dockery & Son," by Philip Larkin, from THE WHITSUN WEDDINGS.

"The Essence of Mathematics," by Charles Sanders Peirce, is reprinted by
permission of the publishers from COLLECTED PAPERS OF CHARLES
SANDERS PEIRCE, Volume IV, edited by Charles Hartshorne and Paul Weiss,
Cambridge, Mass.: The Belknap Press of Harvard University Press, Copyright
1933, 1961, by the President and Fellows of Harvard College.

"The Constitution Revisited," by Scott Buchanan, was originally a Center
Occasional Paper published by The Center for the Study of Democratic
Institutions, and is reprinted with the Center's permission. Copyright 1968 by
The Fund for the Republic, Inc.

Printed in the U.S.A. Library of Congress Catalog Number: 61-65561
International Standard Book Number: 0-85229-306-2

Distributed to the trade by Praeger Publishers, Inc., New York, Washington

Contents

A NOTE ON REFERENCE STYLE

In the following pages, passages in *Great Books of the Western World* are referred to by the initials '*GBWW*,' followed by volume, page number, and page section. Thus, '*GBWW*, Vol. 39, p. 210b' refers to page 210 in Adam Smith's *The Wealth of Nations*, which is Volume 39 in *Great Books of the Western World*. The small letter 'b' indicates the page section. In books printed in single column, 'a' and 'b' refer to the upper and lower halves of the page. In books printed in double column, 'a' and 'b' refer to the upper and lower halves of the left column, 'c' and 'd' to the upper and lower halves of the right column. For example, 'Vol. 53, p. 210b' refers to the lower half of page 210, since Volume 53, James's *Principles of Psychology*, is printed in single column. On the other hand, 'Vol. 7, p. 210b' refers to the lower left quarter of the page, since Volume 7, Plato's *Dialogues*, is printed in double column.

Gateway to the Great Books is referred to by the initials '*GGB*,' followed by volume and page number. Thus, '*GGB*, Vol. 10, pp. 39-57' refers to pages 39 through 57 of Volume 10 of *Gateway to the Great Books*, which is James's essay, "The Will to Believe."

The Great Ideas Today is referred to by the initials '*GIT*,' followed by the year and page number. Thus '*GIT* 1968, p. 210' refers to page 210 of the 1968 edition of *The Great Ideas Today*.

The Great Ideas Today, 1961–1975

This year marks the fifteenth anniversary of *The Great Ideas Today*—the fifteenth year in which a substantial volume concerned with contemporary developments in the intellectual tradition of the West has appeared for the special use and benefit of the many owners of *Great Books of the Western World*.

It is a record in which the editors take some pride. There is nothing else quite like the book that for fifteen years they have managed to produce. Subscribers to *The Great Ideas Today* know its annual features—an informed discussion by several persons of some current issue or world event, authoritative surveys in layman's language of the state of the arts and sciences, a special article reviewing current thought on a major idea, and, more recently, a reconsideration by an appropriate person of one of the works in the set of Great Books—features not to be easily found, if they exist at all, in any other publication. To these must be added the essays, stories, poems, and in some cases entire books that various issues of *The Great Ideas Today* have reprinted, until it can be fairly said that whoever owns the whole series, or even a considerable part of it, has acquired a sizable library of minor classics to go with the Great Books themselves.

What has made the venture possible is an underlying truth which it shares with the much larger venture of publishing *Great Books of the Western World* and its unique *Syntopicon*—the truth being that the works in the set of Great Books are themselves really contemporaneous and that serious talk about what is going on today, anywhere in the world, necessarily involves them. It is for this reason that an annual concerned with on-going developments in the same tradition has been a viable enterprise. *The Great Ideas Today* could never have provided a contemporary aspect for the Great Books if they had not had it all along. The task has simply been to point it out.

Inevitably there have been certain changes or at least shifts of focus in the volume over so long a period. For one thing, while still a work of very considerable length it is no longer quite so long as it was at first; if it were, it would have to cost a good deal more than it does, for the price of everything to do with books has risen sharply over the years, in particular the price of paper. On the other hand, after some experimentation, a format has been established which is flexible enough for varying editorial purposes and production needs and yet allows a uniform work to be brought out each year, adding to what has become a handsome set of volumes.

There have been editorial changes, too, not so explicit or so fixed. Neither the symposiums nor the reviews of the arts and sciences which appear each year have the strict annual character with which at first they were designed. Some readers have questioned this, arguing that the chosen symposium subject is not one they recognize as current, or that they cannot count on keeping up each year with developments in one or another of the disciplines that is of special concern to them. Of course, the annual symposium was never really intended to deal with the issues or problems of everyday journalism. It was and is designed as a forum for the discussion of subjects—current, to be sure—in which are to be found underlying questions that require to be clarified if they are to be adequately grasped. For example, the discussion in the present volume of recent attempts to teach language to chimpanzees is not so much an effort to resolve the question whether such attempts have been successful, or can ever be so, but to consider what they imply about the nature of language and, beyond that, what they invite us to recall about human nature and human dignity. Our failure to understand what these last require of us has been the cause of endless suffering and profound injustice to a great portion of the human race in our time.

That the volume no longer reviews each area of the arts and sciences each year, as it bravely started out to do, may be admitted, and will perhaps be understood by anyone who can appreciate the difficulty of finding annually as many as four authorities able and willing to summarize the year's developments in the humanities, the social sciences, the physical sciences, and the speculative disciplines. *The Great Ideas Today* does keep up, so far as possible, with developments in each of these areas, but not in each of them on an annual basis and not, as one might say, from an annual point of view. The result is a kind of essay which, if it is not so current, yet does not quickly date as articles from earlier issues of the volume seem now to have done, and is besides usually of greater depth, since it is not so much of a survey as earlier reviews of such material were required to be. At the same time, it avoids the implication that significant events in the various disciplines always come about, like new cars, according to an annual schedule, or that even when they do they can at once be properly evaluated.

The commitment of *The Great Ideas Today* to learning—or, if such a word carries dismal academic connotations, to intellectual pleasure and insight —has never varied. It is as strong as it ever was. If some of the didactic machinery that early issues carried—long explanatory notes, comparison of one article with another, extended references to the *Syntopicon*—have been dispensed with, it is because after a time, possibly through repetition, these devices seemed likely to put readers off and so to defeat the ends they were designed to achieve. Besides, they were always a little inconsistent with the principle underlying the publication of *Great Books of the Western World*, which was that there would be no editorial attempt to interpret the authors in the set—a principle that seemed worth extending to the contributors to *The Great Ideas Today*. Editorial introductions are still included, of course, to the works each volume reprints. There is often an extended editorial discussion of the symposium topic as treated in the Great Books, and frequently there are Notes to the Reader which serve as guides from the various articles to relevant readings in *Great Books of the Western World*.

Old subscribers to the volume know how useful these Notes can be. So may any student above, say, the third year of high school who is willing to go a little beyond the requirements of a particular class assignment—a research topic, a term paper, a special project or report—to consider the underlying ideas his or her subject contains. An adult reader with a certain amount of curiosity and determination will find such Notes equally helpful for private study.

To be sure, not every issue of *The Great Ideas Today* will contain articles of equal interest, and then not every Note need be followed up. Where an article seems especially absorbing or worthwhile, the Note will point to the appropriate chapters in the *Syntopicon*—the chapters, that is, whose introductory essays summarize the ideas the article invokes as they appear in the tradition of the Great Books. It is easy enough in most cases to perceive what those ideas are. For example, in connection with the symposium in this volume, the *Syntopicon* chapters to read are clearly the ones on ANIMAL, on MAN, on LANGUAGE, and on SIGN AND SYMBOL. On the other hand, if someone is particularly interested in, say, the article by Dr. Short, the relevant chapters would be those on ASTRONOMY, on MATTER, and on SPACE. And so forth.

The chapter essays, in which the tradition of the Great Books is recalled with clarity, conciseness, and complete neutrality, may convey all the information that readers want in many cases. It is when an article in *The Great Ideas Today* is of particular interest, when the ideas it raises are of special concern, that a reader may wish to go further. To go further means to study the outline at the end of the relevant *Syntopicon* essay, to see what the components of the idea are and how many aspects it has, or, as we tend nowadays to say, what its structure is. Again, some of this, however interesting and worth noting, may be clearly beside the point of a given reader's interest. But where the outline's topics strike the reader as comprehending just those aspects of the subject with which an article in *The Great Ideas Today* has dealt, they will be worth following up. Thus Mr. Bayley's essay on "The Poetry of Self-Creation" in the present volume, which would naturally lead one to read Chapter 69, POETRY, would also point, as anyone will see who reads it, to Chapter 56, MEMORY AND IMAGINATION—in particular to Topic 2c, on the association of ideas: controlled and free association: reminiscence and reverie; to Topic 4a, on memory in the life of the individual: personal identity and continuity; and to the various divisions of Topic 5 devoted to the activity of the imagination. The same article would point to Chapter 88, SOUL, especially Topic 1d, on the soul as the principle of personal identity: the doctrine of the self; and also to Topic 5a, dealing with the soul's knowledge of itself by reflection on its acts. These topics indicate that the tradition of the Great Books has a good deal to say about the matters discussed by Mr. Bayley and indicate just where it is said.

No doubt, even such a relatively limited number of topics will contain what may seem an overwhelmingly large number of references to various authors in *Great Books of the Western World*. At this point the reader must sit down at a desk or table within reach of the books in that set and prepare to pull them down so as to look up the indicated passages. He or she will discover that not all of them need be pursued. Some authors will seem less likely to be instructive than others in a given case. Among those who remain, not all the passages indicated in their works will seem equally interesting or important when examined, nor should they.

What anyone is likely to end up with, after a couple of hours' work, are a few passages—half a dozen, a dozen—which seem substantial and suggestive, and at least one or two which clearly require more extended reading in the authors from whom they come. Another evening may have to be devoted to such reading, doubtless more if the subject is a large one. But when this task is done, after an investment of time not perhaps any greater than that required for getting through a longish novel, or what may be taken up by trips to the library to look up more conventional reference material, one will have, if one is a student, the wherewithal for a far more interesting piece of written work than one would otherwise be able to produce, while if one has no occasion of that sort to meet, there will have been acquired the stuff for quiet reflection, good talk among friends, perhaps some private work, and further reading. And this will be seen, if one looks back, as the residue of a kind of sifting process, of an exercise in self-education, which is what *The Great Ideas Today*, like *Great Books of the Western World* and the *Syntopicon*, has all along been designed both to encourage and make possible, and what it still hopes will be attempted by at least a portion of its readers.

It needs only to be added, before we close this retrospect—this prelude, too, as it really is, to future issues of *The Great Ideas Today* which now are in the planning stage—that we feel a debt of gratitude to the great number of very distinguished contributors in both academic and public life who over the years have responded to our request for articles on various subjects. The quality of these contributions and the unvarying cooperativeness and courtesy with which they have been provided have been the source of much satisfaction to us and have insured the success of the volume over so many years, as we have no doubt they will continue to do.

PART ONE

A Symposium on Language and Communication

Introduction

In presenting this year's symposium, the editors of *The Great Ideas Today* have been inspired by recent reports of progress in the teaching of various forms of language to animals, particularly chimpanzees. These experiments, as well as earlier efforts to establish speech communication with bottle-nosed dolphins and the ongoing effort to design a robot that will be able to converse with men, have raised anew the old question of what man is and how he differs from other creatures—whether his distinction is merely one of degree, as a quantity of brainpower greater than but not essentially different from what chimpanzees do, and robots may, exhibit, or a difference of kind, the result of a characteristic or capacity which no other organism possesses to any extent. This question has been raised because, if man's difference is in fact one of kind, it lies to a very great extent in his ability to use language, and, correspondingly, because if other creatures besides himself can be demonstrated to have linguistic ability, it would be hard to maintain that there is any but a difference in degree, however great, between them and human beings. And that perforce raises the further question of just what language is, and how we can determine whether chimpanzees, for instance, are capable of it; for not even their most ardent champions would claim that the linguistic competence of such animals, supposing they have some, is easy to recognize, or that it can be inferred except through painstaking and sophisticated experimental procedures.

It is this more limited question about language, rather than the larger one about species, which the contributors to the symposium were asked to consider. Each of them has some special competence in the field of language and a known concern with it. Roger S. Fouts has himself participated in certain of the chimpanzee experiments, notably those with Washoe, the animal trained by Allen and Beatrice Gardner in the use of Ameslan, or American Sign Language. Professor Lamb is a linguist whose interest is in the character and structure of language; Professor Dance's field is that of speech communication, which is at least of related importance if it is not, as Professor Dance argues, more nearly the heart of the matter; Professor McNeill, a distinguished psychologist, has written on the subject of how language is acquired; Dr. Adler, who some years ago wrote a book called *The Difference of Man and the Difference It Makes*, which was addressed to the larger question just referred to, has recently completed another work also, *Some Questions about Language: A Theory of Human Discourse and Its Objects*, devoted to the subject at hand.

In some respects these contributors are agreed as to what language is; in others, reflecting their different preoccupations, they differ. In any case they hold different opinions as to whether the recent experiments have been successful—whether, that is, language can really be taught to chimpanzees (not whether they are capable of speaking; none of the experiments has been designed to teach speech, which is apparently impossible for chimpanzees to imitate), or whether it is only some astonishingly complex forms of communication, within the power of chimpanzees to grasp, which have been developed. Indeed, the difference between language and communication seems to be central to the discussion, though it is not always directly confronted, and the title which has been given to the symposium points to that fact. But another difference, less clearly defined but more often touched upon, is between language as the symbolic representation of what we perceive as present to our senses and language as conveying, in the words of Joan Robinson, "information about things not present and ... speculation about things not known." This, after all, is perhaps the definitive aspect of language in the human sense.

There are those who may wonder, of course, whether it really matters if a capacity for language is demonstrated in animals or not. Such a question may seem insignificant as compared, say, with the issues inherent in the social crisis and ecological peril which are to be found these days throughout the world, or to reflect a misguided concern with human difference at a time when the full extent of human dependence is just beginning to be understood. Certainly, in conceiving the present discussion, there has been no desire on the part of the editors to deny, nor any tendency to forget, that whatever man's difference is, he is part of a natural order which is the work of something greater than himself, and within which other creatures have, from some perspectives, a power and importance superior to his own.

> *The ant's a centaur in his dragon world,*
> *Pull down thy vanity, it is not man*
> *Made courage, or made order, or made grace;*
>   *Pull down thy vanity, I say pull down!**

What has seemed worth reaffirming, so far as present understanding allows and giving due weight to recent evidence which seeks to prove the

---

* "Canto 81" from *The Cantos* by Ezra Pound (New York: New Directions, 1965).

contrary, is that a difference does exist between man and the rest of nature, a difference which is the result of an evolution that permits no return, and which is decisively indicated, though it is by no means altogether encompassed, by man's capacity for language. This is not so far as it may seem from other current human concerns that appear more pressing. It is precisely our failure to recognize the human difference that underlies the exploitation of some human beings by others in so many parts of the world today, while at the same time it renders arbitrary and erratic the dominion over other creatures which man can exercise well only if he perceives the basis for it and accepts the responsibilities which it entails.

The Development of Human Linguistic Behaviors in Chimpanzees

Roger S. Fouts

Dr. Roger Fouts received his Ph.D. degree from the University of Nevada at Reno under the direction of Dr. R. Allen Gardner and Dr. Beatrice T. Gardner. He was a member of the research team examining two-way communication with an infant chimpanzee using a gestural language as the mode. Dr. Fouts and the chimpanzee, Washoe, went to the Institute of Primate Studies and the Department of Psychology at the University of Oklahoma in 1970. From 1970 to 1973 Dr. Fouts was a research associate and continued the examination of gestural language acquisition and use with several chimpanzees. At present, he is assistant professor of psychology at the University of Oklahoma and is continuing this research, in addition to examining the use of sign language in the treatment of noncommunicating autistic children. He has published a number of papers dealing with aspects of his work in primate studies.

This paper will examine some of the more recent attempts which have been made to find linguistic behaviors in apes. The paper will emphasize the similarities between such behaviors and the human use of language rather than the differences. This is not intended to imply that differences do not exist or that they are less important than the similarities. The present state of the empirical sciences is such that it is possible to demonstrate that a behavior is present in one species but not possible to demonstrate that it is absent in another. If one fails to find comparable behavior in different species, it may be best to withhold judgment as to what the failure signifies, especially if the two species are otherwise extremely close to one another.

The linguistic apes

The title of this section is not original with me, but it is from a section in Roger Brown's *A First Language: The Early Stages,*[1] in which he examines two projects studying whether chimpanzees are capable of acquiring either human or artificial language. I shall review the two projects Brown examined as well as two other projects of a similar kind, and I shall comment on Brown's comments when it seems appropriate to do so.

First, I shall review two projects that have used an artificial language system, one made up of various colors and shaped pieces of plastic representing words and another using a computer as the intermediary for language made up of lines and colors on computer keys. Second, I shall review projects that have used American Sign Language for the Deaf (Ameslan), a gestural language used by the deaf people in North America, as the mode of communication.

Devised language studies

David Premack[2] devised a system for two-way communication with a chimpanzee using pieces of plastic of various shapes, textures, and colors to represent words. These pieces of plastic were metal-backed so that they could be placed in a vertical fashion on a metal board. Using the pieces of plastic, Premack was able to train Sarah, a six-year-old female chimpanzee, to use and understand the negative, the interrogative, "wh" questions (what, who, etc.), the concept of "name of" (a metalinguistic constituent of language), dimensional classes, prepositions (in, on, etc.), hierarchically organized sentences (compound or coordinated), the "if ... then" conditional, yes-no interrogative, and the copula (is, are). Premack and Premack state that "Sarah had managed to learn a code, a simple language that nevertheless included some of the characteristic features of natural language. Each step of the training program was made as simple as possible. The objective was to reduce complex notions to a series of simple and highly learnable steps." They conclude that "compared with a two-year-old child ... Sarah holds her own in language ability."[3]

The use of simple steps to train an animal to learn a particular response is a procedure commonly used in operant methodology. It appears the Premacks assumed that the constituents of language can be derived from operant procedures. By reducing these procedures to simple steps they thought it might be possible to convey linguistic constituents to Sarah. For an example of this procedure, note how training was begun. Initially, some fruit was placed on the board, and Sarah was allowed to eat it. Next, before Sarah could eat the fruit, she had to place a piece of the plastic that represented the fruit on the board. New pieces of plastic were added as new aspects of the situation were added. For example, a new piece of plastic was added if the type of fruit changed. Then pieces of plastic representing the trainer's particular name were added, and Sarah was required to place them on the board. Still later, a piece of plastic representing the English word *give* was added, and finally one representing Sarah's name was added also. In this manner Sarah was taught to form sentences made up of pieces of plastic, and she was also trained to respond to sentences such as "Sarah give apple Mary."

Roger Brown, in the book I have already cited, has voiced concern over the use of the operant procedure to train Sarah. Brown states: "The question always arises whether the paradigm preserves the essential properties of the process it is intended to represent."[4] Referring to Sarah, Brown asks: "Has she really shown comprehension of the sentence, or the copula, of the conditional, and so on?"[5]

Brown's concern stems from his knowledge of a well-known experiment by B. F. Skinner in which Skinner used the operant procedure to train two pigeons to peck ping-pong balls back and forth in a fashion that at one level resembled the game that humans play.[6] Brown notes that there were differences between what the pigeons did and what humans do when playing ping-pong. For example, Brown writes, the pigeons "did not, ... keep score or develop strategies for misleading one another."[7]

In response to this, we could say that given the effectiveness of the operant procedure, a program could probably be developed in which a pigeon was trained to keep score and even to develop a strategy that would, on the surface, appear to mislead its opponent. But that would not

David Premack's system for communication with chimpanzees involved the use of plastic chips of various shapes, textures, and colors to represent words. At left, the chimpanzee Elizabeth responds to the sentence "Elizabeth apple touch," and at right, "Elizabeth give apple Amy [the trainer]."

answer the question whether the essential properties of human ping-pong are being preserved in the behavior. Brown appears to be blaming the problem of different processes occurring in a behavior on the experimental procedure rather than on the subject. Consider the situation in which non-ping-pong playing humans are taught to play ping-pong. Would a person who acquired the skills of ping-pong via operant procedures have the essential properties of the process, or would he have a different process as compared with a person who acquired the skills in the fashion usually found in our species? The former is more likely. Hence Brown, in noting that the former result does not seem to occur, perceives only what any scientist who uses these procedures would allow, i.e., that they are unable to change one species into another. Certainly a pigeon would not become a member of the human species if he learned ping-pong. All that can be said is that the human activity called ping-pong is reducible to operant procedures which are simple enough to be learned by several organisms across the phylogenetic scale.

Rather than concern ourselves with the procedure used in experiments of the sort we are discussing, we should consider the individual species involved and how they are either different or the same. T. C. Schneirla notes that the ant caste system appears to have functional similarities to the human caste system.[8] We may say as much about the pigeon ping-pong

processes and the human ping-pong processes. This does not allow us to forget that pigeons are different from humans, however, nor should it blind us to the difference their difference makes in the kind of ping-pong they play. Of course, the differences that exist between the chimpanzee processes of language and the human processes of language are not so great as the differences between pigeon ping-pong and human ping-pong —precisely because the species difference between chimpanzees and humans is less than that between humans and pigeons.

David Premack was not a biological alchemist who was able to change chimpanzees into pigeons, or even into humans, for that matter. But the procedure Premack used undoubtedly had an effect on his operations, and it was this effect that Brown was probably responding to. To put it simply, if you use procedures designed for rats or pigeons, and if you perceive how the rats and pigeons respond, you tend to define rats and pigeons in terms of that response, and you may overlook aspects of the response that indicate complexities and capacities you had not anticipated in those species. Wolfgang Köhler noted the importance of this in 1921 when he said: "The decisive explanations for the understanding of apes frequently arise from quite unforeseen kinds of behavior, for example, use of tools by the animals in ways very different from human beings. If we arrange all conditions in such a way that, so far as possible, the ape can only show the kinds of behavior in which we are interested in advance, or else nothing essential at all, then it will become less likely that the animal does the unexpected and thus teaches the observer something."[9]

It may be, therefore, that some criticism of David Premack is in order for his decision to arrange the conditions in advance so that Sarah could show only the types of behavior that he was interested in—an arrangement that made it difficult to perceive other capacities that Sarah might possess. But Premack makes it quite clear that he was interested only in the behaviors he decided to study, not in others that Sarah might be capable of. And if she did not in fact seem capable of others, it may be only because the situation was deliberately intended to exclude them. So perhaps Premack should not be criticized for doing exactly what he set out to do.

Brown also criticizes David Premack for not doing enough to control the possibility of a "Clever Hans" error.[10] This refers to a well-known problem in the study of behavior that involves inadvertent cueing of the organism for the correct response to make. The problem was first observed in a horse that apparently could perform mathematical problems involving addition and multiplication.[11] It was found that the horse was responding to the subtle expectant postures of people who knew the correct answer. When given a problem, the horse was supposed to answer by tapping his foot a certain number of times. He learned to tap until someone became expectant, and then stop. If the people around the horse did not know the answer (e.g., if one person gave the horse the one number and another person separately gave the horse another number), or if the horse was wearing blinders, he was unable to solve the problem. Because of Clever Hans, we now recognize that it is very important to control for the possibility of cueing when studying the behavior of organisms.

A control for this *was* used by Premack by having a person who did not know Sarah's language work with her.[12] But Brown points out that the blind observer began to learn the language as testing proceded, and thereafter was not completely blind.[13] However, Premack notes that the partial knowledge of the blind observer could not account for Sarah's success.[14] Brown also notes the deterioration of Sarah's performance in the blind conditions, but Premack attributes this to other aspects of the blind test that made the situation different from the one with which Sarah was familiar.

What may be fairly said is that Premack did not use as effective a control for the Clever Hans problem as he might have used. Once again we are dealing with the kind of procedure employed by the experimenter rather than with the subject's abilities. Certainly, the Clever Hans problem is one that should be considered when studying behavior. Allen and Beatrice Gardner point out in their review[15] of Brown's book, *A First Language: The Early Stages*, that Brown himself did not provide controls for this problem in some of his experiments studying language in children. However, it should be emphasized that the Clever Hans problem *has* been adequately controlled for in the research that has established two-way communication between a chimpanzee and a human using gestural language (Ameslan), which will be reviewed in this article.

Another study examining two-way communication between a human and a chimpanzee using an artificially devised system is reported by Rumbaugh, Gill, and von Glasersfeld.[16] The system involves a PDP-8 computer equipped with two consoles containing twenty-five keys apiece. One console is used by a two-and-a-half-year-old female chimpanzee named Lana, the other by a human experimenter in another room. The language devised for this computer is "Yerkish" and is made up of geometric symbols which are placed on the keys, which have three different colors to use as background either singly or in combination. When a key is available for use by Lana, it is softly backlit, and it becomes fully lit when she presses it. When a key is not available for use by Lana, it is not backlit. When Lana or an experimenter presses the keys, the symbols are projected in serial order on seven projectors above the console. The computer dispenses the appropriate incentives when Lana depresses the keys in the serial order which is determined by the computer to be in accordance with correct Yerkish grammar. Using this, Lana may ask for food, drink, music, movies, toys, to have a trainer come in, and so on.

Lana's training was similar to the procedure used by Premack to train Sarah in that small steps were used, and that it was also an operant procedure. Rumbaugh et al. report that, after six months of training, Lana was able to read the projected characters, to complete incomplete sentences based on the incomplete sentences' meaning and serial order, or to reject them if they were not grammatically correct in terms of. the Yerkish grammar.[17]

Since this study was reported after Brown had published his book, it was not included in his review of the projects. The Clever Hans problem was controlled for in this experiment by using a computer as the intermediary for the communication between the humans and the chimpanzee. The procedure may still be self-limiting, as in the pigeon ping-pong studies. However, this danger is apparently reduced because Lana is allowed access to use keys beyond testing or the training situation. It would be interesting to see how much Lana communicated with the computer when the experimenters were not present.

Rather than criticize the above approaches, it is more appropriate to consider them as a matter of scientific taste. If one is prepared to accept the reduced amount of information that results from using a highly structured experimental paradigm, one may fairly employ these approaches.

But it must be realized that the results are often limited to those behaviors the experimenter is capable of conceiving in advance, and that they may not really illuminate the capacities of the organism being studied.

Human language studies

This section will review those research projects that have used Ameslan as the mode of establishing communication with chimpanzees. Ameslan is made up of two parts. One is finger spelling, in which a certain hand configuration is used for each letter of the alphabet, and words are spelled with the hand. Finger spelling was not used with chimpanzees. The second part is made of gestures that have specific hand configuration, movements, and places where they begin and end in relation to the signer's body. For example, the sign for *spoon* is made by extending the index finger and the middle finger with the rest of the fingers bent (this is the "U" hand), then touching the tips of two extended fingers held palm up to the palm of an open hand, and then moving the "U" hand to the mouth and touching the lips with the tips of the two extended fingers. These individual gestures are analogous to words in a spoken language. This form of Ameslan was taught to the chimpanzees.

Drs. R. Allen Gardner and Beatrice T. Gardner were the first to teach a chimpanzee successfully to use a human gestural language.[18] Their chimpanzee, Washoe, is a female who was estimated to be between eight and fourteen months of age when she arrived in Reno in June 1966. By the time Project Washoe ended, in October 1970, Washoe had acquired over 130 signs.

Washoe was raised in an enriched environment much like a human child's. She lived in a self-contained eight-by-twenty-four-foot house trailer in the 5,000-square-foot backyard of the Gardners' home. The trailer had its own kitchen, bedroom, and bathroom. The yard had a large tree with swings, a sandbox, a "geodesic" climbing dome, and several toys. Throughout the day, the researchers who stayed with Washoe used only Ameslan to communicate with her. Washoe was immersed in an environment of Ameslan from the time she awoke in the morning until she was tucked into her bed at night. The researchers collected data on Washoe's signing while serving as her conversational companions. The data were recorded using a daily diary of the events and sign utterances, sampling signs, combinations of signs, and various vocabulary tests.

Washoe acquired her signs via different methods. The Gardners noted a little manual babbling or finger play, but this began to drop out as Washoe began acquiring signs, just as babbling does with human children. Washoe also had gestures in her repertoire when she arrived in Reno. Some of these were similar to signs in Ameslan. For example, Washoe's open-palm-extended-hand use was interpreted as "come-gimme." She also

Drs. R. Allen Gardner and Beatrice T. Gardner taught their chimpanzee, Washoe, American Sign Language (Ameslan) to name objects. Here, Washoe starts (top) and completes (bottom) the Ameslan sign "cat" for a picture of a cat.

would shake her hands at the wrist when in a hurry, or when frustrated by someone not doing something fast enough, or in excitement. This was similar to the *hurry* sign in Ameslan, which involves shaking at the wrist an "H" hand, which is the index finger and middle finger extended and pointed to the side and away from the signer. The Gardners also shaped natural responses into signs that closely resembled them. For example, Washoe would bang on doors with her two hands when she wanted them opened. The Gardners were able to shape this banging behavior into the *open* sign, which involves placing two open hands next to each other, palm down, and then lifting them up while simultaneously moving them apart and rotating the wrist outwards so that the *open* sign ends with the hands being held palm up. Washoe also acquired several signs by observing them and imitating them. Many of these, such as *smoke* and *toothbrush*, were acquired without any intentional teaching on the researchers' part. In fact, she once invented a sign herself by making the outline of a "bib" on her chest. At the time, since the Gardners were not sure whether or not such a sign for *bib* existed in Ameslan, it was not treated as an acceptable sign for Washoe to use. Another method of teaching signs to Washoe involved putting Washoe's hand(s) through the required movements for the sign in the presence of the object or action to which the sign referred. Roger Fouts compared this method of teaching Washoe a sign to strict imitation, which involved only the experimenter making the sign, and found that putting Washoe's hands through the motion for a sign was a much more efficient method.[19] It has since been found that imitation can be nearly as efficient as other methods.[20]

The Clever Hans problem was controlled for in tests of Washoe's vocabulary. The most efficient of these tests was a double-blind slide test of Washoe's vocabulary that was subject-paced. A picture of a particular object which Washoe had never seen before, but which represented a sign in her vocabulary, was projected onto a backward projecting screen. This was behind a sliding door. In another room an observer recorded Washoe's responses to the picture by looking through a one-way mirror that allowed the observer to view Washoe without seeing the picture to which she was responding. Another person was in the room with Washoe, but he or she was positioned next to a wall which precluded any view of the picture, though the observer was still able to see Washoe. When Washoe wanted to start a trial, she would go to the door, and then the person with her would position himself and unlock the door so that Washoe could open it and see the picture. Both observers recorded the sign Washoe made, thus allowing interobserver reliability to be determined. After Washoe signed, the door was locked, and another person changed the slide while the person with Washoe played with her until she was ready to initiate the next trial. Washoe got fifty-three correct out of ninety-nine presentations; one would expect a chance level of responding of three correct out of ninety-nine. Some of Washoe's errors in this test were conceptual in their nature, since an error for a picture of an animal was usually a sign for another animal, and there were confusions between articles of grooming, and so on.

The Gardners also recorded combinations that evidenced Washoe's rule-following behavior or syntactic qualities. They examined Washoe's use of the signs *you-me* and signs representing action verbs. They found that when Washoe used the *you* sign, it preceded the action verb and the *me* sign over 90 percent of the time. Washoe initially preferred the *you-me* -action verb combination, and then later the format *you*-action verb-*me* became more prevalent.

The Gardners[21] classified 294 different two-sign combinations by using Brown's[22] Stage I categories, with a slight modification. They found that 78 percent of Washoe's combinations fit into these categories. Brown notes that Washoe did not always use the same sign order in her combinations when the semantic role remained the same. He states that: "For children learning English this is definitely not the case. With a few exceptions and complications, to be discussed in Stage I, children speaking English use words in just that order appropriate to the semantic relations which referent circumstances suggest that the child intends to express. This difference of attention to word order is potentially of great significance."[23]

The implication of Brown's statement is that human children do not make errors in their combinations of words when they are acquiring English. Intuitively, I am tempted to say that this makes language acquisition in children a most amazing behavior. I do not mean to imply that Brown is incorrect. However, we will be unable to determine this until the testing of correct word order by children is done in a double-blind condition controlling for the Clever Hans problem. The Gardners note the necessity for using double-blind procedures in examining the word order of children in their review of Brown's *A First Language: The Early Stages*. They state: "The problem is not inherent in the subject matter of child psycholinguistics; we Gardners devised double-blind vocabulary tests for the young chimpanzee, Washoe, that avoid all possibility of Clever Hans errors. In the next phase of our chimpanzee research, we are extending the same double-blind techniques to provide tests for word order and other syntactic devices. If the standards of experimentation in child psycholinguistics do not improve soon, we will find ourselves in the paradoxical situation of having solid experimental evidence for the syntactic abilities of chimpanzees and a complete lack of acceptable evidence for any syntactic ability in young children."[24]

Project Washoe ended in Reno in October 1970, when Washoe went to the Institute for Primate Studies at the University of Oklahoma. Washoe readily demonstrates the ability to combine signs in her vocabulary to form spontaneous combinations in a contextually correct manner. The

Gardners have lately begun a second chimpanzee project raising two young chimpanzees from a few days of age. They are currently using more deaf researchers or researchers of deaf parents who are very proficient in the use of Ameslan. This alone should improve the chimpanzees' acquisition of signs, since the researchers are more proficient in the use of Ameslan than were the participants in the original Project Washoe.

The examination of the acquisition and use of Ameslan by chimpanzees has continued at the Institute for Primate Studies using several chimpanzees who either live at the Institute or who are being home-reared in private homes in the surrounding community.

The first study done at the Institute compared the acquisition of ten signs in four chimpanzees.[25] The signs were taught to the four chimpanzees in the same order, using the same method of teaching. After all the chimpanzees had acquired the signs, they were tested on their signs in a double-blind test. It was found that there were individual differences between the chimpanzees in terms of the amount of time required to teach them a sign, and it was also found that some signs were consistently easy or difficult for the chimpanzees to acquire. This study also demonstrates that Washoe's ability to acquire and use signs was not just a fluke peculiar to her.

Roger Mellgren, Roger Fouts, and William Lemmon did a study examining the conceptual ability of a chimpanzee and the relationship of generic and specific use of signs by that chimpanzee.[26] They used Lucy, a seven-year-old female chimpanzee with a vocabulary of seventy-five signs, as their subject. Lucy has been home-reared in a human home and isolated from other chimpanzees since she was two days old. The object of the study was to determine if Lucy would use a new food-related sign in a generic or specific manner. Just prior to the study, she had five food-related signs in her vocabulary, some that she used in a generic sense (*food, fruit, drink*) and two others that she used in a more specific manner (*candy* and *banana*). In the study, she was presented with twenty-four different fruits and vegetables randomly interspersed with other objects for which she had signs. She could pick these items up and do what she wished with them, and the experimenter asked her *what that* in Ameslan so that she would label them. After four days of baseline data collection using these items, Lucy was taught *berry*, using a cherry as the exemplar. This sign remained highly specific to cherries. After four more days of data collection, she was again taught the *berry* sign, but this time blueberries were used as the exemplar. She referred to the blueberries with the *berry* sign for the next two days and then went back to using the sign she had previously used to refer to blueberries.

More interesting was the manner in which Lucy labeled the other fruit and vegetable items. She showed a clear predisposition to use the *fruit* sign to label the fruit items (85 percent), and a predisposition to use the *food* sign to label vegetable items (65 percent). She also combined signs in her vocabulary in a novel fashion to describe items for which she did not have specific signs. For example, she referred to a one-quarter piece of water-melon as a *candy drink* or a *drink fruit* after the experimenter used signs she did have in her vocabulary (*water* and *melon*) to describe it. She labeled a radish with a *fruit food* or *drink* sign for three days until she took a bite out of it, and then she labeled it a *cry-hurt-food* and continued to use *cry* or *hurt* to describe it for the next eight days. She used the combination *smell-fruit* to describe the four citrus fruits in the twenty-four items.

Lucy clearly demonstrates the ability to combine spontaneously in a novel fashion different signs in her vocabulary to describe her concepts and perceptions of the various fruits and vegetables.

Another study examined the relationship between a chimpanzee's abil-ity to understand spoken English words and his ability to acquire signs that were taught using the vocal English words as exemplars for these words.[27] Ally, a home-reared male chimpanzee, was used as the subject. First, his ability to understand ten spoken English words was tested. After he met a criterion of five consecutive correct responses to vocal English commands, e.g., "Pick up the spoon," training was begun. He was taught a sign using the vocal English words as the exemplar. Then a blind condition was used to test for his transfer of the sign to the physical object that had originally been associated with the English word. Ally was able to transfer these signs to their physical referents. In this manner, he displayed the ability to learn a word in one language and then associate that word to a sign in another language, then to transfer the use of this sign to the physical object that the spoken word represented. This is somewhat analogous to second-language acquisition in humans where they learn a word in another language by associating it with the word in their own language that refers to the same thing.

Several other studies are going on at the Institute. We have examined the ability of a chimpanzee to obey novel commands in sign language using blind procedures to test his ability. For example, Ally was tested on his ability to choose one of five items and put it in one of three places when given a command in sign language such as *Put flower in purse*. His perform-ance seems far above the chance level of responding, but the experiment has not yet been completed.

The researchers at the Institute are at various stages of data collection in examining the ability of a chimpanzee to use prepositions such as *in, on,* and *under* to describe the relationship of physical objects to each other; e.g., a ball under a box. We are also testing a chimpanzee's ability to under-stand vocal English commands using the prepositional *in, on,* and *under*. There is another study examining the human-chimpanzee conversational relationship in which interaction is being observed as to who starts, main-tains, and terminates signing. We also have preliminary observations on chimpanzee-to-chimpanzee communication using Ameslan as the mode of communication.

The study conducted by Mellgren, Fouts, and Lemmon with the chimpanzee Lucy examined the conceptual abilities of chimpanzees as revealed by their use of various generic and specific signs. Here, Lucy makes the signs for toothbrush (top left), key (top right), watch (center left), ball (center right), brush (bottom left), and food (bottom right).

The research using sign language as the mode of communication between chimpanzees and humans has really only just begun. Ameslan is proving useful not only to show the linguistic capacities of chimpanzees but to explore the chimpanzee mentality in a way that was never before possible.

Conclusion

When the data on the linguistic abilities of chimpanzees are compared to data on the linguistic abilities of human beings, one problem is immediately noted: The experiments on humans have not displayed the scientific rigor that would make them comparable to the chimpanzee data. Until this is rectified, no adequate conclusion can be drawn.

Language itself should be examined as if it were a developmental process rather than a grouping of static stages. It is hoped that this approach will help in finding an acceptable definition of language, which does not exist at present. The development of the two species being compared should be taken into consideration as well. This should be done in such a way that the similarities of the two species are considered along with the differences. And these should be emphasized with regard to their relative importance. Also, caution should be taken to avoid the use of negative evidence or the absence of evidence when the similarities and differences between the two species are compared.

One final comparison should be made between the two differing approaches in establishing two-way communication with a chimpanzee. It was noted that a rigid predetermined paradigm derived from the Skinnerian method of operant conditioning tends to restrict the organism's behavior. Thus, only those behaviors that fit into the experimenter's predetermined paradigm are allowed to appear. This approach appears to have the drawback of limiting the organism to the experimenter's preconceived notions, and does not explore the complete capacities of that organism. When this approach is compared to the approach devised by the Gardners, it is easy to see which is more effective. Both approaches use acceptable controls in their testing, but the Gardners' approach does not obscure other important characteristics of the organism.

It is often the case that when an organism displays a behavior which the experimenter did not expect, the experimenter is prone to judge that the behavior is the result of error. But this is not necessarily the case. As a fellow scientist who also studies chimpanzees, Emil Menzel, once advised me: "You must remember that one man's error variance is another man's mean."

[1] Roger Brown, *A First Language: The Early Stages* (Cambridge, Mass.: Harvard University Press, 1973).

[2] David Premack, "A Functional Analysis of Language," *Journal of the Experimental Analysis of Behavior* 14, no. 1 (1970): 107–25.

David Premack, "Language in Chimpanzee?" *Science* 172 (21 May 1971): 808–22.

David Premack, "On the Assessment of Language Competence in the Chimpanzee," chap. 4 in *Behavior of Nonhuman Primates*, vol. 4, ed. Allan M. Schrier and Fred Stollnitz (New York: Academic Press, 1971), 186–228.

A. J. Premack and D. Premack, "Teaching Language to an Ape," *Scientific American* 227 (October 1972): 92–99.

[3] Premack and Premack, "Teaching Language to an Ape," p. 99.

[4] Brown, *A First Language*, p. 45.

[5] Ibid.

[6] B. F. Skinner, "Two 'Synthetic Social Relations,'" *Journal of the Experimental Analysis of Behavior* 5 (1962): 531–33.

[7] Brown, *A First Language*, p. 45.

[8] T. C. Schneirla, "Problems in the Biopsychology of Social Organization," in *Selected Writings of T. C. Schneirla*, ed. Lester R. Aronson et al. (San Francisco: W. H. Freeman & Co., 1972), pp. 417–39.

[9] Wolfgang Köhler, "Methods of Psychological Research with Apes," in *The Selected Papers of Wolfgang Köhler*, ed. Mary Henle (New York: Liveright, 1971), p. 215.

[10] Brown, *A First Language*.

[11] Oskar Pfungst, *Clever Hans (The Horse of Mr. von Osten)* (first English edition, 1911; New York: Holt, Rinehart & Winston, 1965).

[12] Premack, "Language in Chimpanzee?"

[13] Brown, *A First Language*.

[14] Premack, "Language in Chimpanzee?"

[15] R. A. Gardner and B. T. Gardner, Review of R. Brown's *A First Language: The Early Stages*, *American Journal of Psychology* (in press).

[16] D. M. Rumbaugh, T. V. Gill, and E. C. von Glasersfeld, "Reading and Sentence Completion by a Chimpanzee (Pan)," *Science* 182 (16 November 1973): 731–33.

[17] Ibid.

[18] R. A. Gardner and B. T. Gardner, "Teaching Sign Language to a Chimpanzee," *Science* 165 (15 August 1969): 664–72.

R. A. Gardner and B. T. Gardner, "Two-Way Communication with an Infant Chimpanzee," chap. 3 in *Behavior of Nonhuman Primates*, 4 : 117–82.

[19] R. S. Fouts, "The Use of Guidance in Teaching Sign Language to a Chimpanzee," *Journal of Comparative and Physiological Psychology* 80, no. 3 (September 1972): 515–22.

[20] R. S. Fouts and L. Goodin, "Acquisition of Signs in a Chimpanzee: A Comparison of Training Methods" (Paper presented at the Psychonomic Society Meeting in Boston, Mass., November 1974).

[21] Gardner and Gardner, "Two-Way Communication with an Infant Chimpanzee."

[22] Roger Brown, "The First Sentences of Child and Chimpanzee," in *Psycholinguistics: Selected Papers*, ed. R. Brown (New York: Free Press, 1970).

[23] Brown, *A First Language*, p. 41.

[24] Gardner and Gardner, Review of *A First Language*.

[25] R. S. Fouts, "Acquisition and Testing of Gestural Signs in Four Young Chimpanzees," *Science* 180 (1 June 1973): 978–80.

[26] R. Mellgren, R. S. Fouts, and W. Lemmon, "American Sign Language in the Chimpanzee: Semantic and Conceptual Functions of Signs" (Paper presented at the Midwestern Psychological Association Meeting in Chicago, Ill., May 1973).

[27] R. S. Fouts, W. Chown, and L. Goodin, "The Use of Vocal English to Teach American Sign Language (ASL) to a Chimpanzee: Translation from English to ASL" (Paper presented at the Southwestern Psychological Association Meeting in Dallas, Tex., April 1973).

Aspects of Induced Language in Chimpanzees

David McNeill

Professor McNeill, a native of California, received his doctorate from the
University of California at Berkeley, was a research fellow at Harvard, and
taught at the University of Michigan before being appointed professor of
psychology and linguistics at the University of Chicago in 1969. Throughout
his career he has been active in psycholinguistics, especially the field of
language development in children. The author of a standard work called *The
Acquisition of Language: The Study of Developmental Psycholinguistics*
(1970), he has in preparation what he characterizes as "a major theoretical
effort to describe and explain the relationship between thought and speech."
This project was undertaken at the Institute for Advanced Study, Princeton,
where Professor McNeill has just finished a two-year appointment.

Chimpanzees in the wild indulge in noisy outbursts sometimes called "carnivals." They hoot, screech, drum a great deal on logs and trees, uproot saplings, crash through the forest, and in general cause a tremendous uproar. According to Reynolds and Reynolds (1965), a husband and wife who lived in the Budongo Forest of equatorial Africa observing chimpanzees, "carnivals" take place anytime the animals are on the move—two or more groups arriving at the same place, one large group breaking up, a single group moving from one food supply to another one elsewhere. These are not battles. There is nothing antagonistic about them, and a battle would be quite contrary to the overall picture of social amiability that the chimpanzee presents. They are more like celebrations or spontaneous ceremonies. When two groups start to separate there are great waves of sound, backed up by prolonged drumrolls, and a continual coming and going of individuals between the separating groups, as if the animals are trying to decide which one to go with. The impression is indeed that of a "carnival" or festive spirit, albeit a spirit that is rather frighteningly energetic.

Goodall (1965) observed chimpanzees using a tool, a stick, to fish out termites. This use of tools is very limited. The tool is not fabricated in a special place using other tools; it has a single function; it is not used in a particular social context; and it is one of the few implements the wild chimpanzee is known to employ regularly. Nonetheless, sticks clearly function as tools for the chimpanzee. When termites are on the verge of migrating, their nests become riddled with holes in which they wait before emerging. During this time, chimpanzees will carefully insert a stick into one of these holes, hold it motionless for a moment, and then withdraw it coated with the termites, a delicacy they nibble with the lips. The stick is always about twelve inches long and must be stiff at the working end. If a piece is too short it is discarded. A long piece is trimmed. If the tip becomes bent, the chimpanzee will turn the stick around and use the opposite end or will break off the bent tip. In choosing a stick, a chimpanzee will carefully examine many candidates before picking one. One male, unsuccessfully trying to extract termites from an exceptionally deep hole with a stick that was the usual twelve inches long, looked around and selected a long vine that was growing several yards away. Goodall saw another chimpanzee carrying a grass stalk in his mouth for half a mile as he successively examined a half-dozen termite nests, looking for one that was ready.

Goodall also found evidence of what appeared to be a "fad" among the chimpanzees, implying social influence. Chimpanzees make nests in trees for sleeping at night. One year Goodall found a nest built in a palm tree for the first time. A year later, nests in palm trees were being built all over the Gombe Stream Reserve.

I mention these examples because they suggest strongly a generic resemblance to human activities, and we might ask whether we can find similarities between human language and the animal's use of an induced language. The sense in which chimpanzees can be said to have the use of a language system is about the same as the sense in which they have carnivals, make and use tools, or experience the movements of fashion. These general convergences with our own activities should prepare us to find a similar, loose convergence on language as well.

Such a phenomenon would be of great interest. It offers the possibility of using a symbolic communication system to study the mental life of another species, the question of what it is like to be a chimpanzee. And if we assume that language must emerge in any species in more or less the same way, inducing language in chimpanzees gives us a glimpse of language emergence as it might have been in the history of mankind itself.

There are several experiments, now, in which an attempt has been made to introduce a visually presented, manually executed language system to a young chimpanzee subject. These experiments have been remarkably successful in teaching the animals a vocabulary of words, and there clearly has been success as well in inducing some kind of productive language use in the chimpanzees. Nonetheless, the experiments unfortunately have been so limited that it is very difficult at the present stage to determine in what respects chimpanzees have the ability to learn a human language. I do not mean to raise the problem of defining a language. This problem is really a red herring, since satisfactory definitions of language are simply not available. The difficulty with the existing experiments on inducing language in a chimpanzee is not whether the experiments meet some definition or other of language but with the self-imposed limitations on the experiments themselves. It is almost impossible to acquire positive evidence on the question of the chimpanzee's language ability. The experiments seem to have been designed pessimistically, with the possibility of failure very much in the foreground. Given the long history of failed attempts to teach a spoken language to chimpanzees, this pessimistic attitude toward teaching a visual language is not hard to understand. The animals have been exposed to the simplest possible linguistic systems, languages so limited in structure that any success in training inevitably tells us very little

of what the animals are capable of doing. There is just not enough structure in the language itself to make its use very informative. A failure, of
course, would have been extremely informative, since then we could say
that chimpanzees cannot learn even this simple language, whatever it is.
But the problem is, ironically, that the experiments have *not* been failures.
They have been successes. Therefore, we learn only a little from them.

The first of the experiments was conceived and conducted by Gardner
and Gardner (1969, 1971), who taught American Sign Language (ASL) to
Washoe, an infant female chimpanzee. More recently, Rumbaugh, Gill,
and von Glasersfeld (1973) have taught a specially devised experimental
language called Yerkish to another young female chimpanzee, Lana. Further experiments along the lines of the original Washoe experiment are
being conducted elsewhere using ASL, but no generally available account
of results from these investigations has appeared.

A technical description of ASL would be impossible, since the language
itself is not well understood, but it is clear that many of the linguistic
processes that are used in most spoken languages are absent from ASL or
are used only rarely. There is no morphology to speak of, for example.
That is, there are no processes of word inflection (such as plural nouns
and verbs in English), and therefore no possibility of processes of inflec-
tional concord (such as using plural nouns only with plural verbs); there
are no formal means for introducing embedded or conjoined clauses;
there is no tense marking (itself usually a morphological process); there is
said to be little reliance on word order. These missing features do not
mean that Washoe (or deaf people) could not make use of the corresponding ideas, for example, the idea of a subordinate clause or of past tense,
but if Washoe were to use these ideas she would have to rely on the
nonlinguistic context to convey them to her partners in the conversation.
Nonlinguistic context has the inconvenient property (for our purposes as
students of the chimpanzee's language ability) of being present regardless
of what the animal does. Since the animal does not provide anything in a
positive action, we can never tell whether she actually has the ability to use
the particular idea in question for organizing a linguistic construction. The
nonlinguistic context may be meaningful to the observer, but without the
evidence of a positive response from the animal, we cannot conclude that
it is meaningful to the animal as a linguistic operation. Hence, the limitation imposed on the Washoe experiment by the language system itself. For
example, even though Washoe produces an utterance that refers to an
event that occurred in the past, we simply don't know if she would acquire
a past tense inflection, should one be provided to her; the temporal dimension might be quite inaccessible to her as something that could be
conveyed linguistically in every utterance.

In contrast to ASL, the structure of Yerkish is completely understood. It
is a totally artificial language, and all of its properties are known (*see* von
Glasersfeld, 1974). Many of the same comments made above about ASL

apply to Yerkish also. It has no morphology, no way of introducing embedded or conjoined clauses, and no tense system. Unlike ASL, it does have a fixed word order, and Lana has shown herself capable of acquiring that, an accomplishment I will turn to later.

What definitely has been incorporated into these two languages and what, therefore, the experiments can clearly show to be acquirable by chimpanzees is a vocabulary. In the case of Yerkish, there is also the ordering of vocabulary items into strings. A vocabulary may be sufficient to demonstrate language ability for some. But if one's interest extends beyond vocabulary learning, these experiments are capable at best of giving only hints, tantalizing hints, of linguistic processes dimly seen in the limited structures the animals are given in the experimental situation.

So little importance was given to aspects of language other than vocabulary in the Gardners' approach that they did not usually bother to record the order in which Washoe made sequences of signs; and when Washoe repeated signs, only one occurrence of each sign was noted. If Washoe produced two signs in opposite order in different utterances, the two utterances would be counted as the same. This may have been like equating "blind venetian" and "venetian blind." If Washoe produced the same sign more than once—for instance, Gimme Food Gimme—the utterance would be noted as a two-sign utterance. The Gardners apparently assumed that the repetition was part of the same utterance and that it made no difference whether the basic utterance was Gimme Food or Food Gimme (the choice of course would be arbitrary). Thus, not only was the language taught to Washoe lacking in many of the structural devices that one finds in a spoken human language, the Gardners systematically rejected most evidence Washoe might have produced that could show a grasp of structure, so strong was their preoccupation with vocabulary (*see* Gardner and Gardner, 1971, p. 168).

We must, therefore, look very carefully indeed if we want to find evidence of linguistic organization in Washoe's use of ASL. I think there is evidence for a certain kind of organization, some of which appears in Lana's use of Yerkish as well. Viewed in this way, the two experiments complement each other.

First and most unexpected are two rules of word order (if we can call them rules) that are based on *social* and *emotional* processes. These appear to be unique to Washoe. Word order in a human language such as English, Japanese, or French generally depends on the speaker's awareness of particular cognitive conceptions. In English, for example, agents appear before instruments, as in "The burglar (agent) opened the window with a crowbar (instrument)." Agent and instrument are functions defined within the speaker's cognitive understanding of a given situation. Washoe has devised a rule in which word order corresponds to social relationships. In a high proportion of the applicable cases, addressees precede and nonaddressees follow, as in these examples (these utterances and all others cited are taken from a corpus of eighty-five specimens for which the word order is known; *see* McNeill, 1974):

> Naomi hug
> You me out
> You out me
> You tickle me Washoe
> Open key

The chimpanzee is a social sort of animal, and perhaps it is not utterly out of the question that it would find the social distinction between addressee and nonaddressee so important that it would become an organizational basis for utterances. There is nothing directly parallel to this in human languages, unless we consider the little formula for polite conversation, "you before I," as a partial equivalent.

A second "rule" seems to be related to the process of grading in primate communication (Marler and Hamilton, 1966). A graded signal—vocalizations that range from low intensity to high—can change continuously in correspondence with a gradation of emotion. Most natural graded signals vary along a sensory dimension of some kind, such as loudness or duration. Washoe used the number of individual signs in a message as a form of grading as well. The more urgent or important the basic meaning of the message, the longer it tended to become. The utterances seem to have no internal structure in these cases, only the basic meaning (such as "open" or "help-with-the-key") and the length of the utterance itself, corresponding to urgency. For example,

> Please Open Hurry
> Open Key Help Hurry
> More More More Sweet Drink

The "rule" Washoe followed in these utterances can be described as follows,

$$S \rightarrow P^n$$

where S is the sequence of signs, P is the basic message Washoe wants to convey, and n is the number of signs proportional to Washoe's sense of urgency (McNeill, 1974). Little children follow a version of this rule when they repeat utterances over and over out of excitement. Washoe also repeated signs, which the Gardners ignored, as already noted. Unlike Washoe, however, children repeat whole phrases or sentences and do not add on words regardless of grammatical constraints.

In a more cognitive direction, we can find two other principles behind Washoe's utterances. At least one of these appears to be in use by Lana as well. Virtually all of Washoe's utterances describe causal events. No doubt her concern with causation is connected with her life circumstances, her living at the Gardners' home under a certain amount of restraint, where nearly everything that happens of interest to Washoe is under the control of others. Lana's life situation is similar in this regard, and she too seems to organize utterances based on causal events.

In Washoe's case, the following diagram summarizes her word order in nearly all utterances (94 percent):

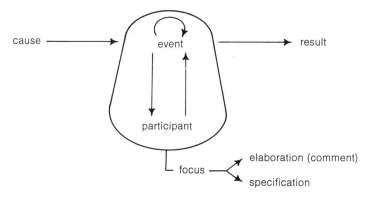

For the central part of the figure, where there is no specific order based on the structure of causal events, the order of words is determined so that a focus is followed by some kind of additional information, either elaborative or specificative (*see* Peters, 1974). Examples of each pair combination in this schema will illustrate most of the patterns Washoe uses:

Cause-Event	Roger You-Tickle
Event-Result	Key Open Please-Blanket
Participant-Event	Baby-Up (means: lift the baby doll up)
Event-Participant	Tickle-Me
Event-Event	Listen-Food (Food refers to the ringing of the dinner bell)
Focus-Elaboration	Baby-Up
Focus-Specification	Listen-Food

The diagram above merely summarizes the patterns that are found among the eighty-five examples in terms of causal events. It is not a picture of what might have been occurring inside Washoe as she produced these utterances. Nevertheless, we can get some feeling for the psychological significance of the patterns if we try to think of parallels with human speech.

There is a strong tendency with us, also, to mention causes early in utterances and effects late (*see* Wason and Johnson-Laird, 1972, for many examples from university students). For whatever reason, people tend to think of causes as preceding their effects, and chimpanzees apparently are no exception to this tendency. Phenomenologically, causes often seem to occur before effects. One sees the hammer raised, then plunging down and striking the nail which is driven into the wood. The cause is seen in the plunging hammer and the effect in the driven nail, corresponding to the temporal sequence of events. If Washoe is capable of forming mental pictures of situations, she could use this same phenomenological sense of cause and effect to arrange words in the cause-first, result-last order.

The occurrence of the focus before and the additional information after, which is the way Washoe organizes utterances about causes that do not have an order otherwise, also exists in human speech. We too tend to start utterances with a semantic focus; e.g., "Bill ... what's wrong with him?" There are even special grammatical devices in English (and other languages) for rearranging sentences so as to place the focus in initial position when it normally would not appear there; for example, "Watermelon is what Bill likes." Washoe's method is perhaps a primitive version of this same process.

A large fraction of Washoe's sequences of signs follow the patterns shown above. It is difficult to deny that these are languagelike performances. Washoe is capable of producing signs in accordance with certain semantic concepts—cause, event, result, etc.—and arranging these within the limits of the causal paradigm to meet her communicative needs. The same process occurs in human languages, using even some of the same patterns. At the same time, however, we must not forget how very limited Washoe's linguistic system is. She has none of the syntactic processes that make human speech flexible. It is not clear, for example, how Washoe could resolve a conflict between her two principles of causation and importance—what if the semantic focus is on the result? Washoe must choose one principle to be secondary in this case, whereas a human speaker generally can find a grammatical construction that will serve both principles simultaneously. Whether or not Washoe can acquire the use of elaborate grammatical operations remains unknown, since there has been no attempt to teach them to her.

Lana, another young female chimpanzee, has been taught to produce messages by pressing buttons on a console that activate a computer. At any given moment, she is faced with an array of buttons, each bearing a distinct symbol and referring to a particular object, action, quality, or semantic operation (such as negation). She must press the buttons in a particular sequence, usually five or six of them, the order determined by the rules of the Yerkish grammar. Her training has emphasized the unalterability of word order. The computer will accept only correct sequences, and each sequence is individually taught. Since the physical arrangement of keys on Lana's console changes from time to time, the possibility is removed of her having merely memorized a sequence of movements. The significance of the keys themselves, of course, never varies.

In the most recent reports (e.g., Rumbaugh and Gill, 1974) Lana is

Lana and her computer.
"Please machine . . ."

"Please machine give . . ."

"Please machine give piece of . . ."
Lana's finger is on the "apple" key.
Her left hand activates the computer.

Lana obtains a slice of apple after
completing the sentence "Please
machine give piece of apple period."

described as regularly producing such utterances as the following (each capitalized word stands for a button on the console):

> ? Lana Drink This Out-of Room (The symbol for a question or request is in initial position.)
> Please Machine Give Coke
> ? Tim Give Cup Which-is Red

She also can correctly complete sequences of symbols her handlers have started. If she is shown Please Machine Give _ _ _, for example, she will press the button for Coke or Milk but not the one for Tim or Music (Rumbaugh, Gill, and von Glasersfeld, 1973).

Of course, the fact that Lana can produce utterances with strict word order sequences is not in itself proof that she has integrated all the semantic ideas a human speaker has with the same sequences. There is a question of what the production units are. This question is not the same as the question of order. At a minimum level, each sequence could itself be a single unit. In this case, there would be no internal structure; the meaning of the utterance would be associated with the string as a whole, and since the chimpanzee has been taught to tap out each sequence in a strict order, she would be able to respond appropriately. At a maximum level, the various semantic components of the meaning of the utterance (Lana, drinking, a substance, a location) are differentially associated with each of the parts of the utterance (the words of the first utterance above, for example). Here, the chimpanzee would construct the utterance in a grammatical way from the semantic parts. Obviously there are intermediate possibilities also, where the production unit is not the whole utterance but neither is it an individual word. There is a construction of the utterance, as in the maximal case, but the building blocks themselves are sequences without an internal structure. Since the training of Lana demanded strict sequentiality, and each string was individually taught, she would produce correctly ordered strings no matter what the size of the production unit was.

The evidence seems to show that this unit is at an intermediate level and in fact is rather similar to the production units involved in some of Washoe's utterances. This evidence takes the form of certain linguistic innovations on Lana's part, where she has gone beyond the language she was taught. These innovations, technically errors, are among the most powerful forms of evidence available to us in trying to understand Lana's true linguistic system. In studying children's language, very similar problems of interpretation arise. For example, if a child says "Billy get it," should we suppose that he knows how to produce pronoun objects in sentences? Our question is answered if we hear the child say "Billy get it my ladder." What appeared at first to be a pronoun object turns out to be a part of the verb for the child, a fact we can discover only from the child's innovative use of the "pronoun" *it*.

Lana produces an innovation in the following "conversation" with T. Gill,

> Lana: Milk Name-of This.
> Tim: Yes.
> Lana: Milk Name-of This.
> Tim: Yes.
> Lana: Milk This.
> Lana: ? Tim Give Lana Coffee.
> Tim: No.
> Lana: ? Tim Move Milk Coffee. (This is the innovation. In Yerkish, and in all Lana's previous experience, Move is used only in an intransitive, noncausative sense. An example would be Tim Move Behind Room, where the object moved and the mover are the same. Here, in contrast, the word is transitive and causative.)
> Tim: Yes.
> Lana: Milk Of This Coffee.
> Lana: ? Tim Move Milk Behind. (The new use of Move again.)
> Tim: ? Behind What.
> Lana: ? Tim Move Milk Behind Room.
> Tim: Yes. (Tim loads the vending device that the computer operates.)
> Lana: Please Machine Give Milk.

Lana's innovative use of a noncausative verb as a causative occurs in the speech of children, also. They will say such things as "I'm gonna fall this on her" or "I'm singing him" (Bowerman, 1974). Whatever the explanation, it is necessary to suppose that the subject (Lana or child) is thinking of utterances in terms of causes. The basic meaning of the word Move in Yerkish in such examples as Tim Move Behind Room does not involve causation. By adding the idea of cause to Move, Lana produced the innovation, Tim Move Milk Behind Room (parallel to children's adding cause to *fall* or *sing*).

The innovation, then, took place at a level of structure suggested by the following:

Cause	Result
Tim Move	Milk Behind Room

Whether Lana differentiated these generic components into smaller components (e.g., into a location, Behind Room) is not clear. The order of words alone tells us nothing about this, since she had been taught to produce just such sequences as the locative Behind Room. Perhaps she did differentiate the utterance into more refined levels. Nevertheless, we can be certain that she formed it at least at the intermediate level of Cause + Result and, in this respect, resembles Washoe in the process of linguistic construction.

Lana's "conversations" show that, whatever the actual level of construction, the animal is able to use the linguistic system she has been taught in a purposive and appropriate way. It is difficult to deny that Lana has the capacity to organize and control novel utterances by manipulating semantic ideas, each associated with a particular verbal formation, and that she does this to achieve definite communicative purposes (e.g., getting Tim to load the computer-operated vending device). This form of activity, and the organization of utterances according to modular semantic units, is the essence of linguistic communication as we understand and expect it within a human language.

In many respects, however, the two chimpanzees' use of language differs profoundly from that of a human's, child or adult. These differences cannot be reduced, because they are built into the linguistic systems the animals are learning. The assumption of the experiments seems to have been that the chimpanzees would find acquiring any sort of grammar or morphology difficult, and consequently these processes were excluded. We have no idea if this belief is justified. It may indeed be true that chimpanzees have difficulty learning how to control, for example, tense marking, plural marking, case marking (as with *she/her* in English), pronominalization, subject-verb inversion, clause embedding, topicalization, compounding, etc.; or they may have no special difficulty with some or all of these. Future experiments on inducing languagelike communication in chimpanzees should give serious thought to incorporating some of the morphological and syntactic processes of a human language in order to produce a more revealing test of the animals' language ability than the simple structures used so far can provide.

To illustrate one such process that has been studied in children, I will describe the acquisition of the distinction in use between *ask* and *tell* in complex sentences with embedded clauses. This remote corner of English is the scene of a great battle children wage on their way to mastery of the language, usually around age seven or eight years. The evidence of their effort, the errors the children make, illustrates the kind of observation that should be sought from chimpanzees as language learners. I do not mean to suggest that chimpanzees should duplicate the performance of children with *ask* and *tell*, but that sufficient structure should be incorporated into the languages they are taught so that observations comparable to these illustrations become at least possible.

The sentences in question are the following:

1. Ask Jill what color this book is.

2. Tell Jill what color this tray is.
3. Ask Jill what's in the box.
4. Tell Jill what's on the table.
5. Ask Jill what to feed the dog.
6. Tell Jill what to feed the horse.

Chomsky (1969) carried out an experiment in which she used sentences like these as directions to child subjects, who followed her instructions as they understood them. The child's response reflects his understanding. There was always another child present, a classmate (Jill in the examples above), and various toy objects—a dog, a horse, articles of food, etc.

With sentences of relatively simple structure such as examples 1 through 4 above, children of seven and eight are generally able to respond correctly:

> Ask Jill what color this book is.
> —What color's that book?
> Tell Jill what color this tray is.
> —Tan

However, with more complicated sentences such as 5 and 6, more complicated because they require the child to work out for himself what the subject is for the second verb (*feed*), the children became confused:

> Ask Jill what to feed the dog.
> —The hot dog

They respond as if the instruction had been *to tell* Jill what to feed the dog. This confusion persists even though the instruction stresses that asking is what is wanted:

> Now I want you to *ask* Jill something. *Ask* her what to feed the dog.
> —The piece of bread

The difficulty with such sentences is specifically linked to the syntactic process by which the child tries to find a subject for the second verb. When the instruction is reworded to provide an explicit grammatical subject, the child is successful:

> Ask Jill what *you* should feed the dog.
> —What should I feed the dog?

It is not the particular words that the child fails to understand. What he does not understand is the role of the words in the structure of the sentence. The child's assumption appears to be that whatever anterior noun is closest to the verb is the subject. Often, this approach to sentence structure works (as it would with "Ask Jill what Mike should eat"), but it misfires with sentences like 5. Such sentences must seem to be misshapen things to a child, but his principle for finding the subject requires that Jill be the performer of the action, and so the child himself is forced to be a teller and not an asker. The same process occurs in sentences produced by children, such as "I promised you to give me a cookie" (said accusingly and meaning "You promised to give me a cookie").

From little mistakes like these, we learn something of the process by which the child assimilates the structure of his language. He begins by thinking that successive words in speech are directly related to each other, and only later discovers that in certain cases words that are not successive can also be directly related. The child must now add a complication to his own language system in order to meet the complexity of the language he is learning, which turns out to be greater than he initially supposed. The process bears a resemblance to hypothesis formation and testing (except that the child is not usually conscious of what he does).

It seems that similar questions are worth asking about the chimpanzee's language learning. Does the chimpanzee also begin with the assumption that successive words are directly related? Can it discover localized exceptions to generalized grammatical rules? Does it form and revise hypotheses? Answering these questions and many others unavoidably requires complicating the language systems taught to the animals. They must go significantly beyond anything now in use. Such work will be tedious and frustrating, for it seeks to produce errors, but I hope I have explained sufficiently the importance of undertaking it.

It is only in this way that we shall find just how these surprising primates, humans, converge onto the chimpanzee and vice versa.

BIBLIOGRAPHY

BOWERMAN, MELISSA. "Learning the Structure of Causative Verbs: A Study in the Relationship of Cognitive, Semantic and Syntactic Development." In *Papers and Reports on Child Language Development*, Committee on Linguistics, Stanford University, June 1974.

CHOMSKY, CAROL. *The Acquisition of Syntax in Children from 5 to 10*. Cambridge, Mass.: M.I.T. Press, 1969.

GARDNER, BEATRICE T., and GARDNER, R. ALLEN. "Two-Way Communication with an Infant Chimpanzee." In *Behavior of Nonhuman Primates*, edited by ALLAN M. SCHRIER and FRED STOLLNITZ. New York: Academic Press, 1971.

GARDNER, R. A., and GARDNER, B. T. "Teaching Sign Language to a Chimpanzee." *Science* 165 (15 August 1969): 664–72.

GOODALL, JANE. "Chimpanzees of the Gombe Stream Reserve." In *Primate Behavior*, edited by IRVEN DE VORE. New York: Holt, Rinehart & Winston, 1965.

MARLER, PETER, and HAMILTON, WILLIAM J., III. *Mechanisms of Animal Behavior*. New York: John Wiley & Sons, 1966.

McNEILL, D. "Sentence Structure in Chimpanzee Communication." In *The Growth of Competence*, edited by K. J. CONNOLLY and J. S. BRUNER. London: Academic Press, 1974.

PETERS, C. R. "On the Possible Contribution of Ambiguity of Expression to the Development of Proto-linguistic Performance." In *Language Origins*, edited by G. W. HEWES, W. C. STOKOE, and R. W. WESCOTT. Silver Spring, Md.: Linstok Press, 1974.

REYNOLDS, V., and REYNOLDS, F. "Chimpanzees in the Budongo Forest." In *Primate Behavior*, edited by I. DE VORE. New York: Holt, Rinehart & Winston, 1965.

RUMBAUGH, D. M., and GILL, T. V. "Language, Apes, and the Apple Which-is Orange, Please." Paper presented at Fifth International Congress of Primatology. Nagoya, Japan, 1974.

RUMBAUGH, D. M., GILL, T. V., and VON GLASERSFELD, E. C. "Reading and Sentence Completion by a Chimpanzee (Pan)." *Science* 182 (16 November 1973): 731–33.

VON GLASERSFELD, E. C. "The Yerkish Language for Non-Human Primates." Unpublished paper. Department of Psychology, University of Georgia, 1974.

WASON, PETER C., and JOHNSON-LAIRD, P. N. *Psychology of Reasoning*. Cambridge, Mass.: Harvard University Press, 1972.

Speech Communication: The Sign of Mankind

Frank E. X. Dance

A native of Brooklyn, Mr. Dance was educated first at Fordham University
and subsequently at Northwestern University, from which he received his
doctorate in 1959. He has held a variety of teaching and advisory positions
in his special area of speech communication, and is now professor of this
subject at the University of Denver, where he has been since 1973. Active in
many academic, professional, and business organizations concerned with
speech and communication, he is the author of *The Citizen Speaks: Speech
Communication for Adults* (1962) as well as coauthor or coeditor of other
works of a similar nature. He has also published more than 40 articles in his
field as well as a number of monographs, has contributed papers to some 80
conferences at various times and in various places, and has given nearly 700
lectures on speech communication theory and education to professional
audiences in the course of his professional career.

One of the problems in any discussion of language, and in particular of speech communication, is that what we are discussing is itself both the instrument and the subject of the discussion. It is difficult to examine an instrument using the very instrument which is the subject of the examination. How does one know whether or not there may be a serious blind spot at the point where the examining instrument touches the examined instrument? This is especially true when we are examining language, because language is the universal human instrument. If I want to measure a screwdriver I can do so using an instrument other than a screwdriver—a pair of calipers, for example—but the only instrument available for examining language is language itself. Highly sophisticated instruments can be used for measuring certain physical qualities of language—wave shape and length, acoustic dimensions, and so forth—but such technical measurements must always be translated back into a natural language before they can be understood.

Given such a difficulty, it helps if we make our examining instrument as precise as possible. Consider the indefiniteness of the terminology ordinarily used when talking about the subject of talking. *Speech communication, language, speech, information, communication, sign,* and *symbol* are all likely to make their appearance in any consideration of man's remarkable and seemingly unique capacity. Even within the essays in this symposium you may find what seems to be a pervasive terminological confusion. If words are viewed as labels or terms which point to concepts, and if we then try to look behind the words so as to locate and understand the concepts to which the words point, we may be able to analyze and understand the points of agreement and disagreement that exist among scholars who are trying to examine man's capacity for spoken symbolic interaction.

In an effort to gain terminological and conceptual precision, we can move from the more general to the more specific term in a deductive manner. The most general term is *stimulus*. For our purposes a stimulus is the smallest unit of sensory input, either internal (such as a stomach twinge) or external (such as the honking of a car horn), that rouses the mind. From among the innumerable stimuli to which we are exposed there are some that cause us to focus our attention; such stimuli cause us to exclude the external or internal world at large and to focus upon some particular thing or things. When this happens the stimulus may be labeled *information*, because it causes us to restrict our focus, to limit our attention, to reduce the variability of our environment by concentrating our attention on a portion of that environment. Information results when a stimulus influences us in such a way as to reduce disorder or uncertainty.

The centering of attention, or the reduction of uncertainty, is not the same thing as the assignment of meaning. Information is the result of the quantitative reduction of disorder. The assignment of meaning to information is *communication*. Obviously stimuli, information, and communication are not restricted to mankind. Living organisms other than man are affected by stimuli, attend to one stimulus or a concentration of stimuli from among all those available, and act upon the information that is perceived. Communication always involves action; that is its peculiar attribute, just as the peculiar attribute of information is that it results in the reduction of uncertainty.

Speech is a genetically determined, individual, psycho-physiological activity consisting of the production of phonated, articulated sound through the interaction and coordination of cortical, laryngeal, and oral structures. So defined, speech will be seen as tied to a specific producing organism and as capable of existing only in concrete actualities. Although it can be developed in some species through training (parrots, mynah birds, etc.), it seems to develop spontaneously only in human beings. Speech is independent of meaning; the sounds produced by a babbling infant, though meaningless to him, can be considered speech.

A *sign* is a stimulus having a fixed and concrete meaning regardless of context. A sign often announces that of which it is a part. Although *human* communication *makes use* of signs, all *nonhuman animal* communication *consists* of signs. In a dog, panting is a sign of physiological effort to restore internal temperature balance, tail wagging is a sign of a pleasant internal state; both the panting and the tail wagging are biologically tied to the activity which they announce. Whereas signs are contextually fixed, symbols are contextually flexible.

A *symbol* is a learned stimulus having a contextually flexible, arbitrary, and abstract meaning. Whereas signs are always used by nonhuman animals and may be used by man, symbols are peculiar to man and may never be used by nonhuman animals. Unlike the sign, which is often biologically tied to that to which it refers, a symbol's meaning is arbitrarily assigned to the symbolic stimulus by its users and is independent of the thing to which the symbol refers. One can often predict the context from the presence of the sign, but a symbol depends upon the specific context for its meaning. ("Flag," a symbol, changes its meaning dependent upon the context in which it is used. "Salute the flag." "Don't flag in your efforts." "Flag the car down.") It needs to be noted that a single stimulus can serve both as a sign and as a symbol, since man can attribute meaning to anything. Thunder, a *sign* of the dissipation of heat in the atmosphere, can also be assigned the *symbolic* meaning of "gods talking." A dog's tail wagging, a *sign* of internal harmony in the dog, can also be a code, "When the dog's tail wags, jump in

When signs are symbols: *"Whereas signs are always used by nonhuman animals and may be used by man, symbols are peculiar to man and may never be used by nonhuman animals."*

"An individual's speech communication first develops as a result of the individual organism being set into relationships with others, principally responding adults."

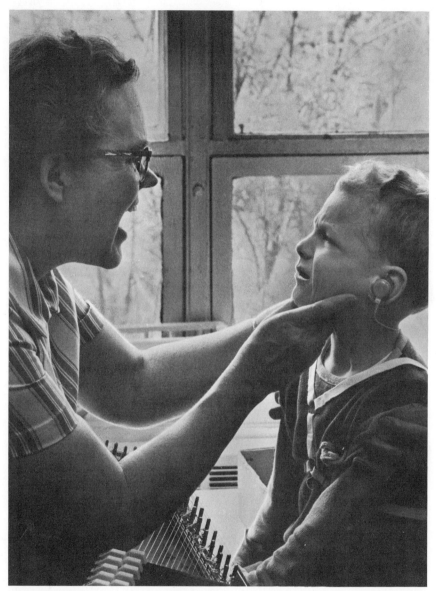

"A child deprived of acoustic perception may, indeed, after arduous labors on his own part as well as on the part of his teachers, acquire some language skill, but that skill always evidences the effects of perceptual deprivation."

your cars and drive to the sea." Once symbols have been initially developed by the individual, symbols can be auditory (a spoken word), visual (thumbs up, a road sign, a logo), tactile ("Two taps on the hand means yes, one means no"), olfactory ("When you smell onions, it's time to go"), gustatory ("The taste of caviar means money") or kinesthetic/proprioceptive, ("When your heart starts racing, you're in love").

When signs or symbols are systematized, we have a *language*. Animal languages are systems of signs. Human languages are systems of signs and symbols. Although the capacity and propensity for the acquisition of human language may be innate in man, the specific languages themselves (English, German, Chinese, etc.) are culturally determined and learned.

There comes a time in human development when genetically determined speech comes into interface with culturally determined language; the product of this contact is a fusion of the two previous behaviors and the resultant emergence of a qualitatively new behavior, a behavior which is more than a simple jointure of the previous behaviors of speech and of language, a behavior which is specifically human, a behavior we call *speech communication*. The individual production of a specific language is the best example of speech communication.

There are differences, then, among such terms as *information, communication, speech, sign, symbol, language,* and *speech communication*. Keeping these differences in mind in our effort to understand man's seemingly unique behavior of spoken symbolic interaction, we shall find it especially useful to discuss speech communication, for it is this act that combines information, communication, speech, and the systematized signs and symbols that comprise language.

An individual's speech communication first develops as a result of the individual organism being set into relationships with others, principally responding adults. Through such relationships the individual infant acquires a self-concept that defines the infant's personhood. This primal self-concept and resultant personhood endures across the multitudinous roles (child, student, parent, employee, employer, et al.) that the individual will fill throughout life. The primal personhood will change and grow, but there will always be maintained the core developed in infancy (unless that core is destroyed by severe physical or psychic trauma). It is for this reason that early developmental experiences are so very important in the shaping of individual character. The infant derives personality from this early communicative interaction.

Once the child has some self-concept, he can proceed to develop his own first level of speech communication, which is intrapersonal. At this first level the individual establishes and maintains symbolic communication within himself. There are those who feel that most, if not all, mental illnesses have their roots in the intrapersonal level of speech communication. In first-level speech communication the individual acts as both sender and receiver of communicative information.

The second level is that of *inter*personal speech communication. Here the sender and receiver are usually two individuals whose human communicative interaction is characterized by the need to focus upon areas of interest or concern with respect to which they are not in total accord. When two people are in total accord about a subject, there is little if any reason for sustained symbolic interaction.

At the third level of speech communication one person communicates with a number of other persons. Public speaking is a typical instance of third-level speech communication; other examples are teaching, lecturing, and entertaining.

All three levels of speech communication are dynamically interrelated. An individual's intrapersonal speech communication (how he talks to himself) affects how he talks to others, whether on the second or third level. On the other hand, the way a person is talked *to* may well affect the way he talks to himself. All of us are familiar with examples, drawn either from our own lives or from the lives of others, wherein a person's behavior and self-concept have been modified as a result of the way others have communicated with him. Religious or political conversion, interrogation techniques, courtship, and other persuasive campaigns work through the levels of speech communication for the alteration of individual attitudes, beliefs, and behavior.

Instruments of mass communication (the press, radio, television, films, et al.) are substitutes for one or more of the primary levels of speech communication. Indeed, as Marshall McLuhan has entertainingly demonstrated,[1] mass communication can and generally does alter the content of the message it conveys by its techniques of dissemination, which become a message of their own, but mass communication is ultimately dependent upon the underlying levels of speech communication.

These levels of speech communication afford investigators a basis for discussion of the ways in which human communicative behavior develops and interacts. The levels are not themselves evidence of the importance of speech communication in human development and behavior.

A mounting body of speculation and supportive evidence indicates that speech communication in the human being performs at least three functions.[2] These are: (1) the linking of the individual with his human environment, (2) the development of higher mental processes, and (3) the regulation of human behavior. It is important to note the stress on *human* in functions one and three, and on *higher* in function two. Animals other than man link themselves with their environment, exhibit some kinds of mental processes, and regulate both their own behavior and the behavior of others. The functions of speech communication serve to make possible a peculiarly *human* kind of linkage and regulation, and the development of *higher* mental processes. Man, being an animal, shares the capacities and capabilities of other animals but adds capacities and capabilities which are peculiarly human, which are indeed species specific. Chief among these

47

"Instruments of mass communication (the press, radio, television, films, et al.) are substitutes for one or more of the primary levels of speech communication."

species-specific capacities and capabilities is the development of spoken symbolic interaction and its derivatives, reading and writing.

The initiation of the first function of speech communication is the process that we earlier discussed as having taken place in the development of the individual's self-concept and personhood. Earlier, the focus was upon the speech communication levels in which this process occurred. Now, we are interested in the process itself. The linking function starts with the emergence of self-concept and continues throughout the life span. It is through speech communication and its attendant symbols that individuals and societies are constituted and maintained. When this linking function is distorted or destroyed, there will always be a corresponding decrement in the integrity of an individual or of a society. It is through the first, linking function that man finds his own individual and social identity and being.

The second, or mentation, function demonstrates the bond between speech communication and thought. It is through speech communication that man develops and maximizes the higher mental processes of memory, thinking, planning and foresight, intelligence, judgment, and the derivatives of speech communication, reading and writing. While serving as a potentiator for the other higher mental processes, speech communication itself serves as the prototype of a higher mental process. Speech communication is the means by which man can transform the perceptual thought of infrahuman organisms into the conceptual thought peculiar to himself.[3] The speech communication instrument underlying this capacity is the spoken symbol. It is the symbol, which is in its human origin spoken, that creates and manifests the primal capacity for decentering or displacement and thus leads, when joined in syntactic structures, to the development of the intentionality that first characterizes speech communication and then is found in all higher mental processes.

Since speech communication defined in this way is species specific, it becomes apparent that speech communication and human communication are coterminous concepts and may be substituted one for another at any time. Communication between humans also includes communicative devices common to other animals, but as such devices are not uniquely human, they do not contribute to uniquely human communication.

The spoken symbol's primal capacity for decentering or displacement may well be the most important quality of symbolization. In the course of a child's development, its external speech communication is gradually internalized. When the child says "mama" aloud, presumably at the same time he also says "mama" silently to himself. As he progresses, he comes to the point where he can say "mama" silently to himself without any external vocalization. When the child has reached the point of complete inner speech communication, he has developed the ability to predicate the existence of "mama" when mama is not within sight or hearing. This interior representation of "mama" or "papa" or "outside" or "bow-wow" elevates the child's capacity for decentering, for displacement, for moving away from the immediacy of the moment or the immediacy of a personally experienced locale. The capacity for decentering potentiates the child's flexibility in adaptation and control of himself and of his environment. It is precisely this decentering afforded by speech communication that allows for the development of a self-concept, of personhood, on the part of the human child. The spoken symbol, the performative instrument of speech communication, allows the human child to step aside from the immediacy of the moment and of his participation in the events of the moment and to see himself from a point outside of himself and thus view himself relating to the events around him. Through speech communication experiences the child forms a concept of himself separate from any specific event or time, a concept which becomes enduring and identifiable, a self-concept.[4]

Such a capacity for "shifting," for "decentering," is also the essential characteristic of intent. To have intent, one must be able to move away from the immediacy of the moment, to shift from the present to the past and to the future. The planning and evaluation which is at the heart of intentionality is created and supported by the capacity to shift arising from speech communication. This shift, which leads to self-concept and intent, may well be the primal shift that enabled man, by combining his animal nature and his decentered intent, to join with other men in the creation of society and civilization. As Susanne K. Langer states it: "The rise of language in the Hominidae marked the completion of the 'Great Shift' from animal to man. The power of speech transformed the genus *Homo* and every aspect of its ambient; for with speech came thought and remembrance, intuition, conception and reason. With words—in dim, distant and very long ages—some strange, unimaginable ancestors of ours built up the human world."* [5]

The derivatives of speech communication (writing, reading, gesture dependent for meaning upon symbolic referents, and so forth) give it a fixture, a permanence which is in contrast to the ephemeral character of its acoustic source. Sound fades rapidly, but print and writing last, and in so doing they give stability to speech communication, allowing human beings to isolate and stabilize ideas in space and time, where they may be objectively studied.

When symbols, either in their original spoken form or as expressed through another modality such as sight, are joined in syntactical structures, intentionality becomes prominent. All speech communication is intentionally constituted. Although Merleau-Ponty assigns intent to bodily action,[6] the intent of such action is a projection (and oftentimes a weak

---

* The mixing of *language, speech,* and *words* in Dr. Langer's writing illustrates the need for a consistent taxonomy. If, in each instance, you substitute *speech communication* and the concept for which the term stands, the quote loses none of its force and gains in its accuracy.

projection) of the intent of speech communication, which sometimes, but not always, directs the action. As far as we now know, through psychophysiological experimentation involving the electrical stimulation of the human cortex, an individual can be artificially excited to the production of grunts, groans, and screams, but he cannot be artificially excited to the production of a single spoken word. He cannot be artificially excited to the production of spoken symbols either in isolation or joined together into a grammatical language. The utterance of a symbol, the performative instrument of speech communication, is always and in all ways volitional and intentional. As we ascend the evolutionary scale, we ascend the scale of degree of intent found in nervous system processes. The evolution of intent manifests ever more consciousness until the consciousness of intent becomes so patent as to result in the organism's self-consciousness, at which point the human organism becomes overtly aware of its own intent. The development of decentering, of intentionality, and of higher mental processes builds in a direct ratio, phylogenetically, ontogenetically, and in discrete individual behaviors.

This discussion of decentering and of intentionality has been part of the consideration of the second function of speech communication, the development of higher mental processes. The social quest for the development of higher mental processes in the individual and in society is realized in formal education and especially in the liberal arts. All of the liberal arts are concerned with the development and augmentation of the individual capacity to use man's unique sign, the symbol. The use of language in general, as embodied in the individual's speech communication, and then the use of specific languages, such as mathematics, philosophy, or chemistry, constitute the liberal arts which allow the individual ever widening control over symbols and their specific applications. Man, through the symbol, decenters first from himself and then from the immediacy of his chronological moment and his geographical space. The liberal arts are those which augment either the first or the second of these decenterings. Man's use of the spoken symbol and the attendant development of conscious intent also leads to the development of choice, and it is choice which is the instrument of freedom, of being liberated.

The third function of speech communication is the regulation of human behavior. This behavior regulation includes the regulation of the self and of others, both internally and externally. When I give myself instructions (how to run a complicated machine for the first time; how to get from one place to another in a new town), I am engaging in the self-regulation of behavior through speech communication. When I give a child instructions, I am engaging in the regulation of the behavior of another through speech communication. Persuasion, exhortation, argument, the writing of textbooks, the preparation of propaganda are all examples of this third function of speech communication.

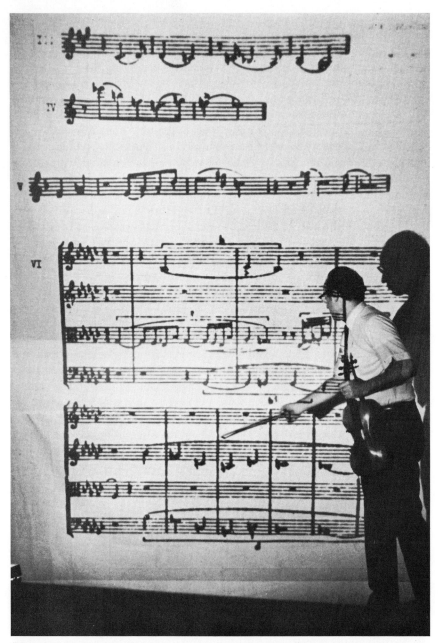

"The use of language in general ... and ... the use of specific languages, such as mathematics, philosophy, or chemistry, constitute the liberal arts which allow the individual ever widening control over symbols and their specific applications."

The three functions of speech communication point directly to the development of what seems to be uniquely human about humanity.

Throughout this essay allusion has been made to the *spoken* mode of symbolic interaction. There are many who believe in what may be called modal equipotentiality. Modal equipotentiality maintains that among the various modes of human symboling (the spoken mode, the written mode, the gestured mode, etc.) all are equally important. Such a position has a surface attraction to it, but it is, in its foundations, erroneous. I speak of its "foundations" because it is at the beginning of life that the spoken word is central and dominant. There is a developmental modal hierarchy that elevates the spoken mode of symbolic interaction to the position of first among equals; however, once the spoken symbol has been developed, modal equipotentiality may exist. The normal acquisition of a culturally defined language is through the aural-oral modality. Writing and gesturing, reading and signing are all derivatives of spoken communication. Although spoken words certainly may be transformed into other modalities such as script, print, or gesture, it is the spoken word that is of primary impact in the development of human communication.

How can this be demonstrated? No one doubts the importance of the spoken word to mankind in general. It is even sufficient in the sense that a person can live a wholly human life without being able to read or write. Literacy is a boon to freedom, but it is not necessary to survival. And where a cultural language such as English exists, it is dependent upon speech communication.

> *Consider, too, that language survives blindness but not deafness. Children who are born blind develop language in a perfectly normal way. Being unable to see the world they talk about is, of course, a terrible handicap, but it does no harm to language. Nor is their language development impaired in any essential way by their inability to read. On the other hand, children who are born deaf suffer a severe linguistic disability. Now it is easy to understand why a deaf child should not learn to speak. Being unable to hear, he cannot properly control and correct the sounds he makes. It is, however, much less obvious why deaf children who do not acquire speech cannot easily be taught to read or write. If speech and writing are but equivalent representations of language, why is the spoken form prerequisite to the written? Why is it, in fact, so very difficult to substitute the optical shapes of an alphabet for the acoustical shapes of Speech?*[7]

There seems to be some kind of acoustic trigger to conceptualization, a trigger extremely sensitive to the kinesthetic-proprioceptive lines of aural-oral stimulation. A child deprived of acoustic perception may, indeed, after arduous labors on his own part as well as on the part of his teachers, acquire some language skill, but that skill always evidences the effects of perceptual deprivation. It is a question of normal wiring. For the normal infant it is the spoken mode that facilitates the development of symbolization and the resultant decentering and intentionality. The functions mentioned earlier are functions of *speech* communication and not of either communication in general or of language in particular. This does not by itself prove the point at issue, of course, nor can such proof be achieved. The closely controlled experimental studies that could help prove the primacy of the spoken modality may be performed on human infants, and such experimentation would be so inhumane as to be unacceptable. The closest kind of empirical evidence we can muster is based upon children who have been born lacking normal perceptual apparatus. The problem with such evidence is that there are always confounding variables which cloud accurate interpretation.

When discussing this problem of modal equipotentiality, a hypothetical choice may be posed. If you were given the choice of sacrificing either sight or hearing, which would you choose to give up? To this question the almost universal answer is "hearing," since adults would feel most deprived by the absence of sight. The second problem may be posed as follows. If you were responsible for a child just about to be born and were told that you must choose, *for the child,* whether he is to be born without sight or without hearing, which would you choose? To this question the almost universal answer is "sight." Why? Because those questioned, basing their answer upon their own experience and introspection, feel that hearing is the more essential perceptual skill for the acquisition of symbolization and all that follows from it. The Soviet psychologist Alexander Romanovich Luria, writing from a lifetime of work with individuals suffering brain damage, states that "the kinesthetic impulses flowing from the speech organs to the cerebral cortex create the 'basal component of the second signal system', and represent a significant factor in the mechanisms of complex intellectual operations."[8] In a much more philosophical vein Heidegger states that "Man is not merely a living being which, in addition to other abilities, also possesses speech. Rather, speech is the home of Being, in which man, while dwelling there, ec-sists by listening to the truth of Being as its shepherd."[9]

The evidence is simply insufficient to *prove* the centrality of the spoken word to human communication, or even to demonstrate experimentally the modal dominance of the spoken word in the acquisition and development of human communication.[10] But even without proof, the hypothesis must be confronted. For if the spoken word *is* central, the focus of current research must necessarily be redirected, and if the spoken word is *not* central, we can get on with the job of developing human language through other modes.

In discussing the various modes of human communication, Lev S. Vygotsky suggested many years ago that rather than trying to teach animals to speak, perhaps we should try to teach them to gesture, since gesticulation, for some animals such as the primates, seemed to come more naturally than did soundmaking.[11] Decades after Vygotsky's original suggestion, comparative psychologists in the United States set out to try to teach what they consider to be a form of human language (American Sign Language) to chimpanzees.[12] At almost the same time, other researchers began trying to teach chimpanzees to learn a form of human language by having an ape manipulate plastic forms designed by the experimenters to represent language elements.[13] In yet another study an effort is being made to teach a form of human language to a chimpanzee through the means of a computer primate interface.[14] All of these studies speak to the inventiveness and imagination of the experimenters. However, at this time the experimental results can all be explained without accepting that language is involved. The studies thus fail to demonstrate unequivocally that experimental animals have been able to acquire what is generally referred to as human communication. Obviously, if the spoken word is central to human communication, these experiments, all of which assiduously avoid the use by the animals of spoken symbols, are pointless. And it is indicative in this connection that the presence of decentering and the corresponding presence of intentionality, both of which seem to have their genesis in the spoken symbol, have not yet been demonstrated in the experimental animals. The animals develop a limited repertoire in what their mentors call a "form of human language" only through the intensive, highly verbal, and technically proficient labors of the skilled researchers conducting the experiment. Human children, on the other hand, acquire and develop sophisticated speech communication ability in the normal course of their growth, and without any special attention being paid to the endeavor on the part of either the child or the responding adults in the child's environment. Nevertheless, whatever the final results of the current effort to teach nonhuman primates a form of human language, we may expect that the studies will contribute to our better understanding of human speech communication, both in its uniqueness and in the commonality of some of its aspects with animal communication.[15]

Recent research in the communication of dolphins and the current studies of chimpanzees are both capable of arousing the most impassioned discussions on the part of scientists and laymen alike. Speech communication and language are important topics for many people, who feel strongly about the issues that appear to them involved in the effort to teach human communication to nonhumans. There are those who consider that the continuum of life allows for no supremacy of the creature called man. Others feel that man is the apex of both the evolutionary process and the creative effort of centuries, and that there is no reason for him either as a species or as an individual to be ashamed of his preeminence. Proponents of both positions find the research into animal performance of what has been considered a uniquely human enterprise to be either threatening or supportive depending on the interpretation of the findings. Although I support the species specificity of speech communication as the determining characteristic of what is peculiarly "human" communication, I cannot help but feel that whatever the ultimate results of the research currently under way, the question is so important that its work deserves our continuing close attention and open minds.

While we await the verdict, we are obliged to accept the moral burden currently placed upon us as human beings by our capacity for spoken symbolic interaction. As of the moment we are unique. We are the only creatures who can name. We are thus also the only creatures who can misname. The Greek word *aretē* refers to an individual's unique excellence. The Greek word *hamartia* refers to an individual's tragic flaw. In many if not most instances an individual's *aretē* defines his *hamartia*. A person's fantastic strength can induce him to do foolish things. Man's ability for speech communication, for spoken symbolic interaction, has led him both to great moral heights and to the depths of degradation. Philosophy, history, architecture, science, art, and all other endeavors dependent on the spoken word for their foundation testify to man working at his limits of excellence for himself and for his fellows. Yet each of these areas of human concern has also been used to justify man's inhumanity to his universe, his planet, and his fellows. Spoken symbolic interaction is not amoral; it has a specific morality which derives from its function in revealing truth. Spoken symbolic interaction which has as its motive the revelation of truth, either the truth of nature, or the truth of individual interiority, is man's species-specific *aretē*. Spoken symbolic interaction which has as its intent the masking of truth, either the truth of nature, or the truth of man as an individual or man in groups, is man's species-specific *hamartia*.

We, as human beings, are not free to use speech communication without concern for the consequences. In human communication there is an internal imperative to truth. Often one's *hamartia* may be discovered by locating one's *aretē*. We in the United States have just gone through a wrenching episode at the highest political level of intentional perversion of spoken symbolic interaction. Distortions and lies abounded in private and public discourse, and in their cumulative effect they posed a threat to the social and political foundations of a great country. This came about through the misspeaking of individuals—Dante's "evil counselors"—who allowed their skill in human communication to become corrupted and then projected this corruption upon the country at large.

Speech communication is species specific, man's unique excellence. Or, in Greek, speech communication is man's social and individual *aretē*. The symbol is the sign of mankind, and the symbol, in its essence and in its practice, must reflect a constant commitment to the truth.

---

[1] Marshall McLuhan, *Understanding Media* (New York: McGraw-Hill Book Co., 1964).

[2] Frank E. X. Dance and Carl E. Larson, *Speech Communication: Concepts and Behavior* (New York: Holt, Rinehart & Winston, 1972), especially chap. 5. In this usage *function* is not the

same as *purpose.* By function is meant something that occurs as the result of the presence of something else without any requirement of subjective and conscious intent. The simplest statement of a functional relationship is, "If A, then B." This connotes a relationship that may or may not be causal but is always necessary.

[3] For a consideration of the distinction between perceptual and conceptual thought, *see* Mortimer J. Adler, *The Difference of Man and the Difference It Makes* (New York: Holt, Rinehart & Winston, 1967).

[4] John H. Flavell et al., *The Development of Role-Taking and Communication Skills in Children* (New York: John Wiley and Sons, 1968).

[5] Susanne K. Langer, *Mind: An Essay on Human Feeling* (Baltimore: Johns Hopkins University Press, 1972), 2 : 316.

[6] Maurice Merleau-Ponty, *The Primacy of Perception*, trans. J. M. Edie (Evanston, Ill.: Northwestern University Press, 1964).

[7] Alvin M. Liberman, "The Speech Code," in *Communication, Language, and Meaning: Psychological Perspectives*, ed. George A. Miller (New York: Basic Books, Inc., 1973), pp. 128–40, especially p. 130.

[8] A. R. Luria, *Human Brain and Psychological Processes*, trans. Basil Haigh (New York: Harper & Row, 1966), p. 295.

[9] Martin Heidegger, *Über den Humanismus* (Frankfurt am Main: Klosterman, 1949), pp. 21 ff.

[10] Frank E. X. Dance, "The Centrality of the Spoken Word," *Central States Speech Journal* 23, no. 3 (Fall 1972): 197–201.

[11] L. S. Vygotsky, *Thought and Language*, trans. and ed. Eugenia Hanfmann and Gertrude Vakar (Cambridge, Mass.: M.I.T. Press, and New York: John Wiley and Sons, 1962), p. 38.

[12] Beatrice T. and R. Allen Gardner, "Two-Way Communication with an Infant Chimpanzee," chap. 3 in *Behavior of Nonhuman Primates*, vol. 4, ed. Allan M. Schrier and Fred Stollnitz (New York: Academic Press, 1971), pp. 117–84.

[13] David Premack, "Language in Chimpanzee?" *Science* 172 (21 May 1971): 808–22.

[14] Duane M. Rumbaugh et al., "Lana (chimpanzee) Learning Language: A Progress Report," *Brain and Language* 1, no. 1 (Spring 1974): 205–12.

[15] Frank E. X. Dance and Carl E. Larson, *The Functions of Human Communication: A Theoretical Approach* (New York: Holt, Rinehart & Winston, in press), *passim.*

Language

Sydney M. Lamb

Professor Lamb is a well-known figure in the field of linguistics. Born in Colorado in 1929, he received his training at the University of California at Berkeley, where he also taught and was director of a machine translation project until his appointment to the Department of Linguistics at Yale University, his present post, in 1964. He is regarded as the chief American proponent of the system of linguistic analysis known as stratificational grammar, a system distinct, for example, from (and by some considered as an alternative to) the better known transformational grammar of Noam Chomsky. Stratificational grammar—which belongs to general structural linguistics insofar as it assumes that there is an abstract relational structure underlying actual utterance, and that this structure is, or ought to be, the primary object of linguistic study—is nevertheless unique in its assumption that every language contains a number of structural layers or strata related in such a way that the units of lower strata "realize" units of strata higher up, and in its conviction that linguistic structure should be described rather as a network of relationships than as a system of rules. Professor Lamb has written the standard American work in this area, *Outline of Stratificational Grammar* (1966), among other works. His other professional interests are cognitive linguistics, semiotics, and cognitive anthropology.

This essay attempts to state what a language is, to outline the more important properties of linguistic structure. If we can specify what the significant properties of human language are, then perhaps we can determine whether or not certain animal communication systems—such as those of porpoises and whales, or the gestural communication systems that have recently been taught to some chimpanzees by humans—deserve to be called languages. We might then be able to either support or challenge the belief that language is an exclusively human faculty.

What is a language? Perhaps to many the most obvious property of a language is its large collection of words. Is a language, then, a set of words? Clearly it is much more than just that. We can't just put together any random combination of words (such as *porpoise tomorrow sleeping the and in helplessly of*) and get an acceptable sentence. There are evidently some fairly definite rules or constructions governing the allowable combinations of words in a language, comprising what is traditionally called *syntax*. A language is no mere collection of signs but is a *system* involving complex interrelationships of signs.

In embarking on this little exploration of the nature of that system, we will do well to clarify first the notion of the *word*. In nontechnical parlance, the term *word* is rather vague. Consider *human* and *humans*: are they two different words, or two forms of the same word? If the latter, how do we explicate the notion "different forms of the same word"? And what about *nonhuman*? It would generally be called a word, yet it appears to contain a word (*human*) within itself; and its meaning is not other than the combination of the meanings of its two parts, *non* and *human*. And what about *give up*? On the one hand it appears to be two words. Yet it requires a dictionary entry in its own right, as a unit, since its meaning is not predictable from the meanings of *give* and *up*. Similarly, *hot dog, English muffin, White House, New York*.

The way out of our difficulty is to recognize that there are two different kinds of "words" which, as our ordinary vocabulary provides only one term for them, are easily confused: the lexical word and the morphological word. *Human* and *humans* are two different morphological words which involve the same lexical word, *human*. The term *lexeme*, coined by B. L. Whorf[1] on the model of *morpheme* and *phoneme* (discussed below), is a convenient designation for the lexical word, an item for which a lexical entry is necessary in a linguistic description; we may therefore restrict the use of *word* as a technical term to mean only the morphological word. In these terms, *nonhuman* is a single (morphological) word representing a combination of two lexemes, *non-* and *human*. Thus lexemes can be shorter than words; they can also be longer, as the examples *give up, hot dog, English muffin* show, each being a single lexeme comprising two words. And lexemes can be longer still: *in spite of, the man in the moon*. These are lexemes in that they exist as units—prefabricated units, as it were—in contrast with, say, *the girl in the taxi*, which for most speakers of English would be formed anew from its parts when a suitable occasion arose. It is, on the other hand, because lexemes are so often coterminous with words that the confusion between these two structurally different units has arisen.

What, then, is a (morphological) word? If we confine our attention for a moment to written language, a word in this sense would appear to be any of those units which occur between spaces or punctuation marks (other than hyphen and apostrophe), as *human, humans, nonhuman*. But how does a person know, when writing a letter, where to put the spaces? What does that knowledge consist of? Is it that (as is the case for lexemes) he has stored in his memory the collection of all the words that it is possible for him to use? This hypothesis hardly seems likely, since such a memory system not only would be grossly uneconomical but would also preclude his constructing a word he has never used before, or recognizing such a word. Surely it is possible for the person who knows English to use a noun in the plural if he has previously encountered it only in the singular: we know how to form plurals of nouns, by following a simple rule. To be sure the rule doesn't apply in the case of irregular plurals (like *women*), so these do somehow have to be learned as units. But they constitute a small minority. Likewise, we have in our English linguistic system a construction that allows us to add *-ness* to adjectives in general, including adjectives which are newly formed by the use of other constructions. Examples of this construction, which can be expressed

Noun / Adj *-ness*,

would be *dimness, dim-wittedness, many-sidedness*. It is possible that some readers will be encountering one or more of these words for the first time here; yet they will have no difficulty at all in accepting them or in knowing what they mean. In fact, so natural is it to accept new words, formed in accordance with standard morphological constructions, that most persons simply wouldn't know, if asked, whether or not they were meeting them for the first time. And, if an occasion arises to use such a word, as in "The dim-wittedness of the chairman was apparent to everyone at the meeting," the person using it does so without stopping to think whether he has used it or heard it before.

We can now return to the question posed above: How does a person writing a letter know where to put the spaces? Evidently it is because, in addition to a set of words which are remembered as units, he has in his linguistic system a set of morphological constructions for forming words. These constructions collectively specify, without enumerating individually, that certain sequences of elementary morphological units constitute words.

Let us take a closer look at these "elementary morphological units." In the terminology of linguistics they are called *morphemes*. Some morphemes are elementary words—that is, words consisting of single morphemes: *porpoise, man, dim, wit*. Other morphemes cannot occur by themselves as words; for example, prefixes (*non-, un-, re-*) and suffixes (*-ness, -ed*). The morphological constructions, together with the rest of the classification of morphemes according to their combinatory potentials (for example, elementary words are distributed among combinatory classes such as "noun," "conjunction," "preposition," etc.), comprise what is known as the *morphotactics*—the tactics (patterns of arrangement) of morphemes. Thus we may say that the reason a person knows what the words of his language are is that he knows the morphotactics of the language. The morphotactics may be considered to include words remembered as units, since it must specify the morphological classes (e.g., noun, preposition) to which they belong, with their membership.

Two further properties of morphotactic structure require mention. First, the morphotactics of language specifies not only the words of a language but also various larger units, such as noun phrases and verb phrases. Second, the morphotactics provides a means for creating new lexemes when the need arises. This feature of a language is one of its most important properties, as it provides the flexibility and adaptability needed for new situations and new ideas. Many of the combinations allowed by morphotactics represent lexemes already present in the vocabulary as "prefabricated units"; for example, *silver-tongued*. To be sure, this lexeme fits the morphotactic construction described above and could thus be generated anew if need be, but most educated speakers of English have heard it so often that it has become stored in their memories as a unit. Most forms generated by the same construction, however, are not lexemes, as *green-bearded*. And in fact, by its ability to generate such new combinations of morphemes, the morphotactics provides a facility for coining new lexemes. A language thus contains within itself the means for its own enrichment and a device allowing any of its users to exercise linguistic creativity.

There are still other units of language that we must consider, namely phonemes. These include the consonants and vowels, as well as, for many languages, prosodic features such as accents or tones. In any language, such units mutually form a structure, which constitutes an independent layer of the linguistic system. This structure has its own tactics: *phonotactics*, the patterns of arrangement of phonemes. Perhaps the most important of the units generated by the phonotactics of a language is the syllable. The ideally simple tactics of syllables, approximated by some of the Polynesian languages, specifies that a syllable consists of a consonant followed by a vowel. English has a very complicated syllable tactics, which provides for syllables as simple as a single vowel but also for complex syllables like *scrounge,* with clusters of consonants before and after a complex vowel nucleus. But even in its complexity, *scrounge* follows quite systematic tactic patterning. For example, the initial cluster conforms to the general pattern for initial three-consonant clusters, seen in *spr(ing), spl(ash), str(ange),* according to which the first is *s,* the second a voiceless stop (*p, t, k*), the third a liquid (*l, r*). The importance of the syllable as a phonotactic unit is comparable to that of the word as a morphotactic unit. Both tactic patterns also generate larger units composed of the basic ones: phrases in morphotactics, phonological words in phonotactics.

The difference between the morphemic and the phonemic layers of the linguistic structure is greater than we would suppose if, for example, we assumed that morphemes are simply composed of phonemes. In fact, a morpheme can have different phonemic forms in different phonological environments. Russian, which like Latin has a system of case endings occurring with noun stems, marking different syntactic functions of nouns, provides a good illustration of this. If we compare the nominative and genitive forms of three typical Russian nouns, written in terms of their constituent phonemes (with stressed vowels marked by acute accent), we have:

Nominative	*durák* 'fool'	*čisnók* 'garlic'	*pʸirók* 'meat pie'
Genitive	*duraká*	*čisnaká*	*pʸiragá*

For nouns of this class, the nominative has no ending, and the genitive is marked with *-a.* These nouns have stress on the endings, or on the last syllable of the stem if there is no ending. The word for 'fool' shows no further difference between the two forms, but 'garlic' has a discrepancy in the vowel of the second syllable, while 'meat pie' has the same vocalic discrepancy as well as the alternation of *k* and *g.* These differences in the forms of the stems are in accord with rules which apply quite generally in the phonological system of Russian. It is a property of Russian phonotactics that the vowel /o/ can occur only in stressed syllables. In unstressed syllables, its close relative /a/ occurs in its stead.[2] Similarly, Russian phonotactics does not allow voiced obstruents in word-final position (unless an immediately following word begins with a voiced obstruent).[3] The pair *k* and *g* differ only in that the former is voiceless while the latter is voiced. In the genitive, where the stem is followed by a vowel, we see a difference between stem-final *k* (for 'fool' and 'garlic') and stem-final *g* (for 'meat pie'), but the stem-final *g* of 'meat pie' cannot appear as such in the nominative, since it would then be in word-final position, and that isn't allowed. So its close relative *k* occurs instead—the consonant with just the same articulatory features as the *g* except for the voicing, the feature which is ruled out in this environment.

The variety of phonemic forms of the stem for 'meat pie,' then, is fully accounted for by the phonotactics, and we are therefore permitted to conclude that this variation has no significance whatever for the morphemic level of Russian. The stem has just one morphemic form, ^{M}/pᶦirog'/, occurring in both the nominative and the genitive, and the different phonemic forms are predictable from the morphemic form together with the general phonological rules. Notice that the morphemic form fails to coincide with either of the two phonemic forms shown above. For this reason, and since it has different phonemic realizations in different phonotactic environments, it would clearly be incorrect to say that the morphemic form in this case is composed of phonemes. Rather, it is composed of units of the morphemic level which are of the same size as phonemes and which can have alternative phonemic realizations. These units can be called *morphons*, in keeping with their status as components of morphemes (cf. the use of *-on* in physics for elementary particles).

But just a little further examination will show that phonemes, too, have components. We have already observed that Russian ^{P}/k/ and ^{P}/g/ — where the superscript P stands for phoneme — differ only in the component of voicing, as in fact is the case also with English. These two phonemes agree in having a component of closure and in the position of closure: the back of the tongue is pressed against the roof of the mouth. Thus ^{P}/k/ may be analyzed into the components *closed* and *back*, while ^{P}/g/ has these same two components plus *voiced*. Similarly, ^{P}/p/ has the components *closed* and *labial*, and ^{P}/b/ has these two plus *voiced*. These phonological components may be called *phonons*, and it will be seen that *phonon* is to *phoneme* as *morphon* is to *morpheme*. All the vowels have the phonon *vocalic*, and they contrast with one another by virtue of components of tongue position and, for some of them, of lip rounding.

The phenomenon of alternation is also found among morphemes. In English, most verbs have the regular past-tense ending, spelled *-d* or *-ed*. At the morphemic level this can be represented as ^{M}/d/. The different pronunciations encountered in, e.g., *loved*, *hated*, and *liked* are accounted for by the phonotactics. The difference between these formations is therefore of no morphological significance. They are realizations of a single morpheme, ^{M}/d/ (which happens to be composed of just one morphon). Other verbs, small in number but generally high in frequency of occurrence, have "irregular" past tense forms: *saw, took, sang, brought,* etc. The conditions for the occurrence of these irregular formations are morphological rather than phonological: they involve the specific verb morphemes involved. Thus we have several past tense morphemes in alternation with one another.

It is not just grammatical endings that find themselves involved in morphemic alternation. In the case of *go* : *went* we have a different stem form for the past. Consider also *good* : *better*. Here the suffix of the comparative is the regular one, -*er*, but the stem is different. That is, it is different in form,[4] but it is somehow the same in syntactic and semantic function. If one asks whether ^{M}/*gud*/ 'good' and ^{M}/*bet*/—where the superscript M stands for morpheme—are the same unit or two different units, we can reply that the question has two correct answers: at the lexemic level we are dealing with one and the same unit—^{L}/*good*/; at the morphemic level, with two different units—its alternate realizations.

With all this in mind, we can see that it would be an oversimplification to say that lexemes are composed of morphemes, since lexemes and morphemes are on two different levels of structure, much like morphemes and phonemes. Rather, we can say that lexemes are composed of lexons, and that lexons are realized as morphemes. For example, the lexemes ^{L}/*under-go*/ and ^{L}/*go-crazy*/ are composed of two lexons each, and the lexeme ^{L}/*go*/ is composed of a single lexon. These three lexemes, like verbal lexemes in general, can occur with or without the past-tense lexeme. When occurring with it, the lexon ^{L}/*go*/ has a different realization from the usual; we may say that ^{L}/*go*/ and ^{L}/*past*/, taken together, have the realization ^{M}/*went*/.

It is very often the case that a lexeme consists of only one lexon; for example, ^{L}/*good*/, ^{L}/*porpoise*/. And it is likewise often the case that a lexon has a single morphemic realization; for example, ^{L}/*porpoise*/. In such cases we don't have to suppose that the linguistic structure engages in unnecessary duplication. Rather, we can say that, e.g., *porpoise*, through its connections in the linguistic system, functions as a lexeme (i.e., is connected to lexotactics and to its meaning) and as a morpheme (i.e., is connected to the morphotactics and to constituent morphons). This type of consideration leads to the conception of language as a network of relations rather than a system whose units are like building blocks. But there is not room here to elaborate on that point.[5]

We are now ready to consider syntax. This term as commonly understood is concerned with the arrangement of words. But, in approaching a more refined view of linguistic structure, we have seen that it is necessary to distinguish the morphological word—a morphotactic unit—from the lexical word or lexeme. With which type of unit is the syntax of traditional grammar concerned? Actually, with both. And indeed, studies of syntax have often become unnecessarily complex in their attempts to deal with both levels at the same time. The larger units which morphological words enter into are specified by the morphotactics, as indicated above. Independently of these constructions there is a tactics of lexemes—lexotactics. The difference between the two tactic patterns may be seen in English verbal expressions. Consider *has taken*. Morphemically, it can be represented as

$$ha\ \text{-}z\ t\bar{a}k\ \text{-}n$$

In terms of morphotactics we have two words, each consisting of a stem and a suffix. But lexemically, it is just the perfect tense of *take;* and the perfect-tense lexeme consists of *have* together with the requirement that the following verb have the past-participle suffix. In addition, we have the third-person-singular element (realized in the ᴹ/z/ of *has*).

Among the most important lexotactic constructions of a language like English are those which specify clauses (subject plus predicate) and sentences (independent clause together with zero or more other clauses plus intonation contour). And just as the morphotactics of a language provides a mechanism for forming new words and phrases, so the lexotactics guides the speakers of a language in constructing clauses and sentences which they have never used before.

We have now identified three systems—phonemic, morphemic, and lexemic—each with its own tactics. Is there more to linguistic structure? The answer depends upon where we draw the boundaries, and unfortunately there is no compelling evidence to indicate where they belong. Below the phonemic system there is further structure, called phonetic or articulatory. But authorities are in disagreement as to whether it is part of linguistic structure or another system closely connected to that structure. For the sake of this brief outline, let us simply bypass consideration of the phonetic system except to mention that more and more linguists are inclined to the view that it lies within the boundaries of linguistic structure.

At the other end—above the lexemic system—lies what can be called the conceptual system, the system which organizes our concepts, ideas, thoughts, our knowledge of ourselves and other people, and of our environments and cultural institutions. Here too there is doubt as to whether a boundary should be recognized. My own current work has turned up evidence indicating that it should. That is, I believe the interface between the lexemic system and the conceptual system is of a different kind from that between the lexemic and morphemic systems and that between the morphemic and phonemic. To describe the difference involves technicalities beyond the scope of this essay, but recognition of a major boundary dividing the conceptual system from the linguistic system would fit in with much of our ordinary parlance, to the effect that language is a device for expressing concepts and thoughts (rather than a system which incorporates concepts and thoughts). On the other hand, investigation of conceptual structure is being undertaken by more and more linguists in the present decade, and such study, if for no other reason, lies within the field of linguistics, even though this part of the field is also being cultivated by some psychologists and computer scientists.

Lexemes have meanings. To say so is different from saying that lexemes are themselves units of meaning. If lexemes and concepts were in a one-to-one correspondence, there would be no justification for making the distinction. But we find lexemes that alternate with other lexemes in expressing meanings. Like the alternating morphemes ᴹ/gud/ and ᴹ/bet/

which occur in different morphemically specifiable environments (viz. ᴹ/*bet*/ with the comparative morpheme ᴹ/-*r*/), alternating lexemes occur in different lexemically specifiable environments. Consider the environments (1) and (2), as in

    1. It is thought that Theodore ... -s ...

    2. Theodore is thought to ...

and let us put *talk softly* in these environments:

    1a. It is thought that Theodore talks softly.

    2a. Theodore is thought to talk softly.

In this case we see no lexemic alternation. But if we say

    1b. It is thought that Theodore can talk.

    2b. Theodore is thought to be able to talk.

we find ᴸ/*can*/ alternating with ᴸ/*be-able-to*/ (a lexeme composed of three lexons). If we say

    1c. It is thought that Theodore has seen the chimp.

    2c. Theodore is thought to have seen the chimp.

there is no lexemic alternation. Both sentences have ᴸ/ ... perfect *see* .../. But if we say

    1d. It is thought that Theodore saw the chimp.

    2d. Theodore is thought to have seen the chimp.

we have a case of alternation, and also neutralization. In (1d) we have ᴸ/ ... past *see* .../, but in (2d) we have ᴸ/ ... perfect *see* .../. The lexeme ᴸ/*past*/ is not allowed in infinitive expressions; instead we get ᴸ/*perfect*/. That is, ᴸ/*past*/ and ᴸ/*perfect*/ are alternating realizations of the same higher-level unit. The neutralization is seen in (2c) and (2d), which are identical. In other words, "Theodore is thought to have seen the chimp" is ambiguous —it can mean either the same as (1c) or the same as (1d).

A person's conceptual system contains his factual knowledge and plays a major role in organizing his perceptions and experiences. The elements of this system include not only abstract concepts such as "love" and "value" but also concrete ones, such as, in the system of a given individual,[6] his internal representations of the members of his family. And of course the concepts cover not only the "things" of one's experience but also processes and relations of various kinds.

The conceptual system also has a tactics, the system of constructions for forming combinations of concepts. The difference between conceptual tactics and lexotactics may be illustrated by such sentences as

    The tuna fishermen were killing porpoises.

    Porpoises were being killed by the tuna fishermen.

Lexotactically these are quite different from each other: different subjects, one with a transitive verb and an object, the other with a passive verbal expression including a prepositional phrase (*by the tuna fishermen*). But conceptually they are almost identical: the same process, and the same participants in that process. In both, *the tuna fishermen* is the agent and *porpoises* is the patient. *Agent* and *patient* identify participant roles in conceptual structure, while *subject* and *object* are terms for lexotactic roles. The conceptual agent is often but not necessarily realized as lexemic subject, and the patient is often realized as lexemic object, though it may be realized as subject by the use of the passive construction of the lexotactics.

A language has two kinds of adaptability that enable it to provide expression for almost the entire range of human experience. One kind has already been touched upon: the creativity furnished by tactic patterns. The other kind is the categorial organization of the system of concepts. Concepts represent not specific things, processes, and relations, but categories thereof. The concept "cat" covers the whole class of cats. Even the narrowest concepts extend beyond specific percepts and experiences. The concept "New York City" spans a range of centuries, hence a variety of cities, which happen to have all had approximately the same location, and which have merged into one another in a continuous line. On the other hand, we have quite broad concepts like "city," even broader ones like "place," and the still broader "thing." Notice that the categories are organized hierarchically ("city"—"place"—"thing"). Thus if a person encounters some new object, so new and different that he has no notion of what it is made of, what it is for, etc., his system is nevertheless able to handle it with no difficulty. A category for it is already present: if nothing else, it is at least a "thing." And of course it can be described, since whatever perceivable properties it has are connected to concepts in the person's system, and these are connected to lexemes.

The categorial organization of the conceptual system is at once its strength and its weakness. By its categorization of experiences it can lead one to the false impression that one has a greater understanding of one's environment than one actually has. When a new object or person or situation is encountered, it automatically gets categorized, gets assigned to one or more concepts on the basis of certain properties, the very perception of which is often selected by the structure of the conceptual system. There is of course a great value in this mechanism. It gives us the ability to deal with new situations and new people without first undertaking an exhaustive survey of all their properties. But there is also a danger, to which we are continually subject: upon assigning the new object or person to a category, on the basis of one or a few properties, we tend to assume unconsciously that it also has other properties to which that concept has connections—properties which the new object or person may not in fact have. In short, we are led by our conceptual systems to think in categories rather than to treat each individual person and situation as an individual, *sui generis*.

We may well ask, at this point, why languages have so much structure. Some of it seems at first glance unnecessary. Couldn't the functions of language be served with fewer strata? Why isn't there just one syntax, instead of several tactic patterns? Why are there two types of structural unit at each stratum (e.g., both morpheme and morphon) rather than just one? To find the answer to such questions, we can consider what it would be like if there were no structure below the lexeme. This would mean that every lexeme would be without structural resemblance to any other lexeme. It would thus be necessary for the speech mechanism to produce many thousands of quite different signals, and for the auditory system to distinguish them. Either that, or the number of lexemes would have to be restricted to the small number of distinct articulations that are possible. Neither situation exists, of course. In language as it is, there are only a very few fundamental signaling elements—the phonons—of which perhaps fifteen are found in the typical language. These occur in different combinations to provide perhaps three dozen phonemes in typical languages. And likewise the (roughly three dozen) morphons join into combinations to provide for a few thousand different morphemes. And at *their* level, the few thousand lexons enter into combinations providing some tens of thousands of lexemes. This general structural principle is like that of physical matter: Neutrons, protons, and electrons combine to provide around a hundred different kinds of atoms, and these atoms enter into combinations to provide a very much larger number of different molecules. Actually, the parallel is even closer: An element may have isotopes; in terms of the level of subatomic particles the isotopes of an element are structurally different from one another. But from the point of view of the chemical behavior of the atoms, the next higher level, the isotopic differences are nonsignificant. The different isotopes of an atom may thus be compared to alternating realizations of a single element of a higher linguistic level.

It will now be apparent why each stratum has two fundamental units. Those named with the suffix *-on* (e.g., morphon, lexon) are the points in the system from which connections extend to the next lower stratum. For example, morphons are the connections to phonemes. In the case of phonons, the connections are to the articulatory mechanism. The units named with the suffix *-eme* are those which connect to the tactics of that stratum and to the higher stratum. Between the *-ons* and the *-emes* of a stratum we have the combinatory structure, which allows a relatively small number of *-ons* to express a relatively large number of *-emes*.

We may also ask why languages indulge in alternating realizations (e.g., M/*gud*/ and M/*bet*/ as realizations of L/*good*/). Unlike the combinatory structures of the various strata, this aspect of linguistic structure appears to have no communicative value. But, upon closer inspection, some instances of alternation do have such value in the functioning of the system. Consider the alternation of P/*t*/ and P/*d*/ as realizations of the regular past tense morpheme M/*-d*/. The former is voiceless while the latter is voiced, and the former occurs only after voiceless consonants, while the latter occurs after voiced consonants and vowels. The alternants are thus seen to blend with their environments. It would be much more difficult to pronounce words if this environmental adaptation were not present. The phonemic system has to some extent a life of its own, and in the course of linguistic history, changes occur to simplify the pronunciation of transitions from one phoneme to the next—but at the expense of introducing morphophonemic alternations into the system.

Alternating morphemic realizations of lexons are not in general rationalizable on any similar grounds. We may identify two major classes of such alternation. In one class, the alternating morphemes are similar in form: M/hav/ and M/ha/, the latter occurring in *has, had*; or the various forms of L/do/ with different vowels, in *do, does, don't, did*. Such cases have resulted from earlier phonological changes which have not survived as productive morphophonemic alternations. Dialect mixture is often also a factor. In the other class, we find alternating morphemes without formal similarity— the alternants having come from different sources. For example, *went* as the past tense of L/go/ is in origin the past of another verb, *wend*. Lexomorphemic alternation can be seen as the price a language pays for its adaptability. This leaves it open to changes in the course of time, changes which often leave it cluttered with useless relics from the past.

Finally, why should there be separate tactic patterns? The answer is to be found in the difference between the conceptual system and the system of expression, i.e., the phonemic system. The latter, in particular the phonotactics, must be adapted to the physical properties of the articulatory mechanism as well as to the auditory system. It is thus markedly different from the conceptual system, for this must be closely related to perception and to the world in general, about which we think and communicate. In addition, the phonotactics provides organization for combinations of a very small number of units, while the conceptual tactics operates with hundreds of thousands of concepts. So different are the two that they can't be directly connected, but must go through two other systems— the lexemic and the morphemic—as intermediaries.

Now let us return to our starting point. Having noted some of the properties of linguistic structure, can we say what a language is in such a way that we can ascertain whether or not certain chimpanzees, for example, have language? To do so, we'd have to stipulate, somehow, that some of the properties are essential or criterial, while others are merely incidental to language as used by humans. On what basis can we do that? Or might we also look outside of language itself to find its defining properties, as some have done: at what it is used for (e.g., interaction of social groups); or at how its expressions are transmitted from one user to another (i.e., by means of sound waves which travel through the air, hence in all directions simultaneously and with the consequence that the signal fades rapidly); or at whether the expressions can deal with situations other than those immediately present ("displacement"); or at how the system is conveyed from one generation to the next (through heredity, as is probably the case for the communication system of bees, or through learning)? The emphasis of this paper reflects its writer's view that one should look at the system itself rather than outside it for its most important properties. But which of these are to be regarded as constituting its defining properties?

Consider that which is usually called *written language*. Now many linguists regard *written language* as a contradiction in terms, since they consider phonological structure to be an essential property of language. Language as represented in written form is derivative from spoken language in both the life of the individual and in the history of civilization, and it is therefore, to such linguists, of little linguistic interest. On the other hand, we have those who claim that certain chimpanzees have language, although these chimps are using expressive media altogether different from speech. This claim obviously rests upon the position that phonological structure is not a defining property of language. Well, is phonological structure an essential part of language or not? It doesn't help to ask the experts, those who specialize in the study of language, for the opinions of the experts vary all the way from those who say "no" to those who consider it the most important property of all.

David Premack's chimp, Sarah, uses plastic objects for lexemes. In her system there is no structure below the lexeme, unless we extract components of color and shape, and the inventory of lexemes is sharply limited. But Sarah does appear to have a rather respectable set of lexotactic constructions. So are we dealing here with language or not? The fact is that we have some properties of human language and not others. It is certainly interesting that she has some lexotactic structure, and we can congratulate her. Can't we be satisfied with that? Does it really mean more if we can somehow define language so that we can say she has language?

I'd like to suggest that the question of whether chimps have language is more artificial than real—it is a question whose semblance of cogency arises from a feature of our conceptual systems discussed above: their categorial organization of all our thinking and experience. Language is itself one of the concepts in our conceptual hierarchy. As with any other concept, its presence leads us to suppose that language is some fairly definite thing, that any system either is a language or is not, that if we can show that some system used by chimps is a language, then we will be permitted to make certain assumptions about chimps, by virtue of conceptual connections from what we now know as "language" to various other concepts, like "intelligence." And the concept of "intelligence" is, for many of us, further connected to something like "deserving of respect." But in reality each communication system is a system of its own kind. It shares some properties with natural human spoken language while differing with respect to other properties. And chimps are deserving of our respect in any case.

Is it, I wonder, appropriate to indulge in a little comparison of our times and thinking to those of a hundred years ago? Then, in the Old West, killing Indians was a popular pastime for the white invaders. The sweet little old ladies would repeat the time-honored maxim, "The only good Indian is a dead Indian," and the young men would occasionally go out hunting Indians as a Saturday night diversion. In the same period, some of the intellectuals, in writing about their travels in the West, would continually demonstrate to their readers, in their descriptions of Indians and their customs, how primitive the Indians were in all respects (including their polysynthetic languages) in contrast to the advanced, civilized, superior white men.

In more recent times, intellectuals still write about the magnificence of human beings in comparison to all other animals. Only humans have language, intelligence, and so forth. Meanwhile, others of our contemporaries are killing whales and porpoises and are mistreating primates in laboratories.

At least we can take note of some progress in the last hundred years.

---

[1] "Language: Plan and Conception of Arrangement" (written in 1938), in *Language, Thought, and Reality: Selected Writings of Benjamin Lee Whorf*, ed. John B. Carroll (Cambridge, Mass.: M.I.T. Press, 1956).

[2] Except after palatalized consonants, where /i/ occurs.

[3] An obstruent is a consonant in whose pronunciation the airstream passing through the mouth is obstructed, either totally (e.g., *k, g*) or almost totally (e.g., *f, s*).

[4] The term *morpheme* is based on the Greek root *morph-*, which means "form."

[5] For elaboration, *see* my "Linguistic and Cognitive Networks" and other papers in *Readings in Stratificational Linguistics*, ed. Adam Makkai and David G. Lockwood (University, Ala.: University of Alabama Press, 1973).

[6] At the conceptual level it is even more necessary than at lower levels to recognize that each member of a speech community has his own individual structure.

The Confusion of the Animalists

Mortimer J. Adler

Dr. Adler's interest in the subject of this symposium goes back at least to 1967, when he published a volume called *The Difference of Man and the Difference It Makes*, which examined the evidence and identified the issues implicit in its title so far as they had been developed to that time.

Dr. Adler, who is, of course, one of the editors in chief of *The Great Ideas Today*, was associate editor of *Great Books of the Western World* and the principal architect of the *Syntopicon*. More recently he was director of planning for the fifteenth edition of the *Encyclopaedia Britannica*, published in 1974, and is now chairman of the Britannica's Board of Editors. He is also director of the Institute for Philosophical Research in Chicago, where he recently completed a book on the philosophy of language that will shortly appear.

A recent book, entitled *Apes, Men, and Language,* bears the subtitle "How teaching chimpanzees to 'talk' alters man's notions of his place in nature."[1] I cite this book, not because it is better or worse than most books of its kind, but because it is the latest in a long line of books and essays that attempt to defend the proposition that men and other animals differ only in degree, not in kind. It does so in the light of the mass of recent evidence concerning the so-called linguistic ability of a number of chimpanzees who have apparently been trained by human experimenters to use signs that appear to function like words and to make what appear to be sentences that are declarative and interrogative in mood as well as imperative. In this essay, I shall attempt to defend the contrary proposition, that man differs in kind from other animals. I will try to explain why recent research on the "speech" of chimpanzees in no way alters the picture. It leaves the question about the difference between men and other animals exactly where it was before these researches were undertaken.[2]

For the sake of brevity, I will use the word *animalist* to refer to those who hold that men differ *only in degree* from other animals, and the word *humanist* for those who hold that men differ *in kind.* To present a perspicuously ordered exposition of a complicated argument within the confines of brevity, I will number the propositions in my argument and state each of them in summary fashion.

1. The animalists do not understand the nature of the problem to which they think scientific evidence affords a solution, nor do they understand the terms in which the problem must be stated or the logic in the light of which the available evidence must be interpreted.

2. The problem of how man differs from other animals—in degree or in kind—is not a purely philosophical problem (like the problem of God's existence and nature or the problem of the distinction between local motion and other forms of change), nor is it a purely scientific problem (like the problem of the existence of certain elementary particles or the problem of the rate of acceleration in free-fall). It is a mixed problem, both scientific and philosophical, the solution to which requires knowledge of

relevant scientific evidence and also philosophical competence in the interpretation of that evidence. With almost no exceptions, the animalists lack the philosophical competence requisite for thinking clearly about the mixed problem of the difference of man. What I have just said applies to animalists who happen to be professors of philosophy just as much as it does to those who are professors or researchers in one or another branch of natural or social science. *A fortiori* it applies to all the journalists who write popular reports of the scientific literature and endorse the animalist position.

3. Having the requisite philosophical competence to think clearly about this problem involves, first of all, an understanding of the distinction between difference in kind and difference in degree.

3a. Men and other animals differ in degree if both possess the same trait but one possesses more of it, the other less. For example, if both men and chimpanzees use signs that function like words, but men have very much larger vocabularies than chimpanzees, then with respect to this trait that they have in common, men and chimpanzees differ in degree.

3b. Men and other animals differ in kind if men either *have certain powers* or *perform certain acts* that are not present in other animals in the slightest degree. For example, if men have the power of conceptual thought and other animals lack this power, or if men use words to refer to unperceived and even imperceptible objects and other animals never use words in this way, then men and other animals differ in kind. Any respect in which men differ in kind from other animals is a trait that only men possess or, what is the same, a uniquely human trait. Differences in kind or degree which are stated in terms of the actions or behavior of men and other animals are directly evidenced in observable behavior, but differences in kind or degree which are stated in terms of powers or abilities which are unobservable (such as the power of perceptual or the power of conceptual thought) cannot be directly evidenced in observable behavior but must be inferred from the observation of behavior.

4. It is a mark of confused thinking to say, on the one hand, that men and other animals differ only in degree and to say, on the other hand, that men do certain things or have certain powers that no other animals do or have to any degree whatsoever. Nevertheless, such eminent scientists as Jacob Bronowski and George Beadle do precisely that.[3]

5. The rule of parsimony in scientific inference, first formulated by William of Ockham and later applied to research on animal behavior by Lloyd

Morgan, proscribes the positing of an unobservable entity unless positing it can be shown to be necessary in order to explain observed phenomena. This rule directs us not to posit the unobservable power of conceptual thought, either in men or in other animals, unless we are unable to explain their observed behavior in any other way. Only if the power of conceptual thought is indispensable to explaining their behavior are we logically justified in positing it as a power they possess.[4]

6. The position of the humanists, which the animalists reject, can be stated in three ways, the second throwing light on the first, and the third on the second.

6a. *Only* man is a person with inherent dignity and inherent rights; all other living organisms, along with inanimate substances, are merely things, having neither inherent dignity nor inherent rights. If other animals have, to some degree, inherent dignity and rights, then man's killing of other animals for the sake of nutriment or clothing is murder and is reprehensible for the same reason that cannibalistic practices are. Similarly, man's use of other animals as beasts of burden or as chattel is enslavement and is reprehensible for the same reason that the enslavement of men is reprehensible. This does not mean, of course, that men cannot do moral damage to *themselves* when they treat animals with cruelty or wantonly destroy them. Many moral imperatives involve the proper use of things and require them to be respected.

6b. *Only* man is a rational animal with free will.

6c. *Only* man has the power of conceptual thought and the power of free choice in selection of means for the accomplishment of a given objective.[5]

7. All three of the foregoing formulations of man's difference in kind state that difference in terms of unobservable traits or properties: "personality," "dignity," "rights," "rationality," "free will," "conceptual thought," and "free choice" all refer to objects that cannot be observed perceptually. They are not objects of sense perception. Of the three statements, the third comes nearest to being stated in terms that permit inferences to be made, either affirmatively or negatively, from observable behavior. We should be able to determine from the observable behavior of men and other animals whether only men have the power of conceptual thought and the power of free choice, or other animals also have these powers, even though to a somewhat diminished degree. If other animals do possess these powers, even to the slightest degree, then men and other animals differ in degree, not in kind.

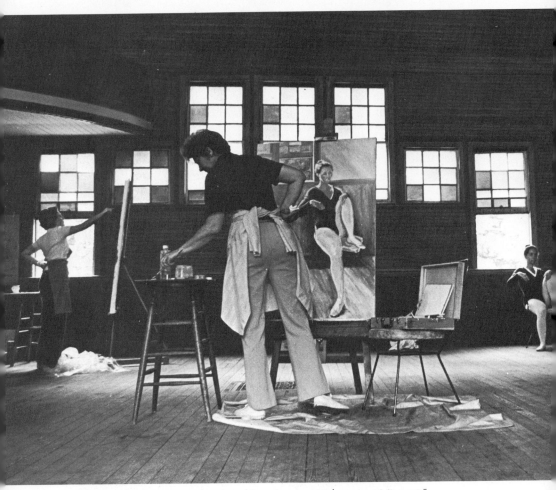

"Only men make totally useless (though enjoyable) works of fine art."

"...the wide range of variability in human productions of every sort, as compared with the uniformity of the productions of other animals."

8. The inference that man uniquely possesses the powers of conceptual thought and of free choice is grounded in part on observations of human and animal behavior in the field of production and social organization. It is important here to note the precision required in stating the point of observable difference to which the evidence turned up by scientific investigation is interpreted as relevant.

8a. To say, for example, that only men make things, or that only men make tools, is false; for beavers make dams, spiders make webs, birds make nests, and apes make tools. However, the following more precise statements are true and are so regarded by leading anthropologists.[6]

8a(i). Only men fashion tools not for immediate use but for future action in remote but foreseeable contingencies. Other so-called tool-making animals improvise instruments that they immediately employ in the same perceptual context which led to the improvisation.

8a(ii). Only men machinofacture products as well as manufacture them; i.e., produce things, first, by making blueprints that incorporate the specifications of the product to be made, and then by creating dies for the reproduction of the specified item out of plastic materials. No other animal machinofactures to any degree.

8a(iii). Only men make totally useless (though enjoyable) works of fine art; the productions of other animals always serve a biological purpose or have some biological utility for the survival of the individual or the species, as human works of fine art do not.

8a(iv). Only man makes artistically, that is, by free choice as well as by conceptual thought. All other animals make instinctively. The observable evidence for this point of difference is the wide range of variability in human productions of every sort, as compared with the uniformity of the productions of other animals, uniform within a given species because instinctively determined and therefore species specific.

8a(v). It is an egregious error, yet one made by eminent scientists, to align the instinctive (and therefore uniform) performances of other species of animals with the voluntary (and therefore variable) performances of men, thereby concluding, for example, that both men and the bowerbirds of Australia make artistically because the latter decorate their nests, or that both men and the dancing bees make complicated statements because the dances of the latter indicate the distance and direction of the place where nectar can be found.[7]

8b. Similarly, to say that only man is a social animal or that only man lives in a highly organized society is false; for many other species of animals are manifestly gregarious, and the social insects, such as wasps, ants, and termites, live in highly organized societies. However, the following more precise statements are true in the light of all available evidence.

8b(i). In addition to being gregarious as other animals are, only man is a political animal; that is, only man frames constitutions and makes laws for the organization and conduct of the societies in which he lives, prescribing right conduct and prohibiting wrong conduct.

8b(ii). Only man associates voluntarily, as is evidenced by the great variability within the human species of the forms of social organization, in families and tribes as well as in states. All other species of gregarious animals associate instinctively (especially those with the highest degree of social organization, such as the social insects), as is evidenced by the uniformity of their species-specific modes of association or patterns of social organization.

8b(iii). Of the two foregoing points, the first is the basis for an inference to man's possession of the power of conceptual thought; the second is the basis for an inference to man's possession of the power of free choice.

8c. To say that only man thinks is as ambiguous and imprecise as to say that only man makes products or that only man is social or lives in organized society. If the word *thinking* covers problem solving of all sorts, then other animals think, for problem solving is not a unique human performance. It is, therefore, false to say that only man thinks, or that only human behavior indicates the possession of a power to think. It might be somewhat truer to say that man and man alone is ever engaged in an effort to solve problems, the solutions of which have no biological utility or survival value, such, for example, as chess problems or metaphysical problems. However, the most precise statement of the difference of man, to which observable behavior can be interpreted as relevant, is as follows: only man has the power of conceptual thought, in addition to the power of perceptual thought; all other species totally lack the power of conceptual thought, while possessing in varying degrees the power of perceptual thought.[8]

8c(i). To interpret correctly the comparative behavior of men and other animals in the sphere of thought, and to make correct inferences from such behavioral evidence, it is necessary to understand precisely the distinction between perceptual and conceptual thought. Most of the animal psychologists and ethologists who have attributed the power of conceptual thought to nonhuman animals have done so with little or no understanding of this distinction. Because of that, they have attributed to nonhuman animals a power that they did not need to posit in order to explain their behavior. In so doing, they have violated Ockham's rule of parsimony. All animal behavior, including not only all forms of animal problem solving and all varieties of delayed reaction but also all forms of animal communication and even the recently observed linguistic behavior of chimpanzees, can be explained in terms of the power of perceptual thought. Nothing more need be posited.[9]

8c(ii). The power of perceptual thought enables an animal to deal thoughtfully with perceptual objects (things that are actually being per-

"Man alone is ... engaged in an effort to solve problems, the solutions of which have no biological utility or survival value, such, for example, as chess problems or metaphysical problems."

"Only man associates voluntarily, as is evidenced by the great variability within the human species of the forms of social organization, in families and tribes as well as in states."

ceived), and even in some cases to a slight degree with perceptible objects (things that are remembered or imagined but are not actually being perceived).

8c(iii). The power of perceptual thought includes the power of perceptual abstraction and the power of perceptual generalization. With the power of perceptual thought, an animal is able to react in the same way to perceptual similars, and to react in different ways to things that are perceptually different.[10]

8c(iv). The power of perceptual thought does not extend to objects that are intrinsically imperceptible—incapable of being perceived by the senses. In order to deal thoughtfully with such objects, it is necessary to have the power of conceptual thought, and with it the powers of conceptual abstraction and conceptual generalization.[11]

9. Unique performances on man's part that have already been mentioned, such as machinofacturing, artistic production, constitution framing, and lawmaking, all justify the inference from observed behavior to man's possession of the power of conceptual thought. These unique performances—things that man and man alone does—cannot be explained in terms of the power of perceptual thought, for all involve reference to imperceptible objects. To explain these performances, it is therefore necessary to posit a power that is distinct from and superior to the power of perceptual thought.

9a. In addition to the unique performances on man's part that have already been mentioned, which justify the inference to man's exclusive possession of the power of conceptual thought, it should also be pointed out that man is the only historical animal, that is, the only species of animal that has a history which involves the cumulative transmission of cultural artifacts from generation to generation—such things as beliefs, customs, laws, and theories. This would be impossible if men possessed only the power of perceptual thought. Hence, to explain cumulative cultural transmission, conceptual thought on man's part must be posited.

9b. Cumulative cultural transmission would also be impossible without human language, especially that aspect of human language which cannot be explained without positing the power of conceptual thought. It is further true that all the other unique performances on man's part (such as those in the sphere of artistic or technological production and in the sphere of social organization) would also be impossible without human language, and especially that aspect of human language which is the basis for inferring man's possession of the power of conceptual thought.[12]

9c. We must, therefore, now consider human language and how it differs from what appears to be language or some form of communication in other species of animals. It is at this point that the recent researches on chimpanzees become critically relevant.

9c(i). The question to be answered is *not* whether chimpanzees can, under human tutelage, acquire a language in some sense of the term *language;* it is *not* whether chimpanzees, dolphins, and other of the higher mammals manifest some form of linguistic ability; it is *not* even whether chimpanzees can, under human instruction, learn to use symbols for the purpose of making statements and asking questions.

9c(ii). The question to be answered is rather whether the linguistic performances of chimpanzees, so far as the record now goes, can be explained entirely in terms of the power of perceptual thought, which apes have to a high degree; and whether, in sharp differentiation, the linguistic performances of human beings cannot be thus explained but require us to posit the presence in man of the power of conceptual thought, over and above the power of perceptual thought which man possesses to an even higher degree.

10. In comparing and contrasting the linguistic performances of men and other animals, especially chimpanzees and bottle-nosed dolphins, precision about the points of comparison is of critical importance.

10a. To say that only men communicate with one another is false. In many other species of animals, intraspecific communication by sound or gesture occurs.

10b. It is also false to say that only men make statements. Honeybees make statements by the dances they perform.

10c. In the light of recent researches on chimpanzees, we now know it is false to say that only men use signs that are designators rather than signals (i.e., signs that function as name-words do in human speech), and that only men use such signs to form declarative sentences or to ask questions.

10d. The recent experimental work on chimpanzees makes it false to say that only men can be taught by men to use designative signs and form sentences. The evidence is clear that chimpanzees can be taught by men to do these things.

10e. However, in the light of all the evidence so far reported, it still remains true to say that only human beings can teach other human beings or chimpanzees to use name-words and make sentences; so far as the record goes, chimpanzees do not teach other chimpanzees or human beings to perform these acts.

10f. Most important of all are the following facts ignored or overlooked by all the animalists in their mistaken supposition that the recent experimental work on chimpanzees *proves* that the difference between men and apes is one of degree, not of kind.

10f(i). In the light of all the recent work on chimpanzees, it still remains true to say that only men use signs that are name-words to refer to imperceptible objects, such as *right* and *wrong*, *just* and *unjust*, *liberty* and *equality*, *infinity* and *eternity*, *perceptual thought* and *conceptual thought*, and so on.

10f(ii). It also still remains true to say that only men make syntactically complete sentences which are grammatically correct in their construction; the recorded sentences of the chimpanzees may have some resemblance to human sentences, but the difference between the apparent and the genuine remains critically significant.

10f(iii). If the word *language* is used equivocally to cover all forms of sign using and all appearances of sentence making, then it cannot be said that man is the only linguistic animal, or that language is a unique property of human beings. But if instead of using the loose word *language*, we substitute the precise phrase *syntactical speech*, and use it unequivocally, then it must be said that man and man alone engages in syntactical speech and that syntactical speech is a unique property of human beings.[13]

11. While the evidence provided by recent work on chimpanzees does not prove, as the animalists claim, that men and apes differ only in degree or that chimpanzees show a capacity for acquiring syntactical speech even to a slight degree, we cannot, therefore, conclude with any finality that the question about the difference of man is demonstrably answered. The recent work on chimpanzees is at most a matter of the last seven or eight years. Given another twenty or another hundred years of experimental investigation in this field, evidence may be forthcoming which decisively disproves the position of the humanist; i.e., makes it false to say that only men have the power of conceptual thought, as to say that would be false if and when chimpanzees ever learn how to engage in genuinely syntactical speech about imperceptible objects.[14]

12. Future experimenters will have the criteria they need to make an accurate appraisal and correct interpretation of their data, and so avoid the confusions rampant among the current animalists, only if two basic distinctions become clear to them.

12a. The first is the distinction between naming by description and naming by acquaintance. These represent two quite distinct ways in which human infants acquire name-words and increase their vocabularies.[15]

12a(i). On the one hand, children do so by direct perceptual acquaintance with the object named, as when the child acquires the word *dog* as the name for the animal that is lying at his feet, or the word *candy* for the sweet being held out to him, or the word *mama* for the person who is holding him tight. These are all perceptual objects, immediately present to the child; he learns the new word by hearing an adult impose it as the name or designative sign for the object with which he is perceptually acquainted.

12a(ii). On the other hand, very young children also acquire new name-words when the object named is not perceptually present and even when they have never had any perceptual acquaintance with the object named. They are able to acquire new name-words, the referential significance of which they can understand as a result of having the object named verbally described to them. For example, when a child asks about the meaning of the word *kindergarten* on being told that he or she is going to be sent to kindergarten before ever having had the experience of being in one, the verbal description of kindergarten as "a place where you go to play with other children" will add the word *kindergarten* to the child's vocabulary as a significant name-word.

12a(iii). The very young child, with whose linguistic performances the animalists compare those of chimpanzees, acquires name-words by verbal description as well as by perceptual acquaintance—not only name-words such as *sister* or *brother* for a perceptual object that has not yet been perceived because the forthcoming sibling has not yet been born, but also name-words for such imperceptible objects as *just* and *unjust*, *right* and *wrong*, *good* and *bad*. Without being able to acquire names by verbal description of the objects named, the human child would be unable to acquire name-words for imperceptible objects.

12b. The second distinction is that between categorematic and syncategorematic words, or name-words and linguistic operators.[16]

12b(i). The categorematic words of human language are the parts of speech traditionally classified as nouns, verbs, adjectives—the words that name or designate both perceptual and also imperceptible objects.

12b(ii). The syncategorematic words of human language are the parts of speech traditionally classified as particles, and subdivided into definite and indefinite articles, prepositions, conjunctions, and disjunctions; they also include such logical operators as "is," "is not," "if ... then ...," "not both," and so on.

12c. As it is true that without the ability to acquire names by verbal description, the use of language to refer to imperceptible objects would be impossible, so it is also true that without the ability to use syncategorematic words, syntactical speech—the construction of grammatically complete and correct sentences—would also be impossible.

13. Recent work on chimpanzees does not include evidence that chimpanzees can acquire names by verbal description as contrasted with acquiring names by perceptual acquaintance, nor does it include evidence that chimpanzees can learn to use syncategorematic words (grammatical and logical operators). Hence we must conclude, so far as experimental results show, that the linguistic performance of chimpanzees does not indicate their possession of the power of conceptual thought, nor does it indicate their ability to engage in syntactical speech. The sentences formed by chimpanzees bear some resemblance to the sentences found in human speech, but that is as far as it goes. In addition, what chimpanzees can talk about (perceptual objects only) indicates a critical deficiency on their part, even as compared with the speech of very young children, who can refer to imperceptible as well as perceptual objects. Future research may change the picture and support the contention of the animalists. But it will do so only if the evidence warrants the animalist in answering the following questions affirmatively—questions which must now, in the light of present evidence, be answered negatively.

13a. Can chimpanzees acquire name-words by verbal description as well as by perceptual acquaintance, and among the name-words thus acquired, do some refer to imperceptible objects or do all refer to perceptual objects?

13b. Can chimpanzees acquire syncategorematic as well as categorematic words, and can they learn to use such words to form syntactically complete and grammatically correct sentences?

13c. The two foregoing questions provide the criteria for judging whether or not chimpanzees have the power of syntactical speech and a range of name-words that requires us to infer that they have the power of conceptual thought. There are, however, two other questions which should be considered by the animalist; and if, now or in the future, he answers them negatively, he should ask himself, "If not, why not?"

13c(i). Do chimpanzees in their native habitat acquire any form of language that involves using signs that function as name-words (restricted to perceptual objects) and involves making sentences that bear some remote resemblance to sentences in human syntactical speech?

13c(ii). In captivity and under human tutelage, can one chimpanzee impart to another chimpanzee the kind of linguistic attainments that it has acquired as a result of being trained by human beings?

14. Even if, now and in the foreseeable future, the evidence remains definitely in favor of the position of the humanist and adverse to the

"The existence of a merely superficial difference in kind between men and apes . . . does [not] raise any new questions about the origin of the human species."

position of the animalist, the difference in kind between men and apes, dolphins, or other animals may be only a superficial rather than a radical difference in kind.

14a. It is superficial if the power of conceptual thought uniquely present in men is possessed by them only because of their vastly superior degree of brain power.

14b. It is a radical difference in kind only if the power of conceptual thought uniquely present in man cannot be adequately explained in terms of brain power but must involve the positing of some other factor, present in man and not present in other animals.[17]

15. The solution of this problem—whether the difference in kind between man and other animals is superficial or radical—will never be found or even approached by means of experimental work on animals, but only through another kind of experimental work (on artificial intelligence) and through the construction of "thinking machines" which will simulate syntactical speech and be able to engage in conversation with human beings.[18]

To sum up: the confusion manifested by the animalists arises from three failures of understanding on their part.

In the first place, they fail to understand that the difference of man does not rest on comparative evidence of human and animal behavior *solely* in the sphere of communication or language.

In the second place, they fail to understand that, even in the sphere of language, the critical question to be answered is whether the linguistic performance of chimpanzees justifies and necessitates the attribution to them of the power of conceptual thought, as the syntactical speech of men does.

In the third place, they fail to understand that, until it can be proved that the difference in kind between men and other animals is radical rather than superficial (which for logical reasons may be forever impossible[19]), the existence of a merely superficial difference in kind between men and apes or other mammals in no way interrupts the continuity of nature (since that continuity remains in the spectrum of degrees of underlying brain power), nor does it raise any new questions about the origin of the human species from ancestors shared with anthropoid apes, by natural causes operating in the evolutionary process.

---

[1] This book, by Eugene Linden (New York: Saturday Review Press, 1974), reports and appraises all the recent work done on the linguistic performances of chimpanzees. It reviews evidence accumulated since I wrote *The Difference of Man and the Difference It Makes* (New York: Holt, Rinehart & Winston, 1967)—hereinafter cited as *DOM*. I will in subsequent footnotes cite chapter and pages in *DOM* in order to acquaint the reader with the state of scientific evidence and opinion prior to the recent researches on chimpanzees, as well as for my own critical appraisal of scientific evidence and opinion at the time I wrote *DOM*.

[2] Although the new evidence accumulated since 1967 does not alter my adherence to the humanist position as defended in *DOM*, it does require me to make a sharper and more precise statement of the argument for the humanist position and against the animalist position than I made in *DOM*. The present essay, therefore, corrects a number of inaccuracies and imprecisions in the earlier statement of the argument.

[3] *See* Jacob Bronowski, *The Identity of Man* (Garden City, N.Y.: Natural History Press, 1965), pp. 11–12, 48; and George and Muriel Beadle, *The Language of Life* (Garden City, N.Y.: Doubleday & Co., 1966), pp. 39, 41.

[4] See *DOM*, pp. 101–2, 106, 110.

[5] These three propositions make man superior to all other living organisms—superior in kind, not just in degree—but that is quite consistent with man's being not only the best but also the worst of animals, either best or worst because of the use he makes of his superior powers. *See* Aristotle *Politics* 1. 2. 1253a 31–34: "Man, when perfected, is the best of animals, but, when separated from law and justice, he is the worst of all; since armed injustice is the more dangerous, and he is equipped at birth with arms, meant to be used by intelligence and virtue, which he may use for the worst ends" (*GBWW*, Vol. 9, p. 446).

[6] See *DOM*, chap. 6.

[7] See *DOM*, pp. 114–18.

[8] See *DOM*, chap. 10.

[9] For a fuller exposition of this matter, see *DOM*, chap. 10, especially pp. 152–64.

[10] Ibid., pp. 160–61.

[11] See *DOM*, chap. 11, pp. 180–90.

[12] "Man is the only animal whom [nature] has endowed with the gift of speech. And whereas mere voice is but an indication of pleasure or pain, and is therefore found in other animals (for their nature attains to the perception of pleasure and pain and the intimation of them to one another, and no further), the power of speech is intended to set forth the expedient and inexpedient, and therefore likewise the just and the unjust" (Aristotle *Politics* 1. 2. 1253a 9–14; *GBWW*, Vol. 9, p. 446). Allowing for some factual inaccuracies in this early statement of the humanist position, the quoted passage can be construed as drawing a sharp line between animal communication about perceptual objects and human speech which extends beyond this to conceptual objects, such as the *expedient* and the *inexpedient*, the *just* and the *unjust*. In addition to such conceptual objects of moral and political discourse, it extends to all the conceptual objects of scientific discourse. Even more distinctive of the uniqué range of human speech is the range of symbolic objects referred to in poetical discourse. On this last point, see the recent book by George Steiner, *After Babel, Aspects of Language and Translation* (New York: Oxford University Press, 1975): "I believe that the communication of information, of ostensive and verifiable 'facts,' constitutes only one part, and perhaps a secondary part, of human discourse. The potentials of fiction, of counterfactuality, of undecidable futurity profoundly characterise both the origins and nature of speech. They differentiate it ontologically from the many signal systems available to the animal world."

[13] Some years ago, after delivering a lecture at the Aspen Institute in which I defended the humanist position concerning the difference of man, Professor Walter Orr Roberts, the astronomer, who was present, asked me how I would respond if a chimpanzee who had listened to the lecture stood up and said, "Professor Adler, I agree with what you have said about the difference between men and chimpanzees." I replied that I would tell the chimpanzee that he was either a fool or a liar—a fool, if he didn't realize that his statement at the end of my lecture showed that the humanist position was wrong; a liar, if he did realize it.

[14] The proposition advanced by Professor Frank E. X. Dance in his contribution to this Symposium parallels the proposition advanced in this paper. Professor Dance and I agree that the linguistic performances of men and other animals are different in kind, not in degree, although he uses the phrase *speech communication* for what uniquely characterizes the human performance, and I use the phrase *syntactical speech* for it.

[15] For a fuller exposition of this matter, see my forthcoming book *Some Questions about Language* (La Salle, Ill.: Open Court, 1975), chap. 3, q. 5.

[16] Ibid., q. 6.

[17] For a fuller exposition of this matter, see *DOM*, pp. 27–35.

[18] Ibid., chaps. 12–14.

[19] Ibid., chap. 15.

Additional Comments

Roger S. Fouts

As man increases his knowledge concerning his place in nature, there is one rule that should be accepted: science is propaedeutic to philosophy. But such a rule has seldom been observed. Man's fascination with man has led to speculative and usually nonheretical statements concerning his paramount place among animals. It is no longer in vogue to separate man entirely from the other beasts; instead, the fashion is to intuit some special feature of man and then to state that it is surely absent in all other species. This is a delightful game to play if one has a well-broken-in armchair, a warm fire, and perhaps a pipe to puff on occasionally whilst lost in deep contemplation. But, an empiricist should hardly have the time to afford such leisurely pursuits. He, as a scientist, is tied to his data and their collection. He may attempt to build a theoretical model based on his data in order to explain them, or he may use a model that is already established.

Since I consider myself to be a comparative psychologist who studies behavior, I have collected data along with other scientists, and speaking only for myself I have found that a Darwinian model best explains the results I have obtained. From my interpretation of this model I will address myself to the essay entitled "The Confusion of the Animalists" written by Mortimer J. Adler.

There is one major point in the Darwinian position that is either explicitly or implicitly misunderstood or overlooked by some individuals when they concern themselves with man's place in nature. The point is quite simple, and yet it is rarely acknowledged. It is the fact that evolution is not directed toward some ultimate goal or perfection. Over and over, the implication is that evolution is so directed and that the paragon of evolution is man—the ultimate in perfection and the final answer in evolution. But, my personal view is that we are part of evolution, part of that continuity of change that keeps on developing. And we as a species have not been around long enough to even begin to make such an egotistical claim. One could make a better argument for the cockroach.

Dr. Adler in his essay has formed a dichotomy between the "animalists," who hold that man differs from other animals in degree, and the "humanists," who hold that man differs from other animals in kind. I will address my rebuttal to some of the numerous propositions he uses in his argument for the "humanist" position.

In his second proposition he states that the problem of how man differs from other animals is neither purely philosophical nor purely scientific but is a mixed problem. I would disagree. It is purely scientific, since this is where the empirical data and proofs will come from. If the data do not agree with a particular philosophy, that philosophy will have to change or go the way of the other philosophies in the past that were not able to adapt to a new factual environment.

In regard to Dr. Adler's third proposition of defining degree and kind, I would agree. But it should be pointed out that *degree* requires continuity and *kind* requires a dichotomy. If something exists in one species and not in another that is closely related, one must explain that difference in kind by resorting to such concepts as saltation, a "hopeful monster" mutation, or divine creation—especially if the subject is a complex structure or behavior. None of these is palatable to my scientific tastes or knowledge of biology—especially when dealing with a highly complex behavior such as conceptual thought.

Another major flaw in postulating a difference in kind is that one must observe the structure or behavior in one animal and *not* observe it in the other. The use of negative evidence or the absence of evidence to make statements is not usually considered good scientific methodology. It has historically served to help careless scientists to put their academic feet in their mouths ("man is the only animal to use tools, to make tools, and so on").

Also in this section of Dr. Adler's essay, it is noted that observed behavior is somehow tied to unobservable powers or abilities. If the observed event is what defines the presence of an unobservable power, then why resort to unnecessary words that serve only to clutter the problem? Obviously, a central nervous system has to be a given in an organism that demonstrates behavior; it is unnecessary to resort to metaphysical terms to explain such behavior.

In regard to the fourth proposition, I heartily agree.

In proposition five the law of parsimony is emphasized. This law has rightly served science in removing some of the overzealous anthropomorphism that occurred during Romanes' times and resulted in making the anecdotal method an unacceptable tool for science. Most assuredly, it is incorrect to ascribe common traits to animals that may well have a different basis and explanation. But, if given a choice between describing a behavior of a chimpanzee by using terms developed for the stickleback fish or by using terms developed for humans, I would choose the terms developed for the humans because the basis for the behavior would be closer to the human basis than to the stickleback's. In other words, the nature of the individual species and its relation to other species must be taken into consideration when making comparisons. The simplest explanation may not always be the best, because *simple* is a relational word. Unfortunately, the baby may have been thrown out with the bathwater: the naive behaviorism of the first part of this century is a prime example.

Dr. Adler's sixth proposition, which defines the "humanistic" position, gave me some second thoughts about the appropriateness of his choice of the word *humanists*. It is here that man's exploitation and misuse of nature may be inferred, and it hardly seems humane. Here it is stated that man is the only thing that has inherent dignity and rights. And if man didn't have these, then he would be nothing more than a murderer and slave owner. My position is that men have rights and dignity by virtue of being animals, and that other animals do also. They may still kill other animals for nutriment and survival, just as we do, and some insects keep other insects as chattel. This is a fact of nature. It appears that there may be a "humanists" confusion between use and abuse.

Dr. Adler defines man as a rational animal with free will, having the power of conceptual thought and the power of free choice. This is moving rapidly into theology, and it is beyond my means to begin to grasp these terms empirically. Without some definitions at a behavioral level, Dr. Adler might as well have defined man as the only animal with a soul. Scientifically, this is at present a meaningless term.

Proposition seven of the essay employs more vague terms used without behavioral operational definitions. So their existence or nonexistence must rest in belief knowledge, and as a result is outside of the realm of empirical science.

In proposition eight, Dr. Adler makes good use of the absence of evidence, but that evidence is no longer absent. For example, in 8a(i) he states that "only men fashion tools not for immediate use but for future action," but in the present group of articles Dr. David McNeill notes this very behavior in chimpanzees. In 8a(ii) the point is made that only man machinofactures products using blueprints and such. But, how long has man been doing this? And what was he before he started machinofacturing? Dr. Adler states that "No other animal machinofactures to any degree." I might add that to my knowledge no other animal is a member of a labor union either.

With respect to 8a(iii), it may be observed that chimpanzees make totally useless designs using clay or other similar substances of that nature, and this observation would seem to allow a challenge also to proposition 8a(iv). I agree with proposition 8a(v). However, since Dr. Adler has made so much use of the absence of evidence to make these statements, it further supports my earlier warning about making statements based on this type of evidence.

In proposition 8b(i) it is stated that man frames constitutions and makes laws for the organization and conduction of his societies. Again, my question would be: How long has he done so, and was he man before he did this?

With respect to proposition 8b(ii) it is stated that man has great variability in his social organization, whereas other animals associate instinctively, as evidenced by the uniformity of their associations. One need only to look at the wealth of data on various social organizations of baboons and Japanese macaques to see that this is in error.

In proposition 8c, again, other animals appear to solve problems which have no biological utility or survival value (if such things exist), just as man does. The chimpanzee's fascination with lockbox problems is one example of such behavior.

Proposition 9a is also in error, since Japanese macaques have demonstrated cultural transmission of learned behaviors, and we have observed chimpanzees acquiring signs from other chimpanzees.

At this point I will close. The final answer to these questions is in the results of future experiments which comparative psychologists or comparative scientists will discover. When a person makes the statement "Man is the only animal who ... ," he has immediately moved into the realm of the comparative scientist. Fortunately, most comparative behaviorists and biologists don't make statements like that. They know differences exist, but most of these are relatively new. The complex structures (e.g., the eye) and behavior took a long time to develop to the point in their evolution where they now exist.

Sydney M. Lamb

The utter simplicity of the quasi-linguistic systems which have (so far) been taught to chimpanzees, in comparison to the richness of human languages, is brought out strikingly by the contrast between the accounts of chimp quasi-language by Drs. Fouts and McNeill and my survey of the organization of human linguistic structure. As McNeill points out, this contrast does not necessarily reflect inability of the chimps to learn more complex systems. The limitations are rather in what has been presented to the chimps by the human investigators.

Perhaps the most obvious difference is the absence of stratification, or layering of structure, in the chimp systems. Both Lana, who learned "Yerkish," and Sarah, who uses the plastic objects designed by Premack, were working with systems having a fixed small number of lexemes. Both of these systems apparently lack any provision for the creation of new lexemes, and there is probably no structure below the level of the lexeme. In other words, the lexemes in these systems are the same as the elementary signaling elements, in contrast to human languages, which have lexons, morphemes, morphons, and phonemes intervening between the lexemes and the elementary signaling units (the phonons), not to mention the separate tactic patterns at each level. It is conceivable that the plastic objects of Premack's system are to be analyzed into components of shape and color, but such components, while they are significant for the *visual* perception of the objects, probably do not also exist, as components, in Sarah's *linguistic* information system.

On the other hand, Sarah has been able to learn some lexotactic structure that has quite a bit of the complexity found in human languages. As Dr. Fouts mentions, she deals successfully with "wh" questions (What ..., Who ..., etc.), yes-no questions, prepositions, "if ... then ..." sentences, hierarchically organized sentences, and so forth.

It is also worthy of note, in connection with beliefs that some have held concerning capabilities supposedly unique to humans, that Sarah was able to use class terms such as *name of* and *color of* to learn new lexemes, and that she gave evidence of displacement. Let me here augment the accounts of Drs. Fouts and McNeill by quoting from Premack himself:

> *In early training, names were produced by repeatedly associating a piece of plastic with its referent in one linguistic context or another. Later, however, names were generated far more directly by instructions of the form "X is the*

name of Y," where X was a so far unused piece of plastic . . . and Y a so far unnamed object. Following instructions of this kind, Sarah used X in all the ways she used names introduced in more standard ways.

"Color of" was also used productively with Sarah, . . . and in a way that provided an example of displacement—the ability to comprehend statements about, or talk about, "things that are not there." Sarah was given the instruction "brown color of chocolate," as a means of introducing the new color name "brown," both "color of" and "chocolate" being established words. She was then given four colored discs, only one of them brown, and when told "take brown," performed correctly. The critical aspect of this example lies in the fact that when the original instructions—"brown color of chocolate"—were given, no chocolate was present. Only the three plastic words were present, and of course the word "brown" was not itself brown any more than any of the plastic words are iconic. . . . Sarah's subsequent choice of the correct disc indicates that she was able to generate a representation of chocolate on the basis of the word "chocolate" alone; able to associate the relevant aspect of this representation with the word "brown"; and capable subsequently of using the word "brown" to generate a representation that, when matched against the discs, enabled her to select the correct one. Thus what has been correctly singled out as a design feature of language has however been incorrectly regarded as uniquely human: displacement is something the chimpanzee can do.*

The other chimp systems are those using hand gestures for expression. In these systems there has been very little development of lexotactic structure, although it is safe to assume from the work of Premack that a chimp could successfully learn to use a gestural system with lexotactics if the investigators would develop their chimps in that direction. The gestures may differ significantly from Premack's plastic objects in that they, as units of expression, perhaps correspond to lexons rather than to lexemes. The distinction between lexons and lexemes is easily overlooked, since most lexons (of most languages) can function by themselves as lexemes (independently meaningful units); examples of English lexons that do not function in this way include *pro-, con-, de-, -fer,* and *-duct,* which combine to provide the lexemes *product, conduct, deduct, confer, defer.* The determination of whether the gestures are lexemes or lexons does not rest upon whether they are individually meaningful but upon whether or not there are in the system any complex lexemes, i.e., lexemes consisting of combinations of lexons. And it appears that there may be. Fouts cites Lucy's *candy-drink* and *drink-fruit* for watermelon, and *smell-fruit* for citrus fruits. Unfortunately, the evidence as presented by Fouts doesn't permit us to be sure of this point. Since Lucy's syntax (lexotactics) is so primitive, we can't tell whether she is using these as labels (in which case they really are lexemes) or

---

* David Premack, "Symbols and Language," in *Horizons of Anthropology,* ed. Sol Tax and Leslie G. Freeman (Chicago: Aldine Publishing Co., 1975).

whether she is merely describing by combining lexemes. The latter interpretation seems likely for her *cry-hurt-food* for radish, since, as Fouts reports, "she labeled it a *cry-hurt-food* and continued to use *cry* or *hurt* to
describe it for the next eight days." But the account is too vague. It was
either a label, *or* a description, when she "said" *cry-hurt-food*. The use of the
word *continued* by Fouts is inappropriate. Consider *blackbird*, a label (lexeme) which is, e.g., appropriately applied to an albino blackbird, and *black
bird*, a descriptive combination of lexemes which can be applied, for instance, to a crow. That Lucy was merely describing the radish with a combination of lexemes is suggested by Fouts's remark that she "continued to
use *cry* or *hurt* to describe it for the next eight days." This interpretation is
also possible for watermelon, since Lucy provided not one but two different designations, *candy-drink* and *drink-fruit*. If she were really inventing a
lexeme, she'd be more likely to be consistent. An essential property of the
lexeme is its fixedness.

One thing that seems rather certain is that Lucy's lexeme formation, if it
is present, does not make use of morphotactic constructions, as most human lexeme formation does. Lucy's system evidently has no morphotactics.
If she is forming lexemes at all, she is doing so more or less willy-nilly.
Human lexeme formation is patterned by morphotactic constructions, so
that we get, e.g., *blackbird, bluebird*, but not *birdblack; woodpecker, sapsucker*, but
not *peckwood*; and so forth.

As Fouts points out, Ameslan, the human gesture-language, has two
general classes of signs: (1) "finger-spelling," in which each sign stands for
a letter of the alphabet; and (2) the lexonic or lexemic gestures, which are
meaningful in themselves. Ironically, it is the signs of class (1) which make
Ameslan resemble a natural language, but it was only signs of class (2) that
were taught to the chimps. The signs of class (1), like letters of the alphabet, correspond to morphons of a spoken language. By themselves they
mean nothing (except by accident, as in the case of "I," a morpheme
composed of just one morphon), but they enter into combinations with
other morphons to form morphemes. Comparing Ameslan to written English, the signs of class (2) are structurally like the written symbols #, %,
&, +, =. (Readers may at this point pause to reflect whether or not they
have been accustomed to regarding such signs as more or less peripheral
to the written English system.)

The importance of the layering of human linguistic structures must not
be underestimated. This feature perhaps more than any other gives language its richness. It allows a language to have tens of thousands of lexemes (for representing hundreds of thousands of concepts) while making
use of only a very small number of signaling units. But the systems which
have been taught to the chimps have only as many lexemes as they have
signs (unless Lucy really does have a few complex lexemes). What would
human spoken language be like if we had to have a different sound for

every lexeme? How many different lexemes could we have under such circumstances?

By having tens of thousands of lexemes, language is able to provide coverage of most of human experience, both breadth of coverage and fineness of discrimination of the infinite variety of possible experiences. Dr. Adler suggests that differences of degree are clearly distinct from differences of kind, and that the latter are more important. Yet in this case we have a difference of kind—the layering of human linguistic structures as opposed to the single-level chimp systems—whose only function is to make possible a quantitative difference—the profoundly important distinction between being able to have a few dozen lexemes and being able to have tens of thousands of lexemes. Without the sheer quantity of lexemes, the range of applicability of language would be narrow rather than general, and it would thus be unable to guide our thinking. How much of Lucy's life can she communicate about, with her few dozen lexemes? So little that, for her, "language" is a relatively peripheral part of life.

For a chimp gesture system to resemble a human language, the chimps would have to be taught to use signs of class (1), which are not in themselves meaningful but must be combined with others to express meanings. And for David Premack's Sarah, how much more interesting it would be if, instead of using a blue triangle for *apple*, she had to use a combination of, say, a blue triangle followed by a red square followed by a brown trapezoid, and if these same objects in the reverse order would signify something quite unrelated conceptually (cf. *net* and *ten* in English).

Frank E. X. Dance

1. In the time passing from its inception to its completion this symposium seems to have undergone a subtle but definite shift of focus. In the beginning it was suggested that the essays center on the possible species specificity of human language. It was hoped that such a focus would, in turn, enable us to consider the import of contemporary research efforts to teach a form of human language to nonhuman primates. As the essays finally evolved, there appeared to be more emphasis on the nonhuman primate research than might have been expected had the question of uniqueness or species specificity remained in the center ring. Of course it is difficult for the relatively esoteric considerations of human linguistic uniqueness to compete with the precocious and engaging behaviors of the chimpanzee subjects. In fact, we are probably fortunate that this whole symposium is in print rather than on film, for on film the chimps are irresistible scene-stealers. Nevertheless, the question of the species specificity of human language must remain the symposium reader's central interest, for his posture on that issue will determine both his interpretation of the results reported by the primate researchers and his response to the methodology they have employed.

Susanne Langer, in her consideration of a coherent act, says that an act's completion is in a real way present in its beginning.[1] Thus, the predispositions and attitudes of all researchers materially affect not only their choice of research questions but their performance of research studies. This is true of Adler and Dance as much as it is of Fouts, McNeill, and Lamb. The essays need to be read with their authors' predispositions in mind and accounted for. They need to be read with the intent to extract any commonalities bearing on the possible species specificity of human language so as to review the nonhuman primate research in the light of those suggested commonalities. Again, it is worthwhile to remember that the questions being discussed in the essays are not about the position of man in the universe but are endeavors to understand the whole and the parts of that fantastic phenomenon designated variously as speech communication, syntactical speech, speech, and language.

2. A question that is inferred but not addressed directly is whether or not, in our considerations of the species specificity of speech communication, we are looking at things phylogenetically—that is, from the viewpoint of the role of speech communication (by whatever term it is called) in the

race—or whether we are looking at things ontogenetically, from the viewpoint of the role of speech communication in the individual. There may well be vast differences in these two viewpoints. The newborn child of the twentieth century is born into a symboling, a speech communicating, a languaging world. The contemporary infant is, from the moment of his conception, surrounded by language and immersed in it. On the other hand, there was presumably a time when men did not have speech communication, a verbal language, and in that time, aeons ago, the emergence of spoken symbols was unimagined and unanticipated. Accounting for the birth of speech communication in the race as it has developed from barely articulate beginnings would thus demand considerations differing in some dramatic ways from accounting for the acquisition of speech communication by a normal child born in today's world. Haeckel's theorem, at least in terms of human language (ontogeny recapitulates phylogeny, or the development of the individual mirrors the development of the race), although suggestive and provocative, does not seem to give us the final insight into the question of uniqueness. Thus, the question whether man originally learned to speak in the same way by which some men now are trying to induce a form of human language in chimps raises some teasing theological questions. Dr. Adler's questions (13a through 13c) could be considered from both a phylogenetic and ontogenetic viewpoint, vis-à-vis the nonhuman primates.

3.   Some of the chimp research has as its original raison d'être the mapping of the cognitive capacities of the subjects. Other such research had as its original raison d'être the teaching of a form of human language to the subjects so as (*a*) to prove it could be done and (*b*) to establish communication with another species. At this time the stated reasons for most if not all of the chimp research is for the purpose of establishing communication between man and another species. In actuality, communication, considered as the interchange of meaningful information between and among individuals, may be a secondary outcome of symboling, and also a rather late development in the evolution of human speech communication. Phylogenetically, symbols are primarily a means of initiating, fostering, and representing conceptual thought; only later were symbols considered to have the *exchange* of thought as a primary utilization. The developmental relationship of conceptual thought and speech communication, or syntactical speech, is another difficult question that is currently being investigated.[2]

4.   When discussing in my essay the question of the centrality of the spoken word, or of modal equipotentiality, I stated that there was almost no experimental evidence available on the topic. However, there have come to my attention a number of studies which do indeed bear directly, but not finally, upon the subject of developmental modal equipotentiality.

99

Both the methodologies and the results of the studies available at this time are unusually interesting.[3] The studies seem to indicate that human infants have a unique response pattern to those sounds which are within the speech spectrum. As this research endeavor continues, we should come ever closer to a full understanding of the role of the *spoken* symbol in human behavior.

---

[1] Susanne K. Langer, *Mind: An Essay on Human Feeling*, 2 vols. (Baltimore: Johns Hopkins Press, 1967, 1972), passim.

[2] R. L. Schiefelbusch and L. L. Lloyd, eds., *Language Perspectives—Acquisition, Retardation and Intervention* (Baltimore: University Park Press, 1974), passim.

[3] P. D. Eimas, E. R. Siqueland, Peter Jusczyk, and James Vigorito, "Speech Perception in Infants," *Science* 171 (22 January 1971): 303–6.

P. D. Eimas and J. D. Corbit, "Selective Adaptation of Linguistic Feature Detectors," *Cognitive Psychology* 4 (1973): 99–109.

P. D. Eimas, W. E. Cooper, and J. D. Corbit, "Some Properties of Linguistic Feature Detectors," *Perception and Psychophysics* 13 (1973): 247–52.

P. D. Eimas, "Linguistic Processing of Speech by Young Infants," in *Language Perspectives*, ed. Schiefelbusch and Lloyd, pp. 55–73.

D. L. Molfese, "Cerebral Asymmetry in Infants, Children and Adults: Auditory Evoked Responses to Speech and Noise Stimuli" (Unpublished doctoral dissertation, Pennsylvania State University, 1972).

P. A. Morse, "The Discrimination of Speech and Nonspeech Stimuli in Early Infancy" (Unpublished doctoral dissertation, University of Connecticut, 1971).

P. A. Morse, "Speech Perception in Six-Week Old Infants" (Paper presented at the meetings of the Society for Research in Child Development, Minneapolis, April 1971).

P. A. Morse, "The Discrimination of Speech and Nonspeech Stimuli in Early Infancy," *Journal of Exceptional Child Psychology* 14 (1972): 477–92.

P. A. Morse, "Infant Speech Perception: A Preliminary Model and Review of the Literature," in *Language Perspectives*, ed. Schiefelbusch and Lloyd, pp. 19–53.

PART TWO

Review
of the
Arts and Sciences

Political Philosophy in Our Time

Maurice Cranston

The following article surveys the political thought of our time, points out some of its intellectual antecedents, and identifies the principal figures who have contributed to it in Europe and America since the end of the Second World War.

Maurice Cranston has taught at the London School of Economics since 1959. In 1968 he was elected to the Chair of Political Science formerly held by Harold Laski and Michael Oakeshott. He was born in London in 1920, and was educated at Oxford, where, after his M.A., he received a B. Litt. for a thesis on the freedom of the will. This was later incorporated in his book *Freedom* (1953), which has since run into several editions, and established his reputation as a political philosopher. In 1957, he published the definitive biography of *John Locke*, which won the James Tait Black Memorial Prize, among other literary awards. His other books include *The Mask of Politics, What Are Human Rights?*, a critical study of Sartre, and a translation of Rousseau's *Social Contract*. He has written a great deal for radio, notably *Political Dialogues*, imaginary conversations between political philosophers, later published in book form. Professor Cranston has several times been a visiting professor at Harvard, Dartmouth College, and the University of British Columbia and other universities in North America. He is currently writing a biographical study of Rousseau.

The revolt against idealism

There are fashions in philosophy as there are fashions in clothes, and events in the real world have their influence on abstract thought no less than elsewhere, the most dramatic events having usually the greatest impact. The Lisbon earthquake of 1755, which left 32,000 people dead or injured, marked the end of the vogue of a certain sort of optimism according to which everything that happened in the universe happened for the best. Revolutions in government sometimes introduce revolutions in thought, quite apart from the desire of the new regimes to impose them. Wars have also brought great changes.

In the preface to his book *The Metaphysical Theory of the State*, the English social theorist L. T. Hobhouse describes how he had sat reading Hegel in his garden overlooking London during the Zeppelin raids of 1917 and had seen behind the bombs the selfsame hand of the philosopher he was reading: "In the bombing of London I had just witnessed the visible and tangible outcome of a false and wicked doctrine, the foundations of which lay, as I believe, in the book before me."[1]

Hobhouse did not speak for himself alone in thus naming Georg Wilhelm Friedrich Hegel as the man who had propelled the German nation on the road to war. He gave voice to what was to become after 1918 the predominant fashion in Anglo-American philosophy—hostility to the whole conception of metaphysics of which Hegel was the greatest modern exponent—speculative, systematic, idealistic, a kind of philosophy which had been held in high esteem in both America and Great Britain before 1914. In ascribing to philosophy such power to influence events, Hobhouse was rather less mindful of the influence of events on philosophy, including his own.

The effect of the Second World War on fashion in philosophy was to intensify in the English-speaking world the reaction against metaphysics. A crucial book of that period was Karl Popper's *The Open Society and Its Enemies*,[2] a brilliant and forceful two-volume treatise written in English by an Austrian-Jewish refugee in New Zealand, indicting not only Hegel but a string of political philosophers from Plato and Aristotle onward as intellectual forerunners of totalitarian communism, Nazism, and fascism. In the United States at about the same time Bertrand Russell was saying similar things in lectures at the Barnes Foundation, afterward published as a *History of Western Philosophy.*

"Hegel's doctrine of state," said Russell, " ... justifies every internal tyranny and every external aggression that can possibly be imagined."[3]

Russell's background was very different from Popper's. A freethinking English aristocrat, he had been an outspoken pacifist during World War I, sternly opposed to the efforts of Hobhouse and others to transform intellectual objections to Hegelian philosophy into an emotional crusade against Germany. Russell remained a pacifist until 1940, when he finally decided that the Nazis were totally unlike the German rulers of 1914 and could be overcome only by force. Thus in the 1940s Russell renounced his pacifism and became a publicist for what he understood as the cause of democracy against totalitarianism. He was later to become more sympathetic to communism, but during World War II he joined Popper in attacking the communists as well as the Nazis, and in naming various metaphysicians, and especially Hegel, as intellectual forerunners of modern totalitarian thought.

It must be said that from a more distant perspective, the peculiar responsibility of Hegel for Hitler is hard to discern. After 1918 Hegelian philosophy had gone out of fashion in Germany no less than in the English-speaking world. Admittedly, it stayed in favor in Italy, and Mussolini was able to recruit as one of his party "theoreticians" a Hegelian philosopher of some distinction, Giovanni Gentile. But Mussolini's ideology was an eclectic, incoherent construction with as many antirationalistic, and therefore anti-Hegelian, elements as there were "Hegelian" fragments. As for the Nazi ideology, its hostility to reason was unambiguous, and the only philosopher of any international repute who rallied to Nazism was Martin Heidegger, an existentialist.

The case against Hegel was never made with that careful attention to detail and that judicious impartiality which is supposed to be the mark of scholarship. In wartime it did not have to be. Besides, a certain antipathy to metaphysics was nothing new in the English-speaking world. A faith in common sense, the empirical, and the practical has long been supposed to distinguish the Anglo-Saxon mind, or temperament, from the rationalistic, systematic, deductive continental European way of thinking. The Lord Chancellor Francis Bacon, at the beginning of the seventeenth century, was the founder of a fashion that has lasted long enough to become a cultural tradition: a preference for science to any kind of speculative thought, including (though Bacon dared not say it) religious thought. Science alone, Bacon believed, could save mankind, because it could be put to use in overcoming natural disabilities and providing material abundance. The kind of knowledge men most needed was scientific knowledge; the rest was unimportant. In more elaborate ways than Bacon, a long line of English-speaking philosophers, from Locke and Hume to Dewey and Peirce, said much the same thing, that the foundation of all our knowledge is experience acquired through the senses, empirical knowledge as opposed to metaphysical, this latter word being taken to refer to all purely rational, abstract constructions or intuitions of the mind, save those of mathematics and logic, which even the most extreme empiricists have been willing to treat as knowledge, albeit of a wholly tautologous kind.

When Hobhouse and the rest so aggressively rejected Hegel, it was to this alternative tradition of empiricism that they turned and brought back into fashion. But however adequate empiricism may be as a philosophy of mind, it is difficult to see how, as an alternative to Hegelianism, it could possibly serve as political philosophy (or, for that matter, as moral philosophy). Some people have been content to say that empiricism in epistemology "goes together" or "has gone together" with liberalism in politics. The leading English champion of logical positivism, Sir Alfred Ayer, made this claim as recently as 1973 in a Dutch television broadcast.[4] And indeed it is true that Locke, Mill, Russell, and Ayer himself have been liberals in one sense or other of that word. On the other hand, Bacon was a firm believer in enlightened despotism precisely because he believed in the supremacy of science, and Bacon's French disciples in the eighteenth century agreed with him; Hume was a conservative on the grounds that no empiricist can logically invoke such metaphysical liberal principles as the rights of man, and most of Ayer's contemporaries in Oxford philosophy are reputed to be conservatives, doubtless for much the same reason as Hume.

So the claim that empiricism in epistemology "goes together" with liberalism in politics is not tenable, and if it were, such a fortuitous conjunction would not be enough to satisfy the expectations of Hobhouse and others that empiricism should yield a political philosophy as coherent as that of Hegel (but true, where his was false).

One rejoinder to this observation would a few years ago have been that empiricism *cannot* produce any political philosophy, and hence that political philosophy has no raison d'être. For between the two wars empiricism had been pushed to extremes; it had been transformed into logical positivism. No longer content to say that scientific knowledge is the most important form of knowledge, the avant-garde of philosophy had started to say that whatever is not science is nonsense.

Paradoxically, the philosopher who led this fashion was one of the most intensely moral and ardent modern thinkers, Ludwig Wittgenstein. The son of a very rich Austrian, Wittgenstein left Vienna in 1908 to study engineering in England at Manchester, where he developed an interest in logic and so moved on to Cambridge, to study under Bertrand Russell, who taught him "all he had to teach." Wittgenstein then withdrew to a life of solitude. As a prisoner of war during World War I, he fell under the spell of Tolstoy; he decided thereupon to give away all his money (a fortune greatly increased by his family having sold arms to both sides in the war) and live in the utmost poverty. During the 1920s Wittgenstein worked as a village schoolmaster in Austria, but was persuaded to return to Cambridge in the 1930s, and though he gave no lectures and published very little, he acquired a small band of devoted followers, who made his ideas known within a limited public. It was Wittgenstein's singular destiny to produce not one but two philosophical theories, each extremely influential.

The first was set forth in his oracular *Tractatus Logico-Philosophicus*[5] of 1922, a book which ended with the assertion that what could not be stated as fact should not be said at all. A less mystical formulation of the same argument was worked out by a group of Wittgenstein's fellow Austrians who came to be known as the Vienna Circle;[6] these were the original logical positivists. They claimed that all the traditional problems of philosophy were "pseudo-problems" based on confusion of language. Only statements which could be verified, or confirmed by public observation, could be counted as either true or false. All other utterances were meaningless or nonsensical. The judgments of ethics and aesthetics were no more than expressions of emotion, and no sense whatever could be attributed to statements about God.

Although the theory of logical positivism was thus evolved by Austrians in Austria, it had an electrifying effect on both American and British readers. Translated into English by such brilliant exponents as A. J. Ayer in his *Language, Truth and Logic*,[7] and transported both to America and the British Isles by the Austrian philosophers themselves when the Nazis drove them into exile, logical positivism found an environment wholly prepared to welcome it. Some leading members of the Vienna Circle had by the time they reached America or England in the late 1930s begun to modify the extremism of their earlier opinions; Wittgenstein himself had wholly rejected the central theory of his *Tractatus* and had begun to work out his second theory; but Wittgenstein kept silent, and it was the uncompromising *brut* doctrine of logical positivism that penetrated the English-speaking world in the years leading up to World War II. The bleakness of the message seemed to fit the bleakness of the times. The tradition of pragmatism in America and the tradition of commonsense empiricism in England had already diminished the importance of philosophy in the cultural life of those nations. Logical positivism almost promised to banish philosophy to the same cloud-cuckoo-land to which earlier empiricists had banished religion. Almost, but not quite; for even logical positivism still offered some work for philosophy to do.

The role of philosophy, according to logical positivism, was to formulate a "grammar of science." Not only the positivists but Karl Popper, who stood apart from both Wittgenstein and the Vienna Circle (though he lived in Vienna) and was a radical critic of the fundamental assertions of logical positivism, could say in an essay on the Hegelian dialectic published as late as 1940:

> *The whole development of dialectic should be a warning against speculative philosophy. It should remind us that philosophy must not be made a basis for any sort of scientific system and that philosophers should be much more modest in their claims. For their task, which they can fulfil quite usefully, is the study of the methods of science.*[8]

A "grammar of science," or, in other words, the study of logic and methodology alone, it seemed, remained of philosophy. Ethics and aesthetics came under the same shadow as metaphysics. Political philosophy was called into question with all the more hostility because so many of its illustrious past practitioners had been indicted as forerunners of fascism and communism.

Political philosophy, the positivists argued, was based on a mistake, the mistake that there could be knowledge of values. From their point of view, there can be knowledge only of facts, and facts belong to a totally different logical category from values. Values are simply matters of personal preference, and assertions of them can therefore be neither true nor false. Only propositions that can be publicly verified can count as true or false; all else is to be ruled out as literally meaningless. Hence the one permissible study of politics is a "scientific" study, that is, political science understood strictly as the study of practices and behavior in the "real world." As for values, they, from this point of view, "can ultimately be reduced to emotional responses conditioned by the individual's life-experiences."[9]

In American universities empirical political science had already become a rapidly growing subject; American interest in political education coupled with the pragmatic tradition of American thought[10] encouraged research of this kind for its own sake, and the rise of positivism helped at the same time to spread the study of empirical political science and to put a brake on the study of political philosophy.

It cannot be said that philosophers themselves did much to defend the subject. In the classical period, philosophers thought of themselves as teaching men how to live; and in their role as political philosophers, they saw themselves as helping men find the way toward a good or just political order. By the twentieth century, this conception of the philosopher's role had come to be assumed by publicists and pamphleteers, by men like Walter Lippmann and Harold Laski, more often than by genuine philosophers on the model of Plato. And as the polemical voice grew louder, the serious philosophers tried all the harder to establish themselves as neutral, academic figures, *au dessus de la mêlée* of political controversy.

For it was not only the empiricists, or positivists, who held that philosophy is correctly understood as a neutral activity directed toward the explanation of theoretical problems rather than the production of practical wisdom. At the outbreak of World War II, this view was being advanced by leading philosophers of most Western schools of thought, including existentialists, phenomenologists, idealists, and scholastics. Among idealists, both Benedetto Croce in Italy and Michael Oakeshott in England asserted the logical separation of what they called the philosophical and the practical modes of experience, and both put politics squarely within the boundaries of the practical. Croce tried to work out some devious way whereby philosophy could influence political understanding, but Oakeshott insisted that philosophy can contribute nothing to practical political knowledge. Existentialism, more fashionable on the Continent than it ever became in the English-speaking world, allowed its adherents each to construct his own political philosophy. Existentialists were generally men who agreed in what they denied, rather than in what they affirmed. They agreed that there was no truth to be discovered by reason in questions of morals or politics, that there were no universal principles of justice or categorical imperatives. Moral principles were whatever principles a man chose for himself and realized in practice: practice was everything. A brave man was a man who acted bravely and an honest man was a man who acted honestly. "Inner principles," whether of conscience or reason, were metaphysical illusions. Only commitment mattered, and the existentialist was left to make whatever commitment he chose. Heidegger in Germany in 1933 chose Nazism; Camus, in Algeria in 1942, made an equally irrationalist choice, as he saw it, of the cause of justice against Nazism. Sartre took no great interest in politics until he was "converted," as he put it, to Marxism during the German Occupation. Gabriel Marcel remained a political conservative, and Karl Jaspers a liberal. No two existentialists had the same conception of politics.

The phenomenologists, inspired by Edmund Husserl, were no less insistent on the "neutrality" of philosophy. "Theorising," wrote one phenomenologist, "does not serve any practical purpose. Its aim is not to master the world, but to observe and possibly to understand it."[11]

Thomism, too, had a very long tradition of concentration on methodology. The method of analysis favored by the positivist philosophers had much in common with the dialectical method and the logical sophistication of the scholastics. Professionalism and rigor were distinguishing marks of both these schools of thought. And here we may notice one significant difference between twentieth-century philosophy at its best and the philosophy of the nineteenth century. A hundred years ago philosophers published much of their work in general literary reviews addressed to the educated public as a whole; John Stuart Mill indeed was the editor of one such review. Twentieth-century philosophers have published most of their work in learned journals, and have more often than not written for a specialized audience, speaking, as it were, from scholar to scholar.

The growth of specialization and academic rigor is one reason why twentieth-century philosophy, including political philosophy, became so withdrawn from what most people believed to be the central problems of lived political experience. This was most marked at the period which witnessed the outbreak of World War II. At a time when the impassioned ideologies of Nazism and communism looked as if they might conquer the world, academic political philosophy appeared to many people to have nothing useful to say; and its practitioners seemed to be mainly absorbed in logic-chopping of one kind or another.

There were, assuredly, a number of exceptions. Certain Thomist philosophers within the Catholic church had for some years been champions of the idea of a Christian democracy as opposed to the conservative, or reactionary, political tendencies that had dominated the church in the nineteenth century. One of the most important of such philosophers was Jacques Maritain.[12] A French Catholic convert (from Protestantism), Maritain was trained in science and turned to philosophy largely because he found the empiricist, or Baconian, account of science an inadequate account of what scientists actually did. This took him back to the tradition of Aristotle and Aquinas against which Bacon had so passionately rebelled, and though Maritain found no complete truth in either, he saw in the classical and the medieval philosophers at least the basis for a modern theory of knowledge. On the other hand, he noted that the condition of man in the modern world was radically different from that of either antiquity or the medieval period, and hence that an appropriate social and political theory for the twentieth century could not be derived from classical or medieval conceptions.

Maritain argued that it was wholly proper for modern man to seek a large part of his fulfillment in the present life and in the present world, that freedom on earth was as valid a goal as was salvation in heaven. He did not assert that freedom was in any way a religious ideal; it was a civil or political ideal; indeed, Maritain sought to restore, in modern terminology, the conception of freedom as a natural or human right. While he insisted that such natural rights rest on natural law, which comes in turn from God, Maritain pointed out that the actual enjoyment of the right to liberty depended on the existence of certain political institutions, and he further argued that in the modern world such institutions must be democratic. As democracy was increasingly challenged by the rise of totalitarianism, Maritain moved from France to the United States, where he concentrated more and more on social and political problems, without ever losing the philosophical perspective. An American scholar who undertook a similar task in the immediate prewar period was Mortimer Adler, who in such writings as *A Dialectic of Morals*[13] and "The Theory of Democracy"[14] sought to provide a demonstrative argument in favor of the principles of freedom and democracy.

Then, as we have seen, there were the wartime writings of Bertrand Russell and Karl Popper. Russell, however, drew a line between his work as a philosopher, which was mainly concerned with the theory of mathematics (and which was almost fully complete by the time he was forty), and his work as a political and social theorist, to which he devoted the second half of his life. He claimed that there was no logical connection between the one and the other. Popper, on the other hand, tried to develop his political beliefs on philosophical foundations. The war prompted him to do so. Having published as late as 1940 his article suggesting that the only business of the philosopher was to formulate the methods of science, he went on to write *The Open Society and Its Enemies,* a book of which the principal aim, after demolishing the metaphysical philosophers of the past, was to vindicate the superiority of freedom and democracy over any other kind of political arrangement.

When Popper came to reprint his article of 1940, on the subject of the Hegelian dialectic, he altered the last paragraph, so that it read as follows:

> *The whole development of dialectic should be a warning against the dangers inherent in philosophical system-building. It should remind us that philosophy must not be made the basis for any sort of scientific system and that philosophers should be much more modest in their claims. One task which they can fulfil quite usefully is the study of the critical methods of science.*[15]

Popper's change of words is significant. "Speculative philosophy" is no longer called into question as a whole, and the study of the methods of science (now specified as "critical methods") is named as *one* of the tasks and no longer as the only task of philosophy. The climate of philosophy in the English-speaking world had changed a lot between 1940 and 1963, the year in which Popper reprinted his essay on the dialectic, and Popper himself had done as much as anyone to change it.

Even so, political philosophy was reported as late as 1956 to be dead.[16] Ironically, the very place in which Peter Laslett announced the death of political philosophy was the introduction to a collection of postwar essays in political philosophy, essays which could well have been seen as proof of the vitality of the subject in the English-speaking world. But everyone was afraid of boasting.

Locke, in the preface to the first, the 1689, edition of his *Essay concerning Human Understanding,* says of his own work as a philosopher, "It is ambition enough to be employ'd as an under-labourer in clearing the ground a little, and removing some of the rubbish that lies in the way to knowledge."[17] There is an unmistakable element of false modesty in Locke's claim. He hoped, in fact, to propel philosophy into new channels. But contemporary political philosophers have taken their cue from him. They have spoken of their own job as one of tidying things up, of sorting them out, so that other people can make their decisions more intelligently. Political philosophy, like other departments of modern philosophy, has a deceptive air of humility.

The language of politics

We have seen that the Austrian philosophers—Wittgenstein and Popper in their early days, no less than the members of the Vienna Circle—spoke of reducing philosophy to the status of a handmaiden of empirical science. But the actual activity most of them (all of them indeed with the exception of Popper) assigned to philosophy was something which came to be known as analysis. Analysis meant rather different things to different men, but broadly speaking, it was understood as a process of "breaking down" or "taking apart" linguistic utterances to investigate their logical form. For a time the avant-garde of philosophy used this technique mainly as an attack on traditional philosophy. Gilbert Ryle,[18] for example, incongruously seated in the chair of metaphysics at Oxford, suggested that the main task of the new philosophy was the analysis of those expressions which systematically misled traditional philosophers: the main outcome of such analysis was intended to show that the so-called central problems of philosophy derived from persistent confusions of language.

However, the use of analysis as destructive tool against traditional philosophy was, by its very nature, an activity that could not continue indefinitely, and philosophers soon turned to more constructive uses of their technique. The first of their purposes came to be spoken of as clarification. Analysis could be used, not only to break things down but to set them out in a more coherent, intelligible form, and so to banish misunderstandings. One of the consequences of the development of analysis was, ironically perhaps, to turn the tables against those who had promised to eliminate "traditional philosophy" by means of analysis. Analysis carried far enough had the effect of reinstating a good many of those "central problems of philosophy" which the early analysts had said were simply products of confusion of language.

Analytic political philosophy emerged together with analytic moral philosophy. This is hardly surprising, since political philosophy uses the same method as moral philosophy and has in common with it a certain shared field of interest. Problems of justice, for example, and obligation, goodness, and freedom are equally part of moral philosophy and of political philosophy. Analytic moral philosophy established itself sooner than did analytic political philosophy, but the history of the two disciplines is inseparable.

Analytic moral philosophy began by accepting from the positivists the doctrine that the logical category of fact is totally distinct from that of value, and that no knowledge of value can be derived from knowledge of fact. It was agreed that "what is" was wholly distinct from "what ought to be," and that statements about "what ought to be" could be neither true nor false. But if ethics was thus banished from the realm of knowledge, even the most avant-garde philosophers claimed that there was room for what they called metaethics: not the study of the good and the right but the study of statements *about* the good and the right. Metaethics was a wholly theoretical, ethically neutral enterprise conducted at a higher level of abstraction than moral judgment itself.

A pioneering work of this kind which came out during World War II was *Ethics and Language* by Charles L. Stevenson, a young Yale professor of philosophy. Unlike Popper, Russell, Maritain, Adler, and others who responded to the challenge of World War II by reaffirming their commitment to democracy, Stevenson tried to remain at the level of clinical and detached analysis and to work within the categories he had inherited from logical positivism. He started out with a theory of meaning which corresponded to the positivist bifurcation of fact and value; descriptive meaning, as he called it, was that form of meaning which related to facts, emotive meaning was that form of meaning which related to preferences, values, feelings. The meaning of a word, Stevenson argued, was its "disposition"—its disposition, in the case of descriptive meaning, to convey information and affect cognition, and its disposition, in the case of emotive meaning, "to evoke or directly express attitudes, as distinct from designating them."[19] Thus, for example, a word such as *beautiful* does not merely describe something or somebody; it betrays the favorable attitude, or feelings, of the speaker, and tends to elicit similar feelings in the hearer. *Beautiful* is a hurrah word, *ugly* is a boo word.

In the light of later research on the theory of meaning, Stevenson's work looks somewhat immature, but it does have an interesting bearing on the analysis of political words. For all the central words of political discourse—*justice, liberty, despotism, authority, rights, law,* and so forth—are, in Stevenson's terminology, words rich in emotive as well as descriptive meaning. One of the central points of his argument is that emotive meaning can become independent of descriptive meaning. A word, he suggests, may acquire a favorable emotive meaning because it describes something which is favored; then the descriptive meaning may for one reason or another change and the emotive meaning remain unaltered. Stevenson illustrates this point with reference to the word *democracy*. He says that this word has a pleasing emotive meaning for his fellow Americans because the thing it conventionally describes pleases them—that is to say, "government of the people, by the people" as practiced under the American Constitution pleases them. Thus the word *democracy* becomes a hurrah word, and it tends to remain a hurrah word even when it is used to name something different.

"Suppose, for example," Stevenson writes, "that a group of people disapprove of certain aspects of democracy, but continue to approve of other aspects of it. They might leave the descriptive meaning of 'democracy' unchanged, and gradually let it acquire, for their usage, a much less laudatory emotive meaning. On the other hand, they might keep the strong laudatory meaning unchanged, and let 'democracy' acquire a descriptive sense which made reference only to those aspects of democracy (in the older sense) which they favored."[20]

European history since 1930 provides us with an example of what Stevenson is suggesting. The Nazis and Fascists allowed the word *democracy* to retain its conventional descriptive meaning unaltered, and because they disliked what it named, used it as a pejorative word. The Communists, on the other hand, altered the descriptive meaning of the word *democracy* by adopting it to name their own system of government; they kept it as a hurrah word and assimilated its prestige into their institutions.

Emotive meaning, as Stevenson speaks of it, is never precise, it "suggests" rather than states; he says it is not made definite by the operation of linguistic rules, as is descriptive meaning. And once a word has acquired a disposition to evoke or elicit a sympathetic response, it keeps it. Stevenson goes on to say:

> *Suppose, though quite artificially, that a term's laudatory meaning has arisen solely because its descriptive meaning refers to something which people favor. And suppose that a given speaker succeeds in changing the descriptive meaning of the term, in a way which his audience temporarily sanctions. One might expect that the emotive meaning will undergo a parallel change, automatically. But in fact it often will not. Through inertia, it will survive a change in the descriptive meaning on which it originally depended.*[21]

This suggestion of Stevenson throws light on the success of the Communists in making some people think of their regimes as democratic. What they have done is to seize a word in good repute (possessing what Stevenson calls favorable emotive meaning) and use it to name something altogether different from what it has conventionally named. The Communists say, "Let us promote democracy," and then go on to say that true democracy is not government by the people on the American model, but the dictatorship of the proletariat through the agency of the Party.

Stevenson calls this rhetorical device "persuasive definition"—the attempt to direct a listener's friendly feelings toward a new object by claiming that the true form of what he favors is something different from what he had supposed. In reality, persuasive definitions are a form of stipulative definition, which by its nature is wholly arbitrary and can be neither true nor false.

Persuasive definition is the foundation of the alarming language "Newspeak" invented by George Orwell in *Nineteen Eighty-four*. Orwell's novel is set in a totalitarian Utopia where standard English has been replaced by a language suited to the ideological needs of the state. In Newspeak "war is peace, freedom is slavery, ignorance is strength." The institutions of the state are a Ministry of Truth, which issues lying propaganda, a Ministry of Peace, which deals with war, and a Ministry of Love, which supervises the police and prisons.

George Orwell puts Newspeak in an imaginary future, but it is only an extended form of something which has often been employed in the real world by political and by ideological movements. As long ago as the fifteenth century, when Savonarola tried to set up an ideal city in Florence, he changed the name of the Council of War to the Council of Peace, without in any way changing its military duties. Very much more recently in Western Europe, government offices which authorize the destruction of nature are called Ministries of the Environment. The idea is to hide an ugly fact with a beautiful word.

The value of Stevenson's book is that it was an early attempt to achieve an understanding of moral and political ideas through an examination of language. Its greatest defect is that its method proved to be inadequate to the task. Stevenson could see that moral judgments are logically different from expressions of personal preference. Disapproval differs from dislike, and Stevenson suggested that the difference lies in the following: To say "this is wrong" is to say not only "I disapprove of this" but "Do so as well!" In short, Stevenson recognized something which Immanuel Kant had emphasized two centuries earlier, that moral categories are distinguished both by their imperative and their universal character. But Stevenson was unable to provide a satisfactory account of this imperative and universal quality of moral discourse within a theory of meaning which recognized only descriptive and emotive meaning. Later philosophers were to become acutely aware that we do many more things with words besides describing things, on the one hand, and expressing or evoking feelings on the other.

A book which carried on where Stevenson left off was T. D. Weldon's *The Vocabulary of Politics*, first published in 1953. Weldon, an Oxford philosophy don who had established his reputation as a Kant scholar, was fairly late in accepting the conception of philosophy as linguistic analysis, and his book betrays both the fervor and the simplicity of a convert. His book was published in a series edited by A. J. Ayer, who wrote in his introduction to it: "[Mr. Weldon] is concerned not to defend, or attack any one political system, but to exhibit the logic of statements which characteristically figure in discourse about politics."[22]

Weldon repeats the allegation (which by 1953 had become exceedingly familiar) that traditional political philosophy rests on a mistake: "Most well-known philosophers from Plato onwards who have written on politics have ... taken for granted that 'What is the proper relation between the State and the Individual?' is a significant question." Weldon argues that all these philosophers, "Idealist, Democratic, and Marxist," as he calls them, are equally mistaken. And he goes on to claim that their mistake arises from confusions over the implication of language: "[It] arises from the primitive and generally unquestioned belief that words, and especially the words which normally occur in discussions about politics such as 'State,' 'Citizen,' 'Law,' and 'Liberty,' have intrinsic or essential meanings which it is the aim of political philosophers to discover and explain."[23]

Thus, whereas Stevenson had suggested that political words had descriptive and emotive meaning, Weldon claimed that such words had no meaning at all in the sense of denoting entities (Stevenson's "descriptive meaning"). Rather, said Weldon, such words have certain *uses*, which it is the business of the philosopher to analyze. Such a word as *justice* is used, he suggested, less to describe a state of affairs than to *appraise* it. The man who calls an arrangement "just" appraises that arrangement favorably from his own point of view, and such a man ought to be able to give reasons for his appraisal. The use of political words, Weldon goes on to say, is not precise, like that of some technical terms, but they are serviceable enough for the purposes of communication. Moreover, Weldon rejected as overdogmatic the positivist belief that there could be no "bridge" from an is to an ought. "It is perfectly correct to say," he wrote, "that only by intensive study of facts can we reach sound appraisals and advise other people as to their best course of action." And he went on: "When verbal confusions are tidied up most of the questions of traditional political philosophy are not unanswerable. All of them are confused formulations of purely empirical difficulties. This does not mean that these are themselves easy to deal with, but it does mean that writers on political institutions and statesmen, not philosophers, are the proper people to deal with them."[24]

The main difference between Weldon's book and Stevenson's was that Weldon had been influenced by the later work of Wittgenstein and not by the logical positivists. Between the teaching of the *Tractatus* of 1922 and Wittgenstein's later writings there is a radical break, and this break affects his whole theory of language. The early Wittgenstein had claimed that sentences depict the logical forms of fact, so that language is a "picture of reality." On this interpretation, a sentence is true to the extent that it gives an accurate representation of a state of affairs in the real world. In his later work Wittgenstein repudiates this view altogether.

In his *Philosophical Investigations* (a book published posthumously in 1953) Wittgenstein challenges the belief he ascribes to Saint Augustine that children learn a language by learning which objects are named by different words. On this view, learning a language is a matter of memorizing all the "names" and connecting each name with the thing denoted. Wittgenstein claims that this is not at all how we learn to speak. He says that only a small part of learning a language can be achieved by memorizing the names of things. For knowing a language is not primarily a matter of knowing what things are called, but of knowing how to ask questions, give orders, make promises, understand requests, and much else. Just as learning the names of cards is not enough to enable me to play bridge, so learning the names of objects is not enough to enable me to speak a language, for a sentence is not a string of names.

Wittgenstein goes on to suggest that we learn to speak by discovering the use of words. The meaning of a word, Wittgenstein says, is not "what it stands for"; it is simply "the way a word is used." Wittgenstein still agrees that some sentences may describe facts, but he adds that this is only one of many ways in which sentences may function. He asks: "But how many kinds of sentence are there? Say assertion, question, and command?—There are *countless* kinds: countless different kinds of use of what we call 'symbols,' 'words,' 'sentences.' "[25]

Wittgenstein insists that it is by no means easy to say what job each sentence does. This is one of the reasons why language tends, as Wittgenstein puts it, "to bewitch our intelligence." Analysis puts things right. The purpose of analysis is to clear up the muddles and relieve the bewilderment caused by our failure to understand the logic of language. Philosophy is thus a kind of therapy.

At Oxford after World War II, philosophers such as Gilbert Ryle and John L. Austin developed this technique of "ordinary language analysis" to a high degree of sophistication, and it was by them that Weldon was introduced to the ideas of the later Wittgenstein. Hence, while Stevenson spoke of descriptive and emotive meaning, Weldon discarded as fallacious "the doctrine that words have meanings in the classical sense." He suggested that one should examine the use and not the meaning of political words. Weldon classified the central words of political discourse—words such as *freedom, justice,* and so on—as "appraisal words," and he added:

> *Appraisals of the goodness or badness of political institutions are like all other appraisals in that they are formulated by individuals. They vary because individuals are sometimes biassed, short-sighted, selfish, unintelligent and so on. And since it requires much care and training to overcome such limitations it is not surprising that the variations which we find in these departments are greater than those we find in weighing, counting, and measuring, which are a great deal easier to accomplish. What has to be remembered is that a personal view is not necessarily biassed or dishonest.*[26]

Weldon's book ends with the interesting suggestion that there is a considerable resemblance between appraisals of political institutions and appraisals of works of art, but he does not develop this at any length. Nor indeed does he offer much in the way of a detailed analysis of the use of political words; the chapter devoted to this exercise is only one of six. The greater part of the book is directed toward the attack on "traditional political philosophy" and to the reiteration of the point of view summed up elsewhere thus: "The purpose of philosophy ... is to expose and elucidate linguistic muddles; it has done its job when it has revealed the confusions which have occurred and are likely to recur in inquiries into matter of fact because the structure and use of language are what they are.... 'Modern political philosophers do not preach,' we say. 'That was the heresy of the nineteenth century. We are plain, honest men who tidy up muddles and have no axe to grind.' "[27] In the last chapter of his *Vocabulary of Politics,* Weldon declares: "The purpose of this Chapter is entirely therapeutic."[28]

Weldon thus echoes one of Wittgenstein's claims, and in doing so he betrays a blandness which Wittgenstein himself never exhibited. But it does translate into the realm of political philosophy Wittgenstein's conservatism in the matter of language: "Philosophy may in no way interfere with the actual use of language ... it leaves everything as it is."[29]

Oakeshott and Popper

This conservatism of Weldon has been seen by Ernest Gellner[30] and Dante Germino,[31] and by numerous radical critics of the Oxford "philosophy of ordinary language," as a defect of that school of thought. Such criticism is of course political, and does not constitute a philosophical argument against Weldon's method. It is interesting to note, however, that both political and philosophical parallels can be found in the thinking of Weldon's contemporary and compatriot, Michael Oakeshott, a philosopher in no way influenced by Wittgenstein or logical positivism, but a philosopher who belongs to the alternative and rival tradition of Hegelian idealism.[32]

Oakeshott, no less than Weldon, maintains that abstract thought or theorizing has no bearing on the kind of practical judgment employed in politics, and may indeed be systematically misleading. Both Oakeshott and Weldon are equally scornful of "principles" being invoked as foundations for political programs. The main difference is that whereas Weldon is primarily concerned to banish "metaphysical lumber" and cure the reader of any obstacles to the happy pursuit of commonsense solutions by the methods of empirical political science, Oakeshott is at once more thoroughgoing in his skepticism—having small faith in the fact-finding powers of empirical political science—and in his commitment to philosophy. Oakeshott is more original, more sophisticated, and more constructive a thinker. Whereas Weldon leans heavily on the doctrinal pronouncements of Wittgenstein, Oakeshott's political theory flows from the central argument of his own Hegelian philosophy,[33] as expounded in earlier writings such as *Experience and Its Modes*,[34] a book which was published in 1933 when the author was thirty-two. The argument of this book owes much to the theory of truth as coherence. In its pages, Oakeshott depicts the philosopher's task as "the perpetual reestablishment of coherence" or the resolution of the inconsistency in any set of concrete images so as to make it more intelligible. Ordinary or commonsense views may be used as a point of departure, but they are adopted only to be superseded. They are examined and criticized with the aim of moving beyond them to a more comprehensive perspective. Philosophy, on this view, neither seeks nor desires a stopping place. It is not the construction of a complete system of knowledge but rather a method or way of thinking. Its objective is nothing more ambitious than intelligibility. Philosophy, for Oakeshott, is explanation.

While Oakeshott may try "to achieve on each question which he discusses the most inclusive and concordant view,"[35] he does not imagine that such absolute coherence of concrete ideas is ever actually accomplished; this is simply the criterion of whatever is done. Oakeshott notes that men have an incurable tendency to look at the world in ways which, though wholly consistent and self-contained in their own terms, are not fully satisfactory in experience as a whole. Such limited perspectives Oakeshott speaks of as "modes" of experience; each "mode" constructs a specific and homogeneous picture not of a part of the real world but of the whole of experience as it is seen from a given point of interest. Oakeshott sees no theoretical limit to the number of such abstract worlds, but he distinguishes four as being particularly familiar and fully formed: namely those of practice, science, history, and poetry.

Each of these "modes," Oakeshott suggests, has its own validity, but all are in different ways limited, and none is able, in its own terms, to understand its limitations. Only the philosophical perspective is able to transcend the shortcomings of these several "modes," and reinterpret them from the standpoint of experience as a totality. The philosopher seeks to bring out the logical form of each particular "mode" with a view to perceiving "the degree and limitations of the coherence achieved."

Given that this is the method which Oakeshott applies to the study of politics, his first question becomes: What is the principle of coherence to be sought in the interpretation of political activity? Oakeshott considers, and rejects, two well-known ways of characterizing political behavior. First, he repudiates the notion of politics as an ad hoc activity of "Waking up each morning and considering 'What would I like to do?' ... and doing it." For this, he thinks, is to represent politics as something entirely capricious, which it is not. Secondly, he rejects the more exalted and very fashionable belief that politics is an activity which may be guided by an independently premeditated plan or set of principles. Some of the most telling and often quoted passages in Oakeshott's writings are directed against this vision of politics. It is the one that he likes to call "rationalist."

Since the word *rationalism* has several meanings (or uses), it is hardly surprising that these arguments of Oakeshott have been misunderstood. He is certainly not attacking Reason. He is criticizing rather a kind of intellectualism or what he has sometimes called *philosophisme*. "The Rationalist," writes Oakeshott, "is like a shopkeeper who, having bought an estate, thinks that a correspondence course in estate management will give him all the knowledge necessary to control it and its tenancy."[36] The kind of rationalist Oakeshott has in mind is the man who thinks he can apply intellectual blueprints to the world of politics, who imagines he can solve concrete problems by the light of abstract generalizations, and who seeks, in effect, to introduce into politics the method of the polytechnician or engineer.

Against such belief in the sovereignty of technique, Oakeshott insists on the importance of practical knowledge, which is largely traditional knowledge. He likens the art of politics to that of cookery. "A cook," he writes, "is not a man who first has a vision of a pie and then tries to make it; he is a man skilled in cookery, and both his projects and his achievements spring from that skill." Political understanding comes as a result of being apprenticed to, participating in, and thereby "comprehending all the resources of a tradition of behavior."[37]

It must be said that Oakeshott's analogy between politics and cookery sounds rather odd. Plato and other Greeks likened the politician to the flute player, which is surely a better analogy. If politics is an art, it is one of the performing arts, one in which speech, oratory, rhetoric, persuasion play a very large part. And indeed Oakeshott sees this plainly enough when he goes on to define politics. He defines it as "activity and utterance connected with government and the instruments of government" or, in a famous phrase, "the activity of attending to the general arrangements of a set of people whom chance or choice has brought together." Any group may have its politics, but we use the word primarily in connection with those associations known as states. Like all procedures among men, Oakeshott suggests, the rules and institutions of states are most useful when they are familiar and do not alter excessively. Not that Oakeshott sees anything sacrosanct in such rules and institutions; all are "susceptible of change and improvement." But such possible improvements, he argues, are prompted neither by caprice nor by abstract principles; they derive from the recognition of specific and ascertainable defects in what already obtains. Thus political activity is a matter of "amending existing arrangements to make them more coherent."

This emphasis of Oakeshott's on the "politics of repair"[38] and on statesmanship as "choosing the least evil" has prompted some readers to see him as another Edmund Burke. But this is a mistake. Burke, like most conservative political theorists, was a champion of the Christian order, of natural law, of the right to property, and so forth. Oakeshott, who carries the skepticism of his philosophy into his politics, has no belief in such metaphysical abstractions. His kindred spirit is not Burke but David Hume. Like Hume, Oakeshott is conservative as a result of his doubt. Hume relied on tradition, habit, and custom precisely because he could see nothing else to rely on: no God, no natural law, no elevating custom and tradition into sacred substitutes for God and natural law. His skeptical conservatism was open, undogmatic, and splendidly tolerant.

This is equally true of Oakeshott's conservatism. Opposed to all ideology, he cannot, and does not, share the ideological conservatism of Burke and his successors. This attitude which is required by Oakeshott's theory is clearly also part of his natural disposition. No one can read his writings without being struck by his manifest devotion to freedom. And whatever his debt to Hegel in other fields, Oakeshott owes nothing to Hegel in his understanding of what freedom is. Oakeshott's notion of freedom is the plain man's, or rather the plain Englishman's, notion. Freedom is something to be defended against the regime and against any other great concentration of power. And although Oakeshott has sometimes criticized forms of theoretical individualism, his freedom is the freedom of the individual. This is made strikingly clear in an essay of his which has been published only in Holland but which deserves to be better known: "The Masses in Representative Democracy." In this essay he introduces the concept of the "anti-individual." "The 'masses' as they appear in modern European history," Oakeshott writes, "are not composed of individuals; they are composed of 'anti-individuals' united in revulsion from individuality."[39]

The main argument of the essay is that freedom, as Englishmen understand it, is something that emerged in medieval times with the sense of individuality. Individuality demanded a government strong enough to enable the individual to escape from communal or other established pressures, a government which could maintain order and create new rights and duties appropriate to the interests of individuality, but which at the same time was not so powerful that it would itself constitute a new threat to those interests. Legislative bodies arose to make laws favorable to the individual and to establish spheres of private activities (or liberties) in which the individual could act without interference:

In this condition [Oakeshott writes] every subject was secured of the right to pursue his chosen directions of activity as little hindered as might be by his fellows or by the exactions of government itself, and as little distracted by communal pressures. As an individual he was guaranteed freedom of movement, of initiative, of speech, of belief and religious observance, of association and dissociation, of bequest and inheritance; security of person and property; the right to choose one's own occupation and dispose of one's labor and goods; and over all the "rule of law"—the right to be ruled by a known law, applicable to all subjects alike. These rights, appropriate to individuality, were not the privileges of a single class; they were the property of every subject alike. Each signified the abrogation of some feudal privilege.

On this view, government acted like an umpire, administering the rules of the game without taking part, intervening only to settle collisions of interest among the players. Such is the chief characteristic of what Oakeshott speaks of as "parliamentary government."

The rise of the "anti-individual," he argues, goes together with another view of government: what Oakeshott calls "popular" (as opposed to "parliamentary") government. The popular system looks to the establishment of universal adult suffrage to confirm the authority of mere numbers or the mass man; the parliamentary representative is seen, not as an individual, but as an instructed delegate whose function is to assist the creation of a society appropriate to his masters; mass parties grow up composed of "anti-individuals" and dominated by their leaders. But in all this the mass man does not make his own choice; he does not really give a mandate to his leaders. The so-called representative draws up his own mandate and "by a familiar trick of ventriloquism"[40] puts it into the mouths of his electors. Similarly, the favorite device of "popular" government, the plebiscite, is not a method by which the mass man imposes his choices upon his rulers; it is a method of generating a government with unlimited authority to make choices on his behalf. Through the plebiscite, the mass man finally achieves release from the burden of individuality: he is told emphatically what to choose. Oakeshott adds that the style of general political discourse most suited to "popular" (as opposed to "parliamentary") government tends naturally to be the idiom of ideology or, as he calls it, rationalism.

Oakeshott's belief in the superiority of the parliamentary form of government goes together with his special feeling for England: Oakeshott has more than once spoken of the English system as "the most civilised and effective method of social integration ever created by mankind (for it is not the gift of the Gods)." But Oakeshott's conservatism is for this very reason open to the criticism that was addressed by Voltaire to the conservatism of David Hume, namely, that conservatism was a sensible attitude in a country like England where there was freedom to defend and perpetuate. In eighteenth-century France there was no freedom to conserve: hence the demand for ideas of more universal application.

Voltaire's argument was repeated in the 1950s by Friedrich von Hayek in his book *The Constitution of Liberty*,[41] in which among other things he set forth his reasons for preferring liberalism to conservatism. Hayek wrote from the point of view of an economist, disturbed by the growing tendency for belief in state control of the economy, at the expense of individual liberty, to become a new orthodoxy, and in this sense a part of conservatism. For philosophical arguments in favor of liberalism, Hayek turned to his friend, and fellow Austrian, Karl Popper. Popper's contribution to political philosophy[42] was by no means limited to his wartime work *The Open Society and Its Enemies*, and moreover his political thinking was no less a part of his general philosophy of knowledge than was that of Michael Oakeshott. It so happened that Popper and Oakeshott both held chairs after the war at the London School of Economics, and between them they transformed that former stronghold of left-wing sociology into one of the two most important centers in the English-speaking world of political philosophy (the other being the University of Chicago).

Popper came to philosophy in the first place, as did Wittgenstein and most of the other Austrian philosophers, from a background of science. But he soon reached a radically different conclusion about the nature of science from that of his contemporaries, and this distinctive "Popperian" notion stands at the beginning of his whole system. Popper has recalled[43] that his mind was first exercised about the nature of science when he noticed a certain difference between theories such as that of Freud and theories such as that of Einstein. On the positivists' conception of science, this difference could not be accounted for. According to the positivists, science was a matter of making observations and experiments which suggested and confirmed hypotheses, and this led the positivists to proclaim their doctrine that truth is verification by publicly observable tests.

Popper noticed that theories such as Freud's could be readily "confirmed" by anything which happened, or, rather that anything which happened could be regarded as confirmation of such theories. Theories of the Freudian type could simply not be disproved. On the other hand, a theory such as Einstein's *could* be disproved; unless certain things happened as predicted, the theory could simply not be sustained. This reflection led Popper to conclude that verifiability was not the crucial characteristic of science, but that *falsifiability* was. The test of a genuinely scientific statement was not "can it be confirmed?" but "can it be disproved?" It was because Freudian theory, like astrology, could never be disproved that Popper was able to challenge its pretensions to be a science.

Popper next went on to deny the whole positivist conception of what science is. Science was not, he argued, an enterprise of observing nature so as to discover its laws but rather an enterprise of making conjectures in the mind and then putting those conjectures to the test of trial and error to see if they could be falsified by experiment. What was not falsified after thorough testing could be accepted as provisional knowledge for the time being. Such provisional knowledge was the best one could aspire to; certain or "confirmed" knowledge was unattainable.

Popper published his philosophy of science in 1935 in his *Logik der Forschung*.[44] A year later he was driven into exile by the Nazis, and was impelled by the world situation to turn his mind to politics. Like Hobhouse in the First World War, Popper detected a similarity between the prevailing German ideology and the theories of Hegel; he went even further and saw similarities between the totalitarian ideologies of the modern world and the "total" metaphysical systems of Plato and his successors.

However, Popper's objections to those systems were different from the objections of the positivists. His objection was based on his own conception of possible human knowledge. Having already argued that scientific knowledge is never more than piecemeal and tentative, Popper went on to suggest that knowledge in history, social science, and politics is equally limited, provisional, and incomplete. Social science, from this perspective, was not very different from natural science; but its claim to be a science at all must pass the crucial test: can its formulations be falsified?

Popper applied this test to Marxism and found it wanting. Marxism was shown to be no more scientific than were astrology and Freudianism. The metaphysical systems of Plato and Hegel were likewise said to belong to that class of theory which no test could falsify. They were not only fictions but mischievous fictions.

Up to this point, Popper might not appear to be far removed from the positivists in the conclusions he reached. And as we have seen, he was still suggesting as late as 1940 that the task of philosophy was the formulation of scientific methodology. But what Popper was actually doing at that time was transferring to the realm of morals and politics the philosophy of knowledge he had worked out to explain the nature of science. The result was interesting. Positivism permitted the philosopher, as we have seen, to cultivate metaethics; but ethics itself was ruled out in part by the positivist divorce of fact from value, and in part by the positivist's acceptance of the determinist doctrine that all human behavior, like every other movement in the universe, has causes which are in principle knowable. Popper rejected determinism with the rest of the empiricist package. He was an indeterminist, and, in keeping with his stress on "falsification," he saw moral judgments not so much as appraisals of the good and the right but as recognitions of the bad and the wrong. For Popper, morality is not the pursuit of the good—a visionary, metaphysical ideal—but the avoidance and rectification of evil. Misery and wrong exist, and our duty is to relieve the one and diminish the other. In this sense, Popper is a "negative utilitarian," and the negativism of his utilitarianism follows logically from the negativism of his earlier principle of scientific knowledge.

The implications for politics are not hard to see. Since it is our moral duty as individuals to diminish evils, it must be our common purpose in framing political policies to relieve distress and curb the suffering in the world; there is no corresponding duty to try to construct a happy, contented, or even a perfectly just world, for no one has any idea how such a world can be constructed. Problems of politics can well be approached in a properly scientific manner, and the proper scientific manner is *not* one of utopian engineering but the method of trial and error, or what Popper came to speak of as "piecemeal engineering."

That favorite question of political philosophers—"Who should rule?"— Popper finds inappropriate. The right question to ask, he suggests, is: "How can institutions be devised which will minimize the risks of bad rulers?" The answer that emerges is the liberal answer: a minimal state is likely to do the least harm. Writing at a time when (as Hayek remarked) planning and various forms of Fabian socialism were much in favor as alternatives to fascism and communism, Popper insisted that such a blueprint approach to political problems was unscientific. The correctly scientific approach to social evils, he claimed, was to seek them out one by one and correct them.

This last suggestion had so much of the conservative in it that Popper was obliged in his later writings[45] to say exactly how he differed from such conservative traditionalists as Oakeshott.

Popper agrees that tradition is of the utmost importance in the life of society, but he suggests that a tradition can be accepted either critically or uncritically. He ascribes an uncritical acceptance to such conservatives as Edmund Burke, and claims that his own acceptance is critical. This, he explains, means the acceptance of some elements in a tradition and the

123

rejection of others: we can rid ourselves of the irrational taboos of a tradition by thinking about them.

Popper notes that traditions are not deliberately created; they develop slowly over the years, and he says that tradition is important to people because they need to know what to expect in social life. Regularity saves us from the terror and anxiety we should feel if there were no order in the way other people behaved. Indeed it is because of this that so many people cling so desperately and uncritically to tradition. The emotional intolerance of such "traditionalists" breeds, Popper thinks, an equally emotional antitraditionalism among radical ideologists. Both attitudes have to be avoided.

Popper's defense of democracy is a similar defense of moderation. He shares all Oakeshott's distaste for plebiscitary or populist government; indeed he refuses to give such forms of government the title of democracy. For Popper, democracy is not to be understood in abstract terms as "government of the people, by the people" but as a system under which "the government can be got rid of without bloodshed."[46] Such democracy is to be preferred as a system of government, not because it is the most perfect but because it is the least evil form of government. It confers no benefits on the citizens, but provides a framework within which people can act freely. "The state," Popper writes, "is a necessary evil: its powers are not to be multiplied beyond what is necessary."[47] Again Popper reverts to the idea of tradition; democratic institutions alone, he insists, are not enough; indeed they are not to be relied on at all, for "institutions are always ambivalent in the sense that, in the absence of a strong tradition, they also may serve the opposite purpose to the one intended.... Traditions are needed to form a kind of link between institutions and the intentions and valuations of individual men."[48]

Popper's conception of democracy is thus a decidedly liberal one, in the sense that he sees as the defining virtue of democracy not that it places power in the hands of the people but that it gives them liberty.

However, if Popper reaches conclusions which are to some extent more liberal than either Weldon's or Oakeshott's, the really important difference between them is not this political difference but the fact that Popper's political opinions are connected with his philosophical beliefs in a sense which is true of neither of the others. Weldon, indeed, insists as Bertrand Russell did before him that his personal political preferences have no connection with his philosophy, and Oakeshott's conservatism and Oakeshott's metaphysics have logically to be kept apart. But Popper's moderate liberalism is part of his general theoretical system, his critical rationalism, a system which has much in common with that of an earlier liberal, the eighteenth-century philosopher Immanuel Kant. Ironically, Popper's endeavors to reinstate Kant have contributed in recent years to a diminution of hostility to Popper's old bête noire, Hegel. Indeed it might well be suggested that there is a lot in common between Popper's concept of falsification and Hegel's concept of negation, and also between Popper's method of trial and error and Hegel's method of the dialectic. But this would not readily have been noticed in the intellectual atmosphere of the 1950s.

The revival of political theory

The end of World War II had witnessed the defeat of fascism and Nazism, but it had not been an unequivocal victory for democracy, since the Western powers had won in alliance with totalitarian communism. Assuredly it was a victory for powers which all called themselves "democratic," but as we have seen in discussing the work of C. L. Stevenson, the word *democratic* had come to be used in very different ways by different people. If ever clarification was needed, it was needed here; and some political philosophers sought in one way or another to provide it.

Their work may broadly be divided into two kinds. First, there are those who took the American, British, or Western system of representative government as the authentic embodiment of democracy, and went on to justify that system. Second, there were those philosophers who sought to investigate the idea of democracy, and who used this abstract model as a means to test the claims of existing political systems to be democratic. To the first type belongs the work of Popper and numerous political sociologists such as Schumpeter, Edward Shils, Daniel Bell, and Seymour Martin Lipset. Among the most politically committed of these writers was Thomas Landon Thorson, who attempted, in *The Logic of Democracy*,[49] to argue in an even more direct and systematic way than had Popper that the fallibility of human knowledge is such as to render democratic government (on the Western liberal model), where policies can be revised by the technique of free discussion, the most rational system of government.

The second approach to the theory of democracy was especially favored by French political philosophers, three of whom may be singled out for attention, since they wrote in English as well as French and thus made a direct contribution to the political philosophy of the English-speaking world*: Yves Simon, Bertrand de Jouvenel, and Raymond Aron. The particular perspective which these three theorists brought to the problem of democracy was not only that of the French Cartesian rationalist tradition but that of citizens of a republic where democracy was working badly, where indeed in 1940 democracy collapsed. There was thus no temptation for them to assume, as did so many American and British writers, that democracy was in order as it existed. Simon, Jouvenel, and Aron each

---

* Since the present essay is concerned with Anglo-American political philosophy, I have omitted those theorists who wrote only in foreign languages, even though several such theorists—Lukács, for example, Camus, Sartre, and Simone Weil—were widely read and studied in the English-speaking world.

belonged to a different school of philosophy and had different political sympathies, but they agreed in arguing that liberty would have to be effectively reconciled with authority if democracy was to be restored. Authority appeared to each one of these theorists as the central problem of democracy.

Yves Simon, a Catholic Thomist who emigrated from France to the United States in 1938, was a philosopher with a firm belief in the value of democracy and a profound mistrust for what he called modern liberalism. Bertrand de Jouvenel, a nobleman with a close affinity to Alexis de Tocqueville, is more sympathetic to liberalism, but less confident than Simon of the positive potentialities of democracy. Raymond Aron has always claimed to be a sociologist rather than a philosopher, but he has made a notable contribution both to the theory of democracy and to the defense of political philosophy against the intrusion of ideology.

The death of Yves Simon in 1961 at the age of fifty-eight robbed the Western world of one of its most original and distinguished political theorists. Like Plato and Hobbes, and indeed like most good political philosophers, Simon turned from pure philosophy to the problems of politics because he was disturbed by the events of his own time. Simon often recalled that his grandfather had taken part in a demonstration against Napoleon III, and he himself remained one of the most progressive of Catholic theorists. If he deplored the anarchistic and Marxist tendencies of the French Left in the years between the two world wars, he was equally critical of the readiness of the French conservatives, the traditional custodians of the idea of authority, to yield to fascism. He believed that it was largely because people had lost their understanding of the meaning of authority that democracy had been defeated in France.

Simon's earliest publications, in French, were on the theory of knowledge; next he published, also in French, several more or less journalistic books on the political situation of France in the 1930s and '40s; then in the '50s and '60s, while he was a professor at the University of Chicago, Simon wrote, in English, his works of political philosophy, the most important being *Philosophy of Democratic Government*,[50] *A General Theory of Authority*,[51] *The Tradition of Natural Law*,[52] *Freedom and Community*.[53]

To some extent, Simon's books can be seen as a continuation of the prewar writings on the subject of democracy by Jacques Maritain and Mortimer Adler. Working in the same tradition of Aristotle and Aquinas, Simon built his argument around the conception of civil society as something natural to man, as opposed to the modern liberal notion of the state as a necessary evil. He suggested that civil government had to be understood as being essentially related to the pursuit of the common good and added that if the state was thought of primarily as the monopolizer of force, its character was bound to be misunderstood. The liberal habit of contrasting authority with liberty made it logically impossible to reconcile authority with freedom; yet such a reconciliation was necessary, Simon argued, if the very idea of a democratic system was to be intelligible.

The correct antithesis to a despotic system, Simon suggested, was a "political" system, and a political system, he wrote, "gives the governed a legal power of resistance."[54] Not all political systems, he went on to say, are democratic. There is a clear parallel between Simon's use of the word *political* and Popper's use of the word *democratic* (to name a system where the government can be changed without bloodshed), but Simon maintains that the defining characteristics of democracy are more extensive than these:

> *The ambition of democracy, from the very start, goes beyond the establishment of a political regime. For government to be political, it suffices that the governed be possessed of a legally guaranteed right of resistance; now democracy cannot undertake to accomplish that much without pledging itself to accomplish much more. . . . When the political idea assumes the democratic form, the people asserts, over and above its freedom* from *abusive power, its freedom* to *govern itself. Keeping the government confined within a definite field is no longer held sufficient; the government has been taken over by the people. Such is democratic freedom, the defining feature of democracy.*[55]

In a paper read at a meeting of the American Catholic Philosophical Association in the year of Hitler's victory in France, Simon indicted the educated classes of continental Europe for having "added to the impatience of the masses the wickedness of their ideological fanaticism."[56] This early perception of the danger of an ideological approach to politics was developed in detail by Simon's compatriot, Raymond Aron, who had in that same year (1940) rallied to General de Gaulle in London and was working in the information services of the Free French movement. In naming ideology as a source of current evils, Aron and Simon were pointing to something more widespread and deeper than totalitarianism. It was an insight which was resisted by popular political writers at the time either because they sought an alliance with communism in the struggle against fascism or because they wished to develop an "ideology of democracy" to challenge the ideologies of both fascism and communism. Among literary writers of those years, George Orwell was virtually alone in recognizing what Simon and Aron had seen; and, as is now well known, efforts to suppress George Orwell's writings were made by left-wing editors and right-wing publishers alike.

Even at the level of academic discussion, Simon and Aron received a cool welcome when they tried to explain that the whole ideological approach to politics, with its irrationalist fervor, its dogmatism, and its confusion of action and theory, was inimical to freedom and alien to democracy. Simon sought, in several of his writings, to formulate the relationship between liberty and authority in such a manner as to effect a reconciliation. One such formulation was the following:

"*Principle of Authority*. Wherever the welfare of a community requires a common action, the unity of that common action must be assured by the highest organs of that community."

"*Principle of Autonomy (or Liberty)*. Whenever a task can be satisfactorily achieved by the initiative of the individual or that of small social units, the fulfillment of that task must be left to the initiative of the individual or to that of small social units."[57]

In his analysis of the concept of liberty as autonomy, Simon stressed the point that authority is directive rather than coercive; authority rests on persuasion rather than compulsion; although Simon was ready to admit that there are occasions when coercion may have to be employed as "one of the instruments of authority," he added that coercion does not, as many liberals supposed, "pertain to the essence of authority."[58] Hence, although there was a logical antinomy between liberty and coercion, there was no logical antinomy between liberty and authority. Modern liberals, Simon argued, were mistaken in thinking that there was such an antinomy. Their mistake, furthermore, was injurious to the cause of democracy, since it was the essential characteristic of democracy that it combined liberty with law by enabling people to make the laws they lived under.

A rather similar theory of authority was worked out by Bertrand de Jouvenel in his book *Sovereignty*.[59] Jouvenel suggested that the word *authority* had fallen into disrepute because of its association with *authoritarianism*, a fashionable pejorative synonym for *despotism*. He proposed to go back to the origins of the word in order to demonstrate that authority, in itself, was in no way antithetical to liberty. The *auctor* (from which Latin word our word *authority* derives) was, for the Romans, a creator, initiator, or inspirer. The *auctor* was the source of actions, but of actions freely done by others. In the political sphere, Jouvenel argued, authority, correctly understood, is the ability of one man to have his proposals accepted by others, so that it is not just *his* will but the will of the community of the whole which puts those proposals into effect.

Authority, Jouvenel suggested, was totally different from power, since power was something that was imposed on men while authority was something they accepted willingly.

"To follow an authority," Jouvenel wrote, "is a voluntary act. Authority ends where voluntary assent ends."[60]

Later in the same book he added: "Authority is ... the creator of the social tie, and its position is consolidated by the benefits which spring from the social tie."[61]

In an earlier book, *On Power*,[62] which Jouvenel wrote as an exile in Switzerland during World War II, he had set forth a critique of the failure of modern democracy to provide an adequate institutional framework for freedom. A certain nostalgia for the Middle Ages was discernible in Jouvenel's desire to safeguard liberty by balancing the powers within the state; his early preference for a constitutional monarchy over any kind of republican government reflected his belief that a strong centralized state, even though based on universal suffrage, tended quickly to become despotic. Before he turned to political philosophy, Jouvenel had had a varied career in politics and journalism, and made a name for himself as a maverick figure of the nonconservative Right in France. After the war, when he spent a good deal of time in British and American universities, he became more appreciative of the Anglo-Saxon type of representative government, and more optimistic for the prospects of democracy, provided the "populist" element was steadily balanced by the constitutional element.[63]

No less vigorously than Yves Simon did Jouvenel repudiate the idea of plebiscitary or mass rule; he invented the term *totalitarian democracy* for that form of government where the plebiscitary conception of democracy found its fulfillment. But Jouvenel never shared Simon's desire to enlarge democracy in the direction of socialism. Indeed he has always sought to correct centralizing, or *étatiste*, tendencies of democracy by asserting the value of economic freedom, and by establishing some modern alternative to the lost authority of the aristocracy. When Jouvenel speaks of himself as a liberal, he thinks of himself as a liberal on the model of John Locke or the eighteenth-century English Whigs; he does not subscribe to the kind of liberalism which Yves Simon attacked: the liberalism of twentieth-century republican French progressives.

Raymond Aron in his earlier years was one such French-style leftist liberal; indeed, as late as 1945 he collaborated with his close friend Jean-Paul Sartre in founding the review *Les Temps modernes*. But when he found that Sartre and so many other French leftists were unwilling to challenge the intellectual credentials of communism, Aron broke with them. It was not only that he wished to oppose the politics of the Soviet Union and its client parties throughout the world; he thought it equally important to repudiate the theory of Marxism, or what the communists liked to call their "philosophy."

A central part of Aron's argument was that Marxism was not a philosophy at all, but an ideology—not a system of thought directed toward the enlargement of understanding and the discovery of truth, but a doctrine which laid down a ready-made explanation of the nature of the world mainly in order to promote a revolutionary transformation of the world. French intellectuals in the immediate postwar period were much more disposed to adhere to ideologies than were their more "pragmatic" or practical Anglo-Saxon contemporaries, so Aron's argument on this subject did not have the immediate impact on the English-speaking world that it had in France.

However, the 1960s witnessed the emergence of a highly influential and fashionable school of ideological thinkers in America and England, and the relevance of Aron's writings was then more keenly perceived. Among these ideologues were some with philosophical pretentions: Herbert Marcuse, for example, and Erich Fromm, and R. D. Laing. What these ideological writers had in common was a belief in what Aron called "utopianism." They all held out the promise that it was possible to have a civilization without repression—that men had only to overthrow the existing culture (being one based on capitalist exploitation) and introduce a new culture based on love, for "alienation" to be ended.

These theorists achieved immense popularity, but Aron's delineation of the frontiers between philosophy and ideology at least served to make it clear that they were not to be counted as philosophers. In a book called *The Opium of the Intellectuals*[64] Aron had drawn an instructive parallel between ideology and certain forms of religious writing—not theology, which is by nature academic, but that religious literature which holds out the promise of salvation as a reward for faith and action. In a world in which traditional religion is everywhere fading, Aron, the sociologist, saw a danger of ideology filling the emotional void which the decay of religion had left behind it.

Aron, the political philosopher, made a notable contribution toward the clarification of such concepts as liberty, equality, hierarchy, as well as authority. Among these values he gave priority to liberty. "The essence of western culture," he wrote, "the basis of its success, the secret of its wide influence, is liberty."

> *Not universal suffrage, a belated and disputable political institution, not the parliamentary system, which is one democratic procedure among others, but the freedom of research and criticism, gradually won, the freedom whose historical conditions have been the duality of temporal and spiritual power, the limitation of State authority and the autonomy of the universities.*[65]

This reference to "historical conditions" is characteristic of Aron's style and method. He thinks the most significant historical condition of modernity is industrialization: industrialization has made it possible for men to experience equality, for example, in a sense which was previously inconceivable, but it has also limited the choice of governments men can opt for. In the late twentieth century, he suggests, men have to choose between some form of constitutional-pluralist political system and some form of monopolistic-party system. In the first, liberty is combined with authority; in the second there is no liberty at all. Thus, for Aron, the actual experience of liberty depends on the existence of authority embodied in settled institutions.

American and British theorists have, on the whole, been less eager than the French to give precedence to the problem of authority. Two exceptions are the English philosophers Stanley Benn and Richard S. Peters, who in their book *Social Principles and the Democratic State*[66] make the analysis of authority the central feature of their interpretation of democracy.[67] Benn and Peters write:

> *Men ... are rule-following animals; they perform predictably in relation to one another and form what is called a social system to a large extent because they accept systems of rules which are variable and alterable by human decision. Indeed we cannot bring out what we mean by a human action without recourse to standards laying down what are accepted as ends and what are efficient and socially appropriate ways of attaining them. ... And this is very closely linked with the idea of "authority." For such standards, being man-made, alterable, and, to a certain extent, arbitrary, procedures are necessary in some spheres at least, for deciding what standards are to be maintained, who is to originate them, who is to decide about their application to particular cases, and who is to introduce changes. Where we find such an arrangement for originators or umpires in the realm of rules, we are in the sphere of "authority."*[68]

Benn and Peters found themselves swiftly carried by the flow of their discussion from the specific problems of democracy to the nature of politics in general, and thus into the Aristotelian domain of justice and the common good. It is significant that they changed the title of their book when it was reissued in America from *Social Principles and the Democratic State* to *Principles of Political Thought*,[69] a title which gives a better indication of its scope.

Politics, according to Benn and Peters, is the "interplay of pressures" arising from the variety of interests and claims in society. For them, as for Simon, justice is the central political norm, but they offer a distinctive analysis of justice. They suggest that the key to justice lies in the concept of impartiality. And while they say, as Simon says, that the proper end of government may be described as "seeking the common good," they interpret these words as an injunction to approach policymaking in a certain spirit, not an injunction to adopt a determinate policy. For a political society to "seek the common good," they suggest, is simply to attend to the interests of its members in a spirit of impartiality.

Benn and Peters point to a connection between impartiality and reason: insofar as philosophy is itself (like science) a clear example of rational discussion, it must be a discussion conducted in accordance with the norms of impartiality and respect for truth. Morality goes beyond this bare impartial consideration of people as sources of arguments, to the richer impartial consideration of people as sources of claims and interests. Being moral, they suggest, is thus one way of being reasonable, without being a synonym for being reasonable.

When Benn and Peters turn from these generalities to the specific questions of democracy, equality, justice, and so forth, they invoke in each case the same notion of impartiality. To say that justice requires equality is, for them, to say that justice requires discrimination between men to be grounded on relevant differences between men. Equality as an ideal is intelligible only in a given context and as a moral criticism of definite inequalities. Impartiality is a principle, they suggest, which demands the assent as much of the public as of the government. Democracy will work only if enough people want it to work and are willing to make the necessary adjustments that the claims of others demand. This spirit, they think, is much more important than the institutions of democracy. And "spirit," of course, is something which tends to grow up slowly over the years, not something which can be imposed, briskly, like a new constitution.

Besides their joint work on political philosophy in general, Stanley Benn and Richard Peters have written separately on different concepts and problems in political philosophy.[70] Indeed the literature of political philosophy in the English-speaking world since World War II is very largely composed of books devoted each to one such concept as justice, law, liberty, rights, equality, or authority. Nor should it be expected to be otherwise, since it is to the task of analysis in one sense or another that philosophers of various persuasions have agreed in directing their energies.

Analysis as an activity is in any case no new thing. It was a favorite exercise of the Age of Reason, when savants such as Buffon and Jussieu delighted in breaking things down and sorting them out in categories and classes. Taxonomy was their name for this art, and in fields such as botany it constituted the greater part of their science. Political philosophy since 1945 contains substantial elements of such taxonomy, and it is instructive to notice how much more elaborate it has become with each successive book.

Take, for example, the problem of freedom. In 1948, C. I. Lewis published an essay[71] in which he simply listed different types of freedom. In 1953, I myself published a book[72] in which I distinguished three forms of freedom and tried to relate these three forms to four types of liberalism. In 1958, Sir Isaiah Berlin published a lecture entitled "Two Concepts of Liberty,"[73] in which he suggested the grouping together of several theories of freedom under the categories of "negative" and "positive." In 1961 Felix Oppenheim brought out his book *Dimensions of Freedom*,[74] in which he sought to distinguish a concept of social freedom from some dozen other senses in which the word *freedom* is employed. The most extensive taxonomy of the idea of freedom was, however, provided later by Mortimer Adler, on behalf of the Institute for Philosophical Research, in a book[75] which aimed to "take stock of Western thought" on the subject of liberty —both metaphysical and political— and left little room for any more work of a purely classificatory and explanatory kind.[76]

Adler speaks of his method as the "dialectical," but to a large extent it corresponds to the method described by others as "analytical." Wittgenstein, for example, calls the work of philosophy "analytical" although the method he himself actually uses is just as much a dialectical one as it is analytic. For it is not Wittgenstein's method to state and defend an argument, but to proceed by assertion, qualification, contradiction. Some of Wittgenstein's more recent commentators have remarked on the continuity between this method of Wittgenstein and that of the classical philosophers; Renford Bambrough, for example, draws attention to "the dialectical idiom, the conversational exchange that is directly presented by Plato, and whose pattern of suggestions and qualifications is closely followed in the superficially continuous prose of Aristotle and Wittgenstein."[77]

Analysis in the rigid sense of the reduction of linguistic complexes into simpler units of discourse, analysis as some form of definition, had given way to analysis of another kind—analysis as description, criticism, ongoing appraisal conducted by a method of dialogue.

Adler in his introduction to volume 2 of *The Idea of Freedom* writes of his Institute's "method of dealing with differences of opinion in an objective and neutral manner," and he adds: our "standpoint [is that] of an observer rather than a participant.... Our task is to order and clarify a wide diversity of views without taking sides."[78]

In subsequent writings on the problems of freedom, Anglo-Saxon philosophers will almost all be found to be taking sides, committing themselves, indeed in some cases frankly undertaking the construction of a metaphysical system. A significant example here is Stuart Hampshire's *Freedom of the Individual*,[79] a book first published in 1965, which develops in relation to the problem of freedom ideas first adumbrated in an earlier book, *Thought and Action*.[80] Although clearly inspired in the first place by Wittgenstein, Hampshire is another philosopher who can be seen to be moving toward a position akin to that of Immanuel Kant, even that of Hegel.[81] Hampshire discards as mythical the empiricist doctrine that our knowledge is derived from sense impressions passively received. He stresses the primacy of human agency and human will; our knowledge of the world begins, he claims, in our manipulation of things for our practical ends. Hampshire tries to provide a systematic account of human freedom by relating it in turn to a theory of knowledge, a theory of language, a theory of intention, and a theory of goodness. Hampshire's book thus marks a clear departure from purely analytic philosophy toward systematic or constructive metaphysics.

Few other writings on the subject of freedom that have appeared in English in the 1960s and 1970s are as ambitious as this, but most of them show a similar desire to justify, rather than merely to clarify, a certain conception of liberty. Here the work of Herbert Hart is especially worth noting, since it combines analytic work of a high degree of professionalism with an endeavor to restate in twentieth-century terms the arguments used by John Stuart Mill[82] in the nineteenth century to defend a liberal conception of political liberty against conservative criticisms. In his book

Law, Liberty and Morality,[83] and related articles, Hart entered a vigorous controversy with an English jurist, Patrick Devlin, who for his part sought in *The Enforcement of Morals*[84] and other writings to restate in contemporary terms the conservative argument put forward in Victorian times against Mill by Sir James Fitzjames Stephen.[85] These are all polemical writings, but they are polemical in the great tradition of Hobbes and Locke, in which the polemicist and the philosopher are one and the same man.

A similar process of change from the strictly analytic and the neutral toward the systematic and the committed in the postwar years can be detected in the philosophical literature of the problem of justice. A characteristic work of the earlier period is Hans Kelsen's *What Is Justice?*,[86] in which the author, himself once closely connected with the Vienna Circle in Austria, puts forward a dogmatic form of legal positivism: justice is the correct interpretation of law, and law is the command of the sovereign. Law is thus seen as a matter of fact, and having nothing to do with value.

During and after the war Chaim Perelman, in such writings as *De La Justice*[87] and *The Idea of Justice*,[88] moves from this positivist dogmatism to a more subtle analysis of the concept of justice. Hart, in *The Concept of Law*,[89] carries the argument further and suggests that legal positivism is mistaken in regarding law as a form of command. In the same book Hart revives the traditional theory of natural law and puts forward a case in defense of what he calls a "minimal" natural law, not entirely unlike the conception of Hobbes.

At Harvard, John Rawls, in a series of articles which culminated in his book *A Concept of Justice*,[90] also went back to the Age of Reason for his inspiration and revived the notion of a social contract as the basis of a new interpretation of the idea of justice. Rawls's arguments sparked off a great deal of controversy in academic circles and even prompted Brian Barry, a political theorist at Oxford, to write a book-length critique, *The Liberal Theory of Justice*.[91] As in the case of the controversy between Hart and Devlin, the debate between Rawls and Barry was as much political as philosophical.[92] Political philosophers could no longer be accused of shutting themselves up in ivory towers.

Postwar speculative thought

Of course, there were some political philosophers in the English-speaking world to whom this criticism could never have been addressed. Among them were several who came to America as exiles from Germany, philosophers who had been educated in that metaphysical tradition against which Hobhouse, Russell, Popper, and the positivists had reacted so bitterly, and which they so readily blamed for the rise of Hitler. Three such scholars were Hannah Arendt, Leo Strauss, and Eric Voegelin. None of these was a

Hegelian, but all had at least studied Hegel thoroughly; all were deeply immersed in the political philosophy of the Greeks, and all had found inspiration either in Plato or in Aristotle. They did not take root easily in America. For whereas the Austrian positivists, such as Carnap and Kelsen, found the pragmatist intellectual climate of the United States wholly congenial, the German metaphysicians felt less at home.

But times changed. By the late 1950s the passions of war had subsided, and it was no longer enough to attack German metaphysics without spelling out exactly what it was that was being attacked. "Hegel" could no longer be used as a name, like "Satan," by definition pejorative; it could no longer be assumed that the case against idealistic metaphysics had been established. As for Plato, there were still enough good classical scholars left in the universities to demonstrate that the Russell-Popper picture of Plato as a forerunner of Hitler was a philistine caricature; any student who had read a few of Plato's Dialogues would see that it was false.

Hannah Arendt's first book in English was *The Origins of Totalitarianism*, published in 1951,[93] and like Popper's *The Open Society and Its Enemies* it was an attempt by a Jewish refugee from the Third Reich to render intelligible the rise of Nazism and Communism. But Hannah Arendt gave a very different interpretation from Popper's, and she recommended a very different alternative to totalitarianism. Whereas Popper traced the intellectual origins of totalitarian ideologies in the writings of metaphysicians from Plato onward, Hannah Arendt looked to the cultural and political circumstances of the nineteenth and early twentieth centuries in which men found themselves. And whereas Popper, a rationalist (as we have seen) of a distinctly original kind, came out in favor of a fairly conventional form of moderate reformist liberalism, Hannah Arendt, an existentialist, developed a distinctly original kind of revolutionary elitism.

Born like Popper at the turn of the century, Hannah Arendt received in pre-Nazi Germany a classical education very different from the scientific education Popper was given in Austria. At Heidelberg she was the pupil of the existentialist philosopher Karl Jaspers, whose works she later edited, and by the time she went into exile in America in 1941 she was already a mature scholar. Her most substantial contribution to political philosophy is *The Human Condition*, first published in 1958. The title itself is a characteristically existentialist one, since it bears witness to her belief that there is no human nature or human essence but only a human situation or predicament. If there *were* a human nature, Hannah Arendt writes, "then surely only a god could know and define it."[94]

Furthermore, Hannah Arendt builds her whole argument on the existentialist doctrine that man is radically free: determinism is false; man is a free agent, responsible for all he does. The distinctive feature of Hannah Arendt's argument, however, is that she adds to this assertion of metaphysical human freedom (something which everybody has) a theory of political freedom, which is something men have to strive to achieve. While she cannot, on her own principles, admit that the realization of such political freedom is man's natural goal, she does, nevertheless, argue that it is man's highest and noblest goal. Thus the conventional existentialist doctrine that all men are free (have free will) is supplemented by the claim that only the best men are free, that freedom is the prize of heroes.

Her account of the origin of totalitarianism has also a recognizably existentialist starting point. The "loneliness" of modern men, following the "death of God," the rootlessness of the masses in industrialized society, their lack of a shared sense of a place in the world—all this, she suggests, conspired to drive them to seek the shelter of totalitarian ideology, to escape from the burden of their metaphysical freedom in a movement where everyone was told what to do. The rise of nineteenth-century imperialism and bureaucracy also helped, she thinks, to accustom people to the idea of rule by faceless institutions, and the spread of the idea of "race" enabled men to resolve their crisis of identity by seeing themselves, not as individuals or persons, but as members of a mythical collectivity, the *Herrenvolk*.

Hannah Arendt's explanation of totalitarianism is thus as much sociological as historical (although she makes few efforts to separate one type of explanation from another), but the central theme of her narrative is, like Rousseau's, a story of man born free, running away from the anxiety of that condition into ever more elaborate forms of servitude. And like Rousseau she has some definite ideas of her own as to what freedom is.

First she repudiates the whole liberal conception of freedom as a private right of the individual to be preserved against the intrusion of other men, including men in authority. Indeed, for her *privacy* is almost a pejorative word.[95] For Hannah Arendt political freedom is something that can be experienced only in the public realm; freedom is action, freedom is positive participation in the political life of one's city.

The human condition, as she describes it, permits a man only three forms of activity: labor, work, and action. Labor is the meanest way of spending one's life, for labor is the tedious, repetitive effort of producing enough in the way of food and so forth to keep alive. It is an activity dictated by natural need, and so falls squarely within the realm of necessity as opposed to freedom. Work is human activity directed to ends other than those exacted by nature and necessity; its products are not immediately consumed, they are the creations of art and craft, the work of an individual, a master; they do not belong to the realm of necessity, but they do fall within the private as opposed to the public domain. Work is thus inferior to action. Action, the third and highest form of human activity, is that by which man realizes his identity. "With word and deed we insert ourselves into the human world, and this insertion is like a second birth."[96] Man seeks immortality. To realize this end he must affirm his identity through speech and action, and this is precisely where politics comes in. For it is the unique genius of politics that it "teaches men how to bring forth what is great and radiant."[97]

This heroic conception of politics prompts Hannah Arendt sometimes to speak like Sartre, of violence, with a certain romantic yearning: When men die a violent death in the company of others, she writes, "it is as though Life itself, the immortal life of the species, nourished as it were by the sempiternal dying of its individual members ... is actualized in the practice of violence."[98] But Hannah Arendt disapproves of the kind of violence favored by Sartre and many other socialist revolutionaries: "The practice of violence ... changes the world," she writes, "but the most probable change is a more violent world."[99] The truth of the matter is that Hannah Arendt disapproves of most of the revolutions and most of the revolutionary movements that the world has known since 1789, not because of their violence but because they have been directed toward what she regards as the wrong ends, namely the achievement of some social or economic transformation.

It is not only that she repudiates socialism; she rejects the whole category of the social. She notes that the concept of society was unknown to the Greeks, who distinguished a public thing, the *polis*, on the one hand, and a private thing, the household, on the other. What is called "society" today, she argues, is not part of the public domain at all, but the household writ large; and the concerns of socialism are not genuinely public and political matters, but economic, material, domestic concerns, which belong to the realm of nature and necessity. Hence all those revolutions since the French Revolution which have had social objectives are not, from her point of view, political movements at all; she will not even allow them the name of "revolution."[100] The only kind of revolution which Hannah Arendt is willing to regard as a genuine revolution is one directed to establishment of freedom: the events in America in 1775–76 thus count as an authentic revolution, as does the rising of the Commune of Paris in 1871 and the Hungarian Revolution of 1956.

Given her exalted conception of freedom, it is something unlikely to be often found. In ancient Greece and Rome, where at least in some few places and at some few times, citizens participated in politics in the way that she recognizes as *action*, men were free. But there is none of Hannah Arendt's form of freedom to be enjoyed in the liberal, democratic, constitutional, and representative forms of government that are the pride of the modern Western world. In her sense of politics, there can be no politics under such systems. She accepts this conclusion, and she sees the possibility of participatory politics, and hence of freedom, only in revolutionary situations, such as occurred in Russia in 1905 and 1917, when workers formed themselves into councils, or in America in 1775–76, where the citizens (if only the more prominent ones) took an active part in the foundation of a republic. Only in those heroic times, Hannah suggests, has modern man tasted freedom or had any experience of what politics actually is.

One of Hannah Arendt's collections of essays is called *Between Past and Future*,[101] and it is perhaps a defect of her work that it seems to have little to say about, or offer to, the present.

Leo Strauss has, superficially, much in common with Hannah Arendt. He too was born in Germany of Jewish parents at the beginning of the century, published scholarly work in Germany, and emigrated just before World War II to America, where he was to become in time, as she did, a professor at the University of Chicago. There are also some similarities in what they have to say, but it is the differences that are crucial. Whereas Hannah Arendt is a paradoxical mixture of the reactionary and the revolutionary in politics, Strauss can be counted a conservative; and whereas Hannah Arendt is an existentialist in philosophy, Strauss (who died in 1973) must be classed as an essentialist. Strauss maintains that it is possible to have objective knowledge of truth, indeed that it is the central purpose of philosophy to transform belief into knowledge: "political philosophy [is] the attempt to replace opinion about the nature of political things by knowledge of the nature of political things."[102]

Strauss's approach to philosophy is that of a man trained in Jewish theological studies; his first book, published in Germany in 1930, is a study of Spinoza's critique of religion. The perspective of religion is something that Strauss never lost, even when he turned to philosophy and politics. Like others of his generation, he was driven to these concerns by the challenge of totalitarianism. He suggested an explanation for the rise of Hitler which was uniquely his own. The collapse of Weimar (not only the Weimar Republic but the German humanist ideals by which that republic was inspired) he attributed to the influence of modern philosophy, of liberalism and positivism, and especially to the spread of the doctrine that knowledge is possible only of fact and that values are matters of subjective feelings, neither true nor false. The logical consequence of positivism, according to Strauss, is nihilism, and it was just this nihilism in the mind of modern man which had paved the way for totalitarianism in the state.

It was not, however, only the most fashionable and advanced forms of positivism that Strauss indicted; the culprit he named was modernity itself. In the first book of his to be published in English, *The Political Philosophy of Hobbes*,[103] Strauss traced the mischievous errors of modernity back to the early seventeenth century; in later writings[104] Strauss pushed the date back even further and named Machiavelli as the theorist who had made the decisive break with the great tradition of Hebrew, Greek, and Christian thought by which Western civilization had been formed, and directed the mind of man toward scientific materialism, liberal hedonism, nihilism, and totalitarianism. The ancient tradition of natural *right*, which had remained alive throughout the medieval period, was overthrown at the time of the so-called Renaissance to make way for the modern conception of natural *rights*. As distinct from the old conception of a network of fundamental laws and duties imposed on mankind by the divine order, there emerged a conception of competing claims to be asserted by each individual. The whole *ethos* of modernity, according to Strauss, left men exposed to the snares of totalitarianism.

In Strauss, the arguments of Hobhouse, Popper, and Russell are reversed; for whereas those scientifically oriented liberals had blamed metaphysics, and specifically the tradition of Plato, for the evils of the present world, Strauss turned the tables and indicted the liberals themselves. Plato and Aristotle, said Strauss, were the key figures in the great tradition of Jewish, classical, and Christian thought which had reconciled liberty and law in the conception of natural right. The scientific liberal modernists who had tried to destroy that classical tradition were the true originators of our present ills.

Thus, where Popper and the others had sought to banish Plato and Aristotle, Strauss would have them restored to their place of honor as the founders of political philosophy. Strauss's message was, simply, back to the classics; and he believed that the present was a most opportune moment in history to undertake this task.

> *The genuine understanding of the political philosophers which is . . . necessary may be said to have been rendered possible by the shaking of all traditions; the crisis of our time may have the accidental advantage of enabling us to understand in an untraditional or derivative manner. This may apply especially to classical political philosophy which has been seen for a considerable time only through the lenses of modern political philosophy and its various successors.*[105]

Strauss, like Oakeshott, argues that the value of political philosophy lies in the enlargement of political understanding, not in the acquisition of political skills.

"We cannot," he writes, "reasonably expect that a fresh understanding of classical political philosophy will supply us with recipes for today's use. For the relative success of modern political philosophy has brought into being a kind of society wholly unknown to the classics, a kind of society to which classical principles as stated and elaborated by the classics are not immediately applicable. Only we living today can possibly find a solution to the problems of today. But an adequate understanding of the principles as elaborated in the classics may be the indispensable starting point for an adequate analysis, to be achieved by us, of present day society in its peculiar character, and for the wise application, to be achieved by us, of these principles to our tasks."[106]

Strauss's book *On Tyranny*[107] is a good illustration of what he has here in mind. Believing that contemporary "value free" social science has failed to provide any adequate explanation of the nature of totalitarianism, Strauss looks back to an ancient study of tyranny: Xenophon's dialogue entitled *The Hieron*. Strauss prints a translation of this dialogue with a commentary of his own, together with a discussion of his interpretation of Xenophon

with a French Hegelian scholar, Alexandre Kojeve. By means of this dialectical scrutiny of an ancient dialogue, Strauss seeks to deepen our insight
into the nature of tyranny as it exists in the modern world, where it is not
a matter of personal rule but a matter of institutions, parties, science, and
technology with pretensions to universal rule.

Strauss preferred to speak of himself as a historian rather than a
philosopher, but there was at least one technical philosophical problem to
which he devoted particular attention, and that was to so-called fact-value
dichotomy: the assertion, so central to modern positivism, that there can
be no logical derivation of knowledge of what ought to be from knowledge
of what is.

Strauss argued in some detail that facts and values, far from being
mutually impenetrable, were logically fused in our language, that value
judgments are built into the words we use to think with and to communicate our thoughts. The whole idea of a value-free political science was, he
suggested, an absurdity, since science itself rests on the affirmation of a
value, namely truth. Arguing in this way, Strauss found himself in the
company of a number of younger philosophers in both America and
Great Britain. For example, John Searle[108] in California, Charles Taylor[109]
in Canada, and Alasdair MacIntyre[110] in England all produced work
which, from starting points wholly unlike Strauss's, came to the same conclusion that it *is* logically possible to derive a value from a fact.

There had also been certain significant developments within the discipline of positivist political science itself. When that science first began to
flourish in American universities, its avowed aim was to be a *wertfrei*, empirical, and objective social science, designed to explain "all the
phenomena of government in terms of observed and observable behavior
of men."[111] But already by the 1940s, the same science presented itself as a
"policy science" working in the service of democracy. Harold Lasswell, one
of the most brilliant exponents of the empirical discipline, wrote during
World War II that political science was as much directed toward the defense of democracy as was military science itself.[112] Plainly such a science is
not value-free, whatever else it may be.

It has been suggested, with good reason, by David Easton,[113] that
Lasswell's work itself was never really value-free. Easton suggests that
Lasswell simply moved from a veiled and implicit acceptance of the elitist
values of the Italian sociologists Pareto and Mosca to an explicit and
avowed acceptance of the values of American democracy. But there is
something Lasswell shares with the other practitioners of empirical political science. Their conception of science, while said to be based on the
model of physics, was really based on the model of psychopathology, a
science of which the central purpose is not the discovery of truth but the
effecting of a cure, a science which is interested in facts only insofar as
those facts relate to such value-laden concepts as health, satisfaction, adjustment, normality. There is, of course, nothing *wertfrei* here. American

political science was always a science on the therapeutic model, so that when it was proclaimed in the 1940s to be a "policy science" in the service of American democracy, it was really only becoming aware of its own nature. Or perhaps it would be truer to say that it was revealing its own nature to those who chose to recognize it. For, as Popper has pointed out, scientists of all kinds are often unaware of the logical character of their own activity. Hence the need for the philosopher to explain things.

Leo Strauss once said: "The question ... 'what is political?' ... cannot be answered scientifically but only dialectically."[114]

Eric Voegelin is one philosopher who disagrees with this; indeed the main enterprise he has set himself is to work out a political philosophy which is both scientific and dialectical. He is perhaps the most ambitious of living political philosophers, the closest, in this sense, to Hegel. More than either Hannah Arendt or Strauss, Voegelin brought to America from Germany that aspiration toward universal knowledge which was the distinguishing mark of the Hegelian tradition. Moreover, Voegelin has never made that final break with Germany which both Strauss and Hannah Arendt, as Jewish emigrants to America, felt impelled to make. A Lutheran, exiled for political reasons by the Nazis, Voegelin returned to Germany after the war to become a professor at Munich University, and he continued to write in German as often as in English. For this reason, Voegelin's work does not wholly fall within the scope of this present essay.

Nevertheless, Voegelin has written important work in English;[115] he has taught at several American universities and has a number of American disciples. Although his writings are diffuse, dense, and unsystematic, he does bring together a number of the main themes which have exercised the minds of English-speaking political philosophers in the past forty years. Like Maritain and Strauss, Voegelin has tried to effect the reconciliation of reason with faith, and specifically with faith in God; and he does so by arguments which are partly existentialist, like Hannah Arendt's, and partly rationalistic, like the Thomists'. His conception of dialectic, while owing much to Hegel, is in practice close to that of Wittgenstein, since Voegelin rejects all system building in favor of argument by suggestion, qualification, and criticism. Like Strauss, Voegelin believes that the recovery of the classics offers the best way to an understanding of present political problems. Like Hannah Arendt, he seeks at the same time to achieve a historical and philosophical perspective. Like Popper, he seeks to bridge the gulf between philosophy and science.

But if Voegelin seems eager to extend the boundaries of political philosophy so that it has no fixed frontiers with other fields of knowledge, he makes a sharp and crucial distinction between political philosophy and ideology. An ideology is a system of thought which, in Marx's words, seeks to change the world rather than to understand it. Voegelin sees a greater danger to political philosophy in the advances of ideology than in the hostility of empirical political science. And undoubtedly since the death of

Stalin in 1953, there has been something of a boom in ideologies all over the world. In the United States, neo-Marxist ideologues such as Herbert Marcuse and Erich Fromm found themselves carried to fame by the wave of fashionable radical sentiment which swept the American bourgeoisie in the 1960s. Writings by such theorists as these, who combine a polemical attack on existing institutions with a visionary or utopian program for human betterment, can easily be mistaken for philosophy, since they are written at a high level of intellectual abstraction.

Voegelin in America, like Oakeshott and Popper in England (and like Raymond Aron and Albert Camus in France), has been in the forefront of the philosophers who have pointed out that genuine philosophy is not ideology, precisely because philosophy is *not* action-oriented, is *not* utopian, is *not* programmatic, is *not* suited to serve as a substitute for religion, is *not* designed to change the world, but *is* designed to understand it.

Philosophers disagree about what understanding is, and what this understanding entails, but almost all would agree with Hegel when he said, "I am at home in the world when I know it, and still more so when I have understood it."[116]

It is curious how the ghost of Hegel has continued to haunt modern political philosophy, even that of the English language into which his works have never been adequately translated. Condemned, for the most part unread, in two world wars, he has reemerged since 1950[117] not only as an intermediary between modern thought and that of classical antiquity but as a philosopher whose thinking sets the pattern of the argument of those who disagree with him as much as of those who agree with him. Hegel may be refuted, but he cannot be ignored, escaped, or banished.

The history of political philosophy in the English-speaking world in the past half century has been the history of transition from a phase when positivism was triumphant and metaphysics mocked to a time when positivism itself is discredited and démodé, and with the recovery of metaphysics the great speculative theorists of the past from Plato to Hegel have begun to come back into their own.

---

[1] *The Metaphysical Theory of the State* (London: George Allen & Unwin, 1918), p. 7.

[2] *The Open Society and Its Enemies* (London: G. Routledge & Sons, 1945).

[3] *History of Western Philosophy* (New York: Simon and Schuster, 1946), p. 742.

[4] *See* Fons Elders, *Reflexive Water* (London: Souvenir Press, 1974).

[5] *Tractatus Logico-Philosophicus* (New York: Harcourt, Brace & Co., 1922).

[6] Their number included Moritz Schlick (who died in 1936), Rudolf Carnap, Kurt Gödel, Gustav Bergmann, Philipp Frank, and Otto Neurath, who all emigrated to America, and Friedrich Weismann, who went to England.

[7] *Language, Truth and Logic* (New York: Oxford University Press, 1936).

[8] "What Is Dialectic?," *Mind* n.s. 49, no. 196 (October 1940): 426.

[9] David Easton, *The Political System* (New York: Alfred A. Knopf, 1953), p. 221.

[10] *See* Bernard R. Crick, *The American Science of Politics* (Berkeley: University of California Press, 1959).

[11] Alfred Schütz, "On Multiple Realities," *Philosophy and Phenomenological Research* 5, no. 4 (June 1945): 533–76.

[12] *See* especially Maritain's *True Humanism* (New York: Charles Scribner's Sons, 1938); *The Person and the Common Good*, trans. John J. Fitzgerald (New York: Charles Scribner's Sons, 1947); *Man and the State* (Chicago: University of Chicago Press, 1951).

[13] *A Dialectic of Morals, The Review of Politics* (Notre Dame, Ind.: University of Notre Dame, 1941).

[14] A series of articles written in collaboration with Walter Farrell, O.P., in *The Thomist* 3, no. 3 (July 1941)–7, no. 1 (January 1944). *See also* "The Demonstration of Democracy," *Proceedings of the American Catholic Philosophy Association* 15: 122–65.

[15] *Conjectures and Refutations* (London: Routledge & Kegan Paul, 1963), p. 335.

[16] By Peter Laslett in *Philosophy, Politics and Society* (Oxford: Basil Blackwell, 1956). Similar diagnoses were offered by A. Cobban, "The Decline of Political Theory," *Political Science Quarterly* 68, no. 3 (September 1953): 321–37; G. E. G. Catlin, "Political Theory: What Is It?," *Political Science Quarterly* 72 (March 1957): 1–29; Robert A. Dahl, "Political Theory," *World Politics* 11 (October 1958): 89–102; Neal Riemer, *The Revival of Democratic Theory* (New York: Appleton-Century-Crofts, 1962), p. 1. The opposite opinion that political philosophy was very much alive was put forward by P. H. Partridge in "Politics, Philosophy, Ideology," *Political Studies* 9 (October 1961): 217–35, and John Plamenatz, "The Use of Political Theory," *Political Studies* 8 (February 1960): 37–47.

[17] "Epistle to the Reader," *An Essay concerning Human Understanding* (London, 1689); cf. *GBWW*, Vol. 35, p. 89.

[18] *See* especially Ryle's "Systematically Misleading Expressions," *Proceedings of the Aristotelian Society* 32 (1931).

[19] *Ethics and Language* (New Haven: Yale University Press, 1944), p. 33.

[20] Ibid., p. 72.

[21] Ibid.

[22] *The Vocabulary of Politics* (Baltimore: Penguin Books, 1953), p. 7.

[23] Ibid., pp. 11–12. Clearly Weldon was no classical scholar. Plato, having no words in his language for our words *state* and *individual*, would not even have understood this question.

[24] Ibid., p. 192.

[25] *Philosophical Investigations*, trans. G. E. M. Anscombe (Oxford: Basil Blackwell, 1953), p. 11E.

[26] *Vocabulary of Politics*, p. 175.

[27] "Political Principles," in *Philosophy, Politics and Society*, ed. Peter Laslett and W. G. Runciman, 3d ser., vol. 1 (Oxford: Basil Blackwell, 1967).

[28] *Vocabulary of Politics*, p. 192.

[29] *Philosophical Investigations*, p. 49E.

[30] *Words and Things* (London: V. Gollancz, 1959), p. 92.

[31] *Beyond Ideology* (New York: Harper & Row, 1967), p. 78–79.

[32] A similarity studied in some detail by W. H. Greenleaf in "Idealism, Modern Philosophy and Politics," in *Politics and Experience*, ed. Preston King and B. C. Parekh (London: Cambridge University Press, 1968).

[33] *See* W. H. Greenleaf, *Oakeshott's Philosophical Politics* (London: Longmans, Green & Co., 1966).

[34] *Experience and Its Modes* (Cambridge: The University Press, 1933).

[35] Greenleaf, *Oakeshott's Philosophical Politics*, p. 15.

[36] *Cambridge Journal*, vol. 1 (1948–49), p. 91.

[37] *Rationalism in Politics* (London: Methuen & Co., and New York: Basic Books, 1962), p. 91.

[38] Ibid., p. 21.

[39] Albert Hunold, ed., *Freedom and Serfdom*, trans. R. H. Stevens (Dordrecht, The Netherlands: D. Reidel, 1961), p. 160.

[40] Ibid., p. 167.

[41] *The Constitution of Liberty* (Chicago: University of Chicago Press, 1960).

[42] See *The Poverty of Historicism* (London: Routledge & Kegan Paul, 1957) and *Conjectures and Refutations*.

[43] *See* Elders, *Reflexive Water*.

[44] It was not published in English until 1959, when it appeared as *The Logic of Scientific Discovery* (New York: Basic Books; London: Hutchinson).

[45] *See* especially *Conjectures and Refutations*.

[46] Ibid., p. 350.

[47] Ibid.

[48] Ibid., p. 351.

[49] *The Logic of Democracy* (New York: Holt, Rinehart & Winston, 1962).

[50] *Philosophy of Democratic Government* (Chicago: University of Chicago Press, 1951).

[51] *A General Theory of Authority* (Notre Dame, Ind.: University of Notre Dame Press, 1962).

[52] *The Tradition of Natural Law*, ed. Vukan Kuic (New York: Fordham University Press, 1965).

[53] *Freedom and Community*, ed. C. P. O'Donnell (New York: Fordham University Press, 1968).

[54] *Philosophy of Democratic Government*, p. 74.

[55] Ibid., p. 76.

[56] *Freedom and Community*, p. 33.

[57] Ibid., pp. 54–55.

[58] Ibid., p. 121.

[59] *Sovereignty*, trans. J. F. Huntington (Chicago: University of Chicago Press, 1957).

[60] Ibid., p. 33.

[61] Ibid., p. 39.

[62] *On Power*, trans. J. F. Huntington (New York: Viking Press, 1949).

[63] *See* his *Pure Theory of Politics* (New Haven: Yale University Press, 1963). Jouvenel also developed an interest in political science as a "policy science" and set up his own institute in Paris for the study of "futurology" in political and economic planning.

[64] *The Opium of the Intellectuals*, trans. Terence Kilmartin (Garden City, N.Y.: Doubleday & Co., 1957). *See also* his *World Technology and Human Destiny* (Ann Arbor: University of Michigan Press, 1963), *Introduction to the Philosophy of History*, trans. George J. Irwin (Boston: Beacon Press, 1961), and *Main Currents in Sociological Thought*, trans. Richard Howard and Helen Weaver (New York: Basic Books, 1965).

[65] *Opium of the Intellectuals*, p. 269.

[66] *Social Principles and the Democratic State* (London: George Allen & Unwin, 1959).

[67] Mention should also be made of certain American theorists, such as Carl J. Friedrich, Hannah Arendt, and Talcott Parsons, who have also contributed to the discussion of authority.

[68] *Social Principles*, pp. 17–18.

[69] *Principles of Political Thought* (New York: Collier Books, 1964).

[70] *See* especially R. S. Peters, "Authority," and S. I. Benn, "Sovereignty," in *Political Philosophy*, ed. Anthony Quinton (London: Oxford University Press, 1967); R. S. Peters, *The Concept of Motivation* (London: Routledge & Kegan Paul, 1958), *Ethics and Education* (London: George Allen & Unwin, 1966), *Reason and Compassion* (London: Routledge & Kegan Paul, 1973).

[71] "The Meaning of Liberty," *Revue internationale de Philosophie* 2, no. 6 (Brussels, 1948).

[72] *Freedom: A New Analysis* (London and New York: Longmans, Green & Co., 1953).

[73] *Two Concepts of Liberty* (Oxford: Oxford University Press, Clarendon Press, 1958).

[74] *Dimensions of Freedom: An Analysis* (London: Macmillan & Co., 1961).

[75] *The Idea of Freedom*, 2 vols. (Garden City, N.Y.: Doubleday & Co., 1958–61).

[76] This work was, however, intended by Adler as a service, not as an alternative to prescriptive formulations, which he himself subsequently offered as two books of a moral, speculative, and committed kind: *The Time of Our Lives* (New York: Holt, Rinehart & Winston, 1970), setting out a constructive theory of morals, and *The Common Sense of Politics* (New York: Holt, Rinehart & Winston, 1971), which sought to establish normative principles of political wisdom. Both books in Adler's own words "attempt to prescribe ideals that ought to be pursued and the steps that ought to be taken toward their realization" (*The Common Sense of Politics*, p. xi).

[77] "How to Read Wittgenstein," in *Understanding Wittgenstein*, ed. Godfrey Vesey (New York: St. Martin's Press, 1974), p. 126.

[78] *The Idea of Freedom*, 2 : 3.

[79] *Freedom of the Individual* (New York: Harper & Row, 1965).

[80] *Thought and Action* (London: Chatto and Windus, 1959).

[81] Hampshire writes, "A transcendental argument of the kind that Kant and Hegel attempted is always needed to show the necessary connection of art with morality and with political knowledge, and thereby show its necessary place in the development of individuals and human societies" (*Feeling and Expression* [London: H. K. Lewis & Co., 1961], p. 245).

[82] See *On Liberty* (1859); *GBWW*, Vol. 43, pp. 267–323. Whether Mill's other writings in political theory can be regarded as liberal is a matter of dispute among scholars.

[83] *Law, Liberty and Morality* (Stanford, Calif.: Stanford University Press, 1963).

[84] *The Enforcement of Morals* (London: Oxford University Press, 1965).

[85] *Liberty, Equality, Fraternity* (London: Smith, Elder & Co., 1873).

[86] *What Is Justice?* (Berkeley: University of California Press, 1957).

[87] *De La Justice* (Brussels: Office de publicité, 1945).

[88] *The Idea of Justice*, trans. John Petrie (London: Routledge & Kegan Paul, 1963).

[89] *The Concept of Law* (Oxford: Oxford University Press, Clarendon Press, 1961).

[90] *A Concept of Justice* (Cambridge, Mass.: Harvard University Press, Belknap Press, 1971).

[91] *The Liberal Theory of Justice* (London: Oxford University Press, 1973).

[92] Perhaps even more so. Controversy surrounding Rawls should not be allowed to divert attention from other important writings on justice, such as those of Carl Friedrich, D. D. Raphael, L. L. Fuller, S. I. Benn, and John Chapman.

[93] *The Origins of Totalitarianism* (New York: Harcourt, Brace & Co., 1951).

[94] *The Human Condition* (New York: Doubleday Anchor Books, 1959), p. 12.

[95] Almost, but not quite; for while she exalts the public, at the expense of the private, she also speaks of the human need for a private space to shelter from publicity, and in which to acquire some spiritual depth (ibid., p. 99).

[96] Ibid., p. 157.

[97] Ibid., p. 184.

[98] "Reflections on Violence," *The New York Review of Books*, 27 February 1969, p. 29.

[99] Ibid., p. 30.

[100] *On Revolution* (New York: The Viking Press, 1963).

[101] *Between Past and Future* (New York: The Viking Press, 1961).

[102] *What Is Political Philosophy?* (New York: The Free Press, 1959), pp. 11–12.

[103] *The Political Philosophy of Hobbes*, trans. Elsa M. Sinclair (New York: Oxford University Press, 1936).

[104] See especially *Thoughts on Machiavelli* (Glencoe, Ill.: The Free Press, 1958).

[105] *The City and Man* (Chicago: Rand McNally & Co., 1964), p. 9.

[106] Ibid., p. 11. (The use of the word *analysis* in this passage by a philosopher strongly opposed to "analytical philosophy" is significant indication of the extent to which analysis has become less controversial as the word *analysis* has become more and more loosely understood.

[107] *On Tyranny* (Chicago: Free Press, 1948).

[108] "How to Derive an Is from an Ought," in *The Is-Ought Question*, ed. W. D. Hudson (London: Macmillan & Co., 1969).

[109] *The Explanation of Behaviour* (London: Routledge & Kegan Paul, 1964).

[110] *Against the Self-Images of the Age* (New York: Schocken Books, 1971).

[111] Robert A. Dahl, "The Behavioral Approach in Political Science," in the *American Political Science Review* 55, no. 4 (December 1961): 767.

[112] *Democracy through Public Opinion* (Menasha, Wis.: George Banta Publishing Co., 1941).

[113] "Harold Lasswell," *Journal of Politics* 12, no. 3 (August 1950): 450–77.

[114] *What Is Political Philosophy?*, pp. 24–25.

[115] Notably *Order and History*, 3 vol. (Baton Rouge: State University Press, 1956); *The New Science of Politics* (Chicago: University of Chicago Press, 1952). Hannah Arendt, Alois Dempf, and Friedrich Engel-Janosi, eds., *Politische Ordnung und Menschliche Existenz* (Munich: Beck, 1962), has a bibliography of Voegelin's work in both German and English.

[116] Hermann Glockner, ed., *Sämtliche Werke* (Stuttgart: F. Frommann, 1927–40), 7 : 142.

[117] Books which throw light on the new recognition of Hegel in the English-speaking world include: J. N. Findlay, *Hegel: A Re-examination* (New York: The Macmillan Co., 1958); Walter Kaufmann, *Hegel: Reinterpretation, Texts, and Commentary* (Garden City, N.Y.: Doubleday & Co., 1965); Z. A. Pelczynski, ed., *Hegel's Political Writings*, trans. T. M. Knox (Oxford: Oxford University Press, Clarendon Press, 1964), and *Hegel's Political Philosophy* (Cambridge: Cambridge University Press, 1971); Raymond Plant, *Hegel* (London: George Allen & Unwin, 1973).

The Planets Today: The New View from Space

Nicholas M. Short

In this article, Dr. Nicholas M. Short undertakes to summarize what has been learned of our planetary system since rocket-propelled exploration from Earth began some twenty years or so ago, and compares it to what we knew about this system when we were limited to what we could perceive through stationary observation.

Dr. Short is geology discipline leader in the Earth Resources Program for NASA at the Goddard Space Flight Center, Greenbelt, Maryland. Born in St. Louis, he was trained in geology at St. Louis University, Washington University, and M.I.T., where he received his doctorate in 1958. He was staff research geologist in the AEC's Project Plowshare to utilize underground nuclear explosives for engineering and mining applications at the Lawrence Radiation Laboratory and served on the faculty of geology at the University of Houston before going to Goddard in 1967 as a senior research associate in the National Academy of Sciences postdoctoral studies program at NASA installations.

A specialist in the transformation of materials by high pressure transient waves, Dr. Short has written or helped to write more than fifty papers in various subfields of geology during his professional career. He is coeditor of the standard reference work on shock metamorphism of natural materials, is coauthor of a pictorial atlas on volcanic landforms, and has recently published a basic textbook on planetary geology. He has lectured on scientific topics at more than sixty universities and civic organizations.

The planetary bodies of our solar system have orbited continuously around their primary—the sun—since it first became organized as a star more than 4.6 billion years ago. The earliest awareness of these planets can be traced to records less than 10,000 years old left by the ancient peoples of Babylonia, China, the Mayan civilization, and others. Their astronomers recognized that five bright celestial objects—known to us as Mercury, Venus, Mars, Jupiter, and Saturn—shifted systematically against the background of fixed stars in a series of motions that suggested a close tie to Earth. However, the deduction that these tiny round disks of light were spherical bodies having dimensions and properties similar to those of Earth could scarcely have occurred to the ancient philosophers and savants. They were conceived instead by the Romans and Greeks to be bodies of astrological significance; that is, they were part of the world of the gods and could themselves directly exert powerful influences on the temperaments of men and the course of their lives. The five planets of old, along with the sun, the moon, and the stars, were fitted by Pythagoras into a series of concentric spheres that surrounded the central Earth. Later, Hipparchus and then Ptolemy refined these motions of the celestial spheres by determining more precise and elaborate movements of the planets and stars. This mathematically complicated view of the universe persisted through the Middle Ages until the heliocentric system of planetary motions devised by Copernicus in the early 1500s gradually won acceptance over the next century.

It was the observing eye and keen mind of Galileo, aided by a primitive Dutch telescope, that brought the real nature of the planets into perspective. Galileo is credited with the discovery of Saturn's rings and four of the thirteen satellites of Jupiter. He described the phases of Venus and correctly ascribed them to changing illumination of its spherical surface when this is seen from Earth as the two planets move around the sun. Galileo also noted the mountains, craters, and dark plains (which he called maria or "seas") of the moon while deducing that it too must be a planetlike object having some similarities to Earth. As the telescope's power and resolution improved, over the next three centuries, the remaining planetary bodies were eventually located—Uranus in 1781, Neptune in 1846, Pluto in 1930, and the asteroids in 1801 and later.

Modern planetology—the study of planets—began in the nineteenth century as an offshoot of astronomy. The basic tool then, as today, was the telescope. By the present century, that instrument had become coupled with such sophisticated equipment as recording photographic cameras, photometers, spectrographs, and thermal sensors suited to exacting measurements of a variety of physical and chemical properties. After World War II, powerful radar pulses were directed to several planets to define their surface topography and, indirectly, the composition of their topmost layers. Still other planetary properties, such as mass, moments of inertia, density distributions, and gravitational constants, were derived for each planet by application of the principles of celestial mechanics through mathematical analysis of orbital data, using ever more precise observations.

By 1957, the year of Sputnik and the opening of the space age, a large scientific literature relating to the moon and planets existed. This encompassed both hard facts and rampant speculations concerning the composition of solid and gaseous planets and their atmospheres, their accompanying force fields, their interiors and surface features, and their origins and subsequent histories. Still, the list of uncertainties and unanswered questions, inevitable in the absence of first-hand data, far exceeded the established knowledge pertaining to Earth's nearest neighbors in the universe.

Since 1957, and especially in the decade beginning in 1965, most of these uncertainties have been resolved and many of the questions answered during a new "golden age" of planetary exploration. Although no one has actually added up the information acquired during this period, it is reasonable to estimate that at least a tenfold expansion of specific data has occurred for the planets in general following the first successful Russian probe to the moon in 1959. Thereafter, more than a dozen unmanned spacecraft were sent by both the United States and the Soviet Union to the moon, to crash or land on its surface or to orbit while gathering a wide spectrum of data.

The culmination of these lunar investigations took place on July 20, 1969, when a small landing vehicle placed the two Apollo 11 astronauts on the moon's surface to initiate the most exciting and informative exploration program of the twentieth century. This was followed by five more Apollo landings through 1972, interspersed with a sequence of unmanned landings of Russian vehicles from 1970 onward.

Both the Americans and the Soviets have sent instrumented space probes to other planets as well. The U.S. Mariner 2 probe launched into outer space flew past Venus in 1962, followed by several other Mariner flybys. The Russians have placed five Venera spacecraft into the Venusian atmosphere; two actually landed on Venus, surviving long enough to acquire and transmit back to Earth valuable data on the hostile environment at that planet's surface. Another Mariner spacecraft returned the first close-up images of Mars in 1965; three more Mariners and several Russian probes have since visited the "red planet." Mariner 9—a model of success in unmanned exploration—has imaged the entire surface of Mars and has made accurate measurements of temperatures, pressures, and composition of the planet's tenuous atmosphere at its surface. Mariner 10 has reached the vicinity of Mercury, the innermost planet, to photograph, in three passes, more than 50 percent of its surface, and to measure some of its fundamental properties. The Pioneer 10 and 11 probes, in 1973 and 1974 respectively, passed through the intense force fields around Jupiter, collecting a variety of data on the largest planet in the solar system. Pioneer 11 is now moving toward an eventual rendezvous in 1979 with Saturn.

This synopsis of achievements in planetary exploration since the mid-1960s clearly points to a vast increase in the data bank now available to planetologists, who are thus better able than they were formerly to describe, categorize, and understand the major and minor bodies of the solar system. Most of the planets are far better defined today in terms of their physical, chemical, and mineralogical makeup, surface properties, internal state, atmospheric composition, and genetic implications as a consequence of the tremendous technical and scientific efforts resulting from the U.S., Soviet, and other national space programs in recent years.[1] The prime object of this article is to review the current knowledge of the planets in light of the information produced from these space studies of the past decade.

The nature of a planet

There still is no unanimous opinion among scientists as to just what constitutes a planet. It is presumed that those planets in our solar system are representative or typical of the many others which probably orbit countless stars in the myriads of galaxies spread over the universe, but we do not actually know that this is so. Planets normally are not self-luminous (although they may reflect light from nearby sources) and would be too small to be seen as discrete bodies. In some instances their presence around a particular star could be inferred from perturbations in the motions of that star, as demonstrated for Barnard's Star, provided the planets are massive enough to exert a significant gravitational influence. The assumption of planetary bodies associated with many of the stars is based on probabilistic arguments developed from cosmogenic models. If, nevertheless, we consider the nine planets of the solar system as exemplary, we can assign the following characteristics to planets in general:

1. They move in prescribed orbits (nearly circular to moderately elliptical) about a more massive primary which exerts a controlling influence

149

through gravitational forces. This primary is usually a luminous body, such as a star, that produces visible light and other forms of energy through internal processes related to the nuclear fusion of hydrogen.

2. A planet is not itself a source of large quantities of energy generated through high temperature nuclear reactions; it may however emit radiation or particulate energy by other processes, as does Jupiter.

3. Each planet normally organizes its constituent materials into a nearly spherical body such that the mass distribution near its outer limits or discrete surface approaches an equipotential state with respect to the center of its own gravitational field.

4. A planet generally consists of a mixture of solids, liquids, and gases in varying proportions. The four inner or terrestrial planets—Mercury, Venus, Earth, and Mars—are made up mainly of rocky materials, with small, varying amounts of atmospheric gases and liquids. The four outer or giant planets—Jupiter, Saturn, Uranus, and Neptune—are composed primarily of simple gases, such as hydrogen, helium, ammonia, and methane, which become increasingly dense toward the interior, where they may liquefy or even solidify under the higher pressures at great depths, and are increasingly diffuse at their outer limits, which have no definite surfaces.

5. The planets themselves may have satellites revolving around them. Some of these satellites have probably been generated in the immediate region of, and more or less simultaneous with, their parent planets. Others—perhaps the majority—have developed in other regions of the solar system, only to be perturbed from their original orbits and captured by their present primary. At least one satellite may have been pulled from its primary to assume its own orbit—Pluto is so much smaller and chemically unlike the other planets that some think it to be an escaped moon of Neptune which has "moved up" to planetary status.

Most other known bodies within the solar system fail to meet one or more of these criteria. Asteroids, for example, are small and misshapen, though they follow fixed orbital paths around the sun. Comets are spherical and may pursue repeatable (predictable) orbits, but they also are small. Several satellites of the giant planets, on the other hand, are as large as Mercury, but the bodies they revolve around are not fixed stars like the sun. And so forth. The moon may be a special case. It meets all criteria of a planet except for its subservience to Earth as a satellite. Because capture is one reasonable explanation for its present status—although other proposed origins are still being considered—it is convenient to treat the moon as a small planet in discussing the exploration of the solar system.

The exploration of the past ten years has disclosed the recurrence of several "universal" processes acting within or on each of the terrestrial planets. These merit some discussion.

Melting and differentiation

There is direct evidence that Earth and its moon have experienced at least one episode of general melting early in their histories. This evidence comes from the diversity of igneous rocks collected at their surfaces. Such diversity represents a broad pattern of chemical or petrologic differentiation, i.e., a separation of mineral constituents according to crystallization processes so as to form layers or zones of differing composition at varying depths. To accomplish such large-scale changes that would account for the diversity of rock types, the most likely explanation assumes an extensive melting of the outer layers of a planet. If the planet has a well-defined mantle and core, this melting may have been total; that is, it can be assumed to have involved the entire planet at one or more stages of its existence.

Large-scale melting has two important consequences for our knowledge of a planet. First, complete melting of the planet's outer reaches will necessarily have altered the original rock materials accreted during the later stages of planetary growth. With the resulting destruction of rock textures and the separation, redistribution, and partial loss of elemental constituents, the final products that appear in the outer layers of the planet may be so changed as to yield little information about the initial nature and state of its primordial materials. This means that sampling at the surfaces of Mercury, Venus, and Mars with the intent of collecting planetary materials in their primitive or undifferentiated state—a missed goal in the Apollo lunar missions—would be fruitless if indeed melting has been general. That does not fully negate the value of obtaining samples, for many rocks will retain products that serve as clues to planetologists for reconstructing planetary evolution. But the hope of finding large quantities of the primitive materials from which planets develop remains much the same as before the planetary exploration programs began. Meteorites are still the best and perhaps the only surviving samples of these materials likely to fall into our hands.

Second, large-scale melting of a planet assures the development of distinct layers having compositional differences. One or more such layers will form—or will once have formed—a crust or outer shell over the sphere. This crust will completely displace the original surface of the planet, removing any signs of accretionary topography and providing a fresh surface from which to record subsequent events. The crust will normally contain less dense constituents that rise upward in a molten body in which convection also operates. Denser constituents will be redistributed downward under gravitational influence in the planetary interior to form mantle rocks. Melting throughout the entire planet seems a necessary condition for buildup of a core of heavier elements such as iron and nickel. A largely molten planet undergoing widespread differentiation is like a blast furnace. Lighter elements move surfaceward to crystallize

151

in the outer layers; heavier elements settle inward to form the mantle rocks.

Volcanism

This term refers to any surface (or near-surface) manifestation of molten rock in its various stages and processes. Volcanic activities range from outpourings of lavas that flood broad areas to conical buildups of viscous fragments that acquire the characteristic volcano shape. The types of volcanic landforms and surface features developed in a region depend on the composition of the materials extruded, the fracture patterns connecting molten rock at deeper levels (magmas) with that near the surface (called lava), and such modifying factors as the presence of an atmosphere or hydrosphere.

Visual evidence of volcanism is confirmed for Earth, the moon, Mars, and Mercury. The surface of Venus remains shrouded in clouds, but radar images of that planet show a topography that may have volcanic components. It is reasonable to expect volcanic features on each of the inner planets if they have undergone extensive melting at some time in their history. Volcanism is an inevitable consequence of the formation of a crust by magmatic processes. The extent to which signs of volcanism can still be recognized on a planetary surface depends on when the volcanic activity occurred, how frequently it may have recurred after crustal development, and the nature of the degradational or erosive processes acting since the surface features formed.

The greatest diversity of volcanic features is found on Earth. This results from the continuing magmatic activity within the outer layers of our planet and from the considerable differences in composition of the rocks available for melting within the complex, highly differentiated continental crust, or within the less variable oceanic layers and upper mantle. Mars, like Earth, shows constructive volcanic landforms (shield volcanoes), as well as extensive lava flows, but the reduced diversity of volcanic features suggests a simpler, less differentiated crust. The moon's volcanic landforms are dominated by those built from lavas of high fluidity, with stratovolcanoes absent, cinder cones rare, and shield volcanoes uncommon. Calderas analogous to those on the flanks of the island of Hawaii are certainly present among the millions of lunar craters, but they appear to be only a small fraction of the total. Mercury displays many surface features in common with the moon, but only a few of these are clearly revealed as volcanic. Dark lava flows and calderas are presumably present.

Degassing

Current opinion holds that some types of carbonaceous chondrites—meteorites composed of magnesium-iron silicates in chondrules (tiny spheres) held within a matrix enriched in water-bearing silicates and abiotic carbonaceous compounds—are probably close to the kinds of materials that entered into the silicate products condensing out of the cooling nebula from which the sun and its planets evolved. These chondrites also are believed to have made up the principal components of accreting inner planetary bodies. Some of the smallest bodies were never heated up to the melting point; many of the meteorites represent samples of this group. In contrast, those larger than 100–200 kilometers in diameter apparently underwent heating sufficient to bring about some degree of melting and recrystallization. The hydrous and carbonaceous constituents in the matrix were gasified and mobilized during this process. The gases, along with some elements of higher volatility (e.g., nitrogen, argon, potassium, sodium, and their oxides), were carried outward to the surface region. Three possible fates awaited them upon release to this lower temperature-pressure regime: (1) they could recombine chemically to form certain compounds, (2) they could condense as liquids or solids and accumulate at or near the surface or in an enveloping atmosphere, or (3) they could diffuse through that atmosphere to escape into outer space. Much depended on their atomic or molecular weights, their condensation temperatures, their chemical reactivity, the mass and size of the parent planet and hence the strength of its gravity field, and the extent to which melting released and circulated these constituents. But the net effect was a degassing or "drying out."

Each of the planets, and our moon, has undergone this process to some degree. The moon and probably Mercury now consist of refractory silicates, depleted in volatile sodium and potassium, and devoid of water, indigenous carbon compounds, or internally generated atmospheric gases. Degassing as such now has almost ceased on these planets, although it may never have been completed in their deep interiors. Mars, which is larger, and which may still be experiencing some active degassing, has retained small quantities of water and other volatiles of higher molecular weights in a thin atmosphere or frozen within its surface layers. These constituents have been somewhat more abundant in the Martian past, but they probably were never organized into condensed accumulations of oceanic dimensions. Venus, nearly the size of Earth, has a dense envelope of gases above its surface. These are dominated by CO_2 along with small amounts of O_2, N_2, and H_2O. The high temperatures associated with the heat-absorbing CO_2 within the envelope have forced the escape of most lighter weight constituents. Earth also has a thick atmosphere differing from that of Venus in containing mostly N_2, some O_2, lesser but important quantities of H_2O in equilibrium with vast quantities of water in the oceans, and small amounts of CO_2 that nonetheless are essential to the maintenance of life. The evolutionary history of Earth's atmosphere diverged from that of Venus in that, on Earth, primitive life forms eventually developed an ability to utilize CO_2 by photosynthesis as a source of energy that could be converted both into fixed carbon and to released oxygen that in time became a significant constituent of the air.

Structural deformation

A rigid crustal layer or outer mantle of any planet is subject to differential stresses capable of deforming these shells in a variety of ways. The stresses can originate from a variety of causes, most of which have been operative on Earth at one time or another. In some places Earth's crust is patently experiencing tensile stresses, whereas elsewhere it is being deformed by compressive or shear stresses. Earth's crustal units are a complex mixture of igneous, sedimentary, and metamorphic rocks of different densities, strengths, and distributions. This complexity is largely responsible for the many modes of structural deformation that characterize our planet. On the other hand, Mars shows only a few of these internally induced structures, Mercury and the moon even less. This is partially explained by the absence of thin sedimentary layers that can be easily bent into folds. The simpler nature of the crusts of these planets is also a factor. Of prime importance is the absence of conditions that favor the mode of deformation known as *plate tectonics* that, as far as is evident from observation, is peculiar to Earth (*see* p. 200). Instead, the moon and Mars, and probably also Venus, possess crusts subjected primarily to tensile stresses, such as from shrinkage, over most of their histories. Mercury, by contrast, shows clear-cut signs of compressive stresses (*see* p. 193).

Cratering

One deformational process, originating from beyond a planet, causes intense, abrupt, and rapid changes at a planetary surface. This is impact cratering, once considered a rare and special event but now verified as another "universal" process that affects all rocky planets at some stage of their evolution.

Literally millions of craters larger than a meter wide have been impressed on the lunar surface, and many billions more exist in sizes ranging down to the microscopic. An almost identical type of surface was revealed on Mercury by Mariner 10. Parts of Mars show large numbers of craters, but volcanism, erosion, and backfilling with aeolian dust have modified the size, distribution, and extent of these circular depressions. Judging from radar observations, Venus seemingly has a fair number of large craters so that, by inference, a greater frequency of ever smaller craters is to be expected. Earth, by contrast, has few confirmed impact structures owing largely to its very active erosional and deformation processes, and to the comparative youth of the rocks overlying most of its continental and oceanic rock surfaces.

Almost nothing was known before the space age about the characteristics and mechanisms of cratering. The impetus to gain a better understanding of craters was the direct outgrowth of a need to explain these most prominent of features seen on the moon before it was explored *in situ*. Several approaches were followed. First, evidence for the occurrence of bona fide impact structures was sought on Earth. Thanks initially to the work of Canadian scientists, the number of known or probable craters and astroblemes (scars or erosional remnants of ancient impact craters) rose in just fifteen years after Sputnik from about fifteen to more than seventy. Many of these craters have now been mapped, sampled, and drilled so as to give a detailed three-dimensional picture of their diagnostic characteristics. Second, features found at impact craters were also observed at nuclear explosion craters, and a striking similarity of morphology and deformational style between the two structures was noted. The physical and mechanical factors involved in producing an explosion crater can be directly observed and measured. Much has been learned from this, by analogy, about impact craters. Third, experimental impact cratering has been carried out under controlled laboratory conditions. High-velocity projectiles fired into rock and sand targets have produced craters having the dimensional characteristics of those on the moon. The chain of events from start to final growth of a crater and the manner in which excavated materials are distributed to its surroundings can be recorded by high-speed framing cameras.

Such are the characteristics of impact energy dispersal that impact craters have a distinct morphology and underlying structural features, though with certain variations according to size. In plane view, an impact crater is almost perfectly circular in outline (except where segments are controlled locally by joints or fractures); this provides a distinction from volcanic craters and calderas. In cross section, the impact crater is initially bowl-shaped or nearly hemispherical, but it undergoes some modification as steep walls break and slump inward. It also has a raised rim. Faults and other displacements abound in the wall rocks beyond the limits of cratering, and fractures extend more or less radially outward, but this deformation dies out rapidly with distance; by contrast, a volcanic crater has feeder vents and fractures which continue indefinitely in a cylindrical zone below the surface depression.

The rock material fragmented during cratering is mainly ejected from the crater at various angles. Much of the high angle ejecta returns to the vicinity of the crater, with some landing inside and the remainder covering the rim region. This ejecta becomes mixed with broken debris carried into the crater from the slumping walls; on Earth, in larger craters the ejecta then mixes or is covered with lavalike shock-melted rocks. Very large lunar craters and basins are partially filled with lavas derived by melting of hot, deep crustal units owing to offloading pressure reduction. Most of the ejecta tossed out at intermediate to low angle reaches to distances of two to five crater radii. Some of the very low angle ejecta can extend for ten to twenty radii or greater as streaks or rays. Additional fragmental material, dust, rock vapor, and trapped gases (air on Earth) become mobilized as a fast-traveling cloud or base surge that adds new layers and/or scours the earlier deposited ejecta.

The pressure waves accompanying crater growth impose a unique set of changes, known as *shock metamorphism*, on the target rocks. None of these changes has been shown to take place from endogenetic (internal) processes in the upper crust where both static and deformation pressures remain well below 25 kilobars. At shock pressures between 50 and 100 kilobars, the common rock-forming minerals break into networks of tiny fractures. Between 100 and 300 kilobars, these minerals develop multiple sets of lamellae or planar features whose crystallographic orientations are quite distinct from those of lamellae in tectonically stressed rocks. Over the range of 300 to 440 kilobars, some minerals are transformed into an atomically disoriented or glassy state, without loss of their external shapes —a phenomenon that has never been duplicated by any nonshock process. High-pressure forms of quartz, feldspar, and other minerals, unknown in crustal rocks, have also been found in shocked rocks. Discovery of any or a combination of these shock-metamorphic features can be accepted as incontrovertible proof of an event requiring transient pressure waves. In nature, only the exogenic (external) process of impact cratering meets this requirement.

Impacts during the last two billion years are too rare on Earth to affect its surface overall. On the moon, Mercury, and Mars, whose surfaces date back to the first billion years of each planet's existence, impact craters or their ejecta products occupy a large part of the visible area. These surfaces reveal something about the various objects that moved through space in the early history of the solar system. The size distribution of such objects— planets, asteroids, comets, meteorites, and dust particles—follows a negative logarithmic distribution. This means that the number of discrete particles decreases in frequency as the sizes of the particles (diameters) increase, according to some logarithmic increment; thus, hypothetically, if a sampling of 100 million particles smaller than ten centimeters were counted in a sampling, there would also be found a million particles between a tenth and a meter wide, ten thousand between one-tenth and one kilometer in diameter, and only ten larger than ten kilometers—along with other numbers of particles having different size ranges than those mentioned. Data of this kind are conveniently plotted as cumulative frequency curves (fig. 1) in which numbers greater or less than specified size limits are progressively added or accumulated for each new size considered.

Use of such curves allows the size distribution of craters within some large reference area to be determined directly, although the spatial distribution or location of each crater is not specified from the curves. Surfaces having more craters of various sizes are generally considered older; that is, they have been exposed longer to an assumed constant flux. Relative ages of surfaces in different regions of a planet can then be determined by comparison of their respective frequency curves. Two cautions must be raised. First, flux rates since the start of the solar system have probably not

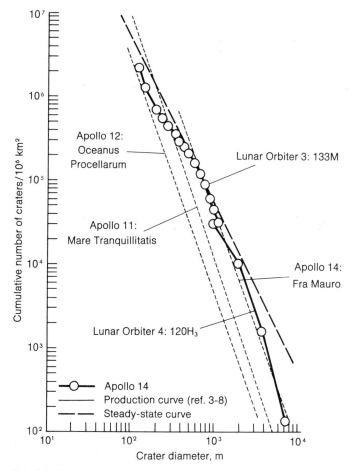

Figure 1. Cumulative size-frequency distribution of craters on the lunar surface at the Apollo 11, 12, and 14 sites and the Lunar Orbiter 3 and 4 sites. Photographs of these sites were used to measure numbers and diameters of craters. The cumulative numbers are normalized to a standard area (1 million square kilometers). For any given crater size, plotted curves on the right refer to areas with larger numbers of craters than those on the left.

been constant either in space (distance from the sun) or in time; hence, differences in crater densities between compared surfaces must be adjusted for variations in incoming particles. Second, given long enough a surface will become saturated in one or more crater sizes. When this happens, new craters cannot be fitted among older ones, and a steady state of formation for those sizes will ensue; continuing bombardment will then obliterate some older craters and will not add any new ones to the count. Complete saturation of all discernible sizes will rule out use of such a surface as an impact counter and make relative-age dating meaningless.

The use of crater frequencies to calculate and map the relative ages of materials units on the moon is further explained on page 166.

Surface modifying processes

Cratering is probably the most effective degradational process acting on ancient planetary surfaces. It is also aggradational, however, in cases where innumerable impacts grind up the crust and redistribute ejecta deposits into interleaving layers that gradually build up thick piles of surficial debris.

Depending on the extent and efficiency of atmospheric protection, several other external processes will also act on the surfaces. Micrometeorite particles, of which millions will strike a small area of surface on the moon or Mercury in periods of days, are extremely effective in wearing away exposed rock fragments or layers by abrasion. Even smaller particles—atomic nuclei, electrons, protons—associated with cosmic rays and the solar wind will induce gradual destruction of surfaces by forming unstable glassy coatings of disorganized atomic layers prone to slough off through thermal stress or further micrometeorite impacts.

Sliding movements of loose materials in response to gravitational pull even on gentle slopes commonly occur on planetary surfaces exposed to a vacuum. Internal seismic disturbances or quakes can hasten such movements. Adjustments of this nature are found on the moon, Mercury, Mars, and Earth. Slope instability is also influenced by the flow of gases (winds) in planets possessed of an atmosphere. Mars and Earth display effects from this process, and a variant of aeolian erosion and transport must also result from the dense gases in motion around Venus. These gases can also react chemically with the surface; the presence of water and other solvents, especially when moving as rain, streams, or oceans, greatly enhances the rates and degree of erosion at planetary surfaces.

Planetary genesis

The first serious efforts to develop models for the origin of planets can be traced to the seventeenth and eighteenth centuries in the theories put forth by the philosopher-scientists Descartes and Kant. Most such ideas through the nineteenth century were based on concepts dealing with the mechanics of moving bodies as developed by Galileo, Kepler, Newton, and others. Two schools of opinion competed. One, which advocated a dualistic model, assumed the planets to have been torn from the sun (whose existence was presupposed without explanation) by gravitational or collision forces exerted by a second stellar companion or a passing star or comet. These views were largely abandoned in the early twentieth century in favor of monistic models, outgrowths of those proposed by Kant and Laplace, in which the sun and its planets originated together from a collapsing cloud or nebula of dust and gases. Variations of this basic notion underlie most of today's cosmological views of planetary genesis.

Through the first half of the twentieth century, modifications of the nebular hypothesis resulted mainly from applications of principles in force-field physics. Gravitational instabilities, turbulence, magnetic forces, atomic ionization, radiation pressures, high velocity nuclear and electronic particles, and thermal energy were all called upon to account for the organization and transfer of different materials into planetary bodies having the variations in composition, size, density, and orbital motions observed in the solar system. In the 1940s and '50s, a new factor was introduced into physical models on the basis of new observations and calculations. This was the recognition that meteorites are important clues to planetary origin. These meteorites—particularly the carbonaceous chondrites, but also ordinary chondrites and the irons—set constraints or boundary conditions on the chemical nature and behavior of the nebular mass that has to be considered in testing any model. In the past twenty years, the approach to understanding planetary genesis has relied more on the chemistry than on the physics of the processes involved to explain the compositional variants of the nine planets and their satellites.

Any model of the solar system must satisfy these confirmed facts:

1. Planetary orbits are regularly spaced around the sun (according to Bode's Law) and are nearly circular—that is, they are slightly elliptical.
2. All planets revolve around the sun in the same direction, prograde or counterclockwise with respect to the celestial north pole, and also rotate in a prograde manner on their own axes.
3. The sun has inherited only about 1 percent of the total angular momentum of the system but possesses almost all its mass.
4. The mass ratios of the sun to its planets, ranging from 1,000 to 1 to 100,000 to 1, are similar to the mass ratios between the planets and their satellites.
5. The inner or terrestrial planets tend to be small, dense, slow in rotating, and have no more than two satellites; the outer or giant planets are much larger, less dense, rotate faster, and have up to thirteen satellites.

Current opinion holds planetary formation to be a common event in the evolution of stars. It follows, then, that planets should abound in the sun's galaxy as well as in the millions of other galaxies throughout the universe. The conditions by which life—and especially intelligent, communicative life—can develop on some planets may be much more rarely fulfilled.

The starting point in most modern hypotheses of planetary genesis lies within any region in a galaxy where nebular material approaches some critical density or concentrations of its principal constituents (mainly gaseous hydrogen, with some helium, ammonia, methane, inert gases, and dust composed of metals, oxides, and silicates). Radiation pressure from neighboring stars keeps the cloud in motion. Dispersed particles begin to collect into denser units by gravitational attraction, condensation from the vapor state, and accretion in parts of the nebula having higher-than-average densities. Local gravitational instabilities foster development of "clots" of matter that grow preferentially. This leads to collapse of the nebula as it organizes into larger bodies that sweep up much of the remaining dust and gases. Most of these clots become protostars, each of which gathers about itself smaller clots of hydrogen-rich, silicate, and frozen gas materials. The entire nebula, upon inception of these local material buildups through collapse, begins to contract and rotate. Rotation speeds up with increasing collapse, causing the nebula to assume a somewhat spiral shape. Individual star clots within it also rotate faster so that nebular matter under their control redistributes into a flattened or discoidal residue of gases and dust whirling about them. Gradually, this material draws closer to the star clots, until the dominant hydrogen it contains reaches a critical density at which fusion by proton-proton reactions to helium then commences. The shrouding dust-gas envelope remains subject to centrifugal forces, radiation pressures, gas and particle streaming, and gravitational attractions. Ionized gases are propelled through the cloud along magnetic lines of force as a star acquires its own magnetic field. Elements of differing masses are thus transferred to varying distances from the central star. For single stars,[2] turbulence and gravitational instabilities within the surrounding gas-dust cloud promote further clotting or accretion of particles into planet-sized and smaller bodies in much the same way as the regional nebula in the galaxy broke up into protostars.

During the final collapse phase around an individual star, temperatures within its nebula rise to 2,000° Kelvin (K)[3] or higher. Above that limit, essentially all dust particles are vaporized and added to the general gas. Cooling proceeds over time during which various chemical constituents begin to condense, each at a characteristic (pressure-dependent) temperature of solidification. A regular condensation sequence is followed by a typical gas mixture containing hydrogen, helium, nitrogen, oxygen, carbon, silicon, magnesium, iron, the alkali metals (sodium and potassium), and other elements in solar proportion. This sequence is described in the equilibrium-condensation model of J. S. Lewis and others. Each condensate remains in chemical equilibrium with the altered gases but will react with it as temperatures fall. Near 1,600° K, refractory oxides of calcium, aluminum, and titanium will be the first to condense out. Metallic iron and nickel appear next at 1,300° K, followed by the magnesium silicate enstatite at 1,200° K, and sodium- and potassium-rich silicates (feldspars) at 1,000° to 800° K. Around 680° K, hydrogen sulfide reacts with available iron to form the dense mineral troilite, a phase of FeS. Between 1,200° and 500° K, some of the iron is oxidized to FeO which enters into pyroxene and olivine minerals during reaction with enstatite. In the interval between 550° and 175° K, water becomes an essential part of the silicates in contact with it to form serpentine and other hydrous minerals. Below 175° K, H_2O will solidify into water ice, and at 150° and 120° K, ammonia and methane gases respectively condense and form hydrates with the water. Finally, at temperatures from 65° to 25° K, the now impoverished gas will lose any argon, neon, and hydrogen by condensation, leaving only helium from its gaseous phase.

As applied to the solar system, this model assumes a decreasing temperature-pressure gradient from the region of the sun to the outermost edge of the nebula. Near the sun, reactions over a narrow temperature range around 1,200° K produced refractory minerals and magnesium pyroxenes that organized into Mercury. The moon, as a minor planet possibly displaced, appears to be even more enriched in refractory oxides and magnesium-rich silicates. Further out, at temperatures near 800°, Venus formed from magnesium silicates along with some alkali feldspars. Earth developed at temperatures in the 650°– 600° K range, from hydrous silicates, among other materials. At a somewhat cooler temperature — 400° K —Mars formed. Each of these inner planets then underwent melting (heated by radioactive elements, short-lived isotopes, gravitational contraction energy, etc.) and differentiation so as to rearrange its particular mineral mixture into an orderly crust, mantle, and core. Jupiter and Saturn are special cases of very large clots of primordial solar gases, but their satellites likely are differentiated mixtures of water-ice and methane or ammonia—what is to be expected at the low-temperature end of the condensation series. Uranus and Neptune, whose compositions are inexactly known, also probably contain considerable methane and ammonia.

All of the planets built up into spheroidal bodies by accretion of small clots or planetesimals held together by frozen gases, solid carbon compounds, electrical charges, and so forth. The last growth stages of the terrestrial planets were accompanied by final accretion of associated planetesimals whose impacts are still recorded as surviving craters on Mercury, the moon, Mars, and probably Venus. Initially, the inner planets may have retained thick atmospheres of remaining solar gases, but these could have been blown off by an explosive, mass-divesting phase of the sun before it reached its present size.

Exploration of the planets

Earth

Ever since Sputnik I in 1957 and Explorer I in 1958 were placed in Earth's orbit to study cosmic rays, much of the space program, particularly in the first ten years, has centered on obtaining hitherto unavailable information about Earth's figure, surface, atmosphere, and radiation fields. Among the more important results have been (1) discovery of the Van Allen radiation belts; (2) definition of the nature and distribution of Earth's magneto-sphere; (3) observations of various solar-terrestrial relations, such as magnetic storm, solar flare, and sunspot effects and development of the aurora; (4) analysis of phenomena in the upper atmosphere including properties of the ozone layer, airglow, and noctilucent clouds and characteristics of the thermosphere; (5) meteorological data on global cloud cover, moisture content, temperature profiles, wind field distribution—especially over previously inaccessible regions; (6) improved world charts of the geoid, mass distributions, gravitational field, and surface magnetic field; and (7) images of Earth's surface from orbital photography and multispectral scanners used to explore, develop, and manage the planet's natural resources and man's modification of the environment.

These terrestrial studies have also provided functional spacecraft and sensor systems, extensive operating experience, and a vast collection of data on planetary environments of immediate benefit to the exploration of the other planets.

The moon

Most cartographic features on the earthward-facing side of our satellite had been named and charted by the mid-seventeenth century. From his telescope studies, Galileo had conveniently subdivided the moon's topography into lower dark areas called the *maria* and lighter upland areas termed the *terrae* or highlands. Superimposed on both were numerous circular depressions considered to be craters; well over a thousand of those larger than two kilometers in diameter had been given names (after astronomers, philosophers, and scientists) by the twentieth century. Two topics dominated the thinking among selenologists up to this time. First was the nature of the dark areas, considered to be seas in Galileo's time but soon thereafter recognized as solid surfaces when more and more craters were found within the maria. Gradually, the idea that the mare surfaces could be lava flows of basaltic composition came to be popular. Second, attempts to explain the origin of lunar craters stirred simmering controversy among the few serious students of the moon. In 1665 the physicist Robert Hooke argued that they were burst bubbles created in a frothing lava. Volcanic views prevailed until 1802 when von Bieberstein advocated meteorite impact as the prime process. Over the next hundred and fifty years the impact hypothesis gained general acceptance, despite some cogent counterarguments from a diehard core of volcanologists.

Prior to the space age, almost all knowledge of the moon came from calculations with celestial mechanics data and through telescope observations. Motions of the moon depend on certain physical properties. The moon's size (3,476 kilometers in diameter) and mass (7.35×10^{25} kilograms) result in an average density of 3.34 grams per cubic centimeter. If surface layers are typical basic igneous rocks of densities near 3.0–3.2 grams per cubic centimeter, the rocks at great depth cannot be much different; that is, a metallic core is either small or absent. The moon's moments of inertia lead to a dimensionless number for a homogeneous sphere that is best fitted to a body without well-defined increases in density with depth. This could mean that the moon does not have sharply delimited layers in its interior, and thus lacks a core or a mantle of high-density minerals. The moon's shape departs from a perfect sphere to that of a triaxial ellipsoid having a small earth-pointing bulge several kilometers above the mean surface elevation. The bulge may have formed when a hotter moon had a plastic or molten interior at a time the satellite was nearer to Earth. The bulge became "frozen in" to a crust now strong enough to support and preserve it at about the time the moon "locked" onto Earth in synchronous rotation. Synchronous rotation, in which periods of lunar rotation are equivalent to lunar revolution about Earth, causes one side of the sphere to face Earth at all times; prior to that condition the moon may have been much closer to Earth, but beyond its Roche limit—that is, the point (2.9 times Earth's radius) closer than which it would have suffered disintegration from tidal forces.

Photographs and visual inspection of the front face provided the basic working data used to describe and interpret the moon's surface features. Enlarged views of the maria and of dark fillings in some larger craters recorded the appearance and distribution of wrinkle ridges, straight to curved rilles (channels), flow fronts, and moundlike protuberances, all of which have analogues on Earth in volcanic terrains associated with basaltic outpourings. The possibility of some still-active volcanism on the moon was raised by sightings of transient events (luminescent red glows and color changes) and by measurements of gas discharges and thermal hotspots. Telescope observations also allowed various crater morphologies to be categorized into several genetic subtypes depending on differences in formation, size, and degree of erosional modification. Variations in crater populations (frequencies) were considered indicative of the relative ages of the surfaces containing them. Photometric measurements of the albedo (ratio of total reflected to incident light) and spectral reflectivity (reflected light intensities as a function of wavelength) of surface materials demonstrated the specific values to be consistent with basic igneous rocks ground up into a porous, granular powder that forms a widespread layer on the surface. From this emerged one now discredited supposition of a dustlike cover on the moon into which any spacecraft might sink as in quicksand if landings were attempted.

Concern with the physical state of the lunar surface and its potential hazards to manned landings outweighed even scientific inquisitiveness in formulating pre-Apollo exploration programs with unmanned probes. Television pictures made by the Ranger probes confirmed the presence of increasing numbers of smaller craters, some of which are only one to ten meters across. The surface thus was rough and likely to challenge any landing attempt. However, discovery of some large rock boulders indicated the surface to be strong and cohesive enough to support heavy weights.

Close looks at the lunar surface came early in 1966 with the touchdown of a Russian Luna probe, followed 119 days later by the landing of the American Surveyor I. Both spacecraft had scanning TV cameras that could pan the scene from the area directly under the mountings to the horizon. The returned pictures revealed a rough, rubbly surface (fig. 2) pockmarked with craters, some many meters in diameter. A mechanical scoop capable of scraping into soft materials verified the surface at each of five Surveyor sites (*see* fig. 3) to consist of unconsolidated rock debris. This forms the *regolith* or rock mantle that is equivalent to the so-called powder or dust layer that was suspected on the moon, but its mechanical properties clearly indicated the soillike material to be compact and capable of maintaining a substantial load. Presence of rock fragments at the surface suggested the regolith to be a thin (one to twenty meters) deposit overlying bedrock. A geochemical instrument on the last three Surveyors accurately determined that the composition of the topmost layers was similar to that of terrestrial basic igneous rocks.

At one time the Apollo program sought to place as many as ten missions on the moon. To select the landing sites, far better details of the lunar surface than could be determined by telescope were required. Accordingly, five Lunar Orbiter spacecraft, each equipped with two scanning photo-cameras, were sent to image the entire surface of the moon as they circled it at various altitudes. The photos were processed onboard, scanned electronically, and reconstituted on Earth from transmitted signals. Maximum resolutions of several meters were achieved in the lower-orbiting missions. The Orbiter series proved fantastically successful and sent back many now-famous views (fig. 4) as well as more prosaic ones (fig. 5) invaluable to mission planners. The achievements of the Orbiter project are still influencing lunar studies. Among the most important are: (1) provision of high-quality photos well-suited to mapping surface "stratigraphic" units, (2) images of unseen parts of the polar regions and of the almost unknown far side of the moon, where highlands dominate and maria are sparse, (3) better definition of structural and volcanic features, along with close looks at phenomena related to cratering, and (4) development of methods based on crater morphology by which to estimate regolith thicknesses. In addition, analysis of perturbations in the orbits of the spacecraft disclosed the presence of large, near-surface, positive (excess) concentrations of mass—referred to as *mascons*—whose gravitational effects caused slight accelerations of the Orbiters during overpasses. The mascons have since been variously explained as the residues of heavy metal meteorites, plugs of denser material pushed up from the upper mantle, or fillings of basins with lavas denser than the surrounding highlands. The mascons imply a lunar crust with considerable strength able to

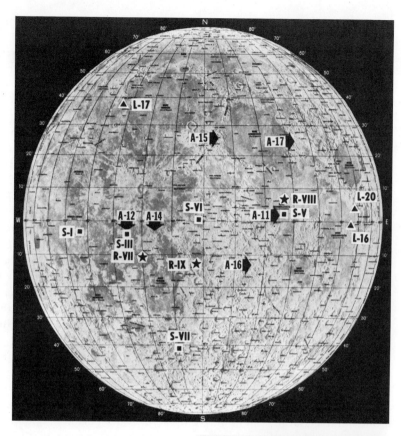

Figure 2 (right). View of the lunar surface produced as a mosaic of individual pictures obtained by the television camera on the Surveyor 5 spacecraft which landed on Mare Tranquillitatis. The entire surface is pitted with craters of varying sizes.

Figure 3 (above). Map of the lunar front side on which the locations of the Ranger impact points, Surveyor probe touchdown sites, Russian Luna landing areas, and Apollo exploration sites have been plotted by the author.

support them and, further, indicate that isostatic balances probably are maintained in the moon's outer shells.

A NASA-supported program to map the moon within a stratigraphic framework was begun by the U.S. Geological Survey even before the Orbiter photos were available. The problems involved in making a geologic map of another planetary body were different in many respects from those encountered for Earth, but the solutions drew upon some of the same principles applied to terrestrial mapping. It was recognized that major map units would consist either of lava flows or of ejecta tossed from basins or large craters. Since neither lithology nor age could be directly determined, the deposits must be treated as *materials* units rather than as *stratigraphic* units. In most cases, the forms or surface expressions of these units were the only visible characteristics, so that a morphological classification became the most practical approach. Different units were perceived as relatively *older* or *younger* than others according to the principles of superposition ("the one on top should be more recent") and transection ("the invaded, crosscut, overlapped, or offset unit is older"). The age of an unsaturated surface was suggested also by the frequency of craters. Cumulative frequency curves were made for selected areas in different regions being mapped. Those of the highlands invariably showed higher crater densities than the maria.

Unlike Earth, where most deposits assigned to a single stratigraphic unit represent sedimentation or accumulation lasting thousands or even millions of years, the moon's surface characteristics are determined by events of very brief duration. Every crater distributed its ejecta in minutes. Even if one hundred large craters were emplaced over a period of one hundred million years, the sum total of time involved in moving the ejecta deposits into their present positions would be only a few hours. Most of the intervening time between impacts would be uneventful and leave no record. The relative order of crater occurrences, reconstructed by noting the overlap relations, freshness of morphology, and crater events associated with each distinct ejecta blanket, does help, however, to decipher the historical development of the region, even though the duration of time may be hard to assess.

Most of the widespread materials units identified on the moon result from the biggest impacts—those associated with basin formation. These impacts sent ejecta outward for long distances, covering older deposits, especially close in. Other materials units can sometimes be established from the combined deposits of smaller craters formed relatively quickly from similar crustal materials; however, after long time intervals, such composite units are likely to become thoroughly mixed and reworked by continuing impacts and constant introduction of new ejecta.

In setting up a time-related classification of lunar materials units, E. M. Shoemaker and R. Hackman in 1962 decided to group ejecta deposits or lava flows into broad subdivisions defined by characteristics of one or

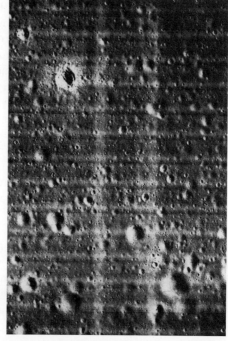

Figure 4 (above). Lunar Orbiter 4 image of part of the moon near and beyond the western limb of the moon's front side produced from a series of individual photostrips. The great bulls-eye feature near the image center is the Orientale Basin, a huge impact crater filled with mare basalts in the center and surrounded by rings of mountains. The outer ring has a diameter of 900 kilometers.

Figure 5 (right). View produced by Lunar Orbiter 3 of a typical mare surface. This high resolution image shows craters as small as two meters. Craters of different "ages" are indicated by the degree of "freshness"; some have ejecta blankets and sharp rims (left of center top), but older ones have subdued rims (bottom right).

more large impacts at type localities. All deposits tied to rayed craters that formed during an extended time interval were placed in the youngest system, the Copernican, named after the rayed crater Copernicus, which itself was produced in just an instant of time about halfway through the interval. The Copernican Period, which is the present one, is now known from dating of Apollo rocks to have lasted for about two billion years. Vast as that time interval may seem, it has not been sufficient to erase the rays around most large craters. Those craters developed early in Copernican time are, of course, more degraded than the fresher, more recent ones, but all of them retain a semblance of rays still best seen on mare surfaces. Craters like Eratosthenes formed after the time of general mare development between about two and somewhat more than three billion years ago but have now lost their ray deposits and are more worn. The oldest craters made in this Eratosthenian Period are thus traced back to the last episodes of lava production but are not invaded by maria. The next older system of materials, represented by the Imbrian Period, extends back in time to a single starting event, the giant impact that created the Imbrium basin and scattered vast volumes of crustal rocks over much of the front face. This event occurred nearly four billion years ago during a late stage of bombardments by planetesimals in which many of the other large basins were also impressed (perhaps over a span of two to three hundred million years). For the next 700 million years the Imbrian Period was marked by lava flows that spread over much of the front side lowlands and basin interiors to make up nearly all the mare units. Big craters in the mare-filled lowlands that formed during or before the Imbrian are normally covered in part or completely by younger lavas. All events prior to the Imbrium basin are relegated to the pre-Imbrian Period which spans an interval from 3.9 billion years to the moon's origin some 4.6 billion years ago. That interval embraces several major activities, including final accretion, first general melting, solidification of a crust, and intense bombardment of that crust. Where the crust survives (between basins and lowlands and over most of the far side), craters on it are far more frequent and generally older than adjacent maria. Few highlands craters are filled with lava, except some large ones which (like many post-mare craters) display impact melt products in their interiors.

In retrospect, then, there was general but not unanimous agreement prior to the Apollo exploration program on these characteristics of the moon:

1. Its figure is nonspherical, with an asymmetric distribution of higher uplands and lower mare plains.
2. The uplands consist of less dense materials.
3. The moon has chemically differentiated, with the maria being the most obvious products of melting and extrusion, but does not have a distinctly layered interior.

4. Volcanic units are most likely basalts and similar basic rocks.
5. The maria are thought to be as old as two or three billion years; the highlands presumably are even older.
6. The outer shell of the moon possesses considerable strength or rigidity.
7. Most major topographic features—basins, craters, arcuate mountain chains, hummocky terrain—result from impact processes; other features—ridges, rilles, domes, and fractures—are related to volcanism.
8. The lunar surface is covered with rubble or fine rock debris in layers retaining sufficient cohesive strength to bear large loads.
9. Materials units associated with various major events in lunar history can be distinguished and mapped.
10. The moon is "dead" or at least dormant with respect to major dynamic activities but is not necessarily "cold" (well below rock melting points) in its interior.

The Apollo program began formally with a commitment in 1961 by President John F. Kennedy to place astronauts on the moon within a decade. The technical, engineering, and scientific feats that brought realization to this promise with the first landing in 1969, and through five more missions in the next three years, surely rank among the outstanding intellectual and spiritual achievements in mankind's brief tenure on Earth. Years of careful mapping, analysis of probe data, and preparation of men and machines paid off handsomely in three circumlunar flights and six successful landings of Apollo missions 8 through 17. Visual and photographic documentation of the moon from orbit and on the ground, the return of more than 380 kilograms of lunar samples, the emplacement of five geophysical instrument stations, and the operation of orbital experiments have together opened a new vista in the exploration of the planets.

The choice of optimum landing sites for the first several Apollo missions was dictated more from considerations of safety during touchdown and subsequent exploration than from scientific reasons. As confidence grew through experience, later sites were selected primarily from criteria that met needs for specific scientific information. The rationale for selection of each site is summarized in the table. The locations of the sites have already been given in figure 3. The appearance of these sites from orbit is presented in figure 6.

A brief résumé of the highlights of each Apollo mission is appropriate. Apollo 11 set down July 20, 1969, on a moderately cratered basalt plain in southwest Mare Tranquillitatis (fig. 7). The astronauts collected twenty-two kilograms of samples and emplaced several geophysical instruments. Apollo 12 landed on Oceanus Procellarum near the large crater Lansberg. Rocks from this site were notably different in composition from those at Apollo 11. Some had been thrown to their locations as part of a ray traced to the crater Copernicus, which had cut into materials within the crust

Site Science Rationale

	type	process	material	age
Apollo 11	mare	basin filling	basaltic lava	older mare filling
Apollo 12	mare	basin filling	basaltic lava	younger mare filling
Apollo 14	hilly upland	ejecta blanket formation	deep-seated crustal material	early history of moon pre-mare material Imbrium basin formation
Apollo 15	mountain front/ rille/mare	mountain scarp basin filling rille formation	deeper-seated crustal material basaltic lava	composition and age of Apennine front material rille origin and age age of Imbrium mare fill
Apollo 16	highland hills and plains	volcanic construction highland basin filling	volcanic highland materials	composition and age of highland construction and modification composition and age of Cayley formation
Apollo 17	highland massifs and dark mantle	massif uplift lowland filling volcanic mantle	crustal material volcanic deposits	composition and age of highland massifs and possibly of lowland filling composition and age of dark mantle nature of a rock landslide

beneath the mare lavas. The Apollo 14 site was picked on hummocky ejecta deposits north of the crater Fra Mauro. This material had been mapped as the Fra Mauro formation, part of the vast deposits tossed across much of the lunar front side by excavation of the Imbrium basin (fig. 8). Apollo 15 touched down along the front of the Apennine Mountains, a segment of the lunar crust carried up during the Imbrium basin event, against which mare lavas had lapped. This mission saw the first use of a Lunar Roving Vehicle or Rover to transport the two astronauts long distances during sampling and observations. The third crew member, remaining in orbit in the command module, busied himself in this and two subsequent missions by conducting a wide range of instrumented experiments. The Apollo 16 mission was designed to explore a part of the lunar highlands near the crater Descartes to determine the nature of crustal materials there and to check on earlier conclusions that true volcanic materials seemed present as well. Both crustal and "volcanic" rocks were found to be a wide variety of breccias (rock bits having sharp corners)

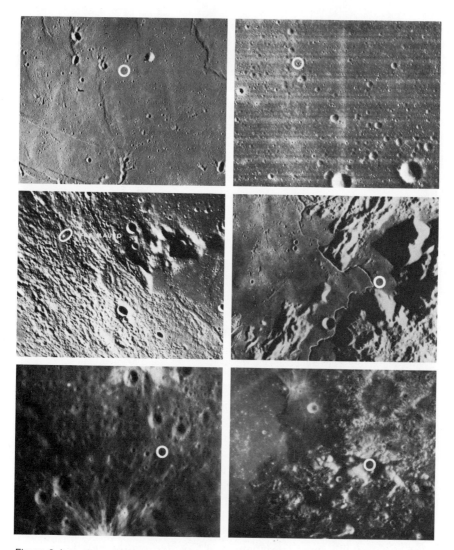

Figure 6. Location and appearance of each of the Apollo landing sites (white circles) as imaged by Lunar Orbiter (strips) or Apollo cameras.
(Top left) Apollo 11, Mare Tranquillitatis.
(Top right) Apollo 12, Oceanus Procellarum.
(Center left) Apollo 14, Fra Mauro.
(Center right) Apollo 15, Hadley-Apennine.
(Bottom left) Apollo 16, Descartes.
(Bottom right) Apollo 17, Littrow-Taurus Mountains.

Figure 7. The approach to the Apollo 11 landing area (just right of center) as viewed by the astronauts from the command module before separation and descent of the landing module.

composed of ejecta transported to the site vicinity from several large, distant basins and from craters elsewhere in the uplands. Apollo 17, the final lunar landing on December 11, 1972, again sought out volcanic products, possibly from nearby cinder cones, deposited in a valley between the rugged Taurus Mountains near the crater Littrow. These mountains proved to be great piles of consolidated ejecta from basins and other sources. The valley floor was underlain by basalts similar to those at the Apollo 11 site. The basalts filled a trough and topped a continuation of the ejecta some two kilometers below. Several orange-colored layers in the overlying regolith caused excitement as possible young volcanic deposits but later were shown to be very old materials of uncertain origin.

Although not typical of most of the moon's outer layers, the crystalline rocks collected at the Apollo 11 site have become the reference norm for lunar materials (fig. 9a). These rocks bear a clear kinship in mineralogy and texture to fissure-erupted basalts on Earth, though at the same time they differ from terrestrial basalts in many essential respects (fig. 9b). All minerals in the Apollo 11 crystalline rocks are remarkably fresh, showing none of the alteration products brought about by oxidation and hydration seen in comparable terrestrial rocks. Chemically, these rocks have high iron, titanium, aluminum, and calcium and low sodium and potassium contents among their major elements. Iron, the prime indicator of the

Figure 8. A boulder composed of breccia (light and dark fragments and matrix) at the Apollo 14 site. This rock is typical of the ejecta material produced by the Imbrium basin-forming event.

degree of oxidation, is present almost exclusively in the reduced form FeO, or as free metal. Water seems totally absent in all lunar rocks except possibly for microscopic amounts of hydrated "rust" compounds in a few. Because of the low silica and high iron contents, the crystalline rocks have lower viscosities than terrestrial basalts and hence spread out as flows for hundreds of kilometers from their emergence points. At times much

Figure 9. (a, left) A lunar rock sample from the Apollo 11 site; this is a mare basalt with light-toned plagioclase and darker crystals of pyroxene, together with small open cavities. (b, right) Texture characteristic of mare basalt as magnified under a microscope; the long, light colored crystals in this Apollo 15 rock are plagioclase, and the darker ones are mostly pyroxene.

of a lunar basin may have been covered with still molten "lava lakes." The basalt units at Apollo 11 were emplaced about 3.7 billion years ago—their time of crystallization as reconstructed from radiogenic age-dating by the rubidium-strontium method.

The regolith—a mixture of crystalline rock blocks, breccias, rock clasts, fine-sized mineral grains, and glass in various forms and proportions— gives strong evidence at Apollo 11 of derivation from underlying basalts by local impacts. Most fragments in the soils and breccias are similar in lithology to the basalts. Many, however, display varying degrees of shock

Figure 10. Profile of the change in velocity (horizontal axis) of seismic primary (P) waves with depth in the outer shells of the moon. The shaded areas are plots of laboratory-determined velocities within several lunar and terrestrial rock types. Those that match the profile segments are presumed to correspond to similar materials within the moon.

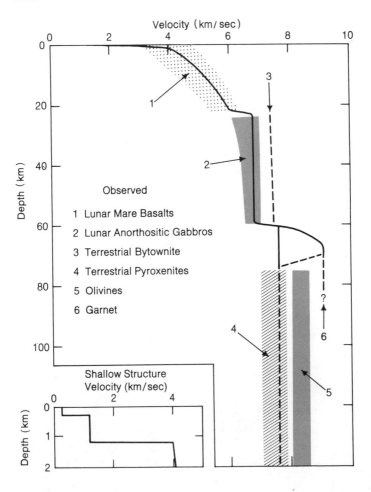

damage imposed by high pressures during impacts that cratered into the bedrock of the mare plains. The pressures were sufficient to convert a fraction of each target into liquid melt or vapor that later condensed as glasses. These glasses, the colors of which—yellow brown, reddish orange, blackish opaque, colorless, green—vary with composition of shock-melted materials, occur in the soils as well-shaped spherules, formless blebs, spray coatings, flow bands, and vesiculated cinders, as well as dispersed as a binder of grains in the breccias.

Nearly all rock samples returned from the moon, be they lavas, breccias, or soils, give *model* ages by the rubidium-strontium method of close to 4.6 billion years. This age is taken as coincident with the initial age of lunar materials as they were being fully organized into the present moon. The age also equates with that of most meteorites. The two rock groups—the oldest datable solid substances in the solar system—are widely assumed to represent some of the primordial materials formed as the sun and its planets came into existence. The moon, then, is among the oldest objects in the system. But it, along with Earth and other units of the solar system, including the sun itself, is much younger than current estimates of the age of the universe, which is thought to be from twelve to sixteen billion years.

A seeming paradox emerges in comparing the ages for breccias or soils with those of the crystalline rocks from which they derive. The mare lavas fall into a 3.1–3.7 billion-year age group. Ages of certain types of crustal layer rocks range from 3.9 to 4.3 billion years. Model ages of regolithic materials containing lava or crustal rocks are 4.6 billion years. The problem is evident: How can soil materials or breccias be apparently older than the crystalline rocks that comprise them? Answers to this seem complex. In part, the discrepancy is apparent, depending on whether the age was determined by whole rock or isochron (individual mineral) radiometric analysis. Other factors, such as contamination with meteoritic materials, or incorporation of components enriched in radiogenic strontium or lead daughter products that boost the calculated ages to older values, are also pertinent.

Radiogenic dating gives age values for initial accretion of lunar materials, development of crustal layers, melting, extrusion, and cooling of lavas, and for the formation of the annealed or ejecta blanket breccias. The regolith has been building up more or less continuously since the lavas or ejecta blankets underlying it were emplaced. A single age for any breccia or soil sample is therefore meaningless. Ages relating to exposure of individual rock or breccia fragments at the lunar surface *at some time* can be calculated by several other techniques. The particle track method examines the density of microscopic streaks that represent crystal structure damage in mineral grains caused by high energy radiation in the incoming solar wind or galactic cosmic rays. Exposure ages of 1–30 million years in surface rocks and 30–500 million years or more in rocks from the top meter of regolith indicate the regolith to be churned up and turned over

Figure 11. Photograph of part of the far side of the moon taken from the orbiting command module of Apollo 16. Most of this side consists of highlands, but darker mare-filled areas (left) lie within the eastern limb region visible from Earth.

in comparable time periods. Ages for core tube samples indicate complete turnover of regolith every 100–200 million years on average. Ray material from Copernicus sampled at Apollo 12 has an exposure age of about 800 million years, provided the ray fragments have resided at or near the surface since arrival.

The lunar rocks have been a treasure-house of information but, as on Earth, such rocks offer only indirect, deduced data on the interior beneath the veneer of the crust. Geophysical devices deployed around the Apollo sites or operated from orbit proved effective in dissecting the moon to reveal its internal structure and composition. Coupled with the revelations from the rock samples, the geophysical experiments have provided the insight into the moon's physical and chemical makeup needed to reconstruct the critical first billion and a half years of its history.

176

One vital question may be asked for every planet: How hot is it today? The answer discloses the extent to which dynamic processes can still act within the planet in its evolutionary course and also indicates the sources of energy that shaped it in the past. An answer for the moon was found in the measurements of heat flow, magnetic properties, and seismic activities obtained by several geophysical instruments in the Apollo Lunar Surface Experiments Package (ALSEP) set up at each site.

Thermal probes were inserted in shallow drill holes at the Apollo 15 and 17 sites. Measurements within the regolith above basalt layers at both sites yielded a heat-flow value almost half that typical of the average for Earth—a surprising result considering the much larger volume of Earth (approximately eighty times) and the concentration of heat-producing radioactive elements in its outer crust—and notably greater than the heat flow expected from a small planetary body of assumed initial chondritic composition. The high value therefore tends to rule out chondrites as the accretionary materials and, further, suggests that the moon is somewhat hotter than once thought. The "excess" heat flow could derive from a still hot (partly melted?) interior but is as readily explained by the production of heat through decay of potassium, uranium, and thorium isotopes in deeper zones.

Unmanned Explorer satellites had previously indicated an absence of a magnetic field around the moon. This should rule out a liquid metal core generating a field from electric currents produced by dynamo motion. However, surface measurements with standing and portable magnetometers demonstrated weak, localized fields ranging from a few to several hundred gammas (one γ is $\sim 0.5 \times 10^{-5}$ the strength of Earth's magnetic field). Other measurements by small satellites dumped into orbit from Apollo command modules confirmed that weak fields up to $1,000\gamma$ occur over the entire surface. The lunar rocks also possess a weak but permanent magnetization residing mostly in metallic iron particles. Taken together, these data all point to a different magnetic state for the moon when most of its crustal rocks were crystallizing. This paleomagnetism could be acquired if the moon then supported an internal magnetic field of $1,000\gamma$ or larger, or if the moon were subjected to an external (solar) magnetic field of about 100 gauss (1 gauss $= 10^{5}\gamma$) or greater.

Variations in the present solar and geomagnetic fields induce a small secondary magnetic field within the moon. Inferred differences in magnetic permeabilities of known or proposed lunar materials can be used to construct models of the temperature-dependent electric conductivity within a moon supporting even a weak field. Two such models lead to temperatures of 750°–800° C (possibly as high as 1,200° C in the inner core) in a core region of dunite (olivine), decreasing to 450°–500° C in a mantle of either peridotite (olivine + pyroxene) in one model or mare basalt in the other.

Placement of seismometers on the surface at the Apollo 11 through 16 sites led to acquisition of data essential to understanding the moon's interior state (fig. 10). At one time, seismometers at four sites operated simultaneously as a network capable of locating seismic epicenters and deep sources. Lunar seismic signals received by these instruments show one striking difference from terrestrial signals: the duration of a lunar signal may be hours instead of the usual minutes on Earth. This results from much-reduced damping factors—particularly the lack of water—in lunar materials such that attenuation of the seismic pulses leads to continued reverberation. One class of signals was soon identified as due to meteorite impacts—verified by comparison of their signals with those caused by the crash of spent third-stage rockets or lunar landers onto the moon. Another class belongs to internal moonquakes. The quakes are weak, stemming from energy releases several orders of magnitude less than those from disturbances in Earth's crust and upper mantle. Moonquakes originate almost exclusively at depths of 800–1,000 kilometers below the surface. Their absence at shallower depths implies that the mantle and crust above are rigid and comparatively cold. Quake epicenters tend to cluster along several surface belts. The quakes increase in frequency during the times of perigee and apogee (positions of closest or farthest distance of the moon from Earth) each month; this indicates an influence by tidal forces in stressing a thick mantle that fails (by minor quake-forming adjustments) at its base.

Other instruments show the moon to have a very tenuous atmosphere. The elements present are mainly helium carried in by the solar wind and argon and other inert gases. Much of the argon derives from decay of radiogenic potassium in lunar materials. During each lunar night, when temperatures drop to $90°$–$100°$ K from a daytime high near $350°$ K, the argon is cold-trapped in the regolith only to be released as a volatile under solar heating.

The orbital experiments began with sightings and other simple tasks by the astronauts in Apollo 11, 12, and 14, and culminated with sophisticated measurements from a Scientific Instrument Module (SIM) bay in the command module during the Apollo 15, 16, and 17 missions. Synoptic photography was an integral part of every mission leading to many outstanding panoramas (fig. 11). A laser altimeter in the SIM bay sent a beam surfaceward to chart accurately a topographic profile along each orbital pass. The readings indicate a higher average altitude for the far-side highlands. When the moon's shape was redetermined from these data, its center of figure was found to be about two kilometers farther from Earth than the center of mass. This is best explained by assuming a thicker crust on the far side and a thinner crust on the Earth side.

As Apollo 11 rock analysis and geophysical data poured in from more than 330 lunar investigators and their teams, some of these scientists began early to offer interpretations or genetic models to satisfy the observations. Interest at first was directed toward the origin of the basalts that had been found, the development of a crust, and the composition of deeper layers. Inevitably, each new mission yielded enough new data to force revision or abandonment of some hypotheses and sometimes formulation of fresh explanations. The recognition of a highlands composed of ejecta piles was a substantial result of the later missions.

In retrospect, three shortcomings of the missions are evident: no deep crustal layers were sampled in place, leaving some uncertainty over the sources and relative sequence of certain kinds of rocks; no bona fide volcanic extrusion fields (such as the Marius Hills, shown in figure 12) were visited; and no *large* impact craters with central peaks and lava infill were directly inspected. Nevertheless, after five years' thoughtful consideration of all data returned from the moon, most scientists have reconciled competing concepts to arrive at a consensus view of the moon's origin and history.

The moon is now generally held to have formed as a companion to Earth, although not necessarily in its immediate vicinity. The materials that accreted into the lunar body were distinctly more refractory than

Figure 12. The Marius Hills, a volcanic region in Oceanus Procellarum, as imaged by Lunar Orbiter 5. Mounds (low cones and domes) five to ten kilometers wide, elongate craters (such as above center), elongate wrinkle ridges, and curved (sinuous) and straight rilles (trenches) are considered evidence of once-active volcanism.

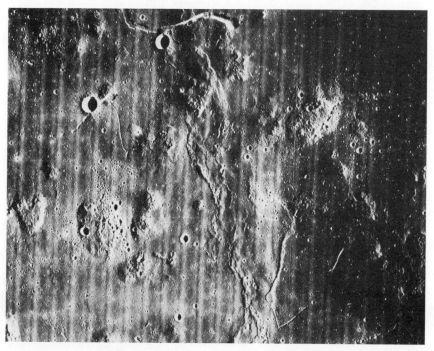

those of Earth. The Ringwood model considers these materials to have been part of a primitive gas cloud "boiled" off Earth as the chondritic masses within it were heated to ~ 2,000° C as total differentiation was completed. The volatiles in that cloud were lost, leaving behind condensates of refractory materials that orbited Earth in a "sediment ring." The ring eventually accreted by attraction and collisions (with the present craters chronicling the last stages). The Anderson model builds the moon from a part of the solar nebula dominated by Type III carbonaceous chondrite material, rich in high-temperature refractory minerals but with a volatile-rich matrix, similar to that making up the Allende meteorite that fell in Mexico shortly before the Apollo 11 launch. Earth formed nearby from another part of the nebula having a somewhat different composition. Both bodies underwent melting and differentiation, but the moon's composition prevented development of a core and a silicic outermost shell such as occurred on Earth, and all volatiles released from it were lost to space.

Almost everyone agrees that the moon heated up and differentiated almost as it accreted, and so began to melt and form crust in its first ten million years. A firm crust had developed by 4.4–4.3 billion years ago. Additional differentiation may have produced layers containing potassium and phosphorus within the first 500 million years of lunar history. Alternative views hold these layers to have formed at the outset of a second

Figure 13. One of the several proposed schemes for differentiation of the outer part of the moon. The starting material is assumed to be an alumina-rich basaltic rock. On melting early in lunar history, denser minerals settled to form a pyroxenite lower layer (100–200 kilometers below present surface), an overlying basaltic layer, and a topmost crustal layer of feldspar-rich rocks (anorthositic gabbro). Subsequent melting at different depths produced younger basaltic rocks of differing composition (KREEP-rich; KREEP-poor).

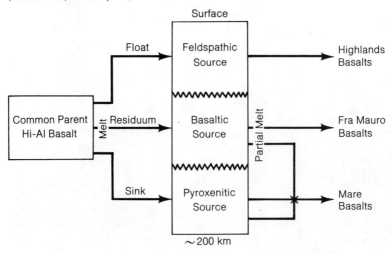

moonwide heating (brought about by heat buildup from radioactive decay of elements in the outer mantle) that culminated in mobilization of mare basalts some 3.8 billion years ago. One of several suggested differentiation schemes is shown in figure 13. The final suite of lunar rock types, despite a variety of names, is far less diverse than those of Earth. Almost all lunar surface rocks can be derived from gabbros (coarse-grained equivalents of basalt). Continued intense bombardment by planetesimals physically altered this crust so as to comminute and fracture its outer layers. In an interval from about 4.25 to 3.85 billion years ago, some asteroid-sized bodies fell into the moon in a series of cataclysmic events that produced the twenty or more large basins on the front side (only a few, mostly mare-free, basins, including the largest on the moon at 1,900 kilometers diameter, occur on the far side). Removal of an overburden load from the thinner Earth-side crust, plus the addition of impact-generated heat, helped to melt deeper layers from which mare basalt differentiates emerged to fill up the basins and spill out into adjacent lowlands. Lavas emplaced in that interval were also impacted, but by then a greatly reduced planetesimal flux caused only a fraction of all larger craters on the moon to form on these younger plains. By 3.1 billion years ago, all volcanic activities presumably had ceased, indicating the moon's heat engine to be incapable of further planetwide melting. The major activity thereafter was sporadic impacting (in which a few large craters like Copernicus and Tycho developed, along with myriads of smaller, fresh Copernican-age craters) and mass-wasting. As determined by the writer and confirmed by Apollo results, the lunar crust in the highlands today is overlain by two to three kilometers of generally consolidated ejecta blanket deposits, and the mare plains are covered by one to fifty meters of regolithic debris.

In closing this section, let us reconsider the list on pages 168–69 of pre-Apollo knowledge of the moon in light of the Apollo results. Almost nothing in the ten points given there requires abandonment or major revision because of the new data acquired from the Apollo missions. In essence, these missions have verified most of what had already been learned by "observation at a distance" through the telescope, and by calculations from principles of celestial mechanics. What the Apollo program accomplished was to provide direct and specific evidence of the composition, internal structure, and age of the moon's materials. The most significant of the results can be summarized as follows:

1. The lunar rock types are relatively few in variety and come from generally simple parents.
2. One or more definite differentiation schemes have now been established for these rocks.
3. Lunar crustal rocks are water-free, in a reduced state, and enriched in refractory elements.
4. The crust consists of a layered assemblage of anorthosites, norites,

and troctolites, called the ANT suite, related to basalts—i.e., volcanic rock.

5. Primordial rocks—unchanged from the moon's earliest days—apparently no longer exist in the moon's outer shells.
6. The highlands are covered with a more or less continuous deposit of breccias derived largely from major cratering events.
7. High heat-flow values indicate a concentration of radioactive elements near the surface.
8. The moon's interior is conveniently subdivided into a thin surface layer of rubble, a crust with one or more compositional layers, a thick mantle with two or more layers, and a core.
9. This core may be liquid or plastic and may once have generated a (now fossil) magnetic field.
10. Almost all major events took place in the first one-and-a-half billion years, starting with accretion, proceeding then to general melting and crust formation simultaneous with and followed by intense cratering, and finishing with selected melting of the outer mantle and extrusion of mare basalts.

Mars

The "red planet" Mars has always fascinated astronomers and science fiction buffs alike. If anything, its space age exploration has greatly increased this fascination. Recognition of a surprising diversity of surface features characteristic of an ancient crust subsequently affected by fracturing, volcanoes, and water and wind erosion heads the list of key discoveries made by the four Mariner probes launched by the United States since 1964.

Telescope observations from Earth provided tantalizing but seldom definitive glimpses of a planet marked by distinctly colored and patterned surfaces. Vast stretches of reddish orange to yellowish brown "desert" regions covered much of Mars. A thin atmosphere, containing identified carbon dioxide, nitrogen, and minor oxygen and water vapor, was assumed to have converted crustal rocks into weathered soils and wind-transported dust having high proportions of limonite (hydrated iron oxide) and hematite (iron oxide). Dark, sometimes bluish green regions were cited as possible indications of simple plant life. Other dark spots or "oases" seemed to telescope viewers to connect along diffuse linear strips. This prompted Giovanni Schiaparelli in 1877 to suppose them to be some kind of channels, which in Italian is given as *canali*—whose misinterpreted meaning led to the popular notion of Martian canals built by intelligent beings. In the scenarios of fiction writers these canals served to bring water from the great polar caps of "ice" that were seen to form alternately at each pole about every two years.

These canals and many other uncertainties about Mars went away after Mariner 4 gave us the first close-ups of this planet. Television cameras in the probe revealed a heavily cratered surface. The craters were generally more flat-floored than those of the moon but otherwise resembled the depressions produced by impacts. The frequency of cratering was intermediate between that of the lunar highlands and maria. Most scientists thought this surface to be old and probably a remnant of a primitive crust. The surfaces scanned by the Mariner 6 and 7 cameras—expanding coverage of the entire planet from 1 to 10 percent—were likewise mostly cratered. Also seen during those flybys were two other types of terrain without craters: a smooth, flat, and featureless surface, and a "chaotic" jumble of knobs, ridges, and valleys. Nothing of the canallike features was seen; it is concluded that these are fortuitous patterns made by chance alignments of craters or by contacts between lighter and darker sections of the surface that take on a linear appearance only in the low-resolution telescope views. The surface was shown to have several kilometers of relief but displayed no features accounting for the maximum relief of seventeen kilometers detected from earlier radar observations.

Sensors on Mariners 4, 6, and 7 found the Martian atmosphere to contain almost entirely CO_2, with traces of water and little nitrogen. Surface pressures averaged six to eight millibars, notably less than anticipated. A dust or haze, visible particularly on the horizon against the limbs of the planet, was picked out. Temperatures at the surface near the equator reached 290° K at Martian noon and dropped to 200° K at night. Air temperatures around the poles were about 230° K in the day, but the ice covering was as cold as 150° K. This is consistent with dry ice (solid CO_2) rather than water ice. This frostlike CO_2 made a veneer less than one meter thick except where piled up to ten meters locally in drifts.

Mariner 4 was unable to detect any magnetic field. This indicates absence of a fluid iron core. Some layering of the planet with a mantle and core and possibly a differentiation-produced crust had been deduced earlier from moments of inertia data. If a metal core does exist, it must be solid or moving sluggishly as a liquid.

Mariner 9's great achievement was to image the entire planet. Like the last two lunar orbiters, this spacecraft was placed in orbit at a high angle to the equator. Mariner 9 took more than 7,300 large- and small-scale pictures of the surface during nearly a year of operation. However, in the early months after arrival, the mission remained in jeopardy. Following launch, Mars experienced one of the severest dust storms on its record, with the entire surface obscured between September and December 1971. Wind velocities reaching 200 kilometers per hour placed particles in the ten-micrometer size range into suspension many kilometers above the surface. An onboard instrument gave spectral data in the thermal infrared consistent with dust compositions equivalent to intermediate silica contents of 60 percent ± 10 percent in terrestrial igneous rocks. While such material may be mixtures of rock types with wider compositional ranges, the *averaged* content is characteristic of andesites—volcanic rocks commonly associated with many of Earth's volcanoes along the continental margins. This is strong evidence for extensive planetary differentiation from an assumed starting material of ultrabasic rocks or carbonaceous chondrites.

As the storm abated and the dust cloud thinned, several high prominences poked through the settling layers. One corresponded to the well-known feature called Nix Olympica, and three others formed a row of peaks named North, Middle, and South Spots.[4] When the surface finally was exposed to view, these four peaks were revealed to be the conical tops of very large volcanoes. Nix Olympica stands some 25 kilometers above the lowest elevations of the Martian surface on a broad base greater than 500 kilometers in diameter (fig. 14a). Its overall shape and slope angles are closely analogous to the great shield volcano complex making up the island of Hawaii, but the Martian version is more than twice as wide. Like the central volcano of Mauna Loa on that island, the top of Nix Olympica is occupied by a large central crater or caldera. The three Spot volcanoes rise 6–8 kilometers above their bases and as much as 17 kilometers above flat, low plains elsewhere on Mars. Other smaller shield-type volcanoes are distributed in several other Martian volcanic provinces.

A second sign of extensive volcanism is the exposure in places of lobate flow fronts comparable to those found in the lunar maria. The dark, low-albedo materials comprising the Martian flows are similar to basalts. Domes with summit craters, aligned craters and small calderas, squeeze-up ridges, and polygonal shrinkage cracks in filled craters all attest to widespread volcanic activities. No stratocones, such as pile up from siliceous volcanic ash on Earth, were imaged by Mariner 9, but the shield volcanoes represent a type not found on the moon.

To the southeast of the cluster of Spot volcanoes is Phoenicis Lacus, a broad high plateau upwarped by swelling of underlying volcanic materials. This plateau is broken by a maze of crisscrossing fractures (fig. 14b). Many are open to widths of several kilometers as fault valleys or grabens extending for tens to hundreds of kilometers in length. This system of wide breaks clearly formed by tensional failure of a warped surface. The fault zone continues eastward to join the largest continuous fracture ever observed on a planetary surface—the 2,700 kilometers long, up to 400–500 kilometers wide, and 6–7 kilometers deep Coprates Canyon in the Tharsis region. Scalloped walls, tributary box canyons, and landslide debris are signs of a widening process related to slope failure, wind action, and possible water erosion. Other sectors of Mars also display major fracture systems.

When the entire Martian surface was finally imaged, it was evident that the earlier Mariners had presented a biased accounting of the extent of cratering. Only about half the total surface area retains evidence of extensive cratering. Much of the southern hemisphere of Mars retains a cratered crust surviving from the early days of the planet. Several large basins, among them Hellas (2,000 kilometers wide), Libya, Argyre, Iapygia, and Edom, remain discernible by virtue of generally circular outlines

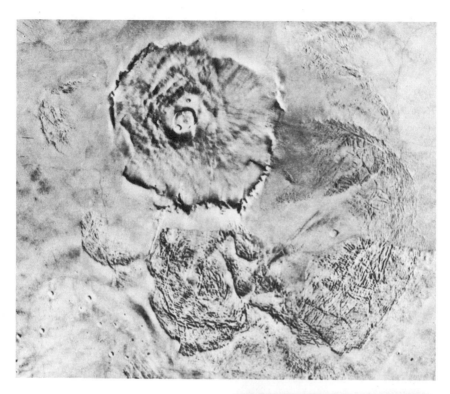

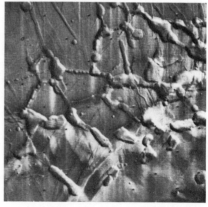

Figure 14. (a, above) Computer-enhanced picture obtained with a television camera on the Mariner 9 spacecraft showing the 24-kilometer-high Nix Olympica on Mars, a huge shield volcano some 500 kilometers wide at its base, and fractured volcanic flow lobes beyond it. (b, right) Crisscrossing fractures (several kilometers wide) in volcanic terrain near the western end of Coprates Canyon; these fractures connect pits and depressions or extend into crater chains.

and smooth-floored interiors. These basins do not seem to have the basaltic fillings of mare character, but dust accumulated in them may now obscure lava bedrock.

Perhaps the most startling and provocative surface features visible in the Mariner 9 images are the many irregular channels that are particularly common in the Chrysae, Mare Erythraeum, Rasena, Memnonia, and Sabaeus Sinus regions. Some resemble the sinuous rilles of the moon and may likewise be related to movements of volcanic gases or ash clouds.

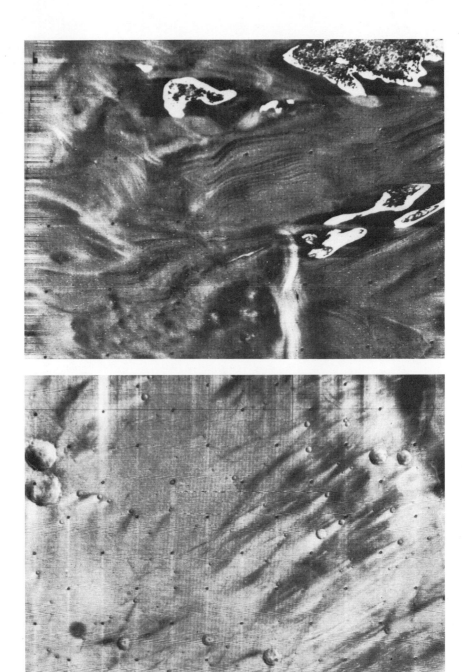

Figure 15. (a, top) Laminated terrain beyond the ice cap around the south pole of Mars. Individual layers are 50 to 100 meters thick. Areas of melting polar ice appear in the upper right quadrant. (b, bottom) Light and dark wind streaks many kilometers in length on the Martian surface.

Others appear to be lava gullies. Many, however, have certain characteristics of dry streambeds that once contained water. Features often associated with terrestrial rivers include headward tributaries, anastomosing or dendritic branches, braided channelways, downstream widening, and terminal distributaries passing over fanlike deposits. The majority of planetologists accept these morphological features as strong evidence of water action in Mars's past. It is postulated that one or more episodes of degassing (particularly during shield volcano activity) released large quantities of water vapor. After condensation, this water either concentrated in shallow ephemeral seas or was locked up in the polar ice caps and in permafrost layers within the Martian regolith. Cyclic melting of the ice cap would free the water again to the atmosphere until precipitated periodically as rain which then collected in the streams. At the present time, Mars has once more lost most of its available water. Ultraviolet spectrometer measurements from Mariner 9 indicate a day-by-day introduction of about 100,000 gallons to the atmosphere and eventual escape. If precipitated all at once, this atmospheric water would cover the planet with a layer no more than ten to twenty micrometers in thickness. Additional water is present in the polar caps and may be buried as frozen layers under the soil and dust covering most of Mars.

Ice layers intermixed with rock material or volcanic ash produce a distinctive laminated terrain (fig. 15*a*) around the polar caps. The polar regions are depressed saucerlike basins in which the alternate light and dark laminae (each about fifty meters thick) form inward-facing ridges arranged in steps. One explanation of the terrain relates it to a 50,000-year cycle of precession or wobble of the Martian rotational axis. Over this period, sublimed CO_2 is gradually transferred from one to the other pole. A residual layer of water-ice is left behind to be covered by dust deposits brought in during major storms. The process is repeated in subsequent cycles. During maximum extent of the CO_2-ice cap, the added weight causes depression of the crust under the laminated terrain (estimated to be four to six kilometers thick now) in response to isostatic adjustment.

Other effects of the growth and retreat of the ice caps are seen in the higher (polar) latitudes. Grooved terrain, smooth terrain, and etch-pitted terrain are possible consequences of glacial action and frost ablation. However, these terrain types are as readily explained by wind deflation and other aeolian processes.

Aeolian features are the one expression of dynamic processes on Mars producing large and rapid enough changes to be detected from Earth and from successive Mariner passes. Variations in surface markings as seen through a telescope, once considered possible vegetation effects, are now identified as shifting dust deposits. Strong winds in a thin atmosphere can pick up only very small particles, but these may be carried long distances. The Mariner 9 cameras have recorded thousands of light and dark "blotches, streaks, plumes, and tails" (fig. 15*b*) which generally taper in toward craters and other surface obstructions. These may orient in several prevailing directions in any scene, as expected from changing winds. The whitish streaks are almost certainly light-colored dust, but the dark streaks are either different materials or exposed (windswept) bare rock surfaces. Aeolian markings recognized in earlier Mariner 6 and 7 images are often wiped out or repositioned. Some markings noted in Mariner 9's first good looks at the surface went through shifts or boundary changes during the next few months. Extensive streak fields are coassociated in several areas with swarms of dunelike hills.

Mars is sovereign over two small "moons." These satellites are extremely small and are presumed to be captured asteroidal bodies. Despite their size, both were photographed by Mariner 9 several times when the probe and satellite orbits brought the satellites into favorable positions for imaging. The elongate Phobos (fig. 16) has visible dimensions of approximately 25 by 21 kilometers; Deimos is more rounded at 13.5 by 12 kilometers. Each satellite has the extremely low albedo characteristic of carbonaceous chondrites. The satellites' surfaces are pockmarked with craters. One crater is near the upper size limit that could be sustained on a small target without its total disruption.

Instruments on Mariner 9 refined some of the data on temperature, atmospheric pressures, and surface profiles obtained in the earlier missions. Two types of infrared instruments measured atmospheric temperature distributions as functions of altitude and latitude. Surface temperatures at different times of the Martian day and over the entire globe were also determined. These sensors, along with the ultraviolet spectrometer

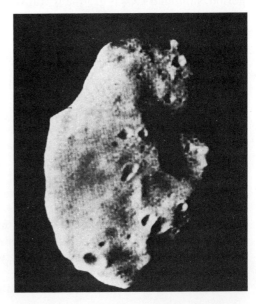

Figure 16. Phobos, the larger of the two "moons" of Mars; this irregularly shaped body (twenty-five kilometers in longest dimension) is pockmarked with craters.

and an S-band radio occultation experiment, provided data used to construct pressure gradients through the atmospheric column. They also found the variation in atmospheric pressure at the surface to range between 3 and 10.5 millibars (average at 5.5 millibars). These variations are largely due to differences in surface topography. By converting pressure variations to elevation differences, topographic profiles have been plotted along many orbit lines across Mars to chart its general relief. The Martian wind field (directions of prevailing winds) has been calculated from temperature and pressure gradient data obtained by the infrared interferometer spectrometer. Information on the gravitational variations within Mars comes from changes in the Mariner 9 orbital paths resulting from slight shifts in acceleration. Most variations appear related to topographic rather than mass differences. A maximum relief of twenty-five kilometers means that Mars has a rougher surface for its size than either Earth or the moon. This implies either lateral near-surface differences in rock composition, or deviations from isostatic equilibrium, or both.

The picture of Mars now emerging after interpretation of the Mariner 9 results is this: Mars, along with the other planets, most likely formed by accretion about 4.6 billion years ago. It soon melted and differentiated into a layered body but may never have produced a magnetically active core. The early history of Mars seems to have paralleled that of the moon. Much as on the moon, planetesimal bombardment peppered the original crust. The Hellas, Argyre, and other basins were sculpted out of this crust together with many thousands of smaller craters. Ancient centers of volcanism then sprang forth in the Hellas and Amazonis regions. Older plains developed at the expense of parts of the cratered terrain. Volcanism thereafter became widespread as basalt flows and some shield volcanoes covered the Nix Olympica, Arcadia, and Alba regions. The Tharsis region experienced broad upwarping with concurrent faulting that culminated in rifting in the adjacent Coprates region. The great shield volcanoes of Nix Olympica and the Three Spots then built up, perhaps as recently as 300–500 million years ago according to some estimates. During this stage, great quantities of gases and water vapor were freed from the heated crustal rocks to collect in an atmospheric envelope. This envelope has gradually dissipated through losses to outer space or reactions with surface rocks. At one period, and possibly continuing on a much reduced scale, water vapor in the gases organized into flowing rivers or as water ice in expanded polar caps. The effects of fluvial and glacial action are well enough preserved to suggest this phase occurred in the last few hundred million years. Frost action or, alternatively, withdrawal of magma, broke up some surficial materials into chaotic terrain. Although it no doubt began as the atmosphere developed, aeolian action has constituted the principal surface-modifying process up to recent times. Much of the terrain was altered by scouring and smoothing from the winds that have worn crater rims and filled their floors, deposited fine sediments in broad plains, and cut grooves and pits into exposed bedrock. Possibly, also, rifting and volcanism are continuing today as an indication of a gradual evolution of a primitive crust into a more diversified one.

Venus

Our sister planet (because of its proximity and similar size) appears as a bright, cloud-covered sphere when viewed by telescope. Prior to direct exploration, the basic facts known about Venus were these: The planet moved in slow retrograde rotation (that is, turned clockwise relative to the north celestial pole) with an annual period of approximately 250 Earth days. A thick atmosphere, supposedly of nitrogen and some carbon dioxide, blanketed the surface; some condensed phase or phases (water, ice, dry ice, or more exotic compounds) produced a continuous cloud layer between fifty and ninety kilometers high. This atmosphere and the surface in contact with it reached temperatures of several hundred degrees centigrade. At intermediate temperatures, silicates in surface rocks would react with CO_2 and H_2O to produce carbonates, but at more elevated temperatures certain metamorphic silicates would form. Radar scans had revealed large circular features (basins and craters?) on an otherwise subdued surface. The high surface and atmospheric temperatures evidenced general differentiation and a currently hot planet in which a core should produce a magnetic field.

Three Mariner spacecraft have flown past Venus, and five Russian Venera probes have attempted landings after gathering data during descent through the atmosphere. The first pair of Mariners and the first trio of Veneras all reported a Venusian atmosphere composed almost entirely of CO_2 ($\sim$ 97 percent) with little nitrogen. Water is scant except as a major constituent of the high clouds. Venera 7, the first Soviet probe to reach the surface and transmit data, measured nighttime temperatures near 320° K at a height of twenty-five kilometers in the atmosphere and 750° K at the surface; the atmospheric pressure on the surface is $\sim$ 90 bars (compared with 1 bar for Earth). Venera 8 found a daytime temperature of 745° K, almost identical with the dark side temperature noted by Venera 7. Lack of a significant temperature difference between day and night sides is indicative of a minimum horizontal temperature gradient, a condition explained by assuming extensive cross-circulation and mixing of a Venusian gas envelope having a high heat capacity. Stratospheric winds of 180 kilometers per hour were sensed by Venera 8 during its parachute descent. Visualization of these circulation patterns was achieved by Mariner 10's television camera, which used an ultraviolet filter to pick out swirling "clouds" of excited carbon monoxide (fig. 17). Venusian clouds eddy around as whorls, spiral streaks, and mottled polygons that result from upward convection and divergent wind flow at velocities of 300 kilometers per hour or more in the equatorial zone.

Figure 17. View of Venus taken at a distance of 720,000 kilometers by a television camera on Mariner 10. Bands of "clouds" of carbon monoxide appear here in this image obtained through an ultraviolet filter.

The atmospheric data support the pre-probe model of C. Sagan and J. V. Pollack for development of high temperatures through a "runaway greenhouse effect." In this model, the atmospheric gases are transparent to visible solar radiation so that the surface becomes heated by insolation. Much of this incoming energy is reflected back to the atmosphere at longer wavelengths, i.e., in the infrared. Because of its abundance, the CO_2 acts as a thermal trap causing a rise in atmospheric temperatures and further release of more CO_2 from surface rocks.

Equipped with a gamma ray spectrometer, Venera 8 on landing telemetered back invaluable data on a surface composition of ~ 4 percent potassium, 200 parts per million uranium, and 650 parts per million thorium. Concentrations at these levels in terrestrial rocks are characteristic of granites and shales. Granite represents an extreme in igneous differentiation. An outer crust of highly differentiated rocks is thus suspected. However, no magnetic evidence of a liquid metal core was detected by the Mariner spacecraft. Surface materials at the Venera site indicate loose particles (porous erosion or chemical reaction products) but not necessarily an impact-produced regolith.

Mercury

At first glance through Mariner 10's television eye, Mercury looks remarkably like the larger twin of Earth's moon. From a distance, the illuminated incoming and outgoing limbs imaged during the March 29, 1974, flyby show a Mercurian surface (fig. 18) containing craters in almost as much profusion as its lunar counterpart. Craters as small as 200 meters or as large as 200 kilometers appear in nearly all of the more than 2,300 pictures returned in the first pass by Mercury or the additional 2,000 received from a second pass in September of 1974 after Mariner 10 had swung around the sun. These craters are identical in most respects to those on the moon now designated as impact in origin. Many Mercurian craters tend to be flat-floored and are without extensive terracing or central peaks. The craters show the same full range of morphological modifications associated with relative age differences as present in the lunar assemblage. Fresh, deep-rayed craters with ejecta blankets (fig. 19) are interspersed with nearly filled, rim-worn craters. The crater frequencies in typical Mercurian terrain are comparable to those of the lunar highlands and therefore must be considered similar in age of development (about

Figure 18 (right). A mosaic of TV-produced images obtained by Mariner 10 showing the surface of Mercury at a distance of 200,000 kilometers.

Figure 19 (above). Closeup view of the surface of Mercury as seen by Mariner 10; the crater on the left is about 100 kilometers wide; bright bands (rays) of ejecta are evident on the right.

3.8–4.4 billion years old). Again, like the moon, only four large basins occur in the most heavily cratered region (analogue to the lunar far side), but thirteen such basins have been identified on the outgoing side. These basins, nearly all less than 440 kilometers in diameter, are best recognized from the two or more sets of topographic arcs that are part of uplifted rings. However, one very large depression—named the Caloris Basin—has an outer ring more than 1,300 kilometers in diameter.

Mercury differs from the moon in two fundamental respects. First, nowhere on its surface were dark, low albedo mare basalt-type outpourings imaged by Mariner 10. While some smooth plains areas could be volcanic deposits, these would have to be different in composition—being perhaps anorthositic gabbros or refractory silicates—to account for albedos characteristic of the lunar highlands. Second, there is a class of linear features on Mercury not generally observed on the moon (one exception may be the Altai Front). Steep-walled, straight scarps rising two to three kilometers above the Mercurian surface extend individually for hundreds of kilometers, often passing indiscriminately through craters and other topographic features. These scarps appear to be compression-induced faults formed as the crust experienced structural adjustments while trying to accommodate the changing volume of a shrinking core.

The surface over much of Mercury is so heavily cratered that many circular features become strongly distorted. The rough, hilly intercratered regions are marked by linear troughs and grooves, knobs, ridges, and irregular elongate depressions. Elsewhere, relatively smooth plains, less cratered than most of Mercury but more so than the lunar maria, have some of the characteristics of the Cayley formation materials on the moon. Like those materials, the Mercurian plains materials were probably emplaced as impact-melted rock, base surge deposits, or ejecta blankets. These plains contain some straight rilles, wrinkle ridges, and polygonal fractures, but domes, cones, and lava flow fronts, such as are found within the moon's Marius Hills, are absent.

The surface of Mercury is heated from the sun to temperatures as high as 700° K. By midafternoon of a Mercurian day (period of rotation is fifty-seven Earth days), the temperature has dropped to ~ 450° K and finally reaches 90° K just before dawn. Above the surface is an extremely thin atmosphere (exerting a pressure of ~ 10^{-12} times that of Earth) consisting mainly of helium, argon, and neon derived from radioactive decay of Mercurian potassium and uranium and from the solar wind.

Particles from the solar wind have been trapped in a magnetosphere by a slight magnetic field of approximately 100–200 gammas strength. This field implies that a metallic iron core—already suspected from Mercury's density of 5.4 grams per cubic centimeter, which would require much of its interior to contain heavy elements—now exists in a melted state. Molten iron is presumably moving too slowly within the core to generate anything more than the present weak field.

Mercury, then, may have the most primitive surface of the inner planets. By analogy to the moon, it melted soon after formation and an iron-rich, refractory silicate crust then formed. Differentiation at that time brought about extreme separation of heavier constituents leading to a thick iron core that still may not be solidified. Massive bombardments by planetesimals persisted thereafter to produce the cratered crust now enveloping much of the planet. The rough intercrater regions may be among the oldest surviving planetary surfaces in the solar system. The heavily cratered nature of the Mercurian surface suggests that large numbers of sizable planetary particles existed near the sun in early solar history.

Jupiter

This giant planet, more than 1,200 times the volume of Earth but containing only 0.001 the mass of the sun, is the first of the outer planets to be visited by spacecraft. After traveling some 800 million kilometers, Pioneer 10 passed to within 130,000 kilometers of the Jovian surface on December 3, 1973. Pioneer 11 approached to almost 43,000 kilometers during its flyby on December 3, 1974, at a maximum velocity of 173,000 kilometers per hour. Despite incredible dangers, by Earth standards, both probes survived intense force fields while sending back data of exceptional quality. Both Pioneer 10 and 11 are moving inexorably toward eventual escape from the solar system, but Pioneer 11 will swing close enough to Saturn in 1979 to return additional data to Earth on that ringed planet.

Because of its great size (diameter about 11.2 times that of Earth), Jupiter's surficial characteristics were reasonably well known from telescope observations before the two Pioneer spacecraft directly measured some of its environmental parameters. The planet's apparent surface was recognized as the visible limits of a gaseous envelope. Prominent color bands (yellow, red brown, blue, grey) were oriented subparallel to the equator (fig. 20). These broad bands and narrower streaks were presumed to be chemically different gases that were smeared out in the direction of planetary rotation. Hydrogen was identified as the principal constituent along with smaller amounts of helium, and some methane and ammonia found mainly in the diffuse hydrogen-helium atmosphere. The Great Red Spot is an anomalous oval feature some 45,000 kilometers in longest dimension embedded in the banded gases.

Jupiter gave evidence of being a hot body which radiated notably more heat energy than would be reflected from the sun's input alone. Pressures calculated for its deep interior (whose state was variously predicted to be solid, liquid, or dense gaseous) reach 100,000,000 atmospheres, and temperatures up to 30,000° K are estimated. However, these conditions are far below critical values needed to initiate nuclear reactions within the massive hydrogen. Some undefined process of internal heat generation, perhaps also responsible for production of the intense magnetic fields associated with Jupiter, must explain the planet's present thermal state.

Figure 20. Jupiter, as seen from Pioneer 10 when it was nearly 2.5 million kilometers away. The bands of hydrogen-rich gases and the Red Spot (left) stand out in this TV image, along with the shadow of the Jovian moon Io (right).

Pioneer 10 and 11 sent back important data on conditions in interplanetary space even before arriving at Jupiter. Neither probe experienced anticipated damage from particles of various sizes in the asteroid belt. Apparently most of the dust, micrometeorites, and small chunks of rock have been swept into larger bodies which are now too few and spread out to be a serious collision hazard. The Pioneers did encounter many more fine particles than were expected in the vicinity of Jupiter, where a dust belt seems to have formed from objects attracted by the planet's strong gravity field.

The Pioneers first detected Jupiter's magnetosphere at a distance of 7.5 million kilometers from the planet. A stronger field, compressed by the solar wind, commences about 2.9 million kilometers from Jupiter. The field strength fluctuates between 2 and 12 gauss and has a reverse polarity relative to Earth. On its outbound journey Pioneer 10 detected the side edge of the magnetosheath some 16.6 million kilometers from Jupiter.

The magnetic field has caused entrapment of protons and electrons from the solar wind in several pancake-shaped radiation belts. These belts exceed the intensities of those of the Van Allen belts around Earth by ten to forty thousand times. Despite bombardment by high-speed electrons with energies up to 30 million electron volts, the instruments onboard both probes survived and are still functioning as the Pioneers head ever deeper into space. Solar radiation penetrating the magnetic field has interacted with Jupiter's atmosphere to form an ionosphere of charged particles which may be the source of pulsed radio waves emanating from the planet.

This atmosphere was shown to consist of about 84 percent hydrogen and 15 percent helium. Temperatures of $\sim 126°$ K within brownish orange bands are slightly warmer than the $\sim 119°$ K of the more bluish belts. The origin of the color banding is still not understood but may be related to condensed sulfur compounds. A purplish haze in the atmosphere above the poles is presumed to result from radiation-excited frozen methane and ammonia. The Red Spot is now explained as a turbulent convection cell (or "hurricane") that rises some nine kilometers above the surrounding nonturbulent atmospheric boundary.

No distinct surface boundary was detected by either Pioneer. The gases simply increase in density from a thin outer atmosphere to a central zone in the planet's interior without any abrupt change from a gaseous to a liquid or solid state. The data do not rule out a rocky core, but there is no substantiating evidence for any solids well below the visible surface. Absence of temperature differences between the day and night sides of Jupiter implies a high heat capacity for its atmosphere. The Pioneer results, however, afford no clear-cut clues to the process by which Jupiter reradiates almost 2.3 times as much energy as it absorbs from the sun. Jupiter seems to be passing through an incipient or low-order stage of energy production by the usual stellar processes but possesses far too little mass ever to evolve into another sun.

Pioneer 11 discovered a new small satellite orbiting Jupiter, bringing to thirteen the number of moons tied to the planet. Better density values were obtained for the four large Galilean satellites: Callisto, 1.65 grams per cubic centimeter; Ganymede, 1.93; Europa, 3.07, and Io, 3.50. These satellites are all surrounded with their own atmospheres. Methane and ammonia gases are principal constituents. Io, a satellite midway between the moon and Mercury in size, has an ionosphere above its atmosphere. Io also is covered with a "snow" of frozen ammonia that vaporizes each time it passes into sunlight. An ice cap covers the poles of the even larger satellite Callisto.

The other planets

Because they have not yet been surveyed by space probes, little that is new has been learned about the other outer planets—Saturn, Uranus, Neptune, and Pluto—during the exploration programs of the last decade. Like Jupiter, Saturn is a great ball of hydrogen and helium gases. Radar studies have disclosed that its rings contain many thousands of objects in the meter-size class associated with much smaller dispersed particles (ices?). A fourth innermost ring was added to the three already known since Galileo's day, after its discovery in long exposure photographs in 1969. Uranus and Neptune are both composed mostly of frozen methane, ammonia, and possibly water ice. Pluto is an abnormally small body, compared with the four giant planets, having a size and density similar to Jupiter's satellite Io. Pluto may be a satellite escaped from Neptune.

Space exploration: feedbacks to Earth

Why have we spent tens of billions of dollars to study the moon, Mars, and the other planets in the solar system? The reply by George Leigh Mallory when asked why he had climbed Mount Everest—"Because it is there"—is almost self-justifying when applied to man's climb to the moon. But there are more practical reasons. One rises above all others: By reconstructing the composition, structure, and history of each planet, we can perhaps then decipher the general nature and sequence of changes for the early Earth—assuming the terrestrial planets all experienced a similar childhood. The ultimate growth pattern of Earth no doubt has been strongly conditioned by events in its formative stages.

Unlike the moon, Mars, and Mercury, Earth retains no traces of the surface materials and morphology extant during the first billion or so years. The oldest terrestrial rocks date back 3.9 billion years, but any extensive rock bodies older than 2.5 billion years are exceedingly rare. No signs of any original crust or even the first igneous differentiates have been recognized in the accessible areas of Earth. Without such rocks in hand, it is impossible to specify with any direct evidence the compositional makeup of the primitive materials accreted into Earth or the nature of a primitive atmosphere which would have altered those rocks. The oldest sedimentary rocks date back 3.2 billion years. In all likelihood a water-bearing atmosphere existed for many millions of years before then, but the origin of any ancient oceans or large water bodies is obscured by the poor record of any preserved stages in their development.

To deduce even indirectly the early history of Earth requires acceptance of the thesis that all rocky planets began in much the same way and thereafter underwent different evolutionary trends that depended on the particulars of initial composition, internal energy, and size of each. As indicated in the section on "The nature of a planet," every terrestrial planet would seem to have been subjected to certain processes. Thus, any inner planet may be assumed to have melted early, formed a crust and probably a core, degassed much of its initial volatiles, been bombarded by countless extraplanetary bodies that imposed a cratered terrain on its surface, and to have been modified surficially thereafter by various erosion processes.

For Mars, Mercury, and the moon, and most likely also for Venus, space exploration has shown that these major steps in planetary evolution took place in the first one to two billion years after birth through accretion.

We have no firm reason to believe that this set of steps actually was followed by the early Earth. Scientific proof simply is lacking, and explicit evidence will probably never be recovered from the now grossly changed terrestrial crust. But, of equal import, we also have no firm reason to discard this set of steps as incorrect or unlikely. If indeed a general principle of similitude applies to Earth as it seems to the moon and the other inner planets, we can state with a high order of confidence that the primitive Earth behaved much like its own moon in the first stages of existence and, more or less, like Mars during the "childhood" years. From then on, however, the other planets have remained "stunted" while Earth has "grown up" insofar as can be judged from its complex surficial environment.

We can visualize, then, an early Earth with a differentiation-produced crust dotted by large numbers of craters and circular basins. Both crust and craters have since been wiped away. As replacements, we now have six large and many smaller continental masses, consisting of a wide variety of generally silica-rich, often intricately layered and folded igneous, sedimentary, and metamorphic rocks, embedded in a compositionally more uniform and continuous lower crust of basic igneous rocks. This crust is underlain at a depth of about 100 kilometers by a hot, plastic asthenosphere some 300 kilometers thick that lies at the top of a thick mantle which in turn overlies a fluid outer core and a solid inner core. The crust and the edges of the continental masses are overlain by a salt-bearing water ocean distributed over the topographically lower 72 percent of Earth's surface. An oxygen-enriched atmosphere covers the entire globe.

These features are unique to Earth. How did such diversity come about? What caused such modifications of the original surface that all vestiges of cratering and early results of the other common planetary processes are now removed?

By comparing our planet to our neighbors, we can see immediately two distinct differences responsible in large part for the present state of Earth. First, Earth seemingly has a more active and efficient heat engine than any other inner planet (excepting Venus?). This results both from its size and its composition. Although inferential, the content of radioactive, heat-releasing elements in the outer shell of Earth is probably higher than the "3M" planets—the moon, Mercury, and Mars. This supply of internal energy continues to drive the solid Earth's near surface processes today, as manifested by crustal plate interaction, continental block movements, mountain building, igneous intrusions, extensive volcanism, and repeated isostatic adjustments, even as it has continuously since well back into the Precambrian Era. Second, Earth has a chemically potent atmosphere, powered by external energy from the sun, that represents an advanced development from a more primitive assemblage of gases. That atmosphere was, and is, the source and carrier of water—the "universal solvent"—which has accumulated into the vast reservoir of the oceans. The size of Earth is responsible for retention of the ingredients of the present atmosphere, but other processes aided in formulating its composition.

Based on recent studies of both Earth and the planets, we can conceptualize this model of Earth's evolution beyond the primitive planetary stage: The original crust—perhaps anorthositic or gabbroic in the lunar sense, or basaltic in the sense of the layers below the ocean floors, or sialic (rich in silica and alumina as characterizes granitic rocks) in the sense of the extreme end product of "blast furnace" differentiation—had formed and was extensively cratered. An atmosphere of hydrogen, ammonia, and methane, similar to the constituents assumed to have surrounded other primitive planets, gradually was altered by released O_2 into H_2O, CO, CO_2, N_2O, and NO_2. In time, with cooling, the water condensed and accumulated in low regions to make the first oceans. Some of the carbon dioxide and nitrogen formed soluble ions in these oceans. The primitive crustal rocks were eventually destroyed either by a new period of general melting (unproved) or, as is more plausible, by chemical attack and physical erosion from the oceans and atmosphere. The resulting alteration products were mostly low-temperature hydrated aluminosilicates (clays) containing fixed sodium and potassium. Thus, water here serves as a differentiation agent, separating iron and magnesium oxides from sodium, potassium, and aluminum oxides. The earliest sediments were probably much like the bulk of those formed today—potassium-rich aluminosilicates—although banded iron beds and carbonates periodically were produced. Because free oxygen had not yet entered the atmosphere, iron was held in the reduced state in the ancient sediments.

The sediments were frequently buried in large, thick wedges or piles. Both uranium and potassium enriched in these sediments acted as a prime heat source that caused them to be metamorphosed and, in many instances, melted into crystalline granites, gneisses, schists, and slates. One view holds that continental nuclei formed by this process of melting and metamorphism. Once developed, the protocontinents rose as clots of less dense sialic materials rooted in the surviving but altered crust. Continued erosion, deposition, and fusion of later sediments laid down on or at the edges of these nuclei led to their gradual enlargement into the continents as seen today. Present continents generally expose ancient granitic shields surrounded by crystalline rocks of younger ages in metamorphic belts, batholiths, and isolated plutons, interspersed with volcanic outpourings and with sedimentary rocks in discontinuous deposits distributed as flat-lying cratonic layers or as folded geosynclinal beds.

The next big change in Earth from those days of the first oceans and sediments involved the modification of the atmosphere. It now is believed that the key to modification was the appearance of primitive single-celled life forms about 3.4 billion years ago. The first forms were anaerobic—capable of living without oxygen. But, in time, multicelled aerobic life forms developed the fundamental ability to photosynthesize inorganic CO_2 and H_2O into starch and free oxygen. This process brought about many essential alterations to Earth's lithosphere, hydrosphere, atmosphere, and biosphere that culminate in the modern world. Oxygen gradually built up in the atmosphere, along with greater amounts of nitrogen. In the upper atmosphere, this oxygen was converted by solar ultraviolet radiation into ozone (O_3^+), which eventually provided an absorbing shield against much of this tissue-damaging ultraviolet radiation reaching Earth's surface. Thus protected, plant life advanced rapidly in the oceans. The oxygen also interacted with surface rocks during weathering to produce oxidized sediments. Red beds, and other rocks containing ferric oxides, mark this transition. Carbonate rocks also became more commonplace.

The above model is straightforward and is probably right in many respects. But recent studies of the crust now demonstrate such a model to be an oversimplification. A great revolution in the earth sciences emerged in the 1960s from the concepts of plate tectonics and continental drift. The subject of the "new global tectonics" and its many ramifications for crustal development are beyond the scope of this article.* Suffice to say, these concepts have been collected into a viable model of crustal development and behavior that seems to explain Earth's geological activities of the last half billion years. With respect to the topics under discussion, the most important conclusions derived from the model are that (1) the present ocean basins are covered with young volcanic rocks, (2) these basins are gradually enlarging or otherwise changing in dimensions, (3) both oceans and continents are shifting as parts of plates that move laterally over the underlying asthenosphere, (4) the continents are mostly older masses of sialic rocks that ride passively along with their supporting plates, and (5) continental as well as oceanic plates may be destroyed at subduction zones or other plate junctures. Two alternative consequences with regard to the fate of a primitive crust can be deduced from the plate tectonics model. First, if not destroyed early in geologic time, this crust may have subsequently been buried by ocean basin-producing volcanic rocks wherever it has not been covered by the continental masses. Or, second, much of the original and the later modified segments of the crust may have subsequently been consumed by downdragging along subduction zones active throughout the geologic past. The consumed materials would thus be converted into new crustal rocks. The continents, in this view, may be decreasing in size as well as splitting up (beginning some 200 million years ago) to drift apart or collide with one another.

Unfortunately, extrapolation of the effects of the new global tectonics into the obscurity of the older Precambrian and Azoic eras becomes an exercise in conceptualization owing to the lack of concrete observations

Figure 21. Photograph of the full Earth taken from the Apollo 17 spacecraft as it returned from the final lunar landing in December 1972. Much of Africa and all of Asia Minor can be seen in the top part of this view of the globe.

and facts. There exists, then, a huge gap between the reasonably well reconstructed picture of Earth's surface in the last one to two billion years and the now totally lost picture of that surface during the first billion years. While the study of the planets has proved invaluable in inferring the state of a primitive Earth, it is highly unlikely that it will offer any direct information whatsoever on Earth's middle years.

Concluding remarks

It seems fitting to close this review article with a direct quote from the final paragraphs of the writer's recent book on planetary geology:

> *In retrospect, as we contemplate the panorama of planets in our solar system, we can marvel at the almost providential fact that each planet seems to provide another set of essential clues for unraveling the mystery of creation. Every planet has proceeded along some peculiar path of evolution all its own yet each still defines a certain stage in a general process. Thus, Jupiter represents a relic of what may be the first stage: accumulation of a dense, reducing atmosphere of hydrogen and helium around a small (silicate?) nucleus. Uranus and Neptune describe a more advanced state in which ammonia and methane are mixed with the hydrogen. Saturn displays orbiting rings similar to those from which the moon and other satellites could have condensed and accreted. Venus and Earth are surrounded by highly evolved atmospheres that severely affect their rocky surfaces. Mars reveals the condition attained by a planet after it has lost most of its gaseous envelope. The Moon and Mercury disclose the fate of planetary surfaces left unprotected by any atmosphere. Finally, a group of small planetoids have conveniently come apart to expose (as meteorites) the kinds of interiors that can develop under varying conditions of heating. To be sure, some of these observed differences among planets depend on their ultimate positions relative to the Sun, or on physicochemical fluctuations in the nebula at the time of their formation. However, taken together the planets make up an elegant picture of what we now believe is a typical system of condensed bodies around a central star.*
>
> *As we move on to new adventures in planetary exploration, we can rightfully ask ourselves what is being accomplished for mankind. The Apollo 17 view of the Earth [fig. 21] suggests a cogent answer. By releasing ourselves from the confines of our planet, we are led to a reawakened appreciation of "Spaceship Earth" and its unique sets of ecological conditions that favor our very existence. Thus, the studies of the planets and stars from outer space itself will inevitably turn back this new knowledge of the universe to us and our own world. And, at the same time, by extending our insatiable desire to fathom the unknown to the surrounding solar system, someday all men may be brought together through this common awareness of their inseparable bond to the Cosmos.[5]*

[1] The reader can gain an appreciation of the scope of these advances in planetology by consulting basic texts in astronomy ca. 1965 or earlier, or the 1963 edition of Fred L. Whipple's *Earth, Moon, and Planets* (Cambridge, Mass.: Harvard University Press), or chap. 2 of N. M. Short's *Planetary Geology* (Englewood Cliffs, N.J.: Prentice-Hall, 1975).

[2] Binary or paired stars tend to remain planetless as remaining nebular matter eventually is carried into the two larger bodies.

[3] Temperatures in degrees Kelvin are simply the sum of degrees Centigrade + 273; e.g., 400° K = 127° C + 273.

[4] These four features have since been renamed Olympus Mons, Arisa Mons, Pavonis Mons, and Ascraeus Mons, using the Latin terms adopted for all Martian landmarks.

[*] *See* Peter J. Wyllie, "Revolution in the Earth Sciences," *GIT* 1971, pp. 169–237.

[5] Short, *Planetary Geology*.

The Poetry of Self-Creation

John Bayley

Mr. Bayley has for a number of years been known on both sides of the Atlantic as one of the most interesting and suggestive of contemporary critics and literary scholars. Educated at Eton and New College, Oxford, he was a fellow of New College in English literature from 1955 to 1974, when he was appointed to the newly created Warton Chair of English at Oxford. Among the books that he has written have been *The Characters of Love* (1960), *Tolstoy and the Novel* (1964), *Pushkin: A Comparative Commentary* (1974), and a recently completed work called *The Use of Division*. Since 1956 he has been married to Iris Murdoch, the novelist.

A recent lead review of a volume of Philip Larkin's poems in the *Times Literary Supplement* led the editors, who were already acquainted with Professor Bayley's other writings, to inquire if he would be willing to submit a more general survey of contemporary literature. Professor Bayley agreed to do so, but asked to be allowed to confine his attention for the most part to the three poets he discusses in the following article. For the benefit of readers who may not know the work of these poets, the editors have, with Professor Bayley's guidance, provided a brief selection of their poems.

M odern poetry is often assumed to be "difficult," in the sense that its subject matter and range of arbitrary reference are so personal to the poet that it is difficult to find out what is going on, even for a reader of goodwill who is prepared to take trouble. It is true that Ezra Pound and T. S. Eliot, often regarded, and with justice, as the founding fathers of modern poetry, created a style deliberately complex and saturated with reminders of other literatures, native and foreign, from Elizabethan drama to the novels of Henry James, from Latin, Provençal, and Chinese poetry to the most fashionable modern French writers. This style made its mark in Eliot's famous poem of 1922, *The Waste Land*, and in the *Cantos* which Pound continued to produce from the period of the First World War up to his death in 1972.

Critics have had plenty to do sorting out the references and elucidating the meaning of such poems, as if each represented a museum full of objects to be identified and cataloged. André Malraux, the French novelist and ideologist, coined the phrase "an imaginary museum" to define the attitudes in modern culture which such a poetry represents and, in a sense, caters to. In the cultural supermarket synthesized by this kind of poetry we can take our choice, of meaning and of reference, in much the same way. All the literary modes of the past have been recreated and packaged for the present.

But another kind of poetry developed in the same era as this modernism of Pound and Eliot, and to some extent in reaction against them. William Carlos Williams distrusted the cosmopolitan and synthetic style, and in his long poem *Paterson*, which concerns the life of an ordinary man in an ordinary American town, he consciously returned to a simpler native tradition, that of Walt Whitman. In "Song of Myself," Whitman had identified himself with every aspect of the national awareness and the nation's history. *Paterson* is a significantly more sober and less ambitious attempt at a kind of personal identification. *Paterson* has never received the widespread notoriety and acclaim accorded to *The Waste Land* and the *Cantos*. But Carlos Williams is a poet's poet: in his quiet way he influenced the subsequent course of American and English poetry as much as if not more than they did. Another great homely poet—in England this time—was

Thomas Hardy; and though his poetry suffered comparative neglect after he died in the twenties, at the end of a long creative life, it has since been growing steadily more admired and more influential. It has had a decisive influence on Philip Larkin, the best English poet writing today.

Robert Lowell and John Berryman are undoubtedly the most impressive of contemporary American poets. They have produced a great deal, and Lowell is still in full flow: Larkin has written comparatively few and slight poems, a slim volume every ten years or thereabouts. It would be no undue simplification to say that both Lowell and Berryman began as followers of the Eliot and Pound eclectic tradition, and gradually grew—as they discovered themselves—into a simplicity that has something in common with *Paterson*, and which depends on the same qualities of self-definition and self-discovery. Larkin, too, is a poet who seems to have tried over the years to define his own state more exactly and more simply. Such a coincidence is remarkable, and significant. At the darkest time of the First World War Wilfred Owen wrote that "all a poet can do today is to warn." These three poets of our time give the impression that all *they* can do is to isolate and create themselves, in relation to the world, and it may be that by concentrating on themselves they define by implication something about the life that the rest of us are experiencing. To create oneself, in our chaotic age, seems for the art of words the only thing that might be done, the only possible thing there remains to do.

Robert Lowell is the most remarkable figure of the three, as he has been the most prolific. He has a distinguished ancestry, and his process of self-making can to some extent be seen as a repudiation of that ancestry. Since it was Puritan and Protestant, he became, in 1940, a Roman Catholic; and since his family formed part of the Boston establishment, he sought his own masters in the poets of the South, John Crowe Ransom, Allen Tate, and Randall Jarrell. In 1944 he published his first collection, *Land of Unlikeness*, having achieved a certain notoriety in the previous year by writing an open letter to President Roosevelt to protest against the Allied bombing policy, and by compelling the authorities to prosecute him for conscientious objection. In 1946 his second book of poetry appeared, *Lord Weary's Castle*, which was followed in 1951 by *The Mills of the Kavanaughs*, its leading poem a lengthy and ambitious dramatic monologue. All these were in many ways a questing and a fumbling around. The poet finds himself in *Life Studies* (1959), an extraordinary breakthrough brought about, it may be, by the violent mental crisis which preceded and accompanied the writing of many of the poems in it. Since then Lowell has remained continuously prolific, adapting and translating from other poets (*Imitations*; 1961) and absorbing them into the pilgrimage of his own creativity as if—to quote one critic—he was "legitimising his progeny, replacing the Lowells and Winslows by Baudelaire, Rimbaud and Rilke." Lowell's latest poetry, the various versions of *Notebook* (1970), *Dolphin*, etc., seem like a determined attempt to revert to incoherency, to absorb daily occurrence, both public and private, into the bloodstream of what might be called continuous program poetry. The experiment does not look promising, but it is too early to say what will become of it.

Both Berryman and Larkin present a less complex history. Berryman's life was one of increasing mental ill health and alcoholism; though for many years he continued to write, and to teach at the University of Minnesota, he finally, in 1972, committed suicide. His long poem *Homage to Mistress Bradstreet* established his reputation in the postwar years, but his real achievement is the sequences of the "Dream Songs"—the first collection, *77 Dream Songs*, was awarded the Pulitzer Prize for poetry in 1965. A last slim collection, *Delusions, Etc*, appeared posthumously. Larkin's first exploratory and uncharacteristic book of poems, *The North Ship*, was published in 1945. Since then three collections, never of more than thirty poems, have appeared at roughly ten-year intervals. None shows much sign of change or development in the conventional sense, but each has increased his reputation. *The Less Deceived* appeared in 1955, *The Whitsun Weddings* in 1964, and *High Windows*, the most recent collection, in 1974. For many years Larkin has been librarian at the University of Hull; he has worked as a librarian since leaving Oxford in 1942. He has also written two novels, *Jill*, published in 1946, and *A Girl in Winter*, which appeared a year later.

Today's poetry is a poetry of contingency. That is to say, poetry has come to terms with what seems most necessary to art now, and to the ways in which art finds it most important to see the world if it is to retain the kinds of authority of which it has always been capable. Such authority rests on an old paradox: the poetry must be itself and like no other thing, but at the same time its engagement with the world must be—or must appear to be—total. In the thirties, Auden's poetry signally demonstrated the paradox and achieved the authority; Auden seemed to be both a man talking to men, briefing his audience with complete confidence, and a magician conjuring a new and unique world into existence. The poets of a comparable achievement today do not create, as Auden did, a world in which political and social tensions are stylized into a myth or charade; their methods of uniting outer contingency and inner essence are in a sense more subtle than his, the space of their creation more random and more relaxed.

Lowell and Berryman are such poets, and their debt to Auden is profound, even though their Americanness, and the tradition of Whitman, makes them seem much more simply communicative than he. And that again is where the contingency comes in. They create the impression of communication as carefully as poets of the past cultivated harmony and order. The whole life of Berryman and Lowell seems to lie about us in their verse. And not only *their* life but *the* life, the sense and the consciousness of the time, sharpened and intensified into the language of poetry.

This is so even though such an intensification seems contradicted by the first appearances of the poetry, which is casual and ordinary, seeming to mime contingency itself, and to open itself to the tedium of living as naturally as does the style of James Joyce, or of Samuel Beckett. The really remarkable thing about such poetry is its capacity to show up prose by transforming into poetry all the idiom, the variety, and the monotony of speech.

To challenge prose almost on its own ground is a dangerous thing to do. But here it has come off. It is instructive to compare the talking verse of Lowell and Berryman, which can seem as dense as lead at one moment and as light as feathers the next, with the brutal monotony of the prose style which Ernest Hemingway evolved, and which Henry Miller, Norman Mailer, William Burroughs, and others have practiced in their various ways. *Life Studies* and "Dream Songs" make this kind of prose appear positively doltish in its limitations. They show that verses, old-fashioned numbers, are still capable of being what Byron wanted—"a form that's large enough to swim in and talk on any subject that I please"—and not only capable but inevitable, commanding complete authority. The poetry of Lowell and Berryman is personal in terms of style, but the form and pressure of their poetry prevent that style from giving the impression of being trapped inside itself. They can always surprise us by appearing to be themselves rather than what the poetry has made them into, and what they have made into poetry.

This use of poetry as a kind of self-creation which yet avoids the constriction and claustrophobia of the self is a remarkable development in the American literary tradition, an extended experiment, in the manner of "Song of Myself," both in verse and prose. "Poetry," said Thoreau, "is a piece of very private history, which unostentatiously lets us into the secret of a man's life." This could only have been said by an American, at once orphan and victim of romanticism. But in modern poetry, to let us in unostentatiously usually means to be *confiding*, so that the poet and the confidence remain at the end beside the poem, and are not wholly extinguished in and identified with it. Elizabeth Bishop's famous poem "The Fish" fails to retain its power on rereading, because it only *seems* to be concentrating with such meticulousness on the phenomenon of the fish: it really turns out to be both confiding and self-justifying, involuntarily defining and enclosing the poet herself. The same is true of such a typical poem of Wallace Stevens's final period as "The Planet on the Table," and, at the other extreme of length and technique, it may be equally true of Carlos Williams's *Paterson*. Stevens himself has defined the impression such a poem makes: it is of the poet in it becoming "a man too exactly himself"; and one can turn those words against him, as against a very different kind of cult poet, Sylvia Plath. She is often coupled with Lowell and Berryman as a poet who explores and exteriorizes personal trauma, but the contrast between her achievement and theirs is in fact total, and is revealed by her extreme *completeness* in a poem, her whole and undivided identity with herself.

Lowell and Berryman seem to be themselves in this sense, but in fact they are very far from it. They have a masterly inability to confide, which is an aspect of the sense in which they are able to appear before us as if with complete abandon. Abandonment with these poets is a formalistic device, and that is what widens their poetic autobiographies into a kind of imperial authority and transports its apparent sprawl of contingencies as far as possible from the actuality of a "case." Because of this formalistic separation from what is real, curiosity has no place in our reception of their experience conveyed as poetry. The medium gives the message a clarity in which there is no room for further speculation. This may well prove the most singular feature of a new breakthrough in the language of poetry: that it leaves no room either for "chatter about Harriet" in the old sense or for its contemporary equivalent, the avid curiosity about the suicide of a Sylvia Plath and about the poems that preceded it as a part of its myth. Berryman's personal "case" was as singular and as desperate as hers, his suicide even more spectacular, but this does not leak into his art, whose convention is to reject any appeal to such things. In spite of all the seeming loose ends of talk, the name-dropping and the facts thrown out, this poetry gives us no need nor excuse to establish details of when, what, where, or with whom. "I perfect my metres," writes Berryman, "until no mosquito can get through." And in an article in *Shenandoah* he remarked that the one essential requirement of a long poem is "the construction of a world rather than the reliance upon one existent." That is certainly true of the long poem before the Romantic era—we have only to think of the *Aeneid*, of *The Faerie Queene*, or *Paradise Lost*—but the examples of *The Prelude*, or *Don Juan*, or *In Memoriam* show us how remarkable, how audacious, indeed, is this new claim to have constructed a poem about the Self which is yet in some way wholly separate from that actual and existing self, the life and progress of the poet, which was natural and indeed necessary to the poets of the Romantic era.

The extreme originality, then, of Lowell and Berryman is to have taken the modern subject, the Self, and to have formalized it along the lines and into the patterns and themes of pre-Romantic poetry, as if it were a subject like the Fall of Man or the Progress of the Soul. So extreme an emphasis on the contingent contrives in the end to dissipate any kind of Romantic or post-Romantic naturalness, the chatty naturalness of Wordsworth and Coleridge in their preface and poetry, as well as the more conventional and more wearisome prose ego of our own century, such as we find in Thomas Wolfe or Malcolm Lowry. Of course this originality does not come out of nothing. The formalization of the Self is an important aspect of what Pound called "making it new" in poetry; and well before that, and influencing it, are the various stylizations of the ego represented by Browning's dramatic method, Rimbaud's "Je suis un autre," and Whitman's claim to a total vicarious experience in "Song of Myself." Yeats's "masks" and Pound's and Eliot's personae—the Tiresias figures who are the mouthpiece for what Eliot himself called the "insignificant" and personal "grumble" of *The Waste Land*—are only the most sophisticated versions in the development of the stylizing process.

The breakthrough of Lowell and Berryman is in showing that no such evident and artificial process of masks and personae is needed at all. They have shown another way for the poet to avoid being "exactly himself." Lowell and Berryman are so present to us in their poetry that the thought of their real live selves is hardly conceivable there. This poetry thus creates the poet, but by an opposite process to that in which character is usually created in a work of imagination. We get to know Macbeth, say, or Leopold Bloom, to the point where we enter into them and they become part of us: like Eurydice in Rilke's poem they are bestowed *wie hundertfacher vorrat*, like the bounty of the weather, and their individuality dissolves in our awareness. But these poets contrive to create themselves as entities so single that we are—as a condition of the formal device—not to share with them or be any part of them. This simplest and most drastic form of avoiding being "exactly themselves" is also, and significantly, a way of avoiding us, and our participation in their poetic being.

In his preface to the "Dream Songs" Berryman showed his awareness of these matters and exaggerated, perhaps deliberately, the convention of a formula.

> *Many opinions and errors in the Songs are to be referred not to the character Henry, still less to the author, but to the title of the work. . . . The poem, then, whatever its wide cast of characters, is essentially about an imaginary character (not the poet, not me) named Henry, a white American in early middle age, who has suffered an irreversible loss and talks about himself sometimes in the first person, sometimes in the third, sometimes even in the second; he has a friend, never named, who addresses him as Mr Bones and variants thereof.*

The tone of this may remind us of Eliot's own demure note on the characters of *The Waste Land*. Such an emphasis is a "kidding on the level" that both distracts the reader and reassures him; other writers, back to Sterne and Pushkin, have sought to deartificialize their formal devices by a comparable candor or jocularity. Nor is this wholly misleading. It is true that "Henry" is not Berryman, in the sense for instance in which Norman Mailer in his books is Norman Mailer; he is Berryman in verse. But this does not mean that he is changed or dramatized; the poem would be much more conventional if he were. All that the poem does is to confer total alienation on the actual being of Berryman, an alienation more aesthetically complete than any social alienation, and perfects as a part of its formalism the partial and dolorous sense of that phenomenon which people today suffer in actual living.

The kind of aesthetic cautery involved in this is even more marked in the shorter poems of Robert Lowell, from *Life Studies* onward. But in both Lowell and Berryman the breakthrough involved in the new freedom, and the new isolation, is exceedingly dramatic and clear-cut. The earlier poems of both, whatever their interest and promise, have a muffled and clangorous quality. In all of them the matter and the manner of "poetry" seems to impede and to falsify the utterance of the poet; and this again is a sign of their originality, for one cannot think of any other poets as good as they for whom the development of what seems a true voice is so important or so long postponed. This again marks them off from Pound or Yeats or Eliot. As the dandy in "Prufrock," Eliot is just as clear and authentic a voice as when he becomes the "aged eagle" of *Ash Wednesday* or the sage of the *Four Quartets*. And Yeats as the dreamer of the *Celtic Twilight* is just as coherent as any of his later remakings, of himself, as the golden songbird of Byzantium or the "foul old man" of the *Last Poems*. But the ambitiousness of Lowell's and Berryman's early poems, the determination to be "great," and to write a great long poem, was for both an obstacle in the way of the form that would reveal and be the true subject, the Self. "The Quaker Graveyard in Nantucket" and *Homage to Mistress Bradstreet* were big projects that would be at the same time American and traditional and impersonally objective, having both the glamour of the old and the significance of the new. Neither is in any sense a masterpiece, at least partly because both are so determined on that status, a pretension which awed or browbeat many readers into taking the fact for granted. Critics too: Hugh Staples calls "The Quaker Graveyard" "a major poem of sustained brilliance which challenges comparison with the great elegies of the language." To challenge such comparison seems indeed the purpose, and the rhetoric of both poems goes about it in an impressive and masterly way that is itself certainly an earnest of major poetic talent. But it is not poetry of the true and overwhelming sort that the mature Lowell and Berryman both write, in which all suggestion of the poetical disappears into a clarity and force unknown to prose, and unhandicapped by the techniques associated with verse.

This could be put in another way, not so favorable, suggesting a loss as well as a gain. Alienation is also a form of verbal cancellation, which cuts off not only reader from poet but reader from poem. Many of Lowell's most impressive poems seem to destroy themselves in the act of creation, like a suicide caught in a camera flash the moment before hitting the ground, and this act of extinction parallels the way in which Berryman as "Henry" removes any contact or intimacy between us while appearing to invite it so completely. Poem and subject with Lowell appear to die at the moment the words hit the paper, a word cut off by the moment of death. With Berryman the same word gives the impression of muttering itself perpetually, between an empty desk and chair.

It seems worth emphasizing again that this cutting of any bond of intimacy shows how much we have come to take it for granted. The writer about meaninglessness today, who deals in what is numb and mad, in the extreme situation, is a commonplace; but the greater the *dérèglement* he describes, the closer he comes to the reader, and the more he depends on a personal relation with him. Like a drunk in a bar, this author needs his finger in our buttonhole; the further off he is from the habitual social and moral world, the more urgent is his need to share this alienation. Professor L. A. Fiedler, in *Partisan Review*, has associated Lowell with writers like Burroughs and Ginsberg, because, as he says, the young respond to the madness in him as they do toward the drugged or freaked-out mental states celebrated by their other favorites. But if this is so, the young are missing the point. The world of madness they respond to has a camaraderie not essentially different from that of surfing or stock-car racing: it has the coziness of a fashion in common. And such a togetherness is not really very far from the more conventional kinds of togetherness in American writing, for instance that of the "poetry workshop," of the well-made "shoal poetry" in which recent American schools have collectively excelled.

As with other schools of poetry, like the "tribe of Ben" or some of the Japanese, these other poets combine a way of writing poetry with a way of life. But being American, and modern, the way of life is both high-minded and overexposed, conventional in the responses it expects and yet almost embarrassingly intimate in the ways it goes about securing them. Most such poems create a moment of being (as in "The Fish") which is designed to last, and which appeals, in that ambition, to what we think of as durable moments in our own existence. There is a poem by William Stafford, for instance, called "Traveling through the Dark," which sets up with some effectiveness such a weighty moment in our social existences. Driving along a mountain road, the poet sees a deer that has been run over and stops to remove it in case it causes another accident. Finding that the wounded creature is a female about to give birth, he stands in indecision—a moment solicitously registered:

> *I thought hard for us all—my only swerving—*
> *then pushed her over the edge into the river.*

In its slighter degree the poem is as much concerned with the social contract as are Rousseau or D. H. Lawrence, and the claim to think hard for us all, though made with suitable understatement, ensures that the poet is attempting not only to assert a social fellowship but also—and as a necessary aspect of it—to establish with the reader his own individual sort of intimacy and collusion.

It is just this kind of self-consciousness about "us all" which is burned out by Lowell. Although his best poems appear to be constructed from the same sort of material—moments of appraisal and consideration—nothing in them is making a social or personal appeal to us. *Life Studies* are not studies in living, or rather in how to live. By exorcising the social bond, they create an authority far deeper and present a self which does not irk us with the desire to make judgments on what Auden called "the guy inside it"—inside the poem, that is. When Lowell tells us in "Skunk Hour":

> *I myself am hell;*
> *Nobody's here. . .*

we believe him not because he is telling us but because the moment of reading seems indeed the last moment before there is nobody there, not even the poem.

> *One dark night,*
> *My Tudor Ford climbed the hill's skull;*
> *I watched for love-cars. Lights turned down,*
> *they lay together, hull to hull,*
> *where the graveyard shelves on the town . . . .*
> *My mind's not right.*

The bald assertion, "my mind's not right," seems neither less nor more than the fact. "What use is my sense of humor?" asks Lowell in another of these poems. He may well ask. But he is not asking us. The kinds of craft and irony which form a comfortable bond between poet and reader, and sustain the tone on its journey into the reader's mind, here seem to fall flat on their faces.

So does what is usually a shared and knowing allusion. "One dark night" echoes the first line of a famous poem by St. John of the Cross, but we get none of the usual pleasure from the literary recognition, because it seems to have given Lowell none to recall it. Nor is there any particular meaning in the fact that the lovers are subsumed into their cars, the human into the mechanical, which in a more social and more diluted kind of poetry would signal a comment on the nature of contemporary society. These are studies of life as the thing that happens before death, no more than that. But they could have been written only in America today, because they afford a peculiarly American style of cancellation, a breakthrough, as it were, into refusal of all that America has stipulated, stood for, and taken for granted. The manic sense of relief involved both glorifies and parodies the challenge of Whitman, the poet who identified America with himself and at the same time renounced in himself any traditional notion of achievement.

> *All that grave weight of America*
> *Cancelled! Like Greece and Rome.*
> *The future in ruins!*

The poem canceled out, alienated as an object, is all the more paradoxical on the face of it because these poems seem to build up a whole world of intimacy with Lowell and with his family and provenance, father and

---

*From Louis Simpson's poem, "Walt Whitman at Bear Mountain."

mother, grandfather and grandmother, their incomes and neuroses, estates and social standing. We hear of the poet's wife and child, job and friends; and the ease with which these facts are alluded to is unique in American literature, reminding us of an earlier class of English memoirists and of Turgenev and Aksakov in Russian. We may feel this about a poem such as "Water 1948," with its masterly and deceptively simple image of the poet's marriage going to pieces through a quiet season in a rented house on the Maine coast, where "In the end, the water was too cold for us." The poet makes no attempt to force his personality and predicament: once again, the absence of confiding is the poet's greatest asset, and for this reason, too, it can afford to be so sparse and clear. Nonetheless, it would not have come off without the roots below it that reach toward the novel, drawing its bare strength from that copious source. As we read, we feel as easily on terms with Lowell as with Yury Zhivago in the poems—such as "Winter Night"—with which Pasternak glosses events in his novel.

This documentation, affable but never familiar, beguiled the first reviewers into enthusing over the poem's "touching" and "human" quality. But the point and the paradox is that such familiar and intimate things—all involuntary, as it might be, with the common good and bad of life—come before us in a context of total depersonalization. Like his son, the poet's father, Commander Lowell, seems caught by the camera just before hitting the deck. The facts of life—how at the age of nineteen he was "old man" of a gunboat on the Yangtze and left Lafcadio Hearn's *Glimpses of Unfamiliar Japan,* a present from his mother, "under an open porthole in a storm"—these facts do not come before us with the Betjeman charm and the queer pathos of a family past: they are nothing but the facts. When Lowell tells us:

> *Father's death was abrupt and unprotesting.*
> *His vision was still twenty-twenty.*
> *After a morning of anxious, repetitive smiling,*
> *his last words to Mother were:*
> *"I feel awful."*

—he is not being smart. Like irony and humor, smartness depends on an eye to and on the reader that is here kept staringly on an object. Lowell can make a statement which in another poet could not avoid coyness and collusion.

> *My Grandfather found*
> *his grandchild's fogbound solitudes*
> *sweeter than human society.*

No doubt it was so. The word *human* there ambushes us with a glassy stare, seemingly unaware of its own charge of meaning. If it is loaded and pointed, it contrives utterly to ignore the fact, and this is what his style of formalization means in Lowell.

The best and most characteristic of these poems thus give the effect of a drama without an audience, even of the poet himself. The intimation is of a life in a state of shock, "remembering the importance of his theme but feeling it no longer," like Wordsworth's Old Man. Perhaps such alienation is the logical and the coming response to the madness of modern society? Perhaps the starkness of Lowell's *Life Studies* indicates and brilliantly exemplifies some general reaction against the Freudian rationale of causation and explanation? Other kinds of social explanation, too. Lowell's danger is in taking over areas of public feeling and estimation which are not susceptible of the formalization treatment. *For the Union Dead* has the wonderful clarity of the *Life Studies* but does not quite succeed in carrying off the contrast between the sundered state of Lowell himself and the high title's public imputation. The voice in it is the triumphantly discovered voice of the formalized Lowell, as the voice in "Dream Songs" is that of Berryman:

> *I often sigh still*
> *For the dark downward and vegetating kingdom*
> *of the fish and the reptile. . .*

—but the big theme is blurred into weakness by over-formalization, as the big theme of "The Quaker Graveyard" was blurred by the lack of a sure individuality in the rhetoric which surged and thrashed about it. The fact is that Lowell cannot speak on behalf of other people. He is as cut off from the dead of the black regiment and their commander, Colonel Shaw, whom he celebrates in over-Whitmanesque lines—

> *He rejoices in man's lovely,*
> *peculiar power to choose*
> *life and die—*

—as he is from the "giant finned cars" of modern America, and its "savage servility." The tone of denunciation and nostalgia in the poem is not quite real, because it claims an open relation to the traditional human world of value which both Lowell's and Berryman's most effective poetry does not and cannot have. We have the impression that Lowell himself is a good man, with the right views on politics, Vietnam, and the race problem— who is, in a word, against sin. But where these topics are concerned he is always on the verge of being poetical, which means in his case "a man too exactly himself," and not the powerful field of force which holds *Life Studies* in its beam.

The New England conscience is, of course, a most important part of Lowell's general poetic apparatus, but it is doubtful whether it is much more than heavy weight to carry round, or at best a matrix for incubating poems which in their exactness of achievement do not seem to owe to it, or own it. "The man really sounds like a prophet," exclaimed Berryman of Lowell's early poetry, apparently without irony. (In their ordinary selves both poets seem completely straightforward, rational, generous, and humane—such at least is the impression, and probably not a misleading one, that we receive from their sayings in print outside their poetry.) Lowell did on occasion *sound* like a prophet, using a rhetoric to do so that for Whitman was the natural voice of prophecy. The prophetic note was implicit in the title of his second volume, *Lord Weary's Castle*, which invoked the Scottish ballad of *Lambkin*.

> *It's Lambkin was a mason good*
> *As ever built wi' stane:*
> *He built Lord Wearie's castle*
> *But payment gat he nane.*

"America," said Berryman, "is Lord Weary's castle, the rich house we use without paying for, which the defrauded one will enter suddenly." It may well be so. But if so, the significance is not one which the real scope of Lowell's poetry can sustain, for the implied judgment has nothing to do with its strength, only with its areas of honorable weakness. The national conscience that occupies an imposing place in the forefront of Lowell's poetics—the distinguished Puritan ancestry accommodating itself to the stresses on the Catholic convert—is in the scale of his real talents mere water under the bridge. Lowell's most ambitious attempt to create a prophetic and moral myth out of the American past—*The Mills of the Kavanaughs*—is an incoherent failure. He has written no poetry which, like *The Waste Land* or *The Second Coming*, increases its power and authority while modulating from the private to the public sphere. The notion of him as "important" in that way, or as a poet of agonized religious symbology, is misleading—importance only as the Ph.D.'s have to discover and proclaim it. But though he is not a prophet, his best poems are themselves prophetic indications of a state that may be becoming increasingly common in Anglo-American society, and to that extent *Life Studies* really does give the effect of nicking the advanced edge of time, giving a peculiar sense of the state of feeling, or the lack of it, in our society.

With that sense goes a remarkable power, which distinguishes Lowell's matured style from Berryman's, of catching the accent of another predicament and giving a quick image of another life. But here too Lowell's touch is uncertain and inclined to be laborious. The Jonathan Edwards poems and "Katherine's Dream" are both incoherent and over-elaborate, attempting too much by way of Browning and the more American tradition of E. A. Robinson. The ones that really come off are brief etches of desperation, and of these one of the very best is "To Speak of Woe That Is in Marriage," a mumbly Chaucerian title for a poem which contradicts in style all leisurely and easygoing Chaucerian narrative.

> *"My hopped-up husband drops his home disputes,*
> *and hits the street to cruise for prostitutes,*

> *free-lancing out along the razor's edge.*
> *This screwball might kill his wife, then take the pledge.*
> *Oh the monotonous meanness of his lust. . . .*
> *It's the injustice . . . he is so unjust—*
> *whiskey-blind, swaggering home at five.*
> *My only thought is how to keep alive.*
> *What makes him tick? Each night now I tie*
> *ten dollars and his car key to my thigh. . . .*
> *Gored by the climacteric of his want,*
> *he stalls above me like an elephant."*

This is Lowell's formalization at its most brilliant: as if the glimpses of his own life-style and matter are fused into one—wholly effective for the given fact, wholly extinguished where the fact ends. Each word makes its precise contact—*lance* and *razor* with *kill*, the seductive *thigh* with the desolating and comic sexual image of the last couplet—and then contact is broken with an almost audible click. Such a way of using words in poetry reminds us of the Augustans, and particularly of Dryden, who also achieves a brilliant and seemingly effortless colloquialism without looking toward us or catching our eye. Not unlike his Zimri, or Pope's Villiers, Lowell's wife in this poem is displayed in a setting of formalized squalor and macabre comedy that has curious affinities with the situation of Berryman's "Henry," who is also, in terms of metaphor, "In the worst inn's worst room ... the floor of plaster and the walls of dung"—the emblematic setting in which Pope places Villiers. Pope's elegant hyperbole has something in common, in terms of sheer style and suggestive preposterousness, with Lowell's couplet

> *Each night now I tie*
> *ten dollars and his car key to my thigh. . . .*

which also seems to exaggerate without specifying a tableau of utter desperation. (Why, after all, in her marital plight, should the wife choose her *thigh* as a hiding place?)

This odd link, in terms of formalization, with the Augustans is a very important aspect of the breakthrough, in terms of the presentation of the self, which Lowell and Berryman have both achieved. That last couplet of the "Woe in Marriage" poem, with its complex image of the husband *stalling* like an elephant (we remember the amorous *cars* of "Skunk Hour") at the beginning of the end of sexual desire, and caught on the horn of his own lust—one can imagine Dryden's bravura execution of such an effect, like the triplet on Jacob Tonson with which he threatened that delinquent publisher—this professional aspect of Lowell fits in oddly well with the alienated aspect of his genius. There is no lingering, no hopeful glance in our direction, only the job in hand and the businesslike cancellation of the account when the job is done. His book of *Imitations* and his translation of

Phaedre are done in this spirit. Dryden would have approved what Lowell says in the preface to the former: "I have tried to write live English and do what my authors would have done if they were writing their poems now and in America." Dryden rewrote Virgil and Chaucer in the Augustan idiom, on the same assumptions. But what was for Dryden a matter of enhancing the accepted civilization of his own time seems in Lowell's case to be the product of some personal and obscurely destructive impulse. Dryden, it might be said, destroys in order to rebuild in the name of the civilization of his time, Lowell in order to reveal the alienation of his time.

This process works well with the poet with whom Lowell has most in common, not in terms of style but of attitude—Rimbaud—for it brings out and emphasizes that poet's disconcerting extensibility and open-endedness. It is possible to add more of the same on to Rimbaud, as Lowell seems to be doing, for this emphasizes and deepens the *dérèglement* which led logically to silence and self-extinction and is in accord with Lowell's own poetic temper. But with Racine or Baudelaire it is another matter. It is an aspect of the formalization of both Lowell and Berryman, their *staring* quality, that they cannot leave the implicit alone. The triumph of Racine is to have enclosed the aberration and lust of Phaedre within the strict limits of a classic poetry. The miracle of the thing is its control, for although Venus is exhibited in all the grossness of her power, she is never allowed to destroy the Apollonian clarity of speech. In destroying this balance, Lowell destroys both the terror and the grandeur of Racine's heroine. "Frothing with desire," his Phaedre is almost as energetically ludicrous a figure as the poisoned Nourmahal in Dryden's *Aurungzebe*. She calls on Hippolytus—in a phrase which mocks the simmering cool of the Racinian confrontation—for his "sword's spasmodic final inch" and converts the unearthly sorrow of Phaedre's statement about the young couple:

> *Tous les jours se levaient clairs et sereins pour eux!*

into a chatty banality—

> *for them each natural impulse was allowed,*
> *each day was summer and without a cloud.*

It seems likely that Lowell's urge to obliterate "all that grave weight," the poetic selfhood of the past, could be connected with his own search for the form as self. A negative inversion would be to take over other poets and compel them, as it were, "to write their poems now and in America," to compel them to surrender their voices in search of Lowell's. Their achievements give a certain sublimity to this apparent effort to expand the ego, to make it a true devourer, which is also a peculiarly American compulsion. But it is also a desolating process. In "The Quaker Graveyard," *Moby Dick* is not so much used as torn to pieces; and in the lengthy playscripts which Lowell based on tales by Hawthorne and Melville—*My Kinsman, Major*

Molineux and *Benito Cereno*—the odd and oblique implicitness of such stories was belabored until it had yielded up its last distinguished drop into the totally obvious.

This need for absolute clarity and obviousness is for both Lowell and Berryman the essential and only way to formalization of the Self, and when it has been achieved there seems—in a manner that seems frightening to themselves and hence to us—nowhere else for either poet to go. The discovery is blank and it is also (Berryman's word) "irreversible." In *Notebook*, Lowell tries to lose himself again, in garrulity and in muddly contact with friends and with the world's problems, but the loss of clarity seems an insult to what has been achieved. After such clarity, what forgiveness can there be in the warm distractions of casual and poetical rhetoric? It seems likely that Lowell knows this perfectly well but knows too that he must go on and be content to ramble and to versify if there is nothing else for it. He once observed to the present critic that one could not just continue to write such poems as *Life Studies*, and this is both reasonable and unassailable. But nothing is easier for a poet today than to be incoherent— incoherence is the contemporary version of Wordsworthian prosiness or Tennysonian high-mindedness: it is the poet simply doing his thing—and though Lowell would never come to resemble all the other and various purveyors of poetic stuff in America, like Theodore Roethke or John Ashbery, Kenneth Fearing or W. D. Snodgrass, he seems now to be back in the position they are in of working in a medium that does not instantly proclaim its necessity, that does not say like Gerard Manley Hopkins's "thing in itself":

> *What I do is me: for that I came.*

—but toils along on an arbitrary and parallel course to speech or prose.

To have discovered such a medium, and to have become themselves so completely and so clearly in it, is, without doubt, what makes Lowell and Berryman the poets they are—head and shoulders above any other American contemporary. But they have become themselves by isolating and dividing themselves from the rest of experience, theirs and ours. When Lowell rejoins his contemporaries in *Notebook* he becomes "exactly himself" in the commonplace way that they are, and the poetry ceases to possess the tension of a true end which it alone can attain and to attain which it has come into existence. It ceases in fact to exert what Berryman calls "imperial sway." Berryman was very conscious of the poets who had exerted this, whose being he had to assume in order to try to exert himself. Pound was not one of them.

> *Not fated like his protégé Tom or drunky Jim*
> *or hard-headed Willie for imperial sway.*

Pound, that is to say, did not achieve in his poetry that particular authority
—acquired by Eliot and Joyce and Yeats—which depersonalizes itself by
discovering and proclaiming its own unique and regal being. That at any
rate was Berryman's view of the matter, and he sought the secret of such
being with an intense and single-minded ferocity until in the "Dream
Songs" and *Love and Fame* he is suddenly there, in apparent total relaxation, and able to look back, from the imperial throne, on the early days of
the power struggle.

> *I didn't want my next poem to be* exactly *like Yeats*
> *or exactly like Auden*
> *since in that case where the hell was* I?
> *but what instead* did *I want it to sound like?*

That was the problem, the urgency of which was peculiarly American
(Thomas Wolfe said something like: "I believe we are lost in America but I
believe we shall be found."), and the means to solve it was bequeathed—as
he saw it—to Berryman by the poets who had written the only truly imperial poetry of the twentieth century.

It could of course be said that I am making far too much out of the
simple fact that a great or even a good poet who survives as a poet is
always growing and changing, casting about and coming back, tinkering
with his style and modifying it in the light of new inspirations from literature. In one sense it is true that both poets "develop" and go through
successive periods and styles, but my contention would be that their real
achievement is not in the conventional sense an aspect of this progress but
depends on what in Berryman's case is an obsession with the idea of a
breakthrough into authority, the transparent authority of himself as poet.
The sign of this having occurred is his own ease about himself and the
past; a seemingly effortless poetry comes as he reflects on the "poetry" he
once tried to write; and there is all the difference in the world between the
relaxed sway of Berryman as himself and the fresh prose of Yeats as he
told us when growing old—

> *Through all the lying days of my youth*
> *I swayed my leaves and flowers in the sun;*
> *Now I may wither into the truth.*

—though it is clear that an intensive schooling in Yeats has led Berryman
to his once-for-all breakthrough. A fine poem in *Love and Fame* called "The
Heroes" shows us most clearly how the process works, the same poem in
which the point is made about "imperial sway" and those recent poets who
have exercised it. The poem begins casually *á propos* Pound, goes on to the
comments on Yeats, Joyce, and Eliot already quoted, and changes into the
celebration of its title.

I had, from my beginning, to adore heroes
& I elected that they witness to,
show forth, transfigure: life-suffering & pure heart
& hardly definable but central weaknesses

for which they were to be enthroned & forgiven by me.
They had come on like revolutionaries,
enemies throughout to accident & chance,
relentless travellers, long used to failure

in tasks that but for them would sit like hanging judges
on faithless & by no means up to it Man.
Humility and complex pride their badges,
every "third thought" their grave.

The Shakespearean reference prepares the way for a return to the sardonic world of mere idea, the last stanza showing us unexpectedly where the first six have come from.

These gathering reflexions, against young women
against seven courses in my final term,
I couldn't sculpt into my helpless verse yet.
I wrote mostly about death.

The ideas come from the poet's "pre-self": imperial sway can be exercised only over the words that make up the self, that can manage, as these do, to stir to awe and delight "faithless & by no means up to it Man."

It is of course the greatest triumph of the formal to seem like a stage entrance into total naturalness, to appear always to be at the point, as Eliot said of Shakespeare, where convention leaves off and naturalism begins. To be under an imperial sway is then the reader's greatest privilege. In terms of its subject we might compare and contrast with "The Heroes" the young Stephen Spender's extraordinarily touching and beautiful and yet by no means "up to it" poem: "I think continually of those who were truly great." As a poem it is all too human, as human as the embarrassment with and for the author that flushes as we read it. What both gives things away and makes the poem is the solemnity with which the author approaches the subject: he brings us up against the whole question of the "truly great" and our response to them. We engage with his response, even by patronage, and by appraising the sentiment of the poem we adjust our own. We control it, rather than it us, because it puts the inadvertent and the contrived together in an unstable state; but precisely for these reasons it is far from being a null poem.

It would be true then to say that Berryman's imperial sway, his "heroism," is won at a considerable cost, the loss of a normal human relation between poet and reader. By failing to become himself in his early poems, Berryman failed also to communicate: and by becoming himself so completely in his later ones he deprives communication of any relevance. And this seems as it should be. Berryman using poets and subjects to find a style is not unlike Lowell's ripping up of the past to make his own rhetoric out of it. The collection called *Berryman's Sonnets* is brilliantly donnish in the way it cavorts around the traditions and idioms of the form, exploiting the Elizabethan sonnet's evasion of any personal and nondramatic reality.

> *Keep your eyes open when you kiss: do: when*
> *You kiss. All silly time else, close them to;*

But in combination with such clever pastiche the gins and limes and love situations of the *Sonnets* strike one as mere modern properties. Berryman used such Donne-like borrowings, one conjectures, as Lowell used his material from *Moby Dick* or the James memoirs, in order to achieve a kind of provisional imperialism before the breakthrough into the real thing. It seems that he understood early, and with unusual clarity, just how formidable were the difficulties ahead, in turning "helpless" verses into an absolute mastery of speech, and he set himself tasks, like the *Sonnets* and *Mistress Bradstreet*, in an effort to learn to be a real person in his poetry from the disciplines of impersonal craft. A kind of macaronic Elizabethan, mixed with the simple pungency of well-chosen modern idiom, finally became the perfect medium of the discovered self, a medium (as we learn from *Love and Fame*) incubated in early days at Cambridge under the influence of Peter Warlock's music, and that of original Elizabethan and sixteenth-century composers like Giles Farnaby, from three pieces by whom—*His Toye, His Dreame*, and *His Reste*—Berryman took the "Dream Song" title.

Berryman's early preoccupation with becoming his own poet takes a particularly American form, but it has also been the problem of all recent poetry. How to avoid the dilution of confidence and intimacy while remaining (as Yeats so often did not) in some sense accessible and human? Hardy did it without even trying, or knowing the problem existed, and this is the basis of his still growing reputation and his great and continuing influence on poetry in England. But an American poet could not learn from Hardy: his idiom is too different and distinct. More complicated than that, he wrote about himself and other things in the same way and with the same lack of the devouring poetic self-consciousness that American poets inherited from Yeats and respond to in him. The poet whom Berryman could use, and whom he much admired in the early days, was Dylan Thomas, and it is significant that for all his admiration of Hardy, Thomas never succeeded in writing convincingly and coherently on the kind of subjects about which Hardy had written—"Fern Hill" is the failure which shows Thomas falling back on Georgian mannerism and relaxing that "imperial sway" over language which his earlier poems had possessed. In some ways, Berryman's progress was the opposite of Thomas's, toward the discovery of the self as a style after a period of rigorous training in techniques of borrowing which made for impersonality. Even after he had achieved his breakthrough into the writing of "big fat fresh original & characteristic poems," Berryman was still liable to go off the air, as it were, when writing about other people, like Tyson and Jo from the mental hospital in *Love and Fame.* In terms of their failure in real communication, in hitting straight at us, these poems have something in common with those early tours de force in which Berryman was not present, like "World-Telegram," and "1 September 1939," and "The Song of the Tortured Girl." Their themes and idiom echoed W. H. Auden, but their inert switched-off quality of accomplished exercises was exactly that of many Thomas poems, not only the late ones but such brilliant short pieces as "The hand that signed the paper." Such poems are not moving, and have no real authority, for they remind us too unavoidably that their authors really acquire the authority to move us only when their style is coincident with their own predicament and being.

D. H. Lawrence spoke of the element of danger in all new utterance, which makes us "prick our ears like an animal in a wood at a strange sound." It is a brilliant and economical point, but it has been too well taken: the attempt at the element of danger, at making us prick our ears, has been responsible for much recent debasement of poetic coinage. It has led, in particular, to clichés about the "daring" use of language. "W. S. Merwin," says Adrienne Rich, "has been working more privately, profoundly and daringly than any other American poet of my generation." We hear of his "daring English, stripped to the bone." But it is difficult to see how English can be used *daringly*, even in the attempt to manufacture "the element of danger in all new utterance." Failure to bring a poem off may show that all art is conceived in the lap of luck, but hardly that dangers were run in the process, or that a poem succeeds if it gives the impression of living dangerously on our behalf. The language of the "Dream Songs" does not seem in the least bit daring, only right, and a poem that strives to give the impression of taking risks with itself and with words cannot succeed. But to some extent both Lowell and Berryman were indeed compelled in their apprenticeship to be daring in this derogatory sense, since neither was born with a style but had to search so hard for one, while the element of "new utterance" in Dylan Thomas gradually relaxed into a facile formula.

Homage to Mistress Bradstreet might well be described as a "daring" poem, but its real achievement has no suggestion of nonsense about it. It is rather a hard and intellectual exercise, embodying an idea which has clearly always-haunted Berryman, and which could be said to reach its final realization in the "Dream Songs." That is the idea of the gap between the poet as a living creature, a huddle of needs, sitting at a desk, and the poet as the author of his poems. Can the two ever become one? In the "Dream Songs" they could be said to do so, as near as can be accomplished. In the case of *Mistress Bradstreet* they fascinated Berryman by seeming about as far apart as they could possibly be.

> *When by me in the dusk my child sits down*
> *I am myself. Simon, if it's that loose,*
> *let me wiggle it out.*
> *You'll get a bigger one there, & bite.*
> *How they loft, how their sizes delight and grate.*
> *The proportioned, spiritless poems accumulate.*
> *And they publish them*
> *away in brutish London, for a hollow crown.*

Berryman brings together his vision of the colonial mother and of the author of so much stilted and painstaking poetry, based on her reading of Quarles and Sylvester ("her favourite poets; unfortunately"). The significance of the vision is his continual awareness of the difference between the poet as a maker and as a person, a gap which the "Henry" poems so triumphantly and remarkably ignore, making the two

> *together lie at once, forever or*
> *so long as I happen.*

There is an echo there from Dylan Thomas's most totally effective poem, "Twenty-four Years," which ends: "I advance for as long as forever is." In *Mistress Bradstreet* Berryman sought to bring together the actual woman and her poems in and as a work of art: in the "Dream Songs" he seeks to unite his perishable and contingent self with the "foreverness" of his poetry.

> *. . . women, cigarettes, liquor, need need need*
> *until he went to pieces.*
> *The pieces sat up and wrote. They did not heed*
> *their piecedom but kept very quietly on*
> *among the chaos.*

In his essay "The Poetry of Confession," M. L. Rosenthal developed the idea that the Americans "are carrying on where Yeats left off," and that the stripping-down process to which they subject themselves in their poetry is a logical development of what Yeats himself wrote at the end of a late poem, "The Circus Animals' Desertion."

> *I must lie down where all the ladders start,*
> *In the foul rag-and-bone shop of the heart.*

But transferring onto paper the living ego as it has to be ("I renounce not even ragged glances, small teeth, nothing") is in fact the reverse of Yeats's self-parodying journey, out of nature into the artifice of eternity. Or so it seems. But Rosenthal is probably right in that the process of making poetry's central symbol out of the irreducible and unaccommodated self is a preoccupation which Yeats can be seen as inaugurating, suggesting guidelines for those who followed. And it is this operation which has led to critics (or to fellow poets) using such words as "daring." The risk of failure is certainly great, because a naturalistic poetry of the contingent self can be only verbal rubbish, and even the controlled "daring" of Anne Sexton and Sylvia Plath comes very quickly to seem circumscribed and banal, a spectacular but ultimately boring form of self-definition rather than a living coincidence of self and poem.

And that coincidence in "Henry" is never boring, partly because the real self lives in a medium of boredom as a fish in water.

> *Life, friends, is boring. We must not say so . . .*

Henry can delight and surprise us by his boredom, as he can surprise and delight us by everything he feels ("He stared at ruin. Ruin stared straight back") and this is all the more remarkable because—as I have said—it is a part of the difficulty and originality of this self-creation that the poet cannot be himself for us in the same sense that a novelist is his characters. The novelist cannot make everything himself—his readers must supply a good deal and will do so; but *we* cannot manage to supply Berryman with anything about himself that *he* does not know and give us. And yet the effect is neither claustrophobic nor confessional but unexpectedly liberating. It is true that such a poetry cannot be "earthed," for it has nothing of the accidental and inadvertent in it, no trace of genuine impurity. The more the poetry seems to ramble and to mention at random names, persons, or events, the more gripped we become by its actual tensions. Berryman has only to mention two rocking chairs, his wife's and his own, for fields of force to be drawn, trembling with a tautness which does not disappear off the edge of the page into our minds, but constitutes in the pattern of the poem a rigid and unending relation. The effect is not dissimilar from Lowell's "Man and Wife,"

> *Tamed by* Miltown, *we lie on Mother's bed;*

and many others, for in both cases the poetry has no wish to communicate with us, or to give us the chance of understanding and filling in the "human" relations involved.

As Americans, Lowell and Berryman cannot avoid the ingrained social imperative not to be "English" in their approach, or lack of it; not to be reticent with the gentlemanly fundamentalism of Auden and Yeats. Their wives and divorces, their neuroses and analyses, drunks and dryings-out, must lie around as open to the neighbor reader as Anne Sexton's orgasms or womb sensations. This is not only the American compulsion but American duty. But the irony and comedy of their achievement is that they contrive to negate by their art all the social implications involved, to achieve the same masterly standoffishness and dominatingness of Auden, while adopting an apparently quite different stance as well as a different legend. In fact, through all the domestic imbroglios of the two poets, all the poetic putting of foot in mouth, we recognize the personal and legendary domain of "the Last Romantic" which Auden had developed from Yeats, that characteristically and ominously centripetal world of stylized meaningfulness, of derelict factories and semidetached houses, and

> *the silent comb*
> *Where dogs have worried or a bird was shot.*

The instant authority of this world was not in the least compromised, for those who recognized poetry's "imperial sway," by the division in it between stern political and social finger pointing and the covert invitation to take part in a private game. Not to share such a game—art forbade that relaxation—but to revel in the ambiguities of a new kind of *paysage moralisée*. And it is really something like such a game—such a *toye* indeed as Berryman called it—that the genius of the American poets found a way to offer. As an achievement it is ambiguous, but it will seem less so as time goes on, just as the world of Auden has become in perspective what he himself called it, "a halcyon structure," with all such a structure's power of showing perspective and inner meaning, rather than a literal contribution to the political and social imagination of its day.

Some unbending critics, like Dr. Frank R. Leavis, never forgave Auden for what they regarded as the confidence trick he had played on the *bien pensants* of the age; and the *bien pensants* of our contemporary culture who have made so much of the honesty, the desolation, and the compassionate sense of life's intolerable pressures in this new poetry may also have to recognize that the matter is not quite like that. Auden never made any bones about it, insisting that the halcyon structure "was useful as structures go, but not to be confused/With anything really important": and Lowell and Berryman have been equally explicit, the former emphasizing the element of extravaganza and burlesque in his work, and the latter commenting in his own poem: "*These songs are not meant to be understood you understand/They are only meant to terrify and comfort.*" In all three cases there is a certain defensiveness in the disclaimer, but the American poets find it harder to persuade readers—and perhaps even to persuade themselves— that their art is not based on new and portentous kinds of social and personal significance. Authority in this modern poetry turns out to rest not on discoveries and pronouncements about the extremities of personal experience but on the invention of a new game with rules so mesmeric that we desire at once to abide by them.

Berryman's master rule is the convention of total insecurity, the pretense—not unlike that of Byron in *Don Juan*—that in completely mastered art the artist may nonetheless suddenly fall off backward into speech, the board collapse, and the pieces be swept off it. And this appearance is achieved by the constant tension exhibited to us between the poet at his desk at the moment of putting down the words, and the words themselves in their arrangement on the page as poetry. The Russian formalists have a term, *pruzhina*—a spring—referring to the bits under tension in a poetic narrative which keep its parts apart and its dimensions open and inviting. Thus, in Pushkin's *Yevgeny Onegin*, Tatyana is a heroine, a "storybook heroine," and the parody of such a heroine, while Yevgeny works the other way round as a storybook hero for her, the parody of such a hero, and the actual hero of the poem. Berryman's device is much more drastic and downright, even crude, but no less effective. Himself as the words on the page confronts in fantastic and formal opposition himself as the bits and pieces, the victim of whiskey bottle and inkbottle, wife, rocking chair, hangover.

The extreme analogy of such a confrontation would be Shakespeare, say, retailing his own immediate sensations and reflections in the course of writing "to be or not to be . . . ." The formal words of such a speech correspond to Berryman's necessity of putting down words which engrave themselves on the page in total separation from the poet and his "huddle of needs." The *sureness* of the performance is linked timelessly with the utter *unsureness* of the performer, never knowing—at any given moment—that he is a poet, so that

> *the paralysed fear that one's not one*
> *is back with us forever . . .*

He explains in a metaphor a reason for the kind of attention we give the process: it is like watching at a birth.

> *My longing, yes, was a woman's*
> *She can't know can she what kind of a baby*
> *she's going with all the will in the world to produce?*
> *I suffered trouble over this.*

A formal comic device is made of the unknown pangs of finding himself about to become a poet, lumbered with an unknown fetus which when it arrives will be himself. It is the exact opposite, in the mirror world of art, of true childbirth, which produces *another person*. But the pains are real enough, and so is the poetry, which, as a birth does, "adds to the stock of available reality."

That is the phrase of R. P. Blackmur, whose comments on poetry came as something of a revelation to the young Berryman ("I was never altogether the same man after *that*"). All major poetry adds to that stock, and

227

during the twentieth century the chief way of making the addition was for the poet not only to see the world as no one else had seen it—that had been done by the great romantics—but to acquire a peculiar and private relation with "available reality," to engage the reader in a kind of oblique and secret drama about the nature of experience. The new reality becomes more and more a question of the ways in which the poet reveals himself, of the idiom he finds in which to do so; and his relation with us thus becomes a hitherto unknown kind of drama. It is an intrinsic part of this new stock of reality—as it was *not* in the cases, say, of Wordsworth or Coleridge or Tennyson—that the poetry itself contains, or seems to, our reactions to the poet. By being himself in a new and peculiar way he binds the reader into an entirely novel and unpredictable relation to him. To do this is to *score*, as Robert Frost would say, and Frost does himself provide a singular and illuminating instance of the complexities of the process, for it is a hidden and subtle specification of his verse world that we in some sense see through it. Frost affects to be a man of a certain sort of meditative and lucidly homely openness: he is actually a man of superb and murderous deviousness, and the effect of his poetry is based on its proclamation of these things and our recognition of them. A kind of drama is played out between us in the actual texture and "reality" of the verse itself.

So it is, *mutatis mutandis*, with Lowell and Berryman; so it was with Eliot. Such poets are remarkable for the ways in which worldliness of a particular sort gets into their poetry, the worldly assiduousness of ambition and the social will. Frost, like Eliot and Yeats, was determined to be a poet in the fullest and most impressive social sense—so are Lowell and Berryman. For it is a paradox that the more inward poetry becomes, and the more specialized its audience, the more it lives and seeks to live by social nuance, fashion, and intrigue. The indifference of the free democratic crowd—and where but in America would such good poets have so minute an audience? —produces a poetry of complex and purposeful worldliness, the determination to succeed in the only sphere in which success is possible. The public status and reception of poets in Russia puts them in a different class: to be a national rhetorician, like Mayakovsky, and still, in our day, Akhmatova or Neruda, is to be in some sense socially stupid and naive. And not to be *taken in*, not to be in any sense socially and nationally innocent, is vital to the working of Western poetry.

In terms of our poetry, to be taken in means a giving of assent that is exterior to the poetry itself. Wilfred Owen, our last great naive poet (if we discount Hardy, who belonged to an earlier generation), made the famous remark that the "poetry [was] in the pity," and that all a poet could do in 1917 was "to warn." Personally, Owen was a prig. He took seriously his poetry and being a poet, but he took even more seriously—he had to—the war situation of the time; and he was always lecturing people about it, as he lectures in much of his poetry—it is ironic that without the war he would not have become a real poet at all. This sort of poetry is genuinely revolutionary, in that it directs our attention not to itself but to what it is urging and saying. It may add to the stock of available reality, but the really important thing is that it "expresses the matter in hand"—Blackmur's other desideratum—and that in doing so it acts as an inspiration. Whether or not the poetry is "in the pity," it is certainly not Owen himself: there is no sense in which he is his own subject, as Rilke and Yeats and Valèry and Lowell and Berryman are theirs. And socially he was as inept as they were adroit; he could not and did not organize the conditions under which he could become his own poet. Owen, in fact, was *taken in,* and it is a great part of his achievement that he was. What mattered to him was revealing to civilians what soldiers suffered in that war, and getting something done about it. To have written great poetry in this way is as remarkable as it is rare; no wonder Yeats refused to admit that it had been done at all.

One could make the point about Owen by comparing the way war appears in his poetry with the way religion appears in Eliot's. No one would question the sincerity of Eliot's religious beliefs, and yet the religion in his poetry is certainly an aspect of the social will that keeps him a poet: it has become himself and his poetry. Our relation to it and to Eliot's use of it is surely very much akin to our relation with Frost or with Yeats in their poetry; we are totally implicated in a unique and homogeneous kind of experience in which we distinguish the separate elements, elements of show-off or subterfuge, of skill and subtlety, but which are all and simply aspects of our dramatic relation with the poet. A "taken in" poet such as Owen is not like this. Our relation to him is much more human, in the sense that it resembles our relation to real people and is for the same reason more potentially embarrassing. No poet who is identified with his own poetry can be as unconscious and inadvertent as Owen can, or as we may feel that Stephen Spender is in the instance I gave from "I think continually...." The Owen who wrote "The Send-Off" and "Insensibility" could write lines like

> *I have perceived much beauty*
> *In the hoarse oaths that kept our courage straight;...*

which amaze us not so much by their callow ineptitude as by their indifference to the cultivation of poetic individuality, and by Owen's readiness to disappear as a poet into an idiom of vulgar poeticism and communal cliché.

Hardy seems also to have been content at times to do that; his writing, perhaps overwriting, of bad relaxed poems keeps him too in the outer world, the world of true contingency. It is this which has made him seem so admirable to other poets who are oppressed by the modern entail of the poet as self, and no one has admired him more than Philip Larkin, who has emphasized his pleasure in and debt to the least and slightest pieces among the great number of Hardy's *Collected Poems.* I believe Larkin to be the most interesting case today of a poet as great as Hardy who is trying to break out of the Lowell/Berryman situation and yet who is undoubtedly in the same boat, for better or for worse. An examination of how this comes about would complete my thesis.

There are few enough of them, but his poems enclose on first impression a large and rather featureless area of our inner and outer geography. Its public vocabulary is usually limited, since it has only to convey the sense that we are not so young as we were, that life has made us and not we ourselves, that we seem to have missed our chances, if any, and that much more in life is to be endured than enjoyed. Pleasures in this area approximate to the moments when, like the man who knocks his head against the wall because it feels so good when he stops, we leave off. The poems seem not so much epiphanies as intermissions, equivalents in art to such moments. If that does not sound much, it would also be true to say that they offer the most refined and accurate expression possible of a national as well as a universal area of this awareness. They are in fact very English, not sentimentally and exuberantly so as John Betjeman's poems deliberately are—it is not in the least a pejorative word to use in praising *him*—and rejecting any kind of eagerness and enthusiasm in the reader. Enthusiasm is emphatically not Larkin's state of mind. His poems have the air of being very meticulously mounted and developed, as if they had spent months in the darkroom or years at the workbench in the garden shed. "In every sense empirically true," like Larkin's young lady in the photograph album, they seem coaxed onto impassive celluloid as if to give the poetic equivalent of its dim candor, as if, too, they would accept with bleak relish the fate of its image:

> *Unvariably lovely there,*
> *Smaller and clearer as the years go by.*

This is not the image of Larkin himself but of his world. Our first impression may be that he is not included in the picture, and as we grow into his poetry it becomes clear that he neither is its center and formal justification, as Lowell and Berryman are of theirs, nor yet has the open and natural relation to it that Hardy has, or that Auden in his different way has. Though Larkin himself is not in the picture, the image of the photograph album gives an important clue to the process of arrest and suspension which determines, as it were, his identity for us. He professes to be boring, as old photos are, and yet absorbing as they also are. Moreover, at one level personality is dissolved in these poems into all our behaviors, while their verbal fastidiousness never seems to patronize the vaguely dolorous nature of humdrum self-awareness but to be its natural secretion. When Berryman tells us that life is boring, he makes it a daring thing to say, as in America it indeed is, as well as the cry of a lost soul kidding on the level. For Larkin the fact is self-evident. He is too English to claim a lost soul or a peculiar wound, and his intimacy is that of the lounge-bar, discreet, impersonal, and occasional, as distinct from American confessional as from the convention of chat among the members of a coterie which is Auden's elegant way of doing it.

Larkin's intimacy depends on its suspension. When we next meet him in that lounge-bar, we are no further advanced in our acquaintance with him; the slate of our previous meeting has been wiped clean. However formalized our acquaintance with Lowell and Berryman may be, we do nonetheless receive from their poems the impression of a developing acquaintance. Theirs is a poetry of natural progression, and in that respect at least they are the heirs in confidence of the early romantics, of Wordsworth and Coleridge. Larkin's poetry of arrest speaks to us in a low clear tone and is silent: the author never lets us know what happens between our meetings. He vanishes, and this in itself stimulates the imagination, as if we had met someone who intrigued us into making up things about him in default of finding out the reality. Continuing the social metaphor, we can say that the poetry of natural progression, however stylized our relations with its speaker, must sooner or later lead to boredom. Wordsworth and Coleridge we have with us always, like Carlos Williams or Berryman or Lowell. They are with us as one of the family, and very tedious their company can be.

The intentions of the poetry of arrest are all internalized; total contingency is focused by the intent gaze of the imagination. Like Lowell and Berryman, Larkin has for subject the nature of contingency itself, but unlike them he distills into verbal essence. And for such a poetry the continuity of ordinary life, of which the American poets contrive so effectively to stylize, is not a possible effect. As Larkin writes, "Nothing, like something, happens anywhere." But the moment of nullity must be enchanted. Keats and Tennyson are the great exponents, though involuntary ones, of such a poetry of arrest. "He will not come," says Mariana, for the poem could not exist if he did. Perhaps he came later? Perhaps: but that is not what either a Tennyson or a Larkin poem can afford to be about. "I choke on such nutritious images," says the poet who is turning the pages of the young lady's photograph album, and these master-images of bygone arrest, of random stillness, are the nourishment that the seeming slow growth of each poem requires.

This is worth emphasizing, because of the assumption that gives Larkin his credentials among students—and not only among them—that he is a poet of today's life-styles, celebrating our common surroundings and customs. A poem such as "Here" led Betjeman to call Larkin "the John Clare of the building estates." This is very misleading, as much so as if on the strength of "The Eve of St. Agnes" Keats were to be labeled the poet of social life in castles. In fact, Larkin's use of his material is not for any purposes of description (though the magic life of *things* in his poems may remind us of many of Auden's) but to achieve those locked, half-concealed intensities of despair which are so much more obviously the formal basis of Berryman's art. Larkin's peculiar vision alienates his people and places precisely by gazing at them so hard when they aren't looking. By surrendering everything at the end of the poem to its own habitual and continuous existence, which the poem has interrupted, he endows that existence with a terrifying poignancy. Many of his poems take such a moment as that in which Keats's lovers of St. Agnes Eve "fled away into the storm." They are starting their honeymoon, and being looked at in a snap of—

> *a past that no one now can share*
> *No matter whose your future*

—but there can be no progress into what Wordsworth called "the world which is the world of all of us." It is by seeing that world in the mirror that the poet gives us such dazzling glimpses of it.

There is thus a droll sense in which Larkin's poems, like the poster girl of "Sunny Prestatyn," whose image was rapidly defaced by being exposed to the public, and who was literally "too good for this life," really are too good for it. They too are not "earthed," cannot mingle with living as the poetry of progression can; they cannot unbend into verbosity or miscalculation, or extend into explanations. Larkin makes us perceive more clearly than the two American poets that poetry has survived and extended its range at the cost of masterly and absolute kinds of aesthetic alienation, which the lucidity and small scale of Larkin shows up. In many of his poems Larkin is concerned with compassion or love or the survival of what is human and traditional, but though these poems ("Church Going," "An Arundel Tomb," "To the Sea," and others) are as nearly perfect as any, they do not "come out" well when mounted like photos in a permanent collection, and when we turn back the pages in search of them. They lack the inner drama, the unease of mirror intimacy, to which we become so addicted in Larkin, and which can no more be lived with on humdrum daily terms than an Englishman's relations with Americans can be. It is indeed possible to feel that the poet is doing it deliberately—giving a fine performance on the Larkin—while his real fans wait for the proper fix, the true flavor by which they know him and for which they have come out of themselves. It is rather significant that the right and proper sentiments in Larkin are not in the least embarrassing (as Spender's enthusing in "I think continually . . ." is) because of the strength of the conspiracy between poet and reader, which appraises it with the approvals of equanimity. We might compare the straight sentiments of Berryman:

> *Working & children & pals are the point of the thing for the grand sea*
> *awaits us which will the us toss and endlessly us undo.*

or

> *We will all die, & the evidence*
> *is: Nothing after that.*

Honey, we don't rejoin.
The thing meanwhile, I suppose, is to be courageous & kind.

The poetry is not trying to impress us with its humanity: we know, and it knows we know, that it hasn't any. And the queer paradox is that for this very reason we can take these poets very seriously at bottom, because none of us—in this queer aesthetic relation—is *taken in*, even by what the poetry is saying. The deepest intimacy, far deeper than anything achievable in normal living, could be said to be involved in this relation, in which we can never seem to feel the discomfort of misunderstanding, inadvertence, or listening to the poet laying down the law. If he lays it down, we understand why, and wait, even though the poem may end in the process, as does "To the Sea" in Larkin's latest collection (1974), called *High Windows.*

> *If the worst*
> *Of flawless weather is our falling short,*
> *It may be that through habit these do best,*
> *Coming to water clumsily undressed*
> *Yearly; teaching their children by a sort*
> *Of clowning; helping the old, too, as they ought.*

Yes, there is that too: but what matters is our relation with the poet, not his comments on decent seaside pieties. Their decency is made possible by their aesthetic relation. The same thing happens in Larkin's novel *A Girl in Winter*, one of the finest and best sustained prose poems in the language. One of the glimpses through its window is of a woman deprived of other human choice by having to look after a bedridden mother, while an extended genre piece, the funniest and most moving in the book, describes taking a sufferer to the dentist. It is the voyeur who sees these things, and the mirrorlike confrontation, in the very act of keeping its back turned on life, shows us almost everything about how life is actually got through.

This conspiracy extends, I would feel, even to poems like "The Building" and "The Old Fools," which are deliberately massive performances— in the case of "The Building" verging on the allegorical—which are seemingly designed to inculcate the utmost gloom and despondency about the nature of living itself. If, like Leopardi, these poems were lucidly mellifluous musings on the horror and the hopelessness of our being here at all, their effect would be rather different—more monotonous—and though not necessarily more impersonal (Leopardi is certainly not that), much less intimately and dramatically absorbing. In practice, however, our relation with Larkin is much too close, even cozy, for the poems to be in any sense horrifying or—as Clive James called "The Building"—"a real chiller." Larkin would not tell us, as Berryman does, that these poems "are meant to terrify and comfort," but as Clive James also perceptively observed, they cannot help "becoming part of life, not death." More than that, our conspiracy with Larkin seems to imply that neither poet nor reader is taken in about the motives that underlie the fashioning of such poems and our reception of them. The clarity of observation, whether it is about what underpins our moral habit, as in "To the Sea," or what speaks to us all, as we come to "that vague age that claims/The end of choice," is made possible only because we are not *there* but elsewhere, in fact in the lucid world of Larkinian art.

This central canon of the Larkinian aesthetic is explored in the wry poem "The Importance of Elsewhere," in which the poet finds himself away from home, but in a place very like home. In that free world we and he are in a foreign country, ticket-of-leave men, licensed to see without taking part. The insistent and utter familiarity of what we are shown ("This is a real girl in a real place,/In every sense empirically true") becomes here a place not only of freedom but where the familiar can be seen for the first time. In the poetry of progression we are, at least by convention, in our daily lives (and never more than when some big deployment of myth or symbolism is going on), but in the Larkinian suspension we are abroad, always knowing our proper place to be back home, where "no elsewhere underwrites my existence." The very practicality and intimacy of Larkin's verse, its almost uncannily reasonable and natural tone, as when he comments on our need for a job, "the toad work"—

> *Give me your arm, old toad;*
> *Help me down Cemetery Road.*

—this is achieved by our *not* being where work and seaside holidays really are. His tone puts us effortlessly in the favored place in which an elsewhere underwrites us, the elsewhere of ordinariness he is apparently talking about.

A triptych poem in *High Windows* called "Livings" shows Larkin's skill at displaying ways of living as an elsewhere; and the last line of "To the Sea" —"helping the old, too, as they ought"—reveals the inwardness of the humor on which the tone is based. For to put it in an Irishism, in Larkin the characteristics of the poetry of arrest have moved a stage further: it is our mutual awareness of what such a poetry is that both makes the joke and makes the poem moving. Of course they ought to help the old, but the tone of the poem acknowledges that the process must take place elsewhere. Larkin manages to get as much relish into good counsel as other poets have got into spiteful satire, and because the poet's humanity is in this humor one does not insult his poetry with clichés about "compassion," any more than one would emphasize the pity in Owen's finest and most withdrawn poems, like "The Send-Off."

> *So secretly, like wrongs hushed-up, they went.*
> *They were not ours:*
> *We never heard to which front these were sent. . . .*

Simple messages in Larkin strike home because they are withdrawn so far from what they speak of, not in any oracular sense, but by the sardonic bleakness of their admission that they have understood the needs of life by avoiding them. "Self's the Man," as another poem's title tells us, and it is self that gives the Larkin attitude to life its shrewd envy and its dispassionate humility. It is instructive to compare "For the Union Dead" with "Going, Going" and "Homage to a Government," the two *O tempora O mores* lamentation poems from *High Windows*; for although those of the English poet are far more subdued and oblique in tone, we may have the same feeling that things have not gone quite right, that none of these poems has the real thrust that its bitterness calls for and seems to vouchsafe. Both Lowell and Larkin are making a statement about society which does not involve their own self-preoccupations, and as in "For the Union Dead" the gap between Lowell's sense of himself and his sense of America's past and present has to be resolved in the speciously violent exclamation of the last stanza—"a savage servility/slides by on grease"—so Larkin's vision of modern England lacks the authority of his own "elsewhere," his own nuance of regrets and rejections.

His humor, too, in these two poems is merely deft, ornamenting without enriching, whereas in "The Whitsun Weddings" it triumphantly determines the whole complex movement of the poem.

> *Just long enough to settle hats and say*
>   I nearly died,
> *A dozen marriages got under way.*

To find himself aboard a trainful of just-married brides would certainly have inspired Hardy, but to something more approaching the ancient observances and jests of folklore. Larkin's response is the more subtle for being more separated, in the modern manner, and for its discreetly humorous emphasis on the anomaly of his own position, for "got under way" is a parody of what the Larkinian moment cannot do. The point is explored and emphasized in the marvelous close.

> *it was nearly done, this frail*
> *Travelling coincidence; and what it held*
> *Stood ready to be loosed with all the power*
> *That being changed can give. We slowed again,*
> *And as the tightened brakes took hold, there swelled*
> *A sense of falling, like an arrow-shower*
> *Sent out of sight, somewhere becoming rain.*

"All the power that being changed can give ...": the power of the poem— and the poet knows it—is in the function of *not* being changed. The tension between the standing ready to be loosed, and the not being, is poignantly and discreetly hilarious, a kind of humor that exactly goes with the old-fashioned aura of magic and sentiment, just as it does in those miniature masterpieces of Hardy like "The Parasol" and "The Self-Unseeing." The difference is in the sad comedy exploited by the poetry of arrest: for what Keats called the "swelling into reality" goes on out of sight, where the rain it raineth every day, and this poetry would be dissolved if it followed. The romantic beauty of those last images is also packed with a dense and down-to-earth suggestiveness of sex and longing, a Shakespearean inwardness printed in every detail.

Larkin proclaims how much he learned from Hardy, his great love, but Hardy does not limn in the mirror, or does not seem to. His verse is more casually attached to the world than Larkin's can afford to be, and its banality is never so meticulous, so advertently adroit. It has the dilution and the garrulity of unselfconsciousness that goes with the poetry of progression. In this furthest sophistication of the poetry of arrest the poet not only must be a voyeur but must exploit the fact of being one. Keats, in "The Eve of St. Agnes," is far too devoutly intent to be aware of his voyeur status: Larkin quietly accepts it and the refinements he brings to it, which are as important as they are effaced. They appear at their lengthiest and most elaborate in that masterpiece, *A Girl in Winter*. We never discover what country Katherine, the foreign heroine of the novel, comes from; the few clues about her background are almost literally glimpses through a window. In a most ingenious sense we see the action doubly as a voyeur, regarding the foreigner Katherine, who lives "elsewhere," while simultaneously seeing her English experiences with her, as a strange and entertaining pattern that is not her "real" life. This may sound tiresomely theoretical, and in a *nouveau roman* it would certainly be so; but in Larkinian fashion it is done with so much blandness and ease, and so much deadpan social comedy, that it seems as if nothing at all unusual were taking place. Almost everything comparable, like the poetic novels of Virginia Woolf and Stevie Smith, seems by contrast shrilly opaque and self-absorbed.

Profoundly original as it is, *A Girl in Winter* not only seems tranquilly unconcerned with experiment and technique but can also be devoured like a real novel, with total engrossment in what is going to happen. Many of the poems, too, have this "nutritious" richness of the best fiction, and it is a singular thing that both in *A Girl in Winter* and in such poems as "To the Sea" and "The Whitsun Weddings" the author contrives to make humdrum habitual displays of niceness, pleasantness, and goodness seem as completely fascinating and absorbing as the intrigue and wickedness which the normal novel concocts to entertain us, and to justify itself. This rare and remarkable ability of Larkin is partly made possible by the characteristics of the poetry of arrest; happiness is a still life, and vice versa, as the Old Fools have cause to know:

> The blown bush at the window, or the sun's
> Faint friendliness on the wall some lonely

> *Rain-ceased midsummer evening. That is where they live:*
> *Not here and now, but where all happened once.*
> > *This is why they give*
> *An air of baffled absence, trying to be there*
> *Yet being here. . . .*

"Elsewhere" is all, certainly, that underwrites the existence of the old. And our elsewhere, in this context, may be the depth of being that shines in Larkin's Vermeer interiors, still life hallowing the normal and increasing the terrible sense of unending disintegration.

> *At death, you break up: the bits that were you*
> *Start speeding away from each other for ever*
> *With no one to see. It's only oblivion, true:*
> *We had it before, . . .*

And yet, all formalistic questions put by, it should simply be recognized that Larkin is good on goodness because his personality, which appears in his poetry as uncompromisingly as Hardy's in his, is totally sympathetic. That it is so may be owing to the secret humor of his own self-perception and to the peculiarities of his reticence, which, at moments as sudden as they are unemphatic, turns out to be not reticence at all.

> *Parting, after about five*
> *Rehearsals, was an agreement*
> *That I was too selfish, withdrawn,*
> *And easily bored to love.*
> *Well, useful to get that learnt. . . .*

Thus the disclosure of "Wild Oats," and a related point is made less parenthetically in "Dockery and Son."

> > *Dockery, now:*
> *Only nineteen, he must have taken stock*
> *Of what he wanted, and been capable*
> *Of . . . No, that's not the difference: rather, how*
>
> *Convinced he was he should be added to!*
> *Why did he think adding meant increase?*
> *To me it was dilution. Where do these*
> *Innate assumptions come from? Not from what*
> *We think truest, or most want to do:*
> *Those warp tight-shut, like doors. They're more a style*
> *Our lives bring with them: habit for a while,*
> *Suddenly they harden into all we've got*
>
> *And how we got it; . . .*

These are disclosures, not confidences, and what they disclose is not an attempt at intimacy. Because his voice is usually so low, Larkin is in a sense more chameleonic than either Lowell or Berryman, although at such moments we seem far closer to him than we ever are to either of them. But the next time we meet him in the bar his personality may seem to have changed, which theirs never do. The new Larkin is much less pondering: suddenly delphic, even brutally facetious.

> *Sexual intercourse began*
> *In nineteen sixty-three*
> *(Which was rather late for me)—*
> *Between the end of the* Chatterley *ban*
> *And the Beatles' first LP.*

or

> *When I see a couple of kids*
> *And guess he's fucking her and she's*
> *Taking pills or wearing a diaphragm,*
> *I know this is paradise*

Yet our sense of him is not shaken—we know it is the same man, a plain and natural self in whatever guise he appears. So indeed it is, and yet, as Larkin's early poems show, such a self has been stabilized and clarified in and by poetry, just as Lowell's and Berryman's have been. In Larkin's first collection of poems, *The North Ship*, there is a high degree of competence and of effective Yeatsian usage, but no Larkin at all. The parallel with the more prolonged nonarrival in their work of Lowell and Berryman is obvious, and so is the difference between all three poets and their predecessors in this respect. Difficult not to conclude that the dynamic of today's best poetry is a setting up in it of the poet, which, when accomplished, constitutes an aesthetic goal. The poet has arrived, as a new person, in our midst, and his newness is defined by the personal reality of the self he has brought to us in his art.

Once *made* and not involuntarily *defined* (as a man too exactly himself) there can be no question today of any Yeatsian "remaking." Critics have remarked on the absence of development, in any traditional sense, in Larkin's poetry, and have usually concluded—surely rightly—that the notion is irrelevant to his achievement. Allowing for a more prolonged period of search and experiment, the same is true of Berryman and probably of Lowell, too. "Development" in their case would also be toward a particular sort of self-creation which holds off the immense and complex meaninglessness of the modern world by a self-creation outside it, adding to its reality but also separating itself from the rest of the sum. In this sense the work of all three poets could be seen as an admission of defeat by the world and a withdrawal from it, a withdrawal from the imperial confidence of Yeats, who not only confidently "remade himself" but, along the same lines and for the same reasons, turned all about him into a legend—friends, religion, politics, even the cultural policies of the new Irish free state—while Auden, too, made a myth out of the climate of the thirties which had a real and potent poetic authority.

Yeats's famous epigram—"Out of the quarrel with others we make rhetoric: out of the quarrel with ourselves we make poetry"—is an accurate enough humanization of his formal method: the quarrel may be a convenience and a convention, but it is certainly there in the rhetoric of his art. But this kind of artificial division would be unthinkable for Larkin and for the American poets; division with them is between the self they discover and the world they implicitly reject in so doing. Anything as theatrical as a quarrel with the self that the poetry has found would be unthinkable, and for Larkin, one feels, would constitute a kind of pretentiousness which by implication he dislikes in Yeats. "I spent ... three years," he tells us in the preface to *The North Ship*, "trying to write like Yeats, not because I liked his personality or understood his ideas but out of infatuation with his music." In Yeats's poem "The Road at My Door," the meeting with soldiers in the Civil War sends him off into a quarrel with himself about what he could be or might have been.

> *I count those feathered balls of soot*
> *The moor-hen guides upon the stream,*
> *To silence the envy in my thought;*
> *And turn towards my chamber, caught*
> *In the cold snows of a dream.*

That is both musical and moving, even though Larkin would probably have muttered "come off it." In our time we do not really think we could have been different from what we are, and Yeats's nostalgia for the notion of the complete man—"soldier, scholar, horseman"—is not so much self-deception as a kind of playacting to catch hold of a poem. But such playacting implies a confidence in the part, in the audience, and in the theatre which does not exist today. Larkin's version of Yeats's mood has all the determinism, the bleak and behavioral acceptance of accepting what has become of one, which in a curious way, and allowing for the difference in idiom, is equally marked in both Lowell and Berryman. Arrival at oneself for these poets is also—or is made to seem to be—a kind of Calvinistic predestination, a state that is part aesthetic grace and part human desperation, in which all other doors have indeed been "warped tight-shut."

> *though our element is time,*
> *We are not suited to the long perspectives*

> *Open at each instant of our lives.*
> *They link us to our losses . . .*

Yeats's dream is of choice, a possible alternative heroism; Larkin is haunted by the possibilities that he knows—being himself now in the poetry—could never have materialized. Berryman and Lowell convey much more dramatically a similar sense of fate, the inescapable burden of being formed by parents and by early traumas: the suicide of Berryman's father, and his acquisition from a stepfather of a second name and identity. As with so much else, the American sense of destiny is far more spectacular than the British one, where "nothing, like something, happens anywhere," and yet it is a singular thing that the goal of all three poets should be formed by this awareness. The personal destiny makes a subject, a legend, which the outer world is no longer capable of affording. They talk about the outer world, but their poetry center is the shape of their own lives. To make yourself in poetry is indeed a toy, a dream and a rest, both confirming your determined status and liberating you from it. Yet this kind of liberation is a far cry from the more jaunty rationalization of Auden in "New Year Letter," which belongs to a more sanguine epoch of Freudian optimism, creating its own kinds of will and power.

> *Suppose we love, not friends or wives,*
> *But certain patterns in our lives,*
> *Effects that take the cause's name,*
> *Love cannot part them all the same.*

Larkin has no such faith. Love may be no less real to him for being a topic of doleful trench humor (we may remember the subdued ambiguity in "Wild Oats"—

> *That I was too selfish, withdrawn,*
> *And easily bored to love . . .*

—where the verb carries the sense both of loving and being loved), but Larkinian truth can be arrived at only through the medium of self-mockery. The ways of doing this are subtle, so much so that we cannot doubt the genuineness of the process—genuine, that is, in terms of art—whereas most poets who try this difficult feat, like Housman, give an impression only of showing off. What makes Larkin seem so genuine is the impeccable quality and deadpan timing of his performance—his feint of shying away from the specter of sexual inadequacy in "Dockery and Son" (. . . he must have taken stock/Of what he wanted, and been capable/Of . . . No, that's not the difference: rather . . .) is a good example—and better still is the comic business of a superlative poem in *High Windows* called "Sympathy in

White Major." The poet speaks of making for himself a Lucullan gin and tonic and then

> *I lift the lot in private pledge:*
> He devoted his life to others.

He creates a cliché of himself as "*a brick, a trump, a proper sport,*" feigning that the poems he writes for others put him in the same class as those worthies whose labors on behalf of cricket club or Oddfellows' Union are celebrated in fulsome speeches, and concludes:

> Here's to the whitest man I know—
> *Though white is not my favourite colour.*

The equation of poet with do-gooder has the usual Larkinian absurdity but is not all absurd: the image of such a man is one of the losses which the "long perspectives" reveal, and Larkin's love of English life makes the fantasy of belonging to it through the exercise of his art not only absurd but poignant. But the real thrust of the poem is in the second of its three stanzas.

> *While other people wore like clothes*
> *The human beings in their days*
> *I set myself to bring to those*
> *Who thought I could the lost displays;*
> *It didn't work for them or me,*
> *But all concerned were nearer thus*
> *(Or so we thought) to all the fuss*
> *Than if we'd missed it separately.*

Others use or "wear" their fellows through being a part of them, members of one body. Larkin, the benefactor, brings art to those not so wholly involved in this process ("the lost displays" suggests a recreation of something not only gone or going but more fundamentally adrift—the lost and abandoned). Art fails both its audience and dispenser, but—the crucial point—makes both feel closer to life. It is assumed the reader too "misses" life—"all the fuss"—but to feel the writer has missed it, and turned the process into art, produces a species of solidarity and consolation.

This is a lame rendering on one of Larkin's most concentrated and pellucid poetic sentences, but the business of the poem is so complex, so terse, and so funny that it seems worthwhile to labor the point in the interest of our understanding how the poetry works. Several of the most successful "Dream Songs" have the same sort of power of pulling us instantly into the quick world of the poem while not being poetic at us, leaving us breathless with the speed and sureness of the performance. Like Berryman's, Larkin's vocabulary can use words that are almost over-whelmingly poetic and *bien trouvé* (*rain-ceased, sun-comprehending*) while giving no impression of gusto or satisfaction in them—the kind we too often feel in Yeats's choice of what he called "the right word that is also the surprising word." Larkinian eloquence does not seem craftily combined with direct or slangy speech but a natural part of it, and such a rich ease is found only in the greatest performers—is, in fact, Shakespearean. Larkin's English shows how much life there still is in the old thing; it is both less self-conscious and more three-dimensional than the American language, more capable, above all, of kinds of intensely satisfying accuracy, low-key phrases that exactly define an indeterminate state. Interestingly, one of his comparative failures in performance is a burlesque about "Jake Balo-kowsky," a young academic at an American university, and the imaginary future biographer of Larkin, in which the American idiom does not sound quite right by Larkinian standards, and the self-mockery is too much on parade to be revealing.

It is, finally, an index of what we get out of this poetry that if some kind of quick or unexpected peer into the interior is lacking, the poem can remain too much a performance. "Now you see me, now you don't," with its suggestion of pier sideshows and baggy holiday trousers, would be a not inappropriate epigraph. A comparison with the straightforwardness of Hardy is again apposite, for *his* confrontation in a poem with unborn pauper child, or a journeying boy at midnight on the Great Western, is absolute: nothing is needed from inside the poet to complete the picture. A poem from Larkin's collection *The Less Deceived* takes an account from Mayhew's study of Victorian London of a child prostitute who was drugged and raped to fit her for the profession. "Deceptions" contrasts her experience with that of her seducer.

> *Slums, years, have buried you. I would not dare*
> *Console you if I could. What can be said . . .*
> *For you would hardly care*
> *That you were less deceived, out on that bed,*
> *Than he was, stumbling up the breathless stair*
> *To burst into fulfilment's desolate attic.*

The metaphysical point is bound to usurp the actuality, as the poetry knows and needs; it is its way of making "all disagreeables evaporate while retaining a steady image of the fact." And for the lurking self the message is that void is always less deceitful than fulfillment, for all fulfillment cannot help being implied in this hideous form: the breathless stair that led here to the desolate attic leads everywhere in life to Yeats's "cold hill side." But Larkin moves us most by shutting off that lurking conviction, as he shuts off the trench-humor that goes with it, and imposes a real gravity ("For you would hardly care ...") in the necessary gap here between poet and victim.

Larkin does two things which are so uncommon today as to be almost unattainable in poetry and in art generally. First, he makes the disagreeables evaporate: he creates supreme beauty out of ugliness, emptiness, and contingency, the trapped and the doomed. Second, he keeps us continuously interested in himself, always wanting to hear more about him. Both gifts he shares, *mutatis mutandis*, with the American poets, and the second, especially, in our time, is little less than miraculous. For the art market would appear to be utterly sated with the self: on every side the personalities of those who write importune us, shoving into ours—as Auden says of Lust and Shame—"their inflamed faces." In modern writing intrusiveness is all, and privacy mocked and decried; Larkin's poetry is unintrusive, private, and yet totally forthcoming.

But even more important is his updating of the fundamental aesthetic that Keats took as much for granted as Spenser, and T. S. Eliot as Matthew Arnold: that the business of poetry is to delight and console, to calm and to satisfy, above all, to enhance into completeness the inadequacies of living. It is to the interest of many writers now to assume the opposite, that what is boring and squalid—or, worse, merely grossly familiar—should be faithfully reproduced and underlined in any art that is honestly and fearlessly "with it." They do so because they are incapable of producing that paradox of transmutation which these three poets have achieved by finding in poetry the forms and the voices of themselves, and dividing these in words from the rest of our existence.

ROBERT LOWELL

At the Indian Killer's Grave

*"Here, also, are the veterans of King Philip's War,
who burned villages and slaughtered young and old,
with pious fierceness, while the godly souls throughout the land were helping them with prayer."*
                                                    Hawthorne

Behind King's Chapel what the earth has kept
Whole from the jerking noose of time extends
Its dark enigma to Jehoshaphat;
Or will King Philip plait
The just man's scalp in the wailing valley! Friends,
Blacker than these black stones the subway bends
About the dirty elm roots and the well
For the unchristened infants in the waste
Of the great garden rotten to its root;
Death, the engraver, puts forward his bone foot
And Grace-with-wings and Time-on-wings compel
All this antique abandon of the disgraced
to face Jehovah's buffets and his ends.
The dusty leaves and frizzled lilacs gear
This garden of the elders with baroque
And prodigal embellishments but smoke,
Settling upon the pilgrims and their grounds,
Espouses and confounds
Their dust with the off-scourings of the town;

The libertarian crown
Of England built their mausoleum. Here
A clutter of Bible and weeping willows guards
The stern Colonial magistrates and wards
Of Charles the Second, and the clouds
Weep on the just and unjust as they will,—
For the poor dead cannot see Easter crowds
On Boston Common or the Beacon Hill
Where strangers hold the golden Statehouse dome
For good and always. Where they live is home:
A common with an iron railing: here
Frayed cables wreathe the spreading cenotaph
Of John and Mary Winslow and the laugh
Of Death is hacked in sandstone, in their year.

Commander Lowell
1887–1950

There were no undesirables or girls in my set,
when I was a boy at Mattapoisett—
only Mother, still her Father's daughter.
Her voice was still electric
with a hysterical, unmarried panic,
when she read to me from the Napoleon book.
Long-nosed Marie Louise
Hapsburg in the frontispiece
had a downright Boston bashfulness,
where she grovelled to Bonaparte, who scratched his navel,
and bolted his food—just my seven years tall!
And I, bristling and manic,
skulked in the attic,
and got two hundred French generals by name,
from *A* to *V*—from Augereau to Vandamme.
I used to dope myself asleep,
naming those unpronounceables like sheep.

Having a naval officer
for my Father was nothing to shout
about to the summer colony at "Matt."
He wasn't at all "serious,"
when he showed up on the golf course,
wearing a blue serge jacket and numbly cut
white ducks he'd bought

at a Pearl Harbor commissariat. . . .
and took four shots with his putter to sink his putt.
"Bob," they said, "golf's a game you really ought to know how to play,
if you play at all."
They wrote him off as "naval,"
naturally supposed his sport was sailing.
Poor Father, his training was engineering!
Cheerful and cowed
among the seadogs at the Sunday yacht club,
he was never one of the crowd.

"Anchors aweigh," Daddy boomed in his bathtub,
"Anchors aweigh,"
when Lever Brothers offered to pay
him double what the Navy paid.
I nagged for his dress sword with gold braid,
and cringed because Mother, new
caps on all her teeth, was born anew
at forty. With seamanlike celerity,
Father left the Navy,
and deeded Mother his property.

He was soon fired. Year after year,
he still hummed "Anchors aweigh" in the tub—
whenever he left a job,
he bought a smarter car.
Father's last employer
was Scudder, Stevens and Clark, Investment Advisors,
himself his only client.
While Mother dragged to bed alone,
read Menninger,
and grew more and more suspicious,
he grew defiant.
Night after night,
à la clarté déserte de sa lampe,
he slid his ivory Annapolis slide rule
across a pad of graphs—
piker speculations! In three years
he squandered sixty thousand dollars.

Smiling on all,
Father was once successful enough to be lost
in the mob of ruling-class Bostonians.
As early as 1928,
he owned a house converted to oil,

and redecorated by the architect
of St. Mark's School.... Its main effect
was a drawing room, "longitudinal as Versailles,"
its ceiling, roughened with oatmeal, was blue as the sea.
And once
nineteen, the youngest ensign in his class,
he was "the old man" of a gunboat on the Yangtze.

Skunk Hour
(For Elizabeth Bishop)

Nautilus Island's hermit
heiress still lives through winter in her Spartan cottage;
her sheep still graze above the sea.
Her son's a bishop. Her farmer
is first selectman in our village;
she's in her dotage.

Thirsting for
the hierarchic privacy
of Queen Victoria's century,
she buys up all
the eyesores facing her shore,
and lets them fall.

The season's ill—
we've lost our summer millionaire,
who seemed to leap from an L. L. Bean
catalogue. His nine-knot yawl
was auctioned off to lobstermen.
A red fox stain covers Blue Hill.

And now our fairy
decorator brightens his shop for fall;
his fishnet's filled with orange cork,
orange, his cobbler's bench and awl;
there is no money in his work,
he'd rather marry.

One dark night,
my Tudor Ford climbed the hill's skull;
I watched for love-cars. Lights turned down,
they lay together, hull to hull,

where the graveyard shelves on the town....
My mind's not right.

A car radio bleats,
"Love, O careless Love...." I hear
my ill-spirit sob in each blood cell,
as if my hand were at its throat....
I myself am hell;
nobody's here—

only skunks, that search
in the moonlight for a bite to eat.
They march on their soles up Main Street:
white stripes, moonstruck eyes' red fire
under the chalk-dry and spar spire
of the Trinitarian Church.

I stand on top
of our back steps and breathe the rich air—
a mother skunk with her column of kittens swills the garbage pail.
She jabs her wedge-head in a cup
of sour cream, drops her ostrich tail,
and will not scare.

JOHN BERRYMAN

261

Restless, as once in love, he put pen to paper—
a stub point with real ink, he hates ballpoints—
and on a thick pad, on lap—
how many thousands times has this been the caper,
in fear & love, with interest, whom None anoints,
taking instead the fourth rap—

habitual—life sentence—will he see it through?
or will a long vac, at the end of time—
discharge—greet gravid Henry?
Many a one his pen's been bad unto,
which they deserved, some honoured in his rhyme
which they deserved, hee hee!

A stub point: *one* odd way to Paradise
ha ha! but of more dignity than my typewriter,
than my marvellous pencils darker.
We're circling, waiting for the tower & the marker
the radio's out, some runways are brighter
as we break Control & come down with our size.

40

I'm scared a lonely. Never see my son,
easy be not to see anyone,
combers out to sea
know they're goin somewhere but not me.
Got a little poison, got a little gun,
I'm scared a lonely.

I'm scared a only one thing, which is me,
from othering I don't take nothin, see,
for any hound dog's sake.
But this is where I livin, where I rake
my leaves and cop my promise, this' where we
cry oursel's awake.

Wishin was dyin but I gotta make
it all this way to that bed on these feet
where peoples said to meet.
Maybe but even if I see my son
forever never, get back on the take,
free, black & forty-one.

145

Also I love him: me he's done no wrong
for going on forty years—forgiveness time—
I touch now his despair,
he felt as bad as Whitman on his tower
but he did not swim out with me or my brother
as he threatened—

a powerful swimmer, to take one of us along
as company in the defeat sublime,
freezing my helpless mother:
he only, very early in the morning,
rose with his gun and went outdoors by my window
and did what was needed.

I cannot read that wretched mind, so strong
& so undone. I've always tried. I—I'm
trying to forgive
whose frantic passage, when he could not live
an instant longer, in the summer dawn
left Henry to live on.

223

It's wonderful the way cats bound about,
it's wonderful how men are not found out
so far.
It's miserable how many miserable are
over the spread world at this tick of time.
These mysteries that I'm

rehearsing in the dark did brighter minds
much bother through them ages, whom who finds
guilty for failure?
Up all we rose with dawn, springy for pride,
trying all morning. Dazzled, I subside
at noon, noon be my gaoler

and afternoon the deepening of the task
poor Henry set himself long since to ask:
Why? Who? When?
—I don know, Mr Bones. You asks too much
of such as you & me & we & such
fast cats, worse men.

179

A terrible applause pulls Henry's ear,
before the stampede: seats on seats collapse,
they are goring each other,
I donno if we'll get away. Who care?
Why don't we fold us down in our own laps,
long-no-see colleague & brother?

—I don't think's time to, time to, Bones.
Tomorrow be more shows; be special need
for rest & rehearse now.
Let's wander on the sands, with knitting bones,
while the small waves please the poor seaweed
so little.—The grand plough

distorts the Western Sky. Back to lurk!
We cannot rave ourselves. Let's hide. It's well
or ill,—there's a bell—so far,
the history of the Species: work, work, work.
All right, I'll stay. The hell with the true knell,
we'll meander as far as the bar.

PHILIP LARKIN

Dockery and Son

'Dockery was junior to you,
Wasn't he?' said the Dean. 'His son's here now.'
Death-suited, visitant, I nod. 'And do
You keep in touch with — —' Or remember how
Black-gowned, unbreakfasted, and still half-tight
We used to stand before that desk, to give
'Our version' of 'these incidents last night'?
I try the door of where I used to live:

Locked. The lawn spreads dazzlingly wide.
A known bell chimes. I catch my train, ignored.
Canal and clouds and colleges subside
Slowly from view. But Dockery, good Lord,
Anyone up today must have been born
In '43, when I was twenty-one.
If he was younger, did he get this son
At nineteen, twenty? Was he that withdrawn

High-collared public-schoolboy, sharing rooms
With Cartwright who was killed? Well, it just shows
How much ... How little ... Yawning, I suppose
I fell asleep, waking at the fumes
And furnace-glares of Sheffield, where I changed,
And ate an awful pie, and walked along
The platform to its end to see the ranged
Joining and parting lines reflect a strong

Unhindered moon. To have no son, no wife,
No house or land still seemed quite natural.
Only a numbness registered the shock
Of finding out how much had gone of life,
How widely from the others. Dockery, now:
Only nineteen, he must have taken stock
Of what he wanted, and been capable
Of ... No, that's not the difference: rather, how

Convinced he was he should be added to!
Why did he think adding meant increase?
To me it was dilution. Where do these
Innate assumptions come from? Not from what
We think truest, or most want to do:
Those warp tight-shut, like doors. They're more a style
Our lives bring with them: habit for a while,
Suddenly they harden into all we've got

And how we got it; looked back on, they rear
Like sand-clouds, thick and close, embodying
For Dockery a son, for me nothing,
Nothing with all a son's harsh patronage.
Life is first boredom, then fear.
Whether or not we use it, it goes,
And leaves what something hidden from us chose,
And age, and then the only end of age.

Sunny Prestatyn

Come To Sunny Prestatyn
Laughed the girl on the poster,
Kneeling up on the sand
In tautened white satin.
Behind her, a hunk of coast, a
Hotel with palms
Seemed to expand from her thighs and
Spread breast-lifting arms.

She was slapped up one day in March.
A couple of weeks, and her face
Was snaggle-toothed and boss-eyed;
Huge tits and a fissured crotch

Were scored well in, and the space
Between her legs held scrawls
That set her fairly astride
A tuberous cock and balls

Autographed *Titch Thomas*, while
Someone had used a knife
Or something to stab right through
The moustached lips of her smile.
She was too good for this life.
Very soon, a great transverse tear
Left only a hand and some blue.
Now *Fight Cancer* is there.

Vers de Société

My wife and I have asked a crowd of craps
To come and waste their time and ours: perhaps
You'd care to join us? In a pig's arse, friend.
Day comes to an end.
The gas fire breathes, the trees are darkly swayed.
And so *Dear Warlock-Williams: I'm afraid* —

Funny how hard it is to be alone.
I could spent half my evenings, if I wanted,
Holding a glass of washing sherry, canted
Over to catch the drivel of some bitch
Who's read nothing but *Which*;
Just think of all the spare time that has flown

Straight into nothingness by being filled
With forks and faces, rather than repaid
Under a lamp, hearing the noise of wind,
And looking out to see the moon thinned
To an air-sharpened blade.
A life, and yet how sternly it's instilled

All solitude is selfish. No one now
Believes the hermit with his gown and dish
Talking to God (who's gone too); the big wish
Is to have people nice to you, which means
Doing it back somehow.
Virtue is social. Are, then, these routines

Playing at goodness, like going to church?
Something that bores us, something we don't do well
(Asking that ass about his fool research)
But try to feel, because, however crudely,
It shows us what should be?
Too subtle, that. Too decent, too. Oh hell,

Only the young can be alone freely.
The time is shorter now for company,
And sitting by a lamp more often brings
Not peace, but other things.
Beyond the light stand failure and remorse
Whispering *Dear Warlock-Williams: Why, of course* —

PART THREE

The Reconsideration
of a Great Book

The Federalist

Rexford G. Tugwell

Two years ago *The Great Ideas Today* undertook to present what the editors intended as a series of essays, one each year, in which an appropriate person would provide a fresh interpretation or at least a contemporary reading of one or more of the works in *Great Books of the Western World*. The first such essay was by Mark Van Doren and dealt with Chaucer's *Canterbury Tales*. Last year William Wallace analyzed the writings of Gilbert, Galileo, and Harvey in volume 28 of *GBWW*. This year, in the essay that follows, Rexford G. Tugwell takes up *The Federalist*, which appears in *GBWW* volume 43.

   Mr. Tugwell, who was trained originally as an economist but has long since taken eminent place in the larger field of political science, has had a distinguished career of more than half a century in academic life, in practical politics, and in a variety of public service groups and organizations. He is the author of many books, among them *The Economic Basis of Public Interest* (1922), *The Art of Politics* (1958), and *F. D. R., Architect of an Era* (1967). From 1966 to the present year he was a senior fellow at the Center for the Study of Democratic Institutions, where among other works he prepared the draft of a proposed new Constitution for the United States.

Contents

A prefatory note

What follows is a description of and commentary on the compendium called *The Federalist*, published first as a series of papers in 1787–88. The authors, Alexander Hamilton, James Madison, and John Jay, under the pseudonym of "Publius," set out to assure, if they could, ratification of the Constitution proposed by the convention just ended in Philadelphia. That it turned out to be more than successful defense, they cannot have anticipated; but that it has continued to be considered much more is the reason for its reexamination here.

A brief comment is appended, together with abbreviated bibliographical listings. There is also a chronology the reader may find useful; perhaps it should be turned to first if the Papers are not familiar. It is a short guide to the authors' progress as they developed their case.

1. Compound government

Compound was the word used by the authors to describe the government proposed for the United States by the framers of the Constitution. It would have three branches and would be quite separate from the governments of the states. The essays expounding this proposal were addressed to "the people of New York," where acceptance was doubtful. Governor Clinton was fanatically opposed, and he was a popular politician with a powerful machine. He might well dominate the forthcoming proceedings and prevent ratification.

The Clintonian contention was that the "compounding" devised by the delegates would impose an unnecessary second government on ones already in existence. The states would lose vital powers to the national center, and the states were the creation of the people; their officials had been chosen in democratic elections; they were small enough to ensure that democracy would continue; and the convention in Philadelphia had far exceeded its terms of reference by devising an entirely new government. What was needed was merely some strengthening of the Congress's powers to ensure better cooperation among the states. What was *not* needed was the rigorous centralization proposed in the new plan.

Thus the Clintonians, arguing only somewhat more vigorously than their counterparts in such other states as Massachusetts and Virginia. The issue was clearly made: either the separateness of the states would be respected or a general government would be given the requisite powers to operate without state intervention. These powers would involve taxation of citizens to furnish funds for enumerated national purposes, thus destroying the ability of the states to impose vetoes on the federal government's undertakings.

The weakness of the Anti-Federalist argument was that the congressional government they were praising was so enfeebled that it had nearly disappeared. This, indeed, was the reason why the convention had been authorized. It was true that its terms of reference had called merely for amendment of the existing Articles of Confederation, but the delegates had also been charged—in instructions by the states—"to form a more perfect Union." This the nationalists (now calling themselves Federalists) had concluded, during the earliest days of the meeting, could be accomplished only by abandoning the Articles—and its Congress—altogether and establishing an entirely new government.

After considering the matter during the long hot weeks between May and September, they had committed their conclusions to a committee on style and had accepted what that group had written for them. That is to say, thirty-nine of them had; there were a number of refusals, some even at the last minute, for the same reasons now cited by the dissenting publicists. In spite of defections the proposal had been approved and consigned to the states for acceptance or rejection.

Even about this consignment the objectors had a grievance; a majority of the delegates, fearing that some states might simply ignore the proposal (as Rhode Island did), had provided that ratification, instead of being unanimous, need be approved by only nine states to become effective. Moreover, conventions newly chosen, not legislatures, were to decide.

These arrangements had made it more difficult for the politicians in the states to organize effective opposition.

New York continued through the succeeding months to be the most likely of all the large states to refuse ratification. Three delegates had been sent to Philadelphia, but two of them, Robert Yates and John Lansing, had been Clintonians. They had sensed what way things were going and had simply quit the meeting. Their third colleague, however, had been Alexander Hamilton, a noted nationalist, who had a formidable following among the elite in New York City. Because he was only one of three, and so a minority member, he had been unable to speak for his delegation and had continued to attend only sporadically after the first weeks; but he had gone back to be one of the signers.

For reasons quite different from those of Yates and Lansing, Hamilton had reservations about the final draft; but because he thought union essential to prevent the nation from becoming powerless in a hostile world, and because the Constitution was Unionist, he had felt compelled to accept what he could not change. During the days after adjournment, he had decided to go further, and in fact not only to lend his considerable influence to the cause of ratification in New York but to mount an attack on the Anti-Federalist position. After some negotiation James Madison and John Jay agreed to supplement his efforts. The ensuing papers were written under the pseudonym "Publius."

The convention had adjourned about the middle of September 1787; the papers began to be published in October. They entered an already heated pamphleteering controversy. They were brief but in series and appeared in newspapers at close intervals, sometimes three a week. Taken together they became a warning of dangers and a determined defense of the convention's proposal.

The Anti-Federalists were quite right in saying that the Constitution would impose another government on the one already in being, but what the *Federalist* authors thought they were more concerned about was that it threatened Clintonian prerogatives. As things were, the states had the sole taxing power; they could control commerce, even that with the other states, and, having a great port, they could exact revenues from goods passing through to the inland regions. Besides, a large bureaucracy owed its existence to Clinton; so did the largest of the state militias, to be used as he preferred, not as might be preferred by national officials. The new document forbade the imposition by the states of tariffs on exports and on imports as well, unless by permission of the central government. It was proposed that the general government take over all dealings with other nations and that there should be permanent armed forces—an army and a navy—when they should be needed.

The new government would thus no longer be dependent on the states for its revenues; defense of the Union would not require their approval; and, what was more frightening to the Clintonians, it would have a chief executive whose powers would exceed those of the state governors. True, presidential ascendancy was stated in rather ambiguous terms; but, nevertheless, it had fearsome implications. The legislative branch was to have two separate bodies: a House of Representatives, elected from districts by a majority of eligible voters, and a Senate with equal representation from large and small states. This did not please the politicians. The authors, however, were able to argue that the whole central setup had a familiar cast. The president resembled the governors, and the central government had three departments with assignments similar to those of the corresponding departments of the states. This feature could be claimed as a virtue not only because of familiarity but because support for such an arrangement could be found in the most respected political philosophers. Among these were Locke and other British authorities, but also Montesquieu, who had said that three branches were essential, each having its own constituency, together with suitable assignments.

There did remain, however, the undoubted fact that there would be compounding. The states would continue as they had been, but there would be an entirely new central government. Matters specifically delegated to the national government, however, were explicitly stated and were presumably not expansible. Any amendment of this arrangement would require the consent of three-quarters of the state legislatures, something not likely to be given except for purposes they would find useful to themselves.

These confining provisions detractors preferred to ignore or belittle and, during the winter, as their attacks mounted, the authors could reasonably complain of misrepresentation. The states, they insisted, would still have governors, legislatures, and courts; they would discipline their own citizens and tax them for their own purposes. In matters of everyday life, there would be little change from what had been customary. The new national government would devote itself to preservation of the Union and to matters affecting the whole rather than any one state or region.

Still, convinced Clintonians saw nothing to be gained from approving the new proposal and much to be lost by its adoption. Their conversion, or the gaining of support from others, was recognized as an uncertain enterprise, but the authors felt bound to try. They were profoundly convinced that the country's threatened dissolution was owed to the lack of cohesion and could be halted only by union. Somehow, New Yorkers must be persuaded that their interests were comprehended in those of the whole. Clinton's forces might dominate the ratifying convention when it met in the spring of 1788, but there were independent citizens who might be persuaded that New York could not prosper, or even survive, alone. If they could be convinced of this, they might become numerous enough to make a majority.

This is what, in the end, happened; and in the success the papers had a part.

2. The task in prospect

Why Hamilton made up his mind to undertake a defense of what had been done in Philadelphia can only be conjectured. No one has told of urging, for instance, by Washington, Gouverneur Morris, James Wilson, Franklin, or any of the other prominent nationalists; but then no one told anything much about the proceedings at the convention or about the private consultations that must have taken place. The official secretary, William Jackson, was either incompetent or lazy and left nothing of much use to historians; even diaries and reminiscences were curiously fragmentary and unrevealing. Conversations in the inns and coffeehouses of Philadelphia must have been important in reaching the many bargains among the differing delegates, but they were not recorded. The single useful source of information was notes made faithfully by Madison day by day. These, however, were known only to himself. They would not be made public for many years.

It is no more than speculation that in the closing days of the meeting the convention's majority must have realized that ratification would be strenuously opposed by some experienced politicians and pamphleteers. Whether or not he was urged, Hamilton took coach for New York immediately after the signing and began to organize for a campaign of persuasion he, at least, believed had to be undertaken.

The authors meant both to strengthen the arguments of supporters and to combat those of the opposition. They would contend that the arrangements reached by the convention were essential to the survival of the new nation. If the proposal was not perfect, it was, nevertheless, the best that could have been obtained from the differing company of delegates; besides, the provisions were, if not what was universally approved, much more acceptable than might be thought at first. This they would demonstrate.

As the papers progressed, the authors seemed to convince themselves that what had emerged from the convention was a more fortunate achievement than even they had at first conceived it to be. If it seemed to their readers contrived and complex, all its provisions were necessary to the integrated whole, and the whole was indeed integrated. It would give the nation revived energy and security, and unless these were achieved the nation would certainly not survive.

With the benefit of experience, later critics would be entitled to say of the authors that they glossed over compromises, ambiguities, and weaknesses they must have known about. There would be future trouble in some of these. For instance, the conciliation of the smaller states—generally spoken of as the Connecticut Compromise—would be the cause of a continuing controversy. Other issues caused disputes, even if not such bitter ones. To illustrate, there had been differences about the kind of executive to be proposed, some delegates favoring a single individual, and some favoring a collegial group; some would have had him (or it) chosen by the legislature and some by the electorate. They had differed also about the assignment of powers among the "departments."

The authors did not conceal the disputes among the delegates or that compromises had been necessary to agreement. They merely argued for acceptance of the result as the best that could have been reached. The Constitution in giving the nation a unified structure would ensure respect in a hostile world. If some of its provisions were not acceptable to all, none was intolerable. When they were understood, it would be seen how they emerged from American experience and so need cause no great anxiety among those who really cared about the nation's future.

The compromise with the states' rights advocates gave the authors their worst problem. They met it by continually emphasizing the limited powers of the central government and the almost untouched ones of the states — except for direct taxation needed to correct the worst deficiency experienced by the existing Congress during the preceding few years. This tactic in the months to follow drove their opponents to less and less effective arguments. They were clearly trying to further their own interests and so were open to derision. The authors made use of every opportunity for belittlement, but also they displayed a convincing fund of erudition and related their knowledge to American necessities. They began on a belligerent note but would end in quite a different — a more reasonable — way. The last of the series would be devoted to showing how details of the proposal were nicely calculated to meet the particular problems of a new nation in a hostile world.

3. The work begins

Both of Hamilton's collaborators were in the city. Jay was an established lawyer whose experience in public service had been unhappy. Madison was attending the last session of the old Congress as a representative from Virginia. Both were anxious for ratification but also were experienced pamphleteers. Madison had shaped the Virginia Resolutions introduced at the beginning of the discussions in Philadelphia as the groundwork for what was to follow, and the notes he had made during the convention gave him authentic material. As it turned out, he would write fewer papers than Hamilton, but those he did write would be some of the most memorable. Jay had not been a delegate at the convention, but he had no reservations about the necessity for adopting the new Constitution.

There were interruptions. Jay became ill before the end of November and was unable to contribute again until February. Madison returned to Virginia in early March to be present at the ratification convention there. Hamilton's contributions had to be reconciled with his work as a practicing lawyer. Nevertheless, the series went on, with some interruptions, from

October 1787 until August 1788. The essays were published originally in several different newspapers and were copied in others. Altogether there were eighty-five.

It must be recalled that Publius entered an erupting campaign of publicity for and against the proposed government. Contemporary prints were filled with diatribes signed by such names as Caesar, Cato, Brutus, and Constant Reader. Nevertheless, Publius's views were at once recognized as something more than the usual contentions, and quickly became the subject of discussion wherever citizens met. Since the papers were injected into so fierce a controversy, their comparative fairness and detachment seem now to be all the more creditable. It can be understood why Publius was taken much more seriously than rival pamphleteers.

The series followed, if only roughly, a scheme announced (by Hamilton) in the first number:

> *I propose, in a series of papers, to discuss the following interesting particulars: —The utility of the UNION to your political prosperity—The insufficiency of the present Confederation to preserve that Union—The necessity of a government at least equally energetic with the one proposed, to the attainment of this object—The conformity of the proposed Constitution to the true principles of republican government—Its analogy to your own State constitution—and lastly, The additional security which its adoption will afford to the preservation of that species of government, to liberty, and to property.*[1]

Accordingly, the first essays emphasized the near disappearance of government under the Articles of Confederation and the conviction that if the nation was to survive there must be radical change. The first objective must be the strength to be had only by national unification.

There was, readers were reminded, an ever present threat from foreign forces on all the borders. This, however, was not the only danger; it was also likely that quarrels among the states themselves would lead to interruptions of intercourse or even to open conflicts. Based on regional interests, these might end in several mutually hostile confederacies. The worst weakness of the existing Congress had been that it had rested on voluntary collaboration among the states, each of which had consulted its own interest in contributing or withholding. Congressional "requisitions" had been ignored or rejected, and there had been no penalties. The states had fallen apart. There was no respected government, and other nations were well aware of the weakness.

This opening theme was well chosen. The convention had come about because of governmental failure. That something had to be done was commonly acknowledged, and opponents now had to admit their lack of solutions for what had become an urgent problem. The Constitution, on the other hand, offered a reasonable alternative to impending dissolution.

It is not too difficult, even after the buildings of the late eighteenth century have been buried under the enormous accumulation of structures on lower Manhattan Island, to visualize the authors of *The Federalist* at their desks, writing with the clumsy materials available, pouring out their convictions concerning immediate dangers and the necessity for union. Hamilton's office was next door to his residence, and both were near the corner of Wall Street and Broadway. He had all the practice he could attend to, and the papers were something he must have pushed aside other concerns to complete. We know that often the printer's boy waited while he finished a paragraph or made a final correction. Jay was equally busy, but Madison was perhaps not so pressed, since the Congress was so inactive. For him, too, however, the demands of newspaper publication made reflection and elaboration impossible.

Under such circumstances it was as much as anyone could have anticipated that what was written would emerge with satisfactory coherence; to have expected that it might become a political treatise, to be read for generations, would have been unrealistic. This could only have happened when the writing was being done out of prepared minds ready to commit their convictions to the waiting paper. Such ripeness could overcome the fact that at least Hamilton and Madison were youngish men addressing sober elders who would have the final disposal of their urgings. Jay lent weight, being older and better established in New York. He joined in at number 2 of the series, going on to write numbers 3, 4, and 5. The style in all the papers was so much alike that Publius could have been a single person. Who imitated whom we do not know; perhaps all had emerged from a similar training in political exposition. Later scholars have had to be ingenious about individual identifications.

The first papers were devoted generally to the dangers from foreign aggression and the helplessness of the states unless they developed a common defense. The first consideration in anyone's mind who studied the situation of the former colonies had to be simple safety, these opening papers said. Not only would the uniting of the states and the establishing of a strong national government act as a deterrent to those who were hoping for disintegration, it would reduce the probability of provocation. The United States was in competition with France and Britain, and its carrying trade could not flourish except at the expense of theirs. The Spanish also thought, Jay maintained, that closing the Mississippi to American commerce would be as convenient for them as closing the Saint Lawrence was for the British.

The conflicts likely to arise from these causes could easily lead to actual war, and how could any state alone be expected to prevail against a determined imperial power?

The argument was lucid:

> *One government can collect and avail itself of the talents and experience of the ablest men, in whatever part of the Union they may be found. It can move on*

uniform principles of policy. It can harmonise, assimilate, and protect the several parts and members, and extend the benefit of its foresight and precautions to each. In the formation of treaties, it will regard the interest of the whole, and the particular interests of the parts as connected with that of the whole.[2]

In the same passage Jay went on to speak of something out of his own experience. He had been ambassador to Spain and France and had been one of the negotiators—with John Adams, Benjamin Franklin, and Henry Laurens—of the Treaty of Paris, making peace with Britain. And later, as secretary for foreign affairs, he had found that difficulties increased as the government weakened. In 1786, for instance, he had negotiated a treaty committing the United States not to use the Mississippi for twenty-five years in return for commercial concessions. Southwesterners had been convinced that they had been sacrificed for benefits to the Northeast. This, and other such experiences with regional and state interests, had convinced him that nothing short of a general government would do, one able to establish and enforce national policies.

The last of these early papers (No. 5) was still concerned with safety. Attention was called to the relevance of British history, so well known to all Americans. It was possible, Jay said, to profit from British mistakes without paying the price that Englishmen had had to pay for them. The most obvious lesson was the one Jay had been speaking of. The people of that small island had for centuries been divided into three nations and, as a consequence, had been almost constantly quarreling with one another:

> *Should the people of America divide themselves into three or four nations, would not the same thing happen? . . . Instead of their being "joined in affection" and free from all apprehension of different "interests," envy and jealousy would soon extinguish confidence and affection, and the partial interests of each confederacy . . . would be the only objects of their policy and pursuits. . . . Like most other bordering nations, they would always be either involved in disputes and war, or live in constant apprehension of them.*[3]

What was to be feared most was just this, and the states or "confederacies"—all the authors of the papers referred repeatedly to possible "confederacies" as more likely to be the alternative to one nation than the states as they then existed—would fall to disputing among themselves and exhaust their resources in this way. It would be likely then that each would establish relationships with foreign powers, calling on them for support against neighbors. Jay concluded:

> *. . . let us not forget how much more easy it is to receive foreign fleets into our ports, and foreign armies into our country, than it is to persuade or compel them to depart. How many conquests did the Romans and others make in the characters of allies, and what innovations did they under the same character introduce into the governments of those whom they pretended to protect.*

> *Let candid men judge, then, whether the division of America into any given number of independent sovereignties would tend to secure us against the hostilities and improper interference of foreign nations.*[4]

This, coming as it did from one with his erudition and experience, carried weight. It would be as compelling as any of the Publius arguments.

4. Concurrent jurisdiction

Papers 6 to 9, written by Hamilton, form a connecting link between this warning by Jay about separateness and a dissertation by Madison about human propensities for division and animosity. The least suspicion of weakness, Hamilton said in this interlude, would invite aggression from abroad; but also the available historical examples showed that the states, if not united, would fall into dissension and attack each other.

Madison, resuming at No. 10, dwelt at some length on the necessity for a government able to prevent the divisions likely to occur because of envy on the one hand and fear on the other. Certain passages in this essay have been among the most quoted in the papers. They anticipated Marx by describing the formation of economic classes and their struggles for advantage. Madison warned that one faction might become a majority and, if it did, would sacrifice to a ruling passion "both the public good and the rights of other citizens." For preventing such disasters, he said, democracies were ineffectual. They had "ever been spectacles of turbulence and contention ... and have in general been as short in their lives as they have been violent in their deaths." There was, however, an alternative:

> *A republic, by which I mean a government in which the scheme of representation takes place, opens a different prospect, and promises the cure for which we are seeking.*[5]

This was clearly distinguishable from a democracy:

> *The two great points of difference between a democracy and a republic are: first, the delegation of the government, in the latter, to a small number of citizens elected by the rest; secondly, the greater number of citizens, and the greater sphere of country, over which the latter may be extended.*[6]

For the larger size and increased population in prospect for the American Union, a republic rather than a democracy was preferable.

> *Extend the sphere, and you take in a greater variety of parties and interests; you make it less probable that a majority of the whole will have a common motive to invade the rights of other citizens; or if such a common motive exists,*

> *it will be more difficult for all who feel it to discover their own strength, and to act in unison with each other.*[7]

Madison concluded by saying that in the extension and proper structure of a Union there existed an adequate remedy for the diseases most likely even in a republic. Agitators might kindle flames within their states but would be unable to spread the conflagration to others.

This argument of Madison's was obviously intended for the more responsible citizens. It must be recalled how few at that time could be called prosperous, and how few were even literate. Those who would actually be involved in choosing the delegates to the impending ratification conventions were a small minority, not the common citizenry but professionals, businessmen, planters, and politicians. Madison was appealing to their desire for relief from the fear of disturbance by an unruly populace. Those to whom he spoke were, by this time, not only New Yorkers. Publius's audience was expanding. Before winter it had spread to Virginia, Massachusetts, and Pennsylvania.[8]

It seems curious that Madison should have been the one to make this first attack on "faction" since, after ratification, he would become an ally of Jefferson who would put together, before Washington's presidency ended, the most enduring of all American political parties, one that would defeat John Adams and carry Jefferson and two successors into office: Madison himself, and then Monroe. They described themselves as Democratic-Republicans, but "democrat" prevailed over "republican," at least in Jefferson's mind and presumably in Madison's. The explanation is, of course, that concern for acceptance of the Constitution overrode ideological differences.

It was not until the twentieth paper that dissertations on the necessity for Union evolved into Madison's application of the argument about faction to the states as such. It must be concluded, he said, that if the national government could not "act on" citizens, the states would simply continually disagree about their powers. Some, they simply could not be allowed to possess. These included: the conduct of foreign relations, common defense, preservation of domestic peace, and regulation of commerce with other nations and among the states. These in many instances required interference with individual actions. If the states intervened there would be such conflicts and such attempts to outdo each other that relations would always be strained. It had to be said again that these powers could have no stated limits. Future exigencies could not be known, so there could be no estimate of the means necessary for meeting them. This had been recognized in the Articles of Confederation, but it had been mistakenly thought that the states would honor "requisitions" of the Congress. They had not, and had shown that they never would. The national government must be able to levy troops, build ships, and raise the necessary revenue to maintain them. The proposed Constitution provided for this.

There followed several papers, contributed by Hamilton, having to do with the necessity for this unlimited — if strictly defined — authority. In this connection came the statement which has so often been quoted:

> *A government ought to contain in itself every power requisite to the full accomplishment of the objects committed to its care, and to the complete execution of the trusts for which it is responsible, free from every other control but a regard to the public good and to the sense of the people.*[9]

Hamilton dwelt at some length — as a future secretary of the treasury might be expected to have done — on the need for reliable sources of revenue. He reiterated the truism that neither foreign attacks nor domestic outbreaks could be foreseen; therefore, the necessary revenue could not be estimated, and the power to acquire it must not be limited. These passages were bold attacks on the bulwarks of the opposition. If the Anti-Federalists could contain the national ability to tax, they could perpetuate the old voluntary scheme. They could then go on as they had done, refusing to honor "requisitions" and ignoring national demands.

The opposition could hardly deny the fact of failure openly; it was evaded by citing the so-called supremacy clause to show that the Federalist intention was the total destruction of local government.[10] This was calculated to arouse all the old fears of monarchical centralization. Hamilton met it by saying that the proposed government would have precisely the same authority without such a clause. Supremacy was implied in the act of creating any government at all. He insisted, again, that the power to do a thing implied the power to employ the means necessary for its doing. Laying a tax, for instance, implied the ability to make laws for that purpose; and the same was true of all the other powers. This should not be a cause for fear; supremacy was declared only for "laws made pursuant to the Constitution," not for any others and not, especially, for those reserved to the states.

There followed a further defense of concurrent sovereignty. This departure in the proposed Constitution was hard to accept, even by those who were well disposed. How could two governments operate in the same jurisdiction? Hamilton pointed out that actually their spheres were not identical; there were two, carefully distinguished, and neither interfered with the other. What was consigned to the federal government was specified; what had been left to the states was all the rest. They would lose nothing. It could even be guessed that the central government was the more likely to be restricted in future because so many of its powers had yet to be determined and those of the states already existed.

Another sensitive subject in many minds was security. On this the Anti-Federalists were in a weak position, and Hamilton spoke at length about it, enlarging on Jay's earlier warnings. There were incursions being made with frightening frequency on all the borders. No single state could successfully resist if there should be a determined effort to take away some part—or all—of its territory. The British, especially, were paying scant attention to the terms of the recent peace treaty and would feel no need to do so until the Union could protect its borders with armed forces. Also, if American rights were being violated on land, it was even worse at sea. The commerce of the seaboard cities was constantly being harassed, and nothing would stop it but the organization of a national navy.

Then, too, there were internal weaknesses. These had been shockingly revealed only recently when Shays had led his nearly successful rebellion against the authorities in Massachusetts. The gathering of a militia to suppress this disorder had been slow and almost too late. If property owners feared the invasion of their holdings and the forcing on them of paper money in payment of debts, they would risk the recurrence of these humiliations unless a central government possessed adequate means for prevention.

This carried the number of papers to 36, and to their publication in book form in March 1788. So far, the government proposed to be established had not been discussed in detail. First priority had been the defusing of the Anti-Federalists' attacks and the awakening of common fears that government had practically ceased to operate. It had been insisted that the nation was in jeopardy, and that Union was the only alternative to the dissolution that seemed to impend. The arguments of those who feared for the sovereignty of the states had been met by pointing out that the proposed Constitution gave the Union strictly limited powers yet would furnish the protection needed against threats from abroad and within.

It was now the end of winter; the important ratification conventions in New York and Virginia were still to be held, and controversy continued. The Clintonians in New York were still contentious. In Virginia the situation appeared to be deteriorating as Henry, Mason, and Lee intensified their attacks. Because of this, Madison was persuaded that he must go home. He would be the best prepared of the three to explain and defend the organization proposed for the federal government with its tripartite form, its complicated checks, and its assignment of responsibilities. His leaving New York was a serious loss, but before he left he made a beginning. Hamilton had only to finish what had been so well begun.

5. Madison on government

The papers written at this juncture were, in effect, answers to the continuing deluge of Anti-Federalist pamphlets and editorials picturing the Constitution in fearsome terms. There had been some ratifications. Pennsylvania had finished its work early; so had Connecticut and Georgia. Massachusetts would ratify in February after a stormy meeting and a close vote. New York and Virginia were the real battlegrounds, and their conventions would apparently be delayed until the summer.[11]

The proposed Constitution still had to be explained and its ratification argued for, on strictly practical grounds and in some detail. The general need for Union and the disasters likely to follow from continued separateness having been demonstrated, it must now be shown that the delegates in Philadelphia had put together a workable system of government.

Madison was convinced that they had; he conceded, however, that this result had not been reached easily. Some differences had had to be compromised. These settlements, although deplored alike by those who were convinced that a stronger central government was needed and those who would have made it weaker, had fortunately in the end added to rather than subtracted from practicality. It was these agreements that would allow the states to go on much as they had been. The Union government of limited purposes would simply be superimposed. It was indeed a compound, but it was entirely suitable for the American situation.

In the convention, it was admitted, there had been difficulties caused by a certain indistinctness about the object to be attained, and certain apparently contradictory objectives had had to be considered. To create a "more perfect union" was, after all, an ambiguous directive, and some delegates had stubbornly defended the autonomy of the states. There had been few relevant lessons from the past, because never before had there been a large government with energy and stability that did not threaten the free carrying on of ordinary affairs. Energy seemed to demand that power should be lodged in a few individuals and for a considerable length of time. Liberty demanded that those entrusted with power should be numerous and should have short periods in office.

Madison admitted that this had not been the only difficulty. New provisions were suggested and had had to be assessed. Some had been adopted and some rejected. No one skilled in the science of government had defined with sufficient clarity its three divisions: legislative, executive, and judicial. There had been only vague definitions of all three "departments." Add to this the delicacy of arbitrating the conflict between delegates from the large and small states, and it was no wonder that there had been some deviations from the symmetry a theorist might have preferred.

That the convention had succeeded as well as it had in resolving these problems could only have been, Madison thought, because it enjoyed in a singular degree exemption from the pestilential influence of party animosities. Thus unencumbered, it had reached a conclusion satisfactory to all the deputations. They had finally acknowledged the necessity of sacrificing private opinions to the public good. That they had despaired of reaching any better result by delay or by suggesting further experiments, Madison acknowledged. Thus they had brought discussions to an end and let their conclusions stand.

The harmony to which Madison alluded was somewhat exaggerated. There had been some active delegates—Mason and Randolph, for instance—who had refused to sign, and other delegates had departed before the end. What followed was also a claim that should have been modified. This was that the convention had been different from other attempts to form satisfactory governments. Other constitutions, Madison said, had been imposed by dictators or small elites and had lacked the agreement of many minds. They had established what had been called republics, but this was an inexact name for the governments of Holland, Venice, Poland, or Britain. A republic, Madison asserted, must derive all its powers, directly or indirectly, from the great body of the people and be administered by persons holding their offices for a limited period or during good behavior. Madison's claim was that the convention had conformed to this criterion. What he omitted was an acknowledgment that the convention's delegates had been the elite of their respective states and that their representation of "the people" was actually representation of the small percentage who were voters. Some large percentage (perhaps 85 or 90) of adults were excluded from the electorate. The myopia of the Philadelphia framers and of Publius about so large a proportion of America's inhabitants would furnish later revisionists with an opening for the contention that the Constitution was indeed the product of a small propertied class and was shaped mainly to protect their interests. The historian Charles A. Beard would be prominent among these, but there would be others as well. If the authors of *The Federalist* had any prevision of such criticism, it was nowhere evident, and, in fact, it was not an issue in the controversies concerning ratification. The Anti-Federalists were not themselves concerned with a widened electorate.

Madison passed on to repeating what had been said before—that the government established by the Constitution would be in the pattern already set by the states, something its detractors still preferred to overlook. Much had been made by the Anti-Federalists of the devising, without authorization, of such a novel arrangement, but, he said, the more important question was whether the convention had done what it was charged to do by the Congress: establish a firm national system adequate to preserve the union and to govern. The delegates had indeed been told to amend the Articles of Confederation, but they had been told something further. This was that they might adopt *such further provisions as should appear to be necessary.* That this certainly absolved the convention of guilt for exceeding its terms of reference, Madison insisted. Nothing less than had been done would have reached the indicated objective.

These preliminaries disposed of, Madison examined two more important matters: whether the powers vested in the central government were excessive, and whether the distribution of powers among its departments was practical. The first would include the contention that undue limitations had been imposed on the states; the second would inquire whether the departments of government would possess the means of keeping each other in their proper places.[12]

The first of these questions, being prominent among the Anti-Federalists' arguments, continued to be considered through several essays. Objectors had concentrated on the provisions giving the federal government the ability to lay and collect taxes, duties, imposts, and excises; but, Madison said, these were to pay debts and provide for a common defense and the general welfare; they were therefore indispensable, and they must not be limited. He offered illustrations concerning the army, the navy, and the militia. It had already been pointed out that the need for these would always be fixed by the actions of others. Besides, intercourse with foreign nations had to be considered, including the making of treaties, the appointing of ambassadors, and the punishing of piracy and other offenses against the law of nations. Then there was the consideration that the border states must be prevented from interrupting commerce passing to the interior.

Madison went on to speak of the power "to coin money [and to] regulate the value thereof." This had been an important omission in the Articles of Confederation and was obviously necessary to union. The same could be said about uniform laws of bankruptcy and the maintenance of post-roads.

Certain other necessary powers were cataloged, ones it was convenient to label "miscellaneous." They included the promotion of science and the useful arts by patents and copyrights, exclusive jurisdiction over a federal district, the admission of new states, the punishment of treason, the assumption of debts, rules respecting possessions of the United States, and provisions for amendment. There were also several powers giving effect to others. There had been a good deal of locally voiced suspicion about these, but it was unwarranted. The Congress had merely been given the duty of making all laws necessary and proper for carrying into effect the powers already enumerated. Those who objected to such powers, Madison said, must consider the primary ones to have been improperly granted. He reiterated what had been said by Hamilton: it was a rule of law and of reason that a vital end legitimized the means for its attainment. Here again, the real question was not whether these provisions were necessary but whether the government should be capable of meeting unanticipated but likely exigencies.

As to the "supremacy clause," spoken of earlier, Madison insisted that, without such a provision, existing state constitutions would have made the new federal Constitution inoperative. Senators and representatives, members of state legislatures, and all other legislative and judicial officers would be essential in giving effect to the new system. They must be bound to its support.

This sequence of papers finished by questioning whether the states after all might not prove so strong that the Union would be undermined. They had immense advantages, the most important being that the federal government was a limited one, whereas their own powers were residual and so encompassed all ordinary activities. It even seemed probable that, although the federal government had been empowered to collect taxes, it might never do so since its power to do so was restricted to purposes largely having to do with security. There was also some reason to doubt whether it could rival the states in keeping popular support. In their current contentiousness, Madison said, objectors seemed to have overlooked one thing entirely: the different establishments were not rivals; both were controlled by a common superior—the people who had made the Constitution and could change it.

Once again Madison pointed out the advantages enjoyed by the states. The federal government would deal with matters that would seem remote. The states would have many more administrators with offices and emoluments, and the public would be more familiar with all their activities. They would be more able to command interest and affection. Even among federal congressmen, a local spirit would prevail. Measures would be decided by their effect not on the national interest but on the "prejudices, interests and pursuits of the governments and people of the individual states." It was possible that there might be little interest in national as opposed to local affairs, and congressmen, responsible only to local constituents, would always be mainly concerned with matters affecting them.

What Madison in this way offered as a virtue turned out to be fact, but actually it would be a persistent difficulty in the future. Congressmen would indeed concentrate on their constituents' demands. Madison did not perceive that in neither branch of the legislature were national interests the first concern of members. In a national government, this was a serious defect. The fact, as things were left, was that only the president had a national constituency, and this would be a frequent source of future contention between the president and the Congress.

6. The distribution of powers

If by this time the most voluble Anti-Federalists had not been silenced, they had at least abandoned their earlier contentions and had fallen back on less convincing claims that the functions of the states would be fatally impaired. There was a visible closing of ranks among the politicians who proposed to defeat the move for ratification whatever the merits of the argument for it. In both Virginia and New York, where decisions had yet to be made, the prospect continued to be discouraging. Because of this the essays were continued. Some of their most effective passages were still to come.

Madison, going on to more detailed description, was able to rely on the careful notes he had taken at the convention. He explained (in No. 47) his further intention:

> *Having reviewed the general form of the proposed government and the general mass of power allotted to it, I proceed to examine the particular structure . . . and the distribution of . . . power among its constituent parts.*[13]

He first examined an often-repeated criticism: the supposed violation of the political maxim that the legislative, executive, and judicial departments had not been made sufficiently separate and distinct. In the structure proposed, it was being said, no regard had been paid to this protection against despotism. If this were true, Madison said, it must be admitted to be "the very definition of tyranny." But he insisted that the charge could not be supported. For his political authority, he recurred to the originator of the precept of separated powers. It was well known that Montesquieu considered the British system to be the best of all governmental models, "the mirror of political liberty." Madison pointed out, however, that the three departments in that government were not totally separate and distinct as the Anti-Federalists implied. The British executive formed a part of the legislative branch; he alone, for instance, made treaties with other governments, and, when made, these had the force of legislative acts. All judges were appointed by him and gave him constitutional advice. One branch of the legislative was counsel to the executive and, as well, the supreme appellate court. The judges, again, were intimately connected with the legislature.

It was apparent from this interdependence, Madison argued, that Montesquieu had not meant by separation that the departments should have no *partial agency in*, or no *control over*, the acts of each other. He had meant, rather, that "if the *whole* power of one department should be held by the same hands that held the *whole* power of another, the principles of freedom would be subverted."

> "*. . . When the legislative and executive powers are united in the same person or body, there can be no liberty, because apprehensions may arise lest* the same *monarch or senate should* enact *tyrannical laws [and]* execute *them in a tyrannical manner.*"
>
> *Again:*
>
> "*Were the power of judging joined with the legislative, the life and liberty of the subject would be exposed to arbitrary control, for* the judge *would then be* the legislator. *Were it joined to the executive power,* the judge *might behave with all the violence of* an oppressor."[14]

In the constitutions of the states, Madison reminded his readers, this judicious relationship among the departments had been uniformly recognized. Although there were differences among them, and although some had no specific declaration of adherence to the principle (as did that of

Massachusetts), all had separate departments and some sort of effect on each by the others. This would be as true of the new government.

If the arrangements in the proposed Constitution were carefully examined, Madison thought, it would be clear that the founders had never for a moment turned their eyes from the danger to liberty inherent in "the overgrown and all-grasping prerogative of ... an hereditary branch of the legislative authority." All legislators were to be elected and were to have limited terms of office. In truth, however, there had existed in America a tendency to allow the legislature more power than the other departments, and, if anything, it had been the worst offender in encroaching on the others. Madison did not expand on this point, but obviously his aspersions on legislatures were factual. The excesses had occurred in reaction to the arbitrariness of the British governors, who had been the executives of the colonies.

Madison admitted that the tendency of each department to reach farther than it should posed a difficulty. He recounted how Jefferson, who was a defender of the thesis that there ought to be no intermingling of departments, had in 1783 prepared a model constitution for adoption in Virginia. In it he had sought to solve the problem by providing that whenever any two of the three branches concurred, each by the voices of two-thirds, a convention should be called for altering the constitution or correcting breaches of it. Madison had immense respect for Jefferson, but he found this solution impractical. The way ought always to be kept open for such drastic actions on great and extraordinary occasions, but there were insuperable objections to such referenda in every instance of departmental reluctance to keep within constitutional limits.

One of these objections was the general one that frequent use of such means would disturb public confidence in the government. Constitutional changes had usually taken place in times of universal indignation, not when smaller matters were in question, and this was as it should be. There was, however, a stronger objection to frequent popular voting. The certain result would be to strengthen the legislative department, already stronger than was healthy. This would come about because the other departments would have fewer advocates, and because the legislators would most likely be the judges of their own conduct. The result in the long run would be serious disequilibrium.

After consideration of all suggestions for exterior solutions, the conclusion had been, Madison said, that there was only one reasonable alternative. This was the partition of powers in such a way that the several constituent parts of the government would, by their mutual relations, be the means of keeping each other in check. That, he said, accounted for the omission of a bill of rights such as some state constitutions had. Such a listing of freedoms was not needed.

Madison was deflected at this point to argue that the "departments" should be "so constituted that the members of each should have as little agency as possible in the appointment of the members of the others." Rigorously applied, this would require that the most important officials should come from "the same fountain of authority." This, of course, was the electorate. Such an arrangement would be expensive and, for the judiciary, awkward, because of necessary qualifications; nevertheless, the principle should hold. Members of each department should at least be "as little dependent as possible on ... the others for the emoluments annexed to their offices." And, Madison added, there existed, beyond this, an even more useful precaution. Each department had been given the constitutional means, and its members would also have personal reasons, for resisting encroachments. Opposition and rivalry would supply the lack of better motives.

Something more had had to be thought of, however, in a tripartite arrangement. In a republic the legislature predominated; therefore, it must be divided, by different modes of election and by different principles of action, each half as little connected as possible with the other. This would reduce somewhat the weight of legislative authority; each house would establish a watch on the other.

The executive would be comparatively weak and ought to be fortified, Madison went on. In theory, this could be done by allowing the executive an absolute veto on legislation, but that would be neither altogether wise nor alone sufficient. On ordinary occasions such a veto might not be exerted firmly enough, and on extraordinary ones it might be "perfidiously abused." For an absolute negative, there could be substituted

> some qualified connection between this weaker department and the weaker branch of the stronger department, by which the latter may be led to support the constitutional rights of the former, without being too much detached from the rights of its own department.[15]

If this now seems an intricate and subtle argument for the checks on each branch by each of the others, as they were formulated in the discussions at Philadelphia, it must be said for Madison that it was actually how the devising had been done. Carefully considered, it constituted a reasonable explanation of the arrangements which had been made giving the executive a qualified veto and the Senate a part in appointments through the proceedings of confirmation. And, as Madison went on to point out, there was a further check in the special character of the system the framers had proposed. For in such a compound republic there would be two distinct governments exercising control over each other. This constituted a double protection for the rights of the people. "The different governments," Madison said, "will control each other, at the same time that each will be controlled by itself."

The separation of the branches and the checks of each on the other seemed so important in the constitutional structure that it would be pursued through a further succession of essays. It was, in fact, presented as the second of the two foundation principles the framers had depended on—the other being the federal arrangement for the states and the nation.

It must be said that Madison was not altogether convincing in arguing that the opposing checks were the best that might have been contrived. For one thing, it could not be denied that the Constitution was deficient in enumerating the powers assigned to the president and the judiciary. It did actually appear, as opponents were saying, that these two branches were too sketchily outlined. The presidency was a real novelty. The office was meant to supply the authority lacking in the Articles of Confederation. Yet the executive could not be modeled on the British king; the experience with that monarchy was both too bitter and too recent. Besides, it seemed to have been agreed that the president's powers should be limited to actually executing the laws—"faithfully" the draft said—and apparently he was not to be a determiner of policy beyond giving the Congress the benefit of his advice "from time to time." This was an unrealistic assumption if, indeed, he was to supply the "energy" so much emphasized by the authors.

The lack of enumeration for the duties of the president was in conspicuous contrast with the specifications listed for congressional responsibilities. The president was not a mere figurehead, because he was to have the "executive power"; but what was it? He had a conditional veto—that is, one the Congress could override—and he was to appoint officials, but, again, with a severe limitation represented by the Senate's power to confirm. It was an incomplete description of duties.

As to the Supreme Court, it had the "judicial power," but its jurisdiction could be determined by the legislature; it was to entertain cases "arising under [the] Constitution," but what was it to do about their disposition if they should involve the powers of the other—supposedly independent—branches? These were omissions that the collaborators must have known were serious. We are reminded again by this that throughout the essays admissions of weakness were avoided unless they had been challenged by the critics. The purpose was to expound in order to persuade.

Throughout these descriptive papers, it must be noted, Publius's argument rested on a theoretical base that even opponents would not be likely to question. Officials, like individuals in other pursuits, could be expected to be diligent in pursuing their own interests, and the liberty of the subject was almost entirely dependent on such a dispersal of these interests that each would have active rivals. In this way, none could accumulate enough power to endanger the others. Adam Smith had elaborated the same view in *The Wealth of Nations** (read, apparently, by all those involved in the current discussions). He had said, it will be recalled, that the butcher, the baker, and so on, each pursuing his own interest, would in the end promote that of the public.

---

* *GBWW*, Vol. 39.

It was pointed out that this conception of motive, and the assumption that officials dispensing power would be governed by it, had been relied on when the system of checks and balances was being devised; and the authors had no difficulty with its exposition. What they did have difficulty with was the demonstration that the checks on the uses of power by each were not likely to weaken the government—to reduce the "energy" they had contended was so important. As they went on to speak of the departments in detail, they had to show that separation in the Constitution was a practical arrangement. Madison would first defend the operational logic of having three departments,[16] and Hamilton would return to the "energy" problem in a later essay.

7. The legislature

The next ten papers (52 to 61) were concerned with the proposed House of Representatives. They discussed its numbers, the relation of its members to their constituents, its general sympathies, its future enlargement, and the effect of its partial control over its own election procedures.

Some misconceptions were easily dismissed. One was that the size of the House would not reflect the country's growth. This was quite wrong. There was provision for expansion; it was to be determined by decennial censuses. The House, according to the agreed-upon formula, could be expected to grow from sixty-five members at the beginning to two hundred in twenty-five years, and to four hundred members in fifty years.

There were other objections with more substance. One of these had to do with the members' terms. A popular observation was recalled to the effect that "where annual elections end, tyranny begins." This, said Madison, was one of those reasonable general conclusions so often extended beyond their specific applicability. Only one ground for complaint really existed: that divisions of time—such as a year—had been adopted for no better reason than convenience. Actually, among the various states there were legislatures with terms varying from six months to two years without any noticeable difference in efficiency.

This was not so important as the qualifications established for the electors and for the elected, Madison thought. Those for the electors were to be the same as for "the most numerous branch of the state legislature." This was fundamental to representative government. It could not be left open to occasional regulation by the states. Still, to have established one uniform rule would have offended them. The best alternative that seemed open had been chosen. As for the candidates, the arrangement that they would have to be twenty-five years of age, to have been a citizen for five years, and to be, also, inhabitants of their state, Madison regarded as reasonable.

There were larger considerations. It often seemed to be forgotten that in the American system, the existence of a written constitution would have its own significance. In a government where the legislature could, by a simple act, change the most important laws, as in England, more frequent elections were needed to keep the lawmakers close to their constituents; but where a constitution, made by the people, governed even the government, this was not necessary.

As to the further question whether biennial elections rather than annual ones were best, the answer was that every legislator should add to sound judgment a knowledge of the subject he might have to pass on. This was the reason for the rule that his term ought to "bear some proportion to the extent of practical knowledge requisite to the due performance of the service." It was noted that there was an important difference between state legislators and federal ones. National lawmakers needed to know something of foreign relations and other issues requiring wider experience than could be gained in one year. There was also the inconvenience of travel to a capital in so large a Union; this made longer terms more convenient.

A more serious charge made by critics had to do with the general makeup of the House, whose members, it was said, would have little sympathy for the mass of the people and would "be most likely to aim at an ambitious sacrifice of the many to the aggrandisement of the few." Of all the possible objections, this seemed to Madison the most extraordinary. It went, he said, to the very heart of republicanism. The aim of every constitution—recalling its function as a law above any laws the legislators might make—was to obtain as rulers those who would possess the most wisdom and the most virtue. It ought also to provide proper precautions for keeping them virtuous. For these purposes the elective mode of choosing was essential. The means for maintaining virtue were various, but the most effective was the need to be reelected.

Keeping these requirements in mind, what in the arrangement for the House of Representatives violated sound principles? What, in the proposal, favored "the elevation of the few on the ruins of the many"? Think, Madison said, of the way provided for choosing the representatives. The great body of the people was to elect them, the same ones who exercised the right in every American state. They were not the rich more than the poor, not the learned more than the ignorant, not the "haughty heirs of distinguished names, more than the humble sons of obscurity and unpropitious fortune."

It was not mentioned that there had been a good deal of argument in the convention about this. The provision that qualifications should conform to those of "the most numerous branch of the state legislature" had been a way of assuaging the fears of those who recalled Shays's Rebellion and other manifestations of disgruntlement among debtors and laborers. Especially, recourse to cheapened money was feared if debtors should gain control of the lawmaking processes. It must be kept in mind that the authors had to reassure the prosperous, who had the fears natural to their class, and at the same time to show that the provisions for election were fair to all. Those selected as legislators, the papers contended, would be the wisest that could be found, since they would be freely chosen by their fellow citizens. They would enter into public service under circumstances certain to produce "affection" for their constituents. "There is," said Madison, "in every breast a sensibility to marks of honour, of favour, of esteem," and this would be a "pledge for grateful and benevolent returns." There was, moreover, a third reason for trusting those who would be selected: they would be attached to a form of government favoring their pretensions and giving them honor and distinction. So pride and vanity would reinforce nobler motives.

This was not all. There would, in addition, be the restraint of frequent elections. This would cause representatives to be reminded "habitually" of their dependence on the voters. Also, it had to be recalled that they could make no law that would not have full operation on themselves and their friends as well as on others.

One of the most eloquent paragraphs in the papers supported these assertions:

> Such will be the relation between the House of Representatives and their constituents. Duty, gratitude, interest, ambition itself, are the chords by which they will be bound to fidelity and sympathy with the great mass of the people. It is possible that these may all be insufficient to control the caprice and wickedness of man. But are they not all that government will admit, and that human prudence can devise? Are they not the genuine and the characteristic means by which republican government provides for the liberty and happiness of the people? . . . What are we to say to the men who profess the most flaming zeal for republican government, yet boldly impeach the fundamental principle of it; who pretend to be champions for the right and the capacity of the people to choose their own rulers, yet maintain that they will prefer those only who will immediately and infallibly betray the trust committed to them?[17]

It was shortly after this point in the series that requests for Madison's return became urgent. He was needed to counter the influence of Virginia's famous orators in the approaching decision about ratification. The Senate, the executive, and the judiciary still remained to be described. Before leaving, Madison had time to write Nos. 62 and 63, arguing that a second chamber was a safeguard against sudden passions likely to affect the larger assembly. Then Jay wrote one essay on the Senate's involvement in foreign relations and, specifically, the usefulness of its approval of treaties negotiated by the president. Hamilton wrote the rest.

The Senate, Madison said, should be considered under five heads. These were: (1) the qualification of its members, (2) their appointment by the state legislatures, (3) equality of representation in the body, (4) the number and terms of their service, and (5) its powers.

He at once made the admission that the second chamber owed its existence to a compromise between the delegates from the small states and those from the larger ones. Delegates from New Jersey, Delaware, and Connecticut had been much afraid that if membership in the federal legislature should be based on population alone it would leave them severely restricted in all matters of national interest. They had presented, after several weeks, the Paterson (or New Jersey) plan. This was offered as an alternative to the Virginia Plan, until then accepted as the center of discussion, and compromise had had to be found before the meeting could proceed.

The suggestion, quickly adopted, that there should be a Senate with equal representation from all the states, had served to conciliate the rebellious delegates. Madison made no attempt now to excuse what had been done. He did, however, find some good in the arrangement. It appeared, he said, that in a republic having both a national and a federal character there ought to be a mixture of proportional and equal representation. He acknowledged that it was superfluous to judge, by theoretical standards, something allowed by "all hands to be the result ... of a spirit of amity" — in other words, compromise. The kind of arrangement the larger states would have preferred was not likely to be conceded; their only option had been to accept the "advice of prudence," and "instead of indulging a fruitless anticipation of the possible mischiefs, ... to contemplate rather the advantageous consequences" which might qualify the sacrifice. So they had made the best of a difficult situation.

It could at least be said that the Senate was a recognition of the sovereignty remaining to the individual states. This had not wholly displeased even the delegates from the larger states. They had no wish to see a consolidation into one republic, or most of them did not. Also, there were certain advantages in a second house. For instance, it would furnish an impediment to impetuous acts of the representatives. Actually, since the "facility and excess" of lawmaking seemed to be the diseases governments were most liable to, this arrangement might prove to be more desirable in practice than appeared at first.

Another deficiency the Senate might supply, said Madison, obviously looking hard for justification, was the wider knowledge and greater caution so clearly needed in a republic. Many recent national embarrassments had resulted from blunders. "What indeed," he asked, "are all the repealing, explaining, and amending laws, which fill and disgrace our voluminous codes, but so many monuments of deficient wisdom?" Senators would be more stable than representatives because of their longer terms and older ages. So the calamitous effect of "a mutable policy" would be less. This sacrificed the respect of other nations and, as well, "poisons the blessing of liberty itself" by producing such incoherent legislation that citizens were unable to understand it. Besides, instability had other deplorable consequences. It was responsible for a want of confidence in government, and this damped every undertaking. No "great improvement or laudable enterprise can go forward which requires the auspices of a steady system of national policy."

This thought led to a whole paper devoted to the usefulness of a Senate in creating a "sense of national character," something that could never be furnished by the representatives. Several examples from antiquity were cited; each of them seemed an obvious warning that there could be abuses of liberty as well as abuses of power. Excessive liberties were more to be feared in America than arbitrary authority. The Senate, some said, might become an aloof and aristocratic body, but it could not do that, Madison said, and still retain the support of the people.

Jay at this point supported Madison in a paper extending the argument. He enlarged on the usefulness to the president, in negotiating treaties, of the advice and consent provided in the Constitution. The provision would allow the president to convene the senators at any time if he should need their advice. Moreover, when the process was complete, the consent of a peculiarly well-adapted body would be helpful, one elected for terms long enough to become acquainted with the complicated issues of foreign relations but not all elected at once, so that continuity could be preserved.

Jay recognized that there were those who objected to treaties being given the force of law, since laws ought only to be made by legislatures; the answer to this was that it was nothing new. Critics seemed to forget that the judgments of the courts, and the commissions given to governors, were as binding on those they affected as laws passed by the state legislatures. "All constitutional acts of power," Jay reminded the critics, "whether in the executive or in the judicial department, have as much legal validity" as legislative acts. That the making of laws had been consigned to legislatures did not entitle such bodies to perform every other act of sovereignty affecting citizens.

Jay having disposed of this subject, Hamilton followed with a discussion of impeachment. The Constitution provided (in Article Two, Section 4) that:

> *The President, Vice-President, and all civil officers of the United States shall be removed from office on impeachment for and conviction of treason, bribery, or other high crimes and misdemeanors.*[18]

Also (in Article One, Section 2) that:

> *The House of Representatives . . . shall have the sole power of impeachment.*[19]

And (in Article One, Section 3) that:

> *The Senate shall have the sole power to try all impeachments. When sitting for that purpose, they shall be on oath or affirmation. When the President of the United States is tried, the Chief Justice shall preside: and no person shall be convicted without the concurrence of two-thirds of the members present.*[20]

These were not precise directives, but clearly impeachment was a judicial function, not a legislative one. Purists who objected to this breach of the separation principle were reminded that there had never been an instance of total separation of governmental function and that there was ample reason why there should not be. Where else than in the legislature could impeachment be lodged? In the Supreme Court? The judges would never find the fortitude to withstand the pressures of such a task; anyway, it was obviously necessary that there should be a more numerous trial body than the Court. The nature of the proceeding dictated not only this but also the need of more latitude than a Court could allow itself. There would be no jury to stand between judges and defendant. Also the conviction was not to end the matter. A subsequent trial of the convicted offenders in ordinary criminal proceedings might follow. Separation had its reasons, but on occasion, such as impeachment, it had to be interpreted sensibly.

Hamilton neglected to note, if indeed it occurred to him, that this check was the only one of the system that was absolute. Presidential vetoes could be overcome by two-thirds vote in the legislature, and there could be substitutes for unconfirmed presidential appointees, but a chief executive deprived of office would be a reversal of the voters' judgment. Actually, the provision was so drastic that it would seldom be used, and then mostly for judges. How far it went as a deterrent was something impossible to determine, but it was meant to be a constant reminder that powers were not to be abused. Obviously, Hamilton thought it important. Several essays were principally devoted to its position in the interbranch scheme. He stated the intention: The Court provided by the Senate was to try "those offences which proceed from the misconduct of public men. . . . they relate chiefly to injuries done immediately to the society itself." They would "seldom fail to agitate the passions of the whole community, and to divide it into parties." For this reason, the proceedings must be impartial.

He went on to ask what the true spirit of the institution was. "Is it not designed as a method of *national inquest* into the conduct of public men?" If so, "who can so properly be the inquisitors for the nation as the representatives of the nation themselves?"

Hamilton saw the process not as a criminal trial. There was no punishment involved. The official was being removed from office because he had failed to meet the high standard of public responsibility.

8. The executive

The situation of the legislature having been analyzed in suitable detail, Hamilton, now alone, went on to the other departments—first the executive. Eleven papers were devoted to the subject, and they have the added interest that this, more than any other part of the proposed Constitution,

had been disapproved by the author who was now defending it. A long
and impassioned plea he had made at the opening of the recent convention for the establishment of an executive with powers and immunities
similar in most respects to those of the king of England was inconsistent
with the argument of these papers. But Hamilton seemed to have been
converted to the belief that the presidency envisioned by the Constitution
might serve the same purpose as a limited monarchy. Before the meeting
in Philadelphia, he may have been no more familiar with the possibilities
in the separation principle than other delegates. Now he was convinced—
or if he was not, he seemed to be—that the executive power as proposed
was adequate.

One of his persuasive passages compared the situation of the president
with that of a king. In it Hamilton said flatly that the Constitution's chief
executive was better suited to the American condition. He would be
elected—and for a term—whereas kings held hereditary positions for life.
The president would have no more than a conditional veto power over
legislation, and that of a king would be absolute (in Britain it no longer
really was, but this was glossed over). Then too the president could be
impeached, and afterward, if convicted, he could be tried like any other
citizen. These were notable advantages.

The office, said Hamilton, was being misrepresented by those who insisted that it copied the British monarchy. They had not hesitated to use
"resources even from the regions of fiction." A magistrate who was in fact
much like the governor of New York state had been magnified into a royal
figure. As Hamilton pursued this thought, it seemed to him more and
more perfidious. (The author he was answering here is known now, and
was doubtless known then, to have been Governor Clinton himself.)
Hamilton's indignation elicited a passage notable for rhetorical irony:

> *He [the president] has been decorated with attributes superior in dignity and
> splendour to those of a king of Great Britain. He has been shown to us with the
> diadem sparkling on his brow and the imperial purple flowing in his train. He
> has been seated on a throne surrounded with minions and mistresses, giving
> audience to the envoys of foreign potentates, in all the supercilious pomp of
> majesty. The image of Asiatic despotism and voluptuousness have scarcely been
> wanting to crown the exaggerated scene. We have been taught to tremble at the
> terrific visages of murdering janizaries, and to blush at the unveiled mysteries
> of a future seraglio.*[21]

Elaborate indignation was directed at those in particular who misrepresented the power ascribed to the president of filling vacancies in the Senate. Through several pages of description, Hamilton cited clauses demonstrating that presidents would have no such authority; that, indeed,
vacancies were to be filled by state governors or by elections. He ended by

asking "whether language can furnish epithets of too much asperity for so shameless ... an attempt to impose on the citizens of America."

Clinton thus having been rebuked, the oratorical style was abandoned in favor of more restrained language. But Hamilton faced further difficulties. Hesitations and reconsiderations had been evident at the convention. No such office as the presidency had existed anywhere before. Comparison with the governorship of a state was not very accurate, if less misleading than the example of a king conjured up by opponents. The intention had been to supply the authority missing in the Articles of Confederation without too strongly suggesting the monarchy repudiated by the recent rebellion. One summer had not been enough to bring the office into focus and satisfy those who had doubts of one kind or another. There had been ready agreement that one individual was preferable to a collegium, but there were difficulties about the term and the selection process, as well as the allotted powers. These uncertainties were not apparent in Hamilton's defense.

He first described the election procedure. It was praised for removing the candidate from immediate contact with those who would be his constituents and entrusting the choice to citizens who were not officeholders of any kind. Such electors would be more apt to choose someone who was wise and virtuous. The point was made, too, that such electors would be only transiently involved. Moreover, they would meet in their respective states and so be free from all "byass." It was, indeed, "a moral certainty that the office of President will never fall to the lot of any man who is not in an eminent degree endowed with the requisite qualifications."

Hamilton returned now to the "energy" he had spoken of in earlier papers as so essential. The president, he said, would supply it. Its components were: (1) unity, (2) duration, (3) adequate support, and (4) competent powers. These Hamilton proceeded to describe.

Unity, he contended, was to be found only in a single executive. There were many who thought that one person might accumulate despotic powers without great difficulty. Actually, if responsibility had been dispersed among several officers with equal powers, the danger of arbitrariness would not have been reduced; the capacity of men for jealousy and rivalry being what it was, there would always be contention and confusion. Many examples from history showed this all too clearly. Even in New York State, where, in one function—appointments to office—a council had replaced the governor, the results had been notoriously bad. When the choices had proved especially irresponsible, the council had blamed the governor and the governor had blamed the council, and everyone had escaped responsibility. One individual must be given clear duties; then he would be answerable for his decisions.

This constituted a brief recapitulation of recurring discussions at the convention, but doubtless it seemed so obvious to Hamilton that it needed little elaboration. It was for the legislature to deliberate; it could do nothing else since it was composed of many members. An executive, however, had to administer affairs and must be allowed the freedom necessary to do so with dispatch and without divided counsels or undue delays.

The second requisite for the executive was duration in office. To personal firmness there must be added security. This would be impossible with a precarious tenure. The principle of separation was involved, too. It was one thing for the executive to be governed by a constitution and quite another to be subordinate to a changing legislature or to the judiciary. The tendency in republics for the legislature to absorb all other agencies being almost irresistible, this subordination would certainly happen unless prevented by checks to congressional aggressions.

It could not be proved that the four-year term decided on by the convention was exactly right to give the president confidence and a sense of responsibility to the electorate, but it seemed reasonable enough as a compromise. Anything less would cause interruptions in administration at such close intervals that chaos would result. The changes certain to occur when successors took office not only argued for a term of at least such length but for reeligibility as well. It might seem plausible at first to support the fixing of a term and then the excluding of the incumbent from further service, but this would certainly diminish the inducements to good behavior. There might even be more sinister results in corruption if an incumbent knew that his time in office was limited. Not inconceivably, also, he might be induced to attempt the prolongation of his power by conspiracy and the use of force. Besides, why should the people be deprived arbitrarily of a magistrate who had served well, and who had accumulated about himself an experienced administration?

The constitution-makers must be given credit, Hamilton said, for having acted wisely in fixing a moderate term and making incumbents reeligible, but more than this, they had furnished the third ingredient of energy by making the president indifferent to congressional pressures and reinforcing the principle of separation. For this purpose they had inserted clauses protecting his emoluments (in Article Two, Section 1):

> *The President shall, at stated times, receive for his services a compensation, which shall neither be increased nor diminished during the period for which he shall have been elected, and he shall not receive within that period any other emolument from the United States or any of them.*[22]

There remained a fourth ingredient of the executive office: competent powers. These Hamilton expounded in several short papers. Considering its subsequent importance the treatment accorded this subject seems scanty; still, it has to be recalled here as with other Federalist papers how different the circumstances were in 1788 from what they became very soon afterward. Then it should not be forgotten how complete the agreement was that Washington would be the first president. Consideration of the office was dominated by the supposition that he would in effect create it and would determine its style. Hamilton must have shared this expectation.

As to the provision making the president commander in chief, the propriety of the arrangement seemed so evident as to require no defense at all. Little more had to be said about the Senate's concurrence in treaties the president might negotiate. Jay had already defended this clause. However, the appointive powers needed at least some explanation. Hamilton quoted, and commented on, the relevant passage (Article One, Section 2). The president was:

> . . . *[to] nominate, and, by and with the advice and consent of the Senate, shall appoint ambassadors, other public ministers and consuls, judges of the Supreme Court, and all other officers of the United States, whose appointments are not herein otherwise provided for, and which shall be established by law; but the Congress may by law vest the appointment of such inferior officers, as they think proper, in the President alone, in the courts of law, or in the heads of departments.*
>
> *The President shall have power to fill up all vacancies that may happen during the recess of the Senate, by granting commissions which shall expire at the end of their next session.*[23]

It is notable that the ambiguities in this article were not mentioned. There is, for instance, an apparent difference between appointing and nominating. Nominating calls for confirmation; appointment does not. Also, Hamilton was vague about the presidential establishment. Early in Washington's presidency the Congress would by law set up the president's organization for administration. The power to do this was not granted explicitly. It was an implication that, like others, would remain a cause of controversy among the branches.

It remained to assert that confirmation of nominations by the Senate would assist in stabilization. Hamilton advanced several reasons for this. It would reduce the likelihood that the president might surround himself with personal adherents; also, a second scrutiny for nominees would increase the care used in nominating them. Hamilton avoided the question whether even minor officials could be made subject to confirmation if the Congress so desired. Incidentally he seemed to feel that the Senate would need to concur in dismissals as well as appointments, another omission that caused trouble at the beginning of the new government's operations.

The discussion was ended without mention of such inadequacies. One likely reason for this has been mentioned—the probability that Washington would be the first incumbent and would create the traditions of the office. To an extent this expectation was fulfilled, but Washington was troubled by uncertain assignments and avoided quarreling with Congress only by reluctantly allowing invasions of what he considered to be his prerogatives.

Hamilton, as secretary of the treasury, was involved in certain of these later controversies, and his omission of any reference in *The Federalist* to possible difficulties can be taken as a glossing over of the Constitution's inadequacies. Still, it must be said that anticipation of all the difficulties likely to be encountered by the newly created president would have required more remarkable foresight than could have been expected of anyone, even a future Cabinet member.

9. The judiciary

The remaining papers (from 78 to 85) were all published together in the second compendium volume in May 1788, when the ratification disputes in New York and Virginia were at their most heated.[24] In New York, particularly, where Hamilton was most concerned, the apparent drift was toward rejection. Virginia's convention, already under way, would be the more crucial, since, with a victory there, the necessary nine states would have ratified. New York, however, would still be important; a Union without that state would be unthinkable.

The scheme of the papers, which called for describing and defending the organization of each of the proposed government's three branches, was yet to be completed. The next six essays were devoted to the judiciary. In them the theory of implied powers was restated, but Hamilton seems to have felt less need to defend the judiciary than the other branches. These were, after all, the last papers in the long series, and by then Hamilton may have said most of what he had meant to say. Perhaps, also, he was diverted to other work in support of ratification. Active organization was now becoming necessary. He had been selected as a delegate to the forthcoming New York convention and was much concerned in its preliminaries. Discussion of the judiciary had been anticipated back in December when, in No. 22, the authors had been deploring the existing government's ineffectiveness. In that essay it had been pointed out that laws were "a dead letter without courts to expound and define their true meaning." Treaties had furnished an illustration: they would have no force at all unless they were uniformly interpreted, and this uniformity could only be reached by having one tribunal for the purpose. If the question were left to the state courts, there would be as many interpretations as there were states. On this score alone, all nations had found it necessary to establish a paramount tribunal, Hamilton pointed out—"possessing a general superintendence, and authorised to settle and declare in the last resort a uniform rule of civil justice."

Hamilton now particularized the earlier remarks which had been offered concerning the need for a Supreme Court. He began by describing what confusion there would be if none should be provided, then went on to say that there could be no question about the propriety of such an institution in the abstract; all agreed about that, but it might be necessary to answer questions concerning its makeup and the extent of its authority.

He found the proposal adequate. On the method of appointing judges he did not linger. It was the same as for other officers of the Union, fully discussed in earlier essays. As to tenure, this was more complicated. The Constitution provided that they were to hold office "during good behavior." This had been questioned, but since such an arrangement was so usual the doubts could be regarded as symptoms only of the general opposition among the Anti-Federalists. Anyone must perceive that in a government of separated powers the judiciary would be the weakest. It could never attack, with any hope of success, either of the other branches; consequently, it ought to have any protection likely to assist in maintaining its independent position. For this purpose nothing would be so effective as permanency in office.

There followed further elaboration of the theory advanced earlier, that the court would be the protector of the Constitution. There were specified limitations on the powers of the legislature, Hamilton said, citing the exclusion of bills of attainder and *ex post facto* laws, and these prohibitions could not be preserved in practice unless it was done by the court "whose duty it must be to declare all acts contrary to the manifest tenor of the Constitution void." Sensing that this might be taken as a claim to judicial supremacy, Hamilton denied that because one authority could declare the acts of another void it must therefore be superior. What was superior in this case, he said, was "the people," who in a republic must be served by both the Congress and the Court. If the will of either department should stand in opposition to the will of the people, expressed in the Constitution, the people must prevail.

Because of its later importance, the argument here deserves a close reading;

> If it be said that the legislative body are themselves the constitutional judges of their own powers, and that the construction they put upon them is conclusive upon the other departments, it may be answered that this cannot be the natural presumption where it is not to be collected from any particular provisions in the Constitution. It is not otherwise to be supposed that the Constitution could intend to enable the representatives of the people to substitute their will to that of their constituents. It is far more rational to suppose that the courts were designed to be an intermediate body between the people and the legislature, in order, among other things, to keep the latter within the limits assigned to their authority. The interpretation of the laws is the proper and peculiar province of the courts. A constitution is, in fact, and must be regarded by the judges, as a fundamental law. It therefore belongs to them to ascertain its meaning, as well as the meaning of any particular act proceeding from the legislative body. If there should happen to be an irreconcilable variance between the two, that which has the superior obligation and validity ought, of course, to be preferred;

> *or, in other words, the Constitution ought to be preferred to the statute, the intention of the people to the intention of their agents.*[25]

This would support the decision written by Chief Justice Marshall fifteen years later establishing what, in spite of Hamilton's disclaimer, did become a claim to judicial supremacy.[26] For now, Hamilton could merely argue that from the duty of the judges to determine what the Constitution meant and whether legislative acts—and, although he did not say this, presidential actions—were in conflict with it, there followed the conclusion that judges should have the extraordinary protections of indefinite tenure and fixed provisions for their support, preferences not given to other officials.

As to the extent of the Court's jurisdiction, Hamilton maintained that the descriptive clauses in the Constitution placed this beyond argument. Cases that would come under the Court's authority were (1) those arising out of the laws passed by the Congress, (2) all those concerning the execution of provisions contained in the Constitution, (3) those to which the United States was a party, (4) those involving the peace of the confederacy —both those relating to foreign nations and those relating to conflicts among the states themselves, (5) those of admiralty or maritime jurisdiction, and (6) those in which the state tribunals could not be expected to be impartial. All these were properly covered by the principle that "every government ought to possess the means of executing its own provisions by its own authority."

Hamilton proceeded then to the difficult questions sure to arise concerning the position of the state courts. The federal judiciary had been carefully restricted to those causes manifestly proper for its cognizance. The highest court would have appellate jurisdiction both as to law and facts, but subject to any exceptions and regulations thought to be advisable. Hamilton recalled what had been established in an earlier paper (No. 33): The states would retain all preexisting authority not exclusively delegated to the federal government. In the state cases there would certainly be appeal to the Supreme Court, but this could hardly be objected to considering the restrictions laid down in the Constitution.

This last consideration had to do with the contention that there ought to have been a provision for trial by jury in civil cases. This, he argued, was something only omitted, not prohibited. The power to constitute courts obviously included the power to prescribe the proceedings, and the legislature could do as it liked about that. Hamilton went on at some length about this, evidently to answer the most serious of the objections then current among lawyers. It was a legal matter of little interest to others, and the argument was a lawyer's brief. Hamilton ended, however, by generally denying that the particular omission meant anything to those concerned with liberty. "The truth is," he said, "that the general *genius* of a government is all that can be substantially relied upon for permanent effects.

Particular provisions, though not altogether useless, have far less virtue and efficacy than are commonly ascribed to them."

10. Conclusion

The two final papers were used to meet a few remaining objections, such as the omission of a bill of rights, and to make a last defense of the Constitution as a whole.

As to the bill of rights, Hamilton followed the argument made earlier by Madison; none was needed because all the essential protections were implicit in the very structure of the government. By making it impossible for arbitrary authority to be lodged in any of the branches, the separate enumerations of rights had been made unnecessary. However, Hamilton pointed out, several specific clauses might be cited as indicating that

> Impeachment did not end an official's liability to trial for the offense he had committed.
>
> Writs of *habeas corpus* were to be suspended only in extreme conditions.
>
> No bills of attainder and no *ex post facto* laws could be passed.
>
> No title of nobility could be accepted, and no official could receive any grant or emolument from abroad.
>
> Trial for all crimes (except impeachment) must be by jury.

What was even more important, however, was the phrase "We, the people," at the very beginning. This indicated where sovereignty lay. It was "a better recognition of popular rights than volumes of those aphorisms which make the principal figure in several of our State bills of rights...." Besides, he went on, "a minute detail of particular rights is certainly far less applicable to a Constitution like that under consideration, which is merely intended to regulate the general political interests of the nation, than to a constitution which has the regulation of every species of personal and private concerns." Such specifications belonged in the constitutions of the states.

He would even go further, Hamilton said, and contend that such enumerations were dangerous as well as unnecessary. They would contain various exceptions to powers not granted and so would afford a pretext for claiming more than had been granted. Why prohibit the doing of things that there was no power to do? For instance, why should it be declared that the liberty of the press must not be restrained when no power was granted by which restriction might be imposed? Charging a government not to do what it was given no power to do was likely to afford the implication that restriction might sometime be imposed.

Hamilton also dealt with the objection that the seat of a Union government would be so far removed that it would escape the proper surveillance of its constituents. This, of course, was something of interest to citizens of so undeveloped a land as they now inhabited, but it could be foreseen that as roads, canals, and other means of communication appeared, distance would gradually be reduced in importance. Besides, the vigilance of the state politicians in protecting their interests could be relied on. There would certainly be rapid circulation of anything the federal government might plan that would affect their prerogatives.

This remark displayed, again, a prevailing view among the authors of the papers about human nature. It had been said or implied many times that self-interest could be depended on to be operative everywhere and always. Federal officials would be prevented from offending to any considerable extent simply because they would be closely watched by those who would be vigilant because naturally sensitive to any threat.

To two other recently appearing objections Hamilton obviously attached little importance. One was that no mention had been made of debts owing to the United States. Inflammatory "railings" had appeared in newspapers, he said, representing this lack as a relinquishment of those debts. To these he only answered by quoting authority: "States neither lose any of their rights, nor are discharged from any of their obligations, by a change in the form of their civil government."[27]

Finally, Hamilton dealt with the complaint that the new government would be needlessly expensive. This, he said, had been exaggerated. Much of what had been done by the states would now be done by the federal government—for instance, collecting customs duties—but also, state legislatures had been compelled to attend to much federal business and would now be relieved of it. New judges and a president would indeed be the cause of added expense, but it would not be considerable.

With these answers to minor objections Hamilton went on to his summary:

> *The additional securities to republican government, to liberty, and to property, to be derived from the adoption of the plan under consideration, consist chiefly in the restraints which the preservation of the Union will impose on local factions and insurrections, and on the ambition of powerful individuals in single States who may acquire credit and influence enough, from leaders and favourites, to become the despots of the people; in the diminution of the opportunities to foreign intrigue, which the dissolution of the Confederacy would invite and facilitate; in the prevention of extensive military establishments, which could not fail to grow out of wars between the States in a disunited situation; in the express guaranty of a republican form of government to each; in the absolute and universal exclusion of titles of nobility; and in the precautions against the repetition of those practices on the part of State governments which have undermined the foundations of property and credit, have planted mutual distrust in the breasts of all classes of citizens, and have occasioned an almost universal prostration of morals.*[28]

This was not quite the end. Hamilton reiterated his satisfaction with what had been proposed, saying that it was the best "our political situation, habits, and opinions" would allow. It was true that concessions of error or omission by friends of the plan had afforded its enemies small triumphs. It enabled them to ask why so imperfect a thing should be accepted and to demand prior amendment so that it would be nearer perfection before being irrevocably established. The answer to this, he repeated, was that it would prolong the precarious state of national affairs. It was chimerical to expect something perfect from imperfect man. All results of collective deliberations would be "a compound, as well of the errors and prejudices as of the good sense and wisdom, of the individuals of whom they are composed."

Hamilton then cited "an excellent little pamphlet lately published in this city" as showing the utter impracticability of assembling a new convention.[29] It was easily demonstrable that subsequent amendments would be far easier to obtain than previous ones. The moment any alteration in the plan was made, it would become for the purpose of adoption a new plan and would require conventions in thirteen states, whereas the adopted Constitution could be amended by the votes of nine.

There was more to this argument. It was perhaps precipitated by uneasiness about the ratification conventions in Virginia and New York. The Anti-Federalists were finding the argument for delay to be effective. Henry, Lee, and Mason in Virginia and the Clintonians in New York had by no means given up. They still hoped to defeat ratification.

As we know, the cause of Union succeeded in spite of these efforts, but only by close votes in both states. To this result Hamilton and Madison contributed mightily by their presence. Hamilton, especially, had been at his most effective during the proceedings in Poughkeepsie. He discovered that after all there were delegates who were open to his arguments concerning the dangers of drift and the usefulness of Union. Clinton was an experienced politician, and he held his upstate contingent in a tight grip. The delegates from the city, however, had more to lose. They were mostly business and professional men with substantial reasons for supporting the promise of order and security. It was these men who made up the final close majority for ratification.

The end sought by Publius's addresses to the people of New York was reached: the Union was established; the Constitution began its long regency.

11. Added comment

The year 1788 was an uncertain one for a nation struggling to be born. One effort, after the rebellion, had failed. There was a new endeavor to be defended. In some respects the proposed Constitution was not what any of the authors really wanted. Each in his own degree would have enlarged the authority of the Union and reduced that of the states. They might also have made a different arrangement of the mutual checks among the branches.

In particular, they must have deplored the ambiguity about "executive power," since this was the source of the "energy" they thought so important. The president was to make appointments "not herein otherwise provided for, and which shall be established by law." The clause continued: "but the Congress may by law vest the appointment of such inferior officers, as they think proper, in the President alone, in the courts of law, or in the heads of departments." The president's ability to gather an effective corps of administrators was thus limited. Not only might the Senate refuse confirmation of his nominees but the Congress might provide for appointments to be made by his subordinates. How, with these limitations, could the president "faithfully execute" the laws?

Actually Washington would have immediate problems caused by these constraints, and his successors would make administrative proposals with a wary eye on the legislature, always thinking first how politicians would react. It can hardly be imagined that Hamilton or Madison had agreed to these limitations on the executive without reservation. Many times they did deplore the contemporary preference for legislative supremacy and warn against its dangers, but nowhere in the papers were such objectionable clauses mentioned. Anxiety for ratification overcame a preference for candor.

Some deeper difficulties were ignored. Amendment of any substantive sort had been made almost impossible. This the authors did not mention, although they recognized that changes might be required. These had been left wholly to the legislative branch—state and federal. No change wanted by the executive or judiciary would be entertained without first considering whether it affected some prerogative of Congress or its individual members. There would be times of growth and change when for long intervals there would be no amendment at all.

Worst of all, there were certain clear contradictions. The call the papers made for a government with "energy" could hardly be achieved in a system one of whose chief characteristics was the effective checking of each branch by the others. Nor was there any recognition of the antagonisms hidden in concurrent sovereignty—the compound government the authors praised as the fortunate, if unexpected, result of compromise. Supporters of strict construction, contending that the powers of the central government must be kept to what was specifically enumerated, would carry on a long controversy with those who accepted the doctrine of expansible implied powers. This was stated clearly enough, but that its pursuit might in time erode many residual powers of the states was not admitted.

The authors accepted the implication that the Supreme Court might construe the Constitution to allow the use of any means necessary for carrying out assigned powers. This gave the Court the most decisive position in government. It could say what the Constitution meant. As matters turned out, these assignments of power, together with the uncertain implications following from them, made continually recurring conflict inevitable as the branches reached for the means to enhance their prerogatives.

If these future difficulties were not foreseen, it still has to be said that their essays did achieve the authors' first purpose. The nation was successfully reborn. They convinced their public that what had been done in Philadelphia offered a government much stronger than the existing one. It secured the Union. It offered no such threat to the states or to the liberties of the citizen as Anti-Federalists predicted.

That this could have been accomplished by three authors who wrote for newspapers with little planning or consultation and with almost no time for reflection or revision still seems remarkable. They could have produced a treatise destined to have a profound and lasting influence under such continuous pressure only because they were dedicated, learned, and competent.

Even though the exhausting efforts of the war for independence and the agonizing struggles within the colonies between loyalists and rebels had presumably come to a conclusion with the Treaty of Paris in 1783, acrimonies still remained. Since some popular leaders who had boycotted the convention were opposing the proposed Constitution with all their considerable talents, the authors were writing in a seething atmosphere of controversy. However much or little the essays contributed to ratification, they were at once recognized by contemporaries as an able defense of the unionist cause. Because Union prevailed, the essays have continued to be respected as the first, at least, if not the most complete, exposition of the principles and intentions of the framers. It is in that sense that as a collection they are quite properly spoken of as "classic."

All footnotes, unless otherwise indicated, refer to "The Federalist" papers or "The Constitution of the United States of America" as found in Volume 43 of *Great Books of the Western World*.

[1] Paper 1, p. 30d.

[2] Paper 4, p. 36a.

[3] Paper 5, p. 37c.

[4] Paper 5, p. 38d.

[5] Paper 10, p. 51d.

[6] Paper 10, p. 51d.

[7] Paper 10, p. 52c.

[8] At first this had not appeared likely, but newspapers in other cities were interested. The first seven essays appeared in the *Independent Journal* and were directed "to the people of New York," but a day or two later they were published in the *Pennsylvania Packet* and the *Daily Advertiser*. After thirty-six papers had been written, a collected volume was published by John and Archibald McLean. This appeared in March. Then on May 28 the rest of the essays appeared as *The Federalist, Volume Second*. Various other papers printed the essays in other cities. The sequence as well as the authorship has continued to be the subject of inquiry. Some references to this will be found in an addendum.

[9] Paper 31, p. 104b.

[10] This clause read: "This Constitution and the laws of the United States which shall be made in pursuance thereof and all treaties made, or which shall be made, under the authority of the United States, shall be the supreme law of the land; and the judges in every State shall be bound thereby, anything in the Constitution or laws of any State to the contrary notwithstanding" (p. 16d).

[11] A note concerning the ratification progression will be found appended to this essay.

[12] This, of course, was what came to be called "checks and balances."

[13] Paper 47, p. 153c.

[14] Paper 47, p. 154d.

[15] Paper 51, p. 163d.

[16] It will have been noticed that the authors used the word *departments* to describe what in later usage became *branches*.

[17] Paper 57, p. 178a.

[18] Constitution of the U.S.A., p. 15c.

[19] Constitution of the U.S.A., p. 11d.

[20] Constitution of the U.S.A., p. 12a.

[21] Paper 67, p. 203c.

[22] Constitution of the U.S.A., p. 15a.

[23] Constitution of the U.S.A., p. 15b.

[24] They were later published in various journals, but not until summer.

[25] Paper 78, p. 231a.

[26] In Marbury v. Madison, 1 Cranch 137 (1803).

[27] This authority was Rutherford's *Institutes*, relied on by all contemporary legal practitioners.

[28] Paper 85, p. 256b.

[29] This was the pamphlet referred to earlier, written by Jay because he had been unable to collaborate in the joint enterprise during the winter. It can be considered an extension of the series, arguing mostly against postponement in order to improve the proposal.

Chronology of Federalist Publication and Ratification

September 17, 1787	Constitutional Convention ends in Philadelphia.
September 28, 1787	Continental Congress votes to transmit the Constitution "to the several legislatures."
October 27, 1787	Hamilton, alarmed by opposition, publishes the first *Federalist Paper* in the *Independent Journal* (New York City semiweekly).
End of October 1787	Attempts to persuade Madison, Jay, Gouverneur Morris, and William Duer to join him. Morris refuses; Duer writes a few papers which are excluded for their inadequacy; Madison and Jay accept.
October 31, 1787– November 10, 1787	*Papers* 2–5. Jay writes of foreign dangers and the advantages of Union.

November 14–21, 1787 · *Papers* 6–8. Hamilton writes of domestic conflicts and of their amelioration under the new Constitution.
Paper 9 (Hamilton). Defends the Union as safeguard against faction and insurrection.

November 22, 1787 · *Paper* 10. Madison makes his first contribution. On the sources of faction and party: man is governed by passion and interest; men band together on the basis of such passions and interests, and especially on the basis of property interests. Madison demonstrates the efficacy of the republican form of government for controlling the excesses of faction and party.

November 24–28, 1787 · *Papers* 11–13 (Hamilton). A consideration of the advantage of Union for commerce and revenue.

November 30, 1787 · *Paper* 14 (Madison). Argues the advantages of republicanism over democracy.

December 1–5, 1787 · *Papers* 15–17 (Hamilton). Attacks the insufficiency of the present government.

December 7, 1787 · Delaware ratifies (the first state to do so).

December 7–11, 1787 · *Papers* 18–20 (Madison, with aid of Hamilton's notes). Discusses the defects and weaknesses of ancient and modern confederations.

December 12, 1787 · Pennsylvania ratifies.

December 12–14, 1787 · *Papers* 21–22 (Hamilton). Enlarges on defects of the present confederation.

December 18, 1787 · New Jersey ratifies.
Paper 23 (Hamilton). Argues the necessity of "energy" in government.

December 19, 1787–
January 9, 1788* · *Papers* 24–29 (Hamilton). Urges the necessity of a common defense and of national military strength.

---

* #29 in the first (McLean) edition of the *Papers* was actually #35 in the newspaper sequence. There were changes in the order of the next six papers as well.

December 28, 1787– January 8, 1788	*Papers* 30–36 (Hamilton). Discusses taxation and finance.
January 2, 1788	Georgia ratifies.
January 9, 1788	Connecticut ratifies.
January 11–12, 1788	*Papers* 37–38 (Madison). Discusses the convention's difficulties in devising a proper form for government.
January 16, 1788	*Paper* 39 (Madison). Praises the republican form of the proposed government.
January 18, 1788	*Paper* 40 (Madison). Defends the legitimacy of the Constitutional Convention.
January 19–29, 1788	*Papers* 41–46 (Madison). Discusses the powers of the proposed national government and those of the states.
January 30–February 6, 1788	*Papers* 47–51 (Madison). Discusses the structure, function, and purpose of the separated powers in the proposed government.
February 6, 1788	Massachusetts ratifies.
Early February 1788	Madison is urged by friends to return to Virginia to lead ratification forces there.
February 8–20, 1788	*Papers* 52–58 (Madison). Describes the proposed House of Representatives.
February 22–26, 1788	*Papers* 59–61 (Hamilton). Defends the Congress's regulation of its own elections.
February 27–March 1, 1788	*Papers* 62–63 (Madison). Describes the Senate.
March 4, 1788	Madison leaves for Virginia.
March 5, 1788	*Paper* 64 (Jay). Describes the Senate and foreign affairs.
March 7–8, 1788	*Papers* 65–66 (Hamilton). Defends the impeachment powers.
March 11–April 2, 1788	*Papers* 67–77 (Hamilton). Describes the executive.
March 22, 1788	Publication of volume 1 of *The Federalist* (nos. 1–36) by John and Archibald McLean.
April 2, 1788	Newspaper publication of *Papers* suspended for preparation of volume 2 of *The Federalist*.

April 28, 1788	Maryland ratifies.
May 23, 1788	South Carolina ratifies.
May 28, 1788	Publication of volume 2 of *The Federalist* (nos. 37–85) by McLean.
	Papers 78–83 (Hamilton). The judiciary is described.
	Papers 84–85 (Hamilton). Considers miscellaneous objections.
June 14, 1788	Resumption of newspaper publication.
June 21, 1788	New Hampshire ratifies. It being the ninth state to do so, the Constitution is thereby adopted.
June 25, 1788	Virginia ratifies.
July 26, 1788	New York ratifies.
August 16, 1788	Last newspaper publication.
November 21, 1789	North Carolina ratifies.
May 29, 1790	Rhode Island ratifies.

Brief Bibliography

A. Concerning The Federalist

For the text of the papers, and for notes concerning the references to authorities made by the authors, the edition prepared by Jacob E. Cooke and published by the Wesleyan University Press in 1961 will be found useful. The text, with a brief introduction, was also included in Volume 43 of the *Great Books of the Western World* (Britannica).

B. The Background

BORDEN, MORTON, ed. *The Antifederalist Papers.* East Lansing: Michigan State University Press, 1965.

MCLAUGHLIN, A. C. *The Confederation and the Constitution: 1783–1789.* New York: Collier Books, 1962.

NEVINS, ALLAN. *The American States during and after the Revolution: 1775–1789.* New York: The Macmillan Co., 1924.

ROSSITER, C. L. *1787: The Grand Convention.* New York: The Macmillan Co., 1966.

SPAULDING, E. W. *New York in the Critical Period: 1783–1789.* New York: Columbia University Press, 1932.

C. The Convention and the Ratification

ELLIOT, JONATHAN. *The Debates in the Several State Conventions on the Adoption of the Federal Constitution.* Philadelphia: J. B. Lippincott, 1941.

FARRAND, MAX, ed. *The Records of the Federal Convention of 1787.* New Haven: Yale University Press, 1966.

HUNT, GAILLARD, and SCOTT, J. B., eds. *The Debates in the Federal Convention of 1787.* Reported by James Madison. New York: Oxford University Press, 1920.

PRESCOTT, A. T., comp. *Drafting the Federal Constitution.* University, La.: Louisiana State University Press, 1941.

SCOTT, E. H., ed. *Journal of the Federal Convention, Kept by James Madison.* Freeport, N.Y.: Books for Libraries Press, 1970.

D. The Federalist Papers

COOKE, J. E., ed. *The Federalist.* Middletown, Conn.: Wesleyan University Press, 1961.
EARLE, E. M., ed. *The Federalist Papers.* New York: Modern Library, 1941.
HUTCHINS, R. M., and ADLER, M. J., eds. *GBWW*, Vol. 43. Chicago: Encyclopaedia Britannica, 1952.

E. The Authors

Alexander Hamilton

HACKER, L. M. *Alexander Hamilton in the American Tradition.* New York: McGraw-Hill Book Co., 1957.
MILLER, J. C. *Alexander Hamilton and the Growth of the New Nation.* New York: Harper & Row, 1964.
MITCHELL, BROADUS. *Alexander Hamilton.* 2 vols. New York: The Macmillan Co., 1957–62.
STOURZH, GERALD. *Alexander Hamilton and the Idea of Republican Government.* Stanford, Calif.: Stanford University Press, 1970.
SYRETT, H. C., and COOKE, J. E., eds. *The Papers of Alexander Hamilton.* 20 vols. New York: Columbia University Press, 1961–74.

John Jay

JOHNSTON, H. P., ed. *The Correspondence and Public Papers of John Jay.* 4 vols. New York: Benjamin Franklin Press, 1970.
MONAGHAN, FRANK. *John Jay, Defender of Liberty.* New York and Indianapolis: The Bobbs-Merrill Co., 1935.
MORRIS, R. B. *John Jay, the Nation, and the Court.* Boston: Boston University Press, 1967.
SMITH, D. L. *John Jay: Founder of a State and Nation.* New York: Teachers College Press, Columbia University, 1968.

James Madison

BRANT, IRVING. *James Madison.* 6 vols. Indianapolis: The Bobbs-Merrill Co., 1941–61.
BURNS, E. M. *James Madison: Philosopher of the Constitution.* New York: Octagon Books, 1968.
HUNT, GAILLARD. *The Life of James Madison.* New York: Russell & Russell, 1968.
HUNT, GAILLARD, ed. *The Writings of James Madison.* 9 vols. New York: G. P. Putnam's Sons, 1900–10.

PART FOUR

Additions
to the
Great Books Library

Persuasion

Jane Austen

Editor's Introduction

The position of Jane Austen, whose bicentennial we celebrate this year, is of a kind rare in literary history, being equally established and unassailable in the critical estimate and in the popular mind. Or at least this has been so since her death in 1817, when her identity as the author of the six novels she had published anonymously was first made known. And it is the more remarkable that it has been so in that she has never been without her embarrassing admirers, the devotees of "dear Jane" with all their cozy self-congratulation, and her as-determined detractors, such as Mark Twain, who once grimly remarked that if he were going to make a library he would begin by leaving her out. A less resilient reputation might have been suffocated by such friends, as it might have been shattered by such enemies, but with Jane Austen neither thing has happened. She has maintained her standing as both a master of the literary form—the novel—which she did much to create, and a sure best-seller.

It is this form, and this form only, that seems to express her. Some novelists can also be characterized as writers of stories or tales, but Jane Austen is seldom so described, for all that she employed the historical manner and was accomplished in the techniques of plot and suspense. Other novelists can be seen to have written moral allegories, or to have attacked social convention or defended it, but these were not Jane Austen's aims, though she was certainly very moral and had high regard for custom and tradition. She was strictly a novelist in the sense that she wrote of fundamental human relationships in a social setting that reveals a moral order, and her popularity, like her esteem, reflects her capacity to put these components of her art together in such a way that they cannot be separated, or even separately imagined (she is not the creator of types, in the sense that Dickens is; nor a novelist of ideas, like Melville; nor, for all her Regency relevance, is she the chronicler of a time and place, as Tolstoy was), but serve only as constituent elements of lives which, in her pages, credible human beings seem actually to live.

Her ability to combine the general with the particular, to bring both wit and sympathy to her work, to sustain an equal respect for personal integrity and social dictates, is nowhere better indicated than in the famous sentence with which *Pride and Prejudice*, the best liked of her books, begins:

> *It is a truth universally acknowledged, that a single man in possession of a good fortune, must be in want of a wife.*

What this charming and demonstrably false proposition really means is something quite other than what it says—something of consequence to a world in which money and marriage are closely tied together. In such a world it is necessary to maintain appearances, above all the appearances that disguise a very different proposition, which is never acknowledged by anybody, and which says that a single woman, who is without a good fortune, must be in want of a husband. This latter proposition is not, of course, really amusing to women in that world who do not want or cannot find any husband, and who may be condemned as a result to lives of base dependency or genteel servitude—so much Jane Austen makes clear. Yet that does not justify a loveless marriage in her eyes, any more than it justifies the self-indulgence of living in sin, these being extremes on either side of the equilibrium she thought essential to happiness, which she depicts as involving a balance of desire and duty, character and fortune, personality and society.

Persuasion, the last of her novels—written, in fact, during the last year of her life, when she was slowly dying of kidney disease—is less brilliant, more complex, cooler in its irony than *Pride and Prejudice*, but it is governed by the same view of what happiness requires. The central action of the book is quickly told. Its heroine, Anne Elliot, second daughter of Sir Walter Elliot, a repellently vain and uncomprehending man "who, for his own amusement, never took up any book but the Baronetage," in which his lineage is duly recorded, comes at the age of twenty-seven to a reconciliation with the only man she has ever loved, whose suit she had rejected eight years before on the well-meant but misguided advice of a family friend. This result, which is easy to predict, and which finally occurs almost offhandedly, is not without interest to the reader, who cares whether or not it happens. But what really concerns Jane Austen, and what she makes her reader think about, is the manner in which such a quiet business between a man of chastened expectations and a woman who, having "been forced into prudence in her youth, ... learned romance as she grew older," brings up the question of the worth of human feelings. These, Jane Austen seems to say, can never be judged in and for themselves, but are understood and trusted only as they are affirmed through the development of character and action in the course of people's lives. Nor is it incidental that this takes place in a social context where the relevant population—that is to say, the novel's secondary characters, who exhibit various kinds and degrees of self-regard—provides a moral map by which the central figures find their way. We come to know our own minds and hearts, the indication is, only through the process of living in a world—any world — that in its structure and behavior reflects a larger human experience.

Persuasion

Chapter one

Sir Walter Elliot, of Kellynch-hall, in Somersetshire, was a man who, for his own amusement, never took up any book but the Baronetage; there he found occupation for an idle hour, and consolation in a distressed one; there his faculties were roused into admiration and respect, by contemplating the limited remnant of the earliest patents; there any unwelcome sensations, arising from domestic affairs, changed naturally into pity and contempt, as he turned over the almost endless creations of the last century—and there, if every other leaf were powerless, he could read his own history with an interest which never failed—this was the page at which the favourite volume always opened:

"Elliot of Kellynch-Hall

"Walter Elliot, born March 1, 1760, married, July 15, 1784, Elizabeth, daughter of James Stevenson, Esq. of South Park, in the county of Gloucester; by which lady (who died 1800) he has issue Elizabeth, born June 1, 1785; Anne, born August 9, 1787; a still-born son, Nov. 5, 1789; Mary, born Nov. 20, 1791."

Precisely such had the paragraph originally stood from the printer's hands; but Sir Walter had improved it by adding, for the information of himself and his family, these words, after the date of Mary's birth, "married, Dec. 16, 1810, Charles, son and heir of Charles Musgrove, Esq. of Uppercross, in

the county of Somerset," and by inserting most accurately the day of the month on which he had lost his wife.

Then followed the history and rise of the ancient and respectable family, in the usual terms: how it had been first settled in Cheshire; how mentioned in Dugdale—serving the office of High Sheriff, representing a borough in three successive parliaments, exertions of loyalty, and dignity of baronet, in the first year of Charles II, with all the Marys and Elizabeths they had married; forming altogether two handsome duodecimo pages, and concluding with the arms and motto: "Principal seat, Kellynch hall, in the county of Somerset," and Sir Walter's hand-writing again in this finale:

"Heir presumptive, William Walter Elliot, Esq., great grandson of the second Sir Walter."

Vanity was the beginning and the end of Sir Walter Elliot's character; vanity of person and of situation. He had been remarkably handsome in his youth; and, at fifty-four, was still a very fine man. Few women could think more of their personal appearance than he did; nor could the valet of any new made lord be more delighted with the place he held in society. He considered the blessing of beauty as inferior only to the blessing of a baronetcy; and the Sir Walter Elliot, who united these gifts, was the constant object of his warmest respect and devotion.

His good looks and his rank had one fair claim on his attachment; since to them he must have owed a wife of very superior character to any thing deserved by his own. Lady Elliot had been an excellent woman, sensible and amiable; whose judgment and conduct, if they might be pardoned the youthful infatuation which made her Lady Elliot, had never required indulgence afterwards. She had humoured, or softened, or concealed his failings, and promoted his real respectability for seventeen years; and though not the very happiest being in the world herself, had found enough in her duties, her friends, and her children, to attach her to life, and make it no matter of indifference to her when she was called on to quit them. Three girls, the two eldest sixteen and fourteen, was an awful legacy for a mother to bequeath; an awful charge rather, to confide to the authority and guidance of a conceited, silly father. She had, however, one very intimate friend, a sensible, deserving woman, who had been brought, by strong attachment to herself, to settle close by her, in the village of Kellynch; and on her kindness and advice, Lady Elliot mainly relied for the best help and maintenance of the good principles and instruction which she had been anxiously giving her daughters.

This friend, and Sir Walter, did *not* marry, whatever might have been anticipated on that head by their acquaintance. Thirteen years had passed away since Lady Elliot's death, and they were still near neighbours and intimate friends; and one remained a widower, the other a widow.

That Lady Russell, of steady age and character, and extremely well provided for, should have no thought of a second marriage, needs no apology to the public, which is rather apt to be unreasonably discontented when a woman *does* marry again, than when she does *not*; but Sir Walter's continuing in singleness requires explanation. Be it known then, that Sir Walter, like a good father (having met with one or two private disappointments in very unreasonable applications), prided himself on remaining single for his dear daughters' sake. For one daughter, his eldest, he would really

have given up any thing, which he had not been very much tempted to do. Elizabeth had succeeded, at sixteen, to all that was possible, of her mother's rights and consequence; and being very handsome, and very like himself, her influence had always been great, and they had gone on together most happily. His two other children were of very inferior value. Mary had acquired a little artificial importance, by becoming Mrs. Charles Musgrove; but Anne, with an elegance of mind and sweetness of character, which must have placed her high with any people of real understanding, was nobody with either father or sister: her word had no weight; her convenience was always to give way; she was only Anne.

To Lady Russell, indeed, she was a most dear and highly valued god-daughter, favourite and friend. Lady Russell loved them all; but it was only in Anne that she could fancy the mother to revive again.

A few years before, Anne Elliot had been a very pretty girl, but her bloom had vanished early; and as even in its height, her father had found little to admire in her (so totally different were her delicate features and mild dark eyes from his own); there could be nothing in them now that she was faded and thin, to excite his esteem. He had never indulged much hope, he had now none, of ever reading her name in any other page of his favourite work. All equality of alliance must rest with Elizabeth; for Mary had merely connected herself with an old country family of respectability and large fortune, and had therefore *given* all the honour, and received none: Elizabeth would, one day or other, marry suitably.

It sometimes happens, that a woman is handsomer at twenty-nine than she was ten years before; and, generally speaking, if there has been neither ill health nor anxiety, it is a time of life at which scarcely any charm is lost. It was so with Elizabeth; still the same handsome Miss Elliot that she had begun to be thirteen years ago; and Sir Walter might be excused, therefore, in forgetting her age, or, at least, be deemed only half a fool, for thinking himself and Elizabeth as blooming as ever, amidst the wreck of the good looks of every body else; for he could plainly see how old all the rest of his family and acquaintance were growing. Anne haggard, Mary coarse, every face in the neighbourhood worsting; and the rapid increase of the crow's foot about Lady Russell's temples had long been a distress to him.

Elizabeth did not quite equal her father in personal contentment. Thirteen years had seen her mistress of Kellynch Hall, presiding and directing with a self-possession and decision which could never have given the idea of her being younger than she was. For thirteen years had she been doing the honours, and laying down the domestic law at home, and leading the way to the chaise and four, and walking immediately after Lady Russell out of all the drawing-rooms and dining-rooms in the country. Thirteen winters' revolving frosts had seen her opening every ball of credit which a scanty neighbourhood afforded; and thirteen springs shewn their blossoms, as she travelled up to London with her father, for a few weeks annual enjoyment of the great world. She had the remembrance of all this; she had the consciousness of being nine-and-twenty, to give her some regrets and some apprehensions. She was fully satisfied of being still quite as handsome as ever; but she felt her approach to the years of danger, and would have rejoiced to be certain of being properly solicited by baronet-blood within the next twelvemonth or two. Then might she again take up the book of books with as much enjoyment as in her early youth; but now she liked it not. Always to be presented with the date of her own birth, and see no marriage follow but that of a youngest sister, made the book an evil; and more than once, when her father had left it open on the table near her, had she closed it, with averted eyes, and pushed it away.

She had had a disappointment, moreover, which that book, and especially the history of her own family, must ever present the remembrance of. The heir presumptive, the very William Walter Elliot, Esq. whose rights had been so generously supported by her father, had disappointed her.

She had, while a very young girl, as soon as she had known him to be, in the event of her having no brother, the future baronet, meant to marry him; and her father had always meant that she should. He had not been known to them as a boy, but soon after Lady Elliot's death Sir Walter had sought the acquaintance, and though his overtures had not been met with any warmth, he had persevered in seeking it, making allowance for the modest drawing back of youth; and in one of their spring excursions to London, when Elizabeth was in her first bloom, Mr. Elliot had been forced into the introduction.

He was at that time a very young man, just engaged in the study of the law; and Elizabeth found him extremely agreeable, and every plan in his favour was confirmed. He was invited to Kellynch Hall; he was talked of and expected all the rest of the year; but he never came. The following spring he was seen again in town, found equally agreeable, again encouraged, invited and expected, and again he did not come; and the next tidings were that he was married. Instead of pushing his fortune in the line marked out for the heir of the house of Elliot, he had purchased independence by uniting himself to a rich woman of inferior birth.

Sir Walter had resented it. As the head of the house, he felt that he ought to have been consulted, especially after taking the young man so publicly by the hand: "For they must have been seen together," he observed, "once at Tattersal's, and twice in the lobby of the House of Commons." His disapprobation was expressed, but apparently very little regarded. Mr. Elliot had attempted no apology, and shewn himself as unsolicitous of being longer noticed by the family, as Sir Walter considered him unworthy of it: all acquaintance between them had ceased.

This very awkward history of Mr. Elliot, was still, after an interval of several years, felt with anger by Elizabeth, who had liked the man for himself, and still more for being her father's heir, and whose strong family pride could see only in *him*, a proper match for Sir Walter Elliot's eldest daughter. There was not a baronet from A to Z, whom her feelings could have so willingly acknowledged as an equal. Yet so miserably had he conducted himself, that though she was at this present time (the summer of 1814) wearing black ribbons for his wife, she could not admit him to be worth thinking of again. The disgrace of his first marriage might, perhaps, as there was no reason to suppose it perpetuated by offspring, have been got over, had he not done worse; but he had, as by the accustomary intervention of kind friends they had been informed, spoken most disrespectfully of them all, most slightingly and contemptuously of the very blood he belonged to, and the honours which were hereafter to be his own. This could not be pardoned.

Such were Elizabeth Elliot's sentiments and sensations; such the cares to alloy, the agitations to vary, the sameness and the elegance, the prosperity and the nothingness, of her scene of life—such the feelings to give interest to a long, uneventful residence in one country circle, to fill the vacancies which there were no habits of utility abroad, no talents or accomplishments for home, to occupy.

But now, another occupation and solicitude of mind was beginning to be added to these. Her father was growing distressed for money. She knew, that when he now took up the Baronetage, it was to drive the heavy bills of his tradespeople, and the unwelcome hints of Mr. Shepherd, his agent, from his thoughts. The Kellynch property was good, but not equal to Sir Walter's apprehension of the state required in its possessor. While Lady Elliot lived, there had been method, moderation, and economy, which had just kept him within his income; but with her had died all such right-mindedness, and from that period he had been constantly exceeding it. It had not been possible for him to spend less; he had done nothing but what

Sir Walter Elliot was imperiously called on to do; but blameless as he was, he was not only growing dreadfully in debt, but was hearing of it so often, that it became vain to attempt concealing it longer, even partially, from his daughter. He had given her some hints of it the last spring in town; he had gone so far even as to say, "Can we retrench? does it occur to you that there is any one article in which we can retrench?" and Elizabeth, to do her justice, had, in the first ardour of female alarm, set seriously to think what could be done, and had finally proposed these two branches of economy: to cut off some unnecessary charities, and to refrain from new-furnishing the drawing-room; to which expedients she afterwards added the happy thought of their taking no present down to Anne, as had been the usual yearly custom. But these measures, however good in themselves, were insufficient for the real extent of the evil, the whole of which Sir Walter found himself obliged to confess to her soon afterwards. Elizabeth had nothing to propose of deeper efficacy. She felt herself ill-used and unfortunate, as did her father; and they were neither of them able to devise any means of lessening their expenses without compromising their dignity, or relinquishing their comforts in a way not to be borne.

There was only a small part of his estate that Sir Walter could dispose of; but had every acre been alienable, it would have made no difference. He had condescended to mortgage as far as he had the power, but he would never condescend to sell. No; he would never disgrace his name so far. The Kellynch estate should be transmitted whole and entire, as he had received it.

Their two confidential friends, Mr. Shepherd, who lived in the neighbouring market town, and Lady Russell, were called on to advise them; and both father and daughter seemed to expect that something should be struck out by one or the other to remove their embarrassments and reduce their expenditure, without involving the loss of any indulgence of taste or pride.

Chapter two

Mr. Shepherd, a civil, cautious lawyer, who, whatever might be his hold or his views on Sir Walter, would rather have the *disagreeable* prompted by any body else, excused himself from offering the slightest hint, and only begged leave to recommend an implicit deference to the excellent judgment of Lady Russell, from whose known good sense he fully expected to have just such resolute measures advised, as he meant to see finally adopted.

Lady Russell was most anxiously zealous on the subject, and gave it much serious consideration. She was a woman rather of sound than of quick abilities, whose difficulties in coming to any decision in this instance were great, from the opposition of two leading principles. She was of strict integrity herself, with a delicate sense of honour; but she was as desirous of saving Sir Walter's feelings, as solicitous for the credit of the family, as aristocratic in her ideas of what was due to them, as any body of sense and honesty could well be. She was a benevolent, charitable, good woman, and capable of strong attachments; most correct in her conduct, strict in her notions of decorum, and with manners that were held a standard of good-breeding. She had a cultivated mind, and was, generally speaking, rational and consistent—but she had prejudices on the side of ancestry; she had a value for rank and consequence, which blinded her a little to the faults of those who possessed them. Herself, the widow of only a knight, she gave the dignity of a baronet all its due; and Sir Walter, independent of his claims as an old acquaintance, an attentive neighbour, an obliging landlord, the husband of her very dear friend, the father of Anne and her sisters, was, as being Sir Walter, in her apprehension entitled to a great deal of compassion and consideration under his present difficulties.

They must retrench; that did not admit of a doubt. But she was very anxious to have it done with the least possible pain to him and Elizabeth. She drew up plans of economy, she made exact calculations, and she did what nobody else thought of doing, she consulted Anne, who never seemed considered by the others as having any interest in the question. She consulted, and in a degree was influenced by her, in marking out the scheme of retrenchment, which was at last submitted to Sir Walter. Every emendation of Anne's had been on the side of honesty against importance. She wanted more vigorous measures, a more complete reformation, a quicker release from debt, a much higher tone of indifference for every thing but justice and equity.

"If we can persuade your father to all this," said Lady Russell, looking over her paper, "much may be done. If he will adopt these regulations, in seven years he will be clear; and I hope we may be able to convince him and Elizabeth, that Kellynch-hall has a respectability in itself, which cannot be affected by these reductions; and that the true dignity of Sir Walter Elliot will be very far from lessened in the eyes of sensible people, by his acting like a man of principle. What will he be doing, in fact, but what very many of our first families have done—or ought to do?—There will be nothing singular in his case; and it is singularity which often makes the worst part of our suffering, as it always does of our conduct. I have great hope of our prevailing. We must be serious and decided—for, after all, the person who has contracted debts must pay them; and though a great deal is due to the feelings of the gentleman, and the head of a house, like your father, there is still more due to the character of an honest man."

This was the principle on which Anne wanted her father to be proceeding, his friends to be urging him. She considered it as an act of indispensable duty to clear away the claims of creditors, with all the expedition which the most comprehensive retrenchments could secure, and saw no dignity in any thing short of it. She wanted it to be prescribed, and felt as a duty. She rated Lady Russell's influence highly, and as to the severe degree of self-denial, which her own conscience prompted, she believed there might be little more difficulty in persuading them to a complete, than to half a reformation. Her knowledge of her father and Elizabeth, inclined her to think that the sacrifice of one pair of horses would be hardly less painful than of both, and soon, through the whole list of Lady Russell's too gentle reductions.

How Anne's more rigid requisitions might have been taken, is of little consequence. Lady Russell's had no success at all —could not be put up with—were not to be borne. "What! Every comfort of life knocked off! Journeys, London, servants, horses, table—contractions and restrictions every where. To live no longer with the decencies even of a private gentleman! No, he would sooner quit Kellynch-hall at once, than remain in it on such disgraceful terms."

"Quit Kellynch-hall." The hint was immediately taken up by Mr. Shepherd, whose interest was involved in the reality of Sir Walter's retrenching, and who was perfectly persuaded that nothing would be done without a change of abode. "Since the idea had been started in the very quarter which ought to dictate, he had no scruple," he said, "in confessing his judgment to be entirely on that side. It did not appear to him that Sir Walter could materially alter his style of living in a house which had such a character of hospitality and ancient dignity to support. In any other place, Sir Walter might judge for himself; and would be looked up to, as regulating the modes of life, in whatever way he might choose to model his household."

Sir Walter would quit Kellynch-hall; and after a very few days more of doubt and indecision, the great question of whither he should go, was settled, and the first outline of this important change made out.

There had been three alternatives, London, Bath, or another house in the country. All Anne's wishes had been for the latter. A small house in their own neighbourhood, where they might still have Lady Russell's society, still be near Mary, and still have the pleasure of sometimes seeing the lawns and groves of Kellynch, was the object of her ambition. But the usual fate of Anne attended her, in having something very opposite from her inclination fixed on. She disliked Bath, and did not think it agreed with her—and Bath was to be her home.

Sir Walter had at first thought more of London, but Mr. Shepherd felt that he could not be trusted in London, and had been skilful enough to dissuade him from it, and make Bath preferred. It was a much safer place for a gentleman in his predicament: he might there be important at comparatively little expense. Two material advantages of Bath over London had of course been given all their weight, its more convenient distance from Kellynch, only fifty miles, and Lady Russell's spending some part of every winter there; and to the very great satisfaction of Lady Russell, whose first views on the projected change had been for Bath, Sir Walter and Elizabeth were induced to believe that they should lose neither consequence nor enjoyment by settling there.

Lady Russell felt obliged to oppose her dear Anne's known wishes. It would be too much to expect Sir Walter to descend into a small house in his own neighbourhood. Anne herself would have found the mortifications of it more than she foresaw, and to Sir Walter's feelings they must have been dreadful. And with regard to Anne's dislike of Bath, she considered it as a prejudice and mistake, arising first from the circumstance of her having been three years at school there, after her mother's death, and, secondly, from her happening to be not in perfectly good spirits the only winter which she had afterwards spent there with herself.

Lady Russell was fond of Bath in short, and disposed to think it must suit them all; and as to her young friend's health, by passing all the warm months with her at Kellynch-lodge, every danger would be avoided; and it was, in fact, a change which must do both health and spirits good. Anne had been too little from home, too little seen. Her spirits were not high. A larger society would improve them. She wanted her to be more known.

The undesirableness of any other house in the same neighbourhood for Sir Walter, was certainly much strengthened by one part, and a very material part of the scheme, which had been happily engrafted on the beginning. He was not only to quit his home, but to see it in the hands of others; a trial of fortitude, which stronger heads than Sir Walter's have found too much. Kellynch-hall was to be let. This, however, was a profound secret; not to be breathed beyond their own circle.

Sir Walter could not have borne the degradation of being known to design letting his house. Mr. Shepherd had once mentioned the word, "advertise," but never dared approach it again; Sir Walter spurned the idea of its being offered in any manner, forbad the slightest hint being dropped of his having such an intention; and it was only on the supposition of his being spontaneously solicited by some most unexceptionable applicant, on his own terms, and as a great favour, that he would let it at all.

How quick come the reasons for approving what we like! Lady Russell had another excellent one at hand, for being extremely glad that Sir Walter and his family were to remove from the country. Elizabeth had been lately forming an intimacy, which she wished to see interrupted. It was with a daughter of Mr. Shepherd, who had returned, after an unprosperous marriage, to her father's house, with the additional burthen of two children. She was a clever young woman, who understood the art of pleasing; the art of pleasing, at least, at Kellynch-hall; and who had made herself so acceptable to Miss Elliot, as to have been already staying there more than once, in spite of all that Lady Russell, who thought it a friendship quite out of place, could hint of caution and reserve.

Lady Russell, indeed, had scarcely any influence with Elizabeth, and seemed to love her, rather because she would love her, than because Elizabeth deserved it. She had never received from her more than outward attention, nothing beyond the observances of complaisance; had never succeeded in any point which she wanted to carry, against previous inclination. She had been repeatedly very earnest in trying to get Anne included in the visit to London, sensibly open to all the injustice and all the discredit of the selfish arrangements which shut her out, and on many lesser occasions had endeavoured to give Elizabeth the advantage of her own better judgment and experience, but always in vain; Elizabeth would go her own way, and never had she pursued it in more decided opposition to Lady Russell, than in this selection of Mrs. Clay; turning from the society of so deserving a sister to bestow her affection and confidence on one who ought to have been nothing to her but the object of distant civility.

From situation, Mrs. Clay was, in Lady Russell's estimate, a very unequal, and in her character she believed a very dangerous companion—and a removal that would leave Mrs. Clay behind, and bring a choice of more suitable intimates within Miss Elliot's reach, was therefore an object of first-rate importance.

Chapter three

"I must take leave to observe, Sir Walter," said Mr. Shepherd one morning at Kellynch, as he laid down the newspaper, "that the present juncture is much in our favour. This peace will be turning all our rich Navy Officers ashore. They will be all wanting a home. Could not be a better time, Sir Walter, for having a choice of tenants, very responsible tenants. Many a noble fortune has been made during the war. If a rich Admiral were to come in our way, Sir Walter—"

"He would be a very lucky man, Shepherd," replied Sir Walter, "that's all I have to remark. A prize indeed would Kellynch Hall be to him; rather the greatest prize of all, let him have taken ever so many before—hey, Shepherd?"

Mr. Shepherd laughed, as he knew he must, at this wit, and then added,

"I presume to observe, Sir Walter, that, in the way of business, gentlemen of the navy are well to deal with. I have had a little knowledge of their methods of doing business, and I am free to confess that they have very liberal notions, and are as likely to make desirable tenants as any set of people one should meet with. Therefore, Sir Walter, what I would take leave to suggest is, that if in consequence of any rumours getting abroad of your intention—which must be contemplated as a possible thing, because we know how difficult it is to keep the actions and designs of one part of the world from the notice and curiosity of the other—consequence has its tax—I, John Shepherd, might conceal any family-matters that I chose, for nobody would think it worth their while to observe me, but Sir Walter Elliot has eyes upon him which it may be very difficult to elude—and therefore, thus much I venture upon, that it will not greatly surprise me if, with all our caution, some rumour of the truth should get abroad—in the supposition of which, as I was going to observe, since applications will unquestionably follow, I should think any from our wealthy naval commanders particularly worth attending to—and beg leave to add, that two hours will bring me over at any time, to save you the trouble of replying."

Sir Walter only nodded. But soon afterwards, rising and pacing the room, he observed sarcastically,

"There are few among the gentlemen of the navy, I imagine, who would not be surprised to find themselves in a house of this description."

"They would look around them, no doubt, and bless their good fortune," said Mrs. Clay, for Mrs. Clay was present; her father had driven her over, nothing being of so much use to Mrs. Clay's health as a drive to Kellynch: "but I quite agree with my father in thinking a sailor might be a very desirable tenant. I have known a good deal of the profession; and besides their liberality, they are so neat and careful in all their ways! These valuable pictures of yours, Sir Walter, if you chose to leave them, would be perfectly safe. Every thing in and about the house would be taken such excellent care of! the gardens and shrubberies would be kept in almost as high order as they are now. You need not be afraid, Miss Elliot, of your own sweet flower-garden's being neglected."

"As to all that," rejoined Sir Walter coolly, "supposing I were induced to let my house, I have by no means made up my mind as to the privileges to be annexed to it. I am not particularly disposed to favour a tenant. The park would be open to him of course, and few navy officers, or men of any other description, can have had such a range; but what restrictions I might impose on the use of the pleasure-grounds, is another thing. I am not fond of the idea of my shrubberies being always approachable; and I should recommend Miss Elliot to be on her guard with respect to her flower-garden. I am very little disposed to grant a tenant of Kellynch Hall any extraordinary favour, I assure you, be he sailor or soldier."

After a short pause, Mr. Shepherd presumed to say,

"In all these cases, there are established usages which make every thing plain and easy between landlord and tenant. Your interest, Sir Walter, is in pretty safe hands. Depend upon me for taking care that no tenant has more than his just rights. I venture to hint, that Sir Walter Elliot cannot be half so jealous for his own, as John Shepherd will be for him."

Here Anne spoke,

"The navy, I think, who have done so much for us, have at least an equal claim with any other set of men, for all the comforts and all the privileges which any home can give. Sailors work hard enough for their comforts, we must all allow."

"Very true, very true. What Miss Anne says, is very true," was Mr. Shepherd's rejoinder, and "Oh! certainly," was his daughter's; but Sir Walter's remark was, soon afterwards—

"The profession has its utility, but I should be sorry to see any friend of mine belonging to it."

"Indeed!" was the reply, and with a look of surprise.

"Yes; it is in two points offensive to me; I have two strong grounds of objection to it. First, as being the means of bringing persons of obscure birth into undue distinction, and raising men to honours which their fathers and grandfathers never dreamt of; and secondly, as it cuts up a man's youth and vigour most horribly; a sailor grows old sooner than any other man; I have observed it all my life. A man is in greater danger in the navy of being insulted by the rise of one whose father, his father might have disdained to speak to, and of becoming prematurely an object of disgust himself, than in any other line. One day last spring, in town, I was in company with two men, striking instances of what I am talking of, Lord St. Ives, whose father we all know to have been a country curate, without bread to eat; I was to give place to Lord St. Ives, and a certain Admiral Baldwin, the most deplorable looking personage you can imagine, his face the colour of mahogany, rough and rugged to the last degree, all lines and wrinkles, nine grey hairs of a side, and nothing but a dab of powder at top. 'In the name of heaven, who is that old fellow?' said I, to a friend of mine who was standing near (Sir Basil Morley). 'Old fellow!' cried Sir Basil, 'it is Admiral Baldwin. What do you take his age to be?' 'Sixty,' said I, 'or perhaps sixty-two.' 'Forty,' replied Sir Basil, 'forty, and no more.' Picture to yourselves my amazement; I shall not easily forget Admiral Baldwin. I never saw quite so wretched an example of what a sea-faring life can do; but to a degree, I know it is the same with them all: they are all knocked about, and exposed to every climate, and every weather, till they are not fit to be seen. It is a pity they are not knocked on the head at once, before they reach Admiral Baldwin's age."

"Nay, Sir Walter," cried Mrs. Clay, "this is being severe indeed. Have a little mercy on the poor men. We are not all born to be handsome. The sea is no beautifier, certainly; sailors do grow old betimes; I have often observed it; they soon lose the look of youth. But then, is not it the same with many other professions, perhaps most other? Soldiers, in active service, are not at all better off: and even in the quieter professions, there is a toil and a labour of the mind, if not of the body, which seldom leaves a man's looks to the natural effect of time. The lawyer plods, quite care-worn; the physician is up at all hours, and travelling in all weather; and even the clergyman—" she stopt a moment to consider what might do for the clergyman; "and even the clergyman, you know, is obliged to go into infected rooms, and expose his health and looks to all the injury of a poisonous atmosphere. In fact, as I have long been convinced, though every profession is necessary and honourable in its turn, it is only the lot of those who are not obliged to follow any, who can live in a regular way, in the country, choosing their own hours, following their own pursuits, and living on their own property, without the torment of trying for more; it is only *their* lot, I say, to hold the blessings of health and a good appearance to the utmost: I know no other set of men but what lose something of their personableness when they cease to be quite young."

It seemed as if Mr. Shepherd, in this anxiety to bespeak Sir Walter's goodwill towards a naval officer as tenant, had been gifted with foresight; for the very first application for the house was from an Admiral Croft, with whom he shortly afterwards fell into company in attending the quarter sessions at Taunton; and indeed, he had received a hint of the admiral from a London correspondent. By the report which he hastened over to Kellynch to make, Admiral Croft was a native of Somersetshire, who having acquired a very handsome fortune, was wishing to settle in his own country, and had come down to Taunton in order to look at some advertised places in that immediate neighbourhood, which, however, had not suited him; that accidentally hearing (it was just as he had foretold, Mr. Shepherd observed, Sir Walter's concerns could not be kept a secret), accidentally hearing of the possibility of Kellynch Hall being to let, and understanding his (Mr. Shepherd's) connection with the owner, he had introduced himself to him in order to make particular inquiries, and had, in the course of a pretty long conference, expressed as strong an inclination for the place as man who knew it only by description, could feel; and given Mr. Shepherd, in his explicit account of himself, every proof of his being a most responsible, eligible tenant.

"And who is Admiral Croft?" was Sir Walter's cold suspicious inquiry.

Mr. Shepherd answered for his being of a gentleman's family, and mentioned a place; and Anne, after the little pause which followed, added —

"He is rear admiral of the white.[1] He was in the Trafalgar action, and has been in the East Indies since; he has been stationed there, I believe, several years."

"Then I take it for granted," observed Sir Walter, "that his face is about as orange as the cuffs and capes of my livery."

Mr. Shepherd hastened to assure him, that Admiral Croft was a very hale, hearty, well-looking man, a little weather-beaten, to be sure, but not much; and quite the gentleman in all his notions and behaviour; not likely to make the smallest difficulty about terms; only wanted a comfortable home, and to get into it as soon as possible; knew he must pay for his convenience; knew what rent a ready-furnished house of that consequence might fetch; should not have been surprised if Sir Walter had asked more; had inquired about the manor; would be glad of the deputation,[2] certainly, but made no great point of it; said he sometimes took out a gun, but never killed; quite the gentleman.

Mr. Shepherd was eloquent on the subject; pointing out all the circumstances of the admiral's family, which made him peculiarly desirable as a tenant. He was a married man, and without children; the very state to be wished for. A house was never taken good care of, Mr. Shepherd observed, without a lady: he did not know, whether furniture might not be in danger of suffering as much where there was no lady, as where there were many children. A lady, without a family, was the very best preserver of furniture in the world. He had seen Mrs. Croft, too; she was at Taunton with the admiral, and had been present almost all the time they were talking the matter over.

"And a very well-spoken, genteel, shrewd lady, she seemed to be," continued he; "asked more questions about the house, and terms, and taxes, than the admiral himself, and seemed more conversant with business. And moreover, Sir Walter, I found she was not quite unconnected in this country, any more than her husband; that is to say, she is sister to a gentleman who did live amongst us once; she told me so herself: sister to the gentleman who lived a few years back, at Monkford. Bless me! what was his name? At this moment I cannot recollect his name, though I have heard it so lately. Penelope, my dear, can you help me to the name of the gentleman who lived at Monkford—Mrs. Croft's brother?"

But Mrs. Clay was talking so eagerly with Miss Elliot, that she did not hear the appeal.

"I have no conception whom you can mean, Shepherd; I remember no gentleman resident at Monkford since the time of old Governor Trent."

"Bless me! how very odd! I shall forget my own name soon, I suppose. A name that I am so very well acquainted with; knew the gentleman so well by sight; seen him a hundred times; came to consult me once, I remember, about a trespass of one of his neighbours; farmer's man breaking into his orchard—wall torn down—apples stolen— caught in the fact; and afterwards, contrary

---

[1] "rear admiral of the white." The Royal Navy was at this time divided into Red, White, and Blue squadrons.

[2] "the deputation," i.e., the formal permission of the lord of the manor, in this case Sir Walter, to shoot game on his grounds.

to my judgment, submitted to an amicable compromise. Very odd indeed!"

After waiting another moment—

"You mean Mr. Wentworth, I suppose," said Anne.

Mr. Shepherd was all gratitude.

"Wentworth was the very name! Mr. Wentworth was the very man. He had the curacy of Monkford, you know, Sir Walter, some time back, for two or three years. Came there about the year—5, I take it. You remember him, I am sure."

"Wentworth? Oh! ay, Mr. Wentworth, the curate of Monkford. You misled me by the term *gentleman.* I thought you were speaking of some man of property: Mr. Wentworth was nobody, I remember; quite unconnected; nothing to do with the Strafford family. One wonders how the names of many of our nobility become so common."

As Mr. Shepherd perceived that this connexion of the Crofts did them no service with Sir Walter, he mentioned it no more; returning, with all his zeal, to dwell on the circumstances more indisputably in their favour; their age, and number, and fortune; the high idea they had formed of Kellynch Hall, and extreme solicitude for the advantage of renting it; making it appear as if they ranked nothing beyond the happiness of being the tenants of Sir Walter Elliot: an extraordinary taste, certainly, could they have been supposed in the secret of Sir Walter's estimate of the dues of a tenant.

It succeeded, however; and though Sir Walter must ever look with an evil eye on any one intending to inhabit that house, and think them infinitely too well off in being permitted to rent it on the highest terms, he was talked into allowing Mr. Shepherd to proceed in the treaty, and authorising him to wait on Admiral Croft, who still remained at Taunton, and fix a day for the house being seen.

Sir Walter was not very wise; but still he had experience enough of the world to feel, that a more unobjectionable tenant, in all essentials, than Admiral Croft bid fair to be, could hardly offer. So far went his under-

standing; and his vanity supplied a little additional soothing, in the admiral's situation in life, which was just high enough, and not too high. "I have let my house to Admiral Croft," would sound extremely well; very much better than to any mere Mr.——; *Mr.* (save, perhaps, some half dozen in the nation) always needs a note of explanation. An admiral speaks his own consequence, and, at the same time, can never make a baronet look small. In all their dealings and intercourse, Sir Walter Elliot must ever have the precedence.

Nothing could be done without a reference to Elizabeth; but her inclination was growing so strong for a removal, that she was happy to have it fixed and expedited by a tenant at hand; and not a word to suspend decision was uttered by her.

Mr. Shepherd was completely empowered to act; and no sooner had such an end been reached, than Anne, who had been a most attentive listener to the whole, left the room, to seek the comfort of cool air for her flushed cheeks; and as she walked along a favourite grove, said, with a gentle sigh, "a few months more, and *he*, perhaps, may be walking here."

Chapter four

He was not Mr. Wentworth, the former curate of Monkford, however suspicious appearances may be, but a captain Frederick Wentworth, his brother, who being made commander in consequence of the action off St. Domingo, and not immediately employed, had come into Somersetshire, in the summer of 1806; and having no parent living, found a home for half a year, at Monkford. He was, at that time, a remarkably fine young man, with a great deal of intelligence, spirit and brilliancy; and Anne an extremely pretty girl, with gentleness, modesty, taste, and feeling. Half the sum of attraction, on either side, might have been enough, for he had nothing to do, and she had hardly any body to love; but the encounter of such lavish recommendations could not fail. They were gradually acquainted, and when acquainted, rapidly and deeply in love. It would be difficult to say which had seen highest perfection in the other, or which had been the happiest; she, in receiving his declarations and proposals, or he in having them accepted.

A short period of exquisite felicity followed, and but a short one. Troubles soon arose. Sir Walter, on being applied to, without actually withholding his consent, or saying it should never be, gave it all the negative of great astonishment, great coldness, great silence, and a professed resolution of doing nothing for his daughter. He thought it a very degrading alliance; and Lady Russell, though with more tempered and pardonable pride, received it as a most unfortunate one.

Anne Elliot, with all her claims of birth, beauty, and mind, to throw herself away at nineteen; involve herself at nineteen in an engagement with a young man, who had nothing but himself to recommend him, and no hopes of attaining affluence, but in the chances of a most uncertain profession, and no connexions to secure even his farther rise in that profession; would be, indeed, a throwing away, which she grieved to think of! Anne Elliot, so young; known to so few, to be snatched off by a stranger without alliance or fortune; or rather sunk by him into a state of most wearing, anxious, youth-killing dependance! It must not be, if by any fair interference of friendship, any representations from one who had almost a mother's love, and mother's rights, it would be prevented.

Captain Wentworth had no fortune. He had been lucky in his profession, but spending freely, what had come freely, had realized nothing. But, he was confident that he should soon be rich; full of life and ardour, he knew that he should soon have a ship, and soon be on a station that would lead to every thing he wanted. He had always been lucky; he knew he should be so still. Such confidence, powerful in its own warmth, and

bewitching in the wit which often expressed it, must have been enough for Anne; but Lady Russell saw it very differently. His sanguine temper, and fearlessness of mind, operated very differently on her. She saw in it but an aggravation of the evil. It only added a dangerous character to himself. He was brilliant, he was headstrong. Lady Russell had little taste for wit; and of any thing approaching to imprudence a horror. She deprecated the connexion in every light.

Such opposition, as these feelings produced, was more than Anne could combat. Young and gentle as she was, it might yet have been possible to withstand her father's ill-will, though unsoftened by one kind word or look on the part of her sister; but Lady Russell, whom she had always loved and relied on, could not, with such steadiness of opinion, and such tenderness of manner, be continually advising her in vain. She was persuaded to believe the engagement a wrong thing—indiscreet, improper, hardly capable of success, and not deserving it. But it was not a merely selfish caution, under which she acted, in putting an end to it. Had she not imagined herself consulting his good, even more than her own, she could hardly have given him up. The belief of being prudent, and self-denying principally for *his* advantage, was her chief consolation, under the misery of a parting—a final parting; and every consolation was required, for she had to encounter all the additional pain of opinions, on his side, totally unconvinced and unbending, and of his feeling himself ill-used by so forced a relinquishment. He had left the country in consequence.

A few months had seen the beginning and the end of their acquaintance; but, not with a few months ended Anne's share of suffering from it. Her attachment and regrets had, for a long time, clouded every enjoyment of youth; and an early loss of bloom and spirits had been their lasting effect.

More than seven years were gone since this little history of sorrowful interest had reached its close; and time had softened down much, perhaps nearly all of peculiar attachment to him, but she had been too dependant on time alone; no aid had been given in change of place (except in one visit to Bath soon after the rupture) or in any novelty or enlargement of society. No one had ever come within the Kellynch circle, who could bear a comparison with Frederick Wentworth, as he stood in her memory. No second attachment, the only thoroughly natural, happy, and sufficient cure, at her time of life, had been possible to the nice tone of her mind, the fastidiousness of her taste, in the small limits of the society around them. She had been solicited, when about two-and-twenty, to change her name, by the young man, who not long afterwards found a more willing mind in her younger sister; and Lady Russell had lamented her refusal; for Charles Musgrove was the eldest son of a man, whose landed property and general importance, were second, in that country, only to Sir Walter's, and of good character and appearance; and however Lady Russell might have asked yet for something more, while Anne was nineteen, she would have rejoiced to see her at twenty-two, so respectably removed from the partialities and injustice of her father's house, and settled so permanently near herself. But in this case, Anne had left nothing for advice to do; and though Lady Russell, as satisfied as ever with her own discretion, never wished the past undone, she began now to have the anxiety which borders on hopelessness for Anne's being tempted, by some man of talents and independence, to enter a state for which she held her to be peculiarly fitted by her warm affections and domestic habits.

They knew not each other's opinion, either its constancy or its change, on the one leading point of Anne's conduct, for the subject was never alluded to, but Anne, at seven-and-twenty, thought very differently from what she had been made to think at nineteen. She did not blame Lady Russell, she did not blame herself for having been guided by her; but she felt that were any young person, in similar circumstances, to apply to her for counsel, they would never receive any of such certain immediate wretchedness, such uncertain future good. She was persuaded that under every disadvantage of disapprobation at home, and every anxiety attending his profession, all their probable fears, delays and disappointments, she should yet have been a happier woman in maintaining the engagement, than she had been in the sacrifice of it; and this, she fully believed, had the usual share, had even more than a usual share of all such solicitudes and suspense been theirs, without reference to the actual results of their case, which, as it happened, would have bestowed earlier prosperity than could be reasonably calculated on. All his sanguine expectations, all his confidence had been justified. His genius and ardour had seemed to foresee and to command his prosperous path. He had, very soon after their engagement ceased, got employ; and all that he had told her would follow, had taken place. He had distinguished himself, and early gained the other step in rank—and must now, by successive captures,[3] have made a handsome fortune. She had only navy lists and newspapers for her authority, but she could not doubt his being rich; and, in favour of his constancy, she had no reason to believe him married.

How eloquent could Anne Elliot have been, how eloquent, at least, were her wishes on the side of early warm attachment, and a cheerful confidence in futurity, against that over-anxious caution which seems to insult exertion and distrust Providence! She had been forced into prudence in her youth, she learned romance as she grew older—the natural sequel of an unnatural beginning.

With all these circumstances, recollections and feelings, she could not hear that Captain Wentworth's sister was likely to live at Kellynch, without a revival of former pain; and many a stroll and many a sigh were

---

[3] "by successive captures." Officers received prize money for capturing enemy ships.

317

necessary to dispel the agitation of the idea. She often told herself it was folly, before she could harden her nerves sufficiently to feel the continual discussion of the Crofts and their business no evil. She was assisted, however, by that perfect indifference and apparent unconsciousness, among the only three of her own friends in the secret of the past, which seemed almost to deny any recollection of it. She could do justice to the superiority of Lady Russell's motives in this, over those of her father and Elizabeth; she could honour all the better feelings of her calmness—but the general air of oblivion among them was highly important, from whatever it sprung; and in the event of Admiral Croft's really taking Kellynch-hall, she rejoiced anew over the conviction which had always been most grateful to her, of the past being known to those three only among her connexions, by whom no syllable, she believed, would ever be whispered, and in the trust that among his, the brother only with whom he had been residing, had received any information of their short-lived engagement. That brother had been long removed from the country—and being a sensible man, and, moreover, a single man at the time, she had a fond dependance on no human creature's having heard of it from him.

The sister, Mrs. Croft, had then been out of England, accompanying her husband on a foreign station, and her own sister, Mary, had been at school while it all occurred—and never admitted by the pride of some, and the delicacy of others, to the smallest knowledge of it afterwards.

With these supports, she hoped that the acquaintance between herself and the Crofts, which, with Lady Russell still resident in Kellynch, and Mary fixed only three miles off, must be anticipated, need not involve any particular awkwardness.

Chapter five

On the morning appointed for Admiral and Mrs. Croft's seeing Kellynch-hall, Anne found it most natural to take her almost daily walk to Lady Russell's, and keep out of the way till all was over; when she found it most natural to be sorry that she had missed the opportunity of seeing them.

This meeting of the two parties proved highly satisfactory, and decided the whole business at once. Each lady was previously well disposed for an agreement, and saw nothing, therefore, but good manners in the other; and, with regard to the gentlemen, there was such an hearty good humour, such an open, trusting liberality on the Admiral's side, as could not but influence Sir Walter, who had besides been flattered into his very best and most polished behaviour by Mr. Shepherd's assurances of his being known, by report, to the Admiral, as a model of good breeding.

The house and grounds, and furniture, were approved, the Crofts were approved, terms, time, every thing, and every body, was right; and Mr. Shepherd's clerks were set to work, without there having been a single preliminary difference to modify of all that "This indenture sheweth."

Sir Walter, without hesitation, declared the Admiral to be the best-looking sailor he had ever met with, and went so far as to say, that, if his own man might have had the arranging of his hair, he should not be ashamed of being seen with him any where; and the Admiral, with sympathetic cordiality, observed to his wife as they drove back through the Park, "I thought we should soon come to a deal, my dear, in spite of what they told us at Taunton. The baronet will never set the Thames on fire, but there seems no harm in him"—reciprocal compliments, which would have been esteemed about equal.

The Crofts were to have possession at Michaelmas, and as Sir Walter proposed removing to Bath in the course of the preceding month, there was no time to be lost in making every dependant arrangement.

Lady Russell, convinced that Anne would not be allowed to be of any use, or any importance, in the choice of the house which they were going to secure, was very unwilling to have her hurried away so soon, and wanted to make it possible for her to stay behind, till she might convey her to Bath herself after Christmas; but having engagements of her own, which must take her from Kellynch for several weeks, she was unable to give the full invitation she wished; and Anne, though dreading the possible heats of September in all the white glare of Bath, and grieving to forego all the influence so sweet and so sad of the autumnal months in the country, did not think that, every thing considered, she wished to remain. It would be most right, and most wise, and, therefore, must involve least suffering, to go with the others.

Something occurred, however, to give her a different duty. Mary, often a little unwell, and always thinking a great deal of her own complaints, and always in the habit of claiming Anne when any thing was the matter, was indisposed; and foreseeing that she should not have a day's health all the autumn, entreated, or rather required her, for it was hardly entreaty, to come to Uppercross Cottage, and bear her company as long as she should want her, instead of going to Bath.

"I cannot possibly do without Anne," was Mary's reasoning; and Elizabeth's reply was, "Then I am sure Anne had better stay, for nobody will want her in Bath."

To be claimed as a good, though in an improper style, is at least better than being rejected as no good at all; and Anne, glad to be thought of some use, glad to have any thing marked out as a duty, and certainly not sorry to have the scene of it in the country, and her own dear country, readily agreed to stay.

This invitation of Mary's removed all Lady Russell's difficulties, and it was consequently soon settled that Anne should not go to Bath till Lady Russell took her, and that all the intervening time should be divided between Uppercross Cottage and Kellynch-lodge.

So far all was perfectly right; but Lady Russell was almost startled by the wrong of one part of the Kellynch-hall plan, when it burst on her, which was, Mrs. Clay's being engaged to go to Bath with Sir Walter and Elizabeth, as a most important and valuable assistant to the latter in all the business before her. Lady Russell was extremely sorry that such a measure should have been resorted to at all—wondered, grieved, and feared—and the affront it contained to Anne, in Mrs. Clay's being of so much use, while Anne could be of none, was a very sore aggravation.

Anne herself was become hardened to such affronts; but she felt the imprudence of the arrangement quite as keenly as Lady Russell. With a great deal of quiet observation, and a knowledge, which she often wished less, of her father's character, she was sensible that results the most serious to his family from the intimacy were more than possible. She did not imagine that her father had at present an idea of the kind. Mrs. Clay had freckles, and a projecting tooth, and a clumsy wrist, which he was continually making severe remarks upon, in her absence; but she was young, and certainly altogether well-looking, and possessed, in an acute mind and assiduous pleasing manners, infinitely more dangerous attractions than any merely personal might have been. Anne was so impressed by the degree of their danger, that she could not excuse herself from trying to make it perceptible to her sister. She had little hope of success; but Elizabeth, who in the event of such a reverse would be so much more to be pitied than herself, should never, she thought, have reason to reproach her for giving no warning.

She spoke, and seemed only to offend. Elizabeth could not conceive how such an absurd suspicion should occur to her; and indignantly answered for each party's perfectly knowing their situation.

"Mrs. Clay," she said warmly, "never forgets who she is; and as I am rather better acquainted with her sentiments than you can be, I can assure you, that upon the subject of marriage they are particularly nice; and that she reprobates all inequality of condition and rank more strongly than most people. And as to my father, I really should not have thought that he, who has kept himself single so long for our sakes, need be suspected now. If Mrs. Clay were a very beautiful woman, I grant you, it might be wrong to have her so much with me; not that any thing in the world, I am sure, would induce my father to make a degrading match; but he might be rendered unhappy. But poor Mrs. Clay, who, with all her merits, can never have been reckoned tolerably pretty! I really think poor Mrs. Clay may be staying here in perfect safety. One would imagine you had never heard my father speak of her personal misfortunes, though I know you must fifty times. That tooth of hers! and those freckles! Freckles do not disgust me so very much as they do him: I have known a face not materially disfigured by a few, but he abominates them. You must have heard him notice Mrs. Clay's freckles."

"There is hardly any personal defect," replied Anne, "which an agreeable manner might not gradually reconcile one to."

"I think very differently," answered Elizabeth, shortly; "an agreeable manner may set off handsome features, but can never alter plain ones. However, at any rate, as I have a great deal more at stake on this point than any body else can have, I think it rather unnecessary in you to be advising me."

Anne had done—glad that it was over, and not absolutely hopeless of doing good. Elizabeth, though resenting the suspicion, might yet be made observant by it.

The last office of the four carriage-horses was to draw Sir Walter, Miss Elliot, and Mrs. Clay to Bath. The party drove off in very good spirits; Sir Walter prepared with condescending bows for all the afflicted tenantry and cottagers who might have had a hint to shew themselves: and Anne walked up at the same time, in a sort of desolate tranquillity, to the Lodge, where she was to spend the first week.

Her friend was not in better spirits than herself. Lady Russell felt this break-up of the family exceedingly. Their respectability was as dear to her as her own; and a daily intercourse had become precious by habit. It was painful to look upon their deserted grounds, and still worse to anticipate the new hands they were to fall into; and to escape the solitariness and the melancholy of so altered a village, and be out of the way when Admiral and Mrs. Croft first arrived, she had determined to make her own absence from home begin when she must give up Anne. Accordingly their removal was made together, and Anne was set down at Uppercross Cottage, in the first stage of Lady Russell's journey.

Uppercross was a moderate-sized village, which a few years back had been completely in the old English style; containing only two houses superior in appearance to those of the yeomen and labourers—the mansion of the 'squire, with its high walls, great gates, and old trees, substantial and unmodernized—and the compact, tight parsonage, enclosed in its own neat garden, with a vine and a pear-tree trained round its casements; but upon the marriage of the young 'squire, it had received the improvement of a farmhouse elevated into a cottage for his residence; and Uppercross Cottage, with its veranda, French windows, and other prettiness, was quite as likely to catch the traveller's eye, as the more consistent and considerable aspect and premises of the Great House, about a quarter of a mile farther on.

Here Anne had often been staying. She knew the ways of Uppercross as well as those of Kellynch. The two families were so continually meeting, so much in the habit of running in and out of each other's house at all hours, that it was rather a surprise to her to find Mary alone; but being alone, her being unwell and out of spirits, was almost a matter of course. Though better endowed than the elder sister, Mary had not Anne's understanding or temper. While well, and happy, and properly attended to, she had great good humour and excellent spirits; but any indisposition sunk her completely;

she had no resources for solitude; and inheriting a considerable share of the Elliot self-importance, was very prone to add to every other distress that of fancying herself neglected and ill-used. In person, she was inferior to both sisters, and had, even in her bloom, only reached the dignity of being "a fine girl." She was now lying on the faded sofa of the pretty little drawing-room, the once elegant furniture of which had been gradually growing shabby, under the influence of four summers and two children; and, on Anne's appearing, greeted her with,

"So, you are come at last! I began to think I should never see you. I am so ill I can hardly speak. I have not seen a creature the whole morning!"

"I am sorry to find you unwell," replied Anne. "You sent me such a good account of yourself on Thursday!"

"Yes, I made the best of it; I always do; but I was very far from well at the time; and I do not think I ever was so ill in my life as I have been all this morning—very unfit to be left alone, I am sure. Suppose I were to be seized of a sudden in some dreadful way, and not able to ring the bell! So, Lady Russell would not get out. I do not think she has been in this house three times this summer."

Anne said what was proper, and enquired after her husband. "Oh! Charles is out shooting. I have not seen him since seven o'clock. He would go, though I told him how ill I was. He said he should not stay out long; but he has never come back, and now it is almost one. I assure you, I have not seen a soul this whole long morning."

"You have had your little boys with you?"

"Yes, as long as I could bear their noise; but they are so unmanageable that they do me more harm than good. Little Charles does not mind a word I say, and Walter is growing quite as bad."

"Well, you will soon be better now," replied Anne, cheerfully. "You know I always cure you when I come. How are your neighbours at the Great House?"

"I can give you no account of them. I have not seen one of them to-day, except Mr.

Musgrove, who just stopped and spoke through the window, but without getting off his horse; and though I told him how ill I was, not one of them have been near me. It did not happen to suit the Miss Musgroves, I suppose, and they never put themselves out of their way."

"You will see them yet, perhaps, before the morning is gone. It is early."

"I never want them, I assure you. They talk and laugh a great deal too much for me. O! Anne, I am so very unwell! It was quite unkind of you not to come on Thursday."

"My dear Mary, recollect what a comfortable account you sent me of yourself! You wrote in the cheerfullest manner, and said you were perfectly well, and in no hurry for me; and that being the case, you must be aware that my wish would be to remain with Lady Russell to the last: and besides what I felt on her account, I have really been so busy, have had so much to do, that I could not very conveniently have left Kellynch sooner."

"Dear me! what can *you* possibly have to do?"

"A great many things, I assure you. More than I can recollect in a moment: but I can tell you some. I have been making a duplicate of the catalogue of my father's books and pictures. I have been several times in the garden with Mackenzie, trying to understand, and make him understand, which of Elizabeth's plants are for Lady Russell. I have had all my own little concerns to arrange—books and music to divide, and all my trunks to repack, from not having understood in time what was intended as to the waggons. And one thing I have had to do, Mary, of a more trying nature; going to almost every house in the parish, as a sort of take-leave. I was told that they wished it. But all these things took up a great deal of time."

"Oh! well"—and after a moment's pause, "But you have never asked me one word about our dinner at the Pooles yesterday."

"Did you go then? I have made no enquiries, because I concluded you must have been obliged to give up the party."

"Oh! yes, I went. I was very well yesterday; nothing at all the matter with me till this morning. It would have been strange if I had not gone."

"I am very glad you were well enough, and I hope you had a pleasant party."

"Nothing remarkable. One always knows beforehand what the dinner will be, and who will be there. And it is so very uncomfortable, not having a carriage of one's own. Mr. and Mrs. Musgrove took me, and we were so crowded! They are both so very large, and take up so much room! And Mr. Musgrove always sits forward. So, there was I, crowded into the back seat with Henrietta and Louisa. And I think it very likely that my illness to-day may be owing to it."

A little farther perseverance in patience, and forced cheerfulness on Anne's side, produced nearly a cure on Mary's. She could soon sit upright on the sofa, and began to hope she might be able to leave it by dinner-time. Then, forgetting to think of it, she was at the other end of the room, beautifying a nosegay; then, she ate her cold meat; and then she was well enough to propose a little walk.

"Where shall we go?" said she, when they were ready. "I suppose you will not like to call at the Great House before they have been to see you?"

"I have not the smallest objection on that account," replied Anne. "I should never think of standing on such ceremony with people I know so well as Mrs. and the Miss Musgroves."

"Oh! but they ought to call upon you as soon as possible. They ought to feel what is due to you as *my* sister. However, we may as well go and sit with them a little while, and when we have got that over, we can enjoy our walk."

Anne had always thought such a style of intercourse highly imprudent; but she had ceased to endeavour to check it, from believing that, though there were on each side continual subjects of offence, neither family could now do without it. To the Great House accordingly they went, to sit the full

half hour in the old-fashioned square parlour, with a small carpet and shining floor, to which the present daughters of the house were gradually giving the proper air of confusion by a grand piano forte and a harp, flower-stands and little tables placed in every direction. Oh! could the originals of the portraits against the wainscot, could the gentlemen in brown velvet and the ladies in blue satin have seen what was going on, have been conscious of such an overthrow of all order and neatness! The portraits themselves seemed to be staring in astonishment.

The Musgroves, like their houses, were in a state of alteration, perhaps of improvement. The father and mother were in the old English style, and the young people in the new. Mr. and Mrs. Musgrove were a very good sort of people; friendly and hospitable, not much educated, and not at all elegant. Their children had more modern minds and manners. There was a numerous family; but the only two grown up, excepting Charles, were Henrietta and Louisa, young ladies of nineteen and twenty, who had brought from a school at Exeter all the usual stock of accomplishments, and were now, like thousands of other young ladies, living to be fashionable, happy, and merry. Their dress had every advantage, their faces were rather pretty, their spirits extremely good, their manners unembarrassed and pleasant; they were of consequence at home, and favourites abroad. Anne always contemplated them as some of the happiest creatures of her acquaintance; but still, saved as we all are by some comfortable feeling of superiority from wishing for the possibility of exchange, she would not have given up her own more elegant and cultivated mind for all their enjoyments; and envied them nothing but that seemingly perfect good understanding and agreement together, that good-humoured mutual affection, of which she had known so little herself with either of her sisters.

They were received with great cordiality. Nothing seemed amiss on the side of the Great House family, which was generally, as

Anne very well knew, the least to blame. The half hour was chatted away pleasantly enough; and she was not at all surprised, at the end of it, to have their walking party joined by both the Miss Musgroves, at Mary's particular invitation.

Chapter six

Anne had not wanted this visit to Uppercross, to learn that a removal from one set of people to another, though at a distance of only three miles, will often include a total change of conversation, opinion, and idea. She had never been staying there before, without being struck by it, or without wishing that other Elliots could have her advantage in seeing how unknown, or unconsidered there, were the affairs which at Kellynch-hall were treated as of such general publicity and pervading interest; yet, with all this experience, she believed she must now submit to feel that another lesson, in the art of knowing our own nothingness beyond our own circle, was become necessary for her; for certainly, coming as she did, with a heart full of the subject which had been completely occupying both houses in Kellynch for many weeks, she had expected rather more curiosity and sympathy than she found in the separate, but very similar remark of Mr. and Mrs. Musgrove—"So, Miss Anne, Sir Walter and your sister are gone; and what part of Bath do you think they will settle in?" and this, without much waiting for an answer—or in the young ladies' addition of, "I hope *we* shall be in Bath in the winter; but remember, papa, if we do go, we must be in a good situation—none of your Queen-squares for us!" or in the anxious supplement from Mary, of "Upon my word, I shall be pretty well off, when you are all gone away to be happy at Bath!"

She could only resolve to avoid such self-delusion in future, and think with heightened gratitude of the extraordinary blessing of having one such truly sympathising friend as Lady Russell.

The Mr. Musgroves had their own game to guard, and to destroy; their own horses, dogs, and newspapers to engage them; and the females were fully occupied in all the other common subjects of house-keeping, neighbours, dress, dancing, and music. She acknowledged it to be very fitting, that every little social commonwealth should dictate its own matters of discourse; and hoped, ere long, to become a not unworthy member of the one she was now transplanted into. With the prospect of spending at least two months at Uppercross, it was highly incumbent on her to clothe her imagination, her memory, and all her ideas in as much of Uppercross as possible.

She had no dread of these two months. Mary was not so repulsive and unsisterly as Elizabeth, nor so inaccessible to all influence of hers; neither was there any thing among the other component parts of the cottage inimical to comfort. She was always on friendly terms with her brother-in-law; and in the children, who loved her nearly as well, and respected her a great deal more than their mother, she had an object of interest, amusement, and wholesome exertion.

Charles Musgrove was civil and agreeable; in sense and temper he was undoubtedly superior to his wife; but not of powers, or conversation, or grace, to make the past, as they were connected together, at all a dangerous contemplation; though, at the same time, Anne could believe, with Lady Russell, that a more equal match might have greatly improved him; and that a woman of real understanding might have given more consequence to his character, and more usefulness, rationality, and elegance to his habits and pursuits. As it was, he did nothing with much zeal, but sport; and his time was otherwise trifled away, without benefit from books, or any thing else. He had very good spirits, which never seemed much affected by his wife's occasional lowness; bore with her unreasonableness sometimes to Anne's admiration; and, upon the whole, though there was very often a little disagreement (in which she had sometimes more share than she wished, being appealed to by both parties), they might pass for a happy couple. They were always perfectly agreed in the want of more money, and a strong inclination for a handsome present from his father; but here, as on most topics, he had the superiority, for while Mary thought it a great shame that such a present was not made, he always contended for his father's having many other uses for his money, and a right to spend it as he liked.

As to the management of their children, his theory was much better than his wife's, and his practice not so bad. "I could manage them very well, if it were not for Mary's interference," was what Anne often heard him say, and had a good deal of faith in; but when listening in turn to Mary's reproach of "Charles spoils the children so that I cannot get them into any order," she never had the smallest temptation to say, "Very true."

One of the least agreeable circumstances of her residence there, was her being treated with too much confidence by all parties, and being too much in the secret of the complaints of each house. Known to have some influence with her sister, she was continually requested, or at least receiving hints to exert it, beyond what was practicable. "I wish you could persuade Mary not to be always fancying herself ill," was Charles's language; and, in an unhappy mood, thus spoke Mary, "I do believe if Charles were to see me dying, he would not think there was any thing the matter with me. I am sure, Anne, if you would, you might persuade him that I really am very ill—a great deal worse than I ever own."

Mary's declaration was, "I hate sending the children to the Great House, though their grandmamma is always wanting to see them, for she humours and indulges them to such a degree, and gives them so much trash and sweet things, that they are sure to come back sick and cross for the rest of the day." And Mrs. Musgrove took the first opportunity of being alone with Anne, to say, "Oh! Miss Anne, I cannot help wishing Mrs. Charles had a little of your method with those children. They are quite different creatures with you! But to be sure, in general they are so spoilt! It is a pity you cannot put your sister in the way of managing them. They are as fine healthy children as ever were seen, poor little dears, without partiality; but Mrs. Charles knows no more how they should be treated!—Bless me, how troublesome they are sometimes!—I assure you, Miss Anne, it prevents my wishing to see them at our house so often as I otherwise should. I believe Mrs. Charles is not quite pleased with my not inviting them oftener; but you know it is very bad to have children with one, that one is obliged to be checking every moment: 'don't do this, and don't do that,' or that one can only keep in tolerable order by more cake than is good for them."

She had this communication, moreover, from Mary. "Mrs. Musgrove thinks all her servants so steady, that it would be high treason to call it in question; but I am sure, without exaggeration, that her upper house-maid and laundry-maid, instead of being in their business, are gadding about the village, all day long. I meet them wherever I go; and I declare, I never go twice into my nursery without seeing something of them. If Jemima were not the trustiest, steadiest creature in the world, it would be enough to spoil her; for she tells me, they are always tempting her to take a walk with them." And on Mrs. Musgrove's side, it was, "I make a rule of never interfering in any of my daughter-in-law's concerns, for I know it would not do; but I shall tell *you*, Miss Anne, because you may be able to set things to rights, that I have no very good opinion of Mrs. Charles's nursery-maid: I hear strange stories of her; she is always upon the gad: and from my own knowledge, I can declare, she is such a fine-dressing lady, that she is enough to ruin any servants she comes near. Mrs. Charles quite swears by her, I know; but I just give you this hint, that you may be upon the watch; because, if you see any thing amiss, you need not be afraid of mentioning it."

Again; it was Mary's complaint, that Mrs. Musgrove was very apt not to give her the precedence that was her due, when they dined at the Great House with other families; and she did not see any reason why she was to be considered so much at home as to lose her place. And one day, when Anne was walking with only the Miss Musgroves, one of them, after talking of rank, people of rank, and jealousy of rank, said, "I have no scruple of observing to *you*, how nonsensical some persons are about their place, because, all the world knows how easy and indifferent you are about it: but I wish any body could give Mary a hint that it would be a great deal better if she were not so very tenacious; especially, if she would not be always putting herself forward to take place of mamma. Nobody doubts her right to have precedence of mamma, but it would be more becoming in her not to be always insisting on it. It is not that mamma cares about it the least in the world, but I know it is taken notice of by many persons."

How was Anne to set all these matters to rights? She could do little more than listen patiently, soften every grievance, and excuse each to the other, give them all hints of the forbearance necessary between such near neighbours, and make those hints broadest which were meant for her sister's benefit.

In all other respects, her visit began and proceeded very well. Her own spirits improved by change of place and subject, by being removed three miles from Kellynch: Mary's ailments lessened by having a constant companion; and their daily intercourse with the other family, since there was neither superior affection, confidence, nor employment in the cottage, to be interrupted by it, was rather an advantage. It was certainly carried nearly as far as possible, for they met every morning, and hardly ever spent an evening asunder; but she believed they should not have done so well without the sight of Mr. and Mrs. Musgrove's respectable forms in the usual places, or without the talking, laughing, and singing of their daughters.

She played a great deal better than either of the Miss Musgroves; but having no voice, no knowledge of the harp, and no fond parents to sit by and fancy themselves delighted, her performance was little thought of, only out of civility, or to refresh the others, as she was well aware. She knew that when she played she was giving pleasure only to herself; but this was no new sensation: excepting one short period of her life, she had never, since the age of fourteen, never since the loss of her dear mother, known the happiness of being listened to, or encouraged by any just appreciation or real taste. In music she had been always used to feel alone in the world; and Mr. and Mrs. Musgrove's fond partiality for their own daughters' performance, and total indifference to any other person's, gave her much more pleasure for their sakes, than mortification for her own.

The party at the Great House was sometimes increased by other company. The neighbourhood was not large, but the Musgroves were visited by every body, and had more dinner parties, and more callers, more visitors by invitation and by chance, than any other family. They were more completely popular.

The girls were wild for dancing; and the evenings ended, occasionally, in an unpremeditated little ball. There was a family of cousins within a walk of Uppercross, in less affluent circumstances, who depended on the Musgroves for all their pleasures: they would come at any time, and help play at any thing, or dance any where; and Anne, very much preferring the office of musician to a more active post, played country dances to them by the hour together; a kindness which always recommended her musical powers to the notice of Mr. and Mrs. Musgrove more than any thing else, and often drew this compliment: "Well done, Miss Anne! very well done indeed! Lord bless me! how those little fingers of yours fly about!"

So passed the first three weeks. Michaelmas came; and now Anne's heart must be in Kellynch again. A beloved home made over to others; all the precious rooms and furniture, groves, and prospects, beginning to own other eyes and other limbs! She could not think of much else on the 29th of September; and she had this sympathetic touch in the evening, from Mary, who, on having occasion to note down the day of the month, exclaimed, "Dear me! is not this the day the Crofts were to come to Kellynch? I am glad I did not think of it before. How low it makes me!"

The Crofts took possession with true naval alertness, and were to be visited. Mary deplored the necessity for herself. "Nobody knew how much she should suffer. She should put it off as long as she could." But was not easy till she had talked Charles into driving her over on an early day; and was in a very animated, comfortable state of imaginary agitation, when she came back. Anne had very sincerely rejoiced in there being no means of her going. She wished, however, to see the Crofts, and was glad to be within when the visit was returned. They came; the master of the house was not at home, but the two sisters were together; and as it chanced that Mrs. Croft fell to the share of Anne, while the admiral sat by Mary, and made himself very agreeable by his good-humoured notice of her little boys, she was well able to watch for a likeness, and if it failed her in the features, to catch it in the voice, or the turn of sentiment and expression.

Mrs. Croft, though neither tall nor fat, had a squareness, uprightness, and vigour of form, which gave importance to her person. She had bright dark eyes, good teeth, and altogether an agreeable face; though her reddened and weather-beaten complexion, the consequence of her having been almost as much at sea as her husband, made her seem to have lived some years longer in the world than her real eight-and-thirty. Her manners were open, easy, and decided, like one who had no distrust of herself, and no doubts of what to do; without any approach to coarseness, however, or any want of good humour. Anne gave her credit, indeed, for feelings of great consideration towards herself, in all that related to Kellynch; and it pleased her: especially, as she had satisfied herself in the very first half minute, in the instant even of introduction, that there was not the smallest symptom of any knowledge or suspicion on Mrs. Croft's side, to give a bias of any sort. She was quite easy on that head, and consequently full of strength and courage, till for a moment electrified by Mrs. Croft's suddenly saying,

"It was you, and not your sister, I find, that my brother had the pleasure of being acquainted with, when he was in this country."

Anne hoped she had outlived the age of blushing; but the age of emotion she certainly had not.

"Perhaps you may not have heard that he is married," added Mrs. Croft.

She could now answer as she ought; and was happy to feel, when Mrs. Croft's next words explained it to be Mr. Wentworth of whom she spoke, that she had said nothing which might not do for either brother. She immediately felt how reasonable it was, that Mrs. Croft should be thinking and speaking of Edward, and not of Frederick; and with shame at her own forgetfulness, applied herself to the knowledge of their former neighbour's present state, with proper interest.

The rest was all tranquillity; till just as they were moving, she heard the admiral say to Mary,

"We are expecting a brother of Mrs. Croft's here soon; I dare say you know him by name."

He was cut short by the eager attacks of the little boys, clinging to him like an old friend, and declaring he should not go; and being too much engrossed by proposals of carrying them away in his coat pocket, etc., to have another moment for finishing or recollecting what he had begun, Anne was left to persuade herself, as well as she could, that the same brother must still be in question. She could not, however, reach such a degree of certainty, as not to be anxious to hear whether any thing had been said on the subject at the other house, where the Crofts had previously been calling.

The folks of the Great House were to spend the evening of this day at the Cottage; and it being now too late in the year for such visits to be made on foot, the coach was beginning to be listened for, when the youngest Miss Musgrove walked in. That she was coming to apologize, and that they should have to spend the evening by themselves, was the first black idea; and Mary was quite ready to be affronted, when Louisa made all right by saying, that she only came on foot, to leave more room for the harp, which was bringing in the carriage.

"And I will tell you our reason," she added, "and all about it. I am come on to give you notice, that papa and mamma are out of spirits this evening, especially mamma; she is thinking so much of poor Richard! And we agreed it would be best to have the harp, for it seems to amuse her more than the piano-forte. I will tell you why she is out of spirits. When the Crofts called this morning (they called here afterwards, did not they?), they happened to say, that her brother, Captain Wentworth, is just returned to England, or paid off, or something, and is coming to see them almost directly; and most unluckily it came into mamma's head, when they were gone, that Wentworth, or something very like it, was the name of poor Richard's captain, at one time, I do not know when or where, but a great while before he died, poor fellow! And upon looking over his letters and things, she found it was so; and is perfectly sure that this must be the very man, and her head is quite full of it, and of poor Richard! So we must all be as merry as we can, that she may not be dwelling upon such gloomy things."

The real circumstances of this pathetic piece of family history were, that the Musgroves had had the ill fortune of a very troublesome, hopeless son; and the good fortune to lose him before he reached his twentieth year; that he had been sent to sea, because he was stupid and unmanageable on shore; that he had been very little cared for at any time by his family, though quite as much as he deserved; seldom heard of, and scarcely at all regretted, when the intelligence of his death abroad had worked its way to Uppercross, two years before.

He had, in fact, though his sisters were now doing all they could for him, by calling him "poor Richard," been nothing better than a thick-headed, unfeeling, unprofitable Dick Musgrove, who had never done any thing to entitle himself to more than the abbreviation of his name, living or dead.

He had been several years at sea, and had, in the course of those removals to which all midshipmen are liable, and especially such midshipmen as every captain wishes to get rid, of, been six months on board Captain Frederick Wentworth's frigate, the Laconia; and from the Laconia he had, under the influence of his captain, written the only two letters which his father and mother had ever received from him during the whole of his absence; that is to say, the only two disinterested letters; all the rest had been mere applications for money.

In each letter he had spoken well of his captain; but yet, so little were they in the habit of attending to such matters, so unobservant and incurious were they as to the names of men or ships, that it had made scarcely any impression at the time; and that Mrs. Musgrove should have been suddenly struck, this very day, with a recollection of the name of Wentworth, as connected with her son, seemed one of those extraordinary bursts of mind which do sometimes occur.

She had gone to her letters, and found it all as she supposed; and the reperusal of these letters, after so long an interval, her poor son gone for ever, and all the strength of his faults forgotten, had affected her spirits exceedingly, and thrown her into greater grief for him than she had known on first hearing of his death. Mr. Musgrove was, in a lesser degree, affected likewise; and when they reached the cottage, they were evidently in want, first, of being listened to anew on this subject, and afterwards, of all the relief which cheerful companions could give.

To hear them talking so much of Captain Wentworth, repeating his name so often, puzzling over past years, and at last ascertaining that it *might*, that it probably *would*, turn out to be the very same Captain Wentworth whom they recollected meeting, once or twice, after their coming back from Clifton—a very fine young man; but they could not say whether it was seven or eight years ago—was a new sort of trial to Anne's nerves. She found, however, that it was one to which she must enure herself. Since he actually was expected in the country, she must teach herself to be insensible on such points. And not only did it appear that he was expected, and speedily, but the Musgroves, in their warm gratitude for the kindness he had shewn poor Dick, and very high respect for his character, stamped as it was by poor Dick's having been six months under his care, and mentioning him in strong, though not perfectly well spelt praise, as "a fine dashing felow, only two perticular about the school-master,"[4] were bent on introducing themselves, and seeking his acquaintance, as soon as they could hear of his arrival.

The resolution of doing so helped to form the comfort of their evening.

Chapter seven

A very few days more, and Captain Wentworth was known to be at Kellynch, and Mr. Musgrove had called on him, and come back warm in his praise, and he was engaged with the Crofts to dine at Uppercross, by the end of another week. It had been a great disappointment to Mr. Musgrove, to find that no earlier day could be fixed, so impatient was he to shew his gratitude, by seeing Captain Wentworth under his own roof, and welcoming him to all that was strongest and best in his cellars. But a week must pass; only a week, in Anne's reckoning, and then, she supposed, they must meet; and soon she began to wish that she could feel secure even for a week.

Captain Wentworth made a very early return to Mr. Musgrove's civility, and she was all but calling there in the same half hour! She and Mary were actually setting forward for the great house, where, as she afterwards learnt, they must inevitably have found him, when they were stopped by the eldest boy's being at that moment brought home in consequence of a bad fall. The child's situation put the visit entirely aside, but she could not hear of her escape with indifference, even in the midst of the serious anxiety which they afterwards felt on his account.

His collar-bone was found to be dislocated, and such injury received in the back, as roused the most alarming ideas. It was an afternoon of distress, and Anne had every thing to do at once—the apothecary to send for—the father to have pursued and informed—the mother to support and keep from hysterics—the servants to control—the youngest child to banish, and the poor suffering one to attend and soothe—besides sending, as soon as she recollected it, proper notice to the other house, which brought her an accession rather of frightened, enquiring companions, than of very useful assistants.

Her brother's return was the first comfort; he could take best care of his wife, and the second blessing was the arrival of the apothecary. Till he came and had examined the child, their apprehensions were the worse for being vague; they suspected great injury, but knew not where; but now the collar-bone was soon replaced, and though Mr.

---

[4] "the school-master." Every ship in the navy was required to have a schoolmaster to teach writing, arithmetic, and navigation to the midshipmen. Most such figures were not very competent and were given little support by their commanders, who unlike Captain Wentworth took no interest in them.

Robinson felt and felt, and rubbed, and looked grave, and spoke low words both to the father and the aunt, still they were all to hope the best, and to be able to part and eat their dinner in tolerable ease of mind; and then it was, just before they parted, that the two young aunts were able so far to digress from their nephew's state, as to give the information of Captain Wentworth's visit; staying five minutes behind their father and mother, to endeavour to express how perfectly delighted they were with him, how much handsomer, how infinitely more agreeable they thought him than any individual among their male acquaintance, who had been at all a favourite before—how glad they had been to hear papa invite him to stay dinner—how sorry when he said it was quite out of his power—and how glad again, when he had promised in reply to papa and mamma's farther pressing invitations, to come and dine with them on the morrow, actually on the morrow!—And he had promised it in so pleasant a manner, as if he felt all the motive of their attention just as he ought! —And, in short, he had looked and said every thing with such exquisite grace, that they could assure them all, their heads were both turned by him!—And off they ran, quite as full of glee as of love, and apparently more full of Captain Wentworth than of little Charles.

The same story and the same raptures were repeated, when the two girls came with their father, through the gloom of the evening, to make enquiries; and Mr. Musgrove, no longer under the first uneasiness about his heir, could add his confirmation and praise, and hope there would be now no occasion for putting Captain Wentworth off, and only be sorry to think that the cottage party, probably, would not like to leave the little boy, to give him the meeting. "Oh, no! as to leaving the little boy!"—both father and mother were in much too strong and recent alarm to bear the thought; and Anne, in the joy of the escape, could not help adding her warm protestations to theirs.

Charles Musgrove, indeed, afterwards shewed more of inclination; "the child was going on so well—and he wished so much to be introduced to Captain Wentworth, that, perhaps, he might join them in the evening; he would not dine from home, but he might walk in for half an hour." But in this he was eagerly opposed by his wife, with "Oh, no! indeed, Charles, I cannot bear to have you go away. Only think, if any thing should happen!"

The child had a good night, and was going on well the next day. It must be a work of time to ascertain that no injury had been done to the spine, but Mr. Robinson found nothing to increase alarm, and Charles Musgrove began consequently to feel no necessity for longer confinement. The child was to be kept in bed, and amused as quietly as possible; but what was there for a father to do? This was quite a female case, and it would be highly absurd in him, who could be of no use at home, to shut himself up. His father very much wished him to meet Captain Wentworth, and there being no sufficient reason against it, he ought to go; and it ended in his making a bold public declaration, when he came in from shooting, of his meaning to dress directly, and dine at the other house.

"Nothing can be going on better than the child," said he, "so I told my father just now that I would come, and he thought me quite right. Your sister being with you, my love, I have no scruple at all. You would not like to leave him yourself, but you see I can be of no use. Anne will send for me if any thing is the matter."

Husbands and wives generally understand when opposition will be vain. Mary knew, from Charles's manner of speaking, that he was quite determined on going, and that it would be of no use to teaze him. She said nothing, therefore, till he was out of the room, but as soon as there was only Anne to hear,

"So! You and I are to be left to shift by ourselves, with this poor sick child—and not a creature coming near us all the evening! I knew how it would be. This is always my luck! If there is any thing disagreeable going on, men are always sure to get out of it, and Charles is as bad as any of them. Very unfeeling! I must say it is very unfeeling of him, to be running away from his poor little boy; talks of his being going on so well! How does he know that he is going on well, or that there may not be a sudden change half an hour hence? I did not think Charles would have been so unfeeling. So, here he is to go away and enjoy himself, and because I am the poor mother, I am not to be allowed to stir; and yet, I am sure, I am more unfit than any body else to be about the child. My being the mother is the very reason why my feelings should not be tried. I am not at all equal to it. You saw how hysterical I was yesterday."

"But that was only the effect of the suddenness of your alarm—of the shock. You will not be hysterical again. I dare say we shall have nothing to distress us. I perfectly understand Mr. Robinson's directions, and have no fears; and indeed, Mary, I cannot wonder at your husband. Nursing does not belong to a man, it is not his province. A sick child is always the mother's property, her own feelings generally make it so."

"I hope I am as fond of my child as any mother—but I do not know that I am of any more use in the sick-room than Charles, for I cannot be always scolding and teazing a poor child when it is ill; and you saw, this morning, that if I told him to keep quiet, he was sure to begin kicking about. I have not nerves for the sort of thing."

"But, could you be comfortable yourself, to be spending the whole evening away from the poor boy?"

"Yes; you see his papa can, and why should not I?—Jemima is so careful! And she could send us word every hour how he was. I really think Charles might as well have told his father we would all come. I am not more alarmed about little Charles now than he is. I was dreadfully alarmed yesterday, but the case is very different to-day."

"Well—if you do not think it too late to give notice for yourself, suppose you were to

go, as well as your husband. Leave little Charles to my care. Mr. and Mrs. Musgrove cannot think it wrong, while I remain with him."

"Are you serious?" cried Mary, her eyes brightening. "Dear me! that's a very good thought, very good indeed. To be sure I may just as well go as not, for I am of no use at home—am I? and it only harasses me. You, who have not a mother's feelings, are a great deal the properest person. You can make little Charles do any thing; he always minds you at a word. It will be a great deal better than leaving him with only Jemima. Oh! I will certainly go; I am sure I ought if I can, quite as much as Charles, for they want me excessively to be acquainted with Captain Wentworth, and I know you do not mind being left alone. An excellent thought of yours, indeed, Anne! I will go and tell Charles, and get ready directly. You can send for us, you know, at a moment's notice, if any thing is the matter; but I dare say there will be nothing to alarm you. I should not go, you may be sure, if I did not feel quite at ease about my dear child."

The next moment she was tapping at her husband's dressing-room door, and as Anne followed her up stairs, she was in time for the whole conversation, which began with Mary's saying, in a tone of great exultation,

"I mean to go with you, Charles, for I am of no more use at home than you are. If I were to shut myself up for ever with the child, I should not be able to persuade him to do any thing he did not like. Anne will stay; Anne undertakes to stay at home and take care of him. It is Anne's own proposal, and so I shall go with you, which will be a great deal better, for I have not dined at the other house since Tuesday."

"This is very kind of Anne," was her husband's answer, "and I should be very glad to have you go; but it seems rather hard that she should be left at home by herself, to nurse our sick child."

Anne was now at hand to take up her own cause, and the sincerity of her manner being soon sufficient to convince him, where conviction was at least very agreeable, he had no farther scruples as to her being left to dine alone, though he still wanted her to join them in the evening, when the child might be at rest for the night, and kindly urged her to let him come and fetch her; but she was quite unpersuadable; and this being the case, she had ere long the pleasure of seeing them set off together in high spirits. They were gone, she hoped, to be happy, however oddly constructed such happiness might seem; as for herself, she was left with as many sensations of comfort, as were, perhaps, ever likely to be hers. She knew herself to be of the first utility to the child; and what was it to her, if Frederick Wentworth were only half a mile distant, making himself agreeable to others!

She would have liked to know how he felt as to a meeting. Perhaps indifferent, if indifference could exist under such circumstances. He must be either indifferent or unwilling. Had he wished ever to see her again, he need not have waited till this time; he would have done what she could not but believe that in his place she should have done long ago, when events had been early giving him the independence which alone had been wanting.

Her brother and sister came back delighted with their new acquaintance, and their visit in general. There had been music, singing, talking, laughing, all that was most agreeable; charming manners in Captain Wentworth, no shyness or reserve; they seemed all to know each other perfectly, and he was coming the very next morning to shoot with Charles. He was to come to breakfast, but not at the Cottage, though that had been proposed at first; but then he had been pressed to come to the Great House instead, and he seemed afraid of being in Mrs. Charles Musgrove's way, on account of the child; and therefore, somehow, they hardly knew how, it ended in Charles's being to meet him to breakfast at his father's.

Anne understood it. He wished to avoid seeing her. He had enquired after her, she found, slightly, as might suit a former slight acquaintance, seeming to acknowledge such as she had acknowledged, actuated, perhaps, by the same view of escaping introduction when they were to meet.

The morning hours of the Cottage were always later than those of the other house; and on the morrow the difference was so great, that Mary and Anne were not more than beginning breakfast when Charles came in to say that they were just setting off, that he was come for his dogs, that his sisters were following with Captain Wentworth, his sisters meaning to visit Mary and the child, and Captain Wentworth proposing also to wait on her for a few minutes, if not inconvenient; and though Charles had answered for the child's being in no such state as could make it inconvenient, Captain Wentworth would not be satisfied without his running on to give notice.

Mary, very much gratified by this attention, was delighted to receive him; while a thousand feelings rushed on Anne, of which this was the most consoling, that it would soon be over. And it was soon over. In two minutes after Charles's preparation, the others appeared; they were in the drawing-room. Her eye half met Captain Wentworth's; a bow, a curtsey passed; she heard his voice—he talked to Mary, said all that was right; said something to the Miss Musgroves, enough to mark an easy footing: the room seemed full—full of persons and voices—but a few minutes ended it. Charles shewed himself at the window, all was ready, their visitor had bowed and was gone; the Miss Musgroves were gone too, suddenly resolving to walk to the end of the village with the sportsmen: the room was cleared, and Anne might finish her breakfast as she could.

"It is over! it is over!" she repeated to herself again, and again, in nervous gratitude. "The worst is over!"

Mary talked, but she could not attend. She had seen him. They had met. They had been once more in the same room!

Soon, however, she began to reason with

herself, and try to be feeling less. Eight years, almost eight years had passed, since all had been given up. How absurd to be resuming the agitation which such an interval had banished into distance and indistinctness! What might not eight years do? Events of every description, changes, alienations, removals—all, all must be comprised in it; and oblivion of the past—how natural, how certain too! It included nearly a third part of her own life.

Alas! with all her reasonings, she found, that to retentive feelings eight years may be little more than nothing.

Now, how were his sentiments to be read? Was this like wishing to avoid her? And the next moment she was hating herself for the folly which asked the question.

On one other question, which perhaps her utmost wisdom might not have prevented, she was soon spared all suspense; for after the Miss Musgroves had returned and finished their visit at the Cottage, she had this spontaneous information from Mary:

"Captain Wentworth is not very gallant by you, Anne, though he was so attentive to me. Henrietta asked him what he thought of you, when they went away; and he said you were so altered he should not have known you again."

Mary had no feelings to make her respect her sister's in a common way; but she was perfectly unsuspicious of being inflicting any peculiar wound.

"Altered beyond his knowledge!" Anne fully submitted, in silent, deep mortification. Doubtless it was so; and she could take no revenge, for he was not altered, or not for the worse. She had already acknowledged it to herself, and she could not think differently, let him think of her as he would. No; the years which had destroyed her youth and bloom had only given him a more glowing, manly, open look, in no respect lessening his personal advantages. She had seen the same Frederick Wentworth.

"So altered that he should not have known her again!" These were words which could not but dwell with her. Yet she soon began to rejoice that she had heard them. They were of sobering tendency; they allayed agitation; they composed, and consequently must make her happier.

Frederick Wentworth had used such words, or something like them, but without an idea that they would be carried round to her. He had thought her wretchedly altered, and, in the first moment of appeal, had spoken as he felt. He had not forgiven Anne Elliot. She had used him ill; deserted and disappointed him; and worse, she had shewn a feebleness of character in doing so, which his own decided, confident temper could not endure. She had given him up to oblige others. It had been the effect of overpersuasion. It had been weakness and timidity.

He had been most warmly attached to her, and had never seen a woman since whom he thought her equal; but, except from some natural sensation of curiosity, he had no desire of meeting her again. Her power with him was gone for ever.

It was now his object to marry. He was rich, and being turned on shore, fully intended to settle as soon as he could be properly tempted; actually looking round, ready to fall in love with all the speed which a clear head and quick taste could allow. He had a heart for either of the Miss Musgroves, if they could catch it; a heart, in short, for any pleasing young woman who came in his way, excepting Anne Elliot. This was his only secret exception, when he said to his sister, in answer to her suppositions,

"Yes, here I am, Sophia, quite ready to make a foolish match. Any body between fifteen and thirty may have me for asking. A little beauty, and a few smiles, and a few compliments to the navy, and I am a lost man. Should not this be enough for a sailor, who has had no society among women to make him nice?"

He said it, she knew, to be contradicted. His bright, proud eye spoke the conviction that he was nice; and Anne Elliot was not out of his thoughts, when he more seriously described the woman he should wish to meet with. "A strong mind, with sweetness of manner," made the first and the last of the description.

"This is the woman I want," said he. "Something a little inferior I shall of course put up with, but it must not be much. If I am a fool, I shall be a fool indeed, for I have thought on the subject more than most men."

Chapter eight

From this time Captain Wentworth and Anne Elliot were repeatedly in the same circle. They were soon dining in company together at Mr. Musgrove's, for the little boy's state could no longer supply his aunt with a pretence for absenting herself; and this was but the beginning of other dinings and other meetings.

Whether former feelings were to be renewed, must be brought to the proof; former times must undoubtedly be brought to the recollection of each; *they* could not but be reverted to; the year of their engagement could not but be named by him, in the little narratives or descriptions which conversation called forth. His profession qualified him, his disposition led him, to talk; and "*That* was in the year six"; "*That* happened before I went to sea in the year six," occurred in the course of the first evening they spent together: and though his voice did not falter, and though she had no reason to suppose his eye wandering towards her while he spoke, Anne felt the utter impossibility, from her knowledge of his mind, that he could be unvisited by remembrance any more than herself. There must be the same immediate association of thought, though she was very far from conceiving it to be of equal pain.

They had no conversation together, no intercourse but what the commonest civility required. Once so much to each other! Now nothing! There *had* been a time, when of all the large party now filling the drawing-room at Uppercross, they would have found it most difficult to cease to speak to one another. With the exception, perhaps, of Admiral and Mrs. Croft, who seemed particularly attached and happy (Anne could allow no other exception even among the married couples), there could have been no two hearts so open, no tastes so similar, no feelings so in unison, no countenances so beloved. Now they were as strangers; nay, worse than strangers, for they could never become acquainted. It was a perpetual estrangement.

When he talked, she heard the same voice, and discerned the same mind. There was a very general ignorance of all naval matters throughout the party; and he was very much questioned, and especially by the two Miss Musgroves, who seemed hardly to have any eyes but for him, as to the manner of living on board, daily regulations, food, hours, etc.; and their surprise at his accounts, at learning the degree of accommodation and arrangement which was practicable, drew from him some pleasant ridicule, which reminded Anne of the early days when she too had been ignorant, and she too had been accused of supposing sailors to be living on board without any thing to eat, or any cook to dress it if there were, or any servant to wait, or any knife and fork to use.

From thus listening and thinking, she was roused by a whisper of Mrs. Musgrove's, who, overcome by fond regrets, could not help saying.

"Ah! Miss Anne, if it had pleased Heaven to spare my poor son, I dare say he would have been just such another by this time."

Anne suppressed a smile, and listened kindly, while Mrs. Musgrove relieved her heart a little more; and for a few minutes, therefore, could not keep pace with the conversation of the others. When she could let her attention take its natural course again, she found the Miss Musgroves just fetching the navy-list (their own navy-list, the first that had ever been at Uppercross), and sitting down together to pore over it, with the professed view of finding out the ships which Captain Wentworth had commanded.

"Your first was the Asp, I remember; we will look for the Asp."

"You will not find her there. Quite worn out and broken up. I was the last man who commanded her. Hardly fit for service then. Reported fit for home service for a year or two, and so I was sent off to the West Indies."

The girls looked all amazement.

"The admiralty," he continued, "entertain themselves now and then, with sending a few hundred men to sea, in a ship not fit to be employed. But they have a great many to provide for; and among the thousands that may just as well go to the bottom as not, it is impossible for them to distinguish the very set who may be least missed."

"Phoo! phoo!" cried the admiral, "what stuff these young fellows talk! Never was a better sloop than the Asp in her day. For an old built sloop, you would not see her equal. Lucky fellow to get her! He knows there must have been twenty better men than himself applying for her at the same time. Lucky fellow to get any thing so soon, with no more interest than his."

"I felt my luck, admiral, I assure you," replied Captain Wentworth, seriously. "I was as well satisfied with my appointment as you can desire. It was a great object with me, at that time, to be at sea, a very great object. I wanted to be doing something."

"To be sure you did. What should a young fellow, like you, do ashore for half a year together? If a man has not a wife, he soon wants to be afloat again."

"But, Captain Wentworth," cried Louisa, "how vexed you must have been when you came to the Asp, to see what an old thing they had given you."

"I knew pretty well what she was, before that day," said he, smiling. "I had no more discoveries to make, than you would have as to the fashion and strength of any old pelisse, which you had seen lent about among half your acquaintance, ever since you could remember, and which at last, on some very

wet day, is lent to yourself. Ah! she was a dear old Asp to me. She did all that I wanted. I knew she would. I knew that we should either go to the bottom together, or that she would be the making of me; and I never had two days of foul weather all the time I was at sea in her; and after taking privateers enough to be very entertaining, I had the good luck, in my passage home the next autumn, to fall in with the very French frigate I wanted. I brought her into Plymouth; and here was another instance of luck. We had not been six hours in the Sound, when a gale came on, which lasted four days and nights, and which would have done for poor old Asp, in half the time; our touch with the Great Nation not having much improved our condition. Four-and-twenty hours later, and I should only have been a gallant Captain Wentworth, in a small paragraph at one corner of the newspapers; and being lost in only a sloop, nobody would have thought about me."

Anne's shudderings were to herself alone: but the Miss Musgroves could be as open as they were sincere, in their exclamations of pity and horror.

"And so then, I suppose," said Mrs. Musgrove, in a low voice, as if thinking aloud, "so then he went away to the Laconia, and there he met with our poor boy. Charles, my dear" (beckoning him to her), "do ask Captain Wentworth where it was he first met with your poor brother. I always forget."

"It was at Gibraltar, mother, I know. Dick had been left ill at Gibraltar, with a recommendation from his former captain to Captain Wentworth."

"Oh!—but, Charles, tell Captain Wentworth, he need not be afraid of mentioning poor Dick before me, for it would be rather a pleasure to hear him talked of, by such a good friend."

Charles, being somewhat more mindful of the probabilities of the case, only nodded in reply, and walked away.

The girls were now hunting for the Laconia; and Captain Wentworth could not deny himself the pleasure of taking the precious volume into his own hands to save them the trouble, and once more read aloud the little statement of her name and rate and present non-commissioned class, observing over it, that she too had been one of the best friends man ever had.

"Ah! those were pleasant days when I had the Laconia! How fast I made money in her. A friend of mine, and I, had such a lovely cruise together off the Western Islands. Poor Harville, sister! You know how much he wanted money—worse than myself. He had a wife. Excellent fellow! I shall never forget his happiness. He felt it all, so much for her sake. I wished for him again the next summer, when I had still the same luck in the Mediterranean."

"And I am sure, Sir," said Mrs. Musgrove, "it was a lucky day for *us*, when you were put captain into that ship. *We* shall never forget what you did."

Her feelings made her speak low; and Captain Wentworth, hearing only in part, and probably not having Dick Musgrove at all near his thoughts, looked rather in suspense, and as if waiting for more.

"My brother," whispered one of the girls; "mamma is thinking of poor Richard."

"Poor dear fellow!" continued Mrs. Musgrove; "he was grown so steady, and such an excellent correspondent, while he was under your care! Ah! it would have been a happy thing, if he had never left you. I assure you, Captain Wentworth, we are very sorry he ever left you."

There was a momentary expression in Captain Wentworth's face at this speech, a certain glance of his bright eye, and curl of his handsome mouth, which convinced Anne, that instead of sharing in Mrs. Musgrove's kind wishes, as to her son, he had probably been at some pains to get rid of him; but it was too transient an indulgence of self-amusement to be detected by any who understood him less than herself; in another moment he was perfectly collected and serious; and almost instantly afterwards coming up to the sofa, on which she and Mrs. Musgrove were sitting, took a place by the latter, and entered into conversation with her, in a low voice, about her son, doing it with so much sympathy and natural grace, as shewed the kindest consideration for all that was real and unabsurd in the parent's feelings.

They were actually on the same sofa, for Mrs. Musgrove had most readily made room for him—they were divided only by Mrs. Musgrove. It was no insignificant barrier indeed. Mrs. Musgrove was of a comfortable substantial size, infinitely more fitted by nature to express good cheer and good humour, than tenderness and sentiment; and while the agitations of Anne's slender form, and pensive face, may be considered as very completely screened, Captain Wentworth should be allowed some credit for the self-command with which he attended to her large fat sighings over the destiny of a son, whom alive nobody had cared for.

Personal size and mental sorrow have certainly no necessary proportions. A large bulky figure has as good a right to be in deep affliction, as the most graceful set of limbs in the world. But, fair or not fair, there are unbecoming conjunctions, which reason will patronize in vain—which taste cannot tolerate—which ridicule will seize.

The admiral, after taking two or three refreshing turns about the room with his hands behind him, being called to order by his wife, now came up to Captain Wentworth, and without taking any observation of what he might be interrupting, thinking only of his own thoughts, began with,

"If you had been a week later at Lisbon, last spring, Frederick, you would have been asked to give a passage to Lady Mary Grierson and her daughters."

"Should I? I am glad I was not a week later then."

The admiral abused him for his want of gallantry. He defended himself; though professing that he would never willingly admit any ladies on board a ship of his, excepting for a ball, or a visit, which a few hours might comprehend.

"But, if I know myself," said he, "this is from no want of gallantry towards them. It is rather from feeling how impossible it is, with all one's efforts, and all one's sacrifices, to make the accommodations on board, such as women ought to have. There can be no want of gallantry, admiral, in rating the claims of women to every personal comfort *high*—and this is what I do. I hate to hear of women on board, or to see them on board; and no ship, under my command, shall ever convey a family of ladies any where, if I can help it."

This brought his sister upon him.

"Oh Frederick!—But I cannot believe it of you. All idle refinement!—Women may be as comfortable on board, as in the best house in England. I believe I have lived as much on board as most women, and I know nothing superior to the accommodations of a man of war. I declare I have not a comfort or an indulgence about me, even at Kellynch-hall" (with a kind bow to Anne), "beyond what I always had in most of the ships I have lived in; and they have been five altogether."

"Nothing to the purpose," replied her brother. "You were living with your husband; and were the only woman on board."

"But you, yourself, brought Mrs. Harville, her sister, her cousin, and the three children, round from Portsmouth to Plymouth. Where was this superfine, extraordinary sort of gallantry of yours, then?"

"All merged in my friendship, Sophia. I would assist any brother officer's wife that I could, and I would bring any thing of Harville's from the world's end, if he wanted it. But do not imagine that I did not feel it an evil in itself."

"Depend upon it they were all perfectly comfortable."

"I might not like them the better for that, perhaps. Such a number of women and children have no *right* to be comfortable on board."

"My dear Frederick, you are talking quite idly. Pray, what would become of us poor sailors' wives, who often want to be conveyed to one port or another, after our husbands, if every body had your feelings?"

"My feelings, you see, did not prevent my taking Mrs. Harville, and all her family, to Plymouth."

"But I hate to hear you talking so, like a fine gentleman, and as if women were all fine ladies, instead of rational creatures. We none of us expect to be in smooth water all our days."

"Ah! my dear," said the admiral, "when he has got a wife, he will sing a different tune. When he is married, if we have the good luck to live to another war, we shall see him do as you and I, and a great many others, have done. We shall have him very thankful to any body that will bring him his wife."

"Ay, that we shall."

"Now I have done," cried Captain Wentworth—"When once married people begin to attack me with, 'Oh! you will think very differently, when you are married.' I can only say, 'No, I shall not,' and then they say again, 'Yes, you will,' and there is an end of it."

He got up and moved away.

"What a great traveller you must have been, ma'am!" said Mrs. Musgrove to Mrs. Croft.

"Pretty well, ma'am, in the fifteen years of my marriage; though many women have done more. I have crossed the Atlantic four times, and have been once to the East Indies, and back again; and only once, besides being in different places about home—Cork, and Lisbon, and Gibraltar. But I never went beyond the Streights—and never was in the West Indies. We do not call Bermuda or Bahama, you know, the West Indies."

Mrs. Musgrove had not a word to say in dissent; she could not accuse herself of having ever called them any thing in the whole course of her life.

"And I do assure you, ma'am," pursued Mrs. Croft, "that nothing can exceed the accommodations of a man of war; I speak, you know, of the higher rates. When you come to a frigate, of course, you are more confined—though any reasonable woman may be perfectly happy in one of them; and I can safely say, that the happiest part of my life has been spent on board a ship. While we were together, you know, there was nothing to be feared. Thank God! I have always been blessed with excellent health, and no climate disagrees with me. A little disordered always the first twenty-four hours of going to sea, but never knew what sickness was afterwards. The only time that I ever really suffered in body or mind, the only time that I ever fancied myself unwell, or had any ideas of danger, was the winter that I passed by myself at Deal, when the Admiral (*Captain* Croft then) was in the North Seas. I lived in perpetual fright at that time, and had all manner of imaginary complaints from not knowing what to do with myself, or when I should hear from him next; but as long as we could be together, nothing ever ailed me, and I never met with the smallest inconvenience."

"Ay, to be sure. Yes, indeed, oh yes, I am quite of your opinion, Mrs. Croft," was Mrs. Musgrove's hearty answer. "There is nothing so bad as a separation. I am quite of your opinion. I know what it is, for Mr. Musgrove always attends the assizes, and I am so glad when they are over, and he is safe back again."

The evening ended with dancing. On its being proposed, Anne offered her services, as usual, and though her eyes would sometimes fill with tears as she sat at the instrument, she was extremely glad to be employed, and desired nothing in return but to be unobserved.

It was a merry, joyous party, and no one seemed in higher spirits than Captain Wentworth. She felt that he had every thing to elevate him, which general attention and deference, and especially the attention of all the young women could do. The Miss Hayters, the females of the family of cousins already mentioned, were apparently admitted to the honour of being in love with him; and as for Henrietta and Louisa, they both seemed so entirely occupied by him, that

nothing but the continued appearance of the most perfect good-will between themselves, could have made it credible that they were not decided rivals. If he were a little spoilt by such universal, such eager admiration, who could wonder?

These were some of the thoughts which occupied Anne, while her fingers were mechanically at work, proceeding for half an hour together, equally without error, and without consciousness. *Once* she felt that he was looking at herself—observing her altered features, perhaps, trying to trace in them the ruins of the face which had once charmed him; and *once* she knew that he must have spoken of her; she was hardly aware of it, till she heard the answer; but then she was sure of his having asked his partner whether Miss Elliot never danced? The answer was, "Oh! no, never; she has quite given up dancing. She had rather play. She is never tired of playing." Once, too, he spoke to her. She had left the instrument on the dancing being over, and he had sat down to try to make out an air which he wished to give the Miss Musgroves an idea of. Unintentionally she returned to that part of the room; he saw her, and, instantly rising, said, with studied politeness,

"I beg your pardon, madam, this is your seat"; and though she immediately drew back with a decided negative, he was not to be induced to sit down again.

Anne did not wish for more of such looks and speeches. His cold politeness, his ceremonious grace, were worse than any thing.

Chapter nine

Captain Wentworth was come to Kellynch as to a home, to stay as long as he liked, being as thoroughly the object of the Admiral's fraternal kindness as of his wife's. He had intended, on first arriving, to proceed very soon into Shropshire, and visit the brother settled in that county, but the attractions of Uppercross induced him to put this off.

There was so much of friendliness, and of flattery, and of every thing most bewitching in his reception there; the old were so hospitable, the young so agreeable, that he could not but resolve to remain where he was, and take all the charms and perfections of Edward's wife upon credit a little longer.

It was soon Uppercross with him almost every day. The Musgroves could hardly be more ready to invite than he to come, particularly in the morning, when he had no companion at home, for the Admiral and Mrs. Croft were generally out of doors together, interesting themselves in their new possessions, their grass, and their sheep, and dawdling about in a way not endurable to a third person, or driving out in a gig, lately added to their establishment.

Hitherto there had been but one opinion of Captain Wentworth, among the Musgroves and their dependencies. It was unvarying, warm admiration every where. But this intimate footing was not more than established, when a certain Charles Hayter returned among them, to be a good deal disturbed by it, and to think Captain Wentworth very much in the way.

Charles Hayter was the eldest of all the cousins, and a very amiable, pleasing young man, between whom and Henrietta there had been a considerable appearance of attachment previous to Captain Wentworth's introduction. He was in orders, and having a curacy in the neighbourhood where residence was not required, lived at his father's house, only two miles from Uppercross. A short absence from home had left his fair one unguarded by his attentions at this critical period, and when he came back he had the pain of finding very altered manners, and of seeing Captain Wentworth.

Mrs. Musgrove and Mrs. Hayter were sisters. They had each had money, but their marriages had made a material difference in their degree of consequence. Mr. Hayter had some property of his own, but it was insignificant compared with Mr. Musgrove's; and while the Musgroves were in the first class of society in the country, the young Hayters would, from their parents' inferior, retired, and unpolished way of living, and their own defective education, have been hardly in any class at all, but for their connexion with Uppercross; this eldest son of course excepted, who had chosen to be a scholar and a gentleman, and who was very superior in cultivation and manners to all the rest.

The two families had always been on excellent terms, there being no pride on one side, and no envy on the other, and only such a consciousness of superiority in the Miss Musgroves, as made them pleased to improve their cousins. Charles's attentions to Henrietta had been observed by her father and mother without any disapprobation. "It would not be a great match for her; but if Henrietta liked him—and Henrietta *did* seem to like him."

Henrietta fully thought so herself, before Captain Wentworth came; but from that time Cousin Charles had been very much forgotten.

Which of the two sisters was preferred by Captain Wentworth was as yet quite doubtful, as far as Anne's observation reached. Henrietta was perhaps the prettiest, Louisa had the higher spirits; and she knew not *now*, whether the more gentle or the more lively character were most likely to attract him.

Mr. and Mrs. Musgrove, either from seeing little, or from an entire confidence in the discretion of both their daughters, and of all the young men who came near them, seemed to leave every thing to take its chance. There was not the smallest appearance of solicitude or remark about them, in the Mansion-house; but it was different at the Cottage: the young couple there were more disposed to speculate and wonder; and Captain Wentworth had not been above four or five times in the Miss Musgroves' company, and Charles Hayter had but just reappeared, when Anne had to listen to the opinions of her brother and sister, as to *which* was the one liked best. Charles gave it for Louisa, Mary for Henrietta, but quite agreeing that to have him marry either would be extremely delightful.

Charles "had never seen a pleasanter man in his life; and from what he had once heard Captain Wentworth himself say, was very sure that he had not made less than twenty thousand pounds by the war. Here was a fortune at once; besides which, there would be the chance of what might be done in any future war; and he was sure Captain Wentworth was as likely a man to distinguish himself as any officer in the navy. Oh! it would be a capital match for either of his sisters."

"Upon my word it would," replied Mary. "Dear me! If he should rise to any very great honours! If he should ever be made a Baronet! 'Lady Wentworth' sounds very well. That would be a noble thing, indeed, for Henrietta! She would take place of me then, and Henrietta would not dislike that. Sir Frederick and Lady Wentworth! It would be but a new creation, however, and I never think much of your new creations."

It suited Mary best to think Henrietta the one preferred on the very account of Charles Hayter, whose pretensions she wished to see put an end to. She looked down very decidedly upon the Hayters, and thought it would be quite a misfortune to have the existing connection between the families renewed—very sad for herself and her children.

"You know," said she, "I cannot think him at all a fit match for Henrietta; and considering the alliances which the Musgroves have made, she has no right to throw herself away. I do not think any young woman has a right to make a choice that may be disagreeable and inconvenient to the *principal* part of her family, and be giving bad connections to those who have not been used to them. And, pray, who is Charles Hayter? Nothing but a country curate. A most improper match for Miss Musgrove, of Uppercross."

Her husband, however, would not agree with her here; for besides having a regard for his cousin, Charles Hayter was an eldest son, and he saw things as an eldest son himself.

"Now you are talking nonsense, Mary," was therefore his answer. "It would not be a *great* match for Henrietta, but Charles has a very fair chance, through the Spicers of getting something from the Bishop in the course of a year or two; and you will please to remember, that he is the eldest son; whenever my uncle dies, he steps into very pretty property. The estate at Winthrop is not less than two hundred and fifty acres, besides the farm near Taunton, which is some of the best land in the country. I grant you, that any of them but Charles would be a very shocking match for Henrietta, and indeed it could not be; he is the only one that could be possible; but he is a very good-natured, good sort of a fellow; and whenever Winthrop comes into his hands, he will make a different sort of place of it, and live in a very different sort of way; and with that property, he will never be a contemptible man. Good, freehold property. No, no; Henrietta might do worse than marry Charles Hayter; and if she has him, and Louisa can get Captain Wentworth, I shall be very well satisfied."

"Charles may say what he pleases," cried Mary to Anne, as soon as he was out of the room, "but it would be shocking to have Henrietta marry Charles Hayter; a very bad thing for *her*, and still worse for *me;* and therefore it is very much to be wished that Captain Wentworth may soon put him quite out of her head, and I have very little doubt that he has. She took hardly any notice of Charles Hayter yesterday. I wish you had been there to see her behaviour. And as to Captain Wentworth's liking Louisa as well as Henrietta, it is nonsense to say so; for he certainly *does* like Henrietta a great deal the best. But Charles is so positive! I wish you had been with us yesterday, for then you might have decided between us; and I am sure you would have thought as I did, unless

341

you had been determined to give it against me."

A dinner at Mr. Musgrove's had been the occasion, when all these things should have been seen by Anne; but she had staid at home, under the mixed plea of a head-ache of her own, and some return of indisposition in little Charles. She had thought only of avoiding Captain Wentworth; but an escape from being appealed to as umpire, was now added to the advantages of a quiet evening.

As to Captain Wentworth's views, she deemed it of more consequence that he should know his own mind, early enough not to be endangering the happiness of either sister, or impeaching his own honour, than that he should prefer Henrietta to Louisa, or Louisa to Henrietta. Either of them would, in all probability, make him an affectionate, good-humoured wife. With regard to Charles Hayter, she had delicacy which must be pained by any lightness of conduct in a well-meaning young woman, and a heart to sympathize in any of the sufferings it occasioned; but if Henrietta found herself mistaken in the nature of her feelings, the alteration could not be understood too soon.

Charles Hayter had met with much to disquiet and mortify him in his cousin's behaviour. She had too old a regard for him to be so wholly estranged, as might in two meetings extinguish every past hope, and leave him nothing to do but to keep away from Uppercross; but there was such a change as became very alarming, when such a man as Captain Wentworth was to be regarded as the probable cause. He had been absent only two Sundays; and when they parted, had left her interested even to the height of his wishes, in his prospect of soon quitting his present curacy, and obtaining that of Uppercross instead. It had then seemed the object nearest her heart, that Dr. Shirley, the rector, who for more than forty years had been zealously discharging all the duties of his office, but was now growing too infirm for many of them, should be quite fixed on engaging a curate; should make his curacy quite as good as he could afford, and should give Charles Hayter the promise of it. The advantage of his having to come only to Uppercross, instead of going six miles another way; of his having, in every respect, a better curacy; of his belonging to their dear Dr. Shirley, and of dear, good Dr. Shirley's being relieved from the duty which he could no longer get through without most injurious fatigue, had been a great deal, even to Louisa, but had been almost every thing to Henrietta. When he came back, alas! the zeal of the business was gone by. Louisa could not listen at all to his account of a conversation which he had just held with Dr. Shirley: she was at window, looking out for Captain Wentworth; and even Henrietta had at best only a divided attention to give, and seemed to have forgotten all the former doubt and solicitude of the negociation.

"Well, I am very glad indeed, but I always thought you would have it; I always thought you sure. It did not appear to me that—In short, you know, Dr. Shirley *must* have a curate, and you had secured his promise. Is he coming, Louisa?"

One morning, very soon after the dinner at the Musgroves, at which Anne had not been present, Captain Wentworth walked into the drawing-room at the Cottage, where were only herself and the little invalid Charles, who was lying on the sofa.

The surprise of finding himself almost alone with Anne Elliot, deprived his manners of their usual composure: he started, and could only say, "I thought the Miss Musgroves had been here—Mrs. Musgrove told me I should find them here," before he walked to the window to recollect himself, and feel how he ought to behave.

"They are up stairs with my sister—they will be down in a few moment, I dare say," had been Anne's reply, in all the confusion that was natural; and if the child had not called her to come and do something for him, she would have been out of the room the next moment, and released Captain Wentworth as well as herself.

He continued at the window; and after calmly and politely saying, "I hope the little boy is better," was silent.

She was obliged to kneel down by the sofa, and remain there to satisfy her patient; and thus they continued a few minutes, when, to her very great satisfaction, she heard some other person crossing the little vestibule. She hoped, on turning her head, to see the master of the house; but it proved to be one much less calculated for making matters easy—Charles Hayter, probably not at all better pleased by the sight of Captain Wentworth, than Captain Wentworth had been by the sight of Anne.

She only attempted to say, "How do you do? Will not you sit down? The others will be here presently."

Captain Wentworth, however, came from his window, apparently not ill-disposed for conversation; but Charles Hayter soon put an end to his attempts, by seating himself near the table, and taking up the newspaper; and Captain Wentworth returned to his window.

Another minute brought another addition. The younger boy, a remarkable stout, forward child, of two years old, having got the door opened for him by some one without, made his determined appearance among them, and went straight to the sofa to see what was going on, and put in his claim to any thing good that might be giving away.

There being nothing to be eat, he could only have some play; and as his aunt would not let him teaze his sick brother, he began to fasten himself upon her, as she knelt, in such a way that, busy as she was about Charles, she could not shake him off. She spoke to him—ordered, intreated, and insisted in vain. Once she did contrive to push him away, but the boy had the greater pleasure in getting upon her back again directly.

"Walter," said she, "get down this moment. You are extremely troublesome. I am very angry with you."

"Walter," cried Charles Hayter, "why do you not do as you are bid? Do not you hear your aunt speak? Come to me, Walter, come to cousin Charles."

But not a bit did Walter stir.

In another moment, however, she found herself in the state of being released from him; some one was taking him from her, though he had bent down her head so much, that his little sturdy hands were unfastened from around her neck, and he was resolutely borne away, before she knew that Captain Wentworth had done it.

Her sensations on the discovery made her perfectly speechless. She could not even thank him. She could only hang over little Charles, with most disordered feelings. His kindness in stepping forward to her relief—the manner—the silence in which it had passed—the little particulars of the circumstance—with the conviction soon forced on her by the noise he was studiously making with the child, that he meant to avoid hearing her thanks, and rather sought to testify that her conversation was the last of his wants, produced such a confusion of varying, but very painful agitation, as she could not recover from, till enabled by the entrance of Mary and the Miss Musgroves to make over her little patient to their cares, and leave the room. She could not stay. It might have been an opportunity of watching the loves and jealousies of the four; they were now all together, but she could stay for none of it. It was evident that Charles Hayter was not well inclined towards Captain Wentworth. She had a strong impression of his having said, in a vext tone of voice, after Captain Wentworth's interference, "You ought to have minded *me*, Walter; I told you not to teaze your aunt," and could comprehend his regretting that Captain Wentworth should do what he ought to have done himself. But neither Charles Hayter's feelings, nor any body's feelings, could interest her, till she had a little better arranged her own. She was ashamed of herself, quite ashamed of being so nervous, so overcome by such a trifle; but so it was; and it required a long application of solitude and reflection to recover her.

Chapter ten

Other opportunities of making her observations could not fail to occur. Anne had soon been in company with all the four together often enough to have an opinion, though too wise to acknowledge as much at home, where she knew it would have satisfied neither husband nor wife; for while she considered Louisa to be rather the favourite, she could not but think, as far as she might dare to judge from memory and experience, that Captain Wentworth was not in love with either. They were more in love with him; yet there it was not love. It was a little fever of admiration; but it might, probably must, end in love with some. Charles Hayter seemed aware of being slighted, and yet Henrietta had sometimes the air of being divided between them. Anne longed for the power of representing to them all what they were about, and of pointing out some of the evils they were exposing themselves to. She did not attribute guile to any. It was the highest satisfaction to her, to believe Captain Wentworth not in the least aware of the pain he was occasioning. There was no triumph, no pitiful triumph in his manner. He had, probably, never heard, and never thought of any claims of Charles Hayter. He was only wrong in accepting the attentions (for accepting must be the word) of two young women at once.

After a short struggle, however, Charles Hayter seemed to quit the field. Three days had passed without his coming once to Uppercross; a most decided change. He had even refused one regular invitation to dinner; and having been found on the occasion by Mr. Musgrove with some large books before him, Mr. and Mrs. Musgrove were sure all could not be right, and talked, with grave faces, of his studying himself to death. It was Mary's hope and belief, that he had received a positive dismissal from Henrietta, and her husband lived under the constant dependance of seeing him to-morrow. Anne could only feel that Charles Hayter was wise.

One morning, about this time, Charles Musgrove and Captain Wentworth being gone a shooting together, as the sisters in the cottage were sitting quietly at work, they were visited at the window by the sisters from the mansion-house.

It was a very fine November day, and the Miss Musgroves came through the little grounds, and stopped for no other purpose than to say, that they were going to take a *long* walk, and, therefore, concluded Mary could not like to go with them; and when Mary immediately replied, with some jealousy, at not being supposed a good walker, "Oh, yes, I should like to join you very much, I am very fond of a long walk," Anne felt persuaded, by the looks of the two girls, that it was precisely what they did not wish, and admired again the sort of necessity which the family-habits seemed to produce, of every thing being to be communicated, and every thing being to be done together, however undesired and inconvenient. She tried to dissuade Mary from going, but in vain; and that being the case, thought it best to accept the Miss Musgroves' much more cordial invitation to herself to go likewise, as she might be useful in turning back with her sister, and lessening the interference in any plan of their own.

"I cannot imagine why they should suppose I should not like a long walk!" said Mary, as she went up stairs. "Every body is always supposing that I am not a good walker! And yet they would not have been pleased, if we had refused to join them. When people come in this manner on purpose to ask us, how can one say no?"

Just as they were setting off, the gentlemen returned. They had taken out a young dog, who had spoilt their sport, and sent them back early. Their time and strength, and spirits, were, therefore, exactly ready for this walk, and they entered into it with pleasure. Could Anne have foreseen such a junction, she would have staid at home; but, from some feelings of interest and curiosity, she fancied now that it was too late to retract, and the whole six set forward together in the direction chosen by the Miss Musgroves, who evidently considered the walk as under their guidance.

Anne's object was, not to be in the way of any body, and where the narrow paths across the fields made many separations necessary, to keep with her brother and sister. Her *pleasure* in the walk must arise from the exercise and the day, from the view of the last smiles of the year upon the tawny leaves and withered hedges, and from repeating to herself some few of the thousand poetical descriptions extant of autumn, that season of peculiar and inexhaustible influence on the mind of taste and tenderness, that season which has drawn from every poet, worthy of being read, some attempt at description, or some lines of feeling. She occupied her mind as much as possible in such like musings and quotations; but it was not possible, that when within reach of Captain Wentworth's conversation with either of the Miss Musgroves, she should not try to hear it; yet she caught little very remarkable. It was mere lively chat, such as any young persons, on an intimate footing, might fall into. He was more engaged with Louisa than with Henrietta. Louisa certainly put more forward for his notice than her sister. This distinction appeared to increase, and there was one speech of Louisa's which struck her. After one of the many praises of the day, which were continually bursting forth, Captain Wentworth added,

"What glorious weather for the Admiral and my sister! They meant to take a long drive this morning; perhaps we may hail them from some of these hills. They talked of coming into this side of the country. I wonder whereabouts they will upset to-day. Oh! it does happen very often, I assure you —but my sister makes nothing of it—she would as lieve be tossed out as not."

"Ah! You make the most of it, I know," cried Louisa, "but if it were really so, I should do just the same in her place. If I loved a man, as she loves the Admiral, I would be always with him, nothing should ever separate us, and I would rather be overturned by him, than driven safely by anybody else."

It was spoken with enthusiasm.

"Had you?" cried he, catching the same tone; "I honour you!" And there was silence between them for a little while.

Anne could not immediately fall into a quotation again. The sweet scenes of autumn were for a while put by—unless some tender sonnet, fraught with the apt analogy of the declining year, with declining happiness, and the images of youth and hope, and spring, all gone together, blessed her memory. She roused herself to say, as they struck by order into another path, "Is not this one of the ways to Winthrop?" But nobody heard, or, at least, nobody answered her.

Winthrop, however, or its environs—for young men are, sometimes, to be met with, strolling about near home—was their destination; and after another half mile of gradual ascent through large enclosures, where the ploughs at work, and the fresh-made path spoke the farmer, counteracting the sweets of poetical despondence, and meaning to have spring again, they gained the summit of the most considerable hill, which parted Uppercross and Winthrop, and soon commanded a full view of the latter, at the foot of the hill on the other side.

Winthrop, without beauty and without dignity, was stretched before them; an indifferent house, standing low, and hemmed in by the barns and buildings of a farm-yard.

Mary exclaimed, "Bless me! here is Winthrop—I declare I had no idea!—well, now I think we had better turn back; I am excessively tired."

Henrietta, conscious and ashamed, and seeing no cousin Charles walking along any path, or leaning against any gate, was ready to do as Mary wished; but "No," said Charles Musgrove, and "No, no," cried Louisa more eagerly, and taking her sister aside, seemed to be arguing the matter warmly.

Charles, in the meanwhile, was very decidedly declaring his resolution of calling on his aunt, now that he was so near; and very evidently, though more fearfully, trying to induce his wife to go too. But this was one of the points on which the lady shewed her strength, and when he recommended the advantage of resting herself a quarter of an hour at Winthrop, as she felt so tired, she resolutely answered, "Oh! no, indeed!—walking up that hill again would do her more harm than any sitting down could do her good," and, in short, her look and manner declared, that go she would not.

After a little succession of these sort of debates and consultations, it was settled between Charles and his two sisters, that he, and Henrietta, should just run down for a few minutes, to see their aunt and cousins, while the rest of the party waited for them at the top of the hill. Louisa seemed the principal arranger of the plan; and, as she went a little way with them, down the hill, still talking to Henrietta, Mary took the opportunity of looking scornfully around her, and saying to Captain Wentworth,

"It is very unpleasant, having such connexions! But I assure you, I have never been in the house above twice in my life."

She received no other answer, than an artificial, assenting smile, followed by a contemptuous glance, as he turned away, which Anne perfectly knew the meaning of.

The brow of the hill, where they remained, was a cheerful spot; Louisa returned, and Mary finding a comfortable seat for herself, on the step of a stile, was very well satisfied so long as the others all stood about her; but when Louisa drew Captain Wentworth away, to try for a gleaning of nuts in an adjoining hedge-row, and they were gone by degrees quite out of sight and sound, Mary was happy no longer; she quarrelled with her own seat, was sure Louisa had got a much better somewhere, and nothing could prevent her from going to look for a better also. She turned through the same gate, but could not see them. Anne found a nice seat for her, on a dry sunny bank, under the hedge-row, in which she had no doubt of their still being—in some spot or other. Mary sat down for a moment, but it would not do; she was sure Louisa had

found a better seat somewhere else, and she would go on, till she overtook her.

Anne, really tired herself, was glad to sit down; and she very soon heard Captain Wentworth and Louisa in the hedge-row, behind her, as if making their way back, along the rough, wild sort of channel, down the centre. They were speaking as they drew near. Louisa's voice was the first distinguished. She seemed to be in the middle of some eager speech. What Anne first heard was,

"And so, I made her go. I could not bear that she should be frightened from the visit by such nonsense. What!—would I be turned back from doing a thing that I had determined to do, and that I knew to be right, by the airs and interference of such a person?—or, of any person I may say. No, I have no idea of being so easily persuaded. When I have made up my mind, I have made it. And Henrietta seemed entirely to have made up hers to call at Winthrop today—and yet, she was as near giving it up, out of nonsensical complaisance!"

"She would have turned back then, but for you?"

"She would indeed. I am almost ashamed to say it."

"Happy for her, to have such a mind as yours at hand!—After the hints you gave just now, which did but confirm my own observations, the last time I was in company with him, I need not affect to have no comprehension of what is going on. I see that more than a mere dutiful morning-visit to your aunt was in question; and woe betide him, and her too, when it comes to things of consequence, when they are placed in circumstances, requiring fortitude and strength of mind, if she have not resolution enough to resist idle interference in such a trifle as this. Your sister is an amiable creature; but *yours* is the character of decision and firmness, I see. If you value her conduct or happiness, infuse as much of your own spirit into her, as you can. But this, no doubt, you have been always doing. It is the worst evil of too yielding and indecisive a character, that no influence over it can be depended on. You are never sure of a good impression being durable. Every body may sway it; let those who would be happy be firm. Here is a nut," said he, catching one down from an upper bough. "To exemplify —a beautiful glossy nut, which, blessed with original strength, has outlived all the storms of autumn. Not a puncture, not a weak spot any where. This nut," he continued, with playful solemnity, "while so many of its brethren have fallen and been trodden under foot, is still in possession of all the happiness that a hazel-nut can be supposed capable of." Then, returning to his former earnest tone: "My first wish for all, whom I am interested in, is that they should be firm. If Louisa Musgrove would be beautiful and happy in her November of life, she will cherish all her present powers of mind."

He had done, and was unanswered. It would have surprised Anne, if Louisa could have readily answered such a speech— words of such interest, spoken with such serious warmth!—she could imagine what Louisa was feeling. For herself—she feared to move, lest she should be seen. While she remained, a bush of low rambling holly protected her, and they were moving on. Before they were beyond her hearing, however, Louisa spoke again.

"Mary is good-natured enough in many respects," said she, "but she does sometimes provoke me excessively, by her nonsense and her pride; the Elliot pride. She has a great deal too much of the Elliot pride. We do so wish that Charles had married Anne instead. I suppose you know he wanted to marry Anne?"

After a moment's pause, Captain Wentworth said,

"Do you mean that she refused him?"

"Oh! yes, certainly."

"When did that happen?"

"I do not exactly know, for Henrietta and I were at school at the time; but I believe about a year before he married Mary. I wish she had accepted him. We should all have liked her a great deal better; and papa and mamma always think it was her great friend Lady Russell's doing, that she did not. They think Charles might not be learned and bookish enough to please Lady Russell, and that therefore, she persuaded Anne to refuse him."

The sounds were retreating, and Anne distinguished no more. Her own emotions still kept her fixed. She had much to recover from, before she could move. The listener's proverbial fate was not absolutely hers; she had heard no evil of herself, but she had heard a great deal of very painful import. She saw how her own character was considered by Captain Wentworth; and there had been just that degree of feeling and curiosity about her in his manner, which must give her extreme agitation.

As soon as she could, she went after Mary, and having found, and walked back with her to their former station, by the stile, felt some comfort in their whole party being immediately afterwards collected, and once more in motion together. Her spirits wanted the solitude and silence which only numbers could give.

Charles and Henrietta returned, bringing, as may be conjectured, Charles Hayter with them. The minutiae of the business Anne could not attempt to understand; even Captain Wentworth did not seem admitted to perfect confidence here; but that there had been a withdrawing on the gentleman's side, and a relenting on the lady's, and that they were now very glad to be together again, did not admit a doubt. Henrietta looked a little ashamed, but very well pleased; Charles Hayter exceedingly happy, and they were devoted to each other almost from the first instant of their all setting forward for Uppercross.

Every thing now marked out Louisa for Captain Wentworth; nothing could be plainer; and where many divisions were necessary, or even where they were not, they walked side by side, nearly as much as the other two. In a long strip of meadowland, where there was ample space for all, they were thus divided—forming three distinct parties; and to that party of the three which boasted least animation, and least complaisance, Anne necessarily belonged. She joined Charles and Mary, and was tired enough to be very glad of Charles's other arm; but Charles, though in very good humour with her, was out of temper with his wife. Mary had shewn herself disobliging to him, and was now to reap the consequence, which consequence was his dropping her arm almost every moment, to cut off the heads of some nettles in the hedge with his switch; and when Mary began to complain of it, and lament her being ill-used, according to custom, in being on the hedge side, while Anne was never incommoded on the other, he dropped the arms of both to hunt after a weasel which he had a momentary glance of; and they could hardly get him along at all.

This long meadow bordered a lane, which their footpath, at the end of it, was to cross; and when the party had all reached the gate of exit, the carriage advancing in the same direction, which had been some time heard, was just coming up, and proved to be Admiral Croft's gig. He and his wife had taken their intended drive, and were returning home. Upon hearing how long a walk the young people had engaged in, they kindly offered a seat to any lady who might be particularly tired; it would save her full a mile, and they were going through Uppercross. The invitation was general, and generally declined. The Miss Musgroves were not at all tired, and Mary was either offended, by not being asked before any of the others, or what Louisa called the Elliot pride could not endure to make a third in a one horse chaise.

The walking-party had crossed the lane, and were surmounting an opposite stile; and the admiral was putting his horse into motion again, when Captain Wentworth cleared the hedge in a moment to say something to his sister. The something might be guessed by its effects.

"Miss Elliot, I am sure *you* are tired," cried Mrs. Croft. "Do let us have the pleasure of taking you home. Here is excellent room for

three, I assure you. If we were all like you, I believe we might sit four. You must, indeed, you must."

Anne was still in the lane; and though instinctively beginning to decline, she was not allowed to proceed. The admiral's kind urgency came in support of his wife's; they would not be refused; they compressed themselves into the smallest possible space to leave her a corner, and Captain Wentworth, without saying a word, turned to her, and quietly obliged her to be assisted into the carriage.

Yes, he had done it. She was in the carriage, and felt that he had placed her there, that his will and his hands had done it, that she owed it to his perception of her fatigue, and his resolution to give her rest. She was very much affected by the view of his disposition towards her which all these things made apparent. This little circumstance seemed the completion of all that had gone before. She understood him. He could not forgive her, but he could not be unfeeling. Though condemning her for the past, and considering it with high and unjust resentment, though perfectly careless of her, and though becoming attached to another, still he could not see her suffer, without the desire of giving her relief. It was a remainder of former sentiment; it was an impulse of pure, though unacknowledged friendship; it was a proof of his own warm and amiable heart, which she could not contemplate without emotions so compounded of pleasure and pain, that she knew not which prevailed.

Her answers to the kindness and the remarks of her companions were at first unconsciously given. They had travelled half their way along the rough lane, before she was quite awake to what they said. She then found them talking of "Frederick."

"He certainly means to have one or other of those two girls, Sophy," said the admiral; "but there is no saying which. He has been running after them, too, long enough, one would think, to make up his mind. Ay, this comes of the peace. If it were war, now, he

would have settled it long ago. We sailors, Miss Elliot, cannot afford to make long courtships in time of war. How many days was it, my dear, between the first time of my seeing you, and our sitting down together in our lodgings at North Yarmouth?"

"We had better not talk about it, my dear," replied Mrs. Croft, pleasantly; "for if Miss Elliot were to hear how soon we came to an understanding, she would never be persuaded that we could be happy together. I had known you by character, however, long before."

"Well, and I had heard of you as a very pretty girl; and what were we to wait for besides?—I do not like having such things so long in hand. I wish Frederick would spread a little more canvas, and bring us home one of these young ladies to Kellynch. Then, there would always be company for them. And very nice young ladies they both are; I hardly know one from the other."

"Very good humoured, unaffected girls, indeed," said Mrs. Croft, in a tone of calmer praise, such as made Anne suspect that her keener powers might not consider either of them as quite worthy of her brother; "and a very respectable family. One could not be connected with better people. My dear admiral, that post!—we shall certainly take that post."

But by coolly giving the reins a better direction herself, they happily passed the danger; and by once afterwards judiciously putting out her hand, they neither fell into a rut, nor ran foul of a dung-cart; and Anne, with some amusement at their style of driving, which she imagined no bad representation of the general guidance of their affairs, found herself safely deposited by them at the cottage.

Chapter eleven

The time now approached for Lady Russell's return; the day was even fixed, and Anne, being engaged to join her as soon as she was resettled, was looking forward to an early removal to Kellynch, and beginning to think how her own comfort was likely to be affected by it.

It would place her in the same village with Captain Wentworth, within half a mile of him; they would have to frequent the same church, and there must be intercourse between the two families. This was against her; but, on the other hand, he spent so much of his time at Uppercross, that in removing thence she might be considered rather as leaving him behind, than as going towards him; and, upon the whole, she believed she must, on this interesting question, be the gainer, almost as certainly as in her change of domestic society, in leaving poor Mary for Lady Russell.

She wished it might be possible for her to avoid ever seeing Captain Wentworth at the hall; those rooms had witnessed former meetings which would be brought too painfully before her; but she was yet more anxious for the possibility of Lady Russell and Captain Wentworth never meeting any where. They did not like each other, and no renewal of acquaintance now could do any good; and were Lady Russell to see them together, she might think that he had too much self-possession, and she too little.

These points formed her chief solicitude in anticipating her removal from Uppercross, where she felt she had been stationed quite long enough. Her usefulness to little Charles would always give some sweetness to the memory of her two months visit there, but he was gaining strength apace, and she had nothing else to stay for.

The conclusion of her visit, however, was diversified in a way which she had not at all imagined. Captain Wentworth, after being unseen and unheard of at Uppercross for two whole days, appeared again among them to justify himself by a relation of what had kept him away.

A letter from his friend, Captain Harville, having found him out at last, had brought intelligence of Captain Harville's being settled with his family at Lyme for the winter; of their being therefore, quite unknowingly, within twenty miles of each other. Captain Harville had never been in good health since a severe wound which he received two years before, and Captain Wentworth's anxiety to see him had determined him to go immediately to Lyme. He had been there for four-and-twenty hours. His acquittal was complete, his friendship warmly honoured, a lively interest excited for his friend, and his description of the fine country about Lyme so feelingly attended to by the party, that an earnest desire to see Lyme themselves, and a project for going thither was the consequence.

The young people were all wild to see Lyme. Captain Wentworth talked of going there again himself; it was only seventeen miles from Uppercross; though November, the weather was by no means bad; and, in short, Louisa, who was the most eager of the eager, having formed the resolution to go, and besides the pleasure of doing as she liked, being now armed with the idea of merit in maintaining her own way, bore down all the wishes of her father and mother for putting it off till summer; and to Lyme they were to go—Charles, Mary, Anne, Henrietta, Louisa, and Captain Wentworth.

The first heedless scheme had been to go in the morning and return at night, but to this Mr. Musgrove, for the sake of his horses, would not consent; and when it came to be rationally considered, a day in the middle of November would not leave much time for seeing a new place, after deducting seven hours, as the nature of the country required, for going and returning. They were consequently to stay the night there, and not to be expected back till the next day's dinner. This was felt to be a considerable amendment; and though they all met at the Great House at rather an early breakfast hour, and set off very punctually, it was so much past noon before the two carriages, Mr. Musgrove's coach containing the four ladies, and Charles's curricle, in which he drove Captain Wentworth, were descending the long hill into Lyme, and entering upon

the still steeper street of the town itself, that it was very evident they would not have more than time for looking about them, before the light and warmth of the day were gone.

After securing accommodations, and ordering a dinner at one of the inns, the next thing to be done was unquestionably to walk directly down to the sea. They were come too late in the year for any amusement or variety which Lyme, as a public place, might offer; the rooms were shut up, the lodgers almost all gone, scarcely any family but of the residents left—and, as there is nothing to admire in the buildings themselves, the remarkable situation of the town, the principal street almost hurrying into the water, the walk to the Cobb, skirting round the pleasant little bay, which in the season is animated with bathing machines and company, the Cobb itself, its old wonders and new improvements, with the very beautiful line of cliffs stretching out to the east of the town, are what the stranger's eye will seek; and a very strange stranger it must be, who does not see charms in the immediate environs of Lyme, to make him wish to know it better. The scenes in its neighbourhood, Charmouth, with its high grounds and extensive sweeps of country, and still more its sweet retired bay, backed by dark cliffs, where fragments of low rock among the sands make it the happiest spot for watching the flow of the tide, for sitting in unwearied contemplation; the woody varieties of the cheerful village of Up Lyme, and, above all, Pinny, with its green chasms between romantic rocks, where the scattered forest trees and orchards of luxuriant growth declare that many a generation must have passed away since the first partial falling of the cliff prepared the ground for such a state, where a scene so wonderful and so lovely is exhibited, as may more than equal any of the resembling scenes of the far-famed Isle of Wight: these places must be visited, and visited again, to make the worth of Lyme understood.

The party from Uppercross passing down

by the now deserted and melancholy looking rooms, and still descending, soon found themselves on the sea shore, and lingering only, as all must linger and gaze on a first return to the sea, who ever deserve to look on it at all, proceeded towards the Cobb, equally their object in itself and on Captain Wentworth's account; for in a small house, near the foot of an old pier of unknown date, were the Harvilles settled. Captain Wentworth turned in to call on his friend; the others walked on, and he was to join them on the Cobb.

They were by no means tired of wondering and admiring; and not even Louisa seemed to feel that they had parted with Captain Wentworth long, when they saw him coming after them, with three companions, all well known already by description to be Captain and Mrs. Harville, and a Captain Benwick, who was staying with them.

Captain Benwick had some time ago been first lieutenant of the Laconia; and the account which Captain Wentworth had given of him, on his return from Lyme before; his warm praise of him as an excellent young man and an officer, whom he had always valued highly, which must have stamped him well in the esteem of every listener, had been followed by a little history of his private life, which rendered him perfectly interesting in the eyes of all the ladies. He had been engaged to Captain Harville's sister, and was now mourning her loss. They had been a year or two waiting for fortune and promotion. Fortune came, his prize-money as lieutenant being great—promotion, too, came at *last*; but Fanny Harville did not live to know it. She had died the preceding summer, while he was at sea. Captain Wentworth believed it impossible for man to be more attached to woman than poor Benwick had been to Fanny Harville, or to be more deeply afflicted under the dreadful change. He considered his disposition as of the sort which must suffer heavily, uniting very strong feelings with quiet, serious, and retiring manners, and a decided taste for reading, and sedentary pursuits. To finish the interest of the story, the friendship between him and the Harvilles seemed, if possible, augmented by the event which closed all their views of alliance, and Captain Benwick was now living with them entirely. Captain Harville had taken his present house for half a year, his taste, and his health, and his fortune all directing him to a residence unexpensive, and by the sea; and the grandeur of the country, and the retirement of Lyme in the winter, appeared exactly adapted to Captain Benwick's state of mind. The sympathy and good-will excited towards Captain Benwick was very great.

"And yet," said Anne to herself, as they now moved forward to meet the party, "he has not, perhaps, a more sorrowing heart than I have. I cannot believe his prospects so blighted for ever. He is younger than I am; younger in feeling, if not in fact; younger as a man. He will rally again, and be happy with another."

They all met, and were introduced. Captain Harville was a tall, dark man, with a sensible, benevolent countenance; a little lame; and from strong features, and want of health, looking much older than Captain Wentworth. Captain Benwick looked and was the youngest of the three, and, compared with either of them, a little man. He had a pleasing face and a melancholy air, just as he ought to have, and drew back from conversation.

Captain Harville, though not equalling Captain Wentworth in manners, was a perfect gentleman, unaffected, warm, and obliging. Mrs. Harville, a degree less polished than her husband, seemed however to have the same good feelings; and nothing could be more pleasant than their desire of considering the whole party as friends of their own, because the friends of Captain Wentworth, or more kindly hospitable than their entreaties for their all promising to dine with them. The dinner, already ordered at the inn, was at last, though unwillingly, accepted as an excuse; but they seemed almost hurt that Captain Wentworth should have brought any such party to Lyme, without considering it as a thing of course that they should dine with them.

There was so much attachment to Captain Wentworth in all this, and such a bewitching charm in a degree of hospitality so uncommon, so unlike the usual style of give-and-take invitations, and dinners of formality and display, that Anne felt her spirits not likely to be benefited by an increasing acquaintance among his brother-officers. "These would have been all my friends," was her thought; and she had to struggle against a great tendency to lowness.

On quitting the Cobb, they all went indoors with their new friends, and found rooms so small as none but those who invite from the heart could think capable of accommodating so many. Anne had a moment's astonishment on the subject herself; but it was soon lost in the pleasanter feelings which sprang from the sight of all the ingenious contrivances and nice arrangements of Captain Harville, to turn the actual space to the best possible account, to supply the deficiencies of lodging-house furniture, and defend the windows and doors against the winter storms to be expected. The varieties in the fitting-up of the rooms, where the common necessaries provided by the owner, in the common indifferent plight, were contrasted with some few articles of a rare species of wood, excellently worked up, and with something curious and valuable from all the distant countries Captain Harville had visited, were more than amusing to Anne: connected as it all was with his profession, the fruit of its labours, the effect of its influence on his habits, the picture of repose and domestic happiness it presented, made it to her a something more, or less, than gratification.

Captain Harville was no reader; but he had contrived excellent accommodations, and fashioned very pretty shelves, for a tolerable collection of well-bound volumes, the property of Captain Benwick. His lameness prevented him from taking much exercise; but a mind of usefulness and ingenuity seemed to furnish him with constant employment within. He drew, he varnished, he carpentered, he glued; he made toys for the children, he fashioned new netting-needles and pins with improvements; and if every thing else was done, sat down to his large fishing-net at one corner of the room.

Anne thought she left great happiness behind her when they quitted the house; and Louisa, by whom she found herself walking, burst forth into raptures of admiration and delight on the character of the navy—their friendliness, their brotherliness, their openness, their uprightness; protesting that she was convinced of sailors having more worth and warmth than any other set of men in England; that they only knew how to live, and they only deserved to be respected and loved.

They went back to dress and dine; and so well had the scheme answered already, that nothing was found amiss; though its being "so entirely out of season," and the "no-thorough-fare of Lyme," and the "no expectation of company," had brought many apologies from the heads of the inn.

Anne found herself by this time growing so much more hardened to being in Captain Wentworth's company than she had at first imagined could ever be, that the sitting down to the same table with him now, and the interchange of the common civilities attending on it (they never got beyond) was become a mere nothing.

The nights were too dark for the ladies to meet again till the morrow, but Captain Harville had promised them a visit in the evening; and he came, bringing his friend also, which was more than had been expected, it having been agreed that Captain Benwick had all the appearance of being oppressed by the presence of so many strangers. He ventured among them again, however, though his spirits certainly did not seem fit for the mirth of the party in general.

While Captains Wentworth and Harville led the talk on one side of the room, and, by recurring to former days, supplied anecdotes in abundance to occupy and entertain the others, it fell to Anne's lot to be placed rather apart with Captain Benwick; and a very good impulse of her nature obliged her to begin an acquaintance with him. He was shy, and disposed to abstraction; but the engaging mildness of her countenance, and gentleness of her manners, soon had their effect; and Anne was well repaid the first trouble of exertion. He was evidently a young man of considerable taste in reading, though principally in poetry; and besides the persuasion of having given him at least an evening's indulgence in the discussion of subjects, which his usual companions had probably no concern in, she had the hope of being of real use to him in some suggestions as to the duty and benefit of struggling against affliction, which had naturally grown out of their conversation. For, though shy, he did not seem reserved; it had rather the appearance of feelings glad to burst their usual restraints; and having talked of poetry, the richness of the present age, and gone through a brief comparison of opinion as to the first-rate poets, trying to ascertain whether *Marmion* or *The Lady of the Lake* were to be preferred, and how ranked the *Giaour* and *The Bride of Abydos*; and moreover, how the *Giaour* was to be pronounced, he shewed himself so intimately acquainted with all the tenderest songs of the one poet, and all the impassioned descriptions of hopeless agony of the other; he repeated, with such tremulous feeling, the various lines which imaged a broken heart, or a mind destroyed by wretchedness, and looked so entirely as if he meant to be understood, that she ventured to hope he did not always read only poetry; and to say, that she thought it was the misfortune of poetry, to be seldom safely enjoyed by those who enjoyed it completely; and that the strong feelings which alone could estimate it truly, were the very feelings which ought to taste it but sparingly.

His looks shewing him not pained, but pleased with this allusion to his situation, she was emboldened to go on; and feeling in herself the right of seniority of mind, she ventured to recommend a larger allowance of prose in his daily study; and on being requested to particularize, mentioned such works of our best moralists, such collections of the finest letters, such memoirs of characters of worth and suffering, as occurred to her at the moment as calculated to rouse and fortify the mind by the highest precepts, and the strongest examples of moral and religious endurances.

Captain Benwick listened attentively, and seemed grateful for the interest implied; and though with a shake of the head, and sighs which declared his little faith in the efficacy of any books on grief like his, noted down the names of those she recommended, and promised to procure and read them.

When the evening was over, Anne could not but be amused at the idea of her coming to Lyme, to preach patience and resignation to a young man whom she had never seen before; nor could she help fearing, on more serious reflection, that, like many other great moralists and preachers, she had been eloquent on a point in which her own conduct would ill bear examination.

Chapter twelve

Anne and Henrietta, finding themselves the earliest of the party the next morning, agreed to stroll down to the sea before breakfast. They went to the sands, to watch the flowing of the tide, which a fine southeasterly breeze was bringing in with all the grandeur which so flat a shore admitted. They praised the morning; gloried in the sea; sympathized in the delight of the fresh-feeling breeze—and were silent; till Henrietta suddenly began again, with,

"Oh! yes, I am quite convinced that, with very few exceptions, the sea-air always does good. There can be no doubt of its having been of the greatest service to Dr. Shirley, after his illness, last spring twelvemonth. He declares himself, that coming to Lyme for a month, did him more good than all the medicine he took; and, that being by the sea, always makes him feel young again. Now, I cannot help thinking it a pity that he does not live entirely by the sea. I do think he had better leave Uppercross entirely, and fix at Lyme. Do not you, Anne? Do not you agree with me, that it is the best thing he could do, both for himself and Mrs. Shirley? She has cousins here, you know, and many acquaintance, which would make it cheerful for her, and I am sure she would be glad to get to a place where she could have medical attendance at hand, in case of his having another seizure. Indeed I think it quite melancholy to have such excellent people as Dr. and Mrs. Shirley, who have been doing good all their lives, wearing out their last days in a place like Uppercross, where, excepting our family, they seem shut out from all the world. I wish his friends would propose it to him. I really think they ought. And, as to procuring a dispensation,[5] there could be no difficulty at his time of life, and with his character. My only doubt is, whether any thing could persuade him to leave his parish. He is so very strict and scrupulous in his notions; over-scrupulous, I must say. Do not you think, Anne, it is being over-scrupulous? Do not you think it is quite a mistaken point of conscience, when a clergyman sacrifices his health for the sake of duties, which may be just as well performed by another person? And at Lyme too—only seventeen miles off—he would be near enough to hear, if people thought there was any thing to complain of."

Anne smiled more than once to herself during this speech, and entered into the subject, as ready to do good by entering into the feelings of a young lady as of a young man, though here it was good of a lower standard, for what could be offered but general acquiescence? She said all that was reasonable and proper on the business; felt the claims of Dr. Shirley to repose, as she ought; saw how very desirable it was that he should have some active, respectable young man, as a resident curate, and was even courteous enough to hint at the advantage of such resident curate's being married.

"I wish," said Henrietta, very well pleased with her companion, "I wish Lady Russell lived at Uppercross, and were intimate with Dr. Shirley. I have always heard of Lady Russell, as a woman of the greatest influence with every body! I always look upon her as able to persuade a person to any thing! I am afraid of her, as I have told you before, quite afraid of her, because she is so very clever; but I respect her amazingly, and wish we had such a neighbour at Uppercross."

Anne was amused by Henrietta's manner of being grateful, and amused also, that the course of events and the new interests of Henrietta's views should have placed her friend at all in favour with any of the Musgrove family; she had only time, however, for a general answer, and a wish that such another woman were at Uppercross, before all subjects suddenly ceased, on seeing Louisa and Captain Wentworth coming towards them. They came also for a stroll till breakfast was likely to be ready; but Louisa recollecting, immediately afterwards, that she had something to procure at a shop, invited them all to go back with her into the town. They were all at her disposal.

When they came to the steps, leading upwards from the beach, a gentleman at the same moment preparing to come down, politely drew back, and stopped to give them way. They ascended and passed him; and as they passed, Anne's face caught his eye, and he looked at her with a degree of earnest admiration, which she could not be insensible of. She was looking remarkably well; her very regular, very pretty features, having the bloom and freshness of youth restored by the fine wind which had been blowing on her complexion, and by the animation of eye which it had also produced. It was evident that the gentleman (completely a gentleman in manner) admired her exceedingly. Captain Wentworth looked round at her instantly in a way which shewed his no-

---

[5] "dispensation," i.e., a clerical living, often of an absentee kind in a distant parish. Many country clerics were less scrupulous than Charles Hayter and were content to allow others to do the duties for which they were paid.

ticing of it. He gave her a momentary glance, a glance of brightness, which seemed to say, "That man is struck with you, and even I, at this moment, see something like Anne Elliot again."

After attending Louisa through her business, and loitering about a little longer, they returned to the inn; and Anne in passing afterwards quickly from her own chamber to their dining-room, had nearly run against the very same gentleman, as he came out of an adjoining apartment. She had before conjectured him to be a stranger like themselves, and determined that a well-looking groom, who was strolling about near the two inns as they came back, should be his servant. Both master and man being in mourning assisted the idea. It was now proved that he belonged to the same inn as themselves; and this second meeting, short as it was, also proved again by the gentleman's looks, that he thought hers very lovely, and by the readiness and propriety of his apologies, that he was a man of exceedingly good manners. He seemed about thirty, and, though not handsome, had an agreeable person. Anne felt that she should like to know who he was.

They had nearly done breakfast, when the sound of a carriage (almost the first they had heard since entering Lyme) drew half the party to the window. "It was a gentleman's carriage—a curricle—but only coming round from the stable-yard to the front door—Somebody must be going away. It was driven by a servant in mourning."

The word curricle made Charles Musgrove jump up, that he might compare it with his own, the servant in mourning roused Anne's curiosity, and the whole six were collected to look, by the time the owner of the curricle was to be seen issuing from the door amidst the bows and civilities of the household, and taking his seat, to drive off.

"Ah!" cried Captain Wentworth, instantly, and with half a glance at Anne; "it is the very man we passed."

The Miss Musgroves agreed to it; and

having all kindly watched him as far up the hill as they could, they returned to the breakfast-table. The waiter came into the room soon afterwards.

"Pray," said Captain Wentworth, immediately, "can you tell us the name of the gentleman who is just gone away?"

"Yes, Sir, a Mr. Elliot; a gentleman of large fortune—came in last night from Sidmouth—dare say you heard the carriage, Sir, while you were at dinner; and going on now for Crewkherne, in his way to Bath and London."

"Elliot!"—Many had looked on each other, and many had repeated the name, before all this had been got through, even by the smart rapidity of a waiter.

"Bless me!" cried Mary; "it must be our cousin—it must be our Mr. Elliot, it must, indeed!—Charles, Anne, must not it? In mourning, you see, just as our Mr. Elliot must be. How very extraordinary! In the very same inn with us! Anne, must not it be our Mr. Elliot; my father's next heir? Pray Sir" (turning to the waiter), "did not you hear—did not his servant say whether he belonged to the Kellynch family?"

"No, ma'am, he did not mention no particular family; but he said his master was a very rich gentleman, and would be a baronight some day."

"There! you see!" cried Mary, in an ecstasy, "Just as I said! Heir to Sir Walter Elliot!—I was sure that would come out, if it was so. Depend upon it, that is a circumstance which his servants take care to publish wherever he goes. But, Anne, only conceive how extraordinary! I wish I had looked at him more. I wish we had been aware in time, who it was, that he might have been introduced to us. What a pity that we should not have been introduced to each other!—Do you think he had the Elliot countenance? I hardly looked at him, I was looking at the horses; but I think he had something of the Elliot countenance. I wonder the arms did not strike me! Oh!—the great-coat was hanging over the panel, and hid the arms; so it did, otherwise, I am sure,

I should have observed them, and the livery too; if the servant had not been in mourning, one should have known him by the livery."

"Putting all these very extraordinary circumstances together," said Captain Wentworth, "we must consider it to be the arrangement of Providence, that you should not be introduced to your cousin."

When she could command Mary's attention, Anne quietly tried to convince her that their father and Mr. Elliot had not, for many years, been on such terms as to make the power of attempting an introduction at all desirable.

At the same time, however, it was a secret gratification to herself to have seen her cousin, and to know that the future owner of Kellynch was undoubtedly a gentleman, and had an air of good sense. She would not, upon any account, mention her having met with him the second time; luckily Mary did not much attend to their having passed close by him in their early walk, but she would have felt quite ill-used by Anne's having actually run against him in the passage, and received his very polite excuses, while she had never been near him at all; no, that cousinly little interview must remain a perfect secret.

"Of course," said Mary, "you will mention our seeing Mr. Elliot, the next time you write to Bath. I think my father certainly ought to hear of it; do mention all about him."

Anne avoided a direct reply, but it was just the circumstance which she considered as not merely unnecessary to be communicated, but as what ought to be suppressed. The offence which had been given her father, many years back, she knew; Elizabeth's particular share in it she suspected; and that Mr. Elliot's idea always produced irritation in both, was beyond a doubt. Mary never wrote to Bath herself; all the toil of keeping up a slow and unsatisfactory correspondence with Elizabeth fell on Anne.

Breakfast had not been long over, when they were joined by Captain and Mrs. Har-

ville, and Captain Benwick, with whom they had appointed to take their last walk about Lyme. They ought to be setting off for Uppercross by one, and in the meanwhile were to be all together, and out of doors as long as they could.

Anne found Captain Benwick getting near her, as soon as they were all fairly in the street. Their conversation, the preceding evening, did not disincline him to seek her again; and they walked together some time, talking as before of Mr. Scott and Lord Byron, and still as unable, as before, and as unable as any other two readers, to think exactly alike of the merits of either, till something occasioned an almost general change amongst their party, and instead of Captain Benwick, she had Captain Harville by her side.

"Miss Elliot," said he, speaking rather low, "you have done a good deed in making that poor fellow talk so much. I wish he could have such company oftener. It is bad for him, I know, to be shut up as he is; but what can we do? we cannot part."

"No," said Anne, "that I can easily believe to be impossible; but in time, perhaps—we know what time does in every case of affliction, and you must remember, Captain Harville, that your friend may yet be called a young mourner—Only last summer, I understand."

"Ay, true enough," (with a deep sigh) "only June."

"And not known to him, perhaps, so soon."

"Not till the first week in August, when he came home from the Cape—just made into the Grappler. I was at Plymouth, dreading to hear of him; he sent in letters, but the Grappler was under orders for Portsmouth. There the news must follow him, but who was to tell it? not I. I would as soon have been run up to the yard-arm. Nobody could do it, but that good fellow (pointing to Captain Wentworth). The Laconia had come into Plymouth the week before; no danger of her being sent to sea again. He stood his chance for the rest—wrote up for leave of absence, but without waiting the return, travelled night and day till he got to Portsmouth, rowed off to the Grappler that instant, and never left the poor fellow for a week; that's what he did, and nobody else could have saved poor James. You may think, Miss Elliot, whether he is dear to us!"

Anne did think on the question with perfect decision, and said as much in reply as her own feelings could accomplish, or as his seemed able to bear, for he was too much affected to renew the subject—and when he spoke again, it was of something totally different.

Mrs. Harville's giving it as her opinion that her husband would have quite walking enough by the time he reached home, determined the direction of all the party in what was to be their last walk; they would accompany them to their door, and then return and set off themselves. By all their calculations there was just time for this; but as they drew near the Cobb, there was such a general wish to walk along it once more, all were so inclined, and Louisa soon grew so determined, that the difference of a quarter of an hour, it was found, would be no difference at all, so with all the kind leave-taking, and all the kind interchange of invitations and promises which may be imagined, they parted from Captain and Mrs. Harville at their own door, and still accompanied by Captain Benwick, who seemed to cling to them to the last, proceeded to make the proper adieus to the Cobb.

Anne found Captain Benwick again drawing near her. Lord Byron's "dark blue seas" could not fail of being brought forward by their present view, and she gladly gave him all her attention as long as attention was possible. It was soon drawn per force another way.

There was too much wind to make the high part of the new Cobb pleasant for the ladies, and they agreed to get down the steps to the lower, and all were contented to pass quietly and carefully down the steep flight, excepting Louisa; she must be jumped down them by Captain Wentworth. In all

their walks, he had had to jump her from the stiles; the sensation was delightful to her. The hardness of the pavement for her feet, made him less willing upon the present occasion; he did it, however; she was safely down, and instantly, to shew her enjoyment, ran up the steps to be jumped down again. He advised her against it, thought the jar too great; but no, he reasoned and talked in vain; she smiled and said, "I am determined I will"; he put out his hands; she was too precipitate by half a second, she fell on the pavement on the Lower Cobb, and was taken up lifeless!

There was no wound, no blood, no visible bruise; but her eyes were closed, she breathed not, her face was like death. The horror of that moment to all who stood around!

Captain Wentworth, who had caught her up, knelt with her in his arms, looking on her with a face as pallid as her own, in an agony of silence. "She is dead! she is dead!" screamed Mary, catching hold of her husband, and contributing with his own horror to make him immoveable; and in another moment, Henrietta, sinking under the conviction, lost her senses too, and would have fallen on the steps, but for Captain Benwick and Anne, who caught and supported her between them.

"Is there no one to help me?" were the first words which burst from Captain Wentworth, in a tone of despair, and as if all his own strength were gone.

"Go to him, go to him," cried Anne, "for heaven's sake go to him. I can support her myself. Leave me, and go to him. Rub her hands, rub her temples; here are salts—take them, take them."

Captain Benwick obeyed, and Charles at the same moment, disengaging himself from his wife, they were both with him; and Louisa was raised up and supported more firmly between them, and every thing was done that Anne had prompted, but in vain; while Captain Wentworth, staggering against the wall for his support, exclaimed in the bitterest agony,

"Oh God! her father and mother!"

"A surgeon!" said Anne.

He caught the word; it seemed to rouse him at once, and saying only "True, true, a surgeon this instant," was darting away, when Anne eagerly suggested,

"Captain Benwick, would not it be better for Captain Benwick? He knows where a surgeon is to be found."

Every one capable of thinking felt the advantage of the idea, and in a moment (it was all done in rapid moments) Captain Benwick had resigned the poor corpse-like figure entirely to the brother's care, and was off for the town with the utmost rapidity.

As to the wretched party left behind, it could scarcely be said which of the three, who were completely rational, was suffering most, Captain Wentworth, Anne, or Charles, who, really a very affectionate brother, hung over Louisa with sobs of grief, and could only turn his eyes from one sister, to see the other in a state as insensible, or to witness the hysterical agitations of his wife, calling on him for help which he could not give.

Anne, attending with all the strength and zeal, and thought, which instinct supplied, to Henrietta, still tried, at intervals, to suggest comfort to the others, tried to quiet Mary, to animate Charles, to assuage the feelings of Captain Wentworth. Both seemed to look to her for directions.

"Anne, Anne," cried Charles, "what is to be done next? What, in heaven's name, is to be done next?"

Captain Wentworth's eyes were also turned towards her.

"Had not she better be carried to the inn? Yes, I am sure, carry her gently to the inn."

"Yes, yes, to the inn," repeated Captain Wentworth, comparatively collected, and eager to be doing something. "I will carry her myself. Musgrove, take care of the others."

By this time the report of the accident had spread among the workmen and boatmen about the Cobb, and many were collected near them, to be useful if wanted, at any rate, to enjoy the sight of a dead young lady, nay, two dead young ladies, for it proved twice as fine as the first report. To some of the best-looking of these good people Henrietta was consigned, for, though partially revived, she was quite helpless; and in this manner, Anne walking by her side, and Charles attending to his wife, they set forward, treading back with feelings unutterable, the ground, which so lately, so very lately, and so light of heart, they had passed along.

They were not off the Cobb, before the Harvilles met them. Captain Benwick had been seen flying by their house, with a countenance which shewed something to be wrong; and they had set off immediately, informed and directed, as they passed, towards the spot. Shocked as Captain Harville was, he brought senses and nerves that could be instantly useful; and a look between him and his wife decided what was to be done. She must be taken to their house—all must go to their house—and await the surgeon's arrival there. They would not listen to scruples: he was obeyed; they were all beneath his roof; and while Louisa, under Mrs. Harville's direction, was conveyed up stairs, and given possession of her own bed, assistance, cordials, restoratives were supplied by her husband to all who needed them.

Louisa had once opened her eyes, but soon closed them again, without apparent consciousness. This had been a proof of life, however, of service to her sister; and Henrietta, though perfectly incapable of being in the same room with Louisa, was kept, by the agitation of hope and fear, from a return of her own insensibility. Mary, too, was growing calmer.

The surgeon was with them almost before it had seemed possible. They were sick with horror while he examined; but he was not hopeless. The head had received a severe contusion, but he had seen greater injuries recovered from: he was by no means hopeless; he spoke cheerfully.

That he did not regard it as a desperate case—that he did not say a few hours must

end it—was at first felt, beyond the hope of most; and the ecstasy of such a reprieve, the rejoicing, deep and silent, after a few fervent ejaculations of gratitude to Heaven had been offered, may be conceived.

The tone, the look, with which "Thank God!" was uttered by Captain Wentworth, Anne was sure could never be forgotten by her; nor the sight of them afterwards, as he sat near a table, leaning over it with folded arms, and face concealed, as if overpowered by the various feelings of his soul, and trying by prayer and reflection to calm them.

Louisa's limbs had escaped. There was no injury but to the head.

It now became necessary for the party to consider what was best to be done, as to their general situation. They were now able to speak to each other, and consult. That Louisa must remain where she was, however distressing to her friends to be involving the Harvilles in such trouble, did not admit a doubt. Her removal was impossible. The Harvilles silenced all scruples; and, as much as they could, all gratitude. They had looked forward and arranged every thing, before the others began to reflect. Captain Benwick must give up his room to them, and get a bed elsewhere—and the whole was settled. They were only concerned that the house could accommodate no more; and yet perhaps by "putting the children away in the maids' room, or swinging a cot somewhere," they could hardly bear to think of not finding room for two or three besides, supposing they might wish to stay; though, with regard to any attendance on Miss Musgrove, there need not be the least uneasiness in leaving her to Mrs. Harville's care entirely. Mrs. Harville was a very experienced nurse; and her nursery-maid, who had lived with her long and gone about with her every where, was just such another. Between those two, she could want no possible attendance by day or night. And all this was said with a truth and sincerity of feeling irresistible.

Charles, Henrietta, and Captain Wentworth were the three in consultation, and for a little while it was only an interchange of perplexity and terror. "Uppercross—the necessity of some one's going to Uppercross—the news to be conveyed—how it could be broken to Mr. and Mrs. Musgrove—the lateness of the morning—an hour already gone since they ought to have been off—the impossibility of being in tolerable time." At first, they were capable of nothing more to the purpose than such exclamations; but, after a while, Captain Wentworth, exerting himself, said,

"We must be decided, and without the loss of another minute. Every minute is valuable. Some must resolve on being off for Uppercross instantly. Musgrove, either you or I must go."

Charles agreed; but declared his resolution of not going away. He would be as little incumbrance as possible to Captain and Mrs. Harville; but as to leaving his sister in such a state, he neither ought, nor would. So far it was decided; and Henrietta at first declared the same. She, however, was soon persuaded to think differently. The usefulness of her staying!—She, who had not been able to remain in Louisa's room, or to look at her, without sufferings which made her worse than helpless! She was forced to acknowledge that she could do no good; yet was still unwilling to be away, till touched by the thought of her father and mother, she gave it up; she consented, she was anxious to be at home.

The plan had reached this point, when Anne, coming quietly down from Louisa's room, could not but hear what followed, for the parlour door was open.

"Then it is settled, Musgrove," cried Captain Wentworth, "that you stay, and that I take care of your sister home. But as to the rest—as to the others—If one stays to assist Mrs. Harville, I think it need be only one. Mrs. Charles Musgrove will, of course, wish to get back to her children; but, if Anne will stay, no one so proper, so capable as Anne!"

She paused a moment to recover from the emotion of hearing herself so spoken of. The other two warmly agreed to what he said, and she then appeared.

"You will stay, I am sure; you will stay and nurse her," cried he, turning to her and speaking with a glow, and yet a gentleness, which seemed almost restoring the past. She coloured deeply; and he recollected himself, and moved away. She expressed herself most willing, ready, happy to remain. "It was what she had been thinking of, and wishing to be allowed to do. A bed on the floor in Louisa's room would be sufficient for her, if Mrs. Harville would but think so."

One thing more, and all seemed arranged. Though it was rather desirable that Mr. and Mrs. Musgrove should be previously alarmed by some share of delay; yet the time required by the Uppercross horses to take them back, would be a dreadful extension of suspense; and Captain Wentworth proposed, and Charles Musgrove agreed, that it would be much better for him to take a chaise from the inn, and leave Mr. Musgrove's carriage and horses to be sent home the next morning early, when there would be the farther advantage of sending an account of Louisa's night.

Captain Wentworth now hurried off to get every thing ready on his part, and to be soon followed by the two ladies. When the plan was made known to Mary, however, there was an end of all peace in it. She was so wretched, and so vehement, complained so much of injustice in being expected to go away, instead of Anne; Anne, who was nothing to Louisa, while she was her sister, and had the best right to stay in Henrietta's stead! Why was not she to be as useful as Anne? And to go home without Charles, too —without her husband! No, it was too unkind! And, in short, she said more than her husband could long withstand; and as none of the others could oppose when he gave way, there was no help for it: the change of Mary for Anne was inevitable.

Anne had never submitted more reluctantly to the jealous and ill-judging claims of Mary; but so it must be, and they set off for the town, Charles taking care of his sister, and Captain Benwick attending to her. She gave a moment's recollection, as they hurried along, to the little circumstances which the same spots had witnessed earlier in the morning. There she had listened to Henrietta's schemes for Dr. Shirley's leaving Uppercross; farther on, she had first seen Mr. Elliot; a moment seemed all that could now be given to any one but Louisa, or those who were wrapt up in her welfare.

Captain Benwick was most considerately attentive to her; and, united as they all seemed by the distress of the day, she felt an increasing degree of good-will towards him, and a pleasure even in thinking that it might, perhaps, be the occasion of continuing their acquaintance.

Captain Wentworth was on the watch for them, and a chaise and four in waiting, stationed for their convenience in the lowest part of the street; but his evident surprise and vexation, at the substitution of one sister for the other—the change of his countenance—the astonishment—the expressions begun and suppressed, with which Charles was listened to, made but a mortifying reception of Anne; or must at least convince her that she was valued only as she could be useful to Louisa.

She endeavoured to be composed, and to be just. Without emulating the feelings of an Emma towards her Henry,[6] she would have attended on Louisa with a zeal above the common claims of regard, for his sake; and she hoped he would not long be so unjust as to suppose she would shrink unnecessarily from the office of a friend.

In the meantime she was in the carriage. He had handed them both in, and placed himself between them; and in this manner, under these circumstances full of astonishment and emotion to Anne, she quitted Lyme. How the long stage would pass; how it was to affect their manners; what was to be their sort of intercourse, she could not foresee. It was all quite natural, however. He was

---

[6] "the feelings of an Emma towards her Henry." The reference is to a poem by Matthew Prior in which Emma professes her willingness to serve a rival with whom Henry pretends to be in love.

devoted to Henrietta; always turning towards her; and when he spoke at all, always with the view of supporting her hopes and raising her spirits. In general, his voice and manner were studiously calm. To spare Henrietta from agitation seemed the governing principle. Once only, when she had been grieving over the last ill-judged, ill-fated walk to the Cobb, bitterly lamenting that it ever had been thought of, he burst forth, as if wholly overcome—

"Don't talk of it, don't talk of it," he cried. "Oh God! that I had not given way to her at the fatal moment! Had I done as I ought! But so eager and so resolute! Dear, sweet Louisa!"

Anne wondered whether it ever occurred to him now, to question the justness of his own previous opinion as to the universal felicity and advantage of firmness of character; and whether it might not strike him, that, like all other qualities of the mind, it should have its proportions and limits. She thought it could scarcely escape him to feel, that a persuadable temper might sometimes be as much in favour of happiness, as a very resolute character.

They got on fast. Anne was astonished to recognise the same hills and the same objects so soon. Their actual speed, heightened by some dread of the conclusion, made the road appear but half as long as on the day before. It was growing quite dusk, however, before they were in the neighbourhood of Uppercross, and there had been total silence among them for some time, Henrietta leaning back in the corner, with a shawl over her face, giving the hope of her having cried herself to sleep; when, as they were going up their last hill, Anne found herself all at once addressed by Captain Wentworth. In a low, cautious voice, he said,

"I have been considering what we had best do. She must not appear at first. She could not stand it. I have been thinking whether you had not better remain in the carriage with her, while I go in and break it to Mr. and Mrs. Musgrove. Do you think this a good plan?"

She did: he was satisfied, and said no more. But the remembrance of the appeal remained a pleasure to her—as a proof of friendship, and of deference for her judgment, a great pleasure; and when it became a sort of parting proof, its value did not lessen.

When the distressing communication at Uppercross was over, and he had seen the father and mother quite as composed as could be hoped, and the daughter all the better for being with them, he announced his intention of returning in the same carriage to Lyme; and when the horses were baited, he was off.

Chapter thirteen

The remainder of Anne's time at Uppercross, comprehending only two days, was spent entirely at the mansion-house, and she had the satisfaction of knowing herself extremely useful there, both as an immediate companion, and as assisting in all those arrangements for the future, which, in Mr. and Mrs. Musgrove's distressed state of spirits, would have been difficulties.

They had an early account from Lyme the next morning. Louisa was much the same. No symptoms worse than before had appeared. Charles came a few hours afterwards, to bring a later and more particular account. He was tolerably cheerful. A speedy cure must not be hoped, but every thing was going on as well as the nature of the case admitted. In speaking of the Harvilles, he seemed unable to satisfy his own sense of their kindness, especially of Mrs. Harville's exertions as a nurse. "She really left nothing for Mary to do. He and Mary had been persuaded to go early to their inn last night. Mary had been hysterical again this morning. When he came away, she was going to walk out with Captain Benwick, which, he hoped, would do her good. He almost wished she had been prevailed on to come home the day before; but the truth was, that

Mrs. Harville left nothing for any body to do."

Charles was to return to Lyme the same afternoon, and his father had at first half a mind to go with him, but the ladies could not consent. It would be going only to multiply trouble to the others, and increase his own distress; and a much better scheme followed and was acted upon. A chaise was sent for from Crewkherne, and Charles conveyed back a far more useful person in the old nursery-maid of the family, one who having brought up all the children, and seen the very last, the lingering and long-petted master Harry, sent to school after his brothers, was now living in her deserted nursery to mend stockings, and dress all the blains and bruises she could get near her, and who, consequently, was only too happy in being allowed to go and help nurse dear Miss Louisa. Vague wishes of getting Sarah thither, had occurred before to Mrs. Musgrove and Henrietta; but without Anne, it would hardly have been resolved on, and found practicable so soon.

They were indebted, the next day, to Charles Hayter for all the minute knowledge of Louisa, which it was so essential to obtain every twenty-four hours. He made it his business to go to Lyme, and his account was still encouraging. The intervals of sense and consciousness were believed to be stronger. Every report agreed in Captain Wentworth's appearing fixed in Lyme.

Anne was to leave them on the morrow, an event which they all dreaded. "What should they do without her? They were wretched comforters for one another!" And so much was said in this way, that Anne thought she could not do better than impart among them the general inclination to which she was privy, and persuade them all to go to Lyme at once. She had little difficulty; it was soon determined that they would go, go to-morrow, fix themselves at the inn, or get into lodgings, as it suited, and there remain till dear Louisa could be moved. They must be taking off some trouble from the good people she was with; they might at least relieve Mrs. Harville from the care of her own children; and in short they were so happy in the decision, that Anne was delighted with what she had done, and felt that she could not spend her last morning at Uppercross better than in assisting their preparations, and sending them off at an early hour, though her being left to the solitary range of the house was the consequence.

She was the last, excepting the little boys at the cottage, she was the very last, the only remaining one of all that had filled and animated both houses, of all that had given Uppercross its cheerful character. A few days had made a change indeed!

If Louisa recovered, it would all be well again. More than former happiness would be restored. There could not be a doubt, to her mind there was none, of what would follow her recovery. A few months hence, and the room now so deserted, occupied but by her silent, pensive self, might be filled again with all that was happy and gay, all that was glowing and bright in prosperous love, all that was most unlike Anne Elliot!

An hour's complete leisure for such reflections as these, on a dark November day, a small thick rain almost blotting out the very few objects ever to be discerned from the windows, was enough to make the sound of Lady Russell's carriage exceedingly welcome; and yet, though desirous to be gone, she could not quit the mansion-house, or look an adieu to the cottage, with its black, dripping, and comfortless veranda, or even notice through the misty glasses the last humble tenements of the village, without a saddened heart. Scenes had passed in Uppercross, which made it precious. It stood the record of many sensations of pain, once severe, but now softened; and of some instances of relenting feeling, some breathings of friendship and reconciliation, which could never be looked for again, and which could never cease to be dear. She left it all behind her; all but the recollection that such things had been.

Anne had never entered Kellynch since

her quitting Lady Russell's house, in September. It had not been necessary, and the few occasions of its being possible for her to go to the hall she had contrived to evade and escape from. Her first return, was to resume her place in the modern and elegant apartments of the lodge, and to gladden the eyes of its mistress.

There was some anxiety mixed with Lady Russell's joy in meeting her. She knew who had been frequenting Uppercross. But happily, either Anne was improved in plumpness and looks, or Lady Russell fancied her so; and Anne, in receiving her compliments on the occasion, had the amusement of connecting them with the silent admiration of her cousin, and of hoping that she was to be blessed with a second spring of youth and beauty.

When they came to converse, she was soon sensible of some mental change. The subjects of which her heart had been full on leaving Kellynch, and which she had felt slighted, and been compelled to smother among the Musgroves, were now become but of secondary interest. She had lately lost sight even of her father and sister and Bath. Their concerns had been sunk under those of Uppercross, and when Lady Russell reverted to their former hopes and fears, and spoke her satisfaction in the house in Camden-place, which had been taken, and her regret that Mrs. Clay should still be with them, Anne would have been ashamed to have it known, how much more she was thinking of Lyme, and Louisa Musgrove, and all her acquaintance there; how much more interesting to her was the home and the friendship of the Harvilles and Captain Benwick, than her own father's house in Camden-place, or her own sister's intimacy with Mrs. Clay. She was actually forced to exert herself, to meet Lady Russell with any thing like the appearance of equal solicitude, on topics which had by nature the first claim on her.

There was a little awkwardness at first in their discourse on another subject. They must speak of the accident at Lyme. Lady Russell had not been arrived five minutes the day before, when a full account of the whole had burst on her; but still it must be talked of, she must make enquiries, she must regret the imprudence, lament the result, and Captain Wentworth's name must be mentioned by both. Anne was conscious of not doing it so well as Lady Russell. She could not speak the name, and look straight forward to Lady Russell's eye, till she had adopted the expedient of telling her briefly what she thought of the attachment between him and Louisa. When this was told, his name distressed her no longer.

Lady Russell had only to listen composedly, and wish them happy; but internally her heart revelled in angry pleasure, in pleased contempt, that the man who at twenty-three had seemed to understand somewhat of the value of an Anne Elliot, should, eight years afterwards, be charmed by a Louisa Musgrove.

The first three or four days passed most quietly, with no circumstance to mark them excepting the receipt of a note or two from Lyme, which found their way to Anne, she could not tell how, and brought a rather improving account of Louisa. At the end of that period, Lady Russell's politeness could repose no longer, and the fainter self-threatenings of the past, became in a decided tone, "I must call on Mrs. Croft; I really must call upon her soon. Anne, have you courage to go with me, and pay a visit in that house? It will be some trial to us both."

Anne did not shrink from it; on the contrary, she truly felt as she said, in observing,

"I think you are very likely to suffer the most of the two; your feelings are less reconciled to the change than mine. By remaining in the neighbourhood, I am become inured to it."

She could have said more on the subject; for she had in fact so high an opinion of the Crofts, and considered her father so very fortunate in his tenants, felt the parish to be so sure of a good example, and the poor of the best attention and relief, that however sorry and ashamed for the necessity of the removal, she could not but in conscience feel that they were gone who deserved not to stay, and that Kellynch-hall had passed into better hands than its owners'. These convictions must unquestionably have their own pain, and severe was its kind; but they precluded that pain which Lady Russell would suffer in entering the house again, and returning through the well-known apartments.

In such moments Anne had no power of saying to herself, "These rooms ought to belong only to us. Oh, how fallen in their destination! How unworthily occupied! An ancient family to be so driven away! Strangers filling their place!" No, except when she thought of her mother, and remembered where she had been used to sit and preside, she had no sigh of that description to heave.

Mrs. Croft always met her with a kindness which gave her the pleasure of fancying herself a favourite; and on the present occasion, receiving her in that house, there was particular attention.

The sad accident at Lyme was soon the prevailing topic; and on comparing their latest accounts of the invalid, it appeared that each lady dated her intelligence from the same hour of yester morn, that Captain Wentworth had been in Kellynch yesterday (the first time since the accident), had brought Anne the last note, which she had not been able to trace the exact steps of, had staid a few hours and then returned again to Lyme—and without any present intention of quitting it any more. He had enquired after her, she found, particularly; had expressed his hope of Miss Elliot's not being the worse for her exertions, and had spoken of those exertions as great. This was handsome, and gave her more pleasure than almost any thing else could have done.

As to the sad catastrophe itself, it could be canvassed only in one style by a couple of steady, sensible women, whose judgments had to work on ascertained events; and it was perfectly decided that it had been the consequence of much thoughtlessness and much imprudence; that its effects were most alarming, and that it was frightful to think, how long Miss Musgrove's recovery might yet be doubtful, and how liable she would still remain to suffer from the concussion hereafter! The Admiral wound it all up summarily by exclaiming,

"Ay, a very bad business indeed. A new sort of way this, for a young fellow to be making love, by breaking his mistress's head!—is not it, Miss Elliot?—This is breaking a head and giving a plaister truly!"

Admiral Croft's manners were not quite of the tone to suit Lady Russell, but they delighted Anne. His goodness of heart and simplicity of character were irresistible.

"Now, this must be very bad for you," said he, suddenly rousing from a little reverie, "to be coming and finding us here. I had not recollected it before, I declare, but it must be very bad. But now, do not stand upon ceremony. Get up and go over all the rooms in the house if you like it."

"Another time, Sir, I thank you, not now."

"Well, whenever it suits you. You can slip in from the shrubbery at any time. And there you will find we keep our umbrellas, hanging up by that door. A good place, is not it? But" (checking himself) "you will not think it a good place, for yours were always kept in the butler's room. Ay, so it always is, I believe. One man's ways may be as good as another's, but we all like our own best. And so you must judge for yourself, whether it would be better for you to go about the house or not."

Anne, finding she might decline it, did so, very gratefully.

"We have made very few changes either!" continued the Admiral, after thinking a moment. "Very few. We told you about the laundry-door, at Uppercross. That has been a very great improvement. The wonder was, how any family upon earth could bear with the inconvenience of its opening as it did, so long! You will tell Sir Walter what we have done, and that Mr. Shepherd thinks it the greatest improvement the house ever had. Indeed, I must do ourselves the justice to say, that the few alterations we have made have been all very much for the better. My wife should have the credit of them, however. I have done very little besides sending away some of the large looking-glasses from my dressing-room, which was your father's. A very good man, and very much the gentleman I am sure—but I should think, Miss Elliot" (looking with serious reflection) "I should think he must be rather a dressy man for his time of life. Such a number of looking-glasses! oh Lord! there was no getting away from oneself. So I got Sophy to lend me a hand, and we soon shifted their quarters; and now I am quite snug, with my little shaving glass in one corner, and another great thing that I never go near."

Anne, amused in spite of herself, was rather distressed for an answer, and the Admiral, fearing he might not have been civil enough, took up the subject again, to say,

"The next time you write to your good father, Miss Elliot, pray give him my compliments and Mrs. Croft's, and say that we are settled here quite to our liking, and have no fault at all to find with the place. The breakfast-room chimney smokes a little, I grant you, but it is only when the wind is due north and blows hard, which may not happen three times a winter. And take it altogether, now that we have been into most of the houses hereabouts and can judge, there is not one that we like better than this. Pray say so, with my compliments. He will be glad to hear it."

Lady Russell and Mrs. Croft were very well pleased with each other; but the acquaintance which this visit began, was fated not to proceed far at present; for when it was returned, the Crofts announced themselves to be going away for a few weeks, to visit their connexions in the north of the county, and probably might not be at home again before Lady Russell would be removing to Bath.

So ended all danger to Anne of meeting Captain Wentworth at Kellynch-hall, or of seeing him in company with her friend. Every thing was safe enough, and she smiled over the many anxious feelings she had wasted on the subject.

Chapter fourteen

Though Charles and Mary had remained at Lyme much longer after Mr. and Mrs. Musgrove's going, than Anne conceived they could have been at all wanted, they were yet the first of the family to be at home again, and as soon as possible after their return to Uppercross, they drove over to the lodge. They had left Louisa beginning to sit up; but her head, though clear, was exceedingly weak, and her nerves susceptible to the highest extreme of tenderness; and though she might be pronounced to be altogether doing very well, it was still impossible to say when she might be able to bear the removal home; and her father and mother, who must return in time to receive their younger children for the Christmas holidays, had hardly a hope of being allowed to bring her with them.

They had been all in lodgings together. Mrs. Musgrove had got Mrs. Harville's children away as much as she could, every possible supply from Uppercross had been furnished, to lighten the inconvenience to the Harvilles, while the Harvilles had been wanting them to come to dinner every day; and in short, it seemed to have been only a struggle on each side as to which should be most disinterested and hospitable.

Mary had had her evils; but upon the whole, as was evident by her staying so long, she had found more to enjoy than to suffer. Charles Hayter had been at Lyme oftener than suited her, and when they dined with the Harvilles there had been only a maidservant to wait, and at first, Mrs. Harville had always given Mrs. Musgrove precedence; but then, she had received so very handsome an apology from her on finding out whose daughter she was, and there had been so much going on every day, there had been so many walks between their lodgings and the Harvilles, and she had got books from the library and changed them so often, that the balance had certainly been much in favour of Lyme. She had been taken to Charmouth too, and she had bathed, and she had gone to church, and there were a great many more people to look at in the church at Lyme than at Uppercross, and all this, joined to the sense of being so very useful, had made really an agreeable fortnight.

Anne enquired after Captain Benwick. Mary's face was clouded directly. Charles laughed.

"Oh! Captain Benwick is very well, I believe, but he is a very odd young man. I do not know what he would be at. We asked him to come home with us for a day or two; Charles undertook to give him some shooting, and he seemed quite delighted, and for my part, I thought it was all settled; when behold! on Tuesday night, he made a very awkward sort of excuse; 'he never shot' and he had 'been quite misunderstood,' and he had promised this and he had promised that, and the end of it was, I found, that he did not mean to come. I suppose he was afraid of finding it dull; but upon my word I should have thought we were lively enough at the Cottage for such a heart-broken man as Captain Benwick."

Charles laughed again and said, "Now Mary, you know very well how it really was. It was all your doing" (turning to Anne). "He fancied that if he went with us, he should find you close by; he fancied every body to be living in Uppercross; and when he discovered that Lady Russell lived three miles off, his heart failed him, and he had not courage to come. That is the fact, upon my honour. Mary knows it is."

But Mary did not give into it very graciously; whether from not considering Captain Benwick entitled by birth and situation to be in love with an Elliot, or from not wanting to believe Anne a greater attraction to Uppercross than herself, must be left to be guessed. Anne's good-will, however, was not to be lessened by what she heard. She boldly acknowledged herself flattered, and continued her enquiries.

"Oh! he talks of you," cried Charles, "in such terms,"—Mary interrupted him. "I declare, Charles, I never heard him mention Anne twice all the time I was there. I declare, Anne, he never talks of you at all."

"No," admitted Charles, "I do not know that he ever does, in a general way—but however, it is a very clear thing that he admires you exceedingly. His head is full of some books that he is reading upon your recommendation, and he wants to talk to you about them; he has found out something or other in one of them which he thinks—Oh! I cannot pretend to remember it, but it was something very fine—I overheard him telling Henrietta all about it—and then 'Miss Elliot' was spoken of in the highest terms!—Now Mary, I declare it was so, I heard it myself, and you were in the other room.—'Elegance, sweetness, beauty,' Oh! there was no end of Miss Elliot's charms."

"And I am sure," cried Mary warmly, "it was very little to his credit, if he did. Miss Harville only died last June. Such a heart is very little worth having; is it, Lady Russell? I am sure you will agree with me."

"I must see Captain Benwick before I decide," said Lady Russell, smiling.

"And that you are very likely to do very soon, I can tell you, ma'am," said Charles. "Though he had not nerves for coming away with us and setting off again afterwards to pay a formal visit here, he will make his way over to Kellynch one day by himself, you may depend on it. I told him the distance and the road, and I told him of the church's being so very well worth seeing, for as he has a taste for those sort of things, I thought that would be a good excuse, and he listened with all his understanding and soul; and I am sure from his manner that you will have him calling here soon. So, I give you notice, Lady Russell."

"Any acquaintance of Anne's will always be welcome to me," was Lady Russell's kind answer.

"Oh! as to being Anne's acquaintance," said Mary, "I think he is rather my acquaintance, for I have been seeing him every day this last fortnight."

"Well, as your joint acquaintance, then, I shall be very happy to see Captain Benwick."

"You will not find any thing very agreeable in him, I assure you, ma'am. He is one of the dullest young men that ever lived. He has walked with me, sometimes, from one end of the sands to the other, without saying a word. He is not at all a well-bred young man. I am sure you will not like him."

"There we differ, Mary," said Anne. "I think Lady Russell would like him. I think she would be so much pleased with his mind, that she would very soon see no deficiency in his manner."

"So do I, Anne," said Charles. "I am sure Lady Russell would like him. He is just Lady Russell's sort. Give him a book, and he will read all day long."

"Yes, that he will!" exclaimed Mary, tauntingly. "He will sit poring over his book, and not know when a person speaks to him, or when one drops one's scissors, or any thing that happens. Do you think Lady Russell would like that?"

Lady Russell could not help laughing. "Upon my word," said she, "I should not have supposed that my opinion of any one could have admitted of such difference of conjecture, steady and matter of fact as I may call myself. I have really a curiosity to see the person who can give occasion to such directly opposite notions. I wish he may be induced to call here. And when he does, Mary, you may depend upon hearing my opinion; but I am determined not to judge him before-hand."

"You will not like him, I will answer for it."

Lady Russell began talking of something else. Mary spoke with animation of their meeting with, or rather missing, Mr. Elliot so extraordinarily.

"He is a man," said Lady Russell, "whom I have no wish to see. His declining to be on cordial terms with the head of his family, has left a very strong impression in his disfavour with me."

This decision checked Mary's eagerness, and stopped her short in the midst of the Elliot countenance.

With regard to Captain Wentworth, though Anne hazarded no enquiries, there was voluntary communication sufficient. His spirits had been greatly recovering lately, as might be expected. As Louisa improved, he had improved; and he was now quite a different creature from what he had been the first week. He had not seen Louisa; and was so extremely fearful of any ill consequence to her from an interview, that he did not press for it at all; and, on the contrary, seemed to have a plan of going away for a week or ten days, till her head were stronger. He had talked of going down to Plymouth for a week, and wanted to persuade Captain Benwick to go with him; but, as Charles maintained to the last, Captain Benwick seemed much more disposed to ride over to Kellynch.

There can be no doubt that Lady Russell and Anne were both occasionally thinking of Captain Benwick, from this time. Lady Russell could not hear the door-bell without feeling that it might be his herald; nor could Anne return from any stroll of solitary indulgence in her father's grounds, or any visit of charity in the village, without wondering whether she might see him or hear of him. Captain Benwick came not, however. He was either less disposed for it than Charles had imagined, or he was too shy; and after giving him a week's indulgence, Lady Russell determined him to be unworthy of the interest which he had been beginning to excite.

The Musgroves came back to receive their happy boys and girls from school, bringing with them Mrs. Harville's little children, to improve the noise of Uppercross, and lessen that of Lyme. Henrietta remained with Louisa; but all the rest of the family were again in their usual quarters.

Lady Russell and Anne paid their compliments to them once, when Anne could not but feel that Uppercross was already quite alive again. Though neither Henrietta, nor Louisa, nor Charles Hayter, nor Captain Wentworth were there, the room presented as strong a contrast as could be wished, to the last state she had seen it in.

Immediately surrounding Mrs. Musgrove were the little Harvilles, whom she was sedulously guarding from the tyranny of the two children from the Cottage, expressly arrived to amuse them. On one side was a table, occupied by some chattering girls, cutting up silk and gold paper; and on the other were tressels and trays, bending under the weight of brawn and cold pies, where riotous boys were holding high revel; the whole completed by a roaring Christmas fire, which seemed determined to be heard, in spite of all the noise of the others. Charles and Mary also came in, of course, during their visit; and Mr. Musgrove made a point of paying his respects to Lady Russell, and sat down close to her for ten minutes, talking with a very raised voice, but, from the clamour of the children on his knees, generally in vain. It was a fine family-piece.

Anne, judging from her own temperament, would have deemed such a domestic hurricane a bad restorative of the nerves, which Louisa's illness must have so greatly shaken; but Mrs. Musgrove, who got Anne near her on purpose to thank her most cordially, again and again, for all her attentions to them, concluded a short recapitulation of what she had suffered herself, by observing, with a happy glance round the room, that after all she had gone through, nothing was so likely to do her good as a little quiet cheerfulness at home.

Louisa was now recovering apace. Her mother could even think of her being able to join their party at home, before her brothers and sisters went to school again. The Harvilles had promised to come with her and stay at Uppercross, whenever she returned. Captain Wentworth was gone, for the present, to see his brother in Shropshire.

"I hope I shall remember, in future," said Lady Russell, as soon as they were reseated in the carriage, "not to call at Uppercross in the Christmas holidays."

Every body has their taste in noises as well as in other matters; and sounds are quite innoxious, or most distressing, by their sort rather than their quantity. When Lady Russell, not long afterwards, was entering Bath on a wet afternoon, and driving through the long course of streets from the Old Bridge to Camden-place, amidst the dash of other carriages, the heavy rumble of carts and drays, the bawling of newsmen, muffin-men and milkmen, and the ceaseless clink of pattens, she made no complaint. No, these were noises which belonged to the winter pleasures; her spirits rose under their influence; and, like Mrs. Musgrove, she was feeling, though not saying, that, after being long in the country, nothing could be so good for her as a little quiet cheerfulness.

Anne did not share these feelings. She persisted in a very determined, though very silent, disinclination for Bath; caught the first dim view of the extensive buildings, smoking in rain, without any wish of seeing them better; felt their progress through the streets to be, however disagreeable, yet too rapid; for who would be glad to see her when she arrived? And looked back, with fond regret, to the bustles of Uppercross and the seclusion of Kellynch.

Elizabeth's last letter had communicated a piece of news of some interest. Mr. Elliot was in Bath. He had called in Camden-place; had called a second time, a third; had been pointedly attentive: if Elizabeth and her father did not deceive themselves, had been taking as much pains to seek the acquaintance, and proclaim the value of the connection, as he had formerly taken pains to shew neglect. This was very wonderful, if it were true; and Lady Russell was in a state of very agreeable curiosity and perplexity about Mr. Elliot, already recanting the sentiment she had so lately expressed to Mary, of his being "a man whom she had no wish to see." She had a great wish to see him. If he really sought to reconcile himself like a dutiful branch, he must be forgiven for having dismembered himself from the paternal tree.

Anne was not animated to an equal pitch by the circumstance; but she felt that she would rather see Mr. Elliot again than not, which was more than she could say for many other persons in Bath.

She was put down in Camden-place; and Lady Russell then drove to her own lodgings, in Rivers-street.

Chapter fifteen

Sir Walter had taken a very good house in Camden-place, a lofty, dignified situation, such as becomes a man of consequence; and both he and Elizabeth were settled there, much to their satisfaction.

Anne entered it with a sinking heart, anticipating an imprisonment of many months, and anxiously saying to herself, "Oh! when shall I leave you again?" A degree of unexpected cordiality, however, in the welcome she received, did her good. Her father and sister were glad to see her, for the sake of shewing her the house and furniture, and met her with kindness. Her making a fourth, when they sat down to dinner, was noticed as an advantage.

Mrs. Clay was very pleasant, and very, smiling; but her courtesies and smiles were more a matter of course. Anne had always felt that she would pretend what was proper on her arrival; but the complaisance of the others was unlooked for. They were evidently in excellent spirits, and she was soon to listen to the causes. They had no inclination to listen to her. After laying out for some compliments of being deeply regretted in their old neighbourhood, which Anne could not pay, they had only a few faint enquiries to make, before the talk must be all their own. Uppercross excited no interest, Kellynch very little, it was all Bath.

They had the pleasure of assuring her that Bath more than answered their expectations in every respect. Their house was undoubtedly the best in Camden-place; their drawing-rooms had many decided advantages over all the others which they had either seen or heard of; and the superiority was not less in the style of the fitting-up, or the taste of the furniture. Their acquaintance was exceedingly sought after. Every body was wanting to visit them. They had drawn back from many introductions, and still were perpetually having cards left by people of whom they knew nothing.

Here were funds of enjoyment! Could Anne wonder that her father and sister were happy? She might not wonder, but she must sigh that her father should feel no degradation in his change; should see nothing to regret in the duties and dignity of the resident land-holder; should find so much to be vain of in the littlenesses of a town; and she must sigh, and smile, and wonder too, as Elizabeth threw open the folding-doors, and walked with exultation from one drawing-room to the other, boasting of their space, at the possibility of that woman, who had been mistress of Kellynch Hall, finding extent to be proud of between two walls, perhaps thirty feet asunder.

But this was not all which they had to make them happy. They had Mr. Elliot, too. Anne had a great deal to hear of Mr. Elliot. He was not only pardoned, they were delighted with him. He had been in Bath about a fortnight (he had passed through Bath in November, in his way to London, when the intelligence of Sir Walter's being settled there had of course reached him, though only twenty-four hours in the place, but he had not been able to avail himself of it); but he had now been a fortnight in Bath, and his first object, on arriving, had been to leave his card in Camden-place, following it up by such assiduous endeavours to meet, and, when they did meet, by such great openness of conduct, such readiness to apologize for the past, such solicitude to be received as a relation again, that their former good understanding was completely re-established.

They had not a fault to find in him. He had explained away all the appearance of neglect on his own side. It had originated in misapprehension entirely. He had never had an idea of throwing himself off; he had feared that he was thrown off, but knew not why; and delicacy had kept him silent. Upon the hint of having spoken disrespectfully or carelessly of the family, and the family honours, he was quite indignant. He, who had ever boasted of being an Elliot, and whose feelings, as to connection, were only too strict to suit the unfeudal tone of the present day! He was astonished, indeed! But his character and general conduct must refute it. He could refer Sir Walter to all who knew him; and, certainly, the pains he had been taking on this, the first opportunity of reconciliation, to be restored to the footing of a relation and heir-presumptive, was a strong proof of his opinions on the subject.

The circumstances of his marriage too were found to admit of much extenuation. This was an article not to be entered on by himself; but a very intimate friend of his, a Colonel Wallis, a highly respectable man, perfectly the gentleman (and not an ill-looking man, Sir Walter added), who was living in very good style in Marlborough Buildings, and had, at his own particular request, been admitted to their acquaintance through Mr. Elliot, had mentioned one or two things relative to the marriage, which made a material difference in the discredit of it.

Colonel Wallis had known Mr. Elliot long, had been well acquainted also with his wife, had perfectly understood the whole story. She was certainly not a woman of family, but well educated, accomplished, rich, and excessively in love with his friend. There had been the charm. She had sought him. Without that attraction, not all her money would have tempted Elliot, and Sir Walter was, moreover, assured of her having been a very fine woman. Here was a great deal to soften the business. A very fine woman, with a large fortune, in love with him! Sir Walter seemed to admit it as complete apology, and though Elizabeth could not see the circumstance in quite so favourable a light, she allowed it be a great extenuation.

Mr. Elliot had called repeatedly, had dined with them once, evidently delighted by the distinction of being asked, for they gave no dinners in general; delighted, in short, by every proof of cousinly notice, and placing his whole happiness in being on intimate terms in Camden-place.

Anne listened, but without quite understanding it. Allowances, large allowances, she knew, must be made for the ideas of those who spoke. She heard it all under embellishment. All that sounded extravagant or irrational in the progress of the reconciliation might have no origin but in the language of the relators. Still, however, she had the sensation of there being something more than immediately appeared, in Mr. Elliot's wishing, after an interval of so many years, to be well received by them. In a worldly view, he had nothing to gain by being on terms with Sir Walter, nothing to risk by a state of variance. In all probability he was already the richer of the two, and the Kellynch estate would as surely be his hereafter as the title. A sensible man! and he had looked like a *very* sensible man, why should it be an object to him? She could only offer one solution; it was, perhaps, for Elizabeth's sake. There might really have been a liking formerly, though convenience and accident had drawn him a different way, and now that he could afford to please himself, he might mean to pay his addresses to her. Elizabeth was certainly very handsome, with well-bred, elegant manners, and her character might never have been penetrated by Mr. Elliot, knowing her but in public, and when very young himself. How her temper and understanding might bear the investigation of his present keener time of life was another concern, and rather a fearful one. Most earnestly did she wish that he might not be too nice, or too observant, if Elizabeth were his object; and that Elizabeth was disposed to believe herself so, and that her friend Mrs. Clay was encouraging the idea, seemed apparent by a glance or two between them, while Mr. Elliot's frequent visits were talked of.

Anne mentioned the glimpses she had had of him at Lyme, but without being much attended to. "Oh! yes, perhaps, it had been Mr. Elliot. They did not know. It might be him, perhaps." They could not listen to her description of him. They were describing him themselves; Sir Walter especially. He did justice to his very gentlemanlike appearance, his air of elegance and fashion, his good shaped face, his sensible eye, but, at the same time, "must lament his being very much under-hung, a defect which time seemed to have increased; nor could he pretend to say that ten years had not altered almost every feature for the worse. Mr. Elliot appeared to think that he (Sir Walter) was looking exactly as he had done when they last parted," but Sir Walter had "not been able to return the compliment entirely, which had embarrassed him. He did not mean to complain, however. Mr. Elliot was better to look at than most men, and he had no objection to being seen with him any where."

Mr. Elliot, and his friends in Marlborough Buildings, were talked of the whole evening. "Colonel Wallis had been so impatient to be introduced to them! and Mr. Elliot so anxious that he should!" And there was a Mrs. Wallis, at present only known to them by description, as she was in daily expectation of her confinement; but Mr. Elliot spoke of her as "a most charming woman, quite worthy of being known in Camden-place," and as soon as she recovered, they were to be acquainted. Sir Walter thought much of Mrs. Wallis; she was said to be an excessively pretty woman, beautiful. He longed to see her. He hoped she might make some amends for the many very plain faces he was continually passing in the streets. The worst of Bath was, the number of its plain women. He did not mean to say that there were no pretty women, but the number of the plain was out of all proportion. He had frequently observed, as he walked, that one handsome face would be followed by thirty, or five and thirty frights; and once, as he had stood in a shop in Bond-street he had counted eighty-seven women go by, one after another, without there being a tolerable face among them. It had been a frosty morning, to be sure, a sharp frost, which hardly one woman in a thousand could stand the test of. But still, there certainly were a dreadful multitude of ugly women in Bath; and as for the men! they were infinitely worse. Such scare-crows as the streets were full of! It was evident how little the women were used to the sight of any thing tolerable, by the effect which a man of decent appearance produced. He had never walked any where arm in arm with Colonel Wallis (who was a fine military figure, though sandy-haired), without observing that every woman's eye was upon him; every woman's eye was sure to be upon Colonel Wallis. Modest Sir Walter! He was not allowed to escape, however. His daughter and Mrs. Clay united in hinting that Colonel Wallis's companion might have as good a figure as Colonel Wallis, and certainly was not sandy-haired.

"How is Mary looking?" said Sir Walter, in the height of his good humour. "The last time I saw her, she had a red nose, but I hope that may not happen every day."

"Oh! no, that must have been quite accidental. In general she has been in very good health, and very good looks since Michaelmas."

"If I thought it would not tempt her to go out in sharp winds, and grow coarse, I would send her a new hat and pelisse."

Anne was considering whether she should venture to suggest that a gown, or a cap, would not be liable to any such misuse, when a knock at the door suspended every thing. "A knock at the door! and so late! It was ten o'clock. Could it be Mr. Elliot? They knew he was to dine in Lansdown Crescent. It was possible that he might stop in his way home, to ask them how they did. They could think of no one else. Mrs. Clay decidedly thought it Mr. Elliot's knock." Mrs. Clay was right. With all the state which a butler and foot-boy could give, Mr. Elliot was ushered into the room.

It was the same, the very same man, with no difference but of dress. Anne drew a little back, while the others received his compliments, and her sister his apologies for calling at so unusual an hour, but "he could not be so near without wishing to know that neither she nor her friend had taken cold the day before, etc. etc." which was all as politely done, and as politely taken as possible, but her part must follow then. Sir Walter talked of his youngest daughter; "Mr. Elliot must give him leave to present him to his youngest daughter"—(there was no occasion for remembering Mary) and Anne, smiling and blushing, very becomingly shewed to Mr. Elliot the pretty features which he had by no means forgotten, and instantly saw, with amusement at his little start of surprise, that he had not been at all aware of who she was. He looked completely astonished, but not more astonished than pleased; his eyes brightened, and with the most perfect alacrity he welcomed the relationship, alluded to the past, and entreated to be received as an acquaintance already. He was quite as good-looking as he had appeared at Lyme, his countenance improved by speaking, and his manners were so exactly what they ought to be, so polished, so easy, so particularly agreeable, that she could compare them in excellence to only one person's manners. They were not the same, but they were, perhaps, equally good.

He sat down with them, and improved their conversation very much. There could be no doubt of his being a sensible man. Ten minutes were enough to certify that. His tone, his expressions, his choice of subject, his knowing where to stop—it was all the operation of a sensible, discerning mind. As soon as he could, he began to talk to her of Lyme, wanting to compare opinions respecting the place, but especially wanting to speak of the circumstance of their happening to be guests in the same inn at the same time, to give his own route, understand something of hers, and regret that he should have lost such an opportunity of paying his respects to her. She gave him a short account of her party, and business at Lyme. His regret increased as he listened. He had spent his whole solitary evening in the room adjoining theirs; had heard voices—mirth continually; thought they must be a most delightful set of people—longed to be with them; but certainly without the smallest suspicion of his possessing the shadow of a right to introduce himself. If he had but asked who the party were! The name of Musgrove would have told him enough. "Well, it would serve to cure him of an absurd practice of never asking a question at an inn, which he had adopted, when quite a young man, on the principle of its being very ungenteel to be curious.

"The notions of a young man of one or two and twenty," said he, "as to what is necessary in manners to make him quite the thing, are more absurd, I believe, than those of any other set of beings in the world. The folly of the means they often employ is only to be equalled by the folly of what they have in view."

But he must not be addressing his reflections to Anne alone; he knew it; he was soon diffused again among the others, and it was only at intervals that he could return to Lyme.

His enquiries, however, produced at length an account of the scene she had been engaged in there, soon after his leaving the place. Having alluded to "an accident," he must hear the whole. When he questioned, Sir Walter and Elizabeth began to question also; but the difference in their manner of doing it could not be unfelt. She could only compare Mr. Elliot to Lady Russell, in the wish of really comprehending what had passed, and in the degree of concern for what she must have suffered in witnessing it.

He staid an hour with them. The elegant little clock on the mantel-piece had struck "eleven with its silver sounds," and the watchman was beginning to be heard at a distance telling the same tale, before Mr. Elliot or any of them seemed to feel that he had been there long.

Anne could not have supposed it possible

that her first evening in Camden-place could have passed so well!

Chapter sixteen

There was one point which Anne, on returning to her family, would have been more thankful to ascertain, even than Mr. Elliot's being in love with Elizabeth, which was, her father's not being in love with Mrs. Clay; and she was very far from easy about it, when she had been at home a few hours. On going down to breakfast the next morning, she found there had just been a decent pretence on the lady's side of meaning to leave them. She could imagine Mrs. Clay to have said, that "now Miss Anne was come, she could not suppose herself at all wanted"; for Elizabeth was replying, in a sort of whisper, "That must not be any reason, indeed. I assure you I feel it none. She is nothing to me, compared with you"; and she was in full time to hear her father say, "My dear Madam, this must not be. As yet, you have seen nothing of Bath. You have been here only to be useful. You must not run away from us now. You must stay to be acquainted with Mrs. Wallis, the beautiful Mrs. Wallis. To your fine mind, I well know the sight of beauty is a real gratification."

He spoke and looked so much in earnest, that Anne was not surprised to see Mrs. Clay stealing a glance at Elizabeth and herself. Her countenance, perhaps, might express some watchfulness; but the praise of the fine mind did not appear to excite a thought in her sister. The lady could not but yield to such joint entreaties, and promise to stay.

In the course of the same morning, Anne and her father chancing to be alone together, he began to compliment her on her improved looks; he thought her "less thin in her person, in her cheeks; her skin, her complexion, greatly improved—clearer, fresher. Had she been using any thing in particular!" "No, nothing." "Merely Gowland,"[7] he supposed. "No, nothing at all." "Ha! he was surprised at that," and added, "Certainly you cannot do better than continue as you are; you cannot be better than well; or I should recommend Gowland, the constant use of Gowland, during the spring months. Mrs. Clay has been using it at my recommendation, and you see what it has done for her. You see how it has carried away her freckles."

If Elizabeth could but have heard this! Such personal praise might have struck her, especially as it did not appear to Anne that the freckles were at all lessened. But every thing must take its chance. The evil of the marriage would be much diminished, if Elizabeth were also to marry. As for herself, she might always command a home with Lady Russell.

Lady Russell's composed mind and polite manners were put to some trial on this point, in her intercourse in Camden-place. The sight of Mrs. Clay in such favour, and of Anne so overlooked, was a perpetual provocation to her there; and vexed her as much when she was away, as a person in Bath who drinks the water, gets all the new publications, and has a very large acquaintance, has time to be vexed.

As Mr. Elliot became known to her, she grew more charitable, or more indifferent, towards the others. His manners were an immediate recommendation; and on conversing with him she found the solid so fully supporting the superficial, that she was at first, as she told Anne, almost ready to exclaim, "Can this be Mr. Elliot?" and could not seriously picture to herself a more agreeable or estimable man. Every thing united in him; good understanding, correct opinions, knowledge of the world, and a warm heart. He had strong feelings of family-attachment and family-honour, without pride or weakness; he lived with the liberality of a man of fortune, without display; he judged for himself in every thing essential, without defying public opinion in any point of worldly decorum. He was steady, observ-

---

[7] "Gowland." A lotion for the complexion much favored in Bath.

ant, moderate, candid; never run away with by spirits or by selfishness, which fancied itself strong feeling; and yet, with a sensibility to what was amiable and lovely, and a value for all the felicities of domestic life, which characters of fancied enthusiasm and violent agitation seldom really possess. She was sure that he had not been happy in marriage. Colonel Wallis said it, and Lady Russell saw it; but it had been no unhappiness to sour his mind, nor (she began pretty soon to suspect) to prevent his thinking of a second choice. Her satisfaction in Mr. Elliot outweighed all the plague of Mrs. Clay.

It was now some years since Anne had begun to learn that she and her excellent friend could sometimes think differently; and it did not surprise her, therefore, that Lady Russell should see nothing suspicious or inconsistent, nothing to require more motives than appeared, in Mr. Elliot's great desire of a reconciliation. In Lady Russell's view, it was perfectly natural that Mr. Elliot, at a mature time of life, should feel it a most desirable object, and what would very generally recommend him, among all sensible people, to be on good terms with the head of his family; the simplest process in the world of time upon a head naturally clear, and only erring in the heyday of youth. Anne presumed, however, still to smile about it; and at last to mention "Elizabeth." Lady Russell listened, and looked, and made only this cautious reply: "Elizabeth! Very well. Time will explain."

It was a reference to the future, which Anne, after a little observation, felt she must submit to. She could determine nothing at present. In that house Elizabeth must be first; and she was in the habit of such general observance as "Miss Elliot," that any particularity of attention seemed almost impossible. Mr. Elliot, too, it must be remembered, had not been a widower seven months. A little delay on his side might be very excusable. In fact, Anne could never see the crape round his hat, without fearing that she was the inexcusable one, in attributing to him such imaginations; for though his marriage had not been very happy, still it had existed so many years that she could not comprehend a very rapid recovery from the awful impression of its being dissolved.

However it might end, he was without any question their pleasantest acquaintance in Bath; she saw nobody equal to him; and it was a great indulgence now and then to talk to him about Lyme, which he seemed to have as lively a wish to see again, and to see more of, as herself. They went through the particulars of their first meeting a great many times. He gave her to understand that he had looked at her with some earnestness. She knew it well; and she remembered another person's look also.

They did not always think alike. His value for rank and connexion she perceived to be greater than hers. It was not merely complaisance, it must be a liking to the cause, which made him enter warmly into her father and sister's solicitudes on a subject which she thought unworthy to excite them. The Bath paper one morning announced the arrival of the Dowager Viscountess Dalrymple, and her daughter, the Honourable Miss Carteret; and all the comfort of No.—, Camden-place, was swept away for many days; for the Dalrymples (in Anne's opinion, most unfortunately) were cousins of the Elliots; and the agony was, how to introduce themselves properly.

Anne had never seen her father and sister before in contact with nobility, and she must acknowledge herself disappointed. She had hoped better things from their high ideas of their own situation in life, and was reduced to form a wish which she had never foreseen—a wish that they had more pride; for "our cousins Lady Dalrymple and Miss Carteret," "our cousins, the Dalrymples," sounded in her ears all day long.

Sir Walter had once been in company with the late Viscount, but had never seen any of the rest of the family, and the difficulties of the case arose from there having been a suspension of all intercourse by letters of ceremony, ever since the death of that said late Viscount, when, in consequence of a dangerous illness of Sir Walter's at the same time, there had been an unlucky omission at Kellynch. No letter of condolence had been sent to Ireland. The neglect had been visited on the head of the sinner, for when poor Lady Elliot died herself, no letter of condolence was received at Kellynch, and, consequently, there was but too much reason to apprehend that the Dalrymples considered the relationship as closed. How to have this anxious business set to rights, and be admitted as cousins again, was the question; and it was a question which, in a more rational manner, neither Lady Russell nor Mr. Elliot thought unimportant. "Family connexions were always worth preserving, good company always worth seeking; Lady Dalrymple had taken a house, for three months, in Laura-place, and would be living in style. She had been at Bath the year before, and Lady Russell had heard her spoken of as a charming woman. It was very desirable that the connexion should be renewed, if it could be done, without any compromise of propriety on the side of the Elliots."

Sir Walter, however, would choose his own means, and at last wrote a very fine letter of ample explanation, regret and entreaty, to his right honourable cousin. Neither Lady Russell nor Mr. Elliot could admire the letter; but it did all that was wanted, in bringing three lines of scrawl from the Dowager Viscountess. "She was very much honoured, and should be happy in their acquaintance." The toils of the business were over, the sweets began. They visited in Laura-place, they had the cards of Dowager Viscountess Dalrymple, and the Hon. Miss Carteret, to be arranged wherever they might be most visible; and "Our cousins in Laura-place,"—"Our cousin, Lady Dalrymple and Miss Carteret," were talked of to every body.

Anne was ashamed. Had Lady Dalrymple and her daughter even been very agreeable, she would still have been ashamed of the agitation they created, but they were noth-

ing. There was no superiority of manner, accomplishment, or understanding. Lady Dalrymple had acquired the name of "a charming woman," because she had a smile and a civil answer for every body. Miss Carteret, with still less to say, was so plain and so awkward, that she would never have been tolerated in Camden-place but for her birth.

Lady Russell confessed that she had expected something better; but yet "it was an acquaintance worth having," and when Anne ventured to speak her opinion of them to Mr. Elliot, he agreed to their being nothing in themselves, but still maintained that as a family connexion, as good company, as those who would collect good company around them, they had their value. Anne smiled and said,

"My idea of good company, Mr. Elliot, is the company of clever, well-informed people, who have a great deal of conversation; that is what I call good company."

"You are mistaken," said he gently, "that is not good company, that is the best. Good company requires only birth, education and manners, and with regard to education is not very nice. Birth and good manners are essential; but a little learning is by no means a dangerous thing in good company, on the contrary, it will do very well. My cousin, Anne, shakes her head. She is not satisfied. She is fastidious. My dear cousin (sitting down by her), you have a better right to be fastidious than almost any other woman I know; but will it answer? Will it make you happy? Will it not be wiser to accept the society of these good ladies in Laura-place, and enjoy all the advantages of the connexion as far as possible? You may depend upon it, that they will move in the first set in Bath this winter, and as rank is rank, your being known to be related to them will have its use in fixing your family (our family let me say) in that degree of consideration which we must all wish for."

"Yes," sighed Anne, "we shall, indeed, be known to be related to them!"—then recollecting herself, and not wishing to be answered, she added, "I certainly do think there has been by far too much trouble taken to procure the acquaintance. I suppose (smiling) I have more pride than any of you; but I confess it does vex me, that we should be so solicitous to have the relationship acknowledged, which we may be very sure is a matter of perfect indifference to them."

"Pardon me, dear cousin, you are unjust to your own claims. In London, perhaps, in your present quiet style of living, it might be as you say: but in Bath, Sir Walter Elliot and his family will always be worth knowing, always acceptable as acquaintance."

"Well," said Anne, "I certainly am proud, too proud to enjoy a welcome which depends so entirely upon place."

"I love your indignation," said he; "it is very natural. But here you are in Bath, and the object is to be established here with all the credit and dignity which ought to belong to Sir Walter Elliot. You talk of being proud, I am called proud I know, and I shall not wish to believe myself otherwise, for our pride, if investigated, would have the same object, I have no doubt, though the kind may seem a little different. In one point, I am sure, my dear cousin (he continued, speaking lower, though there was no one else in the room), in one point, I am sure, we must feel alike. We must feel that every addition to your father's society, among his equals or superiors, may be of use in diverting his thoughts from those who are beneath him."

He looked, as he spoke, to the seat which Mrs. Clay had been lately occupying, a sufficient explanation of what he particularly meant; and though Anne could not believe in their having the same sort of pride, she was pleased with him for not liking Mrs. Clay; and her conscience admitted that his wishing to promote her father's getting great acquaintance, was more than excusable in the view of defeating her.

Chapter seventeen

While Sir Walter and Elizabeth were assiduously pushing their good fortune in Laura-place, Anne was renewing an acquaintance of a very different description.

She had called on her former governess, and had heard from her of there being an old school-fellow in Bath, who had the two strong claims on her attention, of past kindness and present suffering. Miss Hamilton, now Mrs. Smith, had shewn her kindness in one of those periods of her life when it had been most valuable. Anne had gone unhappy to school, grieving for the loss of a mother whom she had dearly loved, feeling her separation from home, and suffering as a girl of fourteen, of strong sensibility and not high spirits, must suffer at such a time; and Miss Hamilton, three years older than herself, but still from the want of near relations and a settled home, remaining another year at school, had been useful and good to her in a way which had considerably lessened her misery, and could never be remembered with indifference.

Miss Hamilton had left school, had married not long afterwards, was said to have married a man of fortune, and this was all that Anne had known of her, till now that their governess's account brought her situation forward in a more decided but very different form.

She was a widow, and poor. Her husband had been extravagant; and at his death, about two years before, had left his affairs dreadfully involved. She had had difficulties of every sort to contend with, and in addition to these distresses, had been afflicted with a severe rheumatic fever, which finally settling in her legs, had made her for the present a cripple. She had come to Bath on that account, and was now in lodgings near the hot-baths, living in a very humble way, unable even to afford herself the comfort of a servant, and of course almost excluded from society.

Their mutual friend answered for the

satisfaction which a visit from Miss Elliot would give Mrs. Smith, and Anne therefore lost no time in going. She mentioned nothing of what she had heard, or what she intended, at home. It would excite no proper interest there. She only consulted Lady Russell, who entered thoroughly into her sentiments, and was most happy to convey her as near to Mrs. Smith's lodgings in Westgate-buildings, as Anne chose to be taken.

The visit was paid, their acquaintance re-established, their interest in each other more than re-kindled. The first ten minutes had its awkwardness and its emotion. Twelve years were gone since they had parted, and each presented a somewhat different person from what the other had imagined. Twelve years had changed Anne from the blooming, silent, unformed girl of fifteen, to the elegant little woman of seven-and-twenty, with every beauty excepting bloom, and with manners as consciously right as they were invariably gentle; and twelve years had transformed the fine-looking, well-grown Miss Hamilton, in all the glow of health and confidence of superiority, into a poor, infirm, helpless widow, receiving the visit of her former protegée as a favour; but all that was uncomfortable in the meeting had soon passed away, and left only the interesting charm of remembering former partialities and talking over old times.

Anne found in Mrs. Smith the good sense and agreeable manners which she had almost ventured to depend on, and a disposition to converse and be cheerful beyond her expectation. Neither the dissipations of the past—and she had lived very much in the world, nor the restrictions of the present; neither sickness nor sorrow seemed to have closed her heart or ruined her spirits.

In the course of a second visit she talked with great openness, and Anne's astonishment increased. She could scarcely imagine a more cheerless situation in itself than Mrs. Smith's. She had been very fond of her husband—she had buried him. She had been used to affluence—it was gone. She had no child to connect her with life and happiness

again, no relations to assist in the arrangement of perplexed affairs, no health to make all the rest supportable. Her accommodations were limited to a noisy parlour, and a dark bed-room behind, with no possibility of moving from one to the other without assistance, which there was only one servant in the house to afford, and she never quitted the house but to be conveyed into the warm bath. Yet, in spite of all this, Anne had reason to believe that she had moments only of languor and depression, to hours of occupation and enjoyment. How could it be? —She watched—observed—reflected—and finally determined that this was not a case of fortitude or of resignation only. A submissive spirit might be patient, a strong understanding would supply resolution, but here was something more: here was that elasticity of mind, that disposition to be comforted, that power of turning readily from evil to good, and of finding employment which carried her out of herself, which was from Nature alone. It was the choicest gift of Heaven; and Anne viewed her friend as one of those instances in which, by a merciful appointment, it seems designed to counterbalance almost every other want.

There had been a time, Mrs. Smith told her, when her spirits had nearly failed. She could not call herself an invalid now, compared with her state on first reaching Bath. Then, she had indeed been a pitiable object —for she had caught cold on the journey, and had hardly taken possession of her lodgings, before she was again confined to her bed, and suffering under severe and constant pain; and all this among strangers —with the absolute necessity of having a regular nurse, and finances at that moment particularly unfit to meet any extraordinary expense. She had weathered it however, and could truly say that it had done her good. It had increased her comforts by making her feel herself to be in good hands. She had seen too much of the world, to expect sudden or disinterested attachment any where, but her illness had proved to her that her landlady had a character to preserve, and would not use her ill; and she had been particularly fortunate in her nurse, as a sister of her landlady, a nurse by profession, and who had always a home in that house when unemployed, chanced to be at liberty just in time to attend her. "And she," said Mrs. Smith, "besides nursing me most admirably, has really proved an invaluable acquaintance. As soon as I could use my hands, she taught me to knit, which has been a great amusement; and she put me in the way of making these little thread-cases, pin-cushions and card-racks, which you always find me so busy about, and which supply me with the means of doing a little good to one or two very poor families in this neighbourhood. She has a large acquaintance, of course professionally, among those who can afford to buy, and she disposes of my merchandize. She always takes the right time for applying. Every body's heart is open, you know, when they have recently escaped from severe pain, or are recovering the blessing of health, and nurse Rooke thoroughly understands when to speak. She is a shrewd, intelligent, sensible woman. Hers is a line for seeing human nature; and she has a fund of good sense and observation which, as a companion, make her infinitely superior to thousands of those who having only received 'the best education in the world,' know nothing worth attending to. Call it gossip if you will; but when nurse Rooke has half an hour's leisure to bestow on me, she is sure to have something to relate that is entertaining and profitable, something that makes one know one's species better. One likes to hear what is going on, to be *au fait* as to the newest modes of being trifling and silly. To me, who live so much alone, her conversation I assure you is a treat."

Anne, far from wishing to cavil at the pleasure, replied, "I can easily believe it. Women of that class have great opportunities, and if they are intelligent may be well worth listening to. Such varieties of human nature as they are in the habit of witnessing! And it is not merely in its follies, that they are well read; for they see it occasionally under every circumstance that can be most interesting or affecting. What instances must pass before them of ardent, disinterested, self-denying attachment, of heroism, fortitude, patience, resignation—of all the conflicts and all the sacrifices that ennoble us most. A sick chamber may often furnish the worth of volumes."

"Yes," said Mrs. Smith more doubtingly, "sometimes it may, though I fear its lessons are not often in the elevated style you describe. Here and there, human nature may be great in times of trial, but generally speaking it is its weakness and not its strength that appears in a sick chamber; it is selfishness and impatience rather than generosity and fortitude, that one hears of. There is so little real friendship in the world!—and unfortunately" (speaking low and tremulously) "there are so many who forget to think seriously till it is almost too late."

Anne saw the misery of such feelings. The husband had not been what he ought, and the wife had been led among that part of mankind which made her think worse of the world, than she hoped it deserved. It was but a passing emotion however with Mrs. Smith, she shook it off, and soon added in a different tone,

"I do not suppose the situation my friend Mrs. Rooke is in at present, will furnish much either to interest or edify me. She is only nursing Mrs. Wallis of Marlborough-buildings—a mere pretty, silly, expensive, fashionable woman, I believe—and of course will have nothing to report but of lace and finery. I mean to make my profit of Mrs. Wallis, however. She has plenty of money, and I intend she shall buy all the high-priced things I have in hand now."

Anne had called several times on her friend, before the existence of such a person was known in Camden-place. At last, it became necessary to speak of her. Sir Walter, Elizabeth and Mrs. Clay returned one morning from Laura-place, with a sudden invitation from Lady Dalrymple for the same evening, and Anne was already engaged, to spend that evening in Westgate-buildings. She was not sorry for the excuse. They were only asked, she was sure, because Lady Dalrymple being kept at home by a bad cold, was glad to make use of the relationship which had been so pressed on her, and she declined on her own account with great alacrity—"She was engaged to spend the evening with an old school-fellow." They were not much interested in any thing relative to Anne, but still there were questions enough asked, to make it understood what this old school-fellow was; and Elizabeth was disdainful, and Sir Walter severe.

"Westgate-buildings!" said he; "and who is Miss Anne Elliot to be visiting in Westgate-buildings?—A Mrs. Smith. A widow Mrs. Smith—and who was her husband? One of the five thousand Mr. Smiths whose names are to be met with every where. And what is her attraction? That she is old and sickly. Upon my word, Miss Anne Elliot, you have the most extraordinary taste! Every thing that revolts other people, low company, paltry rooms, foul air, disgusting associations are inviting to you. But surely, you may put off this old lady till to-morrow. She is not so near her end, I presume, but that she may hope to see another day. What is her age? Forty?"

"No, Sir, she is not one-and-thirty; but I do not think I can put off my engagement, because it is the only evening for some time which will at once suit her and myself. She goes into the warm bath to-morrow, and for the rest of the week you know we are engaged."

"But what does Lady Russell think of this acquaintance?" asked Elizabeth.

"She sees nothing to blame in it," replied Anne; "on the contrary, she approves it; and has generally taken me, when I have called on Mrs. Smith."

"Westgate-buildings must have been rather surprised by the appearance of a carriage drawn up near its pavement!" observed Sir Walter. "Sir Henry Russell's widow, indeed, has no honours to distinguish her arms; but still, it is a handsome equipage, and no doubt is well known to convey a Miss Elliot. A widow Mrs. Smith, lodging in Westgate-buildings!—A poor widow, barely able to live, between thirty and forty—a mere Mrs. Smith, an every day Mrs. Smith, of all people and all names in the world, to be the chosen friend of Miss Anne Elliot, and to be preferred by her, to her own family connections among the nobility of England and Ireland! Mrs. Smith, such a name!"

Mrs. Clay, who had been present while all this passed, now thought it advisable to leave the room, and Anne could have said much and did long to say a little, in defence of *her* friend's not very dissimilar claims to theirs, but her sense of personal respect to her father prevented her. She made no reply. She left it to himself to recollect, that Mrs. Smith was not the only widow in Bath between thirty and forty, with little to live on, and no sirname of dignity.

Anne kept her appointment; the others kept theirs, and of course she heard the next morning that they had had a delightful evening. She had been the only one of the set absent; for Sir Walter and Elizabeth had not only been quite at her ladyship's service themselves, but had actually been happy to be employed by her in collecting others, and had been at the trouble of inviting both Lady Russell and Mr. Elliot; and Mr. Elliot had made a point of leaving Colonel Wallis early, and Lady Russell had fresh arranged all her evening engagements in order to wait on her. Anne had the whole history of all that such an evening could supply, from Lady Russell. To her, its greatest interest must be, in having been very much talked of between her friend and Mr. Elliot, in having been wished for, regretted, and at the same time honoured for staying away in such a cause. Her kind, compassionate visits to this old school-fellow, sick and reduced, seemed to have quite delighted Mr. Elliot. He thought her a most extraordinary young woman; in her temper, manners, mind, a model of female excellence. He could meet even Lady Russell in a discussion of her merits; and Anne could not be given to understand so much by her friend, could not know herself to be so highly rated by a sensible man, without many of those agreeable sensations which her friend meant to create.

Lady Russell was now perfectly decided in her opinion of Mr. Elliot. She was as much convinced of his meaning to gain Anne in time, as of his deserving her; and was beginning to calculate the number of weeks which would free him from all the remaining restraints of widowhood, and leave him at liberty to exert his most open powers of pleasing. She would not speak to Anne with half the certainty she felt on the subject, she would venture on little more than hints of what might be hereafter, of a possible attachment on his side, of the desirableness of the alliance, supposing such attachment to be real, and returned. Anne heard her, and made no violent exclamations. She only smiled, blushed, and gently shook her head.

"I am no match-maker, as you well know," said Lady Russell, "being much too well aware of the uncertainty of all human events and calculations. I only mean that if Mr. Elliot should some time hence pay his addresses to you, and if you should be disposed to accept him, I think there would be every possibility of your being happy together. A most suitable connection every body must consider it—but I think it might be a very happy one."

"Mr. Elliot is an exceedingly agreeable man, and in many respects I think highly of him," said Anne; "but we should not suit."

Lady Russell let this pass, and only said in rejoinder, "I own that to be able to regard you as the future mistress of Kellynch, the future Lady Elliot—to look forward and see you occupying your dear mother's place, succeeding to all her rights, and all her popularity, as well as to all her virtues, would be the highest possible gratification to me. You are your mother's self in countenance and disposition; and if I might be allowed to fancy you such as she was, in situation, and name, and home, presiding and blessing in the same spot, and only superior to her in being more highly valued! My dearest Anne, it would give me more delight than is often felt at my time of life!"

Anne was obliged to turn away, to rise, to walk to a distant table, and, leaning there in pretended employment, try to subdue the feelings this picture excited. For a few moments her imagination and her heart were bewitched. The idea of becoming what her mother had been; of having the precious name of "Lady Elliot" first revived in herself; of being restored to Kellynch, calling it her home again, her home for ever, was a charm which she could not immediately resist. Lady Russell said not another word, willing to leave the matter to its own operation; and believing that, could Mr. Elliot at that moment with propriety have spoken for himself!—She believed, in short, what Anne did not believe. The same image of Mr. Elliot speaking for himself, brought Anne to composure again. The charm of Kellynch and of "Lady Elliot" all faded away. She never could accept him. And it was not only that her feelings were still adverse to any man save one; her judgment, on a serious consideration of the possibilities of such a case, was against Mr. Elliot.

Though they had now been acquainted a month, she could not be satisfied that she really knew his character. That he was a sensible man, an agreeable man, that he talked well, professed good opinions, seemed to judge properly and as a man of principle, this was all clear enough. He certainly knew what was right, nor could she fix on any one article of moral duty evidently transgressed; but yet she would have been afraid to answer for his conduct. She distrusted the past, if not the present. The names which occasionally dropt of former associates, the allusions to former practices and pursuits, suggested suspicions not favourable of what he had been. She saw that there had been bad habits; that Sunday-travelling had been a common thing; that there had been a period of his life (and probably not a short one) when he had been, at least, careless on all serious matters; and, though he might now think very differently, who could answer for the true sentiments of a clever, cautious man, grown old enough to appreciate a fair character? How could it ever be ascertained that his mind was truly cleansed?

Mr. Elliot was rational, discreet, polished —but he was not open. There was never any burst of feeling, any warmth of indignation or delight, at the evil or good of others. This, to Anne, was a decided imperfection. Her early impressions were incurable. She prized the frank, the open-hearted, the eager character beyond all others. Warmth and enthusiasm did captivate her still. She felt that she could so much more depend upon the sincerity of those who sometimes looked or said a careless or a hasty thing, than of those whose presence of mind never varied, whose tongue never slipped.

Mr. Elliot was too generally agreeable. Various as were the tempers in her father's house, he pleased them all. He endured too well, stood too well with everybody. He had spoken to her with some degree of openness of Mrs. Clay; had appeared completely to see what Mrs. Clay was about, and to hold her in contempt; and yet Mrs. Clay found him as agreeable as anybody.

Lady Russell saw either less or more than her young friend, for she saw nothing to excite distrust. She could not imagine a man more exactly what he ought to be than Mr. Elliot; nor did she ever enjoy a sweeter feeling than the hope of seeing him receive the hand of her beloved Anne in Kellynch church, in the course of the following autumn.

Chapter eighteen

It was the beginning of February; and Anne, having been a month in Bath, was growing very eager for news from Uppercross and Lyme. She wanted to hear much more than Mary communicated. It was three weeks since she had heard at all. She only knew that Henrietta was at home again; and that

Louisa, though considered to be recovering fast, was still at Lyme; and she was thinking of them all very intently one evening, when a thicker letter than usual from Mary was delivered to her, and, to quicken the pleasure and surprise, with Admiral and Mrs. Croft's compliments.

The Crofts must be in Bath! A circumstance to interest her. They were people whom her heart turned to very naturally.

"What is this?" cried Sir Walter. "The Crofts arrived in Bath? The Crofts who rent Kellynch? What have they brought you?"

"A letter from Uppercross Cottage, Sir."

"Oh! those letters are convenient passports. They secure an introduction. I should have visited Admiral Croft, however, at any rate. I know what is due to my tenant."

Anne could listen no longer; she could not even have told how the poor Admiral's complexion escaped; her letter engrossed her. It had been begun several days back.

"February 1st,——.
"My dear Anne,

"I make no apology for my silence, because I know how little people think of letters in such a place as Bath. You must be a great deal too happy to care for Uppercross, which, as you well know, affords little to write about. We have had a very dull Christmas; Mr. and Mrs. Musgrove have not had one dinner-party all the holidays. I do not reckon the Hayters as any body. The holidays, however, are over at last: I believe no children ever had such long ones. I am sure I had not. The house was cleared yesterday, except of the little Harvilles; but you will be surprised to hear they have never gone home. Mrs. Harville must be an odd mother to part with them so long. I do not understand it. They are not at all nice children, in my opinion; but Mrs. Musgrove seems to like them quite as well, if not better, than her grand-children. What dreadful weather we have had! It may not be felt in Bath, with your nice pavements; but in the country it is of some consequence. I have not had a creature call on me since the second week in January, except Charles Hayter, who has been calling much oftener than was welcome. Between ourselves, I think it a great pity Henrietta did not remain at Lyme as

long as Louisa; it would have kept her a little out of his way. The carriage is gone to-day, to bring Louisa and the Harvilles to-morrow. We are not asked to dine with them, however, till the day after, Mrs. Musgrove is so afraid of her being fatigued by the journey, which is not very likely, considering the care that will be taken of her; and it would be much more convenient to me to dine there to-morrow. I am glad you find Mr. Elliot so agreeable, and wish I could be acquainted with him too; but I have my usual luck, I am always out of the way when any thing desirable is going on; always the last of my family to be noticed. What an immense time Mrs. Clay has been staying with Elizabeth! Does she never mean to go away? But perhaps if she were to leave the room vacant we might not be invited. Let me know what you think of this. I do not expect my children to be asked, you know. I can leave them at the Great House very well, for a month or six weeks. I have this moment heard that the Crofts are going to Bath almost immediately; they think the admiral gouty. Charles heard it quite by chance: they have not had the civility to give me any notice, or offer to take any thing. I do not think they improve at all as neighbours. We see nothing of them, and this is really an instance of gross inattention. Charles joins me in love, and every thing proper. Yours, affectionately,

"Mary M——."

"I am sorry to say that I am very far from well; and Jemima has just told me that the butcher says there is a bad sore-throat very much about. I dare say I shall catch it; and my sore-throats, you know, are always worse than anybody's."

So ended the first part, which had been afterwards put into an envelop, containing nearly as much more.

"I kept my letter open, that I might send you word how Louisa bore her journey, and now I am extremely glad I did, having a great deal to add. In the first place, I had a note from Mrs. Croft yesterday, offering to convey any thing to you; a very kind, friendly note indeed, addressed to me, just as it ought; I shall therefore be able to make my letter as long as I like. The admiral does not seem very ill, and I sincerely hope Bath will do him all the good he wants. I shall be truly glad to have them back

again. Our neighbourhood cannot spare such a pleasant family. But now for Louisa. I have something to communicate that will astonish you not a little. She and the Harvilles came on Tuesday very safely, and in the evening we went to ask her how she did, when we were rather surprised not to find Captain Benwick of the party, for he had been invited as well as the Harvilles; and what do you think was the reason? Neither more nor less than his being in love with Louisa, and not choosing to venture to Uppercross till he had had an answer from Mr. Musgrove; for it was all settled between him and her before she came away, and he had written to her father by Captain Harville. True, upon my honour. Are not you astonished? I shall be surprised at least if you ever received a hint of it, for I never did. Mrs. Musgrove protests solemnly that she knew nothing of the matter. We are all very well pleased, however; for though it is not equal to her marrying Captain Wentworth, it is infinitely better than Charles Hayter; and Mr. Musgrove has written his consent, and Captain Benwick is expected to-day. Mrs. Harville says her husband feels a good deal on his poor sister's account; but, however, Louisa is a great favourite with both. Indeed Mrs. Harville and I quite agree that we love her the better for having nursed her. Charles wonders what Captain Wentworth will say; but if you remember, I never thought him attached to Louisa; I never could see any thing of it. And this is the end, you see, of Captain Benwick's being supposed to be an admirer of yours. How Charles could take such a thing into his head was always incomprehensible to me. I hope he will be more agreeable now. Certainly not a great match for Louisa Musgrove; but a million times better than marrying among the Hayters."

Mary need not have feared her sister's being in any degree prepared for the news. She had never in her life been more astonished. Captain Benwick and Louisa Musgrove! It was almost too wonderful for belief; and it was with the greatest effort that she could remain in the room, preserve an air of calmness, and answer the common questions of the moment. Happily for her, they were not many. Sir Walter wanted to know whether the Crofts travelled with four horses, and whether they were likely to be situated in such a part of Bath as it might suit Miss Elliot and himself to visit in; but had little curiosity beyond.

"How is Mary?" said Elizabeth; and without waiting for an answer, "And pray what brings the Crofts to Bath?"

"They come on the Admiral's account. He is thought to be gouty."

"Gout and decrepitude!" said Sir Walter. "Poor old gentleman."

"Have they any acquaintance here?" asked Elizabeth.

"I do not know; but I can hardly suppose that, at Admiral Croft's time of life, and in his profession, he should not have many acquaintance in such a place as this."

"I suspect," said Sir Walter coolly, "that Admiral Croft will be best known in Bath as the renter of Kellynch-hall. Elizabeth, may we venture to present him and his wife in Laura-place?"

"Oh! no, I think not. Situated as we are with Lady Dalrymple, cousins, we ought to be very careful not to embarrass her with acquaintance she might not approve. If we were not related, it would not signify; but as cousins, she would feel scrupulous as to any proposal of ours. We had better leave the Crofts to find their own level. There are several odd-looking men walking about here, who, I am told, are sailors. The Crofts will associate with them!"

This was Sir Walter and Elizabeth's share of interest in the letter; when Mrs. Clay had paid her tribute of more decent attention, in an enquiry after Mrs. Charles Musgrove, and her fine little boys, Anne was at liberty.

In her own room she tried to comprehend it. Well might Charles wonder how Captain Wentworth would feel! Perhaps he had quitted the field, had given Louisa up, had ceased to love, had found he did not love her. She could not endure the idea of treachery or levity, or any thing akin to ill-usage between him and his friend. She could not endure that such a friendship as theirs should be severed unfairly.

Captain Benwick and Louisa Musgrove! The high-spirited, joyous, talking Louisa Musgrove, and the dejected, thinking, feeling, reading Captain Benwick, seemed each of them every thing that would not suit the other. Their minds most dissimilar! Where could have been the attraction? The answer soon presented itself. It had been in situation. They had been thrown together several weeks; they had been living in the same small family party; since Henrietta's coming away, they must have been depending almost entirely on each other, and Louisa, just recovering from illness, had been in an interesting state, and Captain Benwick was not inconsolable. That was a point which Anne had not been able to avoid suspecting before; and instead of drawing the same conclusion as Mary, from the present course of events, they served only to confirm the idea of his having felt some dawning of tenderness toward herself. She did not mean, however, to derive much more from it to gratify her vanity, than Mary might have allowed. She was persuaded that any tolerably pleasing young woman who had listened and seemed to feel for him, would have received the same compliment. He had an affectionate heart. He must love somebody.

She saw no reason against their being happy. Louisa had fine naval fervour to begin with, and they would soon grow more alike. He would gain cheerfulness, and she would learn to be an enthusiast for Scott and Lord Byron; nay, that was probably learnt already; of course they had fallen in love over poetry. The idea of Louisa Musgrove turned into a person of literary taste, and sentimental reflection, was amusing, but she had no doubt of its being so. The day at Lyme, the fall from the Cobb, might influence her health, her nerves, her courage, her character to the end of her life, as thoroughly as it appeared to have influenced her fate.

The conclusion of the whole was, that if the woman who had been sensible of Captain Wentworth's merits could be allowed to prefer another man, there was nothing in the engagement to excite lasting wonder; and if Captain Wentworth lost no friend by it, certainly nothing to be regretted. No, it was not regret which made Anne's heart beat in spite of herself, and brought the colour into her cheeks when she thought of Captain Wentworth unshackled and free. She had some feelings which she was ashamed to investigate. They were too much like joy, senseless joy!

She longed to see the Crofts, but when the meeting took place, it was evident that no rumour of the news had yet reached them. The visit of ceremony was paid and returned, and Louisa Musgrove was mentioned, and Captain Benwick too, without even half a smile.

The Crofts had placed themselves in lodgings in Gay-street, perfectly to Sir Walter's satisfaction. He was not at all ashamed of the acquaintance, and did, in fact, think and talk a great deal more about the Admiral, than the Admiral ever thought or talked about him.

The Crofts knew quite as many people in Bath as they wished for, and considered their intercourse with the Elliots as a mere matter of form, and not in the least likely to afford them any pleasure. They brought with them their country habit of being almost always together. He was ordered to walk, to keep off the gout, and Mrs. Croft seemed to go shares with him in every thing, and to walk for her life, to do him good. Anne saw them wherever she went. Lady Russell took her out in her carriage almost every morning, and she never failed to think of them, and never failed to see them. Knowing their feelings as she did, it was a most attractive picture of happiness to her. She always watched them as long as she could; delighted to fancy she understood what they might be talking of, as they walked along in happy independence, or equally delighted to see the Admiral's hearty shake of the hand when he encountered an old friend, and observe their eagerness of conversation when occasionally forming into a little knot of the navy, Mrs. Croft looking as intelligent and keen as any of the officers around her.

Anne was too much engaged with Lady Russell to be often walking herself, but it so happened that one morning, about a week or ten days after the Crofts' arrival, it suited her best to leave her friend, or her friend's carriage, in the lower part of the town, and return alone to Camden-place; and in walking up Milsom-street, she had the good fortune to meet with the Admiral. He was standing by himself, at a printshop window, with his hands behind him, in earnest contemplation of some print, and she not only might have passed him unseen, but was obliged to touch as well as address him before she could catch his notice. When he did perceive and acknowledge her, however, it was done with all his usual frankness and good humour. "Ha! is it you? Thank you, thank you. This is treating me like a friend. Here I am, you see, staring at a picture. I can never get by this shop without stopping. But what a thing here is, by way of a boat. Do look at it. Did you ever see the like? What queer fellows your fine painters must be, to think that any body would venture their lives in such a shapeless old cockleshell as that. And yet, here are two gentlemen stuck up in it mightily at their ease, and looking about them at the rocks and mountains, as if they were not to be upset the next moment, which they certainly must be. I wonder where that boat was built!" (laughing heartily) "I would not venture over a horsepond in it. Well," (turning away) "now, where are you bound? Can I go any where for you, or with you? Can I be of any use?"

"None, I thank you, unless you will give me the pleasure of your company the little way our road lies together. I am going home."

"That I will, with all my heart, and farther too. Yes, yes, we will have a snug walk together; and I have something to tell you as we go along. There, take my arm; that's right: I do not feel comfortable if I have not a woman there. Lord! what a boat it is!" taking a last look at the picture, as they began to be in motion.

"Did you say that you had something to tell me, sir?"

"Yes, I have. Presently. But here comes a friend, Captain Brigden; I shall only say, 'How d'ye do,' as we pass, however. I shall not stop. 'How d'ye do.' Brigden stares to see anybody with me but my wife. She, poor soul, is tied by the leg. She has a blister on one of her heels, as large as a three shilling piece. If you look across the street, you will see Admiral Brand coming down and his brother. Shabby fellows, both of them! I am glad they are not on this side of the way. Sophy cannot bear them. They played me a pitiful trick once—got away some of my best men. I will tell you the whole story another time. There comes old Sir Archibald Drew and his grandson. Look, he sees us; he kisses his hand to you; he takes you for my wife. Ah! the peace has come too soon for that younker. Poor old Sir Archibald! How do you like Bath, Miss Elliot? It suits us very well. We are always meeting with some old friend or other; the streets full of them every morning; sure to have plenty of chat; and then we get away from them all, and shut ourselves into our lodgings, and draw in our chairs, and are as snug as if we were at Kellynch, ay, or as we used to be even at North Yarmouth and Deal. We do not like our lodgings here the worse, I can tell you, for putting us in mind of those we first had at North Yarmouth. The wind blows through one of the cupboards just in the same way."

When they were got a little farther, Anne ventured to press again for what he had to communicate. She had hoped, when clear of Milsom-street, to have her curiosity gratified; but she was still obliged to wait, for the Admiral had made up his mind not to begin, till they had gained the greater space and quiet of Belmont, and as she was not really Mrs. Croft, she must let him have his own way. As soon as they were fairly ascending Belmont, he began,

"Well, now you shall hear something that will surprise you. But first of all, you must tell me the name of the young lady I am going to talk about. That young lady, you know, that we have all been so concerned for. The Miss Musgrove, that all this has been happening to. Her christian name—I always forget her christian name."

Anne had been ashamed to appear to comprehend so soon as she really did; but now she could safely suggest the name of "Louisa."

"Ay, ay, Miss Louisa Musgrove, that is the name. I wish young ladies had not such a number of fine christian names. I should never be out, if they were all Sophys, or something of that sort. Well, this Miss Louisa, we all thought, you know, was to marry Frederick. He was courting her week after week. The only wonder was, what they could be waiting for, till the business at Lyme came; then, indeed, it was clear enough that they must wait till her brain was set to right. But even then, there was something odd in their way of going on. Instead of staying at Lyme, he went off to Plymouth, and then he went off to see Edward. When we came back from Minehead, he was gone down to Edward's, and there he has been ever since. We have seen nothing of him since November. Even Sophy could not understand it. But now, the matter has taken the strangest turn of all; for this young lady, this same Miss Musgrove, instead of being to marry Frederick, is to marry James Benwick. You know James Benwick."

"A little. I am a little acquainted with Captain Benwick."

"Well, she is to marry him. Nay, most likely they are married already, for I do not know what they should wait for."

"I thought Captain Benwick a very pleasing young man," said Anne, "and I understand that he bears an excellent character."

"Oh! yes, yes, there is not a word to be said against James Benwick. He is only a commander, it is true, made last summer, and these are bad times for getting on, but he has not another fault that I know of. An excellent, good-hearted fellow, I assure you, a very active, zealous officer too, which is more than you would think for, perhaps, for that soft sort of manner does not do him justice."

"Indeed you are mistaken there, sir. I should never augur want of spirit from Captain Benwick's manners. I thought them particularly pleasing, and I will answer for it they would generally please."

"Well, well, ladies are the best judges; but James Benwick is rather too piano for me, and though very likely it is all our partiality, Sophy and I cannot help thinking Frederick's manners better than his. There is something about Frederick more to our taste."

Anne was caught. She had only meant to oppose the too-common idea of spirit and gentleness being incompatible with each other, not at all to represent Captain Benwick's manners as the very best that could possibly be, and, after a little hesitation, she was beginning to say, "I was not entering into any comparison of the two friends," but the Admiral interrupted her with,

"And the thing is certainly true. It is not a mere bit of gossip. We have it from Frederick himself. His sister had a letter from him yesterday, in which he tells us of it, and he had just had it in a letter from Harville, written upon the spot, from Uppercross. I fancy they are all at Uppercross."

This was an opportunity which Anne could not resist; she said, therefore, "I hope, Admiral, I hope there is nothing in the style of Captain Wentworth's letter to make you and Mrs. Croft particularly uneasy. It did certainly seem, last autumn, as if there were an attachment between him and Louisa Musgrove; but I hope it may be understood to have worn out on each side equally, and without violence. I hope his letter does not breathe the spirit of an ill-used man."

"Not at all, not at all; there is not an oath or a murmur from beginning to end."

Anne looked down to hide her smile.

"No, no; Frederick is not a man to whine and complain; he has too much spirit for that. If the girl likes another man better, it is very fit she should have him."

"Certainly. But what I mean is, that I hope there is nothing in Captain Wentworth's manner of writing to make you suppose he thinks himself ill-used by his friend, which might appear, you know, without its being absolutely said. I should be very sorry that such a friendship as has subsisted between him and Captain Benwick should be destroyed, or even wounded, by a circumstance of this sort."

"Yes, yes, I understand you. But there is nothing at all of that nature in the letter. He does not give the least fling at Benwick; does not so much as say, 'I wonder at it, I have a reason of my own for wondering at it.' No, you would not guess, from his way of writing, that he had ever thought of this Miss (what's her name?) for himself. He very handsomely hopes they will be happy together, and there is nothing very unforgiving in that, I think."

Anne did not receive the perfect conviction which the Admiral meant to convey, but it would have been useless to press the enquiry farther. She, therefore, satisfied herself with commonplace remarks, or quiet attention, and the Admiral had it all his own way.

"Poor Frederick!" said he at last. "Now he must begin all over again with somebody else. I think we must get him to Bath. Sophy must write, and beg him to come to Bath. Here are pretty girls enough, I am sure. It would be of no use to go to Uppercross again, for that other Miss Musgrove, I find, is bespoke by her cousin, the young parson. Do not you think, Miss Elliot, we had better try to get him to Bath?"

Chapter nineteen

While Admiral Croft was taking this walk with Anne, and expressing his wish of getting Captain Wentworth to Bath, Captain Wentworth was already on his way thither. Before Mrs. Croft had written, he was arrived; and the very next time Anne walked out, she saw him.

Mr. Elliot was attending his two cousins

and Mrs. Clay. They were in Milsom-street. It began to rain, not much, but enough to make shelter desirable for women, and quite enough to make it very desirable for Miss Elliot to have the advantage of being conveyed home in Lady Dalrymple's carriage, which was seen waiting at a little distance; she, Anne, and Mrs. Clay, therefore, turned into Molland's, while Mr. Elliot stepped to Lady Dalrymple, to request her assistance. He soon joined them again, successful, of course; Lady Dalrymple would be most happy to take them home, and would call for them in a few minutes.

Her ladyship's carriage was a barouche, and did not hold more than four with any comfort. Miss Carteret was with her mother; consequently it was not reasonable to expect accommodation for all the three Camden-place ladies. There could be no doubt as to Miss Elliot. Whoever suffered inconvenience, she must suffer none, but it occupied a little time to settle the point of civility between the other two. The rain was a mere trifle, and Anne was most sincere in preferring a walk with Mr. Elliot. But the rain was also a mere trifle to Mrs. Clay; she would hardly allow it even to drop at all, and her boots were so thick! much thicker than Miss Anne's; and, in short, her civility rendered her quite as anxious to be left to walk with Mr. Elliot, as Anne could be, and it was discussed between them with a generosity so polite and so determined, that the others were obliged to settle it for them; Miss Elliot maintaining that Mrs. Clay had a little cold already, and Mr. Elliot deciding on appeal, that his cousin Anne's boots were rather the thickest.

It was fixed accordingly that Mrs. Clay should be of the party in the carriage; and they had just reached this point when Anne, as she sat near the window, descried, most decidedly and distinctly, Captain Wentworth walking down the street.

Her start was perceptible only to herself; but she instantly felt that she was the greatest simpleton in the world, the most unaccountable and absurd! For a few minutes she saw nothing before her. It was all confusion. She was lost; and when she had scolded back her senses, she found the others still waiting for the carriage, and Mr. Elliot (always obliging) just setting off for Union-street on a commission of Mrs. Clay's.

She now felt a great inclination to go to the outer door; she wanted to see if it rained. Why was she to suspect herself of another motive? Captain Wentworth must be out of sight. She left her seat, she would go, one half of her should not be always so much wiser than the other half, or always suspecting the other of being worse than it was. She would see if it rained. She was sent back, however, in a moment by the entrance of Captain Wentworth himself, among a party of gentlemen and ladies, evidently his acquaintance, and whom he must have joined a little below Milsom-street. He was more obviously struck and confused by the sight of her, than she had ever observed before; he looked quite red. For the first time, since their renewed acquaintance, she felt that she was betraying the least sensibility of the two. She had the advantage of him, in the preparation of the last few moments. All the overpowering, blinding, bewildering, first effects of strong surprise were over with her. Still, however, she had enough to feel! It was agitation, pain, pleasure, a something between delight and misery.

He spoke to her, and then turned away. The character of his manner was embarrassment. She could not have called it either cold or friendly, or any thing so certainly as embarrassed.

After a short interval, however, he came towards her and spoke again. Mutual enquiries on common subjects passed; neither of them, probably, much the wiser for what they heard, and Anne continuing fully sensible of his being less at ease than formerly. They had, by dint of being so very much together, got to speak to each other with a considerable portion of apparent indifference and calmness; but he could not do it now. Time had changed him, or Louisa had changed him. There was consciousness of some sort or other. He looked very well, not as if he had been suffering in health or spirits, and he talked of Uppercross, of the Musgroves, nay, even of Louisa, and had even a momentary look of his own arch significance as he named her; but yet it was Captain Wentworth not comfortable, not easy, not able to feign that he was.

It did not surprise, but it grieved Anne to observe that Elizabeth would not know him. She saw that he saw Elizabeth, that Elizabeth saw him, that there was complete internal recognition on each side; she was convinced that he was ready to be acknowledged as an acquaintance, expecting it, and she had the pain of seeing her sister turn away with unalterable coldness.

Lady Dalrymple's carriage, for which Miss Elliot was growing very impatient, now drew up; the servant came in to announce it. It was beginning to rain again, and altogether there was a delay, and a bustle, and a talking, which must make all the little crowd in the shop understand that Lady Dalrymple was calling to convey Miss Elliot. At last Miss Elliot and her friend, unattended but by the servant (for there was no cousin returned), were walking off; and Captain Wentworth, watching them, turned again to Anne, and by manner, rather than words, was offering his services to her.

"I am much obliged to you," was her answer, "but I am not going with them. The carriage would not accommodate so many. I walk. I prefer walking."

"But it rains."

"Oh! very little. Nothing that I regard."

After a moment's pause he said, "Though I came only yesterday, I have equipped myself properly for Bath already, you see" (pointing to a new umbrella), "I wish you would make use of it, if you are determined to walk; though, I think, it would be more prudent to let me get you a chair."

She was very much obliged to him, but declined it all, repeating her conviction, that the rain would come to nothing at present, and adding, "I am only waiting for Mr. El-

liot. He will be here in a moment, I am sure."

She had hardly spoken the words, when Mr. Elliot walked in. Captain Wentworth recollected him perfectly. There was no difference between him and the man who had stood on the steps at Lyme, admiring Anne as she passed, except in the air and look and manner of the privileged relation and friend. He came in with eagerness, appeared to see and think only of her, apologised for his stay, was grieved to have kept her waiting, and anxious to get her away without further loss of time, and before the rain increased; and in another moment they walked off together, her arm under his, a gentle and embarrassed glance, and a "good morning to you," being all that she had time for, as she passed away.

As soon as they were out of sight, the ladies of Captain Wentworth's party began talking of them.

"Mr. Elliot does not dislike his cousin, I fancy?"

"Oh! no, that is clear enough. One can guess what will happen there. He is always with them; half lives in the family, I believe. What a very good-looking man!"

"Yes, and Miss Atkinson, who dined with him once at the Wallises, says he is the most agreeable man she ever was in company with."

"She is pretty, I think; Anne Elliot; very pretty, when one comes to look at her. It is not the fashion to say so, but I confess I admire her more than her sister."

"Oh! so do I."

"And so do I. No comparison. But the men are all wild after Miss Elliot. Anne is too delicate for them."

Anne would have been particularly obliged to her cousin, if he would have walked by her side all the way to Camden-place, without saying a word. She had never found it so difficult to listen to him, though nothing could exceed his solicitude and care, and though his subjects were principally such as were wont to be always interesting—praise, warm, just, and discriminating, of Lady Russell, and insinuations highly rational against Mrs. Clay. But just now she could think only of Captain Wentworth. She could not understand his present feelings, whether he were really suffering much from disappointment or not; and till that point were settled, she could not be quite herself.

She hoped to be wise and reasonable in time; but alas! alas! she must confess to herself that she was not wise yet.

Another circumstance very essential for her to know, was how long he meant to be in Bath; he had not mentioned it, or she could not recollect it. He might be only passing through. But it was more probable that he should be come to stay. In that case, so liable as every body was to meet every body in Bath, Lady Russell would in all likelihood see him somewhere. Would she recollect him? How would it all be?

She had already been obliged to tell Lady Russell that Louisa Musgrove was to marry Captain Benwick. It had cost her something to encounter Lady Russell's surprise; and now, if she were by any chance to be thrown into company with Captain Wentworth, her imperfect knowledge of the matter might add another shade of prejudice against him.

The following morning Anne was out with her friend, and for the first hour, in an incessant and fearful sort of watch for him in vain; but at last, in returning down Pulteney-street, she distinguished him on the right hand pavement at such a distance as to have him in view the greater part of the street. There were many other men about him, many groups walking the same way, but there was no mistaking him. She looked instinctively at Lady Russell; but not from any mad idea of her recognising him so soon as she did herself. No, it was not to be supposed that Lady Russell would perceive him till they were nearly opposite. She looked at her however, from time to time, anxiously; and when the moment approached which must point him out, though not daring to look again (for her own countenance she knew was unfit to be seen), she was yet perfectly conscious of Lady Rus-

sell's eyes being turned exactly in the direction for him, of her being in short intently observing him. She could thoroughly comprehend the sort of fascination he must possess over Lady Russell's mind, the difficulty it must be for her to withdraw her eyes, the astonishment she must be feeling that eight or nine years should have passed over him, and in foreign climes and in active service too, without robbing him of one personal grace!

At last, Lady Russell drew back her head. "Now, how would she speak of him?"

"You will wonder," said she, "what has been fixing my eye so long; but I was looking after some window-curtains, which Lady Alicia and Mrs. Frankland were telling me of last night. They described the drawing-room window-curtains of one of the houses on this side of the way, and this part of the street, as being the handsomest and best hung of any in Bath, but could not recollect the exact number, and I have been trying to find out which it could be; but I confess I can see no curtains hereabouts that answer their description."

Anne sighed and blushed and smiled, in pity and disdain, either at her friend or herself. The part which provoked her most, was that in all this waste of foresight and caution, she should have lost the right moment for seeing whether he saw them.

A day or two passed without producing any thing. The theatre or the rooms, where he was most likely to be, were not fashionable enough for the Elliots, whose evening amusements were solely in the elegant stupidity of private parties, in which they were getting more and more engaged; and Anne, wearied of such a state of stagnation, sick of knowing nothing, and fancying herself stronger because her strength was not tried, was quite impatient for the concert evening. It was a concert for the benefit of a person patronised by Lady Dalrymple. Of course. they must attend. It was really expected to be a good one, and Captain Wentworth was very fond of music. If she could only have a few minutes conversation with him again, she fancied she should be satisfied; and as to the power of addressing him she felt all over courage if the opportunity occurred. Elizabeth had turned from him, Lady Russell overlooked him; her nerves were strengthened by these circumstances; she felt that she owed him attention.

She had once partly promised Mrs. Smith to spend the evening with her; but in a short hurried call she excused herself and put it off, with the more decided promise of a longer visit on the morrow. Mrs. Smith gave a most good-humoured acquiescence.

"By all means," said she; "only tell me all about it, when you do come. Who is your party?"

Anne named them all. Mrs. Smith made no reply; but when she was leaving her, said, and with an expression half serious, half arch, "Well, I heartily wish your concert may answer; and do not fail me to-morrow if you can come; for I begin to have a foreboding that I may not have many more visits from you."

Anne was startled and confused, but after standing in a moment's suspense, was obliged, and not sorry to be obliged, to hurry away.

Chapter twenty

Sir Walter, his two daughters, and Mrs. Clay, were the earliest of all their party, at the rooms in the evening; and as Lady Dalrymple must be waited for, they took their station by one of the fires in the octagon room. But hardly were they settled, when the door opened again, and Captain Wentworth walked in alone. Anne was the nearest to him, and making yet a little advance, she instantly spoke. He was preparing only to bow and pass on, but her gentle "How do you do?" brought him out of the straight line to stand near her, and make enquiries in return, in spite of the formidable father and sister in the back ground. Their being in the back ground was a support to Anne; she knew nothing of their looks, and felt equal

to everything which she believed right to be done.

While they were speaking, a whispering between her father and Elizabeth caught her ear. She could not distinguish, but she must guess the subject; and on Captain Wentworth's making a distant bow, she comprehended that her father had judged so well as to give him that simple acknowledgment of acquaintance, and she was just in time by a side glance to see a slight curtsey from Elizabeth herself. This, though late and reluctant and ungracious, was yet better than nothing, and her spirits improved.

After talking however of the weather and Bath and the concert, their conversation began to flag, and so little was said at last, that she was expecting him to go every moment; but he did not; he seemed in no hurry to leave her; and presently with renewed spirit, with a little smile, a little glow, he said,

"I have hardly seen you since our day at Lyme. I am afraid you must have suffered from the shock, and the more from its not overpowering you at the time."

She assured him that she had not.

"It was a frightful hour," said he, "a frightful day!" and he passed his hand across his eyes, as if the remembrance were still too painful; but in a moment half smiling again, added, "The day has produced some effects however—has had some consequences which must be considered as the very reverse of frightful. When you had the presence of mind to suggest that Benwick would be the properest person to fetch a surgeon, you could have little idea of his being eventually one of those most concerned in her recovery."

"Certainly I could have none. But it appears—I should hope it would be a very happy match. There are on both sides good principles and good temper."

"Yes," said he, looking not exactly forward—"but there I think ends the resemblance. With all my soul I wish them happy, and rejoice over every circumstance in favour of it. They have no difficulties to contend with at home, no opposition, no caprice, no delays. The Musgroves are behaving like themselves, most honourably and kindly, only anxious with true parental hearts to promote their daughter's comfort. All this is much, very much in favour of their happiness; more than perhaps—"

He stopped. A sudden recollection seemed to occur, and to give him some taste of that emotion which was reddening Anne's cheeks and fixing her eyes on the ground. After clearing his throat, however, he proceeded thus,

"I confess that I do think there is a disparity, too great a disparity, and in a point no less essential than mind. I regard Louisa Musgrove as a very amiable, sweet-tempered girl, and not deficient in understanding; but Benwick is something more. He is a clever man, a reading man—and I confess that I do consider his attaching himself to her, with some surprise. Had it been the effect of gratitude, had he learnt to love her, because he believed her to be preferring him, it would have been another thing. But I have no reason to suppose it so. It seems, on the contrary, to have been a perfectly spontaneous, untaught feeling on his side, and this surprises me. A man like him, in his situation! With a heart pierced, wounded, almost broken! Fanny Harville was a very superior creature; and his attachment to her was indeed attachment. A man does not recover from such a devotion of the heart to such a woman!—He ought not—he does not."

Either from the consciousness, however, that his friend had recovered, or from other consciousness, he went no farther; and Anne, who, in spite of the agitated voice in which the latter part had been uttered, and in spite of all the various noises of the room, the almost ceaseless slam of the door, and ceaseless buzz of persons walking through, had distinguished every word, was struck, gratified, confused, and beginning to breathe very quick, and feel an hundred things in a moment. It was impossible for her to enter on such a subject; and yet, after a pause, feeling the necessity of speaking,

and having not the smallest wish for a total change, she only deviated so far as to say,

"You were a good while at Lyme, I think?"

"About a fortnight. I could not leave it till Louisa's doing well was quite ascertained. I had been too deeply concerned in the mischief to be soon at peace. It had been my doing—solely mine. She would not have been obstinate if I had not been weak. The country round Lyme is very fine. I walked and rode a great deal; and the more I saw, the more I found to admire."

"I should very much like to see Lyme again," said Anne.

"Indeed! I should not have supposed that you could have found any thing in Lyme to inspire such a feeling. The horror and distress you were involved in—the stretch of mind, the wear of spirits!—I should have thought your last impressions of Lyme must have been strong disgust."

"The last few hours were certainly very painful," replied Anne: "but when pain is over, the remembrance of it often becomes a pleasure. One does not love a place the less for having suffered in it, unless it has been all suffering, nothing but suffering—which was by no means the case at Lyme. We were only in anxiety and distress during the last two hours; and, previously, there had been a great deal of enjoyment. So much novelty and beauty! I have travelled so little, that every fresh place would be interesting to me —but there is real beauty at Lyme: and in short" (with a faint blush at some recollections) "altogether my impressions of the place are very agreeable."

As she ceased, the entrance door opened again, and the very party appeared for whom they were waiting. "Lady Dalrymple, Lady Dalrymple," was the rejoicing sound; and with all the eagerness compatible with anxious elegance, Sir Walter and his two ladies stepped forward to meet her. Lady Dalrymple and Miss Carteret, escorted by Mr. Elliot and Colonel Wallis, who had happened to arrive nearly at the same instant, advanced into the room. The others joined them, and it was a group in which Anne found herself also necessarily included. She was divided from Captain Wentworth. Their interesting, almost too interesting conversation must be broken up for a time; but slight was the penance compared with the happiness which brought it on! She had learnt, in the last ten minutes, more of his feelings towards Louisa, more of all his feelings, than she dared to think of! and she gave herself up to the demands of the party, to the needful civilities of the moment, with exquisite, though agitated sensations. She was in good humour with all. She had received ideas which disposed her to be courteous and kind to all, and to pity every one, as being less happy than herself.

The delightful emotions were a little subdued, when, on stepping back from the group, to be joined again by Captain Wentworth, she saw that he was gone. She was just in time to see him turn into the concert room. He was gone—he had disappeared: she felt a moment's regret. But "they should meet again. He would look for her—he would find her out long before the evening were over—and at present, perhaps, it was as well to be asunder. She was in need of a little interval for recollection."

Upon Lady Russell's appearance soon afterwards, the whole party was collected, and all that remained, was to marshal themselves, and proceed into the concert room; and be of all the consequence in their power, draw as many eyes, excite as many whispers, and disturb as many people as they could.

Very, very happy were both Elizabeth and Anne Elliot as they walked in. Elizabeth, arm in arm with Miss Carteret, and looking on the broad back of the dowager Viscountess Dalrymple before her, had nothing to wish for which did not seem within her reach; and Anne—but it would be an insult to the nature of Anne's felicity, to draw any comparison between it and her sister's; the origin of one all selfish vanity, of the other all generous attachment.

Anne saw nothing, thought nothing of the brilliancy of the room. Her happiness was from within. Her eyes were bright, and her cheeks glowed, but she knew nothing about it. She was thinking only of the last half hour, and as they passed to their seats, her mind took a hasty range over it. His choice of subjects, his expressions, and still more his manner and look, had been such as she could see in only one light. His opinion of Louisa Musgrove's inferiority, an opinion which he had seemed solicitous to give, his wonder at Captain Benwick, his feelings as to a first, strong attachment—sentences begun which he could not finish—his half averted eyes, and more than half expressive glance—all, all declared that he had a heart returning to her at least; that anger, resentment, avoidance, were no more; and that they were succeeded, not merely by friendship and regard, but by the tenderness of the past; yes, some share of the tenderness of the past. She could not contemplate the change as implying less. He must love her.

These were thoughts, with their attendant visions, which occupied and flurried her too much to leave her any power of observation; and she passed along the room without having a glimpse of him, without even trying to discern him. When their places were determined on, and they were all properly arranged, she looked round to see if he should happen to be in the same part of the room, but he was not, her eye could not reach him; and the concert being just opening, she must consent for a time to be happy in an humbler way.

The party was divided, and disposed of on two contiguous benches: Anne was among those on the foremost, and Mr. Elliot had manoeuvred so well, with the assistance of his friend Colonel Wallis, as to have a seat by her. Miss Elliot, surrounded by her cousins, and the principal object of Colonel Wallis's gallantry, was quite contented.

Anne's mind was in a most favourable state for the entertainment of the evening: it was just occupation enough: she had feelings for the tender, spirits for the gay, attention for the scientific, and patience for the wearisome; and had never liked a concert better, at least during the first act. Towards the close of it, in the interval succeeding an Italian song, she explained the words of the song to Mr. Elliot. They had a concert bill between them.

"This," said she, "is nearly the sense, or rather the meaning of the words, for certainly the sense of an Italian love-song must not be talked of, but it is as nearly the meaning as I can give; for I do not pretend to understand the language. I am a very poor Italian scholar."

"Yes, yes, I see you are. I see you know nothing of the matter. You have only knowledge enough of the language, to translate at sight these inverted, transposed, curtailed Italian lines, into clear, comprehensible, elegant English. You need not say anything more of your ignorance. Here is complete proof."

"I will not oppose such kind politeness; but I should be sorry to be examined by a real proficient."

"I have not had the pleasure of visiting in Camden-place so long," replied he, "without knowing something of Miss Anne Elliot; and I do regard her as one who is too modest, for the world in general to be aware of half her accomplishments, and too highly accomplished for modesty to be natural in any other woman."

"For shame! for shame!—this is too much flattery. I forget what we are to have next," turning to the bill.

"Perhaps," said Mr. Elliot, speaking low, "I have had a longer acquaintance with your character than you are aware of."

"Indeed!—How so? You can have been acquainted with it only since I came to Bath, excepting as you might hear me previously spoken of in my own family."

"I knew you by report long before you came to Bath. I had heard you described by those who knew you intimately. I have been acquainted with you by character many years. Your person, your disposition, accomplishments, manner—they were all present to me."

Mr. Elliot was not disappointed in the in-

terest he hoped to raise. No one can withstand the charm of such a mystery. To have been described long ago to a recent acquaintance, by nameless people, is irresistible; and Anne was all curiosity. She wondered, and questioned him eagerly—but in vain. He delighted in being asked, but he would not tell.

"No, no—some time or other perhaps, but not now. He would mention no names now; but such, he could assure her, had been the fact. He had many years ago received such a description of Miss Anne Elliot, as had inspired him with the highest idea of her merit, and excited the warmest curiosity to know her."

Anne could think of no one so likely to have spoken with partiality of her many years ago, as the Mr. Wentworth, of Monkford, Captain Wentworth's brother. He might have been in Mr. Elliot's company, but she had not courage to ask the question.

"The name of Anne Elliot," said he, "has long had an interesting sound to me. Very long has it possessed a charm over my fancy; and, if I dared, I would breathe my wishes that the name might never change."

Such she believed were his words; but scarcely had she received their sound, than her attention was caught by other sounds immediately behind her, which rendered every thing else trivial. Her father and Lady Dalrymple were speaking.

"A well-looking man," said Sir Walter, "a very well-looking man."

"A very fine young man indeed!" said Lady Dalrymple. "More air than one often sees in Bath. Irish, I dare say."

"No, I just know his name. A bowing acquaintance. Wentworth—Captain Wentworth of the navy. His sister married my tenant in Somersetshire—the Croft, who rents Kellynch."

Before Sir Walter had reached this point, Anne's eyes had caught the right direction, and distinguished Captain Wentworth standing among a cluster of men at a little distance. As her eyes fell on him, his seemed to be withdrawn from her. It had that appearance. It seemed as if she had been one moment too late; and as long as she dared observe, he did not look again: but the performance was re-commencing, and she was forced to seem to restore her attention to the orchestra, and look straight forward.

When she could give another glance, he had moved away. He could not have come nearer to her if he would; she was so surrounded and shut in: but she would rather have caught his eye.

Mr. Elliot's speech too distressed her. She had no longer any inclination to talk to him. She wished him not so near her.

The first act was over. Now she hoped for some beneficial change; and, after a period of nothing-saying amongst the party, some of them did decide on going in quest of tea. Anne was one of the few who did not choose to move. She remained in her seat, and so did Lady Russell; but she had the pleasure of getting rid of Mr. Elliot; and she did not mean, whatever she might feel on Lady Russell's account, to shrink from conversation with Captain Wentworth, if he gave her the opportunity. She was persuaded by Lady Russell's countenance that she had seen him.

He did not come however. Anne sometimes fancied she discerned him at a distance, but he never came. The anxious interval wore away unproductively. The others returned, the room filled again, benches were reclaimed and re-possessed, and another hour of pleasure or of penance was to be set out, another hour of music was to give delight or the gapes, as real or affected taste for it prevailed. To Anne, it chiefly wore the prospect of an hour of agitation. She could not quit that room in peace without seeing Captain Wentworth once more, without the interchange of one friendly look.

In re-settling themselves, there were now many changes, the result of which was favourable for her. Colonel Wallis declined sitting down again, and Mr. Elliot was invited by Elizabeth and Miss Carteret, in a manner not to be refused, to sit between them; and by some other removals, and a little scheming of her own, Anne was enabled to place herself much nearer the end of the bench than she had been before, much more within reach of a passer-by. She could not do so, without comparing herself with Miss Larolles,[8] the inimitable Miss Larolles, but still she did it, and not with much happier effect; though by what seemed prosperity in the shape of an early abdication in her next neighbours, she found herself at the very end of the bench before the concert closed.

Such was her situation, with a vacant space at hand, when Captain Wentworth was again in sight. She saw him not far off. He saw her too; yet he looked grave, and seemed irresolute, and only by very slow degrees came at last near enough to speak to her. She felt that something must be the matter. The change was indubitable. The difference between his present air and what it had been in the octagon room was strikingly great. Why was it? She thought of her father—of Lady Russell. Could there have been any unpleasant glances? He began by speaking of the concert, gravely; more like the Captain Wentworth of Uppercross; owned himself disappointed, had expected better singing; and, in short, must confess that he should not be sorry when it was over. Anne replied, and spoke in defence of the performance so well, and yet in allowance for his feelings, so pleasantly, that his countenance improved, and he replied again with almost a smile. They talked for a few minutes more; the improvement held; he even looked down towards the bench, as if he saw a place on it well worth occupying; when, at that moment, a touch on her shoulder obliged Anne to turn round. It came from Mr. Elliot. He begged her pardon, but she must be applied to, to explain Italian again. Miss Carteret was very anxious to have a general idea of what was next to be

---

[8] "Miss Larolles." In Fanny Burney's novel *Cecilia*, Miss Larolles, who is head of the Voluble sect of fashionable society, tries to attract the attention of Mr. Meadows, the head of the Insensiblists, by sitting on the outside of the benches.

sung. Anne could not refuse; but never had she sacrificed to politeness with a more suffering spirit.

A few minutes, though as few as possible, were inevitably consumed; and when her own mistress again, when able to turn and look as she had done before, she found herself accosted by Captain Wentworth, in a reserved yet hurried sort of farewell. "He must wish her good night. He was going—he should get home as fast as he could."

"Is not this song worth staying for?" said Anne, suddenly struck by an idea which made her yet more anxious to be encouraging.

"No!" he replied impressively, "there is nothing worth my staying for," and he was gone directly.

Jealousy of Mr. Elliot! It was the only intelligible motive. Captain Wentworth jealous of her affection! Could she have believed it a week ago—three hours ago! For a moment the gratification was exquisite. But alas! there were very different thoughts to succeed. How was such jealousy to be quieted? How was the truth to reach him? How, in all the peculiar disadvantages of their respective situations, would he ever learn her real sentiments? It was misery to think of Mr. Elliot's attentions. Their evil was incalculable.

Chapter twenty-one

Anne recollected with pleasure the next morning her promise of going to Mrs. Smith; meaning that it should engage her from home at the time when Mr. Elliot would be most likely to call; for to avoid Mr. Elliot was almost a first object.

She felt a great deal of good will towards him. In spite of the mischief of his attentions, she owed him gratitude and regard, perhaps compassion. She could not help thinking much of the extraordinary circumstances attending their acquaintance; of the right which he seemed to have to interest her, by every thing in situation, by his own sentiments, by his early prepossession. It was

altogether very extraordinary. Flattering, but painful. There was much to regret. How she might have felt, had there been no Captain Wentworth in the case, was not worth enquiry; for there was a Captain Wentworth: and be the conclusion of the present suspense good or bad, her affection would be his for ever. Their union, she believed, could not divide her more from other men, than their final separation.

Prettier musings of high-wrought love and eternal constancy, could never have passed along the streets of Bath, than Anne was sporting with from Camden-place to Westgate-buildings. It was almost enough to spread purification and perfume all the way.

She was sure of a pleasant reception; and her friend seemed this morning particularly obliged to her for coming, seemed hardly to have expected her, though it had been an appointment.

An account of the concert was immediately claimed; and Anne's recollections of the concert were quite happy enough to animate her features, and make her rejoice to talk of it. All that she could tell, she told most gladly; but the all was little for one who had been there, and unsatisfactory for such an enquirer as Mrs. Smith, who had already heard, through the short cut of a laundress and a waiter, rather more of the general success and produce of the evening than Anne could relate; and who now asked in vain for several particulars of the company. Every body of any consequence or notoriety in Bath was well known by name to Mrs. Smith.

"The little Durands were there, I conclude," said she, "with their mouth open to catch the music; like unfledged sparrows ready to be fed. They never miss a concert."

"Yes. I did not see them myself, but I heard Mr. Elliot say they were in the room."

"The Ibbotsons—were they there? and the two new beauties, with the tall Irish officer, who is talked of for one of them."

"I do not know. I do not think they were."

"Old Lady Mary Maclean? I need not ask after her. She never misses, I know; and you

must have seen her. She must have been in your own circle, for as you went with Lady Dalrymple, you were in the seats of grandeur; round the orchestra, of course."

"No, that was what I dreaded. It would have been very unpleasant to me in every respect. But happily Lady Dalrymple always chooses to be farther off; and we were exceedingly well placed—that is for hearing; I must not say for seeing, because I appear to have seen very little."

"Oh! you saw enough for your own amusement. I can understand. There is a sort of domestic enjoyment to be known even in a crowd, and this you had. You were a large party in yourselves, and you wanted nothing beyond."

"But I ought to have looked about me more," said Anne, conscious while she spoke, that there had in fact been no want of looking about; that the object only had been deficient.

"No, no—you were better employed. You need not tell me that you had a pleasant evening. I see it in your eye. I perfectly see how the hours passed—that you had always something agreeable to listen to. In the intervals of the concert, it was conversation."

Anne half smiled and said, "Do you see that in my eye?"

"Yes, I do. Your countenance perfectly informs me that you were in company last night with the person, whom you think the most agreeable in the world, the person who interests you at this present time, more than all the rest of the world put together."

A blush overspread Anne's cheeks. She could say nothing.

"And such being the case," continued Mrs. Smith, after a short pause, "I hope you believe that I do know how to value your kindness in coming to me this morning. It is really very good of you to come and sit with me, when you must have so many pleasanter demands upon your time."

Anne heard nothing of this. She was still in the astonishment and confusion excited by her friend's penetration, unable to imagine how any report of Captain Wentworth could have reached her. After another short silence—

"Pray," said Mrs. Smith, "is Mr. Elliot aware of your acquaintance with me? Does he know that I am in Bath?"

"Mr. Elliot!" repeated Anne, looking up surprised. A moment's reflection shewed her the mistake she had been under. She caught it instantaneously; and, recovering courage with the feeling of safety, soon added, more composedly, "are you acquainted with Mr. Elliot?"

"I have been a good deal acquainted with him," replied Mrs. Smith, gravely, "but it seems worn out now. It is a great while since we met."

"I was not at all aware of this. You never mentioned it before. Had I known it, I would have had the pleasure of talking to him about you."

"To confess the truth," said Mrs. Smith, assuming her usual air of cheerfulness, "that is exactly the pleasure I want you to have. I want you to talk about me to Mr. Elliot. I want your interest with him. He can be of essential service to me; and if you would have the goodness, my dear Miss Elliot, to make it an object to yourself, of course it is done."

"I should be extremely happy—I hope you cannot doubt my willingness to be of even the slightest use to you," replied Anne; "but I suspect that you are considering me as having a higher claim on Mr. Elliot—a greater right to influence him, than is really the case. I am sure you have, somehow or other, imbibed such a notion. You must consider me only as Mr. Elliot's relation. If in that light, if there is any thing which you suppose his cousin might fairly ask of him, I beg you would not hesitate to employ me."

Mrs. Smith gave her a penetrating glance, and then, smiling, said,

"I have been a little premature, I perceive. I beg your pardon. I ought to have waited for official information. But now, my dear Miss Elliot, as an old friend, do give me a hint as to when I may speak. Next week? To be sure by next week I may be allowed to think it all settled, and build my own selfish schemes on Mr. Elliot's good fortune."

"No," replied Anne, "nor next week, nor next, nor next. I assure you that nothing of the sort you are thinking of will be settled any week. I am not going to marry Mr. Elliot. I should like to know why you imagine I am."

Mrs. Smith looked at her again, looked earnestly, smiled, shook her head, and exclaimed,

"Now, how I do wish I understood you! How I do wish I knew what you were at! I have a great idea that you do not design to be cruel, when the right moment comes. Till it does come, you know, we women never mean to have any body. It is a thing of course among us, that every man is refused —till he offers. But why should you be cruel? Let me plead for my—present friend I cannot call him—but for my former friend. Where can you look for a more suitable match? Where could you expect a more gentlemanlike, agreeable man? Let me recommend Mr. Elliot. I am sure you hear nothing but good of him from Colonel Wallis; and who can know him better than Colonel Wallis?"

"My dear Mrs. Smith, Mr. Elliot's wife has not been dead much above half a year. He ought not to be supposed to be paying his addresses to any one."

"Oh! if these are your only objections," cried Mrs. Smith, archly, "Mr. Elliot is safe, and I shall give myself no more trouble about him. Do not forget me when you are married, that's all. Let him know me to be a friend of yours, and then he will think little of the trouble required, which it is very natural for him now, with so many affairs and engagements of his own, to avoid and get rid of as he can—very natural, perhaps. Ninety-nine out of a hundred would do the same. Of course, he cannot be aware of the importance to me. Well, my dear Miss Elliot, I hope and trust you will be very happy. Mr. Elliot has sense to understand the value of such a woman. Your peace will not be shipwrecked as mine has been. You are safe in all worldly matters, and safe in his character. He will not be led astray, he will not be misled by others to his ruin."

"No," said Anne, "I can readily believe all that of my cousin. He seems to have a calm, decided temper, not at all open to dangerous impressions. I consider him with great respect. I have no reason, from any thing that has fallen within my observation, to do otherwise. But I have not known him long; and he is not a man, I think, to be known intimately soon. Will not this manner of speaking of him, Mrs. Smith, convince you that he is nothing to me? Surely, this must be calm enough. And, upon my word, he is nothing to me. Should he ever propose to me (which I have very little reason to imagine he has any thought of doing), I shall not accept him. I assure you I shall not. I assure you Mr. Elliot had not the share which you have been supposing, in whatever pleasure the concert of last night might afford—not Mr. Elliot; it is not Mr. Elliot that—"

She stopped, regretting with a deep blush that she had implied so much; but less would hardly have been sufficient. Mrs. Smith would hardly have believed so soon in Mr. Elliot's failure, but from the perception of there being a somebody else. As it was, she instantly submitted, and with all the semblance of seeing nothing beyond; and Anne, eager to escape farther notice, was impatient to know why Mrs. Smith should have fancied she was to marry Mr. Elliot, where she could have received the idea, or from whom she could have heard it.

"Do tell me how it first came into your head."

"It first came into my head," replied Mrs. Smith, "upon finding how much you were together, and feeling it to be the most probable thing in the world to be wished for by everybody belonging to either of you; and you may depend upon it that all your acquaintance have disposed of you in the same way. But I never heard it spoken of till two days ago."

"And has it indeed been spoken of?"

"Did you observe the woman who opened

the door to you, when you called yesterday?"

"No. Was not it Mrs. Speed, as usual, or the maid? I observed no one in particular."

"It was my friend, Mrs. Rooke—Nurse Rooke, who, by the by, had a great curiosity to see you, and was delighted to be in the way to let you in. She came away from Marlborough-buildings only on Sunday; and she it was who told me you were to marry Mr. Elliot. She had had it from Mrs. Wallis herself, which did not seem bad authority. She sat an hour with me on Monday evening, and gave me the whole history."

"The whole history!" repeated Anne, laughing. "She could not make a very long history, I think, of one such little article of unfounded news."

Mrs. Smith said nothing.

"But," continued Anne, presently, "though there is no truth in my having this claim on Mr. Elliot, I should be extremely happy to be of use to you, in any way that I could. Shall I mention to him your being in Bath? Shall I take any message?"

"No, I thank you: no, certainly not. In the warmth of the moment, and under a mistaken impression, I might, perhaps, have endeavoured to interest you in some circumstances. But not now: no, I thank you, I have nothing to trouble you with."

"I think you spoke of having known Mr. Elliot many years?"

"I did."

"Not before he married, I suppose?"

"Yes; he was not married when I knew him first."

"And—were you much acquainted?"

"Intimately."

"Indeed! Then do tell me what he was at that time of life. I have a great curiosity to know what Mr. Elliot was as a very young man. Was he at all such as he appears now?"

"I have not seen Mr. Elliot these three years," was Mrs. Smith's answer, given so gravely that it was impossible to pursue the subject farther; and Anne felt that she had gained nothing but an increase of curiosity. They were both silent—Mrs. Smith very thoughtful. At last,

"I beg your pardon, my dear Miss Elliot," she cried, in her natural tone of cordiality, "I beg your pardon for the short answers I have been giving you, but I have been uncertain what I ought to do. I have been doubting and considering as to what I ought to tell you. There were many things to be taken into the account. One hates to be officious, to be giving bad impressions, making mischief. Even the smooth surface of family-union seems worth preserving, though there may be nothing durable beneath. However, I have determined; I think I am right; I think you ought to be made acquainted with Mr. Elliot's real character. Though I fully believe that, at present, you have not the smallest intention of accepting him, there is no saying what may happen. You might, some time or other, be differently affected towards him. Hear the truth, therefore, now, while you are unprejudiced. Mr. Elliot is a man without heart or conscience; a designing, wary, cold-blooded being, who thinks only of himself; who, for his own interest or ease, would be guilty of any cruelty, or any treachery, that could be perpetrated without risk of his general character. He has no feeling for others. Those whom he has been the chief cause of leading into ruin, he can neglect and desert without the smallest compunction. He is totally beyond the reach of any sentiment of justice or compassion. Oh! he is black at heart, hollow and black!"

Anne's astonished air, and exclamation of wonder, made her pause, and in a calmer manner she added,

"My expressions startle you. You must allow for an injured, angry woman. But I will try to command myself. I will not abuse him. I will only tell you what I have found him. Facts shall speak. He was the intimate friend of my dear husband, who trusted and loved him, and thought him as good as himself. The intimacy had been formed before our marriage. I found them most intimate friends; and I, too, became excessively pleased with Mr. Elliot, and entertained the highest opinion of him. At nineteen, you know, one does not think very seriously, but Mr. Elliot appeared to me quite as good as others, and much more agreeable than most others, and we were almost always together. We were principally in town, living in very good style. He was then the inferior in circumstances, he was then the poor one; he had chambers in the Temple, and it was as much as he could do to support the appearance of a gentleman. He had always a home with us whenever he chose it; he was always welcome; he was like a brother. My poor Charles, who had the finest, most generous spirit in the world, would have divided his last farthing with him; and I know that his purse was open to him; I know that he often assisted him."

"This must have been about that very period of Mr. Elliot's life," said Anne, "which has always excited my particular curiosity. It must have been about the same time that he became known to my father and sister. I never knew him myself, I only heard of him, but there was a something in his conduct then with regard to my father and sister, and afterwards in the circumstances of his marriage, which I never could quite reconcile with present times. It seemed to announce a different sort of man."

"I know it all, I know it all," cried Mrs. Smith. "He had been introduced to Sir Walter and your sister before I was acquainted with him, but I heard him speak of them for ever. I know he was invited and encouraged, and I know he did not choose to go. I can satisfy you, perhaps, on points which you would little expect; and as to his marriage, I knew all about it at the time. I was privy to all the fors and againsts, I was the friend to whom he confided his hopes and plans, and though I did not know his wife previously (her inferior situation in society, indeed, rendered that impossible), yet I knew her all her life afterwards, or, at least, till within the last two years of her life, and can answer any question you wish to put."

"Nay," said Anne, "I have no particular enquiry to make about her. I have always understood they were not a happy couple.

But I should like to know why, at that time of his life, he should slight my father's acquaintance as he did. My father was certainly disposed to take very kind and proper notice of him. Why did Mr. Elliot draw back?"

"Mr. Elliot," replied Mrs. Smith, "at that period of his life, had one object in view—to make his fortune, and by a rather quicker process than the law. He was determined to make it by marriage. He was determined, at least, not to mar it by an imprudent marriage; and I know it was his belief (whether justly or not, of course I cannot decide), that your father and sister, in their civilities and invitations, were designing a match between the heir and the young lady; and it was impossible that such a match should have answered his ideas of wealth and independence. That was his motive for drawing back, I can assure you. He told me the whole story. He had no concealments with me. It was curious, that having just left you behind me in Bath, my first and principal acquaintance on marrying, should be your cousin; and that, through him, I should be continually hearing of your father and sister. He described one Miss Elliot, and I thought very affectionately of the other."

"Perhaps," cried Anne, struck by a sudden idea, "you sometimes spoke of me to Mr. Elliot?"

"To be sure I did, very often. I used to boast of my own Anne Elliot, and vouch for your being a very different creature from—"

She checked herself just in time.

"This accounts for something which Mr. Elliot said last night," cried Anne. "This explains it. I found he had been used to hear of me. I could not comprehend how. What wild imaginations one forms, where dear self is concerned! How sure to be mistaken! But I beg your pardon; I have interrupted you. Mr. Elliot married, then, completely for money? The circumstance, probably, which first opened your eyes to his character."

Mrs. Smith hesitated a little here. "Oh! those things are too common. When one lives in the world, a man or woman's marrying for money is too common to strike one as it ought. I was very young, and associated only with the young, and we were a thoughtless, gay set, without any strict rules of conduct. We lived for enjoyment. I think differently now; time and sickness, and sorrow, have given me other notions; but, at that period, I must own I saw nothing reprehensible in what Mr. Elliot was doing. 'To do the best for himself,' passed as a duty."

"But was not she a very low woman?"

"Yes; which I objected to, but he would not regard. Money, money, was all that he wanted. Her father was a grazier, her grandfather had been a butcher, but that was all nothing. She was a fine woman, had had a decent education, was brought forward by some cousins, thrown by chance into Mr. Elliot's company, and fell in love with him; and not a difficulty or a scruple was there on his side, with respect to her birth. All his caution was spent in being secured of the real amount of her fortune, before he committed himself. Depend upon it, whatever esteem Mr. Elliot may have for his own situation in life now, as a young man he had not the smallest value for it. His chance of the Kellynch estate was something, but all the honour of the family he held as cheap as dirt. I have often heard him declare, that if baronetcies were saleable, any body should have his for fifty pounds, arms and motto, name and livery included; but I will not pretend to repeat half that I used to hear him say on that subject. It would not be fair. And yet you ought to have proof; for what is all this but assertion? and you shall have proof."

"Indeed, my dear Mrs. Smith, I want none," cried Anne. "You have asserted nothing contradictory to what Mr. Elliot appeared to be some years ago. This is all in confirmation, rather, of what we used to hear and believe. I am more curious to know why he should be so different now?"

"But for my satisfaction; if you will have the goodness to ring for Mary—stay, I am sure you will have the still greater goodness of going yourself into my bed-room, and bringing me the small inlaid box which you will find on the upper shelf of the closet."

Anne, seeing her friend to be earnestly bent on it, did as she was desired. The box was brought and placed before her, and Mrs. Smith, sighing over it as she unlocked it, said,

"This is full of papers belonging to him, to my husband, a small portion only of what I had to look over when I lost him. The letter I am looking for, was one written by Mr. Elliot to him before our marriage, and happened to be saved; why, one can hardly imagine. But he was careless and immethodical, like other men, about those things; and when I came to examine his papers, I found it with others still more trivial from different people scattered here and there, while many letters and memorandums of real importance had been destroyed. Here it is. I would not burn it, because being even then very little satisfied with Mr. Elliot, I was determined to preserve every document of former intimacy. I have now another motive for being glad that I can produce it."

This was the letter, directed to "Charles Smith, Esq. Tunbridge Wells," and dated from London, as far back as July, 1803.

"Dear Smith,

"I have received yours. Your kindness almost overpowers me. I wish nature had made such hearts as yours more common, but I have lived three-and-twenty years in the world, and have seen none like it. At present, believe me, I have no need of your services, being in cash again. Give me joy: I have got rid of Sir Walter and Miss. They are gone back to Kellynch, and almost made me swear to visit them this summer, but my first visit to Kellynch will be with a surveyor, to tell me how to bring it with best advantage to the hammer. The baronet, nevertheless, is not unlikely to marry again; he is quite fool enough. If he does, however, they will leave me in peace, which may be a decent equivalent for the reversion. He is worse than last year.

"I wish I had any name but Elliot. I am sick of it. The name of Walter I can drop, thank God! and I desire you will never insult me with my second W.

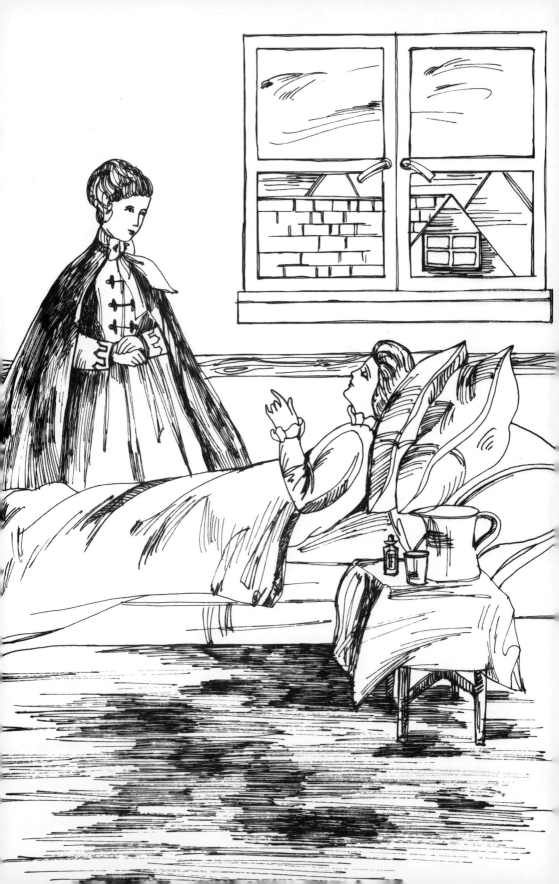

again, meaning, for the rest of my life, to be only yours truly,

"*Wm. Elliot.*"

Such a letter could not be read without putting Anne in a glow; and Mrs. Smith, observing the high colour in her face, said,

"The language, I know, is highly disrespectful. Though I have forgot the exact terms, I have a perfect impression of the general meaning. But it shews you the man. Mark his professions to my poor husband. Can any thing be stronger?"

Anne could not immediately get over the shock and mortification of finding such words applied to her father. She was obliged to recollect that her seeing the letter was a violation of the laws of honour, that no one ought to be judged or to be known by such testimonies, that no private correspondence could bear the eye of others, before she could recover calmness enough to return the letter which she had been meditating over, and say,

"Thank you. This is full proof undoubtedly, proof of every thing you were saying. But why be acquainted with us now?"

"I can explain this too," cried Mrs. Smith, smiling.

"Can you really?"

"Yes. I have shewn you Mr. Elliot, as he was a dozen years ago, and I will shew him as he is now. I cannot produce written proof again, but I can give as authentic oral testimony as you can desire, of what he is now wanting, and what he is now doing. He is no hypocrite now. He truly wants to marry you. His present attentions to your family are very sincere, quite from the heart. I will give you my authority; his friend Colonel Wallis."

"Colonel Wallis! you are acquainted with him?"

"No. It does not come to me in quite so direct a line as that; it takes a bend or two, but nothing of consequence. The stream is as good as at first; the little rubbish it collects in the turnings, is easily moved away. Mr. Elliot talks unreservedly to Colonel Wallis of his views on you—which said Colonel Wallis I imagine to be in himself a sensible, careful, discerning sort of character; but Colonel Wallis has a very pretty silly wife, to whom he tells things which he had better not, and he repeats it all to her. She, in the overflowing spirits of her recovery, repeats it all to her nurse; and the nurse, knowing my acquaintance with you, very naturally brings it all to me. On Monday evening my good friend Mrs. Rooke let me thus much into the secrets of Marlborough-buildings. When I talked of a whole history therefore, you see, I was not romancing so much as you supposed."

"My dear Mrs. Smith, your authority is deficient. This will not do. Mr. Elliot's having any views on me will not in the least account for the efforts he made towards a reconciliation with my father. That was all prior to my coming to Bath. I found them on the most friendly terms when I arrived."

"I know you did; I know it all perfectly, but—"

"Indeed, Mrs. Smith, we must not expect to get real information in such a line. Facts or opinions which are to pass through the hands of so many, to be misconceived by folly in one, and ignorance in another, can hardly have much truth left."

"Only give me a hearing. You will soon be able to judge of the general credit due, by listening to some particulars which you can yourself immediately contradict or confirm. Nobody supposes that you were his first inducement. He had seen you indeed, before he came to Bath, and admired you, but without knowing it to be you. So says my historian at least. Is this true? Did he see you last summer or autumn, 'somewhere down in the west,' to use her own words, without knowing it to be you?"

"He certainly did. So far it is very true. At Lyme; I happened to be at Lyme."

"Well," continued Mrs. Smith triumphantly, "grant my friend the credit due to the establishment of the first point asserted. He saw you then at Lyme, and liked you so well as to be exceedingly pleased to meet with you again in Camden-place, as Miss

Anne Elliot, and from that moment, I have no doubt, had a double motive in his visits there. But there was another, and an earlier; which I will now explain. If there is any thing in my story which you know to be either false or improbable, stop me. My account states, that your sister's friend, the lady now staying with you, whom I have heard you mention, came to Bath with Miss Elliot and Sir Walter as long ago as September (in short when they first came themselves), and has been staying there ever since; that she is a clever, insinuating, handsome woman, poor and plausible, and altogether such in situation and manner, as to give a general idea among Sir Walter's acquaintance, of her meaning to be Lady Elliot, and as general a surprise that Miss Elliot should be apparently blind to the danger."

Here Mrs. Smith paused a moment; but Anne had not a word to say, and she continued,

"This was the light in which it appeared to those who knew the family, long before your return to it; and Colonel Wallis had his eye upon your father enough to be sensible of it, though he did not then visit in Camden-place; but his regard for Mr. Elliot gave him an interest in watching all that was going on there, and when Mr. Elliot came to Bath for a day or two, as he happened to do a little before Christmas, Colonel Wallis made him acquainted with the appearance of things, and the reports beginning to prevail. Now you are to understand that time had worked a very material change in Mr. Elliot's opinions as to the value of a baronetcy. Upon all points of blood and connexion, he is a completely altered man. Having long had as much money as he could spend, nothing to wish for on the side of avarice or indulgence, he has been gradually learning to pin his happiness upon the consequence he is heir to. I thought it coming on, before our acquaintance ceased, but it is now a confirmed feeling. He cannot bear the idea of not being Sir William. You may guess therefore that the news he heard from his friend,

could not be very agreeable, and you may guess what it produced; the resolution of coming back to Bath as soon as possible, and of fixing himself here for a time, with the view of renewing his former acquaintance and recovering such a footing in the family, as might give him the means of ascertaining the degree of his danger, and of circumventing the lady if he found it material. This was agreed upon between the two friends, as the only thing to be done; and Colonel Wallis was to assist in every way that he could. He was to be introduced, and Mrs. Wallis was to be introduced, and every body was to be introduced. Mr. Elliot came back accordingly; and on application was forgiven, as you know, and re-admitted into the family; and there it was his constant object, and his only object (till your arrival added another motive) to watch Sir Walter and Mrs. Clay. He omitted no opportunity of being with them, threw himself in their way, called at all hours—but I need not be particular on this subject. You can imagine what an artful man would do; and with this guide, perhaps, may recollect what you have seen him do."

"Yes," said Anne, "you tell me nothing which does not accord with what I have known, or could imagine. There is always something offensive in the details of cunning. The manoeuvres of selfishness and duplicity must ever be revolting, but I have heard nothing which really surprises me. I know those who would be shocked by such a representation of Mr. Elliot, who would have difficulty in believing it; but I have never been satisfied. I have always wanted some other motive for his conduct than appeared. I should like to know his present opinion, as to the probability of the event he has been in dread of; whether he considers the danger to be lessening or not."

"Lessening, I understand," replied Mrs. Smith. "He thinks Mrs. Clay afraid of him, aware that he sees through her, and not daring to proceed as she might do in his absence. But since he must be absent some time or other, I do not perceive how he can ever be secure, while she holds her present influence. Mrs. Wallis has an amusing idea, as nurse tells me, that it is to be put into the marriage articles when you and Mr. Elliot marry, that your father is not to marry Mrs. Clay. A scheme, worthy of Mrs. Wallis's understanding, by all accounts; but my sensible nurse Rooke sees the absurdity of it. 'Why, to be sure, ma'am,' said she, 'it would not prevent his marrying any body else.' And indeed, to own the truth, I do not think nurse in her heart is a very strenuous opposer of Sir Walter's making a second match. She must be allowed to be a favourer of matrimony you know, and (since self will intrude) who can say that she may not have some flying visions of attending the next Lady Elliot, through Mrs. Wallis's recommendation?"

"I am very glad to know all this," said Anne, after a little thoughtfulness. "It will be more painful to me in some respects to be in company with him, but I shall know better what to do. My line of conduct will be more direct. Mr. Elliot is evidently a disingenuous, artificial, worldly man, who has never had any better principle to guide him than selfishness."

But Mr. Elliot was not yet done with. Mrs. Smith had been carried away from her first direction, and Anne had forgotten, in the interest of her own family concerns, how much had been originally implied against him; but her attention was now called to the explanation of those first hints, and she listened to a recital which, if it did not perfectly justify the unqualified bitterness of Mrs. Smith, proved him to have been very unfeeling in his conduct towards her, very deficient both in justice and compassion.

She learned that (the intimacy between them continuing unimpaired by Mr. Elliot's marriage) they had been as before always together, and Mr. Elliot had led his friend into expenses much beyond his fortune. Mrs. Smith did not want to take blame to herself, and was most tender of throwing any on her husband; but Anne could collect that their income had never been equal to their style of living, and that from the first,

there had been a great deal of general and joint extravagance. From his wife's account of him, she could discern Mr. Smith to have been a man of warm feelings, easy temper, careless habits, and not strong understanding, much more amiable than his friend, and very unlike him—led by him, and probably despised by him. Mr. Elliot, raised by his marriage to great affluence, and disposed to every gratification of pleasure and vanity which could be commanded without involving himself (for with all his self-indulgence he had become a prudent man), and beginning to be rich, just as his friend ought to have found himself to be poor, seemed to have had no concern at all for that friend's probable finances, but, on the contrary, had been prompting and encouraging expenses, which could end only in ruin. And the Smiths accordingly had been ruined.

The husband had died just in time to be spared the full knowledge of it. They had previously known embarrassments enough to try the friendship of their friends, and to prove that Mr. Elliot's had better not be tried; but it was not till his death that the wretched state of his affairs was fully known. With a confidence in Mr. Elliot's regard, more creditable to his feelings than his judgment, Mr. Smith had appointed him the executor of his will; but Mr. Elliot would not act, and the difficulties and distresses which this refusal had heaped on her, in addition to the inevitable sufferings of her situation, had been such as could not be related without anguish of spirit, or listened to without corresponding indignation.

Anne was shewn some letters of his on the occasion, answers to urgent applications from Mrs. Smith, which all breathed the same stern resolution of not engaging in a fruitless trouble, and, under a cold civility, the same hard-hearted indifference to any of the evils it might bring on her. It was a dreadful picture of ingratitude and inhumanity; and Anne felt at some moments, that no flagrant open crime could have been worse. She had a great deal to listen to; all the particulars of past sad scenes, all the minutiae of distress upon distress, which in former conversations had been merely hinted at, were dwelt on now with a natural indulgence. Anne could perfectly comprehend the exquisite relief, and was only the more inclined to wonder at the composure of her friend's usual state of mind.

There was one circumstance in the history of her grievances of particular irritation. She had good reason to believe that some property of her husband in the West Indies, which had been for many years under a sort of sequestration for the payment of its own incumbrances, might be recoverable by proper measures; and this property, though not large, would be enough to make her comparatively rich. But there was nobody to stir in it. Mr. Elliot would do nothing, and she could do nothing herself, equally disabled from personal exertion by her state of bodily weakness, and from employing others by her want of money. She had no natural connexions to assist her even with their counsel, and she could not afford to purchase the assistance of the law. This was a cruel aggravation of actually streightened means. To feel that she ought to be in better circumstances, that a little trouble in the right place might do it, and to fear that delay might be even weakening her claims, was hard to bear!

It was on this point that she had hoped to engage Anne's good offices with Mr. Elliot. She had previously, in the anticipation of their marriage, been very apprehensive of losing her friend by it; but on being assured that he could have made no attempt of that nature, since he did not even know her to be in Bath, it immediately occurred, that something might be done in her favour by the influence of the woman he loved, and she had been hastily preparing to interest Anne's feelings, as far as the observances due to Mr. Elliot's character would allow, when Anne's refutation of the supposed engagement changed the face of every thing, and while it took from her the new-formed hope of succeeding in the object of her first

anxiety, left her at least the comfort of telling the whole story her own way.

After listening to this full description of Mr. Elliot, Anne could not but express some surprise at Mrs. Smith's having spoken of him so favourably in the beginning of their conversation. "She had seemed to recommend and praise him!"

"My dear," was Mrs. Smith's reply, "there was nothing else to be done. I considered your marrying him as certain, though he might not yet have made the offer, and I could no more speak the truth of him, than if he had been your husband. My heart bled for you, as I talked of happiness. And yet, he is sensible, he is agreeable, and with such a woman as you, it was not absolutely hopeless. He was very unkind to his first wife. They were wretched together. But she was too ignorant and giddy for respect, and he had never loved her. I was willing to hope that you must fare better."

Anne could just acknowledge within herself such a possibility of having been induced to marry him, as made her shudder at the idea of the misery which must have followed. It was just possible that she might have been persuaded by Lady Russell! And under such a supposition, which would have been most miserable, when time had disclosed all, too late?

It was very desirable that Lady Russell should be no longer deceived; and one of the concluding arrangements of this important conference, which carried them through the greater part of the morning, was, that Anne had full liberty to communicate to her friend every thing relative to Mrs. Smith, in which his conduct was involved.

Chapter twenty-two

Anne went home to think over all that she had heard. In one point, her feelings were relieved by this knowledge of Mr. Elliot. There was no longer any thing of tenderness due to him. He stood, as opposed to

Captain Wentworth, in all his own unwelcome obtrusiveness; and the evil of his attentions last night, the irremediable mischief he might have done, was considered with sensations unqualified, unperplexed. Pity for him was all over. But this was the only point of relief. In every other respect, in looking around her, or penetrating forward, she saw more to distrust and to apprehend. She was concerned for the disappointment and pain Lady Russell would be feeling, for the mortifications which must be hanging over her father and sister, and had all the distress of foreseeing many evils, without knowing how to avert any one of them. She was most thankful for her own knowledge of him. She had never considered herself as entitled to reward for not slighting an old friend like Mrs. Smith, but here was a reward indeed springing from it!—Mrs. Smith had been able to tell her what no one else could have done. Could the knowledge have been extended through her family!—But this was a vain idea. She must talk to Lady Russell, tell her, consult with her, and having done her best, wait the event with as much composure as possible; and after all, her greatest want of composure would be in that quarter of the mind which could not be opened to Lady Russell, in that flow of anxieties and fears which must be all to herself.

She found, on reaching home, that she had, as she intended, escaped seeing Mr. Elliot; that he had called and paid them a long morning visit; but hardly had she congratulated herself, and felt safe till to-morrow, when she heard that he was coming again in the evening.

"I had not the smallest intention of asking him," said Elizabeth, with affected carelessness, "but he gave so many hints; so Mrs. Clay says, at least."

"Indeed I do say it. I never saw any body in my life spell harder for an invitation. Poor man! I was really in pain for him; for your hard-hearted sister, Miss Anne, seems bent on cruelty."

"Oh!" cried Elizabeth, "I have been rather too much used to the game to be soon overcome by a gentleman's hints. However, when I found how excessively he was regretting that he should miss my father this morning, I gave way immediately, for I would never really omit an opportunity of bringing him and Sir Walter together. They appear to so much advantage in company with each other! Each behaving so pleasantly! Mr. Elliot looking up with so much respect!"

"Quite delightful!" cried Mrs. Clay, not daring, however, to turn her eyes towards Anne. "Exactly like father and son! Dear Miss Elliot, may I not say father and son?"

"Oh! I lay no embargo on any body's words. If you will have such ideas! But, upon my word, I am scarcely sensible of his attentions being beyond those of other men."

"My dear Miss Elliot!" exclaimed Mrs. Clay, lifting up her hands and eyes, and sinking all the rest of her astonishment in a convenient silence.

"Well, my dear Penelope, you need not be so alarmed about him. I did invite him, you know. I sent him away with smiles. When I found he was really going to his friends at Thornberry-park for the whole day to-morrow, I had compassion on him."

Anne admired the good acting of the friend, in being able to shew such pleasure as she did, in the expectation, and in the actual arrival of the very person whose presence must really be interfering with her prime object. It was impossible but that Mrs. Clay must hate the sight of Mr. Elliot; and yet she could assume a most obliging, placid look, and appear quite satisfied with the curtailed license of devoting herself only half as much to Sir Walter as she would have done otherwise.

To Anne herself it was most distressing to see Mr. Elliot enter the room; and quite painful to have him approach and speak to her. She had been used before to feel that he could not be always quite sincere, but now she saw insincerity in every thing. His attentive deference to her father, contrasted with his former language, was odious; and when she thought of his cruel conduct towards Mrs. Smith, she could hardly bear the sight of his present smiles and mildness, or the sound of his artificial good sentiments. She meant to avoid any such alteration of manners as might provoke a remonstrance on his side. It was a great object with her to escape all enquiry or eclat; but it was her intention to be as decidedly cool to him as might be compatible with their relationship, and to retrace, as quietly as she could, the few steps of unnecessary intimacy she had been gradually led along. She was accordingly more guarded, and more cool, than she had been the night before.

He wanted to animate her curiosity again as to how and where he could have heard her formerly praised; wanted very much to be gratified by more solicitation; but the charm was broken: he found that the heat and animation of a public room were necessary to kindle his modest cousin's vanity; he found, at least, that it was not to be done now, by any of those attempts which he could hazard among the too-commanding claims of the others. He little surmised that it was a subject acting now exactly against his interest, bringing immediately into her thoughts all those parts of his conduct which were least excusable.

She had some satisfaction in finding that he was really going out of Bath the next morning, going early, and that he would be gone the greater part of two days. He was invited again to Camden-place the very evening of his return; but from Thursday to Saturday evening his absence was certain. It was bad enough that a Mrs. Clay should be always before her; but that a deeper hypocrite should be added to their party, seemed the destruction of every thing like peace and comfort. It was so humiliating to reflect on the constant deception practised on her father and Elizabeth; to consider the various sources of mortification preparing for them! Mrs. Clay's selfishness was not so complicate nor so revolting as his; and Anne would have compounded for the marriage at once, with all its evils, to be clear of Mr. Elliot's subtleties, in endeavouring to prevent it.

On Friday morning she meant to go very early to Lady Russell, and accomplish the necessary communication; and she would have gone directly after breakfast but that Mrs. Clay was also going out on some obliging purpose of saving her sister trouble, which determined her to wait till she might be safe from such a companion. She saw Mrs. Clay fairly off, therefore, before she began to talk of spending the morning in Rivers-street.

"Very well," said Elizabeth, "I have nothing to send but my love. Oh! you may as well take back that tiresome book she would lend me, and pretend I have read it through. I really cannot be plaguing myself for ever with all the new poems and states of the nation that come out. Lady Russell quite bores one with her new publications. You need not tell her so, but I thought her dress hideous the other night. I used to think she had some taste in dress, but I was ashamed of her at the concert. Something so formal and *arrangé* in her air! and she sits so upright! My best love, of course."

"And mine," added Sir Walter. "Kindest regards. And you may say, that I mean to call upon her soon. Make a civil message. But I shall only leave my card. Morning visits are never fair by women at her time of life, who make themselves up so little. If she would only wear rouge, she would not be afraid of being seen; but last time I called, I observed the blinds were let down immediately."

While her father spoke, there was a knock at the door. Who could it be? Anne, remembering the preconcerted visits, at all hours, of Mr. Elliot, would have expected him, but for his known engagement seven miles off. After the usual period of suspense, the usual sounds of approach were heard, and "Mr. and Mrs. Charles Musgrove" were ushered into the room.

Surprise was the strongest emotion raised by their appearance; but Anne was really glad to see them; and the others were not so sorry but that they could put on a decent air of welcome; and as soon as it became clear that these, their nearest relations, were not arrived with any views of accommodation in that house, Sir Walter and Elizabeth were able to rise in cordiality, and do the honours of it very well. They were come to Bath for a few days with Mrs. Musgrove, and were at the White Hart. So much was pretty soon understood; but till Sir Walter and Elizabeth were walking Mary into the other drawing-room, and regaling themselves with her admiration, Anne could not draw upon Charles's brain for a regular history of their coming, or an explanation of some smiling hints of particular business, which had been ostentatiously dropped by Mary, as well as of some apparent confusion as to whom their party consisted of.

She then found that it consisted of Mrs. Musgrove, Henrietta, and Captain Harville, beside their two selves. He gave her a very plain, intelligible account of the whole; a narration in which she saw a great deal of most characteristic proceeding. The scheme had received its first impulse by Captain Harville's wanting to come to Bath on business. He had begun to talk of it a week ago; and by way of doing something, as shooting was over, Charles had proposed coming with him, and Mrs. Harville had seemed to like the idea of it very much, as an advantage to her husband; but Mary could not bear to be left, and had made herself so unhappy about it that, for a day or two, every thing seemed to be in suspense, or at an end. But then, it had been taken up by his father and mother. His mother had some old friends in Bath, whom she wanted to see; it was thought a good opportunity for Henrietta to come and buy wedding-clothes for herself and her sister; and, in short, it ended in being his mother's party, that every thing might be comfortable and easy to Captain Harville; and he and Mary were included in it, by way of general convenience. They had arrived late the night before. Mrs. Harville, her children, and Captain Benwick, remained with Mr. Musgrove and Louisa at Uppercross.

Anne's only surprise was, that affairs should be in forwardness enough for Hen-rietta's wedding-clothes to be talked of: she had imagined such difficulties of fortune to exist there as must prevent the marriage from being near at hand; but she learned from Charles that, very recently (since Mary's last letter to herself), Charles Hayter had been applied to by a friend to hold a living for a youth who could not possibly claim it under many years; and that, on the strength of his present income, with almost a certainty of something more permanent long before the term in question, the two families had consented to the young people's wishes, and that their marriage was likely to take place in a few months, quite as soon as Louisa's. "And a very good living it was," Charles added, "only five-and-twenty miles from Uppercross, and in a very fine country—fine part of Dorsetshire. In the centre of some of the best preserves in the kingdom, surrounded by three great proprietors, each more careful and jealous than the other; and to two of the three, at least, Charles Hayter might get a special recommendation. Not that he will value it as he ought," he observed, "Charles is too cool about sporting. That's the worst of him."

"I am extremely glad, indeed," cried Anne, "particularly glad that this should happen: and that of two sisters, who both deserve equally well, and who have always been such good friends, the pleasant prospects of one should not be dimming those of the other—that they should be so equal in their prosperity and comfort. I hope your father and mother are quite happy with regard to both."

"Oh! yes. My father would be well pleased if the gentlemen were richer, but he has no other fault to find. Money, you know, coming down with money—two daughters at once—it cannot be a very agreeable operation, and it streightens him as to many things. However, I do not mean to say they have not a right to it. It is very fit they should have daughters' shares; and I am sure he has always been a very kind, liberal father to me. Mary does not above half like Henrietta's match. She never did, you know.

But she does not do him justice, nor think enough about Winthrop. I cannot make her attend to the value of the property. It is a very fair match, as times go; and I have liked Charles Hayter all my life, and I shall not leave off now."

"Such excellent parents as Mr. and Mrs. Musgrove," exclaimed Anne, "should be happy in their children's marriages. They do every thing to confer happiness, I am sure. What a blessing to young people to be in such hands! Your father and mother seem so totally free from all those ambitious feelings which have led to so much misconduct and misery, both in young and old! I hope you think Louisa perfectly recovered now?"

He answered rather hesitatingly, "Yes, I believe I do—very much recovered; but she is altered: there is no running or jumping about, no laughing or dancing; it is quite different. If one happens only to shut the door a little hard, she starts and wriggles like a young dab chick in the water; and Benwick sits at her elbow, reading verses, or whispering to her, all day long."

Anne could not help laughing. "That cannot be much to your taste, I know," said she; "but I do believe him to be an excellent young man."

"To be sure he is. Nobody doubts it; and I hope you do not think I am so illiberal as to want every man to have the same objects and pleasures as myself. I have a great value for Benwick; and when one can but get him to talk, he has plenty to say. His reading has done him no harm, for he has fought as well as read. He is a brave fellow. I got more acquainted with him last Monday than ever I did before. We had a famous set-to at rat-hunting all the morning, in my father's great barns; and he played his part so well, that I have liked him the better ever since."

Here they were interrupted by the absolute necessity of Charles's following the others to admire mirrors and china; but Anne had heard enough to understand the present state of Uppercross, and rejoice in its happiness; and though she sighed as she rejoiced, her sigh had none of the ill-will of envy in it. She would certainly have risen to their blessings if she could, but she did not want to lessen theirs.

The visit passed off altogether in high good humour. Mary was in excellent spirits, enjoying the gaiety and the change; and so well satisfied with the journey in her mother-in-law's carriage with four horses, and with her own complete independence of Camden-place, that she was exactly in a temper to admire every thing as she ought, and enter most readily into all the superiorities of the house, as they were detailed to her. She had no demands on her father or sister, and her consequence was just enough increased by their handsome drawing-rooms.

Elizabeth was, for a short time, suffering a good deal. She felt that Mrs. Musgrove and all her party ought to be asked to dine with them, but she could not bear to have the difference of style, the reduction of servants, which a dinner must betray, witnessed by those who had been always so inferior to the Elliots of Kellynch. It was a struggle between propriety and vanity; but vanity got the better, and then Elizabeth was happy again. These were her internal persuasions.—"Old fashioned notions—country hospitality—we do not profess to give dinners—few people in Bath do—Lady Alicia never does; did not even ask her own sister's family, though they were here a month: and I dare say it would be very inconvenient to Mrs. Musgrove—put her quite out of her way. I am sure she would rather not come—she cannot feel easy with us. I will ask them all for an evening; that will be much better—that will be a novelty and a treat. They have not seen two such drawing rooms before. They will be delighted to come to-morrow evening. It shall be a regular party—small, but most elegant." And this satisfied Elizabeth: and when the invitation was given to the two present, and promised for the absent, Mary was as completely satisfied. She was particularly asked to meet Mr. Elliot, and be introduced to Lady Dalrymple and Miss Carteret, who were fortunately already engaged to come;

and she could not have received a more gratifying attention. Miss Elliot was to have the honour of calling on Mrs. Musgrove in the course of the morning, and Anne walked off with Charles and Mary, to go and see her and Henrietta directly.

Her plan of sitting with Lady Russell must give way for the present. They all three called in Rivers-street for a couple of minutes; but Anne convinced herself that a day's delay of the intended communication could be of no consequence, and hastened forward to the White Hart, to see again the friends and companions of the last autumn, with an eagerness of good will which many associations contributed to form.

They found Mrs. Musgrove and her daughter within, and by themselves, and Anne had the kindest welcome from each. Henrietta was exactly in that state of recently-improved views, of fresh-formed happiness, which made her full of regard and interest for every body she had ever liked before at all; and Mrs. Musgrove's real affection had been won by her usefulness when they were in distress. It was a heartiness, and a warmth, and a sincerity which Anne delighted in the more, from the sad want of such blessings at home. She was intreated to give them as much of her time as possible, invited for every day and all day long, or rather claimed as a part of the family; and in return, she naturally fell into all her wonted ways of attention and assistance, and on Charles's leaving them together, was listening to Mrs. Musgrove's history of Louisa, and to Henrietta's of herself, giving opinions on business, and recommendations to shops; with intervals of every help which Mary required, from altering her ribbon to settling her accounts, from finding her keys, and assorting her trinkets, to trying to convince her that she was not ill used by any body; which Mary, well amused as she generally was in her station, at a window overlooking the entrance to the pump-room, could not but have her moments of imagining.

A morning of thorough confusion was to be expected. A large party in an hotel ensured a quick-changing, unsettled scene. One five minutes brought a note, the next a parcel, and Anne had not been there half an hour, when their dining-room, spacious as it was, seemed more than half filled: a party of steady old friends were seated round Mrs. Musgrove, and Charles came back with Captains Harville and Wentworth. The appearance of the latter could not be more than the surprise of the moment. It was impossible for her to have forgotten to feel, that this arrival of their common friends must be soon bringing them together again. Their last meeting had been most important in opening his feelings; she had derived from it a delightful conviction; but she feared from his looks, that the same unfortunate persuasion, which had hastened him away from the concert room, still governed. He did not seem to want to be near enough for conversation.

She tried to be calm, and leave things to take their course; and tried to dwell much on this argument of rational dependance—"Surely, if there be constant attachment on each side, our hearts must understand each other ere long. We are not boy and girl, to be captiously irritable, misled by every moment's inadvertence, and wantonly playing with our own happiness." And yet, a few minutes afterwards, she felt as if their being in company with each other, under their present circumstances, could only be exposing them to inadvertencies and misconstructions of the most mischievous kind.

"Anne," cried Mary, still at her window, "there is Mrs. Clay, I am sure, standing under the colonnade, and a gentleman with her. I saw them turn the corner from Bath-street just now. They seem deep in talk. Who is it?—Come, and tell me. Good heavens! I recollect. It is Mr. Elliot himself."

"No," cried Anne quickly, "it cannot be Mr. Elliot, I assure you. He was to leave Bath at nine this morning, and does not come back till to-morrow."

As she spoke, she felt that Captain Wentworth was looking at her; the consciousness of which vexed and embarrassed her, and

made her regret that she had said so much, simple as it was.

Mary, resenting that she should be supposed not to know her own cousin, began talking very warmly about the family features, and protesting still more positively that it was Mr. Elliot, calling again upon Anne to come and look herself; but Anne did not mean to stir, and tried to be cool and unconcerned. Her distress returned, however, on perceiving smiles and intelligent glances pass between two or three of the lady visitors, as if they believed themselves quite in the secret. It was evident that the report concerning her had spread; and a short pause succeeded, which seemed to ensure that it would now spread farther.

"Do come, Anne," cried Mary, "come and look yourself. You will be too late, if you do not make haste. They are parting, they are shaking hands. He is turning away. Not know Mr. Elliot, indeed!—You seem to have forgot all about Lyme."

To pacify Mary, and perhaps screen her own embarrassment, Anne did move quietly to the window. She was just in time to ascertain that it really was Mr. Elliot (which she had never believed), before he disappeared on one side, as Mrs. Clay walked quickly off on the other; and checking the surprise which she could not but feel at such an appearance of friendly conference between two persons of totally opposite interests, she calmly said, "Yes, it is Mr. Elliot certainly. He has changed his hour of going, I suppose, that is all—or I may be mistaken; I might not attend," and walked back to her chair, recomposed, and with the comfortable hope of having acquitted herself well.

The visitors took their leave; and Charles, having civilly seen them off, and then made a face at them, and abused them for coming, began with—

"Well, mother, I have done something for you that you will like. I have been to the theatre, and secured a box for to-morrow night. A'n't I a good boy? I know you love a play; and there is room for us all. It holds nine. I have engaged Captain Wentworth.

Anne will not be sorry to join us, I am sure. We all like a play. Have not I done well, mother?"

Mrs. Musgrove was good humouredly beginning to express her perfect readiness for the play, if Henrietta and all the others liked it, when Mary eagerly interrupted her by exclaiming,

"Good heavens, Charles! how can you think of such a thing? Take a box for to-morrow night! Have you forgot that we are engaged to Camden-place to-morrow night? and that we were most particularly asked on purpose to meet Lady Dalrymple and her daughter, and Mr. Elliot—all the principal family connexions—on purpose to be introduced to them? How can you be so forgetful?"

"Phoo! phoo!" replied Charles, "what's an evening party? Never worth remembering. Your father might have asked us to dinner, I think, if he had wanted to see us. You may do as you like, but I shall go to the play."

"Oh! Charles, I declare it will be too abominable if you do! when you promised to go."

"No, I did not promise. I only smirked and bowed, and said the word 'happy.' There was no promise."

"But you must go, Charles. It would be unpardonable to fail. We were asked on purpose to be introduced. There was always such a great connexion between the Dalrymples and ourselves. Nothing ever happened on either side that was not announced immediately. We are quite near relations, you know: and Mr. Elliot too, whom you ought so particularly to be acquainted with! Every attention is due to Mr. Elliot. Consider, my father's heir—the future representative of the family."

"Don't talk to me about heirs and representatives," cried Charles. "I am not one of those who neglect the reigning power to bow to the rising sun. If I would not go for the sake of your father, I should think it scandalous to go for the sake of his heir. What is Mr. Elliot to me?"

The careless expression was life to Anne,

who saw that Captain Wentworth was all attention, looking and listening with his whole soul; and that the last words brought his enquiring eyes from Charles to herself.

Charles and Mary still talked on in the same style; he, half serious and half jesting, maintaining the scheme for the play; and she, invariably serious, most warmly opposing it, and not omitting to make it known, that however determined to go to Camden-place herself, she should not think herself very well used, if they went to the play without her. Mrs. Musgrove interposed.

"We had better put it off. Charles, you had much better go back, and change the box for Tuesday. It would be a pity to be divided, and we should be losing Miss Anne too, if there is a party at her father's; and I am sure neither Henrietta nor I should care at all for the play, if Miss Anne could not be with us."

Anne felt truly obliged to her for such kindness; and quite as much so, moreover, for the opportunity it gave her of decidedly saying—

"If it depended only on my inclination, ma'am, the party at home (excepting on Mary's account) would not be the smallest impediment. I have no pleasure in the sort of meeting, and should be too happy to change it for a play, and with you. But, it had better not be attempted, perhaps."

She had spoken it; but she trembled when it was done, conscious that her words were listened to, and daring not even to try to observe their effect.

It was soon generally agreed that Tuesday should be the day, Charles only reserving the advantage of still teasing his wife, by persisting that he would go to the play to-morrow, if nobody else would.

Captain Wentworth left his seat, and walked to the fire-place; probably for the sake of walking away from it soon afterwards, and taking a station, with less barefaced design, by Anne.

"You have not been long enough in Bath," said he, "to enjoy the evening parties of the place."

"Oh! no. The usual character of them has nothing for me. I am no card-player."

"You were not formerly, I know. You did not use to like cards; but time makes many changes."

"I am not yet so much changed," cried Anne, and stopped, fearing she hardly knew what misconstruction. After waiting a few moments he said—and as if it were the result of immediate feeling—"It is a period, indeed! Eight years and a half is a period!"

Whether he would have proceeded farther was left to Anne's imagination to ponder over in a calmer hour; for while still hearing the sounds he had uttered, she was startled to other subjects by Henrietta, eager to make use of the present leisure for getting out, and calling on her companions to lose no time, lest somebody else should come in.

They were obliged to move. Anne talked of being perfectly ready, and tried to look it; but she felt that could Henrietta have known the regret and reluctance of her heart in quitting that chair, in preparing to quit the room, she would have found, in all her own sensations for her cousin, in the very security of his affection, wherewith to pity her.

Their preparations, however, were stopped short. Alarming sounds were heard; other visitors approached, and the door was thrown open for Sir Walter and Miss Elliot, whose entrance seemed to give a general chill. Anne felt an instant oppression, and, wherever she looked, saw symptoms of the same. The comfort, the freedom, the gaiety of the room was over, hushed into cold composure, determined silence, or insipid talk, to meet the heartless elegance of her father and sister. How mortifying to feel that it was so!

Her jealous eye was satisfied in one particular. Captain Wentworth was acknowledged again by each, by Elizabeth more graciously than before. She even addressed him once, and looked at him more than once. Elizabeth was, in fact, revolving a great measure. The sequel explained it. After the waste of a few minutes in saying the proper nothings, she began to give the invitation which was to comprise all the remaining dues of the Musgroves. "To-morrow evening, to meet a few friends, no formal party." It was all said very gracefully, and the cards with which she had provided herself, the "Miss Elliot at home," were laid on the table, with a courteous, comprehensive smile to all; and one smile and one card more decidedly for Captain Wentworth. The truth was, that Elizabeth had been long enough in Bath, to understand the importance of a man of such an air and appearance as his. The past was nothing. The present was that Captain Wentworth would move about well in her drawing-room. The card was pointedly given, and Sir Walter and Elizabeth arose and disappeared.

The interruption had been short, though severe; and ease and animation returned to most of those they left, as the door shut them out, but not to Anne. She could think only of the invitation she had with such astonishment witnessed; and of the manner in which it had been received, a manner of doubtful meaning, of surprise rather than gratification, of polite acknowledgment rather than acceptance. She knew him; she saw disdain in his eye, and could not venture to believe that he had determined to accept such an offering, as atonement for all the insolence of the past. Her spirits sank. He held the card in his hand after they were gone, as if deeply considering it.

"Only think of Elizabeth's including every body!" whispered Mary very audibly. "I do not wonder Captain Wentworth is delighted! You see he cannot put the card out of his hand."

Anne caught his eye, saw his cheeks glow, and his mouth form itself into a momentary expression of contempt, and turned away, that she might neither see nor hear more to vex her.

The party separated. The gentlemen had their own pursuits, the ladies proceeded on their own business, and they met no more while Anne belonged to them. She was earnestly begged to return and dine, and give them all the rest of the day; but her spirits had been so long exerted, that at present she felt unequal to more, and fit only for home, where she might be sure of being as silent as she chose.

Promising to be with them the whole of the following morning, therefore, she closed the fatigues of the present, by a toilsome walk to Camden-place, there to spend the evening chiefly in listening to the busy arrangements of Elizabeth and Mrs. Clay for the morrow's party, the frequent enumeration of the persons invited, and the continually improving detail of all the embellishments which were to make it the most completely elegant of its kind in Bath, while harassing herself in secret with the never-ending question, of whether Captain Wentworth would come or not? They were reckoning him as certain, but, with her, it was a gnawing solicitude never appeased for five minutes together. She generally thought he would come, because she generally thought he ought; but it was a case which she could not so shape into any positive act of duty or discretion, as inevitably to defy the suggestions of very opposite feelings.

She only roused herself from the broodings of this restless agitation, to let Mrs. Clay know that she had been seen with Mr. Elliot three hours after his being supposed to be out of Bath; for having watched in vain for some intimation of the interview from the lady herself, she determined to mention it; and it seemed to her that there was guilt in Mrs. Clay's face as she listened. It was transient, cleared away in an instant, but Anne could imagine she read there the consciousness of having, by some complication of mutual trick, or some overbearing authority of his, been obliged to attend (perhaps for half an hour) to his lectures and restrictions on her designs on Sir Walter. She exclaimed, however, with a very tolerable imitation of nature,

"Oh dear! very true. Only think, Miss Elliot, to my great surprise I met with Mr. Elliot in Bath-street! I was never more astonished. He turned back and walked with me to the Pump-yard. He had been prevented setting off for Thornberry, but I really forget by what—for I was in a hurry, and could not much attend, and I can only answer for his being determined not to be delayed in his return. He wanted to know how early he might be admitted to-morrow. He was full of 'to-morrow,' and it is very evident that I have been full of it too ever since I entered the house, and learnt the extension of your plan, and all that had happened, or my seeing him could never have gone so entirely out of my head."

Chapter twenty-three

One day only had passed since Anne's conversation with Mrs. Smith; but a keener interest had succeeded, and she was now so little touched by Mr. Elliot's conduct, except by its effects in one quarter, that it became a matter of course the next morning, still to defer her explanatory visit in Rivers-street. She had promised to be with the Musgroves from breakfast to dinner. Her faith was plighted, and Mr. Elliot's character, like the Sultaness Scheherazade's head, must live another day.

She could not keep her appointment punctually, however; the weather was unfavourable, and she had grieved over the rain on her friends' account, and felt it very much on her own, before she was able to attempt the walk. When she reached the White Hart, and made her way to the proper apartment, she found herself neither arriving quite in time, nor the first to arrive. The party before her were Mrs. Musgrove, talking to Mrs. Croft, and Captain Harville to Captain Wentworth, and she immediately heard that Mary and Henrietta, too impatient to wait, had gone out the moment it had cleared, but would be back again soon, and that the strictest injunctions had been left with Mrs. Musgrove, to keep her there till they returned. She had only to submit, sit down, be outwardly composed,

and feel herself plunged at once in all the agitations which she had merely laid her account of tasting a little before the morning closed. There was no delay, no waste of time. She was deep in the happiness of such misery, or the misery of such happiness, instantly. Two minutes after her entering the room, Captain Wentworth said,

"We will write the letter we were talking of, Harville, now, if you will give me materials."

Materials were all at hand, on a separate table; he went to it, and nearly turning his back on them all, was engrossed by writing.

Mrs. Musgrove was giving Mrs. Croft the history of her eldest daughter's engagement, and just in that inconvenient tone of voice which was perfectly audible while it pretended to be a whisper. Anne felt that she did not belong to the conversation, and yet, as Captain Harville seemed thoughtful and not disposed to talk, she could not avoid hearing many undesirable particulars, such as "how Mr. Musgrove and my brother Hayter had met again and again to talk it over; what my brother Hayter had said one day, and what Mr. Musgrove had proposed the next, and what had occurred to my sister Hayter, and what the young people had wished, and what I said at first I never could consent to, but was afterwards persuaded to think might do very well," and a great deal in the same style of open-hearted communication—Minutiae which, even with every advantage of taste and delicacy which good Mrs. Musgrove could not give, could be properly interesting only to the principals. Mrs. Croft was attending with great good humour, and whenever she spoke at all, it was very sensibly. Anne hoped the gentlemen might each be too much self-occupied to hear,

"And so, ma'am, all these things considered," said Mrs. Musgrove in her powerful whisper, "though we could have wished it different, yet altogether we did not think it fair to stand out any longer; for Charles Hayter was quite wild about it, and Henrietta was pretty near as bad; and so we thought they had better marry at once, and make the best of it, as many others have done before them. At any rate, said I, it will be better than a long engagement."

"That is precisely what I was going to observe," cried Mrs. Croft. "I would rather have young people settle on a small income at once, and have to struggle with a few difficulties together, than be involved in a long engagement. I always think that no mutual —"

"Oh! dear Mrs. Croft," cried Mrs. Musgrove, unable to let her finish her speech, "there is nothing I so abominate for young people as a long engagement. It is what I always protested against for my children. It is all very well, I used to say, for young people to be engaged, if there is a certainty of their being able to marry in six months, or even in twelve, but a long engagement!"

"Yes, dear ma'am," said Mrs. Croft, "or an uncertain engagement; an engagement which may be long. To begin without knowing that at such a time there will be the means of marrying, I hold to be very unsafe and unwise, and what, I think, all parents should prevent as far as they can."

Anne found an unexpected interest here. She felt its application to herself, felt it in a nervous thrill all over her, and at the same moment that her eyes instinctively glanced towards the distant table, Captain Wentworth's pen ceased to move, his head was raised, pausing, listening, and he turned round the next instant to give a look—one quick, conscious look at her.

The two ladies continued to talk, to re-urge the same admitted truths, and enforce them with such examples of the ill effect of a contrary practice, as had fallen within their observation, but Anne heard nothing distinctly; it was only a buzz of words in her ear, her mind was in confusion.

Captain Harville, who had in truth been hearing none of it, now left his seat, and moved to a window; and Anne seeming to watch him, though it was from thorough absence of mind, became gradually sensible that he was inviting her to join him where he stood. He looked at her with a smile, and a little motion of the head, which expressed, "Come to me, I have something to say"; and the unaffected, easy kindness of manner which denoted the feelings of an older acquaintance than he really was, strongly enforced the invitation. She roused herself and went to him. The window at which he stood, was at the other end of the room from where the two ladies were sitting, and though nearer to Captain Wentworth's table, not very near. As she joined him, Captain Harville's countenance reassumed the serious, thoughtful expression which seemed its natural character.

"Look here," said he, unfolding a parcel in his hand, and displaying a small miniature painting, "do you know who that is?"

"Certainly, Captain Benwick."

"Yes, and you may guess who it is for. But (in a deep tone) it was not done for her. Miss Elliot, do you remember our walking together at Lyme, and grieving for him? I little thought then—but no matter. This was drawn at the Cape. He met with a clever young German artist at the Cape, and in compliance with a promise to my poor sister, sat to him, and was bringing it home for her. And I have now the charge of getting it properly set for another! It was a commission to me! But who else was there to employ? I hope I can allow for him. I am not sorry, indeed, to make it over to another. He undertakes it—(looking towards Captain Wentworth) he is writing about it now." And with a quivering lip he wound up the whole by adding, "Poor Fanny! she would not have forgotten him so soon!"

"No," replied Anne, in a low feeling voice. "That I can easily believe."

"It was not in her nature. She doated on him."

"It would not be the nature of any woman who truly loved."

Captain Harville smiled, as much as to say, "Do you claim that for your sex?" and she answered the question, smiling also, "Yes. We certainly do not forget you, so soon as you forget us. It is, perhaps, our fate rather than our merit. We cannot help ourselves. We live at home, quiet, confined, and our feelings prey upon us. You are forced on exertion. You have always a profession, pursuits, business of some sort or other, to take you back into the world immediately, and continual occupation and change soon weaken impressions."

"Granting your assertion that the world does all this so soon for men (which, however, I do not think I shall grant), it does not apply to Benwick. He has not been forced upon any exertion. The peace turned him on shore at the very moment, and he has been living with us, in our little family-circle, ever since."

"True," said Anne, "very true; I did not recollect; but what shall we say now, Captain Harville? If the change be not from outward circumstances, it must be from within; it must be nature, man's nature, which has done the business for Captain Benwick."

"No, no, it is not man's nature. I will not allow it to be more man's nature than woman's to be inconstant and forget those they do love, or have loved. I believe the reverse. I believe in a true analogy between our bodily frames and our mental; and that as our bodies are the strongest, so are our feelings; capable of bearing most rough usage, and riding out the heaviest weather."

"Your feelings may be the strongest," replied Anne, "but the same spirit of analogy will authorise me to assert that ours are the most tender. Man is more robust than woman, but he is not longer-lived; which exactly explains my view of the nature of their attachments. Nay, it would be too hard upon you, if it were otherwise. You have difficulties, and privations, and dangers enough to struggle with. You are always labouring and toiling, exposed to every risk and hardship. Your home, country, friends, all quitted. Neither time, nor health, nor life, to be called your own. It would be too hard indeed" (with a faltering voice) "if woman's feelings were to be added to all this."

"We shall never agree upon this question" —Captain Harville was beginning to say,

when a slight noise called their attention to Captain Wentworth's hitherto perfectly quiet division of the room. It was nothing more than that his pen had fallen down, but Anne was startled at finding him nearer than she supposed, and half inclined to suspect that the pen had only fallen, because he had been occupied by them, striving to catch sounds, which yet she did not think he could have caught.

"Have you finished your letter?" said Captain Harville.

"Not quite, a few lines more. I shall have done in five minutes."

"There is no hurry on my side. I am only ready whenever you are. I am in very good anchorage here" (smiling at Anne), "well supplied, and want for nothing. No hurry for a signal at all. Well, Miss Elliot" (lowering his voice), "as I was saying, we shall never agree I suppose upon this point. No man and woman would, probably. But let me observe that all histories are against you, all stories, prose and verse. If I had such a memory as Benwick, I could bring you fifty quotations in a moment on my side the argument, and I do not think I ever opened a book in my life which had not something to say upon woman's inconstancy. Songs and proverbs, all talk of woman's fickleness. But perhaps you will say, these were all written by men."

"Perhaps I shall. Yes, yes, if you please, no reference to examples in books. Men have had every advantage of us in telling their own story. Education has been theirs in so much higher a degree; the pen has been in their hands. I will not allow books to prove any thing."

"But how shall we prove any thing?"

"We never shall. We never can expect to prove any thing upon such a point. It is a difference of opinion which does not admit of proof. We each begin probably with a little bias towards our own sex, and upon that bias build every circumstance in favour of it which has occurred within our own circle; many of which circumstances (perhaps those very cases which strike us the most) may be precisely such as cannot be brought forward without betraying a confidence, or in some respect saying what should not be said."

"Ah!" cried Captain Harville, in a tone of strong feeling, "if I could but make you comprehend what a man suffers when he takes a last look at his wife and children, and watches the boat that he has sent them off in, as long as it is in sight, and then turns away and says, 'God knows whether we ever meet again!' And then, if I could convey to you the glow of his soul when he does see them again; when, coming back after a twelvemonth's absence perhaps, and obliged to put into another port, he calculates how soon it be possible to get them there, pretending to deceive himself, and saying, 'They cannot be here till such a day,' but all the while hoping for them twelve hours sooner, and seeing them arrive at last, as if Heaven had given them wings, by many hours sooner still! If I could explain to you all this, and all that a man can bear and do, and glories to do for the sake of these treasures of his existence! I speak, you know, only of such men as have hearts!" pressing his own with emotion.

"Oh!" cried Anne eagerly, "I hope I do justice to all that is felt by you, and by those who resemble you. God forbid that I should undervalue the warm and faithful feelings of any of my fellow-creatures. I should deserve utter contempt if I dared to suppose that true attachment and constancy were known only by woman. No, I believe you capable of every thing great and good in your married lives. I believe you equal to every important exertion, and to every domestic forbearance, so long as—if I may be allowed the expression, so long as you have an object. I mean, while the woman you love lives, and lives for you. All the privilege I claim for my own sex (it is not a very enviable one, you need not covet it) is that of loving longest, when existence or when hope is gone."

She could not immediately have uttered another sentence; her heart was too full, her breath too much oppressed.

"You are a good soul," cried Captain Har-

ville, putting his hand on her arm quite affectionately. "There is no quarrelling with you. And when I think of Benwick, my tongue is tied."

Their attention was called towards the others. Mrs. Croft was taking leave.

"Here, Frederick, you and I part company, I believe," said she. "I am going home, and you have an engagement with your friend. To-night we may have the pleasure of all meeting again, at your party" (turning to Anne). "We had your sister's card yesterday, and I understood Frederick had a card too, though I did not see it—and you are disengaged, Frederick, are you not, as well as ourselves?"

Captain Wentworth was folding up a letter in great haste, and either could not or would not answer fully.

"Yes," said he, "very true; here we separate, but Harville and I shall soon be after you, that is, Harville, if you are ready, I am in half a minute. I know you will not be sorry to be off. I shall be at your service in half a minute."

Mrs. Croft left them, and Captain Wentworth, having sealed his letter with great rapidity, was indeed ready, and had even a hurried, agitated air, which shewed impatience to be gone. Anne knew not how to understand it. She had the kindest "Good morning, God bless you," from Captain Harville, but from him not a word, nor a look. He had passed out of the room without a look!

She had only time, however, to move closer to the table where he had been writing, when footsteps were heard returning; the door opened; it was himself. He begged their pardon, but he had forgotten his gloves, and instantly crossing the room to the writing table, and standing with his back towards Mrs. Musgrove, he drew out a letter from under the scattered paper, placed it before Anne with eyes of glowing entreaty fixed on her for a moment, and hastily collecting his gloves, was again out of the room, almost before Mrs. Musgrove was aware of his being in it—the work of an instant!

The revolution which one instant had made in Anne, was almost beyond expression. The letter, with a direction hardly legible, to "Miss A. E.—." was evidently the one which he had been folding so hastily. While supposed to be writing only to Captain Benwick, he had been also addressing her! On the contents of that letter depended all which this world could do for her! Any thing was possible, any thing might be defied rather than suspense. Mrs. Musgrove had little arrangements of her own at her own table; to their protection she must trust, and sinking into the chair which he had occupied, succeeding to the very spot where he had leaned and written, her eyes devoured the following words:

"I can listen no longer in silence. I must speak to you by such means as are within my reach. You pierce my soul. I am half agony, half hope. Tell me not that I am too late, that such precious feelings are gone for ever. I offer myself to you again with a heart even more your own, than when you almost broke it eight years and a half ago. Dare not say that man forgets sooner than woman, that his love has an earlier death. I have loved none but you. Unjust I may have been, weak and resentful I have been, but never inconstant. You alone have brought me to Bath. For you alone I think and plan. Have you not seen this? Can you fail to have understood my wishes?—I had not waited even these ten days, could I have read your feelings, as I think you must have penetrated mine. I can hardly write. I am every instant hearing something which overpowers me. You sink your voice, but I can distinguish the tones of that voice, when they would be lost on others. Too good, too excellent creature! You do us justice indeed. You do believe that there is true attachment and constancy among men. Believe it to be most fervent, most undeviating in

"F. W.

"I must go, uncertain of my fate; but I shall return hither, or follow your party, as soon as possible. A word, a look will be enough to decide whether I enter your father's house this evening or never."

Such a letter was not to be soon recovered from. Half an hour's solitude and reflection might have tranquillized her; but the ten minutes only, which now passed before she was interrupted, with all the restraints of her situation, could do nothing towards tranquillity. Every moment rather brought fresh agitation. It was an overpowering happiness. And before she was beyond the first stage of full sensation, Charles, Mary, and Henrietta all came in.

The absolute necessity of seeming like herself produced then an immediate struggle; but after a while she could do no more. She began not to understand a word they said, and was obliged to plead indisposition and excuse herself. They could then see that she looked very ill—were shocked and concerned—and would not stir without her for the world. This was dreadful! Would they only have gone away, and left her in the quiet possession of that room, it would have been her cure; but to have them all standing or waiting around her was distracting, and, in desperation, she said she would go home.

"By all means, my dear," cried Mrs. Musgrove, "go home directly and take care of yourself, that you may be fit for the evening. I wish Sarah was here to doctor you, but I am no doctor myself. Charles, ring and order a chair. She must not walk."

But the chair would never do. Worse than all! To lose the possibility of speaking two words to Captain Wentworth in the course of her quiet, solitary progress up the town (and she felt almost certain of meeting him) could not be borne. The chair was earnestly protested against; and Mrs. Musgrove, who thought only of one sort of illness, having assured herself, with some anxiety, that there had been no fall in the case; that Anne had not, at any time lately, slipped down, and got a blow on her head; that she was perfectly convinced of having had no fall, could part with her cheerfully, and depend on finding her better at night.

Anxious to omit no possible precaution, Anne struggled, and said,

"I am afraid, ma'am, that it is not perfectly understood. Pray be so good as to mention to the other gentlemen that we hope to see your whole party this evening. I am afraid there has been some mistake; and I wish you particularly to assure Captain Harville, and Captain Wentworth, that we hope to see them both."

"Oh! my dear, it is quite understood, I give you my word. Captain Harville has no thought but of going."

"Do you think so? But I am afraid; and I should be so very sorry! Will you promise me to mention it, when you see them again? You will see them both again this morning, I dare say. Do promise me."

"To be sure I will, if you wish it. Charles, if you see Captain Harville any where, remember to give Miss Anne's message. But indeed, my dear, you need not be uneasy. Captain Harville holds himself quite engaged, I'll answer for it; and Captain Wentworth the same, I dare say."

Anne could do no more; but her heart prophesied some mischance, to damp the perfection of her felicity. It could not be very lasting, however. Even if he did not come to Camden-place himself, it would be in her power to send an intelligible sentence by Captain Harville.

Another momentary vexation occurred. Charles, in his real concern and good-nature, would go home with her; there was no preventing him. This was almost cruel! But she could not be long ungrateful; he was sacrificing an engagement at a gun-smith's to be of use to her; and she set off with him, with no feeling but gratitude apparent.

They were in Union-street, when a quicker step behind, a something of familiar sound, gave her two moments preparation for the sight of Captain Wentworth. He joined them; but, as if irresolute whether to join or to pass on, said nothing—only looked. Anne could command herself enough to receive that look, and not repulsively. The cheeks which had been pale now glowed, and the movements which had hesitated were decided. He walked by her side. Presently, struck by a sudden thought, Charles said,

"Captain Wentworth, which way are you going? only to Gay-street, or farther up the town?"

"I hardly know," replied Captain Wentworth, surprised.

"Are you going as high as Belmont? Are you going near Camden-place? Because if you are, I shall have no scruple in asking you to take my place, and give Anne your arm to her father's door. She is rather done for this morning, and must not go so far without help. And I ought to be at that fellow's in the market-place. He promised me the sight of a capital gun he is just going to send off; said he would keep it unpacked to the last possible moment, that I might see it; and if I do not turn back now, I have no chance. By his description, a good deal like the second-sized double-barrel of mine, which you shot with one day, round Winthrop."

There could not be an objection. There could be only a most proper alacrity, a most obliging compliance for public view; and smiles reined in and spirits dancing in private rapture. In half a minute, Charles was at the bottom of Union-street again, and the other two proceeding together; and soon words enough had passed between them to decide their direction towards the comparatively quiet and retired gravel-walk, where the power of conversation would make the present hour a blessing indeed; and prepare it for all the immortality which the happiest recollections of their own future lives could bestow. There they exchanged again those feelings and those promises which had once before seemed to secure every thing, but which had been followed by so many, many years of division and estrangement. There they returned again into the past, more exquisitely happy, perhaps, in their re-union, than when it had been first projected; more tender, more tried, more fixed in a knowledge of each other's character, truth, and attachment; more equal to act, more justified in acting. And there, as they slowly paced the gradual ascent, heedless of every group around them, seeing neither saunter-

425

ing politicians, bustling house-keepers, flirting girls, nor nursery-maids and children, they could indulge in those retrospections and acknowledgments, and especially in those explanations of what had directly preceded the present moment, which were so poignant and so ceaseless in interest. All the little variations of the last week were gone through; and of yesterday and to-day there could scarcely be an end.

She had not mistaken him. Jealousy of Mr. Elliot had been the retarding weight, the doubt, the torment. That had begun to operate in the very hour of first meeting her in Bath; that had returned, after a short suspension, to ruin the concert; and that had influenced him in every thing he had said and done, or omitted to say and do, in the last four-and-twenty hours. It had been gradually yielding to the better hopes which her looks, or words, or actions occasionally encouraged; it had been vanquished at last by those sentiments and those tones which had reached him while she talked with Captain Harville; and under the irresistible governance of which he had seized a sheet of paper, and poured out his feelings.

Of what he had then written, nothing was to be retracted or qualified. He persisted in having loved none but her. She had never been supplanted. He never even believed himself to see her equal. Thus much indeed he was obliged to acknowledge—that he had been constant unconsciously, nay unintentionally; that he had meant to forget her, and believed it to be done. He had imagined himself indifferent, when he had only been angry; and he had been unjust to her merits, because he had been a sufferer from them. Her character was now fixed on his mind as perfection itself, maintaining the loveliest medium of fortitude and gentleness; but he was obliged to acknowledge that only at Uppercross had he learnt to do her justice, and only at Lyme had he begun to understand himself.

At Lyme, he had received lessons of more than one sort. The passing admiration of Mr. Elliot had at least roused him, and the scenes on the Cobb, and at Captain Harville's, had fixed her superiority.

In his preceding attempts to attach himself to Louisa Musgrove (the attempts of angry pride), he protested that he had for ever felt it to be impossible; that he had not cared, could not care for Louisa; though, till that day, till the leisure for reflection which followed it, he had not understood the perfect excellence of the mind with which Louisa's could so ill bear a comparison; or the perfect, unrivalled hold it possessed over his own. There, he had learnt to distinguish between the steadiness of principle and the obstinacy of self-will, between the darings of heedlessness and the resolution of a collected mind. There, he had seen every thing to exalt in his estimation the woman he had lost, and there begun to deplore the pride, the folly, the madness of resentment, which had kept him from trying to regain her when thrown in his way.

From that period his penance had become severe. He had no sooner been free from the horror and remorse attending the first few days of Louisa's accident, no sooner begun to feel himself alive again, than he had begun to feel himself, though alive, not at liberty.

"I found," said he, "that I was considered by Harville an engaged man! That neither Harville nor his wife entertained a doubt of our mutual attachment. I was startled and shocked. To a degree, I could contradict this instantly; but, when I began to reflect that others might have felt the same—her own family, nay, perhaps herself, I was no longer at my own disposal. I was hers in honour if she wished it. I had been unguarded. I had not thought seriously on this subject before. I had not considered that my excessive intimacy must have its danger of ill consequence in many ways; and that I had no right to be trying whether I could attach myself to either of the girls, at the risk of raising even an unpleasant report, were there no other ill effects. I had been grossly wrong, and must abide the consequences."

He found too late, in short, that he had

entangled himself; and that precisely as he became fully satisfied of his not caring for Louisa at all, he must regard himself as bound to her, if her sentiments for him were what the Harvilles supposed. It determined him to leave Lyme, and await her complete recovery elsewhere. He would gladly weaken, by any fair means, whatever feelings or speculations concerning him might exist; and he went, therefore, to his brother's, meaning after a while to return to Kellynch, and act as circumstances might require.

"I was six weeks with Edward," said he, "and saw him happy. I could have no other pleasure. I deserved none. He enquired after you very particularly; asked even if you were personally altered, little suspecting that to my eye you could never alter."

Anne smiled, and let it pass. It was too pleasing a blunder for a reproach. It is something for a woman to be assured, in her eight-and-twentieth year, that she has not lost one charm of earlier youth: but the value of such homage was inexpressibly increased to Anne, by comparing it with former words, and feeling it to be the result, not the cause of a revival of his warm attachment.

He had remained in Shropshire, lamenting the blindness of his own pride, and the blunders of his own calculations, till at once released from Louisa by the astonishing and felicitous intelligence of her engagement with Benwick.

"Here," said he, "ended the worst of my state; for now I could at least put myself in the way of happiness, I could exert myself, I could do something. But to be waiting so long in inaction, and waiting only for evil, had been dreadful. Within the first five minutes I said, 'I will be at Bath on Wednesday,' and I was. Was it unpardonable to think it worth my while to come? and to arrive with some degree of hope? You were single. It was possible that you might retain the feelings of the past, as I did; and one encouragement happened to be mine. I could never doubt that you would be loved and sought by others, but I knew to a certainty that you had refused one man at least, of better pretensions than myself: and I could not help often saying, Was this for me?"

Their first meeting in Milsom-street afforded much to be said, but the concert still more. That evening seemed to be made up of exquisite moments. The moment of her stepping forward in the octagon-room to speak to him, the moment of Mr. Elliot's appearing and tearing her away, and one or two subsequent moments, marked by returning hope or increasing despondence, were dwelt on with energy.

"To see you," cried he, "in the midst of those who could not be my well-wishers, to see your cousin close by you, conversing and smiling, and feel all the horrible eligibilities and proprieties of the match! To consider it as the certain wish of every being who could hope to influence you! Even, if your own feelings were reluctant or indifferent, to consider what powerful supports would be his! Was it not enough to make the fool of me which I appeared? How could I look on without agony? Was not the very sight of the friend who sat behind you, was not the recollection of what had been, the knowledge of her influence, the indelible, immoveable impression of what persuasion had once done—was it not all against me?"

"You should have distinguished," replied Anne. "You should not have suspected me now; the case so different, and my age so different. If I was wrong in yielding to persuasion once, remember that it was to persuasion exerted on the side of safety, not of risk. When I yielded, I thought it was to duty; but no duty could be called in aid here. In marrying a man indifferent to me, all risk would have been incurred, and all duty violated."

"Perhaps I ought to have reasoned thus," he replied, "but I could not. I could not derive benefit from the late knowledge I had acquired of your character. I could not bring it into play: it was overwhelmed, buried, lost in those earlier feelings which I had been smarting under year after year. I could think of you only as one who had yielded, who had given me up, who had been influenced by any one rather than by me. I saw you with the very person who had guided you in that year of misery. I had no reason to believe her of less authority now. The force of habit was to be added."

"I should have thought," said Anne, "that my manner to yourself might have spared you much or all of this."

"No, no! your manner might be only the ease which your engagement to another man would give. I left you in this belief; and yet—I was determined to see you again. My spirits rallied with the morning, and I felt that I had still a motive for remaining here."

At last Anne was at home again, and happier than any one in that house could have conceived. All the surprise and suspense, and every other painful part of the morning dissipated by this conversation, she re-entered the house so happy as to be obliged to find an alloy in some momentary apprehensions of its being impossible to last. An interval of meditation, serious and grateful, was the best corrective of every thing dangerous in such high-wrought felicity; and she went to her room, and grew steadfast and fearless in the thankfulness of her enjoyment.

The evening came, the drawing-rooms were lighted up, the company assembled. It was but a card-party, it was but a mixture of those who had never met before, and those who met too often—a common-place business, too numerous for intimacy, too small for variety; but Anne had never found an evening shorter. Glowing and lovely in sensibility and happiness, and more generally admired than she thought about or cared for, she had cheerful or forbearing feelings for every creature around her. Mr. Elliot was there; she avoided, but she could pity him. The Wallises; she had amusement in understanding them. Lady Dalrymple and Miss Carteret; they would soon be innoxious cousins to her. She cared not for Mrs. Clay, and had nothing to blush for in the public manners of her father and sister. With the Musgroves, there was the happy chat of perfect ease; with Captain Harville, the kind-hearted intercourse of brother and sister; with Lady Russell, attempts at conversation, which a delicious consciousness cut short; with Admiral and Mrs. Croft, every thing of peculiar cordiality and fervent interest, which the same consciousness sought to conceal; and with Captain Wentworth, some moments of communication continually occurring, and always the hope of more, and always the knowledge of his being there!

It was in one of these short meetings, each apparently occupied in admiring a fine display of green-house plants, that she said—

"I have been thinking over the past, and trying impartially to judge of the right and wrong, I mean with regard to myself; and I must believe that I was right, much as I suffered from it, that I was perfectly right in being guided by the friend whom you will love better than you do now. To me, she was in the place of a parent. Do not mistake me, however. I am not saying that she did not err in her advice. It was, perhaps, one of those cases in which advice is good or bad only as the event decides; and for myself, I certainly never should, in any circumstance of tolerable similarity, give such advice. But I mean, that I was right in submitting to her, and that if I had done otherwise, I should have suffered more in continuing the engagement than I did even in giving it up, because I should have suffered in my conscience. I have now, as far as such a sentiment is allowable in human nature, nothing to reproach myself with; and if I mistake not, a strong sense of duty is no bad part of a woman's portion."

He looked at her, looked at Lady Russell, and looking again at her, replied, as if in cool deliberation,

"Not yet. But there are hopes of her being forgiven in time. I trust to being in charity with her soon. But I too have been thinking over the past, and a question has suggested itself, whether there may not have been one person more my enemy even than that lady? My own self. Tell me if, when I returned to

England in the year eight, with a few thousand pounds, and was posted into the Laconia, if I had then written to you, would you have answered my letter? would you, in short, have renewed the engagement then?"

"Would I!" was all her answer; but the accent was decisive enough.

"Good God!" he cried, "you would! It is not that I did not think of it, or desire it, as what could alone crown all my other success. But I was proud, too proud to ask again. I did not understand you. I shut my eyes, and would not understand you, or do you justice. This is a recollection which ought to make me forgive every one sooner than myself. Six years of separation and suffering might have been spared. It is a sort of pain, too, which is new to me. I have been used to the gratification of believing myself to earn every blessing that I enjoyed. I have valued myself on honourable toils and just rewards. Like other great men under reverses," he added with a smile, "I must endeavour to subdue my mind to my fortune. I must learn to brook being happier than I deserve."

Chapter twenty-four

Who can be in doubt of what followed? When any two young people take it into their heads to marry, they are pretty sure by perseverance to carry their point, be they ever so poor, or ever so imprudent, or ever so little likely to be necessary to each other's ultimate comfort. This may be bad morality to conclude with, but I believe it to be truth; and if such parties succeed, how should a Captain Wentworth and an Anne Elliot, with the advantage of maturity of mind, consciousness of right, and one independent fortune between them, fail of bearing down every opposition? They might in fact have borne down a great deal more than they met with, for there was little to distress them beyond the want of graciousness and warmth. Sir Walter made no objection, and Elizabeth did nothing worse than look cold and unconcerned. Captain Wentworth, with

five-and-twenty thousand pounds, and as high in his profession as merit and activity could place him, was no longer nobody. He was now esteemed quite worthy to address the daughter of a foolish spendthrift baronet, who had not had principle or sense enough to maintain himself in the situation in which Providence had placed him, and who could give his daughter at present but a small part of the share of ten thousand pounds which must be hers hereafter.

Sir Walter indeed, though he had no affection for Anne, and no vanity flattered, to make him really happy on the occasion, was very far from thinking it a bad match for her. On the contrary, when he saw more of Captain Wentworth, saw him repeatedly by daylight and eyed him well, he was very much struck by his personal claims, and felt that his superiority of appearance might be not unfairly balanced against her superiority of rank; and all this, assisted by his well-sounding name, enabled Sir Walter at last to prepare his pen with a very good grace for the insertion of the marriage in the volume of honour.

The only one among them, whose opposition of feeling could excite any serious anxiety, was Lady Russell. Anne knew that Lady Russell must be suffering some pain in understanding and relinquishing Mr. Elliot, and be making some struggles to become truly acquainted with, and do justice to Captain Wentworth. This however was what Lady Russell had now to do. She must learn to feel that she had been mistaken with regard to both; that she had been unfairly influenced by appearances in each; that because Captain Wentworth's manners had not suited her own ideas, she had been too quick in suspecting them to indicate a character of dangerous impetuosity; and that because Mr. Elliot's manners had precisely pleased her in their propriety and correctness, their general politeness and suavity, she had been too quick in receiving them as the certain result of the most correct opinions and well regulated mind. There was nothing less for Lady Russell to do, than to admit that she had been pretty completely wrong, and to take up a new set of opinions and of hopes.

There is a quickness of perception in some, a nicety in the discernment of character, a natural penetration, in short, which no experience in others can equal, and Lady Russell had been less gifted in this part of understanding than her young friend. But she was a very good woman, and if her second object was to be sensible and well-judging, her first was to see Anne happy. She loved Anne better than she loved her own abilities; and when the awkwardness of the beginning was over, found little hardship in attaching herself as a mother to the man who was securing the happiness of her other child.

Of all the family, Mary was probably the one most immediately gratified by the circumstance. It was creditable to have a sister married, and she might flatter herself with having been greatly instrumental to the connexion, by keeping Anne with her in the autumn; and as her own sister must be better than her husband's sisters, it was very agreeable that Captain Wentworth should be a richer man than either Captain Benwick or Charles Hayter. She had something to suffer perhaps when they came into contact again, in seeing Anne restored to the rights of seniority, and the mistress of a very pretty landaulette; but she had a future to look forward to, of powerful consolation. Anne had no Uppercross-hall before her, no landed estate, no headship of a family; and if they could but keep Captain Wentworth from being made a baronet, she would not change situations with Anne.

It would be well for the eldest sister if she were equally satisfied with her situation, for a change is not very probable there. She had soon the mortification of seeing Mr. Elliot withdraw; and no one of proper condition has since presented himself to raise even the unfounded hopes which sunk with him.

The news of his cousin Anne's engagement burst on Mr. Elliot most unexpectedly. It deranged his best plan of domestic happiness, his best hope of keeping Sir Walter single by the watchfulness which a son-in-law's rights would have given. But, though discomfited and disappointed, he could still do something for his own interest and his own enjoyment. He soon quitted Bath; and on Mrs. Clay's quitting it likewise soon afterwards, and being next heard of as established under his protection in London, it was evident how double a game he had been playing, and how determined he was to save himself from being cut out by one artful woman, at least.

Mrs. Clay's affections had overpowered her interest, and she had sacrificed, for the young man's sake, the possibility of scheming longer for Sir Walter. She has abilities, however, as well as affections; and it is now a doubtful point whether his cunning, or hers, may finally carry the day; whether, after preventing her from being the wife of Sir Walter, he may not be wheedled and caressed at last into making her the wife of Sir William.

It cannot be doubted that Sir Walter and Elizabeth were shocked and mortified by the loss of their companion, and the discovery of their deception in her. They had their great cousins, to be sure, to resort to for comfort; but they must long feel that to flatter and follow others, without being flattered and followed in turn, is but a state of half enjoyment.

Anne, satisfied at a very early period of Lady Russell's meaning to love Captain Wentworth as she ought, had no other alloy to the happiness of her prospects than what arose from the consciousness of having no relations to bestow on him which a man of sense could value. There she felt her own inferiority keenly. The disproportion in their fortune was nothing; it did not give her a moment's regret; but to have no family to receive and estimate him properly; nothing of respectability, of harmony, of good-will to offer in return for all the worth and all the prompt welcome which met her in his brothers and sisters, was a source of as lively pain as her mind could well be sensible of, under circumstances of otherwise strong felicity. She had but two friends in the world to add to his list, Lady Russell and Mrs. Smith. To those, however, he was very well disposed to attach himself. Lady Russell, in spite of all her former transgressions, he could now value from his heart. While he was not obliged to say that he believed her to have been right in originally dividing them, he was ready to say almost every thing else in her favour; and as for Mrs. Smith, she had claims of various kinds to recommend her quickly and permanently.

Her recent good offices by Anne had been enough in themselves; and their marriage, instead of depriving her of one friend, secured her two. She was their earliest visitor in their settled life; and Captain Wentworth, by putting her in the way of recovering her husband's property in the West Indies; by writing for her, acting for her, and seeing her through all the petty difficulties of the case, with the activity and exertion of a fearless man and a determined friend, fully requited the services which she had rendered, or ever meant to render, to his wife.

Mrs. Smith's enjoyments were not spoiled by this improvement of income, with some improvement of health, and the acquisition of such friends to be often with, for her cheerfulness and mental alacrity did not fail her; and while these prime supplies of good remained, she might have bid defiance even to greater accessions of worldly prosperity. She might have been absolutely rich and perfectly healthy, and yet be happy. Her spring of felicity was in the glow of her spirits, as her friend Anne's was in the warmth of her heart. Anne was tenderness itself, and she had the full worth of it in Captain Wentworth's affection. His profession was all that could ever make her friends wish that tenderness less; the dread of a future war all that could dim her sunshine. She gloried in being a sailor's wife, but she must pay the tax of quick alarm for belonging to that profession which is, if possible, more distinguished in its domestic virtues than in its national importance.

The Constitution Revisited

Scott Buchanan

Editor's Introduction

Since the time of Hobbes, Locke, and—somewhat later—Rousseau, and as set forth also by certain ancient writers, notably Aristotle, it has come to be accepted that any human community which is regarded as a state must be so constituted by its members. Today there is no such community anywhere in the world—large or small, absolutist or democratic, modern or traditional—that does not have a constitution, or claim to have one, from which it derives its political being. This means different things, of course, in different cases. In some, it provides nothing more (or less) than a nominal sanction for those already in command to rule in whatever way they please. In others, the constitution really creates and regulates the government, with the result that an order is created in which, as Aristotle says, "the citizens rule and are ruled in turn." But in every instance there is at least the implication of restraints upon governmental acts—stated limits within which they may be exercised, given principles from which they are said to proceed, fixed forms for them to follow, and so forth.

That constitutions may have a positive aspect, apart from such restraints or in true fulfillment of them, is not so widely recognized. Even in the United States, where constitutionalism as an idea is firmly established and where the Constitution itself is venerated, there is a tendency to regard constitutional provisions as the source of a structure that, when created, serves only as a kind of theatre within which the real business of government, the true exercise of power, is carried on. The assumption is that this has its own life, that it reflects and accommodates competing interests or serves common needs through a "politics" that is remote from constitutional provisions except as these provide limits to legislation or its enforcement, and save also as, on occasion, the courts may in their name declare laws or administration measures to be prohibited. How a constitution functions in this manner is suggested by the article on *The Federalist* that appears elsewhere in this volume.

But a constitution may provide something more than limits and conditions of government. Where it reflects a real intention on the part of the community to govern itself, through whatever forms of representation, it may assist that intention to be realized, and may even become the embodiment of its realization, in profound and pervasive ways. Or at least that is the point made by Scott Buchanan in the following essay, which maintains that the Constitution of the United States is designed to work, and at its best does work, to further the rational processes that operate whenever self-government is successfully practiced.

This contention, which in effect retraces the famous argument of Plato's *Republic,* and instead of finding the state in man, finds man in the state, reflects a sober reading of one of America's Founding Fathers, Alexander Hamilton, who in the first of the Federalist papers wrote that "it seems to have been reserved to the people of this country, by their conduct and example, to decide the important question, whether societies of men are really capable or not of establishing good government from reflection and choice, or whether they are forever destined to depend for their political constitutions on accident and force." What Hamilton is taken to have implied is that the Constitution of the United States contains the answer to this question insofar as it provides machinery for the reflection and choice upon which good government is said to depend. The Constitution is thus seen as a kind of riddle which reveals its meaning only when it is used for the purposes it was designed to achieve, and which remains mysterious—a relic, a piety, perhaps simply a warning—when it is not so used.

Such a view assumes the possibility of a different sort of politics from the one that is commonly thought to prevail—the one best indicated, perhaps, by the title of a celebrated book on the subject by Harold Lasswell called *Politics: Who Gets What, When, How,* which appeared many years ago. That this sort of politics exists cannot be doubted. But there can also be a politics of the sort that Robert M. Hutchins had in mind when he wrote once that "politics . . . is the science of the common good." By the common good Mr. Hutchins meant, as he went on to say, "a good that accrues to every member of the community because he belongs to it; he would not have it if he did not belong to it." And Mr. Hutchins added, "The task of politics is to define the common good and to organize the community to achieve it." It is this sort of politics, the essay that follows seems to say, that the Constitution makes possible, though it does not guarantee their realization.

Scott Buchanan (1895–1968), whose *Poetry and Mathematics* appeared in last year's *Great Ideas Today,* was educated at Amherst and as a Rhodes scholar at Oxford before going on to teach philosophy at Harvard, the College of the City of New York, and the University of Virginia. From 1937 to 1947 he was dean of St. John's College, Annapolis, where he was the creative spirit of the Great Books Program. Subsequently he became interested in the speculative aspects of government and wrote a book, *Essay in Politics* (1953), concerned with what he thought of as the withering of consent that had overtaken republican institutions since the end of the eighteenth century. At the time of his death he was a Fellow of the Center for the Study of Democratic Institutions in Santa Barbara, California, where this essay was written. It is reprinted with the Center's kind permission.

The Constitution Revisited

The Preamble

The words and phrases of the Preamble to the Constitution are not accidents, and the statement that results from their composition is not a work of idle rhetoric or propaganda. "We the People . . . do ordain and establish this Constitution" condenses into a few words the essence of the revolution that gave birth to the United States of America; it confirms the principle of self-government, that governments derive their just powers from the consent of the governed. It was a resolution written in the eighteenth century, but it was the announcement of a discovery of a principle that had always been true. Kings as well as the newly made citizens had known the deep practical truth of the principle, no matter how far they may have been from conformity to it.

Something similar can be said about the other phrases in the Preamble. They are authentic in the language of the eighteenth century, but they are stating truths that had been hard-won in previous revolutions and had been confirmed in long experience of the vicissitudes of government. They are variations of the traditional conditions for the existence of a political community. Through long usage they had been formulated in the brief abstract language of the common good as the purpose of all government: order, justice, peace, and freedom. The authors of the Constitution knew that they were building on the foundation stones of a long tradition. When they added "com-

mon defence" and "general welfare," they were merely adding some implications of the traditional formula, and they could have added others, as if to say "and so forth."

It is fashionable today to read these phrases as the statement of ideals or values, and then to think of other possible purposes and "goods" that ought to be added and thus constitutionalized. For example, in some more recently written constitutions world peace or a guaranteed income for each citizen has been added. But it would seem that such additions, though worthy of common concern, are subsumable under the terms of the traditional constitutional formula. They specify things that would be brought about if the laws and politics of the time conformed to the principles of justice, freedom, peace, and order.

It would take a long and complicated demonstration to show that the traditional formula is both necessary and sufficient as the statement of our highest political purpose. Part of such a demonstration would consist in showing that the rest of the Constitution supplies the specific means that the grand purpose implies. Another part would try to show that any needed amendment or improvement of the Constitution is authorized by the preambulatory declaration. It may be recalled that some years ago there was an attempt to conduct a great debate about our national goals. It is noteworthy that none of the contributions to that discussion reached any novel purposes that transcend the statement of the Preamble; most of them fell far below. This is not to say that the Preamble contains all the possibilities that will ever be discovered in the common good; it is to say that novel proposals should be tested to see if they are equal to or more universal or more profound than those we have inherited.

The logic of the common good and its formulations is worthy of note. Its terms—justice, peace, freedom, order—are mutually implied. Each one requires the others if it is to be realized. None can be suppressed or ignored if the others are to be saved. It is therefore not possible to treat them as alternative ideals or values to be balanced or bargained away. There may be times when one of them is deficiently cultivated or realized, or it may be that a new problem may throw one into a higher immediate priority, but both in formal thought and in the logic of events the realization of one entails the realization of all the others. It has been guessed that the cold war is a rivalry based on the apparent fact that the Russians are devoting themselves to social justice and that the United States is devoting itself to freedom. As the cold war wears on, it appears that both countries are bringing these concerns into balance; the Russians are discovering the claims of freedom and we are discovering new depths in our failures of justice. And this is happening not merely because of the pressures of competition and propaganda. It is a part of justice to recognize the freedom of men and it is a part of freedom to will that justice is done.

It may be true that the Preamble would be more effective pedagogically if it spelled out some of its implications so that the officers of government as well as the citizens would be continually reminded of the high functions of the laws they make and use. But by the same token a citizenry well educated in the law might better read and understand the formula in its present elegant expression and in its perennial truth. The Preamble may not be the best possible statement of American goals, but its brevity and comprehension stand as a challenge and a warning to those who are ambitious to improve it. For those who find it formal and cold, it may be noted that the general welfare clause has enabled and continues to enable an infusion of charity into the community's concern for the good of its members.

Another clause in the Preamble, "in order to form a more perfect union," had a very special meaning when the Constitution was drafted. The Articles of Confederation had not provided the unity that the new nation needed. The need had become pressing for the purpose of ordering the commerce of the thirteen colonies. When the drafters met, they were known as a committee of commercial gentlemen. But it took little deliberation for them to discover that unity or union had more extensive implications. It contained the need for a basic political order. Meeting this need raised the question of federation to the level of primary attention. The War of Independence had led the colonies to recognize themselves as sovereign states, and this recognition was so vivid that they feared that submission to even a federal union would result in the loss of the independence for which they had fought. Thus, the very purpose of the Constitutional Convention seemed to threaten the thirteen common goods of the constituent parties, and the principle that had gone by various names, usually called states rights, but now amplified and called pluralism, was uncovered. The tension between this principle and the principle of union made the politics of the young republic and came to a crucial climax in the Civil War. The tension has risen and fallen since then, because resort to arms was not a resolution but rather a hardening of the convictions on both sides. Because modern political science and the behavioral sciences have been pursuing politics by other means, the federal problem has come to be thought of, in diminished terms, as a need to preserve what is called our pluralistic society, which calls forth only a weak, pragmatic defense of the federal system.

The revival of politics depends to a great extent on finding both the theoretical and the practical meaning of the purpose expressed in the clause "in order to form a more perfect union." The theoretical issues can be seen in recognizing that there is a necessary counterpart of *e pluribus unum* in a reversal of the phrase, something like *ex uno plures*. We cannot establish a "many" without laying the basis for founding a unity, and this is a continual process. In a living society the finding of the unions and of the relevant "manys" is the life of politics. It comes down to Lincoln's principle that what needs to be done but cannot be done by the individual or the parts by themselves can and must be done by the government as a whole. Finding the units of government and legitimizing their respective functions is the main business of government. And this is begun and continues by making and remaking of the Constitution.

The recent use by the Supreme Court of the Fourteenth Amendment to give uniformity to the provisions of the Civil Rights Act, the reapportionment of electoral districts, and the procedural codes for criminal trials in the states has the appearance of imposed unity, but it has not yet been stated that these will lay the ground for an increased variability in these matters. New problems have been posed by these judgments of the Court, and they will blossom in many diverse solutions of local problems. The codification of law by the Romans forced local invention and variety of interpretation. Thus, also, new achievements in legal justice provide new liberties and rights. The perfection of union is a permanent dedication of the Constitution to the process of political progress as history poses new questions for political solution. This suggests the evolutionary order over which the Constitution presides. Order as an imperative of the common good implies the continual ordering of the parts of the community, the perennial dividing and ruling that government requires.

So much for the Preamble. Much, much more could be said about it as laying the foundation for the complicated provisions of the Constitution. The comments I have chosen will serve as an introduction to the discussion of two principles that pervade these provisions, the principle of representation and the principle of federation.

Representation and federation

Representation of one kind or another has always been a necessary and pervasive principle of government. In most general terms it is the solution of the many diverse problems of the political union; it is always the guide in the process of making a more perfect union. Thus in the direct democracy of the Greek city state it was necessary to elect officers to carry out the decisions of the assembled citizens. Even in Rousseau's radical proposals for the expression of the general will without intermediaries there had to be magistrates who would think and act as agents of the people. But representation in the experience of less democratic regimes had been a more complicated and subtle device. The many things that have to be done for the people, but that cannot be done by merely individual effort, require many different kinds of representation, and some of them involve functions that are not adequately described as carrying out orders or executing the will of the people. At a crucial stage in the development of parliamentary institutions Edmund Burke seemed to invert the notion of representation when he pointed out that his duty as a member of parliament was to ignore the literal expressions of the will of the electorate in order to discover his and their responsibilities to the common good. In fact he was not denying his responsibility to his constituency, but rather demonstrating his and their common, underlying search for the general good of the community.

Representation has its roots in the distinguishable powers of the individual human being, most particularly in what is known as the reflective power of reason. We sense, think, feel, and will, but we also know that we do these things. At first, in children and adolescents, this knowledge can be confused and confusing. It takes years of sophistication and education to bring it to focus and articulation in the mature adult. When it reaches a kind of stability and clarity, it becomes the means by which the individual teaches himself, and the base from which all the rational powers realize themselves in the playing of games, in customs and rituals, in dramas, in institutions, and, of course, in politics.

As a corollary, the arts, the institutions, and the organization of society provide the individual with the occasions for observation of himself and others in which roles are imitated, propagated, and invented, and are internalized in habits. The sociologists have recently abstracted role-playing for the understanding and ordering of all social behavior. Such theories are obviously borrowed from two familiar institutions, the theatre and the political state, both of which in their respective styles enable men to see themselves as others see them—that is, to represent themselves to themselves.

When a man becomes an actor, the playwright gives him a role in speech and in action. The actor has to learn his part and to make it his second, or third, nature. His performance holds a mirror up to himself and other men; he holds a mirror up to society and re-presents it. Of course, all the fine arts partake in this representative function, and they, including the theatre, are subject to the familiar criticism of simply representative art. But they are highly selective in what they represent and their projections are full of imaginative extensions and distortions; and as they distort what they represent, they also transform it.

In the sociological theory based on role-playing the long history of social, economic, and political institutions appears as the interaction between dramatic models and individuals and groups. The family, the market, and government are continually making

and re-making roles for individuals to play. Before the young take on the stations and duties of adult life, they play roles in both formal and informal education and thus acquire the habits on the basis of which they graduate and are initiated into the responsibilities of adult life. If this education is truly liberal and has awakened the intellect to its many dimensions of sophistication and insight, adult life will retain the capacity of playing roles, but it will also include some of the detachment that will enable it to invent alternative roles and therefore to shift roles easily and freely. Since the liberal arts deal in symbols and universal ideas, the playwright in every man not only will reflect these separate roles but will reach theories and make rules for action. The exercise of the liberal arts will transcend the merely dramatic and find laws of society, and even of natural objects.

Dramaturgy and government may seem to be pretty distant analogues of one another, and the reduction of political representation to play-acting would seem to be a satirical trick. But if the liberal artistry of the playwright is taken into account, it is not too difficult to see a constitution and its attendant laws as a plot writ large. It is possible to see a benevolent despot or a fanatical dictator as the playwright and director of a great drama; we have in fact seen such spectacles in our time. It is possible to see a constitutional monarch as the protagonist in a living drama; historians have often used this dramatic machinery to give force to their narratives. John Stuart Mill, though he does not use dramatic terms, shows how these forms of government have fitted the stages of development in historic or backward societies; he seems to say that these forms fit not only because they adapt themselves to the respective conditions of men but because they also have led to more adequate forms of self-government.

The dramatic analogy would seem to get confused and to break down as democracy develops, for the citizen is not only an actor playing a role but also playwright and director as he is elected or appointed to public office. It would seem that the political life of the community as a whole becomes the improvisation of many author-actors. On second thought, however, this means that the drama has become genuine politics under a developing constitution, and confusion is avoidable if the citizen-actors understand their parts in the thickening plot, in other words their offices and their duties.

I have taken this detour into dramaturgy in order to suggest that the reduction of the notion of representation to a kind of agency, according to which the representative has orders from his constituency which he is obligated to carry out, is a misleading analogy. Representation has many dimensions, and there have been other well-known analogies that reveal them. Plato's laborious roster of the human arts under the master art of government is a classic example, one that we should be reminded of as we try now to see technology redistributing men and work and roles under our Constitution. Likewise, the division of society into classes, and their varying relations to the class of classes, the body politic, has been a perennial reminder of the never-ending problem of representation. As we approach what we like to call the classless society, we ironically discover groups and interests in conflict and requiring decision-makers to resolve the conflicts.

While all these analogies and more that might be adduced warn of the danger of oversimplifying the device of representation, they have recently in the hands of the sociologist tended to displace the political problem that they were originally intended to solve, or at least clarify. Since they are not mere fantasies but describe real political problems, at least partially, and seem amenable to empirical verification and even measurement, they have become the favored materials in political science. But it should not be forgotten that they are analogies and therefore somewhat risky aids to political thought, realistic though they may be. They may be even more risky in the practice of politics since they seem to legitimate many forms of political corruption.

So far, representation has been shown to be the extension of that reflective power of the human mind to know itself, to know itself not merely in its individual mode but also in its articulation with other minds. Society knows itself in its representatives. But political representation proper has another intention. Society by nature wishes to know its goals, its ends, its goods, its common good. Sociology tends to show only the apparent goods, what men think they want. Liberal politics used to be concerned that the representative, the politician, be responsive and responsible to public opinion, but it was also concerned that he should be a statesman too, who would practice the political arts in order to discover the real common good and to make not only himself but also his constituency responsible to that. Politics would then be not mere playing a role in a theatrical representation; it would involve both a practical and a speculative dialectic, as in a Platonic dialogue, to expose sophistry and special interest, to penetrate private and public opinion, to expose the impostorship of group power and interest, and to discover the real common good in the process. This process was not conceived as a pleasant ballet of pure spirits but rather as the most difficult and energetic effort of men of good-will to raise themselves together to the level of political intelligence. As the founding fathers said, if men were angels they would need no government, and if they were beasts, they could not attain it. Being men who could learn, they might achieve it through discipline.

So, in this most difficult of enterprises, the roles that men play must be turned into learning disciplines; there must be a curriculum, and this is supplied by a constitution and laws. A citizen in a self-governing society is enrolled in that school; his rights and duties launch him on a course of life-long learning. But a representative by election or by appointment must both learn and teach. The great comprehensive assignment is to learn and relearn the common good and through the laws to teach it to succeeding generations of citizens.

If we consider the learning that goes on in the daily life of the citizen under the common law, it seems that this learning is concerned chiefly with men's private affairs, but that because of the continual process of development in common law which expands it into the field of public law the individual discovers his public life as a citizen. If, for example, one gives the First Amendment of the Constitution a positive reading, it provides the citizen with the institutional means by which self-government can be generated and continually improved. However, these First Amendment institutions—free speech as practiced in the press, in assemblies, in education, and now in radio and television —are preparatory and subsidiary to the great institutions of public government which draw all roles, all classes, all groups, all arts, all interests together and articulate them for the effective discharge of the citizen's responsibility for justice and the other goods that are common in the community. The Constitution of the United States and the laws penetrate the body politic, give it intelligible form and viability. Through them the government itself is the representative of the people.

In a representative government, constitution is a continual process. On the elementary level it makes citizens out of natural persons. The process is not merely nominal; the citizen is an elementary officer, an epitome of the reflexive relation of self-government. This means that he has a duty and a right to judge his own concerns, his acts and their effects, as they bear on the common good. If they entail the common acts of the community, he again has the duty and right to contribute to the common deliberation by which the acts of the community are decided. Common deliberation, or mutual persuasion, happens on all levels of society, and the common judgments to which it

leads result in agreements, promises, rules, roles to be played, the learning of the useful and liberal arts, and the organization of institutions. On all these levels there are imitations of the offices, the laws, and the constitution of the strictly political government. It is from this political paradigm, which penetrates the whole society, that the preceding analogies derive their plausibility. And to this paradigm—the constitution, the laws, and the offices—the analogues should contribute their meanings.

As political science and philosophy are architectonic to all the social sciences, so is the Constitution architectonic to all subordinate institutions. It names and defines the offices of government and then establishes the procedures by which the officers make, administer, and adjudicate the laws. Although a citizen is already an officer by virtue of the revolutionary transformations of the eighteenth century, his rights and duties have further constitutional implications. He may be elected or appointed to public office, and he undergoes a transformation; or perhaps a stronger word should be used: he is transfigured. Grover Cleveland's aphorism, "public office is a public trust," underlines the transformation. The officer represents the interests of his constituency, but with a difference. He must revise the simple notion of a mandate, or of acting as an agency, so that his essential duty is to make, administer, and judge the laws that serve the common good. He must see the interests and needs of his clients under the aspect of the common good. Justice must be done, freedom extended, peace kept, and order discovered. He must insure the legitimation of power throughout the community. He must always understand that it is through this kind of representation that the citizen participates in self-government.

All of this may seem to be a highly artificial, purist, or idealistic interpretation of constitutional government. But two considerations should be kept in mind. The first of these is the distinction between private and public law. Private law developed its rules primarily in the courts of common law, where the interests and needs of individuals were adjudicated by adversary proceedings. In this setting the lawyers are said to "represent" their clients, and the full power of their pleadings is devoted to the separate interests of their respective clients. It is only the judicial process of the court that reaches anything like the transformation of the case into a general rule of law. But public law under the Constitution is different. It has been invented and supported to meet the need discovered in common law for a different view of society, one that perceives it as continually searching for a more perfect union, a social contract, a super-personal instrument for dealing with crime, a developing general welfare, and a social security— all these being understood as the conditions for its existence.

The second consideration is that the invention of institutions able to fulfill such conditions is rooted in the natural power of the human mind to know its natural social processes. Even when we fail to realize these ends and to provide the proper means, we need the assurance that they are possible of attainment, and that they are in part, at least, continually achieved. The Constitution provides us with the machinery of laws and representative offices which assures us as a people that we can do what we ought to will.

All constitutions break down the whole governmental institution into parts with specific limited powers, but the Constitution of the United States is well known throughout the world for its unusually drastic separation of powers. Although it establishes a national unitary government, it follows Montesquieu in applying the federal principle throughout the structure. Historically this was easily accomplished because the formulation was accepted when many new colonies were jealous of their new independence. They persuaded each other to make a more perfect union on condition that they retain many of their original powers. The language of the Tenth Amendment seems to express a resolve that each new proposal for the delegation of powers to the central government would be scrutinized before it was made. This is usually thought to have reflected the fear of centralized power, a fear that was inherited from the European experience of monarchical imperialism. But there seem to be still other more philosophical reasons which are derived from the application of the principle of the division of labor in economics and psychology.

Adam Smith's argument for the division of labor was not new; it had been made by Plato and often repeated. It claimed that both productivity and skill were progressively enhanced when the product was distinguished sharply from others and the respective skills in production were separately cultivated. It has also been argued that human freedom is increased when the various specializations of human activities are multiplied. We have cause to wonder about where the argument leads since Frederick Taylor applied engineering analysis and broke down work into hand and eye movements and perhaps unknowingly ground down jobs to operations that automatic machines can do better. Freedom in work may result in freedom from work.

But short of the extremes to which the argument leads there seems to be a stage of specialization that fits the human condition. Human beings suffer frustration when they try to do everything at once. Special attention to the product and the operations that its production requires does develop the proper art, and its practice establishes relevant habits and skills. It is an easy inference from this that the practice of an art is the realization of distinguishable natural human powers. And the argument from the arts applies to the understanding and discipline of human conduct in general. It also applies to the art of government. The division of the powers in the Constitution fits and corresponds to the powers of the human being.

To be sure, this view of government is at present under heavy sceptical criticism: The division of powers in the great institutions of government, legislative, executive, and judicial, is held to be too rationalistic; the actual conduct of government does not and cannot respect the distinctions; the living Constitution upon which our political life depends is quite a different thing from the formal written document, and we pay sentimental homage to a myth, while we follow custom and improvise an American way of life in our exploitation of persons and institutions. But these things mean only that we choose not to use all of our powers of intelligence, particularly the higher powers that the Constitution invites us to use. The point can be put crudely and comprehensively by saying that we honor and cultivate the powers of the human mind, even the rational powers, when they are engaged in the invention and tending of the technical processes, while we allow similar powers to wither when they are engaged in the making and tending of the laws.

The reason which the Constitution distinguishes and allocates to the great divisions of government is practical reason. It has some important similarities to theoretical or speculative reason; likewise it is implicated in modern science and technology, which combine the theoretical and the practical. But the aim of practical reason is different from the aims of theory and science, and its criteria of rigor and validity are different. It necessarily aims at the good, and cannot escape questions of value. Although it needs to know how events take place and must take account of causes, it is directly concerned with the ordering of means and ends, with final causes. It has many subject-matters. It deals with human beings, more particularly with individual human beings in ethics and rational psychology, but perhaps its noblest science is politics, which deals with human associations and where the ends are common goods and the means are the rules and the laws of organizations, including the state.

The classical definition of law sets up in most brief and elegant form the field within which practical reason operates as political reason: Law is a rule of reason propagated by an authority and directed to the common good. Our Constitution is such a law or body of laws. "We the people" are the authority that propagates the Constitution, a master law which in turn establishes other authorities or offices which in turn propagate other laws. Following Locke and Montesquieu, the Constitution distinguishes three great offices, powers, or functions: the legislature, the executive, and the judiciary; and to them are assigned respectively three uses of practical reason: the making of laws, the executing or administration of laws, and the adjudication of laws. Furthermore, the Constitution not only divides these functions but also separates them by making the institutions equal and independent. They are, as it were, insulated from one another, on the ground, I am claiming, that their confusion would frustrate their efficient service to the various ends of the common good—not only freedom, as Montesquieu argues, but also justice, order, and peace.

The legislature

For some reason that I am not able to discover, there are no studies of the legislative process comparable with the many studies that have been made of the judicial process. This apparent neglect may have something to do with the current decay and denigration of legislatures all over the world. It would seem that the disappearance of legislatures or the forfeiture of their functions to other branches of government would be a most fateful development. Yet the present tendency in that direction is commonly viewed without alarm, and it seems that it has been observed and condoned for a long time. John Stuart Mill in his *Representative Government** says that no one should expect legislatures to make laws. They should debate issues and inform the public, but the actual making of laws should be assigned to small legislative commissions which would be competent to carry out such a difficult

---

* *GBWW*, Vol. 43, pp. 327–442.

task. This suggests the American solution, which is for Congress to give the major and essential tasks to Congressional committees, who then report out bills for final action.

There can be no doubt of the difficulty and importance of the process. It cannot be concealed or dismissed by saying that it is the function of the legislator to express the will of the people. The reverence given to the heroic law-givers of the past, Moses, Lycurgus, Solon, and the lyrical outburst of Rousseau when he thinks of the miracle of law-making in a self-governing society, are at least reminders that the legislative process needs special attention. The following paragraphs could be another modest reminder, a suggestion of questions that ought to be answered in any adequate study.

To begin with, it should be recalled that laws have other origins than from legislatures, namely courts of common law, and that statutes are often extensions of those laws. But common law courts do not primarily aim at legislation; the laws that result are by-products of the judicial process. Statutes are supposed to result from the deliberations and mutual persuasions of legislative bodies, and the formal procedures are supposed to consummate the massive political processes of the community. The question, then, is what are the intentions and the chosen means by which such a remarkable result, law, is achieved.

On first thought, since law is a rule of reason, it would seem that some kind of induction is involved in law-making, some kind of generalization from concrete facts, events, or actions that need further understanding and direction. This clue could lead to a re-examination of the rules of induction for science, as they have been formulated by John Stuart Mill, David Hume, and Francis Bacon. It is not appropriate here to follow the clue out, since the thorny problem of scientific induction is not my concern, but it may be worth noting that these three philosophers had other careers that immersed them in disciplines more closely related to law and politics than to empirical science. Mill was a civil servant, Hume was an historian, and Bacon was a judge. There may be an important truth in the witticism that Francis Bacon thought about science as a Lord Chancellor; similar comments would be applicable to the other two. Bacon and Mill made observations that have puzzled their followers in the criticism of scientific method. Bacon said that in the observation of facts the form or law of facts leaps to the eye. Mill asked a question that he never answered: why is it that the great discoveries in science are generalizations based on one single observation?

All three men seem to agree implicitly with a later distinction of stages in the process of induction: primary and secondary inductions. They seem to be admitting that the rules they formulated were secondary to an initial intuitive induction such as Aristotle described in a simile. Aristotle saw facts as slippery hard-to-catch data fleeing like a retreating army. The army rallies and falls into order when one soldier turns and takes a stand on a point of vantage, a hypothesis, upon which his fellow-soldiers form ranks. These puzzling remarks do not provide an analytical solution of the problem of induction, but they suggest a crucial stage in law-making.

A law-maker is faced with a mass of slippery, hard-to-catch information, pressures, and troubles that threaten order in a society. He seeks a strategy and a rule that will reduce the chaos to order. He with his legislative colleagues seeks further information and opinion. At some point in the deliberation a legal hypothesis leaps to his eye. He takes a stand and proceeds to persuade his colleagues. His insight may come by way of analogies with other laws, to which he turns as lawyers do in their court pleadings. The process may have started outside the legislative chamber and it may involve hearings of lobbies by one or more committees. Trial drafts are made and amendments considered. The bill may be voted down and re-studied for further action. It may be shelved for later consideration.

We have here only a rough description of a very complicated process, but one feature of it seems to be crucial. That is the first grasp of the legal hypothesis, which corresponds to, if it is not identical with, Aristotle's intuitive induction. Without this there is no deliberation, no persuasion, no vote. (The political computer has no program.) Of course, the legal intuitive induction happens in a context—complaints by citizens, pleadings by lobbies, and the other varieties of persuasions, more or less reasonable. But the crucial elements of the context are the body of other law already passed and operating, and the demands of the common good. These produce something like a conversion in the representative law-maker. Because of the exigencies of election campaigns, the representative starts his career in the role of an agent of his constituency, but he realizes as he deliberates on prospective laws that his assignment is to translate the conflict and strife of citizens into a rule of reason for the common good. His intuitive induction—the generalization of the information—is demanded, but it is also helped by the imperative to do justice, make order under freedom, and restore peace to the community. His agency and his insight are like those of a judge. He must see the justice and injustice in the complex situation and find the law that will discharge the community's responsibility, not only in the instant case but for all similar cases.

This means that a legal hypothesis is not merely a generalization from facts and verifiable by facts; it must meet additional criteria. If it is to become a law, it must transcend the welter of facts and pressures of persuasion and become a rule of reason that will persuade free human beings to cultivate new behaviors, actions, habits, and even new institutions as means to the common good. Too often, legislative reason tries to meet these criteria by simply adding a penalty to the primitive legal hypothesis. There is some semblance of validity in this appeal to force, since behavior and habits can be formed by coercion, and it is said that a political community has a monopoly of power to accomplish that. But for any human community it is a cruel regression to the lower levels of civilization, and it is merely an illusion to suppose that coercion is the basis of law and order.

The leverage of persuasion is the reasonableness that can be imbedded in the law, and it is to this that the consent of the governed is given. Such consent can be reduced to the superficial consent that exists in popular opinion, and it is in this sense that a law seems to be the generalization from particulars. There is an illusion here as there is in the use of coercion. The literal expression of the will of the people processed through agitation and the ballot can be very deceitful. If the law is to take root in the habits of free citizens, it has to be framed so that it is available to the intelligence of everybody. As a good teacher must respect the intelligence of his pupils, so the law must appeal to the sense of justice of the community. But the legislator has to reach for and refine the formulation that amplifies his initial legal hypothesis in order to draw out the consent of the people and win their obedience in the future as well as in the present. The final verification of the law is given only in the settled habits it induces in the citizens. Ultimately, that is the meaning of the consent of the governed; all the preliminary expressions of consent—polls, caucuses, party platforms, citizens' ballots, and votes in legislative chambers—are only external conditions for the generation of the internal substance of legality in the habits of the community.

This distinction between external laws and internal habits comes from two kinds of ethical thought. There is the theory of conduct under rules of reason, or codes of ethics. This reaches its climax in Kantian ethics, where there is a hierarchy of imperatives, culminating in the categorical: make all the maxims of your action laws universal. Under that master rule are hypothetical imperatives that take time, place, and circumstance into account, then imperatives of skill that govern the practice of the arts. These imperatives make further rules under which the individual governs himself as if he were a polity.

Then there are the ethics of the virtues. Adherence or obedience to the imperatives develops habits. When the habits are achieved and are properly ordered to valid ends, which are assured under good laws, the habits are virtues and good conduct is free and accompanied by pleasures.

These two kinds of ethics can be cultivated separately, and independent cultivation is necessary at certain stages of education. But the legislator, he who makes the rules of reason for the common good, must know the reciprocal relations and the influences of each kind on the other. Perhaps the most important knowledge and skill that he exercises in law-making concerns the timing of these relations. It is said in the legends concerning Solon and Lycurgus that when they had drawn up a code of laws for their respective polities they got an agreement from the people that the laws should not be changed for ten years, and during that interval they absented themselves from their communities so that the requisite habits could be generated in the people. Sure enough, they got the promise of the people to abide by this legal stasis, but they were under no illusion that they had thereby gained their substantial consent. That could only be recognized and judged after ten years of practice; only then would they know what new laws or amendments were needed.

Whether such attention is ever actually given to law-making, it always involves this process. In the political thought of the ancients the legends of Solon and Lycurgus were honored by Plato, Aristotle, and Thucydides in their rule that laws should not be changed rapidly. This is often taken to mean that these thinkers were simply conservative; they feared the open society. But the true meaning of the legends is that the real existence of law is not in enactments or books but in the hearts of the citizens. This kind of wisdom was well known to monarchs and aristocrats; it has usually not been known by

democracies. It may be impossible to give it respect under modern conditions, but it would seem that legislators should be aware of the dangers in its neglect. Consent of the governed becomes a mockery if it is interpreted superficially and literally in terms of the mechanics of representation and participation.

This somewhat plaintive appeal to the wisdom of the legislator suggests some other jurisprudential depths that we might wish to invoke. In this country we have become familiar with the eye the legislator has to the likelihood that his work will be reviewed by the Supreme Court. Part of his caution is due to a prudential care to avoid having his law judged unconstitutional. But another part of it appeals to the cultivated wisdom of the justices as they view a new law in relation to the rest of the body of established law. The notorious side-effects of the Prohibition Amendment upon the rest of our body of law illustrate the problem, and similar problems arise around almost any statute that single-mindedly seeks a remedy for clear evil, but at the same time brings unforeseen effects in other branches of law—for instance, the apparent effects of the income tax on corporations-for-profit, which in order to protect themselves from the tax have set up thousands of charitable corporations where their assets are sequestered. This is not to say that side-effects are always evil, but only to raise the question of what might be called legal ecology. The ramification of corporation law raises these questions in great complexity—so great, in fact, that foresight seems overwhelmed.

But it is time to return to one of the basic themes of this essay, namely, that persuasion is the all-pervasive life of the body politic. There are various kinds of persuasion on the low, high, and middle ranges. On the level of production and trade are the adversary proceedings of the courts of common law that formalize the business of the market-place. In the so-called voluntary associations are more or less chartered organizations that practice the arts of debate and management under Roberts' Rules of Order and tables of organization. Under the enabling immunities of the First Amendment free speech is practiced with its elaborations in press, assembly, and petition, and these are further developed in our system of free and compulsory education. In each case the intent is to increase the ratio of reason to force. Contrary to much current theory, truly effective and dependable power is increased as reason prevails. Free speech is the assurance of persuasion, and without it power is evanescent. But in order to bring persuasion to its full realization, it must be transformed into laws or rules of reason, and it is for this consummation of politics that the Constitution establishes the machinery of representation and legislation.

The transformation of persuasion into law, whether begun in the House or the Senate, becomes final by the Congress only after both parties have approved a piece of legislation. Under our bicameral system, members of the Congress have the responsibility to find in mutual persuasion and deliberation the intuitive induction that results in a legal hypothesis—for instance, the insight that leads to a social security law, or to a criminal law. The process is essentially a generalization from problematic conditions and needs of the society in all their variety and complexity. The end result must represent these concrete particulars in a reasonable and just pattern; in this sense it must be responsible to the community and the electorate.

In the normal course of particularly significant legislation, the House and the Senate have their own bills before them, and when the first to act sends its bills to the other for concurrence, agreement is reached through floor discussion and action, or following a recommendation by a joint House-Senate conference committee. In both bodies, the procedure involves the wisdom of legislative experience. It is this wisdom and experience that is employed by the legislators in finding the locus of a prospective law in the general body of existing laws, in considering the constitutionality of the proposed legislation, in judging the power to induce new habits in the community with concern about the side-effects that may result with respect to other laws, and in considering the fitness of the new legislation to serve the common good.

I realize that other reasons are given for a bicameral system; most of them bear on the usual concerns to limit the respective powers of the two houses by allowing them to check and balance each other. But these considerations can and ought to be subsumed under the imperatives of jurisprudence mentioned above.

When the bill passes formally into law, sometimes aided by the joint committees of Congress, a new entity exists, not yet the achievement of a living law existing in the hearts of men, but a relatively permanent power of persuasion. Stated in universal language, it is an entity of reason voicing the will of the whole community. It approximates the positivistic definition of law, the command of the sovereign to be enforced by sanctions. But that formula contains a great temptation to identify a law with the so-called monopoly of force which is supposed to be exercised by the state. This would imply that the legislative art consists in the manipulation of groups and their interests into some kind of coalition so that their combined force can coerce the compliance of the rest of the community. Too often the behavior of politicians seems to verify this account of the legislative process, which however it does not accurately describe.

The political process of persuasion, it is true, has its roots in the play of groups, interests, and forces in the community, but when a bill becomes a law, it has been divested of the powers that went into its making, and the decision has been made to entrust the common good to a rule of reason, the only power that can penetrate and permeate the body politic. It becomes the law of the land. This is the truth that lies behind the myth of the social contract: the citizens have made a contract to surrender their individual rights to the popular assembly or its representative parliament, which in turn has agreed to abide by the process of deliberation and the rules of reason. It does not change this fundamental constitutional process to admit that the results are sometimes imperfect and have to be supplemented by police action. The sanctions are not the basis of law; they are auxiliary aids of law to deal with the gap between reason and habit. If the law turns out to depend for its effectiveness just on force alone, it is not a law.

The executive

The final words of the previous section indicate that the law has passed the line separating the legislative from the executive branch of the government. Austin's phrase, "the command of the sovereign," is in the executive or imperative mode, and the passage to the executive department is recognized in our system in the President's act of signing the bill. This has two effects: it is a final act of legislation and it is the acceptance of his duty to execute or administer the law. That he can veto the bill and return it to the legislature for further deliberation is an indication that the act is not merely formal. By his signature the President certifies that the law has become a command and that he pledges his obedience to it, not only his own obedience as an officer of the government but the obedience of the whole executive branch. He also reasserts the proposition that we have a government of laws, not of men, and this means that the law has reached a moment of independence and superiority; it and no person or combination of persons is sovereign.

It is of course true that the mere promulgation, or publication, of a rule of reason does not by itself constitute effective government, just as it is true that issuing an order, no matter by whatever authority, police or military, is not necessarily effective. Richard Neustadt in his *Presidential Power** tells how Truman pitied Eisenhower when the latter became President. He said that the General would be shocked when he discovered that when he issued an order from the President's office, nothing would happen, that the only power of the President is the power of persuasion. To be sure, the President's power of persuasion is very great because he is acting under law; but it is still only persuasion. So it is throughout the executive branch.

The executive mode of persuasion is different from the legislative mode. Whereas the legislator operates under an assignment to find a universal rule that will bring justice and freedom to the whole community and its many interests and pressures, the executive operates under an assignment to administer a general rule of reason so that it can be carried out by many groups and individual citizens. If the rule merely dealt with inanimate or non-rational things, the persuasion might follow an analogy with formal logic. From the general rule as a premise, succeeding rules of less and less generality might be deduced until they are applicable to concrete particulars. Superior officers could issue orders to inferior officers of administration. Tables of administrative organization would seem to indicate that this is the process. But although ours is a government of laws rather than of men, the laws operate through animate, rational, and therefore free men. The men who fill the offices of government, as well as the men in homes and on the streets and in the factories, have to understand in order to obey, and they have to understand well if they are to enlist the obedience of other men. The sequences of Hegelian logic would thus seem even more to the point: the superior officer issues an order or a thesis; the lower officer or officers assert an antithesis which is more specific and full of circumstantial

---

* *Presidential Power: The Politics of Leadership* (New York: John Wiley & Sons, 1964).

considerations, and these are followed by executive deliberations which result in a synthesis.

However, both these logical models are borrowed from theoretical reason, and although they are relevant as guides in practical reasoning, the actual process of administration is different in several respects. The major premise of practical reason is the statement of an end or purpose that requires the discovery and ordering of means. The law may indicate what these are, but the application may involve the invention of institutional and technical means and their actual management in order to achieve the legal intent. Experts in engineering and administration may have to be enlisted, and each of them will have to find his official duties amidst many contingencies. If the enterprise is novel enough, there may have to be new skills acquired on the job. Know-how will have to be added to expertise. Good-will and morale will have to be added to patience and fortitude.

So, although the executive branch and the President as Chief Executive suggest a hierarchy of offices and lines of command, the business of administering and enforcing the laws is much too complex to be contained in such a scheme. The creation of the President's Cabinet, which was not explicitly provided for in the Constitution but was obviously needed to exercise the powers that it delegated, demonstrates the point. In effect, the President's next act after signing a bill into law is to pass it on to the proper Secretary, who then organizes his department to carry out the legal intent.

In the case of the Department of Justice this may call for the immediate application of the police power, but even in this case the Attorney-General may have to bring a case before a Federal court before he can literally enforce the law, and this may become a recurrent necessity and involve the development of a strategy to deal with a series of novel and difficult cases such as those that have arisen chronically under the Sherman Anti-trust Act. The other members of the Cabinet obviously preside over much more than simple law enforcement, much more even than the appointment of Under-Secretaries and their staffs to promulgate and superintend the carrying out of executive orders. They are involved in kinds of persuasion and deliberation different from those of the legislative branch. They have to build bridges from the law to the citizen, from the office to the institutions that form the infra-structure of the society, and these bridges themselves become large and powerful institutions. The Treasury Department provides currency and collects taxes, but it also has to deal with the banking system and its controls of credit; the Labor Department has to discover the consequences of labor laws that enable the development of labor unions.

But perhaps the Department of Agriculture demonstrates most fully the function of the executive branch. In order to carry out the legislative intent of an Act of Congress, this Department had to initiate the scientific research that has transformed agriculture from the bundles of crafts and trades that make up the small farms into industries and technologies and economies. To aid in this it partook in the development of educational institutions, the land-grant colleges and universities, which would combine research with training for the citizen-farmer. It also aided in the establishment of county agents, who carried information and skills to every village and farm. It has to deal in many variable ways with the Granges, Farm Bureaus, and cooperatives that have sprung from voluntary associations. It has always had most complicated relations with the separate states and their agricultural interests and sovereignties, choosing when to enlist their cooperation, when to check their provincial enterprises, and when to circumvent their jurisdiction and deal directly with concrete problems. Since the agricultural empire has always been a major factor in the national economy, recurrent economic depressions and the disturbance of the market by world wars have induced the government to intervene by varying devices of regulation and control of production, prices, storage, and subsidies. This has generated a body of law and a system of administration to aid the farmer, protect the consumer, and advance the public welfare.

The other departments have had similar if not as extensive developments. They all tend to invent new institutions within the executive branch, and these in turn stimulate the development of responsive institutions in the so-called private sector of society. Sometimes the private sector itself spontaneously generates new institutions that need protection or aid from the government, and the government responds by establishing the so-called independent regulatory agencies, which do not fall under the categories provided by the Cabinet but nevertheless belong to the executive branch and fall under the general powers of the President.

In the early days of the Republic the offices of the executive branch were filled by appointment, some with approval by Congress but many without. There consequently grew up the so-called spoils system, in which the President rewarded the members of his party with executive jobs without too critical an eye to fitness for the office. Although the system cost a good deal in inefficiency and corruption, it made for lively politics both in the election campaigns and in the operation of the executive branch. But as the weight and complexity of governmental affairs increased, this form of political vitality had to be sacrificed for the need of efficiency. So gradually the lower executive offices came to be filled by examinations and judgments of merit in a new system of civil service. As the standards were improved, the executive branch was manned increasingly by persons of experience, education, and training; the offices were filled with experts who could look to careers in government and expect increasing education on the job.

It is common now to refer to the executive departments as bureaus, and this means that a new kind of reason has appeared in the art of government. It is often assumed to be the kind of reason that is customarily imputed to the professions, but it is actually the expert and technical reason that is exercised in management. As the civil servant or bureaucrat is often experienced in business and industry, so the arts of government are now borrowed from the current technology. It would seem that technique has taken the place of both law and politics in governmental administration. This transformation has gone so far, it is said, that the present progressive introduction of computers and automation into the executive offices will not change the present operations except to increase their speed and eliminate the possibility of corruption. It may be recalled that the current word for the combination of automation and computation, cybernation, is derived from the Greek word for government.

But the progression from the spoils system through the civil service and the bureaus to cybernation ignores an aspect of the executive art that is very general throughout the executive branch. This might be called executive legislation because it has produced a vast body of administrative law. Such legislation is implied in the powers and duties of the executive. Statutes that flow from the legislative branch are general in intent and therefore must be made more and more particular as they are applied to cases. In the middle ranges that descend from the President and Secretaries and chiefs of bureaus, each office formulates rules to be followed by lower offices and finally by the citizen. But each step in this quasi-legislative and quasi-judicial process involves persuasion, consultation, even trial and error, to make the rule fit the case. When the persuasion becomes complicated, it develops friction, the lower official or the citizen may challenge it and in acute cases may take the rule to court. The judges and lawyers have trouble in dealing with this kind of adjudication; hence there arises the problem of administrative law.

On first thought, as was noted earlier, it would seem the difficulties in the administration of a law would be merely problems in deductive formal logic: the subordinate rules flowing from the general law are constructed from middle terms in syllogisms, or those long series of syllogisms that are called sorites. But the difficulties come precisely in reducing the complex operations of the law in the society to rigorous terms.

Such reductions are attempted in hearings, say by the regulative agencies, in which representatives of the organizations that are to be regulated appear with briefs before representatives of the bureaus. Something like lobbying takes place in these hearings, something like collective bargaining, something like the adversary proceedings of the courts, something like negotiating for contracts. Sometimes the bureau sets up a court with full judicial formalities, as in the tax courts under the Treasury Department. When the hearings are less formal, it appears that the officers of the bureaus, having been chosen in the first place from the knowledgeable members of the private organizations, are acting in collusion with their former associates, and the regulated are the regulators. Some see in these confusions a creeping bureaucracy hungering for power, and some see a creeping socialism. To those concerned with the rule of law and reason, administrative law presents a vast problem in jurisprudence in an increasingly bureaucratic and technological society. Can technology and organization be brought under law? Shall law become a technology?

These questions have in the last generation been cast in a new form. The large industrial corporations that have rapidly assimilated science and technology to their manufacturing and marketing operations have found it necessary to make comprehensive plans. Likewise the developing economies in the new nations have found it necessary to make plans on a national scale

with the help of their governments. This has resulted in the apparent reduction of most of the problems of both economics and politics to the problems of management and administration, both public and private. As such problems are increasingly turned over to experts and their quasi-professional methods for solution, teams of researchers and developers are assigned to find the facts and to rationalize problematic areas that need organization, direction, regulation, and government aid.

When the plans are drafted, they are recommended to voluntary associations, to corporations, or to various levels of the government for action. But there is no commonly held mode for the acceptance of these plans. A voluntary association may accept a plan as a temporary policy and carry it out. Corporations may hire their own experts and build the plans into management programs. A team of experts may work for many firms in an industrial complex, and the members may agree to follow the plans in cooperation, as if they had made a contract. The government bureau may draw up a plan and offer it to a sector of the economy, or a sector of the economy may make a plan and submit it to the government. In these latter cases there is a question about the legal status of such plans, and possibly about the sanctions that will be used in their enforcement.

Plans have profound effects in the society and in the body of accepted law, but in themselves they do not satisfy the requirements for statute laws. They are sometimes formally made by bureaus that are called "authorities," like the Tennessee Valley Authority or the Port of New York Authority, and are ad hoc edicts or directives. There may be the usual hearings granted to the affected citizens for ascertaining their consent, but the courts have difficulty in dealing with cases that cannot be treated in the customary adversary proceedings unless they are broken down into citizens' suits against the government. Permission may be granted for citizens to sue the government, but such permissions are exceptions to the general rules, and the suits deal with the administrative problems in only a piecemeal way, leaving the problem of general legitimation of the plan untouched. There is, in general, a struggle between the technicians and the lawyers, and there is no procedural solution for this in sight, even though public opinion is slowly coming to accept the necessity of planning. The legislatures have as yet found no way of incorporating plans in conventional statutes, except by delegating more and more authority to the executive agencies. The effect of such delegation is to defunctionalize the legislature and give at least the appearance of plausibility to the widely held opinion that government has now become almost wholly executive, administrative, bureaucratic, and impervious to democratic control.

No doubt there is reason to view these developments with alarm, and there are many signs that the alarms are getting attention. Perhaps there is not attention enough to the political processes that have developed within the bureaus themselves; that is, the mutual persuasions and deliberations that go on inside the bureaus, between the bureaus, both inside and outside the government, and with the general public. It should be remembered that it took many years, even centuries, for the common law to comprehend the phenomena of the industrial revolution and to transform itself into public law. It now should be recognized that public law is only beginning to transform itself to deal adequately with a bureaucratic and technological society.

The judiciary

It is said that no man is worth his salt if he was not in his youth a socialist. In a similar aphoristic style it can be said that no one devoted to the rule of law should be trusted if he is not sympathetic with the anarchist.

These mild paradoxes indicate the judicious temperament and the judicial function in government.

If a law is a rule of reason directed to the common good, its terms will be universals. It will apply to what is equal in men, it will apply equally throughout the community, its jurisdiction will be coterminous with the community, and it will reach to the concrete case. These properties of law provide part of what is meant by the legitimacy of government; they are part of the assurance that law is the means by which the responsibility of the citizen for justice can be discharged. They are assurances that men's potentialities as political animals can be realized in political action.

But, reassuring as these virtues of law are, they also mark the limits of its powers. Rules of reason may penetrate the concrete cases, but since they are abstract they cannot exhaust the infinite variety that exists in the concrete individual, nor can they take full account of the infinity that exists in the contingencies of his place, his time, or his circumstances. No matter how good the law, no matter how imaginative, honest, and diligent the officers, no matter how thorough the legal process, every case will hold a residue of contingent fact and circumstance that is not comprehended in the terms of the law. Such a residue may or may not be relevant to the determination of justice, but when it is relevant, it calls for mercy and even charity. The anarchist sees this discrepancy between law and fact, and on it makes his case against all law and government. The judge in a court of law sees the discrepancy and presides over a process that will reduce it to a minimum and therefore increase to the maximum the degree of justice that is humanly attainable.

The jurist and the anarchist are not alone in recognizing the precarious role that reason plays in human experience. Both the ancient and the modern scientist, who devote themselves to speculative reason, are familiar with the cussedness of empirical fact and the corresponding clumsiness of reason in arranging the data for verification. Measurement, that most characteristic art in the sciences, is accomplished only with increasingly complicated instruments and experiments, and the results are announced with coefficients of tolerance and margins of error. While the laboratory and industry deal with these residues of reason by strict controls, which eliminate irrelevant observation and sharpen what is relevant, their chief reliance is on a kind of second, artificial reason, the calculus of probability.

But in a court of law, as in the medical clinic, the concrete individual case is the focus of attention, and the reason employed is not primarily speculative but practical. In the legislature and in the executive the main objective is the making and administration of general rules that will preserve and improve the life of the community, but in the courts the aim is to provide justice to the individual and the issues are often matters of life and death. Therefore, the fact that most citizens will obey the law or that the law is probably just for the great majority of cases is not enough. The meaning and intention of the law must be found in the particular case, and a judgment must be rendered on it if the common good is to be faithfully served.

Throughout the long history of the courts of law there have been many discoveries, inventions, and accumulations of devices to discharge this most difficult of functions. If the appearance of two parties to a dispute before a judge is the original prototype, the formality of adversary proceedings with the accompanying distinction between the plaintiff and the defendant may well be the guiding thread of the historic development. As in other phases of the political process, competitive interests and partisan pleadings were accepted and encouraged, not for their own sakes, nor for what they would demonstrate of their powers to prevail in the contest, but for what they would provide in the way of relevant and competent fact to aid

the judge in arriving at a just judgment. The court soon discovered that interest and even passion, irrelevant as they may be to the final judgment, can be turned to account as engines for rooting out the details of the situation that are necessary for an objective view of it. The full play of adversary proceedings may complicate the process, but they tend to prevent quick judgment on the prima facie case.

But the need for evidence goes beyond the naked pleadings of the two parties to the dispute. At an early time there had been attempts to acquire evidence from higher and lower sources outside the court, ordeals by fire, water, and even combat. These were bizarre, and they led to bizarre results. Slowly but surely, other more rational procedures were substituted, chiefly the admission of witnesses testifying under oath and the aid of trained legal counsel in questioning the witnesses to educe further information and put their testimony in order. The lawyers were members of the court under the supervision of the judges, as well as agents of the parties. They were allowed to question not only their own witnesses but also the witnesses of the adversary. These additions to the court led to the formulation of rules of procedure for the judge to enforce on the parties and their counsels, particularly the rules that govern the admission and treatment of evidence.

The inquiring amateur, viewing the apparent growth and complication of the court, expects to find some steady improvement in the intelligibility and rationality of the procedure. But this is not obviously the result. Teachers of the law of evidence, for instance, find that the rules have grown like Topsy without rhyme or reason, at least on the surface. They are filled with what appears to be proverbial wisdom, old wives' tales, old men's saws, and scraps of ritual. The young lawyer has to memorize the rules and hope to understand them as he pleads. There have been monumental attempts to see deeper into possible principles of human psychology and morals that would put the fragments together in some rational code, as well as to assimilate them to strictly legal thought. But the treatises that have resulted are heavy tomes that do not yield to systematic consolidation and simplification.

The moral to be drawn from this puzzle should not be unfamiliar to the philosophical critic. It would seem to be that practical reason, the more rigorous it tries to be in dealing with the concrete case, deploys its searching questions in more and more complex patterns. The law is no exception. It gives itself to the so-called system of casuistry and equity as it increases its concern to bring justice down to earth.

Perhaps the most impressive illustration of this general insight is to be found in the development of juries. A court of law, whether it be primitive with merely the adversaries to a quarrel and a judge, or formal and sophisticated in the complex procedures of a politically organized society, is a dramatic microcosm representing the whole community. It differentiates the roles of its members along lines that sharpen rational functions. But the result depends on, and through the jury expresses, the unsharpened—that is, less rational—thought, will, and passion of the immediate social environment. In this respect the court is like Greek drama in which the chorus was so prominent. Classical scholars were at first puzzled by the presence of the chorus. The choral odes and dances could be seen as embellishments of a spectacle, but for the most part they seemed to be dull and functionless additions; they did not advance the action. On further study, however, it became clear that the chorus fed new persons into the drama as it developed and responded on its own to the main action in telling ways. The scholars finally concluded that the chorus was the mainstream of the play in which the actors floated and magnified their roles. In more literal terms the odes and dances provided the context of ritual and custom in the community without which the play itself would have no substance, no persuasive force.

This does not imply that the courts imitated the dramatic model, although the parallel suggests an hypothesis that might be explored. It seems probable that the chief, or king, or the self-appointed judge needed the ritualistic and moral support that a jury provides in order to make the court effective. It seems that there has always been in the Anglo-Saxon tradition something like a jury accompanying the business of the courts. Sometimes they act as witnesses, sometimes in grand juries as advisers to the prosecution, finally as petty juries who make the final judgment and render the verdict.

The Greeks and Romans used juries, but they seem to have been large assemblies of citizens chosen at random to hear the pleadings, presided over by moderators, and they rendered their verdicts by majority votes. They were organs of direct democratic government without the sophistication of later representative government and therefore without the beginnings of the distinction between legislative, administrative, and judicial functions. In the Anglo-Saxon tradition juries seem always to have been small bodies of citizens, twelve, fifteen, or twenty-three members, who serve under oath, and under increasingly formal rules. Perhaps the most striking formality is that they are required to reach unanimous decisions and are given unlimited time for deliberation in achieving their conclusions, a procedure that is considered impractical in any other democratic institution. A court trial with a jury is thus a peculiar combination of highly technical and professional procedure and of submission of the formal result to the collective judgment of untechnical unprofessional men of common sense. The theory now is that the jury judges only the issues of fact, but it is known and expected that it also judges issues of law. Because laws as well as men are being tried, the jury has a quasi-jurisprudential function. And yet the verdict is rendered laconically,

Guilty or Not Guilty, and no reasons are given.

In the present climate of opinion it is not surprising to find the jury viewed by both the lay and professional communities as a peculiar institution. It has never been generally accepted on the European continent; it is gradually being given up in England; it seems to persist in the United States because the right to a jury trial is guaranteed by the Constitution. The thin rational criticism of the social and behavioral sciences is beginning to raise questions about its validity, and it is being proposed that a computer might well be substituted for these mysterious and almost secret procedures. The traditional defense of the jury varies from sentimental appeals to the role it has played in the development of democratic institutions to the general defense of small local institutions against the encroachment of big central government. It would seem wiser to see these as partial statements of a larger concern that is intrinsic to the political use of practical reason.

Law has been called a second, artificial reason, which is partially hypostatized by being formulated. Habit is often called a second nature which has been deposited in the human psyche by practical action and experience. The proper combination of these two entities is essential to the life of law and self-government. A jury judging a case is one of the places where this combination becomes effective. It is true that lawyers appeal to the emotions and passions of the jury; it is true that juries can be deceived by false rhetoric and histrionics, as students can be misled by the subtler arts of teaching in schools and universities. But imagination, emotion, and passion are the concomitants of both habit and formal reasoning, particularly the formal part of practical reason. The fact that a jury of twelve good men and true deliberates behind closed doors that protect their freedom of speech, sifts the noisy expertise and artful pleading of the courtroom, and comes to a unanimous decision,

may be something to remember as we submit our democratic institutions to a relentless critique.

So far we have been commenting on some of the schematic trappings of the court of law. They are fragmentary and external to the judicial process in which they play a part; they are like the stage set, the properties, and the list of dramatis personae of the theatre. Concerning the judicial process itself there is a voluminous literature, which is still growing. But for the amateur critic much of this literature is unavailable because it is written by and for the lawyer whose training and daily practice is the reading and pleading of cases. The best treatises seem to have been written by judges who have heard the cases and rendered opinions, often without the help of juries. But even these more detached commentaries are in the form of legal doctrines, first-order abstractions made from bundles of cases, which aid the legal mind to get from one case to another and build the bodies of law that accumulate like coral reefs and persist as quarries from which precedents are selected and used in further pleadings. Even if I were able to do so, I would not presume to add to these commentaries.

A new venture might perhaps begin with the distinction that a judge makes when he delivers his charge to the jury. He instructs the jury in the law that is relevant to the case and implies that they are to accept his account of the legal issues. Then, separately, he summarizes and comments on the facts as they have presumably been established in the testimony of the witnesses and in the pleadings of the respective counsels. He may go farther and point out the unanswered questions that the jury must consider in their deliberations leading to the verdict. Issues of law and issues of fact may have been distinguished in the pleadings, but the presumption is that these two kinds of issues may have been confused in the minds of the jury. This confusion may be more probable since it is a part of the art of vigorous partisan pleading to anticipate and lead to the final judgment that applies the law to the facts. The chief function of the judge's charge to the jury is to raise the level of rhetoric and mutual persuasion to the level of clear dialectic.

The distinction between law and fact suggests that there have been in the arguments by counsels two kinds of hypotheses, one that acts as a plot and tends to throw the facts into a narrative pattern, and one that selects laws and precedents to make a legal doctrine to fit the instant case. Actually, because of the adversary proceedings, the attorneys for the prosecution and the defense multiply these two into four hypotheses, one of fact and one of law for the prosecution, and one of fact and one of law for the defense. These hypotheses are the threads of thought that are spun by the pleading and lead from the indictment to the verdict. They are often announced at the beginning of the respective pleadings, but they may not be clearly formulated until the counsels deliver their summaries at the end.

In its factual aspect the parties to the litigation appear as characters in search of authors. The attorneys are the authors. Their briefs are preliminary scenarios with blanks to be filled in on the stage of the courtroom by other characters acting as witnesses. They are sworn to tell the truth and their testimony must be "material, relevant, and competent" as it is cross-questioned by the attorneys and scrutinized by the judge for admissibility. Real evidence—that is, physical objects identified by witnesses, signed documents, and expert testimony—may be admitted; much testimony that is offered is not admitted because it is immaterial, irrelevant and incompetent to advance the narrative or eventually to fit under the terms of the legal hypothesis.

Although the rules of evidence are many, complex, and detailed, they are not merely restrictive; in skillful hands they can be powerful tools to search out the facts that will fill in the blanks in the narrative. Much legal history has been made by research on the part of attorneys who have known how to construe their findings not only to gain their admission to the court but also to expand and deepen the judgment of the judge and the jury. But, as historians and fiction writers know, narrative is a very high and difficult art. When it is practiced under the conditions of the courtroom, where the life, liberty, and property of individuals are at stake, the imperative to do justice gives a new depth to the imperative to tell the truth.

Witnesses are sworn to tell "the truth, the whole truth, and nothing but the truth, so help me God." This phrase expresses the heaviest burden placed not only on the witnesses but on the court. It should be remembered that the truth that is sought is in the mode of practical reason, and that its meaning is spelled out in the elaborate rules of evidence. When the many testimonies of the witnesses are put together under the factual hypothesis, it must be clear that the total narrative is something less than the "whole truth," the actuality. It must be the whole truth that is humanly available. Some events must be left out, some must be inferred, and the continuity must be supplied.

Even without the rhetorical and histrionic arts of the respective attorneys, there are many possible openings for argument about the facts, and it is these openings that give the conditions for the competing narratives of the adversaries. In the laboratory, where measurements are plotted on graphs, it is said that an infinite number of curves can be drawn through the plotted points. The rule is to draw a smooth curve. In pleading, the testimonies and other items of evidence are like these points. The counsel can draw many lines that compose the facts into a narrative. The rule here is that the story must be credible and persuasive to the jury, or to the judge when there is no jury. Often, the pleadings result in truths that are stranger than fiction.

So it comes about that a court of law, from

which the words judicious and judicial get their meaning, is the political institution where persuasion reaches its highest passionate, imaginative, and verbal development in rhetorical, dramatic, and dialectical forms. These are most fully developed in the summaries of the attorneys at the end of the trial. These performances seem to confirm the worst suspicions of the layman about the corruption of the legal profession, for they seem to be mockeries of the function of the courts. This, however, is to misunderstand the judicial process. Part of the explosion of argument is due to the pressure of the assignment, to do justice, and part of it is due to the pressure of the formal confines within which the trial takes place; but most of it is not only allowed but encouraged by the court and can be understood as practical reason stretching the whole human being to his utmost powers of comprehensive judgment. There are times when human reason does its best in the cool, even cold, contemplation of its object, but there are also times when the responsibility of reason, particularly practical reason, involves it in the struggle to mastery of human life.

Another part of the judge's charge to the jury deals with the development of the legal hypotheses that have been guiding the pleadings of the lawyers. The beginning of these legal hypotheses is, of course, in the indictment, the allegation that the defendant has violated one or more laws. But the law is general or universal, and the case is concrete and individual. Therefore the application of the law will involve the particularization of the law to fit the case, and this may involve a complicated course of argument. In this the judicial process is like the administrative or executive process. It would seem that both processes could be carried out by syllogisms or sorites, but even if this were the case, the finding of middle terms is a laborious process. In the executive process these middle terms are found in the course of negotiation and experiment, and the result often is rules and edicts that may serve to guide an officer or a bureau in carrying out the intent of the law. But there is often a residue of indeterminacy or ambiguity that has to be taken to court. In effect, the judicial process has to complete the executive process in novel and difficult cases.

Although the philosopher or logician may be able to discern a syllogistic thread in the legal reasoning of the court, this is seldom, if ever, the form that the lawyer sees or follows. Rhetoric, rather than logic, is the legal style, the legalist's habit not merely when he is appealing to a jury but also in his own private study or office. It is hard to justify this. There is no intrinsic reason why a lawyer should not be adept in grammar and logic as well as rhetoric, and there is much to be said for the thesis that he ought to have a comprehensive liberal education in which mathematics as well as the verbal arts play a part. Perhaps the computer will teach the lawyer to acquire and use the whole arsenal of intellectual arts, on pain of having all of the judicial process computerized.

Rhetoric is most often associated with figures of speech, metonymy, synecdoche, metaphor, etc. But the figure that takes the main burden of legal reasoning is the analogy. Those rows of drab books in dull blues, dull reds, brown, and gilt that line the shelves of a lawyer's office, contain cases or abstracts of cases that have been recorded in courtrooms, and the textbooks of the law schools up to fairly recently have been casebooks. To the layman, this is a vast compilation of pedantic detail. But besides the dates and jurisdictions of the cases, the intelligible links between the cases are analogies. Some history-making case contains an archetype, or ruling pattern of relations, to which a later case provides an analogue, and these two points of reference set up a line along which many other cases are assimilated by analogy. When the instant case, for which a brief is being prepared, falls into this line or near it, the whole previous series provides the precedents. Each case will have varied the original and the preceding patterns, but the variance will not be enough to have broken the analogy. The present case may seem to stretch the preceding analogies, and then it will be the task of the lawyer to argue it into the series. The pleading may fail and the case may be lost if the step from the past to the present is too great, or it may be won if the new step is admitted and the law is reinterpreted to cover it. This movement of the reasoning from precedent to precedent constitutes the essence of judicial legislation and the growth of the law. Sometimes the original archetype is given in a statute, but the mediation of precedents will be an aid in making the law effective, in keeping it alive in new circumstances, and in approximating justice in the judgment of the case.

Obviously it would be an oversimplification to see each case falling into a single line of precedents as the last term in the series. This may happen in a simple, easy instance, but the harder cases will have facets that lead to many archetypes and series of precedents. The head-notes that precede the opinion in Supreme Court reports aid the reader in following the legal hypothesis of the case, and these references must reflect the notes from which a pleading lawyer has written his brief. The selection and introduction of precedents are the work of the attorneys, but there are occasions when the judge makes such a contribution, particularly when he completes the legal hypothesis in his summary and charge to the jury. Not all precedents offered in the pleadings are admitted; many are offered and few are chosen. There is something like the struggle for survival of precedents in pleadings, and their persistence through the ordeal is decided first by their fitness in the series of analogies and finally in the credibility of the whole argument.

After the final arguments of the counsels have been made, it is the task of the judge to clarify the issues that have been developed in the course of the trial. Although he may have made rulings in the course of the argu-

ments, taken notice of the laws and precedents cited and the admitted or excluded evidence, and in general kept order in the courtroom, his review at the end will be needed, if only to counterbalance the strong partisan pleadings of the counsels. But actually he must bring into play the means by which a synthesis of the arguments can be made in the minds of the jury. Presumably each counsel will have made in his summary a consolidation of a legal hypothesis and a factual hypothesis together with precedents and evidence, and he will have "rested his case" in a final plea for a verdict. The rule is that the judge must in his charge state the issues that have emerged in the legal hypotheses of the two sides and make his judgment on these; in effect, render a legal, professional judgment on what the relevant law is for the case. He passes this judgment on to the jury for their application to the evidence. Then he has a further legal task to review the evidence and give its items their respective weights insofar as the rules of evidence apply. One might say that he clarifies an additional evidential hypothesis as a part of the major legal hypothesis. Thus, the judge provides the jury with as clearly specified a body of law for the instant case as is possible.

It remains for the jury to make the final judgment, which combines the legal and factual hypotheses together with their own view of the facts, and this pattern may include a revision of the weights that the judge has assigned to the facts. It may seem from the layman's viewpoint that the burden put on the jury is more than twelve good men and true can bear and that the legal profession is defaulting its duties in submitting its laborious preparations and procedures to the final judgment of ordinary men. But this is to miss the function of both the legal profession and the public. The court is a representative institution to which is assigned the most difficult of political functions. It brings its professional aid to the judgment of the public. Compared with the legislative and executive branches it is a model for the bringing of reason and deliberation to the business of self-government.

This account of the judicial process has omitted, so far, a major theme in Anglo-Saxon jurisprudence, one that is most often memorialized in the charge that the judge delivers to the jury. In all criminal cases the defendant is assumed to be innocent until he is proved guilty beyond any reasonable doubt. We often forget that this rule is not honored in non-Anglo-Saxon jurisdictions. Together with other rules that flow from this as a premise—for instance, that no defendant shall be compelled in any criminal case to be witness against himself—it sounds a deep note of warning concerning the precarious nature of the judicial process, and indeed about the total effect of the legal process on society. Montesquieu says that one of the ways to judge the quality of any society is through its criminal code. He is chiefly concerned about the degree of liberty in a society and the connection this has with a limited constitutional government. But he is also thinking about the other aspects of the common good, and the ways in which a society assimilates and distributes the "spirit of the laws." The presumption of innocence and the burden of proof that it throws upon the prosecution is, to be sure, a safeguard of liberty, but it also sets limits on the use of practical reason in general.

In all too brief compass we have been taking a narrow and almost microscopic view of the court of law. If the institution were not so widespread, we would have to call it extraordinary. It is one of the wonders of civilization with respect both to the rational ends that it seeks and the rational means that it invents and maintains to achieve those ends. But we should see the individual court and the individual case in its broader context. We have already noted the part that precedents play in its procedures. These are chosen from centuries of records; by implication the whole body of court records is in principle brought to bear on the instant case. Precedents from foreign jurisdictions may be introduced by lawyers and judges in American courts. If the law in this form is not a brooding omnipresence in the sky, it is a body of world law. The Romans discerned this when they identified the law with the *ius gentium*, and reached beyond it to the law of nature and the logos.

Again, the individual court operates within a context of appellate courts. The supreme courts of both the Federal government and the several states supervise systems of courts to which cases already tried by the lower courts can be appealed, and the Supreme Court itself functions at least in part as a segment of the appellate system. This means that, although the cases in the lower courts are carried through to decisions, the trials can be reviewed and rejudged, and there may be a series of appeals from the lowest courts up through the appeal courts to the highest courts of last appeal. Errors of the lower courts may be found and corrected, decisions may be reversed by taking note of new evidence or even of new precedents, cases may be remanded to the lower courts for retrial.

The appellate court follows the pattern of adversary proceedings. Briefs are submitted and pleadings heard from opposing attorneys, but seldom, if ever, are new witnesses and their evidence directly admitted, unless the amicus curiae briefs can be so construed. No juries are employed, but more than one judge sits on the bench, and their decisions are arrived at by majority vote. Perhaps the most striking difference from the lower courts is in the reasoned opinions that accompany the appellate decisions. These opinions still show a deep concern with the justice that must be brought to the individual case, but it seems that the law as well as the defendant is being judged. Some of these decisions have made legal history and are essays if not small treatises in jurisprudence.

In spite of the fact that the many judges on the bench act as both jury and judge, the whole appellate establishment is made up of legal officers carrying out highly professional functions. It is often said that these appellate courts are the least democratic of any of our governmental institutions, but it can also be said that they are our most trusted representatives. We entrust to them the highest duties of a democratic society. We do this because the courts, particularly the appellate courts, are like the traditional professional guilds. They are made up of men who have a body of practical scientific knowledge, and they belong to a professional society, the Bar, which is devoted to the common good and can protect the individual acting together with his colleagues in doing their duties. There is some such rationale in the trust we grant to juries in courts of first instance, and the higher courts confirm our trust the more they bring professional integrity and independence to the exercise of the authority that has been delegated to them.

The notion of the professional guild is further emphasized in the hierarchical arrangement of the courts of appeals. A lower court knows that its procedures and decisions are subject to review, that its defects and errors can be improved, corrected, and amplified by other members of the guild, that its decisions may be reversed if greater knowledge and wisdom are available and needed. We are aware of this trust in the care we exercise in the selection and appointment of judges, in the life tenure that most appellate judges enjoy, and in the independence that we wish them to maintain. The trust is not only in the persons but also in the Bar and the institutions of the judiciary.

Our own Constitution carries this delegation of authority farther than most modern constitutions do in the establishment of the Supreme Court. In addition to its status as the court of highest appeal or last resort, Chief Justice Marshall, in one of the earliest acts of the Court, conferred on it a power not mentioned in the Constitution, the power to judge the constitutionality of acts of Congress and of administrative laws that arise from the operations of the executive as well as of laws that arise from judicial legislation. He did this under a general principle that he discerned working in our form of government. If the Constitution establishes ends to be achieved, it must also be authorizing the means by which the ends may be gained. The powers to authorize such means are the implied powers of the Constitution. In Justice Marshall's opinion the principle of implied powers acted immediately upon the Court itself. All officers of the government swear to uphold the Constitution, but this oath has a special incidence upon the Supreme Court; it must uphold the Constitution judicially. As the court of last resort, it must affirm all laws that come under its cognizance which are consistent with the Constitution, and it must strike down all those laws which are inconsistent with the Constitution. It does not make declaratory judgments of this sort but judges the laws that are relevant to the case in hand, following the usual judicial process.

Thus, it becomes literally true that the judicial system as a whole is continually judging laws as well as men, and the laws themselves are subject to correction and improvement. The Constitution itself is living and growing in the judicial process, finding its implicit meanings and making them explicit in the cases that develop in a growing society.

The widening perspective that opens out from a given case in terms of the reliance of the courts on precedents and in the system of appeals has a still further dimension. A case may have gone through both the lower and higher courts and reached its final disposition. But similar cases can still arise for such treatment in the future, and the arguments of practical reason may be brought to bear on a continuing theme. Earlier judgments may be reversed or extended to new but similar matters. Although the matter of a given case may be disposed of, the body of law continues and grows. The familiar aphorism of Hippocrates concerning the art of medicine applies to the art of law: Life is short, the Art long, the case fleeting, the trial treacherous, judgment difficult. The judge must be ready not only to do his duty, but also to secure the cooperation of the attorneys, their clients, and the juries. There is the short view of the case, the longer view of the appeals, and the longest view in the growth of the law.

I began with the intention to describe the respective functions of the separated powers of government in order to justify their constitutional separation. I am not sure that the intention has been served, but I seem to see now that the separation shows the progressive clarification and improvement of reason that is intended in the three liberal arts of the trivium: Legislation formulates laws after the fashion of the philosophical grammarian; the executive turns laws into the instruments of persuasion and action after the fashion of the rhetorician; the judiciary generalizes and abstracts the law until it becomes the dialectical mode of understanding not only the law but the whole society. Under our Constitution the law divides itself so that reason can rule.

The Essence of Mathematics

Charles Sanders Peirce

Editor's Introduction

Charles Sanders Peirce is now widely recognized as the most versatile and original philosophical thinker that America has so far produced. Yet at his death in 1914 at the age of seventy-five he was virtually unknown and had passed the last years of his life in poverty, neglect, and much suffering from cancer. William James, his friend and benefactor, prophesied truly when he wrote him, in 1903, that "it is only highly skilled technicians and professionals who will sniff the rare perfume of your thought, and, after you are dead, trace things back to your genius." Some sixty years after his death, now that his voluminous papers have come to be studied, Peirce is acknowledged, not only as the father of the philosophical movement known as pragmatism, but also as a great and original contributor to the history and philosophy of science and of logic, to mathematics, especially to linear algebra, and, above all, to mathematical logic and the theory of signs.

Peirce may have been too far ahead of his time for his work to be appreciated for its true value. Yet he himself must bear some blame for that neglect. Although a close and powerful thinker as well as a hard worker (2,000 words a day for much of his life), he never managed to complete any of the many major books that he projected at various times. Thus his writing, except for occasional published articles, consists for the most part of a great mass of unconnected fragments, of books begun again and again but never completed. Peirce's personal character — James compared it to a nettle — and his proud attitude toward others seem also to have contributed greatly to his failure to obtain, or retain, a post befitting his talent and learning.

Peirce was born September 10, 1839, in Cambridge, Massachusetts, the second son of Benjamin Peirce (1809–80), professor of mathematics and of astronomy at Harvard. His early education was carefully supervised by his father, who saw in his son the makings of a mathematical genius. Peirce graduated from Harvard College in 1859 and in 1863, in chemistry, from the Lawrence Scientific School of Harvard University. By that time, although his major interest already centered upon philosophy, he had embarked upon a scientific career. In 1861 he had begun working as an assistant to his father on the U.S. Coast and Geodetic Survey, and he continued work for the Survey office in various capacities until 1891. In this work, which was mathematical and astronomical, and experimental as well as theoretical, he was mainly concerned with obtaining more nearly accurate measurements of the force of gravity. While in charge of the Office of Weights and Measures, he recommended the expansion of that office, which ultimately led to the establishment of the National Bureau of Standards. His work for the Survey won him an international reputation as a scientist, and he was elected a fellow of the American Academy of Arts and Sciences in 1867, of the National Academy of Sciences in 1877, and of the London Mathematical Society in 1880.

Philosophy, however, remained Peirce's first love, and his work for the Survey was not so demanding that he was prevented from its pursuit. During the 1870s he and James with their friends met frequently in Cambridge to discuss philosophical questions, in a group that Peirce called the Metaphysical Club. He also gave two series of lectures at Harvard on logic. Out of these discussions and lectures he published in 1877–78 a series of six articles on the logic of science—the first of which, on "How to Make Our Ideas Clear," is sometimes referred to as the first formulation of pragmatism. In 1879 he was appointed part-time lecturer in logic at the newly established Johns Hopkins University, where he taught graduate students intensively for five years and seemed well on the way to obtaining a university post. But then, for reasons that were not fully revealed, other than "lack of prudence," and that still remain mysterious, his appointment was not renewed. Meanwhile, his disagreements with the administrators of the Survey were worsening, and, in 1891, upon inheriting a small legacy, he resigned his office and retired, with his second wife, a Frenchwoman, to a farm on the Delaware River near Milford, Pennsylvania, the house of which has now been declared a national monument. He had hoped to supplement his income by writing, but while he wrote many reviews for *The Nation* and many articles for Baldwin's *Dictionary of Philosophy and Psychology* as well as *The Century Dictionary*, the compensation he received was never sufficient for any comfort, and often he was reduced to poverty that was relieved only by aid from James and other friends.

The essay printed here under the title of "The Essence of Mathematics" was written in 1902 and consists of a portion of a longer essay entitled "The Simplest Mathematics," which was intended to be the third chapter in his *Minute Logic*, and which remained uncompleted. The text is reprinted from *Collected Papers of Charles Sanders Peirce*, edited by Charles Hartshorne and Paul Weiss (Cambridge: Harvard University Press, 1933), vol. 4, paragraphs nos. 228–43.

The Essence of Mathematics

It does not seem to me that mathematics depends in any way upon logic. It reasons, of course. But if the mathematician ever hesitates or errs in his reasoning, logic cannot come to his aid. He would be far more liable to commit similar as well as other errors there. On the contrary, I am persuaded that logic cannot possibly attain the solution of its problems without great use of mathematics. Indeed all formal logic is merely mathematics applied to logic.

It was Benjamin Peirce, whose son I boast myself, that in 1870 first defined mathematics as "the science which draws necessary conclusions."* This was a hard saying at the time; but today, students of the philosophy of mathematics generally acknowledge its substantial correctness.

The common definition, among such people as ordinary schoolmasters, still is that mathematics is the science of quantity. As this is inevitably understood in English, it seems to be a misunderstanding of a definition which may be very old,[1] the original meaning being that mathematics is the science of *quantities*, that is, forms possessing quantity. We perceive that Euclid was aware that a large branch of geometry had nothing to do with measurement (unless as an aid in demonstrating); and, therefore, a Greek geometer of his age (early in the third century B.C.) or later could not define mathematics as the science of that which the abstract noun quantity expresses. A line, however, was classed as a quantity, or *quantum*, by Aristotle† and his followers; so that even

perspective (which deals wholly with intersections and projections, not at all with lengths) could be said to be a science of quantities, "quantity" being taken in the concrete sense. That this was what was originally meant by the definition "Mathematics is the science of quantity," is sufficiently shown by the circumstance that those writers who first enunciate it, about A.D. 500, that is Ammonius Hermiae and Boëthius, make astronomy and music branches of mathematics; and it is confirmed by the reasons they give for doing so.[2] Even Philo of Alexandria (100 B.C.), who defines mathematics as the science of ideas furnished by sensation and reflection in respect to their necessary consequences, since he includes under mathematics, besides its more essential parts, the theory of numbers and geometry, also the practical arithmetic of the Greeks, geodesy, mechanics, optics (or projective geometry), music, and astronomy, must be said to take the word 'mathematics'

---

* "Linear Associative Algebra" (1870), sec. 1; see *American Journal of Mathematics*, vol. 4 (1881).

[1] From what is said by Proclus Diadochus, A.D. 485 [*Commentarii in Primum Euclidis Elementorum Librum*, Prologi pars prior, c. 12], it would seem that the Pythagoreans understood mathematics to be the answer to the two questions "how many?" and "how much?"

† Aristotle *Metaphysics* 5. 13. 14–20; *GBWW*, Vol. 8, p. 541b.

[2] I regret I have not noted the passage of Ammonius to which I refer. It is probably one of the excerpts given by Brandis. My MS. note states that he gives reasons showing this to be his meaning.

in a different sense from ours. That Aristotle did not regard mathematics as the science of quantity, in the modern abstract sense, is evidenced in various ways. The subjects of mathematics are, according to him, the how much and the continuous. (See *Metaphysics* 11. 3. 1061a33; *GBWW*, Vol. 8, p. 589c.) He referred the continuous to his category of *quantum*; and therefore he did make *quantum*, in a broad sense, the one object of mathematics.

Plato, in the Sixth book of the *Republic*,[3] holds that the essential characteristic of mathematics lies in the peculiar kind and degree of its abstraction, greater than that of physics but less than that of what we now call philosophy; and Aristotle* follows his master in this definition. It has ever since been the habit of metaphysicians to extol their own reasonings and conclusions as vastly more abstract and scientific than those of mathematics. It certainly would seem that problems about God, Freedom, and Immortality are more exalted than, for example, the question how many hours, minutes, and seconds would elapse before two couriers travelling under assumed conditions will come together; although I do not know that this has been proved. But that the methods of thought of the metaphysicians are, as a matter of historical fact, in any aspect, not far inferior to those of mathematics is simply an infatuation. One singular consequence of the notion which prevailed during the greater part of the history of philosophy, that metaphysical reasoning ought to be similar to that of mathematics, only more so, has been that sundry mathematicians have thought themselves, as mathematicians, qualified to discuss philosophy; and no worse metaphysics than theirs is to be found.

Kant regarded mathematical propositions as synthetical judgments *a priori;*[†] wherein there is this much truth, that they are not, for the most part, what he called analytical judgments; that is, the predicate is not, in the sense he intended, contained in the definition of the subject. But if the propositions of arithmetic, for example, are true cogni-

tions, or even forms of cognition, this circumstance is quite aside from their mathematical truth. For all modern mathematicians agree with Plato and Aristotle that mathematics deals exclusively with hypothetical states of things, and asserts no matter of fact whatever; and further, that it is thus alone that the necessity of its conclusions is to be explained.[4] This is the true essence of mathematics; and my father's definition is in so far correct that it is impossible to reason necessarily concerning anything else than a pure hypothesis. Of course, I do not mean that if such pure hypothesis happened to be true of an actual state of things, the reasoning would thereby cease to be necessary. Only, it never would be known apodictically to be true of an actual state of things. Suppose a state of things of a perfectly definite, general description. That is, there must be no room for doubt as to whether anything, itself determinate, would or would not come under that description. And suppose, further, that this description refers to nothing occult—nothing that cannot be summoned up fully into the imagination. Assume, then, a range of possibilities equally definite and equally subject to the imagination; so that, so far as the given description of the supposed state of things is general, the different ways in which it might be made determinate could never introduce doubtful or occult features. The assumption, for example, must not refer to any matter of fact. For questions of fact are not within the purview of the imagination. Nor must it be such that, for example, it could lead us to ask whether the vowel *OO* can be imagined to be sounded on as high a pitch as the vowel *EE*. Perhaps it would have to be re-

---

[3] 510C to the end [*GBWW*, Vol. 7, pp. 387b–88a]; but in the *Laws* his notion is improved.

* See *Metaphysics* 6. 1, 11. 3–4; *GBWW*, Vol. 8, pp. 547b–48c, 589a–90a.

[†] *The Critique of Pure Reason*; *GBWW*, Vol. 42, pp. 1–250.

[4] A view which J. S. Mill (*Logic* II, V, §2) rather comically calls "the important doctrine of Dugald Stewart."

stricted to pure spatial, temporal, and logical relations. Be that as it may, the question whether in such a state of things, a certain other similarly definite state of things, equally a matter of the imagination, could or could not, in the assumed range of possibility, ever occur, would be one in reference to which one of the two answers, *Yes* and *No*, would be true, but never both. But all pertinent facts would be within the beck and call of the imagination; and consequently nothing but the operation of thought would be necessary to render the true answer. Nor, supposing the answer to cover the whole range of possibility assumed, could this be rendered otherwise than by reasoning that would be apodictic, general, and exact. No knowledge of what actually is, no *positive* knowledge, as we say, could result. On the other hand, to assert that any source of information that is restricted to actual facts could afford us a necessary knowledge, that is, knowledge relating to a whole general range of possibility, would be a flat contradiction in terms.

Mathematics is the study of what is true of hypothetical states of things. That is its essence and definition. Everything in it, therefore, beyond the first precepts for the construction of the hypotheses, has to be of the nature of apodictic inference. No doubt, we may reason imperfectly and jump at a conclusion; still, the conclusion so guessed at is, after all, that in a certain supposed state of things something would necessarily be true. Conversely, too, every apodictic inference is, strictly speaking, mathematics. But mathematics, as a serious science, has, over and above its essential character of being hypothetical, an accidental characteristic peculiarity—a *proprium*, as the Aristotelians used to say—which is of the greatest logical interest. Namely, while all the "philosophers" follow Aristotle in holding no demonstration to be thoroughly satisfactory except what they call a "direct" demonstration, or a "demonstration why"—by which they mean a demonstration which employs only general concepts and concludes noth-

ing but what would be an item of a definition if all its terms were themselves distinctly defined—the mathematicians, on the contrary, entertain a contempt for that style of reasoning, and glory in what the philosophers stigmatize as "mere" indirect demonstrations, or "demonstrations that." Those propositions which can be deduced from others by reasoning of the kind that the philosophers extol are set down by mathematicians as "corollaries." That is to say, they are like those geometrical truths which Euclid did not deem worthy of particular mention, and which his editors inserted with a garland, or corolla, against each in the margin, implying perhaps that it was to them that such honor as might attach to these insignificant remarks was due. In the theorems, or at least in all the major theorems, a different kind of reasoning is demanded. Here, it will not do to confine oneself to general terms. It is necessary to set down, or to imagine, some individual and definite schema, or diagram—in geometry, a figure composed of lines with letters attached; in algebra an array of letters of which some are repeated. This schema is constructed so as to conform to a hypothesis set forth in general terms in the thesis of the theorem. Pains are taken so to construct it that there would be something closely similar in every possible state of things to which the hypothetical description in the thesis would be applicable, and furthermore to construct it so that it shall have no other characters which could influence the reasoning. How it can be that, although the reasoning is based upon the study of an individual schema, it is nevertheless necessary, that is, applicable, to all possible cases, is one of the questions we shall have to consider. Just now, I wish to point out that after the schema has been constructed according to the precept virtually contained in the thesis, the assertion of the theorem is not evidently true, even for the individual schema; nor will any amount of hard thinking of the philosophers' corollarial kind ever render it evident. Thinking in general terms is not enough. It is necessary that something should be DONE. In geometry, subsidiary lines are drawn. In algebra permissible transformations are made. Thereupon, the faculty of observation is called into play. Some relation between the parts of the schema is remarked. But would this relation subsist in every possible case? Mere corollarial reasoning will sometimes assure us of this. But, generally speaking, it may be necessary to draw distinct schemata to represent alternative possibilities. Theorematic reasoning invariably depends upon experimentation with individual schemata. We shall find that, in the last analysis, the same thing is true of the corollarial reasoning, too; even the Aristotelian "demonstration why." Only in this case, the very words serve as schemata. Accordingly, we may say that corollarial, or "philosophical" reasoning is reasoning with words; while theorematic, or mathematical reasoning proper, is reasoning with specially constructed schemata.

Another characteristic of mathematical thought is the extraordinary use it makes of abstractions. Abstractions have been a favorite butt of ridicule in modern times. Now it is very easy to laugh at the old physician who is represented as answering the question, why opium puts people to sleep, by saying that it is because it has a dormitive virtue. It is an answer that no doubt carries vagueness to its last extreme. Yet, invented as the story was to show how little meaning there might be in an abstraction, nevertheless the physician's answer does contain a truth that modern philosophy has generally denied: it does assert that there really is in opium *something* which explains its always putting people to sleep. This has, I say, been denied by modern philosophers generally. Not, of course, explicitly; but when they say that the different events of people going to sleep after taking opium have really nothing in common, but only that the mind classes them together —and this is what they virtually do say in denying the reality of generals—they do implicitly deny that there is any true explana-

tion of opium's generally putting people to sleep.

Look through the modern logical treatises, and you will find that they almost all fall into one or other of two errors, as I hold them to be; that of setting aside the doctrine of abstraction (in the sense in which an abstract noun marks an abstraction) as a grammatical topic with which the logician need not particularly concern himself; and that of confounding abstraction, in this sense, with that operation of the mind by which we pay attention to one feature of a percept to the disregard of others. The two things are entirely disconnected. The most ordinary fact of perception, such as "it is light," involves *precisive* abstraction, or *prescission*. But *hypostatic* abstraction, the abstraction which transforms "it is light" into "there is light here," which is the sense which I shall commonly attach to the word abstraction (since *prescission* will do for precisive abstraction) is a very special mode of thought. It consists in taking a feature of a percept or percepts (after it has already been prescinded from the other elements of the percept), so as to take propositional form in a judgment (indeed, it may operate upon any judgment whatsoever), and in conceiving this fact to consist in the relation between the subject of that judgment and another subject, which has a mode of being that merely consists in the truth of propositions of which the corresponding concrete term is the predicate. Thus, we transform the proposition, "honey is sweet," into "honey possesses sweetness." "Sweetness" might be called a fictitious thing, in one sense. But since the mode of being attributed to it *consists* in no more than the fact that some things are sweet, and it is not pretended, or imagined, that it has any other mode of being, there is, after all, no fiction. The only profession made is that we consider the fact of honey being sweet under the form of a relation; and so we really can. I have selected sweetness as an instance of one of the least useful of abstractions. Yet even this is convenient. It facilitates such thoughts as that the sweetness of honey is particularly cloying; that the sweetness of honey is something like the sweetness of a honeymoon; etc. Abstractions are particularly congenial to mathematics. Everyday life first, for example, found the need of that class of abstractions which we call *collections.* Instead of saying that some human beings are males and all the rest females, it was found convenient to say that *mankind* consists of the male *part* and the female *part.* The same thought makes classes of collections, such as pairs, leashes, quatrains, hands, weeks, dozens, baker's dozens, sonnets, scores, quires, hundreds, long hundreds, gross, reams, thousands, myriads, lacs, millions, milliards, milliasses, etc. These have suggested a great branch of mathematics.[5] Again, a point moves: it is by abstraction that the geometer says that it "describes a line." This line, though an abstraction, itself moves; and this is regarded as generating a surface; and so on. So likewise, when the analyst treats operations as themselves subjects of operations, a method whose utility will not be denied, this is another instance of abstraction. Maxwell's notion of a tension exercised upon lines of electrical force, transverse to them, is somewhat similar. These examples exhibit the great rolling billows of abstraction in the ocean of mathematical thought; but when we come to a minute examination of it, we shall find, in every department, incessant ripples of the same form of thought, of which the examples I have mentioned give no hint.

Another characteristic of mathematical thought is that it can have no success where it cannot generalize. One cannot, for example, deny that chess is mathematics, after a fashion; but, owing to the exceptions which everywhere confront the mathematician in this field—such as the limits of the board; the single steps of king, knight, and pawn; the finite number of squares; the peculiar mode of capture by pawns; the queening of pawns; castling—there results a mathematics whose wings are effectually clipped, and which can only run along the ground. Hence it is that a mathematician often finds what a chess-player might call a gambit to his advantage; exchanging a smaller problem that involves exceptions for a larger one free from them. Thus, rather than suppose that parallel lines, unlike all other pairs of straight lines in a plane, never meet, he supposes that they intersect at infinity. Rather than suppose that some equations have roots while others have not, he supplements real quantity by the infinitely greater realm of imaginary quantity. He tells us with ease how many inflexions a plane curve of any description has; but if we ask how many of these are real, and how many merely fictional, he is unable to say. He is perplexed by three-dimensional space, because not all pairs of straight lines intersect, and finds it to his advantage to use quaternions which represent a sort of four-fold continuum, in order to avoid the exception. It is because exceptions so hamper the mathematician that almost all the relations with which he chooses to deal are of the nature of correspondences; that is to say, such relations that for every relate there is the same number of correlates, and for every correlate the same number of relates.

Among the minor, yet striking characteristics of mathematics, may be mentioned the fleshless and skeletal build of its propositions; the peculiar difficulty, complication, and stress of its reasonings; the perfect exactitude of its results; their broad universality; their practical infallibility. It is easy to speak with precision upon a general theme. Only, one must commonly surrender all ambition to be certain. It is equally easy to be certain. One has only to be sufficiently vague. It is not so difficult to be pretty precise and fairly certain at once about a very narrow subject. But to reunite, like mathematics, perfect exactitude and practical infallibility with unrestricted universality, is remarkable.

---

[5] Of course, the moment a collection is recognized as an abstraction we have to admit that even a percept is an abstraction or represents an abstraction, if matter has parts. It therefore becomes difficult to maintain that all abstractions are fictions.

But it is not hard to see that all these characters of mathematics are inevitable consequences of its being the study of hypothetical truth.

It is difficult to decide between the two definitions of mathematics; the one by its method, that of drawing necessary conclusions; the other by its aim and subject matter, as the study of hypothetical states of things. The former makes or seems to make the deduction of the consequences of hypotheses the sole business of the mathematician as such. But it cannot be denied that immense genius has been exercised in the mere framing of such general hypotheses as the field of imaginary quantity and the allied idea of Riemann's surface, in imagining non-Euclidian measurement, ideal numbers, the perfect liquid. Even the framing of the particular hypotheses of special problems almost always calls for good judgment and knowledge, and sometimes for great intellectual power, as in the case of Boole's logical algebra. Shall we exclude this work from the domain of mathematics? Perhaps the answer should be that, in the first place, whatever exercise of intellect may be called for in applying mathematics to a question not propounded in mathematical form [it] is certainly not pure mathematical thought; and in the second place, that the mere creation of a hypothesis may be a grand work of poietic (from ποιέω) genius, but cannot be said to be scientific, inasmuch as that which it produces is neither true nor false, and therefore is not knowledge. This reply suggests the further remark that if mathematics is the study of purely imaginary states of things, poets must be great mathematicians, especially that class of poets who write novels of intricate and enigmatical plots. Even the reply, which is obvious, that by *studying* imaginary states of things we mean *studying* what is true of them, perhaps does not fully meet the objection. The article *Mathematics* in the ninth edition of the *Encyclopædia Britannica* makes mathematics consist in the study of a particular sort of hypotheses, namely, those that are exact, etc., as there set forth at

some length. The article is well worthy of consideration.

The philosophical mathematician, Dr. Richard Dedekind,* holds mathematics to be a branch of logic. This would not result from my father's definition, which runs, not that mathematics is the science of *drawing* necessary conclusions—which would be deductive logic—but that it is the science which *draws* necessary conclusions. It is evident, and I know as a fact, that he had this distinction in view. At the time when he thought out this definition, he, a mathematician, and I, a logician, held daily discussions about a large subject which interested us both; and he was struck, as I was, with the contrary nature of his interest and mine in the same propositions. The logician does not care particularly about this or that hypothesis or its consequences, except so far as these things may throw a light upon the nature of reasoning. The mathematician is intensely interested in efficient methods of reasoning, with a view to their possible extension to new problems; but he does not, *quâ* mathematician, trouble himself minutely to dissect those parts of this method whose correctness is a matter of course. The different aspects which the algebra of logic will assume for the two men is instructive in this respect. The mathematician asks what value this algebra has as a calculus. Can it be applied to unravelling a complicated question? Will it, at one stroke, produce a remote consequence? The logician does not wish the algebra to have that character. On the contrary, the greater number of distinct logical steps, into which the algebra breaks up an inference, will for him constitute a superiority of it over another which moves more swiftly to its conclusions. He demands that the algebra shall analyze a reasoning into its last elementary steps. Thus, that which is a merit in a logical algebra for one of these students is a demerit in the eyes of the other. The one studies the science of draw-

---

* *Was sind und was sollen die Zahlen; Vorwort* (1888).

ing conclusions, the other the science which draws necessary conclusions.

But, indeed, the difference between the two sciences is far more than that between two points of view. Mathematics is purely hypothetical: it produces nothing but conditional propositions. Logic, on the contrary, is categorical in its assertions. True, it is not merely, or even mainly, a mere discovery of what really is, like metaphysics. It is a normative science. It thus has a strongly mathematical character, at least in its methodeutic division; for here it analyzes the problem of how, with given means, a required end is to be pursued. This is, at most, to say that it has to call in the aid of mathematics; that it has a mathematical branch. But so much may be said of every science. There is a mathematical logic, just as there is a mathematical optics and a mathematical economics. Mathematical logic is formal logic. Formal logic, however developed, is mathematics. Formal logic, however, is by no means the whole of logic, or even its principal part. It is hardly to be reckoned as a part of logic proper. Logic has to define its aim; and in doing so is even more dependent upon ethics, or the philosophy of aims, by far, than it is, in the methodeutic branch, upon mathematics. We shall soon come to understand how a student of ethics might well be tempted to make his science a branch of logic; as, indeed, it pretty nearly was in the mind of Socrates. But this would be no truer a view than the other. Logic depends upon mathematics; still more intimately upon ethics; but its proper concern is with truths beyond the purview of either.

There are two characters of mathematics which have not yet been mentioned, because they are not exclusive characteristics of it. One of these, which need not detain us, is that mathematics is distinguished from all other sciences except only ethics, in standing in no need of ethics. Every other science, even logic—logic, especially—is in its early stages in danger of evaporating into airy nothingness, degenerating, as the Germans say, into an arachnoid film, spun from the stuff that dreams are made of. There is no such danger for pure mathematics; for that is precisely what mathematics ought to be.

The other character—and of particular interest it is to us just now—is that mathematics, along with ethics and logic alone of the sciences, has no need of any appeal to logic. No doubt, some reader may exclaim in dissent to this, on first hearing it said. Mathematics, they may say, is preëminently a science of reasoning. So it is; preëminently a science that reasons. But just as it is not necessary, in order to talk, to understand the theory of the formation of vowel sounds, so it is not necessary, in order to reason, to be in possession of the theory of reasoning. Otherwise, plainly, the science of logic could never be developed. The contrary objection would have more excuse, that no science stands in need of logic, since our natural power of reason is enough. Make of logic what the majority of treatises in the past have made of it, and a very common class of English and French books still make of it— that is to say, mainly formal logic, and that formal logic represented as an art of reasoning—and in my opinion this objection is more than sound, for such logic is a great hindrance to right reasoning. It would, however, be aside from our present purpose to examine this objection minutely. I will content myself with saying that undoubtedly our natural power of reasoning is enough, in the same sense that it is enough, in order to obtain a wireless transatlantic telegraph, that men should be born. That is to say, it is bound to come sooner or later. But that does not make research into the nature of electricity needless for gaining such a telegraph. So likewise if the study of electricity had been pursued resolutely, even if no special attention had ever been paid to mathematics, the requisite mathematical ideas would surely have been evolved. Faraday, indeed, did evolve them without any acquaintance with mathematics. Still it would be far more economical to postpone electrical researches, to study mathematics by itself, and then to apply it to electricity, which was Maxwell's way. In this same manner, the various logical difficulties which arise in the course of every science except mathematics, ethics, and logic, will, no doubt, get worked out after a time, even though no special study of logic be made. But it would be far more economical to make first a systematic study of logic. If anybody should ask what are these logical difficulties which arise in all the sciences, he must have read the history of science very irreflectively. What was the famous controversy concerning the measure of force but a logical difficulty? What was the controversy between the uniformitarians and the catastrophists but a question of whether or not a given conclusion followed from acknowledged premises? . . .

But it may be asked whether mathematics, ethics, and logic have not encountered similar difficulties. Are the doctrines of logic at all settled? Is the history of ethics anything but a history of controversy? Have no logical errors been committed by mathematicians? To that I reply, first, as to logic, that not only have the rank and file of writers on the subject been, as an eminent psychiatrist, Maudsley, declares, men of arrested brain-development, and not only have they generally lacked the most essential qualification for the study, namely mathematical training, but the main reason why logic is unsettled is that thirteen different opinions are current as to the true aim of the science. Now this is not a logical difficulty but an ethical difficulty; for ethics is the science of aims. Secondly, it is true that pure ethics has been, and always must be, a theatre of discussion, for the reason that its study consists in the gradual development of a distinct recognition of a satisfactory aim. It is a science of subtleties, no doubt; but it is not logic, but the development of the ideal, which really creates and resolves the problems of ethics. Thirdly, in mathematics errors of reasoning have occurred, nay, have passed unchallenged for thousands of years. This, however, was simply because they escaped notice. Never, in the whole history of the science, has a question whether a given

conclusion followed *mathematically* from given premises, when once started, failed to receive a speedy and unanimous reply. Very few have been even the apparent exceptions; and those few have been due to the fact that it is only within the last half century that mathematicians have come to have a perfectly clear recognition of what is mathematical soil and what foreign to mathematics. Perhaps the nearest approximation to an exception was the dispute about the use of divergent series. Here neither party was in possession of sufficient pure mathematical reasons covering the whole ground; and such reasons as they had were not only of an extra-mathematical kind, but were used to support more or less vague positions. It appeared then, as we all know now, that divergent series are of the utmost utility.[6]

Struck by this circumstance, and making an inference, of which it is sufficient to say that it was not mathematical, many of the old mathematicians pushed the use of divergent series beyond all reason. This was a case of mathematicians disputing about the

_____

[6] It would not be fair, however, to suppose that every reader will know this. Of course, there are many series so extravagantly divergent that no use at all can be made of them. But even when a series is divergent from the very start, some use might commonly be made of it, if the same information could not otherwise be obtained more easily. The reason is—or rather, one reason is—that most series, even when divergent, approximate at last somewhat to geometrical series, at least, for a considerable succession of terms. The series $\log(1+x) = x - \frac{1}{2}x^2 + \frac{1}{3}x^3 - \frac{1}{4}x^4 +$, etc., is one that would not be judiciously employed in order to find the natural logarithm of 3, which is 1.0986, its successive terms being $2 - 2 + 8/3 - 4 + 32/5 - 32/3+$, etc. Still, employing the common device of substituting for the last two terms that are to be used, say M and N, the expression $M/(1 - N/M)$, the succession of the first six values is 0.667, 1.143, 1.067, 1.128, 1.067, which do show some approximation to the value. The mean of the last two, which any professional computer would use (supposing him to use this series, at all) would be 1.098, which is not very wrong. Of course, the computer would practically use the series $\log 3 = 1 + 1/12 + 1/80 + 1/448+$, etc., of which the terms written give the correct value to four places, if they are properly used.

validity of a kind of inference that is not mathematical. No doubt, a sound logic (such as has not hitherto been developed) would have shown clearly that that non-mathematical inference was not a sound one. But this is, I believe, the only instance in which any large party in the mathematical world ever proposed to rely, in mathematics, upon unmathematical reasoning. My proposition is that true mathematical reasoning is so much more evident than it is possible to render any doctrine of logic proper—without just such reasoning—that an appeal in mathematics to logic could only embroil a situation. On the contrary, such difficulties as may arise concerning necessary reasoning have to be solved by the logician by reducing them to questions of mathematics. Upon those mathematical dicta, as we shall come clearly to see, the logician has ultimately to repose.

PICTURE CREDITS

*Key to abbreviations used to indicate location of pictures on page: r.—right; l.—left; t.—top; b.—bottom; c.—center; *—courtesy. Abbreviations are combined to indicate unusual placement.*

Authors

in Great Books of the Western World

Homer	Nicomachus
Aeschylus	Ptolemy
Sophocles	Marcus Aurelius
Herodotus	Galen
Euripides	Plotinus
Thucydides	Augustine
Hippocrates	Thomas Aquinas
Aristophanes	Dante
Plato	Chaucer
Aristotle	Machiavelli
Euclid	Copernicus
Archimedes	Rabelais
Apollonius	Montaigne
Lucretius	Gilbert
Virgil	Cervantes
Plutarch	Francis Bacon
Tacitus	Galileo
Epictetus	Shakespeare
	Kepler